THE
ANNUAL REGISTER
Vol. 247

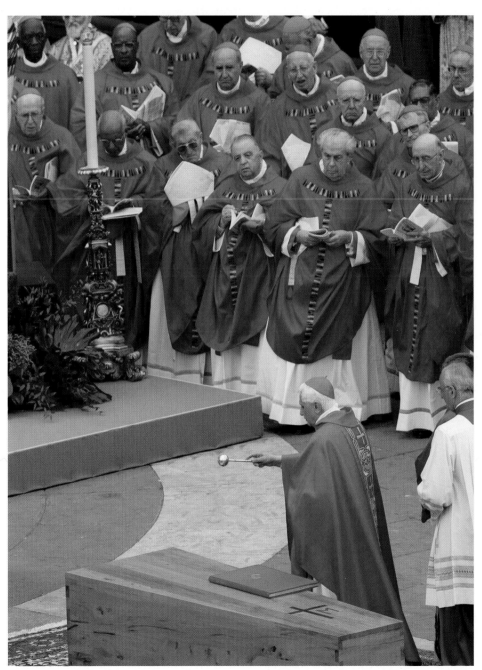

End of an Era (8 April): The future Pope, German Cardinal Joseph Ratzinger, waves an incense burner around the coffin during the funeral of Pope John Paul II. (REUTERS/Alessandro Bianchi).

[Top] *Shattered Lives* (26 October): A young survivor of the Kashmiri earthquake stands amid the rubble of his family home in Muzaffarabad, the capital of Pakistan-administered Kashmir. (REUTERS/Zohra Bensemra).

[Bottom] *After the Storm* (30 August): A man paddles on a door in flooded New Orleans after the city's defences were breached by Hurricane Katrina. (REUTERS/Rick Wilking).

[Top] *Eventual Triumph* (12 November): CDU leader Angela Merkel affirms the agreement that will make her Germany's first female Chancellor, at the head of a coalition government. (REUTERS/Arnd Wiegmann).

[Bottom] *London Bombing* (8 July): The wreckage of a London bus, destroyed by one of four suicide bombers who simultaneously targeted the city's public transport system. (REUTERS/Dylan Martinez).

Commemorating Victory (8 May): A military orchestra performs on a boat passing in front of the Kremlin, Moscow, during the international celebrations of the 60th anniversary of VE Day. (REUTERS/Dima Korotayev).

THE
ANNUAL REGISTER

World Events 2005

Edited by
D.S. LEWIS

Deputy Editor
WENDY SLATER

FIRST EDITED IN 1758
BY EDMUND BURKE

Published by CSA: Cambridge Information Group
7200 Wisconsin Ave.
Bethesda, MD 20814
United States of America and
4640 Kingsgate, Cascade Way
Oxford Business Park South
Oxford, OX4 2ST, England

ISBN: 1-60030-069-3

British Library Cataloguing in Publication Data
The Annual Register-2005
1. History-Periodicals
909.82'8'05 D410

Library of Congress Catalog Card Number: 4-17979

Set in Times Roman by
NEW AGE GRAPHICS, Silver Spring, MD, USA

Printed in the USA by
THE SHERIDAN BOOKS, Chelsea, Michigan, USA

CONTENTS

CONTRIBUTORS

TURKEY

A.J.A. Mango, BA, PhD, Orientalist and writer on current affairs in Turkey and the Near East

PART III

POLAND

A. Kemp-Welch, BSc (Econ), PhD, Senior Lecturer, School of Economic and Social Studies, University of East Anglia

ESTONIA, LATVIA, LITHUANIA

David J. Galbreath, PhD, Lecturer in Politics and International Relations, University of Aberdeen.

CZECH REPUBLIC, SLOVAKIA

Sharon Fisher, MA, Analyst specialising in East European political and economic affairs, Global Insight

HUNGARY

Bill Hayton, MA, Europe Region Planning Editor, BBC World Service

ROMANIA

Gabriel Partos, South-East Europe Analyst, BBC World Service

FORMER YUGOSLAV REPUBLICS
BULGARIA, ALBANIA

Othon Anastasakis, MA, PhD, Director, South East European Studies Programme, St Antony's College, Oxford

RUSSIA, WESTERN CIS

Wendy Slater, MA, PhD, Former Lecturer in Contemporary Russian History, UCL; Deputy Editor, *The Annual Register*

CAUCASUS

Liz Fuller, BA, Caucasus Analyst, Radio Free Europe/Radio Liberty, Prague

PART IV

UNITED STATES OF AMERICA

James Miller, PhD, Associate Professor, Department of History, Carleton University

CANADA

David M.L. Farr, MA, DPhil, LLD, Emeritus Professor of History, Carleton University, Ottawa

MEXICO, CENTRAL AMERICA

Peter Clegg, MSc, PhD, Lecturer in Politics, University of the West of England, Bristol

ARGENTINA, BRAZIL, SOUTH AMERICA
CARIBBEAN

Kurt Perry, Freelance writer on international affairs
Peter Clegg (see Mexico, Central America)

PART V

ISRAEL, PALESTINE, IRAQ

Darren Sagar, MA, Freelance writer specialising in Middle Eastern and South-East Asian affairs

EGYPT, JORDAN, SYRIA, LEBANON

David Butter, MA, Chief Energy Analyst Economist Intelligence Unit; Editor *Business Middle East*; Editor ViewsWire Middle East

SAUDI ARABIA, YEMEN,
ARAB GULF STATES

James Gavin, BA, contributing editor, *Gulf States Newsletter*

SUDAN

Ahmed Al-Shahi, MLitt, DPhil, Former lecturer in Social Anthropology, University of Newcastle Upon Tyne

LIBYA, TUNISIA, ALGERIA,
MOROCCO, WESTERN SAHARA

Richard Lawless, PhD, Emeritus Reader in Modern Middle Eastern Studies, University of Durham; Research Associate, Queen Elizabeth House, University of Oxford.

PART VI

HORN OF AFRICA

KENYA, TANZANIA, UGANDA

NIGERIA, GHANA, SIERRA LEONE,
THE GAMBIA, LIBERIA

FRANCOPHONE AFRICA

CAPE VERDE, SÃO TOMÉ AND PRÍNCIPE

Darren Sagar (see Israel etc)

William Tordoff, MA, PhD, Emeritus Professor of
Government, University of Manchester

Guy Arnold, Writer specialising in Africa and
North-South affairs

Kaye Whiteman, Former publisher, *West Africa*

Christopher Saunders, DPhil, Professor in Department
of Historical Studies, University of Cape Town

PART VII

DEMOCRATIC REPUBLIC OF CONGO,
BURUNDI & RWANDA, MOZAMBIQUE

GUINEA BISSAU, ANGOLA,
ZAMBIA, MALAWI

ZIMBABWE

BOTSWANA, LESOTHO, NAMIBIA,
SWAZILAND, SOUTH AFRICA

Colin Darch, PhD, Senior Information Specialist,
African Studies Library, University of Cape Town

Christopher Saunders (see Cape Verde etc.)

R.W. Baldock, BA, PhD, Editorial Director, Yale
University Press; writer on African affairs

Elizabeth Sidiropoulos, BA Hons, MA, Director of
Studies, South African Institute of International Affairs,
Johannesburg

PART VIII

IRAN

AFGHANISTAN

CENTRAL ASIAN REPUBLICS

INDIA, PAKISTAN, SRI LANKA,
BANGLADESH, NEPAL, BHUTAN

MAURITIUS, SEYCHELLES, COMOROS,
MALDIVES, MADAGASCAR

Keith McLachlan, BA, PhD, Emeritus Professor, School
of Oriental and African Studies, University of London

Matthew Cann, BA

Shirin Akiner, PhD, Lecturer in Central Asian Studies,
School of Oriental and African Studies,
University of London

David Taylor, PhD, Senior Lecturer in Politics with
reference to South Asia, School of Oriental and African
Studies, University of London

Malyn Newitt, BA, PhD, JP, Charles Boxer Professor of
History, Department of Portuguese, King's College, London

PART IX

BURMA (MYANMAR), THAILAND,
MALAYSIA, BRUNEI, SINGAPORE,
VIETNAM, CAMBODIA, LAOS

INDONESIA, EAST TIMOR, PHILIPPINES

CHINA, HONG KONG, TAIWAN

JAPAN

NORTH AND SOUTH KOREA

MONGOLIA

Stephen Levine, PhD, Professor and Head of
School of History, Philosophy, Political Science and
International Relations, Victoria University of Wellington

Norman MacQueen, BA, MSc, DPhil, Head of
Department of Politics, University of Dundee

Phil Deans, BA, PhD, Lecturer in Chinese Politics, School
of Oriental and African Studies, University of London

Ian Nish, PhD, Emeritus Professor of International History,
London School of Economics and Political Science

J.E. Hoare, PhD, Consultant on East Asia; former chargé
d'affaires in Pyongyang

Phil Deans (see China, Hong Kong, Taiwan)

PART X

AUSTRALIA

James Jupp, AM, MSc (Econ), PhD, FASSA, Director, Centre for Immigration and Multicultural Studies, Australian National University, Canberra

PAPUA NEW GUINEA

Norman MacQueen (see Indonesia etc.)

NEW ZEALAND, PACIFIC ISLAND STATES

Stephen Levine (see Burma etc.)

PART XI

UNITED NATIONS

David Travers, BA, Lecturer in Politics and International Relations, Lancaster University; Specialist Advisor on UN to House of Commons' Foreign Affairs Committee

DEFENCE ORGANISATIONS

Paul Cornish, PhD, Peter Carrington Chair in International Security and Head of International Security Programme, Chatham House, London

ECONOMIC ORGANISATIONS

Paul Rayment, MA, Former Director of the Economic Analysis Division of the UN Economic Commission for Europe, Geneva

COMMONWEALTH

Derek Ingram, Consultant Editor of *Gemini News Service*; author and writer on the Commonwealth

FRANCOPHONIE

Kaye Whiteman, (see Francophone Africa)

COMMUNITY OF PORTUGUESE-SPEAKING COUNTRIES

Martin Eaton (see Portugal)

NON-ALIGNED MOVEMENT AND GROUP OF 77

Peter Willets, PhD, Professor of Global Politics, Department of Sociology, The City University, London

ORGANISATION OF THE ISLAMIC CONFERENCE

Darren Sagar (see Israel, Palestine etc.)

EUROPEAN UNION; COUNCIL OF EUROPE

Michael Berendt, Expert on affairs of the European Union

ORGANISATION FOR SECURITY AND CO-OPERATION IN EUROPE; EUROPEAN BANK FOR RECONSTRUCTION AND DEVELOPMENT

Michael Kaser, MA, DLitt, DSocSc, Emeritus Fellow of St Antony's College, Oxford, and Honorary Professor University of Birmingham

OTHER EUROPEAN ORGANISATIONS

Martin Harrison (see France etc.)

ARAB ORGANISATIONS

Darren Sagar (see Israel, Palestine etc.)

AFRICAN ORGANISATIONS AND CONFERENCES

Christopher Saunders (see Guinea Bissau etc.)

ASIA-PACIFIC ORGANISATIONS

Darren Sagar (see Israel, Palestine etc.)

AMERICAN AND CARIBBEAN ORGANISATIONS

Peter Clegg (see Latin America, Caribbean)

PART XII

ECONOMY

Paul Rayment (see Economic Organisations)

PART XIII

MEDICAL, SCIENTIFIC AND INDUSTRIAL RESEARCH

Neil Weir, FRCS, Consultant otolaryngologist and **Lorelly Wilson,** Honorary Teaching Fellow, University of Manchester

INFORMATION TECHNOLOGY

Kristian Saxton, CEO of software consultancy, Aethernet

ENVIRONMENT

Tim Curtis, Regional Editor, *Keesing's Record of World Events*; writer on international affairs

PART XIV

INTERNATIONAL LAW   **Christine Gray,** MA, PhD, Fellow in Law, St John's
                                     College, Cambridge

EUROPEAN COMMUNITY LAW   **N. March Hunnings,** LLM, PhD, Editor, *Encyclopedia
                                     of European Union Law: Constitutional Texts*

LAW IN THE UK   **Jonathan Morgan,** MA, College Lecturer in Law,
                                     Corpus Christi College, Cambridge

LAW IN THE USA   **Robert J. Spjut,** ID, LLD, Member of the State Bars of
                                     California and Florida

PART XV

RELIGION   **Shaunaka Rishi Das,** Director, Oxford Centre for
                                     Hindu Studies, Oxford; **Revd Dr Mark Chapman,**
                                     Vice Principal, Ripon College Cuddesdon, Oxford; **Miri
                                     Freud-Kandel,** MA, PhD, Lecturer in Modern Judaism,
                                     Oxford Centre for Hebrew and Jewish Studies, Junior
                                     Research Fellow, Wolfson College, Oxford; **Peter
                                     Oppenheimer,** MA, President, Oxford Centre for
                                     Hebrew and Jewish Studies; **Timothy Winter,** MA,
                                     Sheikh Zayed Lecturer in Islamic Studies,
                                     University of Cambridge

PART XVI

OPERA   **Rodney Milnes,** OBE, Hon. RAM; Chief Opera Critic,
                                     The Times, 1992-2002

MUSIC   **Francis Routh,** Composer and author; founder director
                                     of the Redcliffe Concerts

BALLET & DANCE   **Jane Pritchard,** Curator of Dance, the Victoria and
                                     Albert Museum of Performing Arts, London

THEATRE   **Matt Wolf,** London theatre critic, *Variety*, the
                                     Associated Press, Bloomberg

CINEMA   **Derek Malcolm,** Cinema critic, *The Guardian*

TV & RADIO   **Raymond Snoddy,** Freelance journalist specialising in
                                     media issues, writing for the *Independent*

VISUAL ARTS   **Anna Somers-Cocks,** Editor, *The Art Newspaper*

ARCHITECTURE   **Patrick Lynch,** RIBA, Lynch Architects, London

LITERATURE   **Alastair Niven,** OBE, Principal, Cumberland Lodge;
                                     formerly Director of Literature, British Council

PART XVI

SPORT   **Paul Newman,** Chief Sports Feature Writer of
                                     The Independent

PART XVIII

DOCUMENTS AND REFERENCE   **AR editorial staff**

PART XIX

OBITUARY

James Bishop, Former Editor of *The Illustrated London News* and Foreign News Editor of *The Times*

PART XX

CHRONICLE OF 2005

MAPS AND DIAGRAMS

Tim Curtis (see the Environment); **AR editorial staff**
Richard Lear, Freelance illustrator

ACKNOWLEDGMENTS

THE editor gratefully acknowledges his debt to a number of individuals and institutions for their help with sources, references and documents. Acknowledgment is also due to the principal sources for the national and IGO data sections (showing the situation at end 2005 unless otherwise stated), namely *Keesing's Record of World Events* (Keesing's Worldwide), the *2005 World Development Report* (Oxford University Press for the World Bank) and the *Financial Times* (London). The Board and the bodies which nominate its members disclaim responsibility for any opinions expressed or the accuracy of facts recorded in this volume.

GNI per capita at PPP is a measure of Gross National Income that allows a standard comparison of real price levels between countries by using the PPP (Purchasing Power Parity) rate. At the PPP rate, one international dollar has the same purchasing power over domestic GNI that the US dollar has over US GNI. PPP GNI per capita is PPP GNI divided by mid-year population

ABBREVIATIONS OF NON-UN INTERNATIONAL ORGANISATIONS

AC	Arctic Council
ACP	African, Caribbean and Pacific states associated with EU
ACS	Association of Caribbean States
AL	Arab League
ALADI	Latin American Integration Association
AMU	Arab Maghreb Union
ANZUS	Australia-New Zealand-US Security Treaty
APEC	Asia-Pacific Economic Co-operation
ASEAN	Association of South-East Asian Nations
AU	African Union
Benelux	Belgium-Netherlands-Luxembourg Economic Union
BSEC	Black Sea Economic Co-operation
CA	Andean Community of Nations
Caricom	Caribbean Community and Common Market
CBSS	Council of the Baltic Sea States
CE	Council of Europe
CEEAC	Economic Community of Central African States
CEFTA	Central European Free Trade Agreement
CEI	Central European Initiative
CIS	Commonwealth of Independent States
COMESA	Common Market of Eastern and Southern Africa
CP	Colombo Plan
CPLP	Community of Portuguese-Speaking Countries
CWTH	The Commonwealth
EBRD	European Bank for Reconstruction and Development
ECO	Economic Co-operation Organisation
ECOWAS	Economic Community of West African States
EEA	European Economic Area
EFTA	European Free Trade Association
EU	European Union
G-8	Group of Eight
GCC	Gulf Co-operation Council
IOC	Indian Ocean Commission
Mercosur	Southern Cone Common Market
NAFTA	North American Free Trade Agreement
NAM	Non-Aligned Movement
NATO	North Atlantic Treaty Organisation
NC	Nordic Council
OAPEC	Organisation of Arab Petroleum Exporting Countries
OAS	Organisation of American States
OECD	Organisation for Economic Co-operation and Development
OECS	Organisation of Eastern Caribbean States
OIC	Organisation of the Islamic Conference
OPEC	Organisation of the Petroleum Exporting Countries
OSCE	Organisation for Security and Co-operation in Europe
PC	Pacific Community
PFP	Partnership for Peace
PIF	Pacific Islands Forum
SAARC	South Asian Association for Regional Co-operation
SADC	Southern African Development Community
SELA	Latin American Economic System
UEMOA	West African Economic and Monetary Union

PREFACE

2005 will be remembered as a year of extreme weather. It began with the world still struggling to come to terms with the scale and aftermath of the Indian Ocean tsunami which had struck in the dying days of 2004. Further calamities were to follow. In Europe during the course of the year there were storms in the north, floods in the east, and extreme drought and forest fires in parts of the west. In July heavy monsoon rains caused fatal floods in India. The USA was battered by a series of hurricanes, including Katrina, which devastated areas of the Gulf coast and laid waste to the historic city of New Orleans. In Kashmir a huge earthquake struck in October, killing tens of thousands and leaving countless others homeless and exposed to a merciless winter.

This sequence of natural disasters was frequently cited as further evidence of the adverse impact of human civilisation upon the global environment. Everywhere, national governments struggled to respond to the disasters: often they were criticised for a lack of foresight in preparing for catastrophe and a failure of organisation in providing an adequate response. While some governments fared better than others in this regard, all were confronted with the diminishing ability of individual nation states to control events in a world which was moving inexorably towards an ever greater degree of globalisation.

Extreme weather—and the environmental concerns with which it was linked—was a dramatic illustration of the increasing interdependence of global civilisation. This was evident too in issues such as the rising global demand for natural resources; questions of international aid and debt; the future of the UN; the ethics associated with accelerating scientific research; and the growing threat of pandemic diseases. In response to this tide of globalisation there were signs of growing resistance in the form of resurgent economic nationalism and, particularly in the developing world, rising popular disaffection with, and opposition towards, encroaching Western culture, neo-liberal economic policies, and international institutions.

This was most apparent in the Islamic world where the gulf with the West seemed to widen still further amid a miasma of incomprehension, mistrust, and intolerance. The spectre of international terrorism continued to stalk the world, with deadly attacks occurring in Pakistan, Egypt, Indonesia, the UK, Jordan, Israel, and Iraq. The core issues of the conflict remained unaddressed. In Iraq there was some progress in the form of free elections, with a high degree of popular participation, but the results were predictably split along ethnic and religious lines. The polls underlined the difficult reality that democracy does not necessarily produce results which are conducive to stability or comfortable for its architects. By the end of the year the country appeared to be fragmenting further amid a rising tide of sectarian violence which threatened to engulf it in civil war.

Meanwhile, Iran, under its new militant President, continued to expand its regional presence and appeared bent on developing a nuclear capability in defiance of the will of the international community. With US military forces still bemired in a crippled Iraq, and public opinion running increasingly against the cost of attritional warfare, Iran seemed willing to ignore Western warnings and continued to develop its nascent nuclear programme with apparent impunity. This nuclear shadow was a stark reminder that increased global interdependence was not synonymous with greater international security.

D.S. Lewis
Aquitaine, April 2005

EXTRACTS FROM PAST VOLUMES

225 years ago

1780. *On the literary education of women.* There are many prejudices entertained against the character of a learned lady; and perhaps if all ladies were profoundly learned, some inconveniences might arise from it; but I must own it does not appear to me, that a woman will be rendered less acceptable in the world, or worse qualified to perform any part of her duty in it, by having employed the time from six to sixteen, in the cultivation of her mind.

200 years ago

1805. *The Battle of Trafalgar, 21 October.* At forty minutes after four all firing ceased, and a complete victory was reported to Lord Nelson, who, having been wounded in the action, survived just long enough to hear the joyful tidings, the fruit of his consummate skill and bravery, and then died, as he had lived, a few minutes before five, with the most heroic resolution. Thus ended the battle of Trafalgar, the most glorious, whether in respect to the science and judgment with which it was conducted, the bravery and spirit with which it was fought, or its fortunate and brilliant result to the conquerors, ever recorded in the naval annals of Great Britain.

175 years ago

1830. *Insurrection in Poland.* Divided and mutilated as Poland now was, it seemed a hopeless prospect for a portion of it to look forward to an unassisted struggle against the gigantic might of Russia, which, in the eyes of Europe, had only to move, in order to crush. To this was to be added the apprehension, that Austria and Prussia, naturally fearing lest their portions of Poland would be endangered if that of Russia was redeemed, would unite with the latter in putting down at once the first efforts of resistance. But Poland prepared for the contest, if it should come, with a stout heart.

150 years ago

1855. *State of the Army in the Crimea.* The unfitness of our military system to cope with the situation in which the army found itself was glaringly exposed. Nothing that was wanted seemed to be forthcoming; everything seemed to be in its wrong place. The troops were perishing from cold, while piles of great coats were lying useless at Balaklava. Porter would have been an invaluable beverage, while rum was pernicious; but nothing but rum was served out to the soldiers, though abundance of porter had been sent out from England.

125 years ago

1880. *The economic progress of China.* During the last forty years its [China's] foreign trade has taken an enormous development, in spite of all that is restrictive, and much that is vexatious, in its provincial administration. Dating only so far back as the year 1865, we find that the foreign trade, then valued at 109,508,686 Haekwan-taels (32,945,620*l*), had advanced to 154,508,686 taels (45,352,606*l*), in 1879, with a corresponding increase of customs revenue. . . . The share in this trade enjoyed by Great Britain, her colonies and India, may be estimated as little short of 40,000,000*l*, or eight-ninths of the whole.

100 years ago

1905. *'Red Sunday' in St. Petersburg.* Next morning [22 January] a huge mass of unarmed men, women and children, with Father Gapon at their head, marched through the streets, singing hymns and carrying crosses and other religious emblems. The approaches to the Winter Palace were guarded by troops, who at first strove to disperse the people with the whips of the Cossacks, but finding this ineffectual used their rifles and swords. The massacre lasted for some hours; unarmed men, women and children were shot or cut down by hundreds as they pushed on towards the palace square.

75 years ago

1930. *Gandhi's salt march.* On March 12 Mr. Gandhi, accompanied by eighty volunteers, began his slow spectacular march of 200 miles on foot from his *ashram* (settlement) near Ahmadabad to Dandi, a village on the sea coast of Surat, to the accompaniment of world-wide newspaper description and comment. In the villages through which he passed he made bitter speeches, and urged the headmen and other minor officials to desert their posts with a view to paralysing the administration. On several occasions he expressed resentment at his non-arrest, which did not accord with his tactical aims. . . Mr. Gandhi and his followers reached Dandi on April 5, and inaugurated their lawless campaign by the making of salt on the seashore. . . He was arrested on May 5.

50 years ago

1955. *The Theatre.* Foreign imports during the year proved both wider in scope and higher in aim than all but a very few of the British products. Outstanding among them was the year's most surprising play-going adventure, *Waiting for Godot*, a piece which lay outside all categories and defied all attempts at definition. Written in French and first presented in Paris, it was the work of an Irishman, Samuel Beckett . . . Deeply symbolic and superficially lacking any coherent meaning, it was produced experimentally at the Arts Theatre (3 August), where it divided the opinions of critics and public, which ranged from ecstasy to contempt.

25 years ago

1980. *The USSR.* Viewed from the Kremlin, 1980 was an exceptionally worrying year. The Soviet leaders probably felt more threatened by events outside Soviet borders than they had done for at least twelve years. The invasion of Afghanistan proved to be a costly and inconclusive business. Among its costs were an almost complete rupture of working relations with the United States, a weakening of Soviet bargaining positions with the West, and an unprecedented volley of abuse from normally compliant Third World countries. Events in Poland opened up the dreadful prospect of independent trade unions and an open opposition flourishing just across Russia's western borders. Given the choice, the Soviet Politburo would no doubt have preferred their neighbours to be visited by the bubonic plague.

THE ANNUAL REGISTER

FOR THE YEAR 2005

I THE YEAR IN REVIEW

THE year 2005 was one of natural disasters. It began with the countries of South-East Asia still struggling with the aftermath of the tsunami which had struck at the end of 2004. In July heavy monsoon rains brought floods in the Indian state of Maharashtra, causing over 1,000 deaths. In August Hurricane Katrina struck Louisiana and neighbouring states in the USA, flooding most of New Orleans. In October there was a massive earthquake in Kashmir, causing over 73,000 deaths and immense damage. Political troubles added to these calamities. A generous world response to the tsunami was partially wasted by muddles and failures in administration. In Maharashtra, the state authorities were criticised for neglecting drainage works and coming too slowly to the rescue of victims. In the USA, the federal, state and city governments were all blamed for inaction before the hurricane and inadequate responses after it, and President George W. Bush was slow to visit the disaster area; though unpublicised private assistance did much to make up for government shortcomings. In Kashmir, the Pakistani and Indian governments co-operated effectively, but tensions persisted on the ground, along the line of control which divided the province.

Less dramatic than these disasters, but perhaps more ominous, was continuing evidence of climate change. The International Climate Change Commission published a report in January, tracing average annual increases in temperature since 1860 and offering gloomy predictions for the next ten years. Permafrost in Siberia was found to be thawing. The British Antarctic Survey reported that glaciers on the continent had shrunk considerably since the 1940s. The report added cautiously that it was too early to say how far these changes were due to human activity; but the consensus of opinion was that climate change was largely caused by man, and the year saw various projects to reduce emissions of greenhouse gases, culminating in an inconclusive world conference in Montreal, Canada, in December.

Oil supplies constituted another focus of anxiety. Optimists pointed out that there were still ample proven reserves of oil; pessimists predicted that production would peak within five years and then decline; everyone knew that supplies were finite. Meanwhile, dependence on natural gas as a source of energy was increasing: for example, Europe was heavily dependent on gas supplies from Russia.

There was also a move back towards nuclear power as a source of energy, despite much public hostility. A less publicised cause for concern lay in increasing demands for water, notably in the USA and China, causing problems which were bound to intensify in coming years.

Another feature of 2005 was certainly man-made: a profusion of terrorist attacks, often by suicide bombers. In Pakistan in March and May there were attacks on Sufi shrines in Islamabad and Baluchistan, and on a Shi'ite mosque in Karachi. In July there were bombs in the UK capital London and Sharm el-Sheikh in Egypt. October brought explosions at holiday resorts in the Indonesian island of Bali. In November there were attacks on hotels in Amman, the capital of Jordan. Throughout the year bomb attacks in Israel were frequent, while in Iraq they were almost ceaseless. Most of these bombings were carried out by Islamic militant groups, a form of religious fanaticism to which the world was becoming grimly accustomed.

Among global institutions, the United Nations had a difficult year. The Volcker Commission investigating corruption in the UN "oil for food" programme for Iraq concluded that senior UN officials had compromised the process of tendering for contracts, and that a former Secretary-General, Boutros Boutros-Ghali, had wrongly influenced the award of a banking contract. The Commission also criticised the current Secretary-General, Kofi Annan, for failing to prevent corruption and mismanagement, but stopped short of finding that he was personally involved in corruption. In September the UN held a special meeting to mark its 60th anniversary and to initiate reforms, but the results were slender. The UN condemned terrorism, but was unable to define it, because a number of states were determined to exclude struggles for national liberation (notably Palestinian actions against Israel) from a definition. Measures to prevent nuclear proliferation and promote disarmament were abandoned, and reform of the UN Security Council was postponed. The UN's desire for reform resembled St Augustine's prayer for chastity: "Lord, make me chaste, but not yet!"

Meanwhile the World Trade Organisation (WTO) was engaged in negotiations for the reduction of agricultural tariffs and subsidies. In October the USA proposed to reduce its subsidies to agriculture by 60 per cent; while the European Commission offered a 70 per cent cut on behalf of the European Union, but was at once reminded by the French that the EU must observe the terms of the Common Agricultural Policy, which had been fixed until 2013. The WTO Conference which met in Hong Kong in December agreed only that farm export subsidies would be phased out by 2013; other decisions were postponed.

The death of Pope John Paul II was a world event of a distinctive kind. He had been a formidable personality, a great communicator and the first truly global Pope, visiting 129 countries during his reign. Conservative in doctrine but radical in politics, he had contributed to the collapse of communism in Eastern Europe, and opposed the Gulf War of 1991, the NATO air bombardment of Serbia in 1995, and the US invasions of Afghanistan (2001) and Iraq (2003). He was the first Pope to visit Israel, and the first to enter a mosque. He left a large pair of shoes for his successor to fill.

Turning to particular countries and regions, Iraq held centre stage. The US government tried hard to keep up a brave front. President Bush declared on 2 February that US forces would remain in Iraq until democracy was secure. The Iraqi elections of 30 January saw voters turning out in encouraging numbers, despite intimidation by insurgents. But the transitional National Assembly then elected was slow to set up a government and draft a constitution, and found it hard to overcome the divisions between Shi'ites, Sunnis, and Kurds. Meanwhile casualties continued to mount, comparatively light among the US and allied forces, but heavy among Iraqi troops, police, and civilians. In June Bush spoke soberly of a time of testing in Iraq, and US Defence Secretary Donald Rumsfeld warned that wars against insurgency in the past had lasted for up to twelve years. It was a grim prospect. Public opinion polls showed declining support for the war, and recruiting for the US Army failed to meet its targets. The opening of the trial of former Iraqi leader Saddam Hussein brought a burst of optimism, but the trial was at once adjourned; and when it resumed the accused seized the opportunity to denounce his accusers. At the end of November, Bush spoke in determined tones of pursuing victory, and of US troops withdrawing at some unspecified time as Iraqi forces took over security responsibilities. Elections for a new National Assembly on 15 December again saw an encouraging turnout, but the results were quickly disputed. The prospects remained gloomy that the USA would yet find a satisfactory way out of its commitment in Iraq.

In Iran, presidential elections in June produced an overwhelming victory for Mahmoud Ahmadinejad, a self-declared heir of the Islamic revolution of 1979 and a violent critic of Israel. On 26 October he made a speech on "A World without Zionism", quoting Ayatollah Khomeini (the leader of the revolution in 1979) declaring that Israel should be wiped from the map; and in December he attacked the Holocaust as a Western myth used to justify the creation of Israel. These speeches carried all the more weight because Iran was potentially a nuclear power. In August the Iranian government resumed the enrichment of its uranium stocks into a form which could be used to produce either nuclear energy or a nuclear bomb. Iran maintained its right to manufacture a nuclear weapon, but disclaimed any present intention of doing so, an enigmatic and possibly ominous position.

Two striking developments took place elsewhere in the Middle East. Syrian troops withdrew from Lebanon, where they had been stationed since 1976. This move followed the assassination in February, in a massive car-bomb explosion, of Rafik al-Hariri, a former Prime Minister of Lebanon, who had at one time worked closely with the Syrians but later opposed their military presence in the country. The responsibility for this crime remained uncertain, but public opinion in Lebanon rapidly concluded that it was the work of Syria and the pro-Syrian Lebanese government. Large-scale demonstrations in the Lebanese capital, Beirut, demanded the withdrawal of Syrian troops, which in fact took place in March and April. Meanwhile, relations between Israel and the Palestinians improved. In January Ariel Sharon, the Israeli Prime Minister, welcomed the election of a new President of the Palestinian National Authority, Mahmoud Abbas; and in February the two leaders met at Sharm el-Sheikh and agreed to end all violence between Israelis and Palestinians. In August the Israeli government removed some 8,500 Israeli settlers from the Gaza Strip, and passed control of the area to the Palestinian National Authority. Hopeful commentators found in these events a turning-point in Middle Eastern affairs and signs of reconciliation between enemies. The reality proved different. Palestinian militants quickly claimed that what happened in Gaza today would be repeated tomorrow in the West Bank and Jerusalem, while Sharon made it amply clear that he would make no compromise over the security of the Israeli state and its people. The Israeli-Palestinian conflict again proved intractable.

The Kashmir dispute between Pakistan and India had lasted for much the same time as the Palestinian problem. In February there was a slight improvement, when the two Foreign Ministers agreed that a direct bus route should be opened between the two zones of Kashmir. The first buses ran on 7 April, despite threats by Islamic militants to turn them into coffins; and thus an apparently prosaic bus service came to symbolise an improvement in relations between India and Pakistan. But the fundamental problem remained, and the claims of the two countries to Kashmir were not resolved.

The most spectacular country of 2005 was China. The Chinese economy had been growing at a remarkable rate, averaging about 9 per cent growth per year from 1997 to 2004, and the IMF forecast 8.5 per cent for 2005. In 1980 Chinese textiles had made up 5 per cent of world production; by 2004 they formed 26 per cent, and still rising. In 2004 Chinese production of computers reached half the world total. This headlong economic growth impinged on other countries, notably in the textile trade. At the beginning of 2005 a World Trade Organisation quota system for textiles expired, and Chinese exports to the USA and the EU increased dramatically, provoking sharp disputes. The EU and the USA both imposed restrictions on Chinese imports, and the US authorities demanded that China should relax the fixed exchange rate for the yuan, which they claimed was undervalued by up to 40 per cent, making Chinese exports artificially cheap. In July the Chinese agreed to revalue the yuan but only by 2 per cent. Rather than pegging the yuan against the dollar, the People's Bank of China announced that the yuan was being allowed to float against a "market basket" of other currencies, whilst keeping it valued in a tight band rather than letting it trade freely. Meanwhile EU negotiations in the Chinese capital, Beijing, produced no agreement. The Chinese were quite prepared to stand up to the heavyweights of the world economy.

China also strengthened its military power. Defence expenditure, on official figures, doubled over five years from 2001. The Chinese had about 700 missiles targeted on Taiwan; and they extended their influence in the Indian Ocean, acquiring port facilities in Pakistan and Bangladesh. They increased their political and economic influence in Africa, notably in Zimbabwe, Sudan, and Angola. In Latin America, China developed its relations with Venezuela, to provide oil for its booming economy. The centre of Chinese foreign policy, however, lay in the country's relations with its Asian neighbours and the USA. In April the Chinese signed an agreement with India on a strategic partnership, and followed up with talks on their frontier disputes. In June China concluded an agreement settling the final section of its frontier with Russia on the Amur river. Relations with Japan were more difficult. The Chinese government denounced new Japanese history textbooks for schools, which presented a favourable view of Japan's role in World War II. The two countries were in dispute over their frontier in the East China Sea, with its undersea gas fields. Behind these current relations stretched a centuries-old rivalry, and ahead lay a potential conflict for the leadership of Asia. Chinese relations with the USA were marked by an uneasy mixture of hostility and interdependence. The two countries were opposed to one another over Taiwan, Korea, North and South, and Iran. They were ideological rivals, and parts of US public opinion denounced China for its communist dictatorship and denial of human rights. Yet at the same time the two countries developed close economic relations. US consumers bought vast quantities of Chinese exports, and the Chinese used some of their dollar earnings to buy US Treasury bonds, thereby helping to finance the US budget deficit in a curious partnership between communist and capitalist regimes. The next few years would doubtless show whether the pace of Chinese economic growth could be sustained, and whether it would prove compatible with what remained an inflexible political system.

Africa attracted attention for very different reasons. Much of the continent was poverty-stricken, and parts were on the verge of famine. The spread of HIV/AIDS continued, afflicting millions of people. In politics, there was a move towards peace in Sudan in January, when a comprehensive agreement was concluded between the government and its opponents in the south, who had sustained a long rebellion. This complex agreement included arrangements for power-sharing and for the distribution of oil revenues between different parts of the country; but even at the start it excluded some opposition groups and failed to settle the conflict in Darfur, where before the month was out government aircraft bombed a village and killed over a hundred people. In June a further national reconciliation agreement was signed in Cairo, Egypt, aimed at setting up a new unified government; but in July this attempt was thrown into confusion by the death, in a helicopter crash, of John Garang, the opposition leader who had just been appointed Vice-President. A new government was finally formed in September, but at the end of the year fighting continued in Darfur and had broken out afresh in the north east. A year's efforts had left peace out of reach.

Elsewhere, several African countries were in a state of unrest. For example, in Somalia a new government was proclaimed in January, with no fewer than forty-seven ministers and forty assistant ministers; yet in practice Somalia had no effective government at all. In Zimbabwe, elections were dominated by intimidation and corruption, and President Robert Mugabe's "land reforms" brought the country to the verge of famine. In Côte d'Ivoire, the South African President Thabo Mbeki negotiated an agreement to end the civil war which had divided the country since 2002; but fighting soon resumed, and in September the northern forces repudiated South African mediation and ended the April agreement.

Other countries professed themselves anxious to help Africa in its difficulties. In June a meeting of the Finance Ministers of the G-7 Group of industrialised countries agreed to cancel large debts owed by fourteen of the poorest countries in Africa, and to arrange for US$25 billion of new aid to the continent. The G-8 Group (the G-7 plus Russia) met in Scotland in July, with aid to Africa as one of its major objectives. A simultaneous public campaign sought to "make poverty history", and a series of rock concerts called "Live-8" heightened public consciousness of Africa's problems. The publicity was intense, but the results were limited. The G-8 countries agreed only to provide US$15-20 billion of new aid between 2005 and 2010; and it was doubtful how much of this aid, even if it was delivered, would achieve its purposes.

In Russia, the conflict between Chechen separatists and the government continued. In March Russian forces killed the Chechen leader, Aslan Maskhadov, removing his body to an unmarked grave to prevent its becoming an object of pilgrimage. President Vladimir Putin of Russia thus demonstrated his determination to win the war; but the resolve of the separatists also remained unbroken. In this battle of wills, Putin secured the tacit support of many outside countries. The EU, often ostentatiously concerned with human rights, allowed the Russian operations against the Chechens to pass with little comment; while the US government welcomed Putin as an ally in its "war" against Islamic terrorism. In domestic affairs, Putin behaved like an elected dictator, looking back nostalgically to the days of a more tightly-controlled society. In his state of the nation address on 25 April he described the collapse of the Soviet Union as "a major geopolitical disaster of the century", separating tens of millions of Russian nationals from their homeland and causing disintegration inside the country. Corruption and violence were endemic, so that a Russian think-tank claimed to calculate that the average bribe paid by businessmen to officials was US$136,000; and when gas canisters exploded in a department store in St Petersburg at the end of December, it was at once assumed that this was an attack by a rival firm.

One of Russia's near neighbours, Ukraine, had until recently been part of the Soviet Union, and now balanced uneasily between Russia and the West. At the end of 2004 it had appeared that the victory of Viktor Yushchenko in the "orange revolution" had shifted Ukraine decisively out of the Russian orbit; but when he became President, Yushchenko was careful to face both ways. He declared Ukraine's intention of seeking to join NATO and the EU; but his first official visit abroad was to Moscow. The Russians had powerful means of influence to hand. In May the Russian companies which supplied most of Ukraine's fuel suddenly reduced their deliveries, forcing the Ukrainian government to abandon a plan to cut prices. The West had economic and political attractions for Ukraine; but Russia could turn off the gas tap.

The Russians also exercised influence in Central Asia, as they had in the past, maintaining military and air bases in Tajikistan and Kyrgyzstan. Russia was not alone. The USA held bases in Kyrgyzstan and Uzbekistan, and China was building an oil pipeline from Kazakhstan to Xinjiang, for which it had signed an agreement in 2004. The area had again become a focus for international rivalry, and Central Asia should be on any list of likely bones of contention in the future.

In Europe, one of the central questions of the year was the fate of the proposed constitution for the European Union, which had been accepted by the member governments in November 2004 and then went for ratification by the individual states, in fifteen by their legislatures and in ten by referendums. By the end of May 2005 nine states had approved the constitution, but on 29 May the French electorate rejected it in a referendum, by 55 to 45 per cent in a high turn-out. On 1 June the Dutch voted even more heavily against, by 62 to 38 per cent. Soon afterwards, the UK government shelved its plans to hold a referendum, so that three important countries had either rejected the constitution or deferred action on it. These events left the EU in disarray. Some members (including Latvia, Cyprus, Malta, and Luxembourg) went ahead and ratified the treaty; while others (including the Czech Republic, Denmark, Finland, and Poland) deferred their votes indefinitely. At the level of public debate, therefore, nothing was decided. Beneath the surface, however, the momentum towards greater integration was maintained, and several of the institutions which were to be established under the constitution simply went ahead. Even so, the future of the European Union looked uncertain, and the gap between elite and popular opinion was dangerously wide.

The EU, uncertain as to its own identity, also faced the long-standing question of Turkey's membership, which raised profound issues of economics, demography, religion, and geography. On 3 October 2005 an EU summit meeting resolved that formal negotiations for Turkish entry should begin at once, though they were likely to be long and difficult. The fundamental questions as to whether Turkey was a European country, and what meaning the European Union attached to its own name, remained unresolved.

In the autumn France was shaken by riots, starting in the northern outskirts of Paris and spreading to cities across the country. There was only one death during the unrest, but thousands of cars were burned, along with many buildings, including primary schools. President Jacques Chirac declared a state of emergency, and gradually the disturbances died down, leaving people wondering what they had signified. Were they no more than random violence, like burning cars on New Year's Eve, or did they mark a crisis for the French model of integration? Other countries watched in dismay, and wondered whether they might face similar difficulties.

Among all these changes, the USA remained the only superpower, with interests across the globe and with economic and military strength greater than any rival. It also claimed to be a power with a directing idea: "the ultimate goal of ending tyranny in our world", as President Bush declared in his second inaugural speech. It was true that the US government was selective in its approach to democracy, regarding street demonstrations in Georgia as a victory for liberty but an election victory in Iran as illegitimate. But the idea ran deep in US politics: Woodrow Wilson went to war in 1917 to make the world safe for democracy; and the impulse it gave to US actions should not be under-rated.

The USA, for all its power, however, also had its weaknesses and limitations. In Iraq, a large US army could do no more than struggle to contain the insurgent forces, with pacification nowhere in sight. Moreover, as long as troops were tied down in Iraq, the USA had no land forces to spare for operations elsewhere. Even in the Western hemisphere the USA had its difficulties, and the "summit of the Americas" held in Argentina at the end of October was far from being a success for Bush. But history showed that the USA had remarkable powers of resilience and adaptability, which might again assert themselves.

The perspective of a single year can be misleading. A Canadian academic report on war and peace in the 21st century published in October 2005 was cautiously optimistic, finding that since the end of the Cold War the number of armed conflicts and casualties in war had diminished substantially, despite events in Iraq and sub-Saharan Africa. Terrorist attacks had been widespread and unsettling, but calculated in cold blood the number of casualties had not been large. This was encouraging news, but we were not likely to be carried away. At the end of 2005 the world remained full of dangers. How was the United States going to get out of Iraq without a serious loss of prestige and influence, not to mention loss of life? How many countries would soon possess nuclear weapons, and what would they do with them? Terrorist attacks might not actually kill large numbers of people, but the prospect of a prolonged struggle by Islamic militants against their enemies in the east as well as the west was a gloomy one. Would the growth of China's power lead to external conflict or internal upheaval, or both? It is hard to end an overview of the year on a note of optimism.

II WESTERN AND SOUTHERN EUROPE

UNITED KINGDOM—SCOTLAND—WALES—NORTHERN IRELAND

UNITED KINGDOM

CAPITAL: London   AREA: 245,000 sq km   POPULATION: 59,400,000
OFFICIAL LANGUAGES: English; Welsh in Wales   POLITICAL SYSTEM: multiparty monarchy
HEAD OF STATE: Queen Elizabeth II (since Feb '52)
RULING PARTY: Labour Party (since May '97)
HEAD OF GOVERNMENT: Tony Blair, Prime Minister (since May '97)
MAIN IGO MEMBERSHIPS (NON-UN): NATO, CWTH, EU, OSCE, CE, PC, OECD, G-8
CURRENCY: pound sterling (end-'05 US$1=£0.58248, €1=£0.68710)
GNI PER CAPITA: US$33,940, US$31,460 at PPP ('04)

THE United Kingdom played a prominent role in world events in 2005, taking over the leadership of both the G-8 and European Council. The Labour government, which won its third term in office in a general election held in May, led a confident nation in celebration at the beginning of July, when it was announced that London had beaten off its competitors to be selected to host the 2012 Olympic Games. The news broke as Prime Minister Tony Blair met leaders of the world's most powerful nations at Gleneagles in Scotland to consider the twin issues of world poverty and climate change. In an instant, the mood of national optimism was destroyed, however, as four young men detonated homemade bombs on public transport during London's rush hour on the morning of 7 July. The remaining months of the year were dominated by the consequences of this event.

POLITICS. As expected, the 5 May general election returned Labour for an unprecedented third successive term in office, but with a substantially reduced majority of sixty-six from its previous unassailable majority of 165 in the House of Commons (the lower chamber of the bicameral Parliament). The swing against Labour, widely attributed to public dissatisfaction with the UK's participation in the Iraq war, left Prime Minister Blair in a weakened position. But while some commentators predicted that the results would inevitably hasten his resignation as Prime Minister, he remained publicly bullish on his determination to serve a full third term in office. Within hours, Blair and his Chancellor of the Exchequer, Gordon Brown, were locked in a power struggle over the composition of the Cabinet, and all seemed back to normal in the "New Labour" government.

Electorally, Labour was hit hardest in London and the south east, while the government fared better than many had expected in other areas. Voters in the West Midlands, for example, were not swayed by the closure of the MG Rover car factory at Longbridge in April. However, Blairite MPs were dealt two decisive blows in traditionally safe seats: loyalist Maggie Jones was defeated by Peter Law in Aneurin Bevan's old constituency of Blaenau Gwent in Wales (see p. 29), and Oona King was defeated by former Labour MP George Galloway, now standing for the anti-war Respect Party, in a bitter campaign at Bethnal Green and Bow in east London. Schools Minister Stephen Twigg unexpectedly lost the Enfield Southgate seat that he had taken so memorably from Conservative Michael Portillo in 1997. Two other ministers, Melanie Johnson and Chris Leslie, were also unseated.

Support for the government had been eroded by a combination of middle-class hostility to the war in Iraq and working-class fear of immigration. The first group turned to the Liberal Democrats, who gained ten seats on their 2001 total, increasing their share of the vote from 18.3 per cent to 23 per cent. Most of this was at the expense of the Labour Party; swings of up to 17 per cent were recorded, for example, in Labour seats in the university areas of Bristol, Manchester, and Cambridge, where opposition to university tuition fees had further eroded support for the government. However, Liberal Democrat leader Charles Kennedy's hopes that the party could "decapitate" leading Tories proved unfounded, and the results fell short of the breakthrough that had been thought possible.

Conservative Party leader Michael Howard attempted to sweep up the second group of disaffected labour support with a populist campaign that focused on the "failure" of Labour's immigration policy. However, it was also the case that the British National Party doubled its share of the vote in some of the 112 seats it contested, doing particularly well in rundown inner city constituencies with no tradition of Conservative politics. The Conservatives gained thirty-three seats on 2001, including Putney, Wimbledon, Hammersmith and Fulham, Hemel Hempstead, and Ilford North. But while targeted effectively at key marginal constituencies, this did not result in an increased share of the vote, which remained the same as in 2001 at 33 per cent. The party notably failed to attract women voters, who voted Tory in significantly lower numbers than did men. Following the election Howard announced on 6 May that he would stand down once the party had had a chance to review the rules regarding the election of the leader. "I am sixty-three years old," he said. "At the time of the next general election in four or five years time I will be sixty-seven or sixty-eight years old, and I believe that is simply too old to lead the party into government." The decision made him the fourth Conservative leader in eight years to resign.

In his own Sedgefield constituency, the Prime Minister was opposed by Reg Keys, the father of a British soldier who had died in Iraq. Speaking on the podium just yards away from Blair after the results were declared, Keys said that the 4,252 votes which he had polled "sent a clear and resounding message about the Iraq war". Distinctly discomfited, Blair acknowledged that the people wanted a Labour government "but with a reduced majority", promising to "respond to that sensibly, wisely and responsibly". He then returned to London for a victory celebration at the National Portrait Gallery.

Blair managed to irritate several senior colleagues in the post-election Cabinet reshuffle; this was the first indication that a reduced majority would make it less easy for the Prime Minister to impose his will on either his government colleagues or Parliament. One indication of the ongoing tension between the Prime Minister's allies and supporters of Chancellor Gordon Brown was the decision of

Labour's election co-ordinator, Alan Milburn, to stand down from Cabinet following the election. The former Health Secretary had resigned in 2003 after a long struggle with the Treasury; this rivalry resurfaced when Milburn returned to run the election campaign. (Brown, who at the outset had felt excluded from electoral strategy, had been brought back to the centre of the campaign—frequently appearing in the company of Blair—in an attempt to ameliorate the high negative personal poll ratings of the Prime Minister.) In other changes, responsibility for combating antisocial behaviour was taken away from Home Secretary Charles Clarke. This area, combined with fostering local government and community cohesion, was to be given to a new Minister of Communities and Local Government, reporting to John Prescott at the Office of the Deputy Prime Minister. Prescott reportedly refused to allow the Prime Minister to appoint David Blunkett to that role, and it was finally given to former Education Minister David Miliband. Ruth Kelly, Secretary at the Department for Education and Skills, was reportedly horrified to hear that unelected political adviser Andrew Adonis was to be given a seat in the House of Lords (the upper chamber) and a position as minister in her department. In his recent role as Blair's education advisor, Adonis had been responsible for the government's most controversial education initiatives, and was widely disliked and mistrusted within the party.

In other major changes, Geoff Hoon was moved from Defence to become Leader of the House of Commons. He was replaced by former Health Secretary John Reid. Patricia Hewitt became Health Secretary. Peter Hain took over as Northern Ireland Secretary at what promised to be a difficult point in the peace process, given the overwhelming defeat of the Ulster Unionist Party in the election (see p. 31). Alan Johnson was promoted to the newly created Department of Productivity, Energy and Industry. The other big winner of the election was David Blunkett, who was brought back into government as Work and Pensions Secretary.

Blunkett's resurrection proved to be short-lived, however. Having resigned as Home Secretary in December 2004 over his affair with Kimberley Quinn (see AR 2004, p. 13), he had played an important role in the election campaign, spearheading the appeal to voters in the Labour heartlands of the north. But doubts remained about his judgement, and despite returning to government, by the autumn he faced multiple allegations of impropriety. These focused on his relationship with DNA Bioscience, and his failure to consult the Cabinet Office's advisory committee on business appointments before taking up a directorship with the company in April. He had simultaneously invested UK£15,000 in the company, transferring ownership of the shares—estimated just months later to be worth UK£300,000 if the company were floated—into a trust for his sons after the election. It was clearly the case, moreover, that Blunkett had been advised on several occasions that the ministerial code of conduct required him to register these interests; but he had failed to do so. This, in combination with further lurid revelations surrounding his personal life, led to his resignation on 2 November.

At long last, the Conservative Party showed signs of life in 2005. Not only did the famous Tory electoral machine appear to enjoy a revival during the campaign, but the subsequent leadership election attracted a wholly unexpected level of interest in the news media. Party insiders initially despaired in September, when Michael Howard's proposal to restore to the parliamentary party the power to select the leader failed to gain the required two-thirds majority to be adopted. The tenure of the disastrous Iain Duncan Smith as leader had been widely attributed to the "one-member, one-vote" method, which placed the decision in the hands of the grassroots members who were increasingly old, reactionary, and out of touch with popular opinion. Yet fears that this mistake would be repeated in 2005 proved unfounded. Five contenders threw their hats into the ring, representing between them a broad spectrum of Conservative opinion. In this sense the race was from the beginning a genuine ballot on the future direction of the party. Shadow Home Secretary David Davis was the frontrunner, a eurosceptic and Thatcherite, who favoured small government and cutting taxes; former Foreign Secretary Malcolm Rifkind, who had only been returned to Westminster in the May election after eight years in the political wilderness, vowed to turn the party back towards the centre of the political spectrum. Kenneth Clarke, former Chancellor, while the most prominent of the contenders and likely to be popular with the electorate, was thought to be too pro-European for most Conservative tastes. Dr Liam Fox, co-chair of the election campaign, was also eurosceptic and a social conservative on the right of the party. Thirty-nine-year-old David Cameron, who had first entered Parliament in 2001, was the most prominent member of the modernising "Notting Hill set" of MPs determined to break with the past, but the least experienced of the candidates.

The big surprise came at the party conference in Blackpool in the first week of October, where Cameron's compelling performance made him a serious contender. His call for modernisation was clear. "There's one thing Gordon Brown fears more than anything else: a Conservative Party that has the courage to change, so let's give him the fright of his life." Davis, by contrast, gave a speech stressing law and order issues, judged by most to be competent but not inspiring. Rifkind was the first candidate to drop out, throwing his support behind Kenneth Clarke in the week before the first ballot of MPs, who according to the party rules had to narrow the field to two candidates to present to the membership. But this was not enough for Clarke to survive the vote on 18 October, putting an end to his political ambitions on his third attempt at gaining the leadership. With the bulk of his support going to Cameron, and the right wing split between Davis and Fox, the outcome of the second ballot two days later was no surprise, and the "two Davids roadshow", taking the campaign to party members around the country, began. They formed an interesting contrast, with the Eton and Oxford educated Cameron promoting an agenda of change and a return to a "one nation" approach in order to recapture the middle ground; while Davis, who grew up on a council estate in London, argued that the party should continue to champion right-wing values. Cameron emerged as the clear winner in the postal vote of 300,000 members, when the result was announced on 6 December.

His first weeks in office were impressive. His reshuffled shadow Cabinet team notably included former leader William Hague, as shadow Foreign Secretary; and Kenneth Clarke, in charge of a new democracy taskforce to examine issues surrounding constitutional reform. David Davis remained in place as shadow Home Secretary and Liam Fox became shadow Defence Secretary. George Osborne remained as Shadow Chancellor. Malcolm Rifkind, miffed at being replaced by William Hague, returned to the backbenches. It was, on the whole, a fairly rightwing bunch. However, it was Cameron's confident and enjoyable first performance at Prime Minister's question time on 8 December that attracted most attention. By offering support for Tony Blair's controversial education bill, he opened the first round in his strategy to reclaim the middle ground by dividing the Prime Minister from his backbench rebels.

Cameron's leadership was very bad news for the Liberal Democrats. While the party's performance in the election was, on paper, the best in eighty years, with nearly one-quarter of the popular vote and a net gain of ten seats, this was less than expected at a time when the party should have had no trouble capitalising on popular mistrust of Blair and the continued rightwing isolation of the Conservatives. Frustration over Charles Kennedy's laid-back style of leadership mounted in the autumn, when the much touted policy review did not appear to get off the ground. It was difficult to see in what direction the party should go once Cameron had entered the frame. With the centre of British political debate increasingly crowded, some members argued for a move to the left. This was by no means a majority view, however. The party was essentially divided and unsure of itself. By mid-December, attention was focusing on Charles Kennedy's future. Disquiet on his front bench was fuelled by long-running whispers in Westminster about his erratic performance, said to be the result of a serious alcohol problem. Kennedy attempted to defend his position, warning senior colleagues that he had no intention of resigning. While speculation continued to mount in the press, it was clear as the year ended that he did not intend to go quietly.

Former Conservative Prime Minister Sir Edward Heath died at the age of eighty-nine in July. Popular former Northern Ireland Secretary Mo Mowlam died on 19 August after a long struggle with cancer, just days after the unexpected death of former Foreign Secretary Robin Cook, who collapsed while hill-walking in Scotland. Cook had resigned from the Cabinet in protest over the decision to invade Iraq. (For obituaries see, respectively, pp. 535; 542-43; 529.)

TERRORISM AND POLITICS. Existing powers of detention without trial of foreign suspects lapsed on 14 March, following a decision of the law lords in December 2004. This imposed an important date by which Home Secretary Charles Clarke needed to get new anti-terror legislation onto the statute book. But even after substantial amendment giving judges a greater role in the decision to impose new "control orders", the government's prevention of terrorism bill only passed after an extraordinary week of confrontation between peers, Parliament and the Home Secretary. The first blow came at the end of February with a vote that cut the Labour majority to just fourteen in the House of Commons. Astonishingly, seventeen Liberal Democrat MPs were absent from the chamber, including Charles Kennedy, in what was acknowledged by the party to be a "cock-up". Critics in the Lords remained unconvinced that revised procedures contained sufficient safeguards to prevent arbitrary detention, and on 8 March peers voted by a 187 majority to impose a "sunset clause" on the bill, meaning that it would expire and be subject to another review in November. This and other amendments were opposed by government but the Lords refused to back down, returning the bill to MPs several times until a deal was finally struck on 11 March—a numbing thirty-one hours into the parliamentary sitting—to reject the sunset clause in favour of a "full re-examination" that the opposition could claim amounted to the same thing. Speculation that the Prime Minister was cynically provoking a rebellion in order to look more "tough on terrorism" than the opposition during the upcoming general election campaign was vigorously denied.

Clarke used emergency powers to impose the new control orders on the ten former Belmarsh prison detainees who were released as the old legislation lapsed. The conditions of their release were strict, including partial house arrest with a night-time curfew, electronic tagging, Internet and mobile telephone restriction, financial controls, and a ban on meeting with any person without prior permission from the Home Office. Official ineptitude surrounding the implementation of the orders, including false allegations that the ten had been linked to a ricin plot in London, led to an apology in April and served to confirm fears from human rights campaigners that the new powers were open to abuse.

14 April saw the collapse of the "ricin" trial, in the middle of an election campaign in which fears over asylum and immigration were already playing an important role. Allegations of an al-Qaida-sponsored plot to poison the capital were based on the testimony of Mohammed Meguerba, an Algerian who had been arrested and interrogated in his native country after leaving the UK in 2002. His allegations centred on his relationship with Kamel Bourgass, an Algerian illegal immigrant in the UK—who was already serving a life sentence for murdering a police officer—and other Algerians based in London. However, Meguerba's evidence was not thought reliable enough to put before a jury, and many of his more far-fetched claims were clearly untrue. Eight other Algerians were set free with no conspiracy found; the jury was deadlocked on Bourgass. It seemed that he was a dangerous but inept loner who had never tried to produce ricin from the recipes which he had discovered on the Internet. The case highlighted concerns about the use of evidence obtained under interrogation from countries with records of torture.

These arguments were pushed aside in the summer, however, with the shocking attacks on London's public transport system perpetrated by four suicide bombers. On the morning of 7 July there were three explosions on the underground system during the morning rush hour, in central London. A fourth bomb was detonated on a bus next to Tavistock Square. In all, the bombers killed fifty-two people and inflicted hundreds of injuries. Timed to coincide with the start of the G-8 summit being hosted by Tony Blair at Gleneagles, the bombings came just a day after Londoners had received the news of the successful bid to hold the 2012 Olympics. G-8 leaders were quick to issue a joint statement expressing unity in the face of terrorism. Interrupting the summit to return to London, the Prime Minister declared from Downing Street that "we will show by our spirit and dignity and by a quiet and true strength that there is in the British people, that our values will long outlast theirs. The purpose of terrorism is just that, it is to terrorise people and we will not be terrorised." Blair attended a meeting of the government's emergency committee, Cobra, with senior ministers and security officials before returning to the summit that evening. As terrible scenes of the disaster were broadcast around the world, London became the focus of international attention and sympathy. The city's vulnerability was underscored two weeks later when, in an echo of the events of 7 July, four incidents involving explosives on public transport occurred in a co-ordinated attack at lunchtime on 21 July. This time there were no casualties. A fifth unexploded device was later discovered abandoned in north London.

In the aftermath of the London bombings police and intelligence services acted quickly to track down the perpetrators and to prevent further attacks. This involved the implementation of "operation kratos", a new shoot-to-kill policy for dealing with suspected suicide bombers. This decision was defended by Metropolitan Police Commissioner Sir Ian Blair, in spite of the killing on 22 July of Jean Charles de Menezes, a twenty-seven-year-old Brazilian resident of London, who had been mistaken by surveillance officers for one of the suspects, Hussain Osman. Completely innocent of any wrongdoing, de Menezes was shot in the head at close range by police on board a tube train at Stockwell in south London. At the inquest on 25 July, it was revealed that he had been shot eight times. The inquiry into the shooting was conducted by the Independent Police Complaints Commission, led by its leader of operations, Roy Clark. The promised "full co-operation" of the police was less than forthcoming, however. A leaked extract from the commission's report revealed on 16 August that initial police accounts of the incident were misleading and sharply at odds with witness statements and closed-circuit television footage. De Menezes was not wearing a bulky jacket and did not flee from armed officers or vault over ticket barriers, stumbling into a train carriage, as had originally been claimed. He had, in fact, walked casually into the station in a denim jacket, with no rucksack, stopping on the way to pick up a free newspaper. At the end of September, it emerged that within hours of the incident, Sir Ian Blair had personally ordered that investigators be denied access to the scene of the shooting, an instruction that was overruled by the Home Office. At the year's end it was thought that the report, due in January 2006, would be handed over to the Crown Prosecution Service so that charges could be considered.

The incident reflected the level of tension among police officers. Events moved quickly in the search for the failed bombers amid fears that they might attempt to launch further attacks. The first, Yasin Hassan Omar, a Somali legally residing in the UK, was arrested in Birmingham on 27 July. The remaining suspects were taken into custody two days later, during raids in London and Rome. Muktar Said-Ibrahim, Hussain Osman, and Ramsi Mohammed were all either naturalised citizens or legally resident in the UK. The suicide bombers who died in the 7 July attacks had meanwhile been identified as Germaine Lindsay, Shehzad Tanweer, and Hasib Hussain. Ringleader Mohammad Sidique Khan was a popular thirty-year-old primary school teaching assistant and youth worker in the deprived Leeds suburb of Beeston, where two of the other bombers also resided. There was widespread shock and sadness that these were British men, with conventional upbringings. A hire car left by them near Luton railway station was subsequently found to have contained a number of home-made bombs containing high explosives, and nails to act as shrapnel. While police and intelligence actions were generally praised in the weeks following the bombings, considerable criticism was nevertheless levelled at the UK security service, MI5, for failing to anticipate the attacks. At the end of July the *New York Times* published details of a leaked assessment written by the UK's Joint Terrorist Analysis Centre shortly before 7 July, which concluded that there was no group with the intent or capability to launch an attack from within the UK, and authorised a downgrading of the security alert status.

By this time, discussions were already under way to formulate the government's response to these atrocities. Meetings of the leaders of the three largest political parties presented a show of unity over the summer. The meetings were convened to consider new measures drawn up by the country's senior police officers, in the hope that a cross-party agreement could be reached before the publication of the new terrorist bill due to be considered by Parliament in the autumn. Before any such agreement, however, and without consultation, on 5 August Tony Blair announced a series of measures designed to strengthen the country's defences against terrorism, including twelve specific points, briefly: new grounds for deportation including fostering hatred or advocating violence to further one's beliefs; a new offence of condoning or "glorifying" terrorism; automatic refusal of asylum for anyone associated with terrorist activity; the possibility of with-drawing citizenship to naturalised citizens engaged in extremist activity; consultation on time limits for extradition cases involving terrorism; a proposal to extend periods of detention without charge; control orders for UK nationals; more special judges to process control orders; a ban on extremist organisations; a review of citizenship ceremonies and advice on integrating isolated parts of the Muslim community; the power to close a place of worship used to promote extremism; and acceleration of proposed new border security measures, including an international database of individuals excluded from entry.

This was the end of any potential consensus. Muslim organisations across the political and theological spectrum were almost united in condemning what were seen as draconian measures aimed entirely at their community and bound to lead to further alienation and radicalisation. In contrast to the government's view, many commentators were quick to point out that it was the country's involvement in the Iraq war that had made the UK a target for attack in the first place. Charles Kennedy accused the Prime Minister of threatening fundamental liberties and many of the government's own backbenchers, including John Denham, chair of the home affairs select committee, argued against the abandonment of a consensual approach, and worried that the Prime Minister was reacting to criticism in the tabloid press. But the government was defiant. At the beginning of September Clarke warned judges not to frustrate plans to deport terror suspects by refusing to accept assurances of good treatment from countries with poor human rights records. This was contrary to European case law on human rights, which was clear on the illegality of deporting persons when there was a reasonable expectation that they would face torture or ill treatment upon arrival. This would apply to all ten suspects currently subject to control orders, nine of whom who were awaiting deportation to Algeria. Clarke also convened an anti-terrorism summit of fifty EU justice and home affairs ministers in September to plead the case for greater European co-operation on anti-terrorism, and to argue in favour of the government's anti-terror package and amending the European Convention on Human Rights.

Opposition mounted when Clarke outlined his draft anti-terror bill on 15 September. Most controversial of the new powers sought was the proposal to extend the maximum period of detention without trial from fourteen days to three months. But other proposals were also subject to criticism, including new offences of indirectly inciting terrorism; of glorifying terrorist acts; of publishing, possessing or disseminating publications that indirectly incited terrorist acts or were likely to be useful to a person preparing to commit a terrorist act; and of attending a terrorist training camp. Some concessions were made when the bill was published formally on 12 October, but Blair insisted that the case for extending the detention period for terrorist suspects was "absolutely compelling".

The government's majority was cut to just one vote when the bill received its second reading on 2 November. Labour MPs were reportedly assured by Clarke at this stage that a compromise would be forthcoming. Blair, however, refused to budge. Controversially, senior police officers made public their support for the Prime Minister, abandoning the convention that they should stay out of political debate. This pressure entirely failed. On 9 November, the Prime Minister was defeated for the first time since 1997, when rebel Labour MPs voted against the bill to defeat the government by 322 votes to 291. Defying a three-line whip, forty-nine backbenchers, including eleven former ministers, voted against; thirteen others abstained. MPs subsequently voted by 323 to 290 to support detention without charge for a reduced period of twenty-eight days, the compromise position advocated by the opposition. While defeat was not surprising on such an extreme proposition, the incident underlined the post-election diminution of the Prime Minister's authority, and also raised questions about his political judgement.

Clarke, who was assumed to have argued in favour of a compromise and lost, took the blame for the defeat, insisting that the judgment had been his alone. Few in Westminster were convinced. The amended bill faced further opposition in the House of Lords on its second reading at the end of the month. Paradoxically, the Association of Chief Police Officers privately opposed four clauses on the grounds that they could damage community relations. Some of the proposals— such as the power to close mosques that were used to foment extremism—were subsequently dropped after widespread criticism from religious leaders as well as the police and opposition peers. As the year ended, the terrorism bill was being scrutinised closely in the House of Lords.

The situation regarding the ten detainees now subject to control orders and await-ing deportation was the subject of one of the most important rulings of recent years on 8 December. In the case of *A and others v Secretary of State for the Home Department*, a panel of seven law lords voted unanimously to overturn a contro-versial Court of Appeal judgment passed in August 2004, that the government was under no obligation to inquire about the origins of evidence obtained in another country that was relevant and otherwise admissible. In other words, the special immigration appeals commission, the body convened to hear the appeals of the detainees, could take account of witness statements obtained under torture abroad, provided none of the torturers were UK citizens. The law lords disagreed, and the ruling was welcomed by human rights advocates as a key victory (see p. 428).

Meanwhile, Sir Ian Blair warned at the end of the year that the terrorist threat to the UK had intensified significantly since 7 July. He reported a 75 per cent increase in counter-terrorism operations and that three conspiracies had been thwarted, resulting in charges and deportations. It was unclear whether this increase was due to more terrorists, better intelligence, or a widening of surveil-lance activities, however. According to police figures, the number of Asian and black people stopped and searched in London by police using anti-terrorism powers increased more than twelve-fold after the bombings. More than 10,000 searches were conducted in the two months following the attacks, none of which resulted in an arrest or a charge related to terrorism.

OTHER DOMESTIC DEVELOPMENTS. The Queen's speech delivered on 17 May set out in a forty-five-bill package the government's "reform and respect" agenda for the following eighteen months. This included measures designed to curb crime and disorder and further modernisation of the public services, notably schools and healthcare. The agenda sent out the clear message that Blair intended to use his final years in government to push through a radical transformation of the public sector, in which the role of the state would shift from the direct provision of serv-ices towards commissioning services that could be purchased from the public, pri-vate, and voluntary sectors.

Healthcare and schools were in the frontline of this revolution, as illustrated by the publication of the controversial education white paper on 25 October. Key points included encouraging all schools to become "trust schools" with greater independence to run their own affairs; these could be sponsored by a variety of bodies including faith groups, charities, universities, and parents. While schools would take over responsibility for admissions, this power would be circumscribed to ensure that children of all abilities were taken into a school. Local education authorities would become commissioners, rather than direct providers of educa-tion. Parental rights would be expanded, with trust schools establishing parents' councils which would have a say in running the schools. It would be easier for private schools to become trust schools in the state sector. Failing schools would be given only one year to improve before a new provider would be sought. There would be encouragement for the "streaming" of teaching by ability, and enhanced powers for teachers to discipline pupils. Discussion of the proposals reportedly marked a sea change in the Cabinet's balance of power in the week before the paper's publication, with the normally loyal John Prescott leading the dissenters who feared that the reforms would disadvantage working-class children by undermining the role of local government in ensuring that provision remained balanced and accessible to all. Reaction in the Labour Party was also deeply divided, and the Education Secretary, Ruth Kelly, was put in the distinctly embarrassing position of having more support from the Conservatives than from within the ranks of her own party. Although technically she was in charge of education, it was widely believed that Lord Adonis was really calling the shots at the department, and the proposed reforms were a vision which he had been promoting since 1997. As scepticism grew among education professionals, Blair was warned that the bill, due to be debated in the new year, would only get through the Commons with Tory support, a further sign that the Prime Minister had become isolated on the right of the mainstream Labour Party.

Legislation to restrict smoking in enclosed public spaces proved to be another source of controversy. While the British Medical Association was insistent upon a total ban, the Cabinet struggled over the best way to proceed. The anti-smoking bill published in October allowed smoking in bars that did not serve food, and in private clubs. This represented a defeat for Health Secretary Patricia Hewitt, who was in favour of a total ban. She was reportedly opposed in the Cabinet's domestic affairs subcommittee by her predecessor and fellow Blairite, Dr John Reid, whose intervention was viewed as particularly inappropriate given the full smoking ban being introduced in his native Scotland in 2006 (see p. 27).

By the end of the year, a total of 150 UK citizens were known to have died in the Indian Ocean tsunami of 26 December 2004, the overwhelming majority of whom had been on holiday in Thailand. The Disasters Emergency Committee (DEC), the umbrella group for large British charities, raised UK£372 million from its tsunami appeal during 2005, with another UK£50 million given directly to member agencies.

The Church of England struggled in 2005 as the Archbishop of Canterbury, Dr Rowan Williams, fought to preserve the unity of the 78 million-strong worldwide Anglican communion of churches. The third strongest Christian denomination, with a presence in 164 countries, was threatened with irreconcilable division over the issue of homosexuality. Conservative evangelicals, who saw the authority of the Biblical tradition as non-negotiable, found themselves increasingly at odds with contemporary Western society and the substantial gay minority within the church. Schism looked increasingly likely as church leaders failed to find a compromise in a series of meetings during the year. By contrast, one of the most joyous images of the year was the sight of Britain's first black archbishop being enthroned in a magnificent celebration at York Minster on 30 November. Dr John Sentamu became the 97th Archbishop of York twenty-six years after he was forced to flee Uganda, where he had been persecuted as a high court judge who dared to defy the brutal dictatorship of Idi Amin.

England rekindled its love of cricket during the test match series with Australia which many claimed was the most exciting in the game's history. After a series of often dramatic and closely fought matches, England scored a two-to-one series win and reclaimed the Ashes for the first time since 1987 (see pp. 470-71).

The wedding of the year took place in a dignified and understated civil ceremony in the 17th-century guildhall lying in the shadow of Windsor Castle. On 22 December the queen of pop music, Sir Elton John, and his partner, David Furnish, were among the first to take advantage of the Civil Partnership Act 2004, which came into force on 5 December and put same-sex civil partnerships on the same legal footing as heterosexual marriages. The ceremony was presided over by the registrar, Clair Williams, who on 9 April had married Prince Charles and Camilla Parker Bowles in the same room.

THE TWO SUMMITEERS: BRITAIN, THE G-8 AND THE EU. The concurrence of the UK's assumption of the chair of the G-8 in January with the British turn at the rotating presidency of the EU from July gave Tony Blair and Gordon Brown a high profile in international affairs. The two were jointly determined to use the opportunity to promote an international consensus on solutions for development, poverty, and environmental issues. In an election year, they were equally determined to promote a united and statesmanlike image to voters at home.

Brown led a series of meetings ahead of the Gleneagles summit in July to build up support for debt relief, and also for his own idea, the international finance facility. His lobbying was backed up by the popular movement, "make poverty history", which culminated in a series of pop concerts collectively known as "Live 8". The agreement that resulted fell far short of what was realistically needed, but it did include a UK£28.8 billion increase in aid by 2010, and the cancellation of debt for fourteen of the world's poorest nations. Agreement was also reached on a new peacekeeping force for Africa and on the need to make access to treatment for HIV/AIDS universal. However, campaigners pointed out that the extent of the aid increase was misleading, and included the figures for debt relief. Not only did the G-8 fail to secure any commitment on trade liberalisation, but it also ignored crucial issues such as capital flight. In the months following the summit, much of the initial optimism of Gleneagles faded as signatories qualified their commitments.

Also in September, Brown unveiled his UK£2.2 billion scheme to improve immunisation in the developing world when he launched the international finance facility for immunisation, his brainchild and the result of months of bargaining. The scheme, which involved borrowing money on the bond markets secured by government pledges to repay, was a pilot which, if successful, Brown hoped would be extended. The ten-year programme, to be delivered by the global alliance for vaccines and immunisation, was expected to be able to save the lives of 5 million children by 2015, in addition to the 1.5 million already protected, thereby halving the number of children who died each year from preventable diseases in developing countries. The scheme was underwritten by France, Italy, Spain, Sweden, and the Bill and Melinda Gates foundation, with the UK contributing the largest share, of 35 per cent. Critics of this mechanism disapproved of the level of interest scheduled over the repayment period.

Climate change was the other issue highlighted by the government during the G-8 presidency. As the Kyoto Protocol came into force in February, Blair's stress on the subject was a politically astute way for him to distance himself from the US administration before the general election in May. But there was little tangible progress, in spite of signs that the issue was being taken more seriously by world leaders by the end of the year. At Gleneagles, Blair appeared to have persuaded US President George W. Bush at least to acknowledge that the issue was a problem, by agreeing to the wording of the final communiqué.

The environment was also one of the key issues that Blair proposed to highlight during the UK's presidency of the EU in the second half of the year, but other matters proved more pressing. Preoccupation with the fate of the EU constitution in the first six months of 2005 threatened to dominate EU relations for the foreseeable future. As the year began, the government's dreaded prospect of a UK referendum seemed to be inevitable, scheduled for the first half of 2006. In February the electoral commission—the independent body that regulated UK elections—approved the wording of the question to be put to British voters: "Should the United Kingdom approve the treaty establishing a constitution for the European Union?". Increasing resistance to the treaty evident among voters in mainland Europe thus came as a relief to the Prime Minister. Coming in the same week as the publication of a bill preparing for a UK referendum, the "non" vote at the end of May was perhaps the biggest favour that the French had ever done for Tony Blair; and when the Dutch followed suit in the following week, it became possible for the government to shelve the constitution issue on 6 June without embarrassment (see pp. 40; 48).

Relations with the other EU member-states were always going to be dominated by the showdown between, on the one hand, demands from partner states that the UK rebate be reviewed in light of changing economic circumstances since its negotiation by Margaret Thatcher in 1984; and, on the other, Blair's demands for radical economic reform and modernisation of the EU. This was certainly evident at the Brussels summit in June, where Blair made compromise on the rebate issue conditional upon renegotiation of the entire EU 2007-13 budget, including agricultural subsidies which were entwined so closely with the issue of assisting the developing world and the success of the World Trade Organisation talks in Hong Kong. Given the accession of ten new and relatively poor countries to the EU in 2004, renegotiation of the rebate was inevitable; the enlargement of the EU to twenty-five members would mean that the overall budget would increase dramatically, sharply increasing the rebate to the point that the UK would become one of the lowest contributors. Blair attempted to use the opportunity as a lever to open a wider discussion. For this reason, he threatened to veto Luxembourg's proposal to freeze the rebate in the budget, unless it was linked to an agreement to reform the common agricultural policy; when French President Jacques Chirac refused to budge, Blair did precisely this, leaving the meeting in disarray with bitter recriminations on all sides. While the Netherlands, Sweden, Spain, and Finland joined the UK in voting against the budget, this was for domestic reasons rather than out of sympathy for Blair's position on the rebate. On this issue he was isolated, and largely responsible for what was widely viewed as the most acrimonious meeting of the European Council's history. This did not augur well for the UK presidency. Blair saw it as his role to build a consensus for reform, but many of his critics believed that he was attempting to export an Anglo-Saxon economic model to the Continent.

With US support, the UK successfully pressed for talks on the accession of Turkey to the EU to begin as planned at the beginning of October, in the face of opposition led by France and Cyprus. This was viewed within the Foreign Office as one of the most effective ways that the West could demonstrate that it was compatible with a democratic Islamic culture.

An informal summit of European leaders hosted at Hampton Court Palace in the last week of October was convened by Blair to consider the larger context of the challenges facing the EU before the formal European Council meeting in December: the response to globalisation, the challenge of growing competition from India and China, and the future of energy supplies. But negotiations to settle the matter of the budget did not resume in earnest until November, nearly at the end of the UK's tenure in office. Unsurprisingly, with no evidence of new support for the UK, the French held firm, and Blair held off on proposing a solution until he had had a chance to meet the new German Chancellor, Angela Merkel, at the end of the month. With no proposal to end the impasse, negotiations soon reached a deadlock, and there was widespread exasperation with the UK government. Finally, Blair began to act at the beginning of December, in a complex series of negotiations. This involved cutting the budget from 1.06 per cent to 1.03 per cent of the EU's GDP, which would cut the size of the rebate without having to agree a new formula upon which to base it. An additional sum was pledged from the UK to make up the cut that this would represent to new members. The verdict was mixed. Blair had failed to persuade the French to discuss subsidies. But then Blair had not changed the rebate formula, and under the terms of the deal the French contribution would be approaching the size of the UK's, a long held objective (see pp. 370-72).

BRITISH OPERATIONS IN IRAQ. The US- and UK-led invasion of Iraq in 2003 continued to be a source of political controversy. The government came under increasing pressure to publish all information concerning the legal advice that it had received about the war, following the disclosure in March that the Attorney General, Lord Goldsmith, had warned only a fortnight before the invasion that it would be unlawful. The full thirteen pages of his advice to the Prime Minister were released at the end of April during the election campaign, leading to accusations that Blair had misled Parliament and the Cabinet over its contents. In May, George Galloway, the newly elected MP for the anti-war Respect Party, testified to the US Senate over allegations that he had benefited personally from the UN's "oil-for-food" programme for Iraq run under Saddam Hussein. Denying the charges, he used the opportunity to deliver a blistering attack upon the legitimacy of the invasion.

Four hundred extra British troops were sent to Iraq ahead of the January elections, as security fears increased. In March Private Johnson Beharry, aged twenty-five, a Grenadian serving in the British Army, became the first soldier to be awarded the Victoria Cross—the highest military honour—since the Falklands War, and the decoration's first living recipient since 1969. The performance of UK forces stationed in Iraq continued to be shaken, however, by allegations of abusive behaviour. In February, three soldiers were convicted of mistreating Iraqi prisoners at the Camp Breadbasket aid camp near Basra in May 2003. Shocking photographs taken by a fourth soldier and released during the proceedings echoed the US scandal at Abu Ghraib prison (see AR 2004, pp. 121; 204-05). In the same month it emerged that seven paratroopers were to be charged with murder and violent disorder, but the nine-week court marshal collapsed in November after a judge accused military police of bungling the investigation. In July, Lord Goldsmith announced that three soldiers would, for the first time, stand trial for war crimes against Iraqi detainees, under the jurisdiction of the International Criminal Court.

Meanwhile, concerns grew over the situation in Basra, where it was admitted in May that radical Shi'ite militias had infiltrated the police force, using their posts to assassinate opponents. In September, after two SAS officers were arrested and held in the custody of militants, a British tank blasted through the walls of Jamiat prison to free them. The action was condemned by the governor of Basra as "barbaric aggression". As hundreds of police officers took to the streets in a demonstration calling for the withdrawal of UK troops, senior Iraqi officials admitted that up to 60 per cent of the police there were infiltrated. Meeting with Iraq's Prime Minister, Ibrahim Jaafari, in London on 21 September, Defence Secretary John Reid insisted that the incidents did not constitute a diplomatic breakdown between Britain and Iraq. In October Tony Blair accused Iran of involvement in supplying sophisticated bombs to insurgents in southern Iraq, thought to have been responsible for the deaths of eight British troops. However, this information was later discounted as inaccurate. By the end of 2005, ninety-five British military personnel had lost their lives in the war and the cost of UK operations in Iraq, at more than UK£5.5 billion, had nearly doubled the government's original estimate. However, with 8,500 troops still stationed there and no easy way out, it was the political cost of the UK's Iraq policy that had proved to be the most disturbing by the end of 2005.

THE ECONOMY IN 2005. The Chancellor of the Exchequer, Gordon Brown, commented in his December pre-budget report that 2005 had been "the toughest and most challenging year for the economy". Brown slashed the predicted rate of economic growth to just 1.75 per cent, down from the 3 to 3.5 per cent he had estimated in his March budget. He further predicted a budget deficit of UK£10 billion, up considerably from the UK£5.7 billion which he had previously forecast, and he estimated that net public borrowing for the year would be UK£37 billion. In the third quarter of the year, the UK's current account deficit rose to UK£10.2 billion, with the deficit on goods and services reaching UK£14.1 billion, partly in consequence of claims of UK£1.9 billion on the British insurance industry arising from Hurricane Katrina.

To help balance his books, the Chancellor imposed a 20 per cent windfall tax on North Sea oil producers, estimated to raise UK£2 billion revenue for the Exchequer. The members of the Offshore Operators Association were disgruntled, but they had all made very substantial profits during the year, with British Petroleum (BP)—the UK's largest firm by market capitalisation—making a UK£12 billion profit, the largest of its corporate history. These profits were achieved as a consequence of escalating international oil prices, driven up by continuing instability in the Middle East and by the disruption to supplies caused by Hurricane Katrina and other storms in the Gulf of Mexico. The high international cost of oil had driven up the price of petrol at UK pumps, reaching UK£1 a litre in September. On 14 September a mass consumer protest against the spiralling prices was scheduled but failed to materialise, probably because petrol prices had by then begun to decline.

For the first time since 1980 the UK was a net importer of oil and gas. Consequently, the UK's trade gap with the rest of the world in goods and services widened in November to UK£5.96 billion, more than UK£1 billion more than originally forecast. A cold snap in that month across Europe, and a dispute between Russia and Ukraine over gas prices, drove up the international wholesale price of gas, leaving the UK vulnerable because the North Sea supplies had begun to run down more quickly than expected.

Other than in the short run, escalating energy prices did not, as many feared, fuel domestic inflation. The consumer price index (CPI), which was the measurement used by the UK government to measure inflation, spiked at 2.5 per cent in September, in the aftermath of Hurricane Katrina, but slipped to 2 per cent by the end of the year. Overall, there were downward pressures on prices through much of the year, with intense competition on the high streets, and with moderate wage demands across most sectors. Core CPI, which excluded items with high price volatility, ended the year at 1.3 per cent. Lower air transport costs—the result of consistently reduced airfares, principally across Europe but also to the rest of the world—and declining oil prices from the middle of the year onward exerted the strongest anti-inflationary influences. Tobacco, food, and drink had an upward pressure on the CPI, as retailers tended to pass on price increases to purchasers. The relative stability of inflation in the UK was one of the key factors that allowed the monetary policy committee of the Bank of England—the UK's central bank—to lower its interest rate from 4.75 per cent to 4.5 per cent in August, where it rested for the rest of the year.

Consumer confidence was low, with people increasingly concerned about their job prospects, the future of the economy and their personal debt. Surveys conducted by Nationwide, a UK bank, showed that confidence began slipping in spring but levelled out in the late autumn. Nationwide also found that appetite for acquiring new debt had fallen to its lowest levels for more than a decade. Nevertheless, consumer spending did pick up in the approach to Christmas, reversing a seven-month decline. Most of the UK's largest retailers—such as Tesco, Marks

& Spencer, Boots, and Sainsburys—posted improved sales. However, the performance of other retailers was less positive. For instance, HMV—the UK's biggest music, videos, DVDs, and computer games retailer—saw its shares slide just before Christmas following reports of sluggish sales, possibly as a result of competition from Internet retailers.

The personal difficulties caused by the high levels of UK personal indebtedness—the greatest in Europe—were seen in days immediately after Christmas. The national debtline, which had been set up by the government in 1987 to assist people in financial trouble, found that it was overwhelmed by a record number of calls from individuals who feared they had so seriously overspent in the previous few weeks that they would be soon facing bankruptcy. The helpline's operators reported that they could not answer over two-thirds of the calls they had received. The Citizens' Advice Bureau and the Consumer Credit Counselling Service reported that they, too, were unable to cope with the numbers of requests for debt advice. The level of UK personal debt had been examined in a report by the Conservative Party, published in March. The report estimated that 15 million people were exposed as result of their collective unsecured debt levels of about UK£1 trillion, and the situation was described in the report as a "time bomb".

According to the Bank of England, consumer borrowing rose by just UK£927 million in November, which was the smallest increase in five years; however, the number of those declaring bankruptcy was soaring. Between July and September 2005 there were 17,562 bankruptcies, representing an almost 50 per cent increase on the year before. This was partly the result of changed rules regarding personal insolvency, which allowed a bankrupt's debts to be discharged after just one year, compared with the previous three-year term. Additionally, a rising number of people chose to use the more lenient individual voluntary arrangements that allowed them to pay back just 30 to 50 pence of each pound owned.

The economic impact of the London bombings in July was difficult to estimate, but it was likely that the long-term consequences would be negligible. However, the effects were very noticeable in London in the short term. Shops in the west end of London—one of the world's leading retail areas by volume—were affected in the immediate aftermath of the incidents and there was a noticeable 30 per cent slump in Thursday shopping, the day of week upon which both the 7 July bombings and the 21 July attempted bombings occurred. Tourist attractions in central London, such as the Tower of London and Madame Tussauds, which were usually amongst the most popular in the UK, recorded a 15 per cent drop in visitor numbers; while attractions on the peripheries of London, like the Royal Botanical Gardens at Kew and the Royal Air Force Museum at Hendon, recorded substantial increases. During the third quarter of 2005 (which corresponded to the period around the July bombings), there was a 4 per cent fall in the number of all visits to London compared with the same quarter of 2004. The numbers of tourists visiting the UK dropped by 2 per cent in September.

Despite these setbacks, the importance of London as the economic powerhouse of the UK economy was consolidated during the year. London's financial services sector, which included banks, insurance, management consultants, and other related services, contributed UK£310.9 billion—or almost one-third—to the UK's wealth, twice that of the manufacturing sector. This represented a significant increase since 1995, when the share of the financial services sector was 24 per cent.

General UK corporate profitability, aside from the oil companies and financial services, was down on earlier estimates. Private non-financial corporations saw profitability of 13.4 per cent in the third quarter of 2005, which was lower than the estimate of 13.8 per cent recorded in the previous quarter. The net rate of return for manufacturing companies in the third quarter of 2005 was estimated at 6.2 per cent, lower than the average of 7.1 per cent for 2004. Towards the end of the year business confidence plummeted to below the European average for the first time in four years.

The UK housing market was unusually flat for much of 2005. According to the Halifax—a leading mortgage-lending bank—the market recovered only towards the end of the year, with house prices rising by 2.1 per cent in the final three months of 2005. The Halifax believed that underpinning the market's recovery was the Bank of England's interest rate cut in August and a relatively stable employment level. However, while the unemployment rate was comparatively low, it slowly increased over consecutive months from the spring onwards, creeping up to 5 per cent in November, which was the highest posted rate in twelve years. At the same time the number of people counted as economically inactive had risen to 7.94 million, the largest number since records began in the early 1970s.

There can be little doubt that 2005 saw the UK economy lose much of its shine. Nevertheless, as the IMF commented in its December annual survey of the world's principal economies, the "macroeconomic stability in the UK remains remarkable".

SCOTLAND

CAPITAL: Edinburgh   AREA: 78,313 sq km   POPULATION: 5,078,400
OFFICIAL LANGUAGES: English, Gaelic   POLITICAL SYSTEM: devolved administration within UK
HEAD OF STATE: Queen Elizabeth II (since Feb '52)
RULING PARTIES: Labour & Liberal Democrats (since May '99)
HEAD OF GOVERNMENT: Jack McConnell (Labour), First Minister (since Nov '01)

CONTROVERSY over the arrangements for controlling the expenses of Members of the Scottish Parliament (MSPs) continued for much of the year. In January Keith Raffan resigned as an MSP, on health grounds, as evidence started to come to light that his high claims for travel expenses included at least one period when he was out of the country. Raffan was the Scottish Liberal Democrat (SLD) list MSP for Mid-Scotland and Fife (i.e. a member not for an individual constituency but selected from a party list to achieve proportional representation). He was succeeded by the next candidate on the list. This process revived disquiet about the democratic credentials of the party list system, because there was no fresh election. Raffan's continuing illness made it impossible during the year to correct his expenses, but a fundamental review of the system was precipitated at the end of

October by the "taxigate" scandal when David McLetchie was forced to resign as leader of the Scottish Conservative Party (though not as an MSP), because he had claimed expenses for taxi journeys taken on private business. McLetchie was succeeded as leader of the Scottish Conservatives by Annabel Goldie. George Reid, the Parliament's Presiding Officer, promised to introduce a much closer scrutiny of the expenses of MSPs.

The Scottish Conservatives were not the only party to change leader during the year. Colin Fox was elected in February to the vacancy as leader of the Scottish Socialist Party and Nicol Stephen was elected in June to succeed Jim Wallace as leader of the Scottish Liberal Democrats.

Tensions between the Scottish and Westminster (UK) Parliaments resurfaced during the year when the Home Secretary sought to act for the whole of the UK without—in the opinion of MSPs—appropriate cognisance of their views or of the distinction between English and Scottish law. Most notably: in framing proposed anti-terror legislation, there was no consultation with senior Scottish law officers; in proposals for the introduction of identity cards, no account was taken of their rejection by MSPs; concerns about the treatment of failed asylum seekers (highlighted by the forced deportation of the Vucaj family to Albania after five years in Scotland) were aggravated by the lack of clarity over what the First Minister, Jack McConnell, had sought to do; and MSPs were upset that their attempts to introduce a ban on the sale of airguns (following the fatal shooting of a two-year-old boy by an airgun pellet) were frustrated because firearms legislation was reserved to Westminster. However, one important addition to the administrative devolution to Scotland was the transfer to the Scottish Executive in October of responsibility for Scotland's rail network. (In September it had been decided to reopen the rail link between Edinburgh and the Borders.)

The most immediately significant change which the Scottish Parliament introduced was a ban on smoking in public places, to be operational from March 2006, coupled with a rise in the minimum legal age for buying tobacco from sixteen to eighteen. Two developments were of major potential importance for the future. The first was the insistence of the Scottish Parliament and Executive that Scotland's population and economic capacity required that it become much more receptive to immigration, at least on a temporary basis, such as by making it easier for overseas students to remain in the country after graduating. Secondly, in December a bill was introduced to bring about a major overhaul of planning law. Aspects of this seemed likely to prove controversial but, even if only partially enacted, it promised to simplify the planning system and reduce delays.

The Westminster general election in May (see pp. 9-10) was conducted in almost entirely new constituencies in Scotland, the number of MPs from Scotland having been reduced from seventy-two to fifty-nine because of Scotland's relative population decline. Analysts had calculated that the effects of the new constituency boundaries were almost neutral, but that compared with the actual 2001 election results the SLD should "gain" a little and all other parties "lose" a little in the "2001 notional" distribution of seats. The "2001 notional" results were Scottish Labour forty-six seats (actual result, fifty-six) (including the Speaker);

SLD nine seats (actual ten); Scottish National Party (SNP) four seats (actual five); and Scottish Conservatives zero seats (actual one). The 2005 results were that Scottish Labour lost five seats—two each to the SLD and the SNP and one to the Scottish Conservatives—from the "2001 notional" position. No party could claim unambiguous success in the election. Scottish Labour lost seats and some of its share of the vote, but remained clearly the biggest force in Scottish politics. The SLD became the second party in terms of share of the vote as well as seats, but had hoped to win more seats. The SNP fell to third position in share of vote but did gain two seats. The Scottish Conservatives lost their only sitting MP, whose seat they had hoped to retain despite its being "notionally" Labour, but had the consolation of gaining a seat from Labour.

Two by-elections were held on 29 September, both seats being retained by Scottish Labour. The Westminster seat of Livingston had been occupied by Robin Cook, former UK Foreign Secretary, who died in August (for obituary see p. 529). The Scottish Parliament seat of Glasgow Cathcart had been held by Lord Watson of Invergowrie. Mike Watson had been MP for the UK parliamentary constituency of Glasgow Central, but his seat had disappeared because of boundary changes in 1995 and he was given a life peerage. In 1999 he was elected to the Scottish Parliament and was re-elected in 2003. In September he admitted fireraising, by setting light to a curtain in an Edinburgh hotel; apparently he was under the influence of alcohol after the November 2004 Scottish Politician of the Year awards ceremony. Watson resigned as MSP and was imprisoned and expelled from the Labour Party.

WALES

CAPITAL: Cardiff   AREA: 20,755 sq km   POPULATION: 2,952,500
OFFICIAL LANGUAGES: Welsh & English   POLITICAL SYSTEM: devolved administration within the UK
HEAD OF STATE: Queen Elizabeth II (since Feb '52)
RULING PARTY: Labour (since May '03)
HEAD OF GOVERNMENT: Rhodri Morgan, First Secretary (since Feb '00)

THE perception that the Welsh people were obsessed with rugby union seemed to have some foundation with the euphoria surrounding Wales's feats on the rugby field during the early part of the year. Wales won the "grand slam" (winning all its games in the Six Nations Championship) for the first time in twenty-seven years, thereby bringing massive satisfaction to a nation which had been starved of sporting success (see p. 471). Both on and off the field, the exploits of Gavin Henson, including his romance with the Welsh singer Charlotte Church, made him a celebrity figure constantly in the news. His harsh punishment for foul play in a match near the end of the year hardly tarnished his reputation in Wales.

In May, the UK general election (see pp. 9-10) saw Labour lose some ground in Wales, with the Conservatives winning three seats (their first in Wales since 1997) and the Liberal Democrats capturing two additional seats. The most astonishing result was that in Blaenau Gwent, traditionally the most solid of Labour strongholds. Peter Law, a long-serving Labour Party member and the constituency's representative at the National Assembly for Wales, stood as an independent and defeated the Labour candidate, Maggie Jones, by a substantial margin. It was considered by many to be a triumph for local democracy over central control, as Jones was seen as an outsider imposed on the constituency through an all-women short list favoured by the Labour Party centrally. The result led to much recrimination and the expulsion of Labour Party stalwarts in the constituency. Nevertheless Labour still dominated the vast majority of UK parliamentary constituencies in Wales, winning twenty-nine of the forty seats.

Plaid Cymru's representation fell from four seats to three, surprisingly losing Ceredigion to the Liberal Democrats. The party also lost its former President, Gwynfor Evans, who died in April. His charismatic leadership was instrumental in the growth of the party after World War II and he was elected Plaid Cymru's first MP in 1966.

The fragile nature of Labour's minority government in the Welsh National Assembly came to the fore in October. Its draft budget for 2006-07 was rejected by the Assembly and only following negotiations with the opposition parties was a revised budget approved in December. The First Minister, Rhodri Morgan, stated that he would not seek a formal coalition with any of the other parties, as had been the case in the past.

Another budget, the European Union budget, which was agreed in December following protracted negotiations (see pp. 370-72), was widely welcomed in Wales since it would allow for further European funding to be claimed for the most deprived parts of Wales. This was considered essential as the economic forecasts were less optimistic following the Chancellor's pre-budget report in early December. Although the increase in the Welsh export figures, particularly to non-EU countries, was encouraging and the unemployment figure for Wales was on average lower than the rest of the UK, there were concerns about the true strength of the economy. Most of the new jobs created in recent years were in the public sector leading to unease that they were not adding value to the economy. There was also evidence of substantial differences in salary levels between regions in Wales, particularly between the prosperous urban areas, such as Cardiff, and rural areas. House prices continued to grow at a higher pace than the rest of the UK, with an increase in average house prices from UK£100,000 in 2003 to UK£150,000 in 2005.

One decision made by Chancellor of the Exchequer Gordon Brown was welcomed in rural Wales when he announced that the SIPPs scheme—whereby wealthy people could buy second homes to top-up their pension plans—was to be abandoned. Had this scheme been implemented, it was predicted that the difficulties experienced by local people buying homes in rural areas of Wales would be exacerbated.

Meanwhile by the end of the year, as the new Assembly building was nearing completion in Cardiff Bay, attention was drawn to the powers that the Assembly might expect in the future (see AR 2004, pp. 31-32). With the main recommendation of the Richard Commission that the Assembly should have primary law-making powers being opposed by Labour MPs, fearful of a loss of power, the government made less ambitious proposals based on the "better governance for Wales" white paper published in June. In a new Government of Wales bill, given its first reading in December, it was proposed that the Assembly government would be given powers to draw up its own legislation, which would then be passed in Westminster using the fast-track procedure of Orders in Council. This process was criticised as a "constitutional fudge", and on the grounds that it would, in effect, allow the Secretary of State for Wales to veto legislation drafted and approved in the Assembly.

The bill did, however, hold out the prospect of full law-making powers being granted to the Assembly, subject to a future referendum, although the Secretary of State for Wales, Peter Hain, stated that such a referendum was unlikely to be held in the near future. The Assembly structure would also change. Instead of an Assembly modelled on old local government lines, it would be reformed into a new parliamentary-type structure with a clear distinction between the Welsh Assembly government and the Assembly acting as a proper legislature, holding government ministers to account. There would also be measures to stop Assembly candidates standing for election in constituencies and at the same time on the proportional representation list. This was seen by opposition parties as a cynical move by Labour to limit the activities of smaller parties. It was expected that the bill would become law in time for the next Assembly elections in 2007.

NORTHERN IRELAND

CAPITAL: Belfast   AREA: 18,843 sq km   POPULATION: 1,702,600
OFFICIAL LANGUAGES: English, Irish & Ulster Scots   POLITICAL SYSTEM: devolved administration within UK
HEAD OF STATE: Queen Elizabeth II (since Feb '52)
RULING PARTIES: Democratic Unionist Party (DUP), Sinn Féin (SF), and Social Democratic and Labour Party (SDLP)
HEAD OF GOVERNMENT: Peter Hain, Secretary of State for Northern Ireland (since May '05)

THE political atmosphere at the start of the year was soured by the Northern Bank robbery and the collapse of the efforts to restore devolution in December 2004 (see AR 2004, p. 36). In January, Hugh Orde, the Chief Constable of the Police Service of Northern Ireland (PSNI), publicly blamed the IRA for the robbery, which it in turn denied. Sectarian tensions remained high. Vicious attacks forced several Catholic families from their homes in Ahoghill, and September witnessed the worst violence for ten years when three days of fierce rioting in loyalist areas followed the re-routing of an Orange parade. The riots reflected the alienation of loyalist working class communities; in September more investment in poorer loyalist areas was pledged.

The summer also witnessed four murders in an escalation of the feud between the paramilitary Ulster Volunteer Force (UVF) and the Loyalist Volunteer Force (LVF). This led the Independent Monitoring Commission (IMC) to recommend continued suspension of financial assistance for the Progressive Unionist Party, with which these groups were linked (see AR 2004, p. 34). It also questioned the

UVF's 1994 ceasefire, which was "de-recognised" by the government following the September riots. In November a truce was agreed to end the feud; shortly afterwards the LVF announced that it had wound up its "military units" and was considering destroying its weapons.

In February a series of raids by Irish police investigating IRA money-laundering led to the arrest of several senior republicans and the seizure of more than UK£2 million, including UK£60,000 in Northern Bank notes. Worried by the implications of such events, the UK and Irish governments threatened to remove Sinn Féin from the political process if IRA criminality continued. In the spring, funding for Sinn Féin members of the UK Parliament at Westminster and for its Northern Ireland Assembly members was suspended. Sinn Féin's difficulties were compounded by the murder of Robert McCartney outside a pub in the staunchly republican area of Belfast on 30 January. This led to a high-profile campaign by the dead man's sisters and fiancée, who accused the IRA of involvement in the murder and a subsequent cover-up of evidence. The campaign included a St Patrick's Day meeting with US President George W. Bush and a visit to the European Parliament. Sinn Féin suspended several members suspected of being involved, and its leader, Gerry Adams, appealed to those responsible to give themselves up. The IRA denied involvement and on 8 March a public offer to shoot the killers was met with general revulsion. However Sinn Féin's chief negotiator, Martin McGuinness, warned the family that their campaign could be open to political manipulation, and Sinn Féin's ambivalent attitude to the affair reflected unwillingness to support any action that could be construed as recognition of the PSNI. In early May, two men were charged with the murder.

In the UK general election (see pp. 9-10), six of the eighteen seats changed hands and the DUP and Sinn Féin consolidated their dominance, a process that was replicated in local government elections on the same day. The Northern Bank and McCartney affairs had little adverse effect on Sinn Féin, which increased its vote from 21.7 to 24.3 per cent, winning five seats and taking Newry and Armagh from the SDLP. Although it won three seats, the SDLP vote fell nearly four points to 17.5 per cent, but party leader Mark Durkan fought off the Sinn Féin challenge in Foyle and the party won South Belfast through a split in the unionist vote. In the battle within unionism, the DUP won 33.7 per cent (up by 11.2 per cent on 2001), gaining four seats and taking its Westminster representation to nine. The UUP was reduced to a single Westminster seat in its worst ever performance, and its vote fell to 17.1 per cent, a loss of nearly ten points. Following his defeat by the DUP in his Upper Bann constituency, UUP leader David Trimble resigned, to be replaced in June by Sir Reg Empey.

In the post-election reshuffle, Peter Hain was appointed Secretary of State (combining the post with responsibility for Wales), and three new faces—David Hanson, Shaun Woodward, and Lord Jeffrey Rooker—joined Angela Smith in the ministerial team. The main policy development was the November announcement of the outcome of the review of public administration. In the first major reform of local administration since 1970, functions such as planning, local roads, regeneration, and local economic development were to be restored to elected councils.

Plans outlined in December saw an increase in public spending of nearly 5 per cent, plus a UK£16 million ten-year programme for capital investment in hospitals, schools, and transport. This was accompanied by rates increases, the introduction of water charges from 2007, and further cuts in civil service jobs. In October it was announced that a total ban on smoking in public places would be introduced by April 2007. In November, an estimated 100,000 people lined the streets and the Stormont estate for the funeral of Belfast-born footballer George Best (for obituary see p. 526). At Belfast City Hall on 19 December two women became the first homosexual couple in the UK to have a full civil partnership ceremony. Also in December, an Algerian national with suspected al-Qaida links became the first international terror suspect to be convicted by a non-jury Diplock Court, when he was jailed for six years for downloading from the Internet information on how to blow up a passenger jet.

Restoration of devolution was the government's main priority but the political process remained deadlocked, despite some important developments. In February the IRA withdrew the offer on decommissioning made in the negotiations in 2004, and warned of a crisis in the peace process. On 6 April, however, Gerry Adams launched an internal debate by calling on the IRA to pursue its goals using exclusively political methods. On 28 July, the IRA formally announced the end to its armed campaign after more than thirty years of violence, committing itself to "exclusively peaceful means" and a fully democratic path to achieve its goals. Although ambiguous, the phrase that "volunteers must not engage in any other activities whatsoever" was interpreted to refer to an end to all criminal activity. On 26 September, General John de Chastelain, head of the independent international commission on decommissioning, announced that the commission was satisfied "beyond any shadow of doubt" that the IRA had decommissioned the "totality" of its arsenal. This was verified by two witnesses from the Catholic and Protestant churches, Father Alex Reid and the Reverend Harold Good, who said that they regarded IRA decommissioning as an "accomplished fact".

In a joint communiqué, the UK and Irish governments noted that if the IRA's words "are borne out by actions, it will be a momentous and historic development". Sinn Féin and the SDLP called for the quick restoration of devolution but unionists remained sceptical. For them, whether all paramilitary activity had indeed ended was to be judged by actions over a "prolonged period": years rather than months. This reflected their discontent about the lack of transparency, notably the absence of an inventory and photographic evidence that weapons had been destroyed. Shaky unionist confidence in the credibility of the Catholic witness was dented in October when Father Reid compared the unionist community's treatment of Catholics to the Nazi's treatment of the Jews, although he later issued an unqualified apology His comments mirrored remarks by Ireland's President Mary McAleese in January (see p. 35).

Following the IRA statement, the UK government restored Sinn Féin's parliamentary allowances and accelerated normalisation and demilitarisation. The government announced that the three Northern Ireland-based battalions of the Royal Irish Regiment (RIR)—comprising 3,000 troops—would be disbanded in August

2007. Contingent on the security situation, troop levels would be reduced from 10,500 to 5,000, the army's support role ended, and counter terrorist laws specific to Northern Ireland repealed. Although welcomed by nationalists, unionists reacted angrily to the announcement. Controversy also surrounded the government's decision in November to introduce legislation to allow "on-the-runs" (those who had committed crimes before 1998, including soldiers and police officers) to have their cases dealt with by a special tribunal and avoid serving a prison sentence. For Peter Hain this was a "painful but necessary" step but all local parties opposed it, albeit for different reasons.

In December the prosecution of three men accused of operating an IRA spy ring at Stormont—central in the collapse of devolution in 2003—was unexpectedly dropped as "not in the public interest". The government denied influencing the decision but refused to give any public explanation. On 16 December it was revealed that one of the accused, Denis Donaldson, a close associate of Gerry Adams, had been working for UK intelligence for twenty years.

So, by the end of the year the government was still struggling to invigorate the political process. Foreshadowing the arguments ahead, on 29 December Hain threatened to cut the salaries of the 108 Assembly members and to cancel elections due in 2007 if Sinn Féin and the DUP did not make progress towards re-establishing power-sharing in 2006.

REPUBLIC OF IRELAND—GERMANY—FRANCE—ITALY—BELGIUM—
THE NETHERLANDS—LUXEMBOURG

REPUBLIC OF IRELAND

CAPITAL: Dublin   AREA: 70,000 sq km   POPULATION: 4,000,000
OFFICIAL LANGUAGES: Irish & English   POLITICAL SYSTEM: multiparty republic
HEAD OF STATE: President Mary McAleese (since Nov '97)
RULING PARTIES: coalition of Fianna Fáil (FF) and Progressive Democrats (PD)
HEAD OF GOVERNMENT: Bertie Ahern (FF), Taoiseach (Prime Minister) (since June '97)
MAIN IGO MEMBERSHIPS (NON-UN): EU, OSCE, CE, OECD, PFP
CURRENCY: euro (end-'05 £1=€1.45540, US$1=€0.84774)
GNI PER CAPITA: US$34,280, US$33,170 at PPP ('04)

THIS was a quiet year politically, but the parties started to jockey for position in advance of the general election due in 2007. In January, the Taoiseach, Bertie Ahern, announced that he intended to complete a full second term in office, then fight a third election as leader of Fianna Fáil, again with the Progressive Democrats, before retiring in 2011. However opinion polls showed a weakening of support for the government as the year progressed. The opposition Fine Gael and Labour parties, which continued efforts to create an alternative government alliance (moves also supported by the Greens), were the preferred government with 36 per cent support, five points ahead of the ruling coalition. This reflected increasing public disillusion with the government's performance, especially over crime, the health service, and the high cost of living in

Ireland, highlighted by the success during the summer of RTE television's *Rip-Off Republic* programme.

In by-elections for the Dáil (the lower house of the bicameral legislature) in March, Fine Gael retained the seat in Meath (vacated by the appointment of its former leader John Bruton as EU ambassador to the USA) with 34 per cent of the vote. In Kildare North, Fianna Fáil's loss of the seat to an independent candidate made the constituency the only one in the country without a representative of either governing party. Much of the interest in Meath centred on the performance of Sinn Féin in its first big electoral test since the murder of Robert McCartney and the Northern Bank robbery (see pp. 30-31). The messages for its future electoral prospects were mixed, however, for while its candidate came third with just over 12 per cent, up nearly three points on 2002, this was an increase of only forty-five votes in a low turnout.

The government's core policy concerns centred on economic management, employment, health, education, affordable housing, crime, and Northern Ireland. Following another outbreak of gangland warfare in November—there were thirteen gangland-style killings in 2005, prompting headlines comparing Dublin to 1930s Chicago—there was another crackdown on the criminal gangs involved in drug dealing, armed robbery, and violence. The basic policy priority remained successful economic management to provide the resources for essential investment in public services. Low inflation and strong economic growth (forecast to reach 5.9 per cent) allowed the government to address the concerns of voters in the December budget, with €4.4 billion of investment in key areas such as childcare, pensions and the elderly.

Several commissions and tribunals continued their work. In October, the Murphy Report revealed evidence of the sexual abuse of young children by priests in County Wexford over a forty-year period; and in June the second report of the Morris Tribunal into the actions of certain Garda (police) members in Donegal was published. The Moriarty Tribunal continued to investigate financial payments to ex-ministers, and in January, former Fianna Fáil Cabinet minister Ray Burke was sentenced to six months in prison for tax evasion in 1993. On the eve of the budget the Minister of State for Transport, Ivor Callely, was forced to resign after a series of scandals, including the disclosure that a construction company had paid for the redecoration of his house. A major controversy erupted at the end of June when five protesters were jailed for refusing to comply with an injunction not to interfere with the construction by Shell of a new gas pipeline in County Mayo. After the men were freed by the High Court in October the government ordered a further safety review of the pipeline, but the issue highlighted public unease about the relationship between the state and multinational companies.

Following rejection in France and the Netherlands of the EU constitution, the government reiterated its support for the document and continued with preparations for its ratification, although no date for the referendum was set. Events pertaining to Northern Ireland remained central, with the government continuing to work with its UK counterpart to revive the 1998 Belfast Agreement (the "Good Friday" Agreement, see AR 1998, pp. 44-51; 556-67). President Mary

McAleese became embroiled in political controversy in January when she infuriated unionists by likening the treatment of Catholics in Northern Ireland to the Nazi genocide against Jews, and subsequently was forced to apologise (see p. 32). In August, the secret return of the three men with Sinn Féin and IRA links accused of training anti-government guerrillas in Colombia (see AR 2004, p. 171) caused difficulties for the government.

GERMANY

CAPITAL: Berlin   AREA: 357,000 sq km   POPULATION: 82,600,000
OFFICIAL LANGUAGE: German   POLITICAL SYSTEM: multiparty republic
HEAD OF STATE: President Horst Köhler (since July '04)
RULING PARTIES: "grand coalition" between Christian Democratic Union/Christian Social Union
   (CDU/CSU) and Social Democratic Party (SPD)
HEAD OF GOVERNMENT: Angela Merkel (CDU), Chancellor (since Nov '05)
MAIN IGO MEMBERSHIPS (NON-UN): NATO, EU, OSCE, CE, CBSS, AC, OECD, G-8
CURRENCY: euro (end-'05 £1=€1.4125, US$1=€0.7357)
GNI PER CAPITA: US$30,120, US$27,950 at PPP ('04)

PUBLIC life in Germany in 2005 was dominated by one unexpected event: the snap election of 18 September. Chancellor Gerhard Schröder's decision to call an election twelve months early transformed an otherwise rather mundane year into one that was characterised by high political drama. In his replacement, Angela Merkel, Germany gained a female Chancellor for the first time in its history. Merkel was also the first eastern German to lead the country since reunification in 1990 (see AR 1990, pp. 150-55). Her path to the Chancellery was not, however, as straightforward as many had expected. Indeed, through the summer months Schröder orchestrated a rousing Social Democratic Party (SPD) comeback, eventually falling a mere one percentage point short of the Christian Democrats (CDU/CSU) on election day. The year ended with a degree of political intrigue as Schröder left representative politics altogether and took up a position, firstly, with Swiss publisher Ringier and then—to widespread consternation—with the North European Gas Pipeline organisation, within which the Russian state-owned energy company, Gazprom, held a 51 per cent stake.

Very few observers saw the September election coming. The German Bundestag (the 603-member lower chamber of the bicameral Parliament) had four-year fixed terms and, therefore, following an election in September 2002, the next federal poll was not scheduled to take place until late 2006. The German President was only authorised to dissolve the Bundestag in extreme circumstances—namely if the Chancellor had lost the support of his legislative majority—and, as 2005 dawned, few would have predicted that any such circumstance was likely to develop. The SPD-Green majority remained small (just four), but manageable. Although the SPD-Green government was unpopular with the population at large, there was little evidence of a groundswell of public opinion in support of the CDU/CSU or the liberal Free Democratic Party (FDP). Popular demonstrations against the SPD-Green programme of labour market and welfare reforms (the so-called "Agenda 2010"), which had been visible throughout the summer of 2004, had largely faded away, and although a new force to the left of the SPD—"The Electoral Alternative: the Party for Employment and Social Justice" (WASG)—was beginning to take shape, there was still little sign that it would seriously destabilise German politics in the short term. A significant number of left-wing SPD members were calling for parts of the "Agenda 2010" programme—specifically those involving unemployment benefit and social support—to be altered, but this seemed to be the normal fare of everyday party politics. There was, therefore, little hint of the drama to come.

The main catalyst for the snap election was the result of the regional election in North-Rhine-Westphalia in May 2005. Given the sheer size of the region— Germany's biggest in terms of population—this particular regional election was always of considerable importance, but it took an even greater significance, first because an SPD defeat would ensure that the Bundesrat (the upper chamber of Parliament) was even more firmly in the hands of the opposition parties; and secondly because North-Rhine-Westphalia had long been an SPD stronghold because of its strong industrial base.

The actual result was, nonetheless, not actually as bad as some social democrats had feared. The Christian Democrats polled 44.8 per cent of the vote (up 7.8 per cent on their showing in the previous election in North-Rhine-Westphalia in 2000), while the SPD came a poor second on 37.1 per cent (down 5.7 per cent). It was also clear that SPD voters had not simply opted to vote Green (the SPD's governing partner at the federal level) as a form of mini-protest: the Green Party also lost votes, polling 6.2 per cent (down 0.9 per cent). SPD voters must, at least to some extent, have left the centre-left camp and supported the CDU. This, above all else, worried the SPD leadership. If something similar happened at the national level then the CDU/CSU and FDP would win the next election at a canter.

One of the reasons for the popular dissatisfaction with the SPD was that most German economic indicators made depressing reading. In February, over 5 million people were officially unemployed—a figure not seen in Germany since the days of deep economic malaise in the early 1930s—and although unemployment came down slightly over the year, to 4.6 million (or 11.2 per cent of the workforce), many Germans remained deeply worried about losing their jobs. Despite a belligerent export sector (exports were up 6.2 per cent), economic growth also remained sluggish, down from 1.6 per cent in 2004 to 0.8 per cent in 2005. Business confidence remained low, there appeared to be an ever expanding hole in federal finances, and Germany suffered—for the fourth year running—the indignity of failing to meet the 3 per cent public deficit criterion set down in the EU's Stability and Growth Pact.

Although faced with a barrage of bleak political and economic indicators, Schröder nonetheless opted for the "nuclear option" of calling an early election, in the knowledge that it could very possibly see his government evicted from office. Speculation abounded as to why he chose this course. One of the reasons was that Schröder was—as he again proved through the summer of 2005— a formidable campaigner. His charm, charisma, quick-wittedness, and statesmanlike demeanour proved considerable electoral assets and he might well have calculated that the excitement of an upcoming election campaign would make his party (and the public at large) forget his contribution to the SPD's disastrous performance in North-Rhine-Westphalia. Schröder may also have calculated that he would be catching the CDU/CSU unprepared, in programmatic, organisational, and strategic terms. The CDU's own agenda was still a point of considerable contention within Christian Democrat ranks; and although Angela Merkel was undoubtedly favourite to be the next chancellor candidate, her enthronement was by no means a foregone conclusion. The opinion polls were also telling a number of stories of which Schröder must have been aware; one of these was that while 66 per cent of voters in May 2005 proclaimed themselves dissatisfied with the work of the SPD/Green government, 50 per cent of them expected a CDU/CSU regime to do no better. Furthermore, 11 per cent actually thought that a CDU/CSU-FDP coalition would actually do a worse job, while only 36 per cent expected a new government to be an improvement on the existing one.

As 18 September dawned, few seriously doubted that Merkel would not be declaring herself Chancellor by the end of the day. Yet on the early evening television talk shows it was Schröder who was belligerently claiming that the election result gave him, and him alone, the authority to lead any future government. Schröder's aggressive performance in the traditional round table debate of party leaders on the evening of the election shocked many Germans, as he bellowed that Merkel "couldn't seriously claim to be Chancellor" after the CDU/CSU and FDP had failed to achieve their expected Bundestag majority. He appeared astoundingly confrontational, uninterested in any form of compromise, and confident to the point of reckless. The SPD may well have achieved one of the poorest election results in its history, but given its forlorn prospects just months, weeks, days and even hours earlier, Schröder was quick to illustrate how close it had come to polling the most votes and how poorly—when compared with its opinion poll showings—the CDU/CSU had performed.

The SPD polled 4.3 per cent less than it had in 2002, but the CDU/CSU also saw its share of the vote drop by 3.3. This left the CDU/CSU with 35.2 per cent—its second worst result since 1949—and the SPD with 34.2 per cent of the popular vote. Little more than half (53 per cent) of all those eligible to vote gave their support to one of the CDU/CSU, or SPD, making this the worst performance by the *Volksparteien* ("people's parties"—the two dominant consensual and mass organisational parties in Germany) since 1949. The CDU/CSU performed particularly poorly in southern Germany, where the CSU lost over 800,000 votes in Bavaria alone (probably because a Bavarian, Edmund Stoiber, had run as the CDU/CSU's candidate for Chancellor in 2002 and had thereby artificially inflated the CDU/CSU's vote). SPD politicians were subsequently much more upbeat about the CDU's failings than they were about their own party's performance.

The real surprise package of the election was the Free Democratic Party. Few within the party can have seriously believed that the liberals would poll 9.8 per cent of the vote. The FDP had attempted to present itself as a much more serious actor than had been the case in the previous election, when it came to be known as the "fun party"; and its quietly efficient reform-orientated campaign—concentrating on the need to lower non-wage labour costs and taxes as well as use market forces to generate economic growth—clearly did it no harm at all. What was most irritating for the CDU/CSU was that the late vote-switchers to the FDP came from within the centre-right camp. Much of the talk in the week before the election was of the possibility of a "grand coalition" of CDU/CSU and SPD, should the FDP not poll enough votes to secure a centre-right coalition with the Christian Democrats. Although opinion polls consistently gave the centre-right a majority, the lead was never large enough to be comfortable, and the danger either of statistical error blurring true feelings or of late swings changing the electoral balance could not be discounted. A significant number of centre-right supporters therefore opted—very late in the day—to support the FDP in an attempt to shore up their preferred coalition partner. The fact that 41 per cent of all FDP supporters stated in exit polls that they "actually preferred the CDU/CSU" was clear evidence of this.

The Party of the Left (Linkspartei) was the other clear winner of the 2005 election, polling 8.7 per cent of the vote and re-entering the Bundestag that it had quit in 2002. Although, in legal terms, the Party of the Left was the old eastern German Party of Democratic Socialism (PDS) under another name, its willingness to put candidates from the new left-wing WASG on its open lists undoubtedly made it more attractive to new electoral groups in western Germany. The Party of the Left maintained its stronghold in the east, polling 25.3 per cent, while registering 4.9 per cent in the west. The party's excellent performance in the west—where it had previously struggled to poll even 1 per cent of the vote—had much to do with former Finance Minister Oskar Lafontaine's talismanic presence as a candidate.

Although very few Germans actually sought a post-election "grand coalition"—a coalition of the two major parties—in the cold light of day the results left very little option but to head down this unconventional route. In the immediate period following the election, politicians from all sides did not shirk from attempting to bring rather more creative coalition possibilities to the negotiating table—the imaginatively known "Jamaica coalition" was frequently discussed in the newspapers in the autumn, such a coalition of CDU/CSU, FDP, and the Greens would have involved parties with the same colours as those of the national flag of the Caribbean island—but to no avail.

Schröder's aggressive post-election tactics enabled the SPD to negotiate a surprisingly powerful range of portfolios within the Cabinet formed in November. Eight of the fifteen Cabinet members came from the SPD, while only seven (plus Merkel) came from the CDU/CSU, despite its having polled more votes in the election. Furthermore, the SPD managed to wrestle a number of important portfolios away from the Christian Democrats; in particular, Frank-Walter Steinmeier was a surprise choice as Foreign Minister, while former North-Rhine-Westphalia prime minister Peer Steinbrück took over from his colleague, Hans Eichel, in the Finance Ministry.

Given that it took almost two months of tough negotiations to construct, the prospects of Merkel's "grand coalition" proving to be a cohesive unit were initially bleak. But the new Chancellor's skilful role as an honest broker in difficult and complex debates on the future funding of the EU in November (see pp. 370-72) proved that she was a calm and composed figure, well suited to leading such an uneasy alliance. Germany remained at heart a consensus society and the "grand coalition" under Angela Merkel was, for the time being, probably the government that best reflected this.

FRANCE

CAPITAL: Paris   AREA: 552,000 sq km   POPULATION: 60,000,000
OFFICIAL LANGUAGE: French   POLITICAL SYSTEM: multiparty republic
HEAD OF STATE AND GOVERNMENT: President Jacques Chirac (UMP) (since May '95)
RULING PARTY: Union for a Popular Movement (UMP) (since Nov '02)
PRIME MINISTER: Dominique de Villepin (since June '05)
MAIN IGO MEMBERSHIPS (NON-UN): NATO, EU, OSCE, CE, OECD, G-8, PC, Francophonie
CURRENCY: euro (end-'05 £1=€1.45540, US$1=€0.84774)
GNI PER CAPITA: US$30,090 (incl DOMs), US$29,320 at PPP ('04)

PRESIDENT Jacques Chirac greeted the new year with a vision of transforming France's economy and industrial base, making it a genuine rival of the USA, and hinting that he might seek a third term in office to bring this about. He envisaged an "agency of industrial innovation" to promote the "national champions" of tomorrow. He also looked forward optimistically to a referendum on the proposed constitution of the European Union, though he had reluctantly accepted the idea after British Prime Minister Tony Blair. Support had dipped slightly recently but all the big mainstream parties and most of the media favoured "Yes", and the polls signalled a comfortable majority. A joint session of the National Assembly and the Senate (the upper and lower chambers of the bicameral legislature) at Versailles in February adopted the requisite amendments to the French constitution by 730 votes to sixty-six. (The gathering also incorporated a new environmental charter, intended to lay the basis for environmental protection and sustainable development.)

However, months of political attrition followed. January brought a succession of public service strikes over a wide range of grievances, from pay and perks to job losses, privatisation, a proposed requirement to maintain skeleton services during industrial action, and plans to relax rules governing the 35-hour week. Many students also took to the streets against proposed modifications to the baccalauréat (the school-leaving examination). Chirac had promised that the legal working week would remain at thirty-five hours, but legislation allowing employers greater flexibility in operating it passed through the National Assembly after heated debate. However, as usual, the government ended by giving ground to the protesters, with concessions on public sector pay, the minimum wage and the "bac".

The public mood was further soured by the revelation that the Minister for the Economy, Finance and Industry, Hervé Gaymard, who preached tight controls on expenditure, was moving into a vast apartment at the taxpayers' expense while owning ample accommodation elsewhere in Paris. He also failed to disclose his ownership of other properties. This was fatal. He was promptly dispatched and replaced in February by the fourth Economy Minister in a year, Thierry Breton, chief executive of France-Télécom.

The political atmosphere was further degraded by continuing high unemployment. The Prime Minister, Jean-Pierre Raffarin, admitted that he had no hope of honouring his pledge to bring it below 10 per cent. March brought polls showing the campaign for a "No" vote to the EU constitution had taken the lead, swelled by hardening opposition to the accession of Turkey, even though Chirac had promised that this would require a separate referendum. There were also fears that France was losing influence within an increasingly "Anglo-Saxon", neo-liberal EU. According to Chirac, this was as great a menace as communism had been in its day.

With the government conducting a belated and lacklustre campaign in favour of ratification, the "No" camp steadily gained ground. The President of the European Commission warned that the government was doing too little to explain the proposals to the electorate. In April Chirac answered questions on television from eighty carefully selected young people. This was not a success. Nor was his final appeal just before polling. On a mediocre turnout of 69.34 percent on 29 May the "No" campaign prevailed, with 15,450,279 votes (54.68 per cent) against 12,806,394 votes (45.32 per cent) for the "Yes". The outcome reflected a mix of objections to the constitution itself—principally over Turkey and neo-liberalism—and unrelated domestic grievances. The "No" votes came predominantly from rural and depressed areas, blue-collar workers, and the unemployed. The "Yes" votes were mainly drawn from the more educated, professionals, and city dwellers. The centre-right Union for a Popular Movement (UMP) and the Union for French Democracy (UDF) were the only parties whose supporters predominantly voted "Yes".

The result was widely seen not only as a serious humiliation for Chirac personally but also as reflecting a gulf between ordinary voters and a distant political elite. It was also a stinging rebuff to the mainstream opposition. Disavowed by a majority of its supporters, the Socialist party ejected the former Prime Minister, Laurent Fabius, from its leadership for campaigning against party policy. Attempts to bring into being a potentially winning electoral alliance on the Left were thrown into disarray.

Raffarin resigned immediately after the referendum and was replaced by Dominique de Villepin, with Nicolas Sarkozy returning to the Interior Ministry, the post from which Chirac had required him to resign upon becoming president of the UMP (see AR 2004, p. 43). Michel Barnier was replaced at the Foreign Ministry by Philippe Douste-Blazy. An elite technocrat who had never run for public office, de Villepin was not an obvious choice to build bridges to disaffected voters. Giving himself one hundred days to "restore the confidence of the people", he acknowledged that the referendum had expressed "their suffering, their impatience, their anger". Employment would be his first priority. He pledged over €4,500 million for job creation and a big increase in expenditure on infrastructure projects. However, there would be a "pause" in delivering the tax cuts that Chirac had promised during his 2002 presidential campaign.

While the need for change was acknowledged, the government's room for manoeuvre was limited by Chirac's insistence on maintaining the traditional French social model, with its high taxes and *dirigisme*, and by the sad plight of the public finances. The public debt was 65.8 per cent of GDP, while current expenditure was already threatening to exceed the EU's limit of 3 per cent. In June, the government introduced incentives for the long-term unemployed and new employment contracts giving small employers freedom to dismiss workers during the first two years of employment. Controls on welfare benefits were tightened and privatisation was accelerated, with a partial sell-off of Gaz de France to be followed by the highly controversial sale of motorway toll companies. "Economic nationalism" was the watchword, with de Villepin vowing to shield ten strategic industries from foreign takeovers. One of these was casinos; another appeared to be Danone, a dairy products firm rumoured to be coveted by PepsiCo. The administrations of both Raffarin and de Villepin fought the European Commission over state aid to ailing companies, liberalisation of energy markets and proposed liberalisation of services, increased textile imports from China, and proposals to cut farm tariffs in the World Trade Organisation's Doha round of trade negotiations. As always, expenditure under the EU's Common Agriculture Policy found an unyielding champion in Chirac. (On the wider world scene relations with the USA showed little improvement and France was not included in US President George W. Bush's European tour. Chirac's persistence in advocating a multi-polar world was never likely to heal the breach with the US administration. His proposal to impose a tax on airline tickets to combat global poverty received a polite reception.)

In the customary bout of social unrest in October, some 1,500,000 workers took to the streets, with wide public support, to protest at worsening social conditions, proposals to close down little-used provincial rail services and to sell off a loss-making ferry line serving Corsica. Seafarers seized one of the ferries, stranding many tourists on the island, until the vessel was spectacularly retrieved by airborne commandos. Always apprehensive of the volatile nature of Corsican politics, the government agreed to retain a 25 per cent stake in the privatised company. Anxieties about "creeping privatisation" and the closure of under-used provincial rail services brought rail strikes in November. The government denied any such intention, though SNCF (the national rail company) had to restructure in preparation for competition for freight in 2006. The strike ended with workers receiving a bonus and a pay rise.

Also during the autumn, the government unveiled fresh proposals to promote growth, get the unemployed back to work, stimulate housing development, and reduce energy consumption. It also increased allowances for women having a third child by up to €1,000 per month. Social unrest took a graver turn in November. Near Paris, two youths, believing that they were being pursued by police, clambered into an electricity sub-station to escape and were electrocuted. This sparked three weeks of rioting, beginning in grim sink estates on the outskirts of Paris. These mainly housed immigrants from North and West Africa. Petty crime and drug dealing were rife, the black economy flourished, and unemployment reached 50 per cent. Some 300 cities and towns became affected by the riots, with nightly clashes with the police and many thousands of vehicles destroyed, though only one further death. Sarkozy denounced the rioters as "rabble". While there was criticism of his harsh and insensitive language, he also had widespread public support. Calling for calm and a firm hand, Chirac acknowledged a "lack of dialogue" and recognised that the riots revealed a "deep malaise", denouncing the "poison" of racism. A "social cohesion" programme was announced, with more social housing, more apprenticeships and scholarships, and the establishment of development zones in affected areas. Such schemes had been urged before, but would they translate into reality this time?

The riots severely shook conventional wisdom about French society and the incorporation of immigrants into it. The traditional approach of expecting immigrants to integrate into French society, espousing traditional republican values, was manifestly not succeeding with people with bitter experiences of discrimination and incomprehension and whose culture was resistant to assimilation. With 5 million or so immigrants or descendants of immigrants, here was the greatest problem facing France, larger even than the challenges of globalisation and economic change, which were also being debated at length.

Much less important, yet a thread that ran right through the year, were the internecine struggles within the government between aspirants to win the presidency in 2007. Initially, Chirac hinted that he might seek a third term. Sarkozy became increasingly overtly critical of the President, attacking "twenty years of immobility, waffle, evading reality and ducking challenges". However, when Chirac was hospitalised for a week with a slight stroke in September, a third term looked increasingly unlikely. His illness gave de Villepin a spell in the limelight. He had already been a more successful Prime Minister than many expected. Now, every political action, notably the handling of the riots, was discussed through the prism of the rivalry between the two men and the tension between Chirac and Sarkozy. In December, to his rivals' anger, Sarkozy arranged for the UMP's rules to be amended to allow members to choose their presidential candidate. (Sarkozy, of course, had strong support among the rank-and-file.) But the fight was far from over. Meanwhile, in November, the Socialists somehow restored a semblance of unity, rallying behind their leader, François Hollande, but at the cost of bringing Fabius back into the fold and adopting policies well to the left of the leadership's inclinations. Here, too, there was a plethora of would-be Presidents.

As ever, the year shed further light on old affairs. June brought final confirmation that, as long suspected, the order to sink the Greenpeace vessel, *Rainbow Warrior*, in Auckland harbour, New Zealand, in 1985, killing one person, had indeed been given by President François Mitterrand (see AR 1985, pp. 130; 313-14). And in October, the trial of forty-seven people, including several former senior allies of the President, ended with most being convicted of involvement in rigging public works contracts worth up some €40 million to finance political parties. This had happened when Chirac was mayor of Paris, but as long as he held office he remained untouchable.

ITALY

CAPITAL: Rome   AREA: 301,000 sq km   POPULATION: 57,600,000
OFFICIAL LANGUAGE: Italian   POLITICAL SYSTEM: multiparty republic
HEAD OF STATE: President Carlo Azeglio Ciampi (since May '99)
RULING PARTY: Casa delle Libertá coalition
HEAD OF GOVERNMENT: Silvio Berlusconi (Forza Italia), Prime Minister (since June '01)
MAIN IGO MEMBERSHIPS (NON-UN): NATO, EU, OSCE, CE, CEI, OECD, G-8
CURRENCY: euro (end-'05 £1=€1.45540, US$1=€0.84774)
GNI PER CAPITA: US$26,120, US$27,860 at PPP ('04)

THE impact of globalisation and the European Union on Italy in 2005 were marked, and concern grew that the country's political institutions were unable to meet the challenges presented. When, in June, the European Commission determined that Italy's budget deficit, which was now on target to exceed 4 per cent in 2005 and 2006, had in 2003 and 2004 already exceeded the 3 per cent limit contained within the EU's Stability and Growth Pact, two ministers from the Northern League suggested that Italy should abandon the euro. Whilst not reflecting government policy, statements hostile to EU regulations and the euro continued to be voiced by senior figures, including Prime Minister Silvio Berlusconi. The weakness of Italian public finances was confirmed in November when Italy's public debt, the second highest in the eurozone, was forecast to grow by 2 per cent in 2005 to reach over 108 per cent, ending the trend of successive reductions achieved in recent years (see pp. 373-74).

Consequently, whilst Berlusconi's coalition, elected in 2001, set a record for longevity and ended the year on track to complete a full legislative term, thus setting another record, many found its achievements wanting. That Italians were not impressed by the government's performance was confirmed by the regional elections held in April. The government lost six of the eight regions it had controlled, from the fourteen contested, provoking a government crisis. More generally, both participants and onlookers were increasingly convinced that the 2006 election would confirm the continuing weakness of government, whoever won. It was thus ever more prominently argued that the bipolar party system that had come into existence following the political crisis of 1993-94 had failed to furnish the robust reformist government that Italy needed, so that a return to centrist government was necessary. Certainly the record of Berlusconi's administration was mixed. Most Italians saw it as having failed to implement its promised reforms, particularly tax cuts, and not even the continuing fall in unemployment—to under 8 per cent by the end of year (below the EU average)—persuaded them differently. International institutions such as the ratings agencies, for their part, were disappointed by the limited nature of those structural reforms that had been achieved, notably in regard to pensions and the labour market.

This pre-election year brought a flurry of legislation to conclusion, including, most notably, the bitterly contested revision of forty-eight of the 139 articles of the 1948 constitution. Since the parliamentary opposition opposed the changes, the reform needed confirmation by referendum, expected soon after the spring 2006 election. Many doubted that sufficient popular support would be mobilised, however, particularly as the government itself was divided over the legislation's merits. How significant it would prove to be, were it confirmed, was also contested. Given intra-governmental wrangling and the resulting compromises, some dismissed it as little more than a protracted exercise in "symbolic politics" reflecting especially the Northern League's need to be seen to have had a major impact on the Italian state. Others regarded the changes as worth keeping, not least given the need to strengthen Italy's core executive. Many more reacted with outrage to what was seen as the violation of a near sacred text.

The reform had two major aspects: "devolution", as the Northern League called it, and a reinforced chief executive. For critics, the former, which provided for regional autonomy over healthcare, education, and the local police, was judged likely to increase significantly the costs of public administration, costs that would be further exacerbated if, as critics also expected, intergovernmental disputes over jurisdiction added to the complexity of the legislative process. Concerns were also expressed about growing regional disparity in the provision of social services and even the long-term integrity of the state, notwithstanding the provision for the government to override regional legislation in the "national interest" insisted upon by the National Alliance (AN) and the Union of Christian Democrats and Centre Democrats (UDC).

The second major aspect of the reform would see the "President of the Council of Ministers" become "Prime Minister", whilst cutting back the powers of the President of the Republic. This aspect of the reform sought to ensure that the electorate played the decisive role in the formation of a government by tying the nomination of the Prime Minister to the candidate indicated by the electoral lists obtaining a legislative majority. It also gave the Prime Minister the formal power to nominate and sack ministers, and to initiate the dissolution of Parliament. This was intended as a disciplinary device in the face of Italy's fragmented and strife-ridden party system. For those most concerned by the anomaly of Berlusconi's accumulation of powers, most but not all of whom were on the Left, these powers amounted to the constitutional ratification of the trend towards the establishment of a plebiscitary, illiberal democracy. And yet, there were strong indications that reformists on Left and Right, including the Left's own prime ministerial candidate, Romano Prodi, favoured the strengthening of the Prime Minister, since coalition conflict otherwise rendered the country all but ungovernable. Thus, whilst Berlusconi had survived a full parliamentary term—unlike Prodi who had lasted only half that (1996-98)—conflict within Berlusconi's Cabinet had led to the resignation of his first Foreign Minister in January 2002, and of his Economics Minister (Giulio Tremonti) in July 2004, as well as the collapse of the government in April 2005, albeit a near identical one replaced it within days. By the end of the year, moreover, electoral reform—again pushed through Parliament by government majority in the face of opposition outrage—had brought the return of proportional representation. This not only exacerbated the likelihood of conflict and government instability on the Left, should it win the election, but encouraged and enabled the leaders of the AN, Gianfranco Fini, and the UDC, Pierferdinando Casini, to compete against Berlusconi, as much as against Prodi, presenting themselves as alternative future leaders for the Right in the event of its defeat.

Other controversial legislation passed in 2005 included reform of the criminal law and of media regulation. The latter, having been returned to Parliament by the President for further consideration after its first passage, enabled a new management board to be appointed, helping to stabilise the administration of the state television and radio services (Radio televisione italiana, RAI). Criminal law reform increased the sentences for re-offenders, leading to forecasts of a one-third increase in the prison population to some 80,000—most of whom would be petty offenders—thus exacerbating the crisis of overcrowding in Italy's prisons. The reform also reduced the statute of limitations for a number of serious crimes, including fraud, leading to estimates by the Court of Cassation that over 40 per cent of current trials would collapse. The bill did not, however, lead to the collapse of the trial against Cesare Previti—one of its key aims, according to its opponents—thanks to a late amendment by the UDC exempting trials already at the appeal stage. Indeed, on 2 December, just days after the passage of the bill, the Appeal Court confirmed the five-year prison sentence imposed on Previti in the so-called "Sme" case, for corrupting judges in 1991 on behalf of Fininvest, Berlusconi's financial holding company. Final appeal decisions regarding this and another ruling against Previti, as well as one against Marcello Dell'Utri—another Berlusconi ally and Defence Minister in Berlusconi's 1994 government—were expected early in 2006.

International events loomed large in both the economic and diplomatic spheres. The end of the World Trade Organisation's Agreement on Textile and Clothing limiting imports from the developing world on 1 January revealed especially Italy's vulnerability to China's booming economy, and Italy strongly supported the EU's negotiation of further voluntary export restraint by that country. Globalising trends had an even more dramatic impact in Italy's financial sector. In December, after five months of domestic and international controversy, the governor of the Bank of Italy, Antonio Fazio, was forced to resign for seeking improperly, and perhaps illegally, to block the take-over of two Italian banks by Dutch and Spanish competitors. In September, the scandal provoked the resignation of the (non-party) Economics Minister, Domenico Siniscalco, who had several other points of conflict with the government, and led to the return of Tremonti to that office. More significantly, the extended nature of the crisis magnified the damage done to the image of one of Italy's most prestigious institutions, already tarnished by a string of savings and investments scandals—the Argentinian default of 2002 and the collapse of Cirio and Parmalat, the canned food and dairy product companies, in late 2002 and late 2003 respectively—in which the Bank was accused of protecting the interests of credit institutions at the expense of savers. The severity of the scandal led to the passage of widely welcomed legislation, hitherto languishing, regulating the protection of savers' interests. Late amendment to that legislation also radically revised the regulation of the Bank of Italy itself.

Diplomatically, the year was a difficult one for the government, not least because of its embroilment in Iraq. The government's weak standing in domestic opinion polls, the unpopularity of the policy, and the Spanish government's high profile withdrawal of its troops in 2004 led the Left, if somewhat contradictorily, to advocate immediate withdrawal, embarrassing the Prime Minister whose strong personal support for US President George W. Bush was well known. The situation was exacerbated by the killing, just outside Baghdad airport on 4 March, of a senior Italian intelligence officer, Nicola Calipari, by a US National Guardsman, whilst rescuing a journalist, Giuliana Sgrena, from her kidnappers (see p. 191). In December, the Rome public prosecutor's office formally indicted the guardsman for murder. In June, meanwhile, press revelations of the alleged kidnapping by the CIA of Milan's imam, in 2003, for the purpose of "extraordinary rendition" to Egypt, added to concerns about the USA's apparent abuse of international law, and of its allies.

Whilst polls consistently showed the Left to have a slight lead in voting intentions, it remained plagued by fragmentation and deep rivalries, not least between its diverse historical identities as they struggled to survive the challenge of unification. This process, indeed, was strenuously resisted. However, it was equally strenuously pursued by Prodi and his supporters, and these won a major victory on 16 October when nationwide "primaries" between competing candidates saw Prodi obtain 74 per cent of the vote on a 4.3 million turnout. Whilst this extraordinary grass-roots mobilisation forced the Left's parties to accept Prodi's leadership, they continued to compete vigorously against each other for support.

At the end of 2005, then, the institutional and political situation was very much in flux. Spring would bring parliamentary elections, the election of a new President of the Republic, and a constitutional referendum, as well as the challenge for the new government of formulating a budget package in circumstances crying out for structural reform.

BELGIUM, THE NETHERLANDS, AND LUXEMBOURG

Belgium

CAPITAL: Brussels　AREA: 33,000 sq km　POPULATION: 10,400,000
OFFICIAL LANGUAGES: French, Flemish & German　POLITICAL SYSTEM: multiparty monarchy
HEAD OF STATE: King Albert II (since Aug. '93)
RULING PARTIES: Flemish Liberals and Democrats (VLD), Socialist Party-Walloon (PS), the Reform
　　Movement (MR), and Social Progressive Alternative Party (SPA)/Spirit Party
HEAD OF GOVERNMENT: Guy Verhofstadt (VLD), Prime Minister (since July '99)
MAIN IGO MEMBERSHIPS (NON-UN): NATO, EU, Benelux, OSCE, CE, OECD, Francophonie
CURRENCY: euro (end-'05 £1=€1.45540, US$1=€0.84774)
GNI PER CAPITA: US$31,030, US$31,360 at PPP ('04)

The Netherlands

CAPITAL: Amsterdam　AREA: 41,000 sq km　POPULATION: 16,300,000
OFFICIAL LANGUAGE: Dutch　POLITICAL SYSTEM: multiparty monarchy
HEAD OF STATE: Queen Beatrix (since April '80)
RULING PARTIES: Christian Democratic Appeal (CDA) in coalition with the People's Party for
　　Freedom and Democracy (VVD) and Democrats '66 (D66) (since May '03)
HEAD OF GOVERNMENT: Jan Pieter Balkenende (CDA), Prime Minister (since July '02)
MAIN IGO MEMBERSHIPS (NON-UN): NATO, EU, Benelux, OSCE, CE, OECD
CURRENCY: euro (end-'05 £1=€1.45540, US$1=€0.84774)
GNI PER CAPITA: US$31,700, US$31,220 at PPP ('04)

Luxembourg

CAPITAL: Luxembourg   AREA: 3,000 sq km   POPULATION: 450,000
OFFICIAL LANGUAGE: Letzeburgish   POLITICAL SYSTEM: multiparty monarchy
HEAD OF STATE: Grand Duke Henri (since Oct '00)
RULING PARTIES: coalition of the Christian Social People's Party (CSV/PCS) and the Luxembourg
   Socialist Workers' Party (LSAP/POSL) (since July '04)
HEAD OF GOVERNMENT: Jean-Claude Juncker (CSV/PCS), Prime Minister (since Jan '95)
MAIN IGO MEMBERSHIPS (NON-UN): NATO, EU, Benelux, OSCE, CE, OECD, Francophonie
CURRENCY: euro (end-'05 £1=€1.45540, US$1=€0.84774)
GNI PER CAPITA: US$56,230, US$61,220 at PPP ('04)

For BELGIUM, 2005 was a festival of national pride, marking the 175th anniversary of freedom from Dutch rule. Some cynics suggested that this anniversary was being celebrated because this deeply divided country might not be in existence by the time of the 200th anniversary. Thus, one of the major political issues of the year was language rights in an electoral district on the edge of the capital, Brussels. After months of unsuccessful negotiations which poisoned the political atmosphere, the government decided to postpone a decision for two years. This enabled it to survive a confidence vote, but at the price of laying down problems for the future.

The country's multiple divisions did nothing to assist solutions to its problems of low growth and high unemployment. Industrial production actually fell and consumption flagged. At times it seemed that the federal government of Guy Verhofstadt would collapse from the enmities between socialists and liberals, and tensions between the different cultural communities over retirement ages and social security benefits. Like so many of her neighbours, Belgium had an aging workforce and lengthening life expectancies. Agreement was finally reached in early October. However, this "generation pact" was immediately rejected by rank and file trade unionists. Two well-supported 24-hour national strikes followed, causing widespread disruption. After further negotiations Parliament approved the pact and the 2006 budget in December. The pact incorporated measures to boost youth employment, pension and social security reforms, and an increase in the retirement age from fifty-eight to sixty. The seventh balanced budget in succession highlighted measures to stimulate the economy and increase employment. Spending would be tightly controlled but the budget included reductions in personal income tax and charges on labour. It introduced taxes on insurance premiums and income from a range of financial instruments. A budget surplus would be ploughed into to a reserve to meet future increases in pension costs.

Terrorism touched Belgium during the year. Thirteen men, all Moroccan or of Moroccan descent, went on trial in November, accused of membership of a militant group linked to the bombings in the Spanish capital, Madrid, in 2004, and in Casablanca, in Morocco, in 2003. A Belgium woman became the first female European suicide bomber in Iraq. There were moves in the Senate (the upper house of the bicameral Parliament) to cut off funds from "liberticide" political parties. Two Rwandans were found guilty of crimes linked to the Rwandan genocide. And in December MPs voted to legalise adoption by homosexual couples.

Three inter-related political preoccupations dominated the year in THE NETHERLANDS: the referendum on the proposed EU constitution, immigration, and terrorism. Long a haven of consensus, compromise, and coalition politics, the country was increasingly uncertain and divided about how to manage a more diverse society, what it now meant to be Dutch, and the place of The Netherlands within an expanded EU. Politics had become more volatile and populist, and the gap between the people and the politicians had widened.

The EU referendum on 1 June was the first for two centuries. It had not been wanted by the centre-right coalition government, which was pressed into it by Parliament. The governing parties' campaign for a "Yes" was belated and uninspired, and it carried the additional handicap of unpopularity over the government's tough economic policies. There was little enthusiasm for EU enlargement and even less for Turkish accession. The scale of the Dutch contribution to the EU budget was resented, while the euro was blamed for inflation. The "No" camp took an early lead in the polls, which desperate efforts by ministers in the closing weeks of the campaign failed to wipe out. Indeed, the gap may have widened. On a mediocre turnout of 63.3 per cent, possibly depressed by the French result three days earlier, the "No" campaign prevailed by an unexpectedly high margin, attracting 4,705,685 votes (61.5 per cent) compared with 2,940,730 (38.5 per cent) in favour. The greatest opposition to the constitution came from young, male, and blue-collar voters. As in France, "Yes" voters were preponderantly more educated and middle-class (see p. 40).

In January a poll found only 19 per cent of Dutch people who did not see the presence of almost one million Muslims (about 6 per cent of the population) as a threat. Such fears were fanned by the July trial of Mohammed Bouyeri, of Moroccan origin, for the murder of the film producer and critic of Islam, Theo van Gogh, in 2004 (see AR 2004, p. 51). Defiantly unrepentant, Bouyeri was sentenced to life imprisonment. In December, the trial opened of fourteen men accused of running a radical terror network. Meanwhile, the government launched a range of schemes for deterring further immigration and better integrating those allowed to settle in The Netherlands. In February a new test was introduced for prospective immigrants. They were required to show proficiency in the Dutch language and knowledge of Dutch society. A campaign was launched to encourage women from ethnic minorities to become more socially involved. July brought a bill to punish people who glorified war crimes, genocide, or terrorist attacks. A number of mosques produced a code of conduct aimed at combating extremism in their congregations. A more rigorous approach was adopted towards resident aliens who broke the law, and the government endorsed a university training scheme for imams. The Immigration Minister introduced a plan to expel young Dutch Antilleans who failed to take work or study. In December Parliament voted by eighty to thirty to ban the burka (the veil worn by some Muslim women) in public places.

The Prime Minister, Jan Pieter Balkenende, termed 2005 economically a "bitter-to-sweet" year. Growth was weak and unemployment edged only minimally down, to 6.5 per cent. Yet there were signs that, at last, the country might be emerging from "one of the worst periods of sluggishness in recent decades", as the OECD put it. With the economy benefiting from high prices for natural gas, the budget for the coming year assumed resumed growth of 2.25 per cent, with the deficit falling from 2.3 per cent to 1.7 per cent. It provided extra funding for child care, reductions in personal taxation and corporation tax, and subsidies for wind energy generation and biomass fuel mixtures while increasing taxation on high-polluting vehicles.

Among other issues, the Minister for Government Reform, Thom de Graaf, resigned in May when his proposed constitutional amendment for mayors to be directly elected failed to win the requisite two-thirds majority in the Senate (the upper house of the bicameral Parliament). The government reacted speedily, perhaps excessively, to the threat of avian influenza (bird 'flu) by ordering all free-range chickens indoors. The restriction was relaxed some weeks later when the pandemic failed to arrive. The Health Ministry submitted new rules to Parliament allowing doctors to end the lives of terminally ill infants. In December a Dutch businessman was jailed for fifteen years for complicity in war crimes by selling the chemicals to Iraq that Saddam Hussein's regime had used against Kurdish villages. Dutch troops withdrew from Iraq in March, but up to 1,400 troops were to be dispatched in 2006 for peacekeeping duties in Afghanistan.

For LUXEMBOURG, the first six months of the year were dominated by running the presidency of the EU, with only modest success despite the well-honed skills as a fixer of the Prime Minister, Jean-Claude Juncker. This was followed by the referendum on the EU constitution in July. On a turnout of 90.44 per cent (Luxembourg had compulsory voting), the "Yes" campaign received 109,494 votes (56.52 per cent) and the "No" camp 84,221 (43.48 per cent). The outcome was no surprise: a founder member of the EU and the highest per capita recipient of EU money, Luxembourg had always been among the EU's staunchest defenders. What was surprising was that the "No" campaign made sufficient inroads for Juncker to threaten resignation in the event of defeat. Only one party, the right-wing populist ADR, came out against the constitution, but there was substantial opposition in areas of high unemployment. Juncker hailed success as "every bit as important" as the votes in France and Germany, and the Chamber of Deputies (the unicameral legislature) went on to complete ratification of the constitution by fifty-seven votes to one. An empty gesture, if ever there was one. Yet the European spirit still burned bright: in October a poll found 80 per cent of favourable judgments on EU membership, the highest rate in Europe.

While, in the customary declaration of policy in October, the Prime Minister emphasised the need for reflection on the future development of Europe, his main concerns were domestic: how to tackle the xenophobia that had surfaced during the referendum campaign, new legislation on immigration and political asylum (there were about 3,000 asylum seekers), and the need for the education system to adapt to an increasingly heterogeneous population. While Luxembourg remained proportionally the wealthiest member of the EU, unemployment had risen to 4.7 per cent. The budget sought to reduce it by increased investment in infrastructure projects through a mixture of public and private finance, including additional funds for housing. The budget deficit would rise from €107 million to €301 million.

DENMARK—ICELAND—NORWAY—SWEDEN—FINLAND—AUSTRIA—
SWITZERLAND—EUROPEAN MINI-STATES

NORDIC COUNTRIES

Denmark

CAPITAL: Copenhagen   AREA: 43,000 sq km   POPULATION: 5,400,000
OFFICIAL LANGUAGE: Danish   POLITICAL SYSTEM: multiparty monarchy
HEAD OF STATE: Queen Margrethe II (since Jan '72)
RULING PARTIES: Liberal Party (V), in coalition with the Conservative People's Party (KF) (since Nov '01)
HEAD OF GOVERNMENT: Anders Fogh Rasmussen (V), Prime Minister (since Dec '01)
MAIN IGO MEMBERSHIPS (NON-UN): NATO, EU, NC, CBSS, AC, OSCE, CE, OECD
CURRENCY: Danish krone (end-'05 £1=DKr10.8558, US$1=DKr6.32350)
GNI PER CAPITA: US$40,650, US$31,550 at PPP ('04)

Iceland

CAPITAL: Reykjavík   AREA: 103,000 sq km   POPULATION: 290,000
OFFICIAL LANGUAGE: Icelandic   POLITICAL SYSTEM: multiparty republic
HEAD OF STATE: President Ólafur Ragnar Grímsson (since Aug '96)
RULING PARTIES: Independence Party (IP) and Progressive Party (PP)
HEAD OF GOVERNMENT: Halldor Asgrimsson (PP) (since Sept '04)
MAIN IGO MEMBERSHIPS (NON-UN): NATO, EFTA/EEA, NC, AC, OSCE, CE, OECD
CURRENCY: Icelandic króna (end-'05 £1=IKr108.576, US$1=IKr63.2450)
GNI PER CAPITA: US$38,620, US$32,360 at PPP ('04)

Norway

CAPITAL: Oslo   AREA: 324,000 sq km   POPULATION: 4,600,000
OFFICIAL LANGUAGE: Norwegian   POLITICAL SYSTEM: multiparty monarchy
HEAD OF STATE: King Harald V (since Jan '91)
RULING PARTIES: coalition of Labour Party (AP), Socialist Left Party (SV), and Centre Party (SP)
HEAD OF GOVERNMENT: Jens Stoltenberg (AP), Prime Minister (since Oct '05)
MAIN IGO MEMBERSHIPS (NON-UN): NATO, EFTA/EEA, NC, CBSS, AC, OSCE, CE, OECD
CURRENCY: Norwegian krone (end-'05 £1=K11.6245, US$1=K6.77130)
GNI PER CAPITA: US$52,030, US$38,550 at PPP ('04)

Sweden

CAPITAL: Stockholm   AREA: 450,000 sq km   POPULATION: 9,000,000
OFFICIAL LANGUAGE: Swedish   POLITICAL SYSTEM: multiparty monarchy
HEAD OF STATE: King Carl XVI Gustav (since Sept '73)
RULING PARTIES: Social Democratic Labour Party (SAP) in coalition with Left Party (Vp) and Green Party (MpG) (since Oct '02)
HEAD OF GOVERNMENT: Göran Persson, Prime Minister (since March '96)
MAIN IGO MEMBERSHIPS (NON-UN): EU, NC, CBSS, AC, PFP, OSCE, CE, OECD
CURRENCY: Swedish krona (end-'05 £1=K13.6629, US$1=K7.95860)
GNI PER CAPITA: US$35,770, US$29,770 at PPP ('04)

Finland
CAPITAL: Helsinki   AREA: 338,000 sq km   POPULATION: 5,200,000
OFFICIAL LANGUAGE: Finnish   POLITICAL SYSTEM: multiparty republic
HEAD OF STATE: President Tarja Halonen (SSDP), since February '00
RULING PARTIES: Centre Party (KESK) in coalition with the Social Democratic Party (SSDP) and
    the Swedish People's Party (SFP) (since April '03)
HEAD OF GOVERNMENT: Matti Vanhanen (KESK) (since June '03)
MAIN IGO MEMBERSHIPS (NON-UN): EU, NC, CBSS, AC, PFP, OSCE, CE, OECD
CURRENCY: euro (end-'05 £1=€1.45540, US$1=€0.84774)
GNI PER CAPITA: US$32,790, US$29,560 at PPP ('04)

As in many other parts of the world, the start of 2005 in the Nordic countries was dominated by the Indian Ocean tsunami catastrophe of 26 December 2004 (see map, p. 296). The beach resorts of Thailand were popular destinations for Nordic tourists and it was soon apparent that many Nordic citizens had been caught up in the tragedy. Original casualty estimates proved to be inflated, but the final death tolls for Nordic citizens, confirmed by the national police forces later in the year, were as follows: 543 Swedes, 178 Finns, eighty-four Norwegians, forty-five Danes (and one person still unaccounted for), making the disaster one of the worst to affect the Nordic countries in modern times. The tragedy had significant political repercussions, especially in SWEDEN. It soon became apparent that the relevant authorities in all four countries had seriously underestimated the scale of the disaster in their initial responses. The Foreign Ministries of DENMARK and NORWAY were criticised for this by the opposition parties, and the Danish Foreign Minister, Friis Arne Petersen, admitted that there had indeed been shortcomings. This self-criticism was also apparent in the Foreign Ministry's official evaluation of its own performance, published in May. A report into the Norwegian Foreign Ministry's handling of the crisis, published in April, severely criticised the department for failures in leadership and communication. The Minister, Jan Petersen, acknowledged these criticisms but refused to resign, stating in his defence that no one could possibly have predicted a catastrophe on such a scale. Public criticism of the authorities was more muted in FINLAND but here, too, the official commission of inquiry chaired by the former President Martti Ahtisaari, which reported in June, found that the state administration was ill-prepared for a major disaster and that there had been problems with the flow of information in particular which had delayed the official response.

The government of SWEDEN was severely affected by the crisis. In the immediate aftermath of the tragedy harsh criticism was directed towards the Prime Minister, Göran Persson, and the Foreign Minister, Laila Freivalds, both of whom blamed in turn civil servants at the Foreign Ministry and the Swedish embassy in Thailand. It was suggested that senior officials had put their Christmas holidays before their responsibility to take charge of the situation. In contrast to the unpopularity of the government, the King and the royal family gained much support for their apparent empathy with the general mood of public mourning. The King, too, appeared to offer a veiled criticism of the government when he let it be known in a newspaper interview that he had learned about the disaster via television reports, whereupon he was criticised by the Social Democratic Party secretary, Marita

Ulvskog, for expressing a political view. A catastrophe commission was appointed to examine the government's handling of the crisis. When this reported in December, as expected the criticism was very severe, indeed to a degree that was unprecedented in modern times. Individuals, including Persson, Freivalds, and her deputy Hans Dahlgren, were singled out for their failure to take overall responsibility; but Persson refused to bow to the mounting pressure and dismiss Freivalds. The opposition parties considered holding a vote of no confidence in the government, but decided to wait until the parliamentary Constitutional Committee had completed its own official enquiry into the crisis, a task with which it had been charged in the immediate aftermath of the disaster and which was expected to be concluded early in 2006.

Early in January SWEDEN faced another natural disaster, albeit not one on the scale of the tsunami. The worst storm for over a hundred years hit southern Scandinavia (and other parts of northern Europe), killing eleven people, causing huge disruption, and leaving hundreds of thousands of households without electricity. The worst consequences were felt in southern Sweden, where many thousands of hectares of forest were destroyed. The government responded with tax breaks and compensation for the forest owners whose livelihoods were affected. On a more positive note, one result of the tsunami was perhaps that it triggered the resumption of the Aceh peace negotiations in Indonesia, and talks were held in FINLAND with Martti Ahtisaari acting as mediator (see p. 298).

The tsunami delayed the expected announcement of the general election in DENMARK by some weeks; it was eventually held on 8 February. The campaign produced few surprises and no change of government. Anders Fogh Rasmussen's ruling Liberal (V) party lost four seats but this was offset by gains for its coalition partners—the Conservative People's Party (KF) and their parliamentary supporters the Danish People's Party (DF)—which gained two seats each. The biggest loser was the Social Democratic Party (SD) which lost five seats, and the biggest gains were made by the Social Liberal Party (RV) which won seven new seats. This party, which had campaigned against the government's restrictive immigration policies, won strong support from students and topped the poll in certain trendy districts of Copenhagen, leading it to be dubbed "de Radicoole" in a play on its Danish name Radikale Venstre. Its success was perhaps partly based on its willingness to discuss issues such as welfare reform and taxation in an election campaign otherwise noted for its lack of political debate. Adopting a tactic borrowed from UK Prime Minister Tony Blair's New Labour, the government emphasised its commitment to "contract politics", asking the electors to vote for it on the basis of a number of specific pledges. Another marked characteristic was the "presidential" nature of the campaign with much media interest in the personalities of the two main party leaders, Anders Fogh Rasmussen and the Social Democrat Mogens Lykketoft.

While Denmark's government remained mostly unchanged, apart from a minor reshuffle, the election did have implications for the opposition parties. Five party leaders resigned following the election, including Lykketoft. The SD leadership was contested by the experienced parliamentarian Frank Jensen and the relatively unknown Helle Thorning-Schmidt, who was eventually elected by a narrow margin following an intensive campaign. Nicknamed "Gucci-Helle" for her love of smart clothes, Thorning-Schmidt was seen as representing a change of style for the party, taking it towards the middle ground. She also became the first woman leader of SD, elected during a year when the reputation of the Nordic countries for the prominence of women in political life seemed to be enhanced. The centre left Alliance Party in ICELAND also held leadership elections, and the former Women's List member Ingibjörg Sólrún Gísladóttir won with two thirds of the vote. Opinion polls suggested that the party was in its strongest position for some years, and that under Gísladóttir's leadership it stood a strong chance of forming the next government. Meanwhile, in SWEDEN there was an intense public debate about feminism and gender equality following the foundation of a new feminist party, Feminist Initiative (Fi). The party, associated in particular with the prominent former Left Party leader Gudrun Schyman, initially attracted a lot of support. But by September it had become riven by factional divides between moderate equal rights feminists and those with more radical views, among them a number of academics engaged with queer theory and "HBT" (homosexual, bisexual and transgender) issues. Several prominent figures resigned and the party's support slumped. Nonetheless, it seemed that gender equality would remain an important issue ahead of the 2006 election campaign, not least in relation to family policy and the question of compulsory paternity leave.

In DENMARK the Social Democrats made up for their disappointing parliamentary election results with success in the November municipal elections when they won control of three out of four of the largest cities (Copenhagen, Ålborg and Århus).

The second parliamentary election in the region was in NORWAY in September, which here produced a change of government. At its congress in March the small Centre Party (SP) had decided to turn away from its traditional centre-right coalition allies and instead enter an alliance with the centre-left Labour Party (AP) and the Socialist Left Party (SV). The election campaign was dominated by the perennial issue of how to manage the country's substantial oil revenues. Advocating more money for welfare, the centre-left group won a clear victory over the sitting minority government—consisting of the Christian People's Party (KFP), the Conservative Party (H) and the Liberals (V)—and formed a new government under the premiership of Jens Stoltenberg (AP). The biggest gain was, however, made by the right wing Progress Party (FRP) which under the leadership of Carl I. Hagen won 22.1 per cent of the vote, making it the second largest party in the Storting (the 169-member legislature). Like its sister party, the DF, the FRP had previously supported the centre-right government in the Storting, but announced in June that it was not prepared to support another Bondevik government, forcing the centre-right parties to face the question whether they would be prepared to consider the FRP, with its controversial views on issues such as immigration, as a partner in possible future coalition negotiations.

The controversial issue of EU membership, which divided the AP from its anti-EU coalition partners, was absent from the election campaign. Elsewhere in the region, the governments of both DENMARK and FINLAND announced that the process of ratifying the EU constitution would be postponed, following the rejection of the treaty in the referendums in France and the Netherlands. DENMARK had been due to hold its own referendum in September 2005.

Politics in FINLAND were strongly affected by the forthcoming presidential election, due to be held in January 2006. By the end of the year there were seven candidates, including the current Prime Minister Matti Vanhanen for the Centre Party (KESK), but opinion polls suggested that the incumbent, Tarja Halonen of the Social Democratic Party (SSDP), was likely to enjoy a comfortable victory. Earlier in the year, FINLAND experienced a protracted industrial conflict between the paperworkers' union and their employers over pay and conditions. The conflict began in March when the union introduced a ban on overtime. This later escalated to strike action, and the employers responded by locking out the paper workers. What was remarkable about the conflict was that the union was able to push the dispute to a transnational level, recognising the extent of multi-national ownership within the Finnish paper industry. It sought and gained public pledges of support from paperworkers' unions in SWEDEN and other EU countries, and in doing so gained some public sympathy for its perceived stance against the forces of globalisation.

Debates about globalisation and international capitalism also continued to dominate public life in ICELAND during the year, especially where ownership of the mass media was concerned. In the aftermath of the previous year's controversy (see AR 2004, p. 58) there were further proposals to restrict ownership of the mass media, but it was not thought likely that legislation would do much to curb the dominance of the Baugur Group, which dominated Icelandic print and broadcast media as well as running substantial retail concerns overseas. In September the chief executive of Baugur, Jón Ásgeir Jóhannesson, was acquitted in a Reykjavík court on charges of fraud and embezzlement, but the case did spark a public debate on how Icelandic corporate life was conducted. Shortly afterwards the former Prime Minister, Davíd Oddsson, announced that he would not be seeking re-election as leader of the Independence Party and would thus be retiring from politics, after a twenty-three year career which had been very influential in reforming the Icelandic economy. In his farewell speech to his party's conference, Oddsson criticised the Baugur Group for its manipulation of the media in the recent court case. In a separate development, the government's proposals for the privatisation of the state telephone company, Síminn, angered many when it was announced that there would be no general release of shares until two years after privatisation: it was alleged that the company was being handed over to a chosen few who had already earned huge sums from earlier privatisations. The suggestion by Agnes Bragadóttir, a journalist from the daily newspaper *Morgunbladid*, that ordinary Icelanders should form a syndicate in order to purchase shares provoked an overwhelming response.

Two important anniversaries were celebrated in the Nordic countries in 2005. Neither was without its controversies. In DENMARK, millions of kroner were spent to mark the bicentenary of the birth of the story writer Hans Christian Andersen, but without the desired results: in October it was reported that the celebrations had failed to attract the expected extra tourists to Denmark, and the proportion of the Danish population who took part in the events was also thought to be disappointing. The chair of the HCA 2005 Foundation, and mayor of Andersen's home city of Odense, Anker Boye, was openly criticised by Culture Minister Brian Mikkelsen in the aftermath of a television show in April which finished 13 million kroner in the red. There was particular criticism of the costly decision to hire Tina Turner as the show's main attraction. Meanwhile, in NORWAY and SWEDEN there was a range of events to mark the centenary of the peaceful end of the union between the two countries in 1905. In SWEDEN, this coincided with the decision to make the official national day, 6 June, a public holiday for the first time, adding further fuel to the perennial debate about what "Swedishness" actually was. In NORWAY, the original board of the centennial commission resigned in April following heavy financial losses. It was suggested that the decision simply to "mark" the centenary rather than to celebrate it had dampened the strength of possible enthusiasm for the project, and that the event itself meant little to most Norwegians.

AUSTRIA

CAPITAL: Vienna   AREA: 84,000 sq km   POPULATION: 8,100,000
OFFICIAL LANGUAGE: German   POLITICAL SYSTEM: multiparty republic
HEAD OF STATE: Federal President Heinz Fischer (since July '04)
RULING PARTIES: The People's Party (ÖVP) in coalition with the Alliance for the Future of Austria (BZÖ)
HEAD OF GOVERNMENT: Wolfgang Schlüssel (ÖVP), Federal Chancellor (since Feb '00)
MAIN IGO MEMBERSHIPS (NON-UN): EU, OSCE, CE, PFP, OECD
CURRENCY: euro (end-'05 £1=€1.45540, US$1=€0.84774)
GNI PER CAPITA: US$32,300, US$31,790 at PPP ('04)

ALTHOUGH 2005 was not an election year in Austria, this did not prevent a degree of political upheaval. Not for the first time, the governor of Carinthia, Jörg Haider, was at the centre of events. Although popular in his home state, Haider's approval ratings—as well as support for the party that he had been instrumental in creating, the Freedom Party (FPÖ)—had been on the wane for quite some time across the rest of Austria. This peaked when the FPÖ lost more than half of its support in municipal elections in March, prompting Haider to flounce out of the FPÖ on 4 April in order to form a new party. The Alliance for the Future of Austria (BZÖ) was formally founded on 17 April, with Haider receiving the support of all but one of the 565 delegates in the leadership election. The new party included the majority of FPÖ legislators as well as all of the party's Cabinet members, and it subsequently replaced the FPÖ in the ruling centre-right coalition (in partnership with the Christian Democratic People's Party, the ÖVP). The FPÖ, meanwhile, elected Heinz-Christian Strache as its new leader on 23 April as it attempted to redefine itself.

Changes in the governing coalition prompted the Greens to attempt a vote of no confidence on 5 April. Their attempts failed, but only narrowly. Nonetheless, belligerent rhetoric about the stability of the new coalition from Chancellor Wolfgang Schüssel could not prevent his government from suffering its first legislative defeat when John Gudenus, an FPÖ member of the Bundesrat (the upper house), voted to support a call for early elections made by the opposition Social Democratic Party (SPÖ) and the Greens. Gudenus gained even greater notoriety when, on 26 April, he was forced to resign from the FPÖ after protests over comments which he made on Austrian television questioning the existence of Nazi gas chambers.

Gudenus's disgrace was quickly followed by that of a member of the newly created BZÖ, Siegfried Kampl. An associate of Haider, Kampl was scheduled to take over the rotating presidency of the Bundesrat in July, but his remarks in late April denouncing as "murderers of comrades" those Austrians who had deserted from the Wehrmacht during World War II forced him to resign his Bundesrat seat. Unsurprisingly, disagreements between the FPÖ and the BZÖ occurred regularly throughout the year and as 2005 closed both parties were hovering on the abyss, registering around 4 per cent (which was also the bare minimum a party needed to poll in order to enter Parliament) in most opinion polls.

In other events, the Bundesrat successfully voted to ratify the EU constitution on 25 May by a margin of by fifty-nine votes to three. Austria therefore became the eighth country to ratify the treaty. The Bundesrat was the stage for more dramatic scenes in late October and early November when Chancellor Wolfgang Schüssel's coalition officially lost its majority in the upper house. The changed circumstances came about as a result of impressive electoral performances by the opposition Social Democrats in regional elections (which affected the composition of the Bundesrat) in Styria, Burgenland, and Vienna. The changed balance of power in the Bundesrat was believed likely to hinder Schüssel as he attempted to push through his agenda of socio-economic reform.

Nor was Austria exempt from the effects of terrorism. On 16 November a bomb exploded outside a mosque in Vienna within which a conference on Islam was being held. The bomb, believed to be the work of the far Right, damaged cars and smashed windows but did not cause any casualties.

SWITZERLAND

CAPITAL: Berne   AREA: 41,000 sq km   POPULATION: 7,400,000
OFFICIAL LANGUAGES: German, French, Italian & Rhaeto-Romanic   POLITICAL SYSTEM: multiparty republic
RULING PARTIES: Coalition of Swiss People's Party (SVP/UDC), Social Democratic Party (SPS/PSS), Radical Democratic Party (FDP/PRD) and the Christian Democratic People's Party (CVP/PDC)
HEAD OF GOVERNMENT: Samuel Schmid (SVP/UDC), 2005 President of Federal Council and Minister of Home Affairs
MAIN IGO MEMBERSHIPS (NON-UN): OECD, OSCE, CE, EFTA, PFP, Francophonie
CURRENCY: Swiss franc (end-'05 £1=SFr2.26260, US$1=SFr1.31790)
GNI PER CAPITA: US$48,230, US$35,370 at PPP ('04)

LIKE a number of other countries across Europe, Switzerland saw referendums make the headlines in 2005. In June the Swiss voted on a challenge to the decision by the government and Federal Assembly (legislature) to take Switzerland into the Schengen area. In addition to greater ease of travel for Swiss citizens, the decision also meant increased information-sharing by the Swiss government on cross-border crime and immigration. Turnout was 56 per cent and the decision to join Schengen was upheld by 55 per cent to 45. The vote also meant that Switzerland signed up to the "Dublin accords", allowing it to refuse entry for asylum claimants travelling from EU countries. Nevertheless, the right-wing populist Swiss People's Party (SVP)—one of the parties within the national governing coalition—continued to suggest that the country was on the verge of being swamped by foreigners. The referendum moved Switzerland in the direction of greater economic integration with the EU, if not towards EU membership, which had been resoundingly rejected in a referendum in 2001. Later in the year, on 25 September, the Swiss approved, by 56 per cent to 44 per cent, a decision to grant citizens of the ten new EU member states the right to work in Switzerland from 2011: the fifteen pre-accession EU countries would already have access to the Swiss labour market from 2007. Even though there remained a widespread suspicion of foreign workers, the overwhelming support of business, politicians, and the media helped secure a majority for the referendum proposal.

A referendum held simultaneously with the Schengen vote saw just under 60 per cent support for a motion to allow same-sex couples legally to declare their relationships as "registered partnerships".

EUROPEAN MINI-STATES

Andorra

CAPITAL: Andorra la Vella   AREA: 445 sq km   POPULATION: 66,000
OFFICIAL LANGUAGE: Catalan   POLITICAL SYSTEM: multiparty monarchy (co-principality)
HEADS OF STATE: President Jacques Chirac of France & Bishop Joan Enric Vives of Urgel (co-princes)
RULING PARTIES: National Andorran Coalition, dominated by Liberal Party of Andorra (PLA)
HEAD OF GOVERNMENT: Albert Pintat Santololària (PLA), President of Executive Council (since May '05)
MAIN IGO MEMBERSHIPS (NON-UN): CE, OSCE
CURRENCY: euro (end-'05 £1=€1.45540, US$1=€0.84774)
GNI PER CAPITA: high income: $10,066 or more ('04 est)

Holy See (Vatican City State)

CAPITAL: Vatican City   AREA: 0.44 sq km   POPULATION: 921 (July '05 est)
OFFICIAL LANGUAGES: Italian & Latin   POLITICAL SYSTEM: non-party papacy
HEAD OF STATE: Pope Benedict XVI (since April '05)
HEAD OF GOVERNMENT: Cardinal Angelo Sodano, Secretary of State (since Dec '90)
MAIN IGO MEMBERSHIPS (NON-UN): OSCE
CURRENCY: euro (end-'05 £1=€1.45540, US$1=€0.84774)
GNI PER CAPITA: equivalent to population of Rome

Liechtenstein

CAPITAL: Vaduz   AREA: 160 sq km   POPULATION: 34,000
OFFICIAL LANGUAGE: German   POLITICAL SYSTEM: multiparty monarchy
HEAD OF STATE: Prince Hans Adam II (since Nov '89)
RULING PARTIES: coalition of the Progressive Citizens' Party (FBP) and the Patriot Union (VU) (since April '05)
HEAD OF GOVERNMENT: Otmar Hasler, Prime Minister (since April '01)
MAIN IGO MEMBERSHIPS (NON-UN): EFTA/EEA, OSCE, CE
CURRENCY: Swiss franc (end-'05 £1=SFr2.26260, US$1=SFr1.31790)
GNI PER CAPITA: high income: US$10,066 or more ('04 est)

Monaco

CAPITAL: Monaco-Ville   AREA: 1.95 sq km   POPULATION: 33,000
OFFICIAL LANGUAGE: French   POLITICAL SYSTEM: non-party monarchy
HEAD OF STATE: Prince Albert II (since April '05)
RULING PARTY: the Union for Monaco (UNAM) (since Feb '03)
HEAD OF GOVERNMENT: Patrick Leclercq, Minister of State (since Jan '00)
MAIN IGO MEMBERSHIPS (NON-UN): OSCE, Francophonie
CURRENCY: euro (end-'05 £1=€1.45540, US$1=€0.84774)
GNI PER CAPITA: high income: US$10,066 or more ('04 est)

San Marino

CAPITAL: San Marino   AREA: 60.5 sq km   POPULATION: 28,000
OFFICIAL LANGUAGE: Italian   POLITICAL SYSTEM: multiparty republic
HEADS OF STATE AND GOVERNMENT: Captains-Regent Claudio Muccioli and Antonello Bacciochi
   (since Oct '05)
RULING PARTIES: Christian Democratic and Socialist parties
MAIN IGO MEMBERSHIPS (NON-UN): OSCE, CE
CURRENCY: euro (end-'05 £1=€1.45540, US$1=€0.84774)
GNI PER CAPITA: high income: US$10,066 or more ('04 est)

In the general election in ANDORRA on 24 April the ruling Liberal Union lost its absolute majority and its leader, Marc Forné Molné, who had been due to retire from the presidency of the executive council, lost his seat. The principality's tight citizenship laws meant that only 13,000 of the 65,000 residents had voting rights; 80.4 per cent voted. The Liberal Party of Andorra (PLA) (formerly the Liberal Union), won 5,100 votes (41.2 per cent) and fourteen seats; the Social Democratic Party won 4,711 votes (38.1 per cent) and eleven seats; Andorran Democratic Centre 1,360 votes (11 per cent) and one seat; and Democratic Renewal 772 votes (6.2 per cent) and one seat. The Greens of Andorra attracted 433 votes (3.5 per cent) but no seats. The resulting National Andorran Coalition government was led by the former Foreign Minister, Albert Pintat Santololària.

At the HOLY SEE (Vatican City State) 2005 was a year of change and continuity. After a long period of failing health Pope John Paul II died on 2 April at the age of eighty-four. While assessments of his pontificate inevitably differed, his tireless travelling and television broadcasting had made him the most widely recognised Pope in history. (For obituary see p. 546; see also p. 433). His funeral, on 8 April, attracted to Rome not only an impressive throng of world leaders and dignitaries of every faith and none, but also huge crowds, including many from his native Poland. He was buried in the crypt of St Peter's Basilica. Large crowds also awaited the outcome of the conclave that elected his successor: Cardinal Joseph Ratzinger, seventy-eight, dean of the Sacred College of Cardinals and henceforth Pope Benedict XVI. It was reported that he had gained the requisite seventy-seven votes on the fourth ballot, with Cardinal Jorge Mario Bergoglio of Buenos Aires, Argentina, receiving the second largest vote.

At his installation Pope Benedict struck a conciliatory note, promising to "listen to the world and the will of the Lord". He would "take up the dialogue" over

Christian unity; he met or corresponded with the leaders of many strands of Christianity and met Muslim leaders during his first journey abroad, to his native Bavaria, in August.

Theologically conservative, the new Pope gave no hint of any intention to move the Catholic Church in new directions. He had, after all, been his predecessor's closest adviser. Addressing the Synod of Bishops in October, he appealed for the real spirit of the second Vatican Council to be kept alive. However, while acknowledging the shortage of priests, the Synod made no changes to its stance on priestly celibacy or shared communion. The Pope also called for improved preparation for the priesthood, and the Vatican subsequently endorsed revised guidelines on admission to the priesthood, insisting that the church would not ordain "those who are actively homosexual, have deep-seated homosexual tendencies or support the so-called gay culture". Welcomed by conservatives, the somewhat more restrictive phrasing drew strong criticism from gay activists. The Pope called for a "positive response" to the November riots in France (see pp. 41-42). The Vatican also reiterated its condemnation of torture, terrorism, and the arms race and was sharply critical of the Iranian President's denial of the Holocaust (see p. 263).

In February, the International Court of Justice threw out the claim by LIECHTENSTEIN for damages for former Liechtenstein assets ceded to Czechoslovakia by Germany in 1945 under the Benes Decrees (see p. 419; AR 2004, p. 77). In April an international team of historians reported that Jewish slave workers had worked on the royal family's estates in Austria under Nazi rule and that in 1938 the royal family had bought property seized from Jews in Austria and Czechoslovakia.

In the March elections the turnout was 86.5 per cent. The Progressive Citizens' Party (FBP) won twelve seats, taking 48.7 per cent of the vote. The Fatherland Union (VU), with 38.2 per cent, took ten seats; and the Free List won three with 13 per cent of the vote. The incumbent Prime Minister, the FBP's Otmar Hasler, now led a coalition of three FBP ministers and two from the VU. He committed himself to securing the country's reputation as a bona fide location for financial services. More down to earth, he had to face farmers angered by a ban on feeding hemp to cattle; the animals were relaxed, they argued, but not stoned.

Prince Rainier III of MONACO, who had been head of state since 1949, died on 19 April at the age of eighty-one after a long illness (for obituary see p. 547). He was succeeded by his son, Prince Albert II, who, at forty-seven, had little experience of public life. (Coincidentally, it emerged that in 2003 Albert had fathered a son, Alexandre Coste, from a relationship with a Franco-Togolese flight attendant.) In his accession speech he pledged to place "morality, honesty and ethics" at the heart of his government's concerns and to clean up Monaco's image as a haven for money-launders and undesirables. Among the first to be affected was Sir Mark Thatcher, son of the former British Prime Minister.

SPAIN—GIBRALTAR—PORTUGAL—MALTA—GREECE—CYPRUS—TURKEY

SPAIN

CAPITAL: Madrid   AREA: 506,000 sq km   POPULATION: 44,100,000 (official Spanish data)
OFFICIAL LANGUAGE: Spanish   POLITICAL SYSTEM: multiparty monarchy
HEAD OF STATE: King Juan Carlos (since Nov '75)
RULING PARTY: Spanish Socialist Workers' Party (PSOE)
HEAD OF GOVERNMENT: José Luís Rodríguez Zapatero, Prime Minister (since April '04)
MAIN IGO MEMBERSHIPS (NON-UN): NATO, EU, OSCE, CE, OECD
CURRENCY: euro (end-'05 £1=€1.45540, US$1=€0.84774)
GNI PER CAPITA: US$21,210, US$25,070 at PPP ('04)

THE year began with the Spanish Socialist Workers' Party (PSOE) government successfully spearheading the European Union's opening of a renewed political dialogue with Cuba. The EU dropped the mild diplomatic sanctions that it had slapped on Cuba in 2003 after the summary execution by firing squad of three people who had hijacked a ferry in an attempt to escape the country. Cuba's leader, Fidel Castro Ruiz, had retaliated by excluding EU embassies from all official contacts. The Spanish government came to the conclusion that this policy was getting nowhere and pressed the need for a more constructive engagement, even though there had been little change in the human rights situation. Spain's leading role in the move, coupled with its friendly overtures towards President Hugo Chávez Frías of Venezuela (the USA's other bête noire in Latin America), complicated its fraught relationship with the US administration of President George W. Bush following the withdrawal by Prime Minister José Luis Rodríguez Zapatero of Spain's 1,300 peacekeeping troops from Iraq after he won the general election in 2004 (see AR 2004, p. 64). The USA was particularly incensed by the government's decision to sell Venezuela eight patrol boats and twelve military aircraft.

One area, however, that helped to establish a modus vivendi with the US government and turn the page on Iraq was Spain's increased military presence in Afghanistan. Around 1,000 peacekeeping troops helped oversee Afghanistan's legislative elections and formed a provincial reconstruction team (PRT) in the western part of the country, enabling NATO to carry out the second phase of its stabilisation mission (see p. 265). Zapatero declared that Spain was in Afghanistan "for the same reasons that we pulled out of Iraq, in order to defend peace, the United Nations and international law". Seventeen Spanish soldiers were killed in the country when their helicopter crashed, leading to accusations by the centre-right Popular Party (PP) that the government was over-reaching in Afghanistan in order to mend fences with the USA. A new National Defence law was passed which required the approval of the Cortes Generales (Spain's bicameral legislature) for sending troops abroad and that these missions were backed by international organisations. The previous centre-right Popular Party (PP) government had sent the troops to Iraq without seeking the Cortes's approval and without UN support.

The reversal of the PP's much more pro-Atlantic foreign policy led Zapatero to forge closer relations with Germany and France. On 20 February, Spain became the first country to approve the EU constitution by referendum, but the turnout was only 42.3 per cent, the lowest participation in all of the country's plebiscites since the restoration of democracy in 1975. The referendum was carried by 77 per cent in favour, 17 per cent against and 6 per cent blank votes.

The issue of regional autonomy, a perennial problem in Spain, also flared up during the year. On 2 February the Cortes Generales rejected by 313 to twenty-nine votes the plan for an "associated free state" between the Basque country, which had suffered the separatist violence of the terrorist group Basque Homeland and Freedom (ETA) for thirty years, and the rest of Spain. The plan included a separate judiciary, financial system, and citizenship. In response Juan José Ibarretxe Markuartu, the Basque premier, brought forward the date of the Basque election to 17 April in a bid to win greater support. But the Basque Nationalist Party (PNV), which had been in power for twenty-five years, did not win an absolute majority. It gained twenty-nine seats, four fewer than in 2001, while the Socialists won five more, the Communist Party of the Basque Lands (EHAK) came from nowhere to win nine, and the PP won fifteen, four fewer than in 2001. EHAK acted as a proxy for Batasuna (EH), a political party outlawed in 2003 because of its ties to ETA. Ibarretxe mustered a working majority in the Basque legislature by receiving support from two EHAK deputies and other smaller parties. For the third year running, ETA did not assassinate any one.

Valencian and Catalan nationalists had better luck than the Basques. The Cortes Generales approved the deal struck between the PSOE and the PP, which governed Valencia. Among other reforms, the new charter gave the region's premier the power to dissolve the Valencian legislature. On 3 November the Cortes Generales voted by 197 to 146 votes in favour of admitting the plan for greater autonomy in Catalonia, presented by the Catalan Socialist Party (PSC), the moderate nationalist coalition Convergence and Union (CiU), and the pro-independence Catalan Republican Left (ERC). However, Zapatero said that the plan, which controversially described Catalonia as a "nation" and called for greater autonomy in tax and judicial issues, would not be approved unless it was watered down. The PP, which voted against it, campaigned for a referendum on the issue. Its leader, Mariano Rajoy Brey, accused Zapatero of giving in to Catalonia because the ERC supported the PSOE in the Cortes Generales.

The storming during October of Spain's North African enclaves of Ceuta and Melilla—over which Morocco claimed sovereignty—by several hundred sub-Saharan Africans, armed with makeshift ladders, highlighted the growing concern over illegal immigration. The assaults, which left eleven people dead as security forces opened fire on the assailants, occurred when the Spanish authorities were doubling the height of the razor sharp fences. Television and newspaper pictures of desperate sub-Saharans with their faces pressed against the fences separating the enclaves from Morocco horrified Spaniards, as did the way in which those who stormed the fences and gained a foothold in the EU were treated. Morocco abandoned hundreds of them in remote desert areas without food or water until, as a result of international pressure, they were rescued and shipped out of the country in buses. Spain's agreement with Morocco on the immediate repatriation of illegal immigrants, which had been dormant since it was signed in 1992, was activated.

The breaching of the fences around the enclaves came after the Spanish government had granted an amnesty to almost 700,000 illegal immigrants. Those who were able to provide some form of employment contract and prove that they had lived in Spain for six months were able to "regularise" their situation between 7 February and 7 May (see AR 2004, p. 67). The move was aimed at ending the exploitation of migrant labour and increasing income tax and social security revenues. Spain's foreign-born population had been growing inexorably and reached close to 9 per cent of the 44.1 million population, more than double the level in 2001. Of the 1.9 million people who arrived in the EU during 2005 (according to Eurostat), one-third came to Spain. The rapid rise in the number began to strain the education and healthcare systems.

In the social sphere, Spain became the fourth country in the world—after Belgium, the Netherlands, and Canada—to allow same-sex marriage. The move was fiercely criticised by the country's powerful Catholic Church with which the government was also at loggerheads over changes to religious education in state schools (see AR 2003, pp. 80-81).

The year-long public inquiry into the placing of ten bombs by Islamist radicals on four crowded commuter trains in Madrid on 11 March, 2004, which killed 191 people and injured more than 1,800, concluded that the PP government had "manipulated" and "twisted" information (see AR 2004, p. 65) . The PP had initially blamed ETA, a move seen as a cynical attempt to gain electoral advantage.

The economy grew by around 3.4 per cent, more than double the pace of other EU members. The unemployment rate (8.7 per cent) was the lowest level since 1978 and, remarkably, this happened despite the huge influx of immigrants. One in every three jobs created in the EU during 2005 was in Spain. But this was at the cost of job precariousness: 34 per cent of salaried employees were on temporary contracts, up from 31 per cent in 2004 and compared with an EU average of 12 per cent. The general government balance was in the black for the first time since 1975 (around 1 per cent of GDP). The main reason for this was the hefty surplus in the social security accounts, largely due to the incorporation into the labour force of many immigrants.

The government claimed a big victory at the EU summit in Brussels on 15-16 December on how to carve up the 2007-13 budget (see pp. 370-72). Spain would remain a net recipient of funds during this period even though its per capita GDP surpassed the threshold for cohesion funds. It would also receive €2 billion to promote research and development—a sector where Spain was a laggard—and would benefit from a fund to combat the growing problem of illegal immigration to the European Union. The Socialists had feared that Spain—the largest net recipient between 1986 and 2005—would abruptly become a net contributor.

This was also the year when Spanish multinationals went on a spending spree abroad. Telefónica, the leading telecoms group, acquired the UK's O2 for €26 billion. It was the largest-ever acquisition of a foreign company by a Spanish firm and made Telefónica the word's fourth largest mobile operator when measured by number of clients. Santander, Spain's largest bank, bought 20 per cent of the Philadelphia-based Sovereign Bancorp—the eighteenth largest US bank by assets—for €2 billion. Both of these acquisitions represented significant shifts in the strategies of Telefónica and Santander, which until then had largely concentrated on Latin America where both of them were major players. Ferrovial, Spain's largest construction group, bought the Webber Group in Texas for €646 million.

The country suffered its worst drought in sixty years. On average, reservoirs were at 45 per cent of their capacity at the end of 2005 (56 per cent a year earlier). Production of cereals was about half that of 2004 and the gap had to be filled by imports. Spaniards took it as an encouraging sign that it poured with rain in Madrid on 31 October, the day that Crown Princess Letizia gave birth to her first child, a daughter. Princess Leonor was the second in line to the throne after her father, Crown Prince Felipe. The 1978 constitution, under which the eldest male was automatically the heir to the throne, was to be changed in order to enable Leonor to be queen.

The year ended with a law banning smoking in the workplace as of 1 January 2006, and the laying to rest of the venerable tradition of the siesta—the extended lunch break that often included a snooze—in the public sector. The law decreed that lunch breaks were limited to one hour (from 12 to 1pm) in order to allow civil servants to clock off at 6pm instead of much later.

GIBRALTAR

CAPITAL: Gibraltar   AREA: 6.5 sq km   POPULATION: 27,884 (July 2005 est.)
OFFICIAL LANGUAGE: English   POLITICAL SYSTEM: semi-autonomous UK overseas territory
HEAD OF STATE: Queen Elizabeth II
GOVERNOR-GENERAL: Sir Francis Richards (since 28 May '03)
RULING PARTY: Gibraltar Social Democrats (GSD)
HEAD OF GOVERNMENT: Peter Caruana, Chief Minister (since May '96)
CURRENCY: Gibraltar pound, at a par with UK pound (end-'05 £1=US$1.71680)
GNI PER CAPITA: US$27,900 at PPP ('00 est.)

As a result of the trilateral forum established by the UK, Spanish, and Gibraltarian governments, longstanding grievances began to be aired directly across the table and not in the form of megaphone diplomacy (see AR 2004, p. 67). Spain had claimed sovereignty over the Rock for some 300 years.

Progress was reportedly made on shared use of the Rock's airport, although no details were announced. (Spain did not allow planes landing there to take off for resort destinations in southern Spain.) Opening up the airport to international use would benefit the tiny Gibraltarian economy as well as resorts on the Costa del Sol. The aim was for its use to be shared without damaging any party's sovereignty.

Other issues discussed were the pensions of retired Spaniards living in Gibraltar and telephone communications with Spain. Co-operation on maritime and port issues was also high on the agenda: the Algeciras port authority and Gibraltar's Ministry for Trade, Industry and Telecommunications signed a framework agreement on collaboration. A sticking point was continued British insistence on sending nuclear-powered submarines to Gibraltar, despite Spanish objections.

The UK government agreed to phase out controversial tax-breaks for companies in Gibraltar by 2010. The exempt company scheme allowed companies to avoid paying corporation tax in return for an annual fee. The European Commission claimed that the tax-breaks were a form of illegal state aid, and Spain had long complained of the "unfair" competition from these companies on its doorstep.

PORTUGAL

CAPITAL: Lisbon   AREA: 92,000 sq km   POPULATION: 10,400,000
OFFICIAL LANGUAGE: Portuguese   POLITICAL SYSTEM: multiparty republic
HEAD OF STATE: President Jorge Sampaio (since March '96)
RULING PARTY: Socialist Party (PS) (since March '05)
HEAD OF GOVERNMENT: José Sócrates (PS), Prime Minister (since March '05)
MAIN IGO MEMBERSHIPS (NON-UN): NATO, OECD, EU, OSCE, CE, CPLP
CURRENCY: euro (end-'05 £1=€1.45540, US$1=€0.84774)
GNI PER CAPITA: US$14,350, US$19,250 at PPP ('04)

A new year ushered in fresh hope for Portugal as the Socialist Party (PS), led by José Sócrates, swept to an electoral victory on 20 February. After three years in opposition, the PS secured 120 seats and 45 per cent of the vote, giving the party its biggest margin of victory since the restoration of democracy in 1974. The landslide win owed much to the incompetence associated with the previous Social Democratic-Popular Party (PSD-PP) coalition government and its incumbent Prime Minister, Pedro Santana Lopes. Notwithstanding its victory, the new government inherited many of the problems that had previously plagued Portugal's recession-hit economy. In 2005 unemployment surged to an eight-year high of 7.5 per cent, productivity remained at less than two-thirds of the EU average, and an over-sized public sector continued to soak up the equivalent of 15 per cent of GDP in wages. Controversial measures aimed at reducing the country's budget deficit were introduced; the issue of abortion re-emerged; and all of these events were played out against the backdrop of the worst drought to afflict Portugal in several decades.

The new PS administration was sworn into office on 12 March and Sócrates's first Cabinet included two independent appointments. Diogo Freitas do Amaral, an outspoken critic of US foreign policy, became Foreign Minister and Luís Campos e Cunha, a former deputy governor of Portugal's Central Bank, was made Minister for the pivotal Finance portfolio. On 22 March, the Assembly of the Republic (the unicameral legislature) approved a package of measures designed to modernise the country's economy. These included the restoration of 150,000 jobs lost under the previous government, achievement of an annual GDP growth rate of 3 per cent, increases in state investment in research, and more teaching of the English language in primary schools. The Prime Minister also called for improvements to Portugal's infrastructure, and as the year unfolded, plans for a second international airport at Lisbon catering for the burgeoning low cost airlines, as well as a new high-speed rail link connecting its two biggest cities with the Spanish capital, Madrid, were announced.

The optimism that greeted this projected wave of modernisation, however, quickly evaporated as the state of the economy again became a topic for heated debate. On 23 May the government admitted that the budget deficit could reach 6.8 per cent of GDP in 2005, more than twice the limit set by the EU in its Stability and Growth Pact. Sócrates blamed previous administrations for not revealing the true extent of the problem and called for more time to control the state finances. In spite of these protestations, the European Commission issued a censure on 22 June and ordered Portugal to cut its budget deficit. In response, Sócrates proposed plans to raise value added tax to 21 per cent and reduce public spending in order to bring the economy into line by 2008. These proposals met with strong domestic opposition on 15 July when up to 500,000 workers staged a national strike. A few days later, Finance Minister Luís Campos e Cunha resigned, citing family reasons and exhaustion for his decision. He was replaced on 20 July by Fernando Teixeira dos Santos who pledged to continue with the proposed tax increases and spending cuts. Almost immediately dos Santos had to contend with the news that Portugal would receive less EU cohesion funding from 2007 onwards. This was a potentially damaging blow to a country that had grown used to euro-largesse and was likely to mean a reduction in the total of €23 billion previously attributed to Portugal between 2000 and 2006.

The problems associated with Portugal's hot political summer were compounded by the calamitous effects of drought-like climatic conditions that persisted for much of the year. Around 97 per cent of the country was officially declared to be suffering from severe or extreme drought during July and August, leading to a 70 per cent decline in cereal production and losses for the agricultural sector amounting to at least €1 billion. A lack of rainfall, high temperatures, and tinderbox conditions meant that major forest fires flared in several regions resulting in fifteen deaths, and the destruction of 100 homes and 210,000 hectares of land. Amid suggestions that several fires had been started deliberately, a state of emergency was declared in the area around Coimbra, whole villages were evacuated, and stretches of the main Lisbon-Oporto motorway were closed for a period of time. Thousands of householders in central and southern Portugal had to be supplied with water by tanker, and tourist complexes in the Algarve began drilling new wells in an attempt to find unexploited water reserves. Meteorologists argued over the nature of the problem with the National Water Institute (INAG), claiming that the drought was an anomaly which occurred just once every 150 years. The announcement did little, however, to calm the anxieties of farmers suffering from an estimated 35 per cent loss in income and the deaths of hundreds of livestock.

At the start of his tenure, Sócrates had called for referendums on the EU constitution and the sensitive issue of abortion. Portugal had one of Europe's strictest abortion laws, deeming the practice illegal except in cases of rape, serious foetal disability, or where the woman's life was in danger. Opinion polls suggested that many Portuguese citizens were in favour of relaxing the legislation and overturning a previous referendum in 1998 when the motion to ease abortion had been narrowly defeated (see AR 1998, p. 97). However, on 29 October the country's Constitutional Court thwarted government plans to hold a referendum in November. Judges ruled that the vote could not be held before September 2006 because the same referendum had been rejected by President Jorge Sampaio earlier in the year.

The only bright spot as the year drew to a close reflected the national obsession with football and Portugal's qualification for the World Cup in 2006. On 9 December they were drawn with Iran, Mexico, and first time qualifiers, Angola, strengthening hopes that the relatively young team could make a strong impression in Germany.

MALTA

CAPITAL: Valletta   AREA: 316 sq km   POPULATION: 401,000
OFFICIAL LANGUAGES: Maltese & English   POLITICAL SYSTEM: multiparty republic in British
   Commonwealth
HEAD OF STATE: President Edward Fenech Adami (since March '04)
RULING PARTY: Nationalist Party (PN)
HEAD OF GOVERNMENT: Lawrence Gonzi, Prime Minister (since March '04)
MAIN IGO MEMBERSHIPS (NON-UN): NAM, CWTH, OSCE, CE, EU
CURRENCY: Maltese lira (end-'05 £1=ML0.62480, US$1=ML0.36400)
GNI PER CAPITA: US$12,250, US$18,720 at PPP ('04)MALTA

THE year saw a constant struggle to maintain employment levels and living standards as Malta registered minimal economic growth. "Competitiveness" was the watchword, as the Nationalist (PN) government negotiated with employers and unions with the aim of forging a social pact, after having failed to produce one the previous year. Again, none was achieved and even the common ground among the unions was lost. In particular, the leadership of the dominant General Workers Union (GWU) drew closer to the Labour (MLP) opposition—a traditional ally— and the two pursued a strategy of sustained criticism and public protest against the government's policies and record, pointing to the sluggish economy and the loss of jobs in the manufacturing sector. Politics and industrial relations crossed paths also when negotiations to privatise Sea Malta, the national maritime line, came to nothing due to a stand-off between the GWU and the Italian buyers, which resulted in the buyers backing out and the government closing down the company.

The government, for its part, maintained that it was on track towards its objectives and, moreover, was about to embark on a large-scale EU-backed investment programme that would enable Malta to reach the Lisbon Treaty employment and economic targets by 2008. As discussions on the EU budget for 2007-13 got underway, there was fear that Malta might lose its "objective one" status, reserved for the EU's least developed regions, but this did not happen and the EU budget that was finally approved in December allocated the island a package of €805 million, retaining roughly the current level of funding (see pp. 370-72). In April, meanwhile, Malta joined the new EU exchange-rate mechanism (ERM II) with a view to adopting the euro in January 2008. In July, the House of Representatives (the unicameral legislature) unanimously ratified the EU constitution, with the MLP having to fend off eurosceptic hard-liners who opposed the party's turn-around from its earlier anti-EU stance, which many believed had lost it the general election in 2003 (see AR 2003, pp. 85-86).

Other than that, the defining feature of the year was the heavily increased influx of migrants and refugees stranded, adrift, or shipwrecked on their journey to mainland Europe. Reacting to foreign criticism over the treatment of migrants in detention centres and to demands that Malta take back migrants who succeeded in proceeding to Italy, the government demanded the EU treat the problem as a European one and share both in patrolling the waters and in absorbing the refugees. Concurrently, Malta appealed to Libya, from where most African migrants seemed to be embarking. The Libyan authorities claimed inability to patrol their 2,000 km coastline, but a meeting of Foreign Ministers of the "Five plus Five" (the institutional forum of five southern European and five North African countries), held in Malta in June, agreed to organise an international conference on the problem in Libya in 2006. Meanwhile, Malta's traditionally amicable relations with that country were further troubled when Libya, in April, unilaterally declared a 62-mile "fishing conservation zone", which included extensive Maltese historical fishing grounds.

GREECE

CAPITAL: Athens   AREA: 132,000 sq km   POPULATION: 11,100,000
OFFICIAL LANGUAGE: Greek   POLITICAL SYSTEM: multiparty republic
HEAD OF STATE: President Karolos Papoulias (since March '05)
RULING PARTY: New Democracy (ND)
HEAD OF GOVERNMENT: Kostas Karamanlis, Prime Minister (since March '04)
MAIN IGO MEMBERSHIPS (NON-UN): NATO, EU, OSCE, CE, BSEC, OECD
CURRENCY: euro (end-'05 £1=€1.45540, US$1=€0.84774)
GNI PER CAPITA: US$16,610, US$22,000 at PPP ('04)

THE theme of the year was undoubtedly corruption. In 2005, the non-governmental organisation, Transparency International, ranked Greece as one of the most corrupt states in the EU, outperformed only by two recent east European entrants.

The focus of domestic debate—the "entangled interests" of media barons influencing the award of public sector contracts—had already been the theme of a 2001 constitutional amendment and a law passed in 2002. Further legislation was passed in January, banning any individual with a 1 per cent share in a media enterprise—or having a relative up to the third degree holding such a share—from participating in bids for public sector tenders. There followed a public battle with the European Commission which reached an inglorious conclusion in April with the Commission's ruling that the law (and the constitutional amendment) violated fundamental principles within the EU's founding treaties. The Commission also challenged the concept behind the legislation, commenting that the media's ability to influence politicians should be irrelevant if public procurement procedures were properly conducted in accordance with EU directives. The law was immediately suspended and subsequently replaced by a vague formulation, permitting scrutiny after the fact only in cases of apparent undue media pressure.

In September, attempting to stem the rising tide of corruption allegations against the government, New Democracy took the startling step of expelling a member of Parliament for acknowledging the existence of improbity within the governing party. To no avail: a series of high level resignations during the year included an Interior Ministry adviser, for running a business sideline fixing public sector hirings; the deputy minister for Finance, whose repeated gaffes included a speech suggesting customs officials should ask for smaller bribes; and former European commissioner Yannis Paleokrassas, who left his post as president of the Public Power Corporation, claiming it was being "ravaged" by an inter-party mafia.

Following persistent claims that news presentation was being shaped by reporters who were secretly on the government payroll, in January the union of journalists published a list of its members employed by the state. Although the catalogue was clearly incomplete, further disclosures were deterred when the union was fined for publishing personal data. In February, revelations of systematic and widespread bribery of judges triggered a crisis within the judiciary, including the subsequent resignation and prosecution of the vice-president of the Supreme Court.

Multi-faceted scandals also erupted within the Orthodox Church, running the gamut from involvement in judicial corruption and peddling stolen antiquities to homosexual relationships among the supposedly celibate higher clergy (see p. 433). While many believed the time had finally come to address the anachronistic state-church relationship, the government chose instead to legislate the establishment of four state-financed ecclesiastical universities, for male students only and with admissions and teaching controlled by the church.

Following the upward revision of national budget deficit figures in 2004, the Greek economy came under close EU scrutiny. In February, the European Council demanded that by 2006 Greece reduce its budget deficit below the 3 per cent of GDP permitted by the Stability and Growth Pact. By the year's end, however, it was clear that this goal was unattainable before 2007.

A central aim of government policy was to reduce the size of the public sector. In May the national telecommunications company negotiated an agreement entailing 6,000 voluntary redundancies, with all future hiring to be based on private sector-style contracts. In December, the government introduced a bill ending tenure for all new public sector employees, immediately triggering a two-day strike. A major setback concerned the cancellation of the fifth attempt to privatise Olympic Airways, after a European Commission ruling that the company repay €700 million of illegal state aid. Changes to the framework governing labour relations also affected the private sector, including the introduction of flexible working hours to cut overtime costs and the extension of shop opening hours. Despite these unpopular economic policies, rising inflation and a tough 2006 budget, opinion polls consistently showed the government ahead of the official opposition. PASOK, still engaged in introspection following its 2004 election defeat, simply seemed unable to offer a convincing alternative.

An economic bright spot was provided by the December EU budget deal, allocating Greece €20.1 billion for the period 2007-13 and granting a one-year extension for the absorption of the funding for 2000-06. That Greece had managed to spend only one-third of the latter by the end of 2005 raised the question how much the country would actually benefit from the new budgetary inflows. On 19 April,

Greece became the sixth EU member-state to ratify the EU constitution, follow-ing a parliamentary vote of 279 for and seventeen against. Ratification, supported by the conservative New Democracy and socialist PASOK, was opposed by the communist party (KKE) and left coalition (SYN). Potential tension over the Macedonian question was postponed, when Greece agreed to the recognition of its northern neighbour as a candidate for EU entry on condition the EU continue to use the appellation of Former Yugoslav Republic of Macedonia rather than the country's constitutional name (see p. 96).

As elsewhere in Europe, human rights violations and the surrender of national sovereignty in the cause of counter-terrorism became a major issue. In Greece, the central focus was on the claim that twenty-eight Pakistanis had been abducted, interrogated, and maltreated by Greek and British undercover agents following the London bombings in July (see pp. 14-15). Although the Minister of Public Order dismissed the claims, on 25 December a newspaper named the Greek secret serv-ice employees and the Athens chief of the UK's intelligence agency, MI6, who were allegedly involved, prompting the public prosecutor to order an investigation.

The worst accident in the history of Greek aviation occurred on 14 August, killing 121 people. Mystery surrounded the episode, with the Cypriot charter plane apparently flying over Greek airspace on automatic pilot for almost two hours, possibly following a loss of cabin pressure which incapacitated the pilots.

For many Greeks, the highlight of the year was the country's victory in the Eurovision song contest. Singing in English, Helena Paparizos, the Swedish-born daughter of Greek migrants, provoked an outburst of national fervour and the highest viewing ratings ever recorded in the history of Greek television.

CYPRUS

CAPITAL: Nicosia   AREA: 9,250 sq km   POPULATION: 928,600: 715,100 Greek Cypriots and others
('02 census); est. 213,500 Turkish Cypriots and Turkish immigrants in the north, of which
87,400 Turkish Cypriots, down from approximately 120,000 in 1974.
POLITICAL SYSTEM: separate multiparty republics: Republic of Cyprus (recognised by UN), Turkish
Republic of Northern Cyprus (TRNC—recognised only by Turkey)
HEAD OF STATE AND GOVERNMENT: President Tassos Papadopoulos (since Feb '03); in the TRNC
President Mehmet Ali Talat (since April '05); Ferdi Sabit Soyer (CTP), Prime Minister (since
April '05)
RULING PARTIES: representatives of the Democratic Party (DIKO), the Communist Party (AKEL)
and the Socialist Party of Cyprus (EDEK) form the Cabinet in the Republic of Cyprus;
Republican Turkish Party (CTP) and Democrat Party (DP) form coalition in TRNC
MAIN IGO MEMBERSHIPS (NON-UN): Republic of Cyprus: EU, OSCE, CE, CWTH; TRNC observer at OIC
CURRENCY: Cyprus pound (end-'05 £1=C£0.83450, US$1=C£0.48610); Turkish new lira in the
north (end -'05 £1=TL2.32020, US$1=TL1.35150)
GNI PER CAPITA: Republic of Cyprus: US$17,580, US$22,330 ('04, based on regression); TRNC:
GNP per capita US$6,850

DESPITE the election in April of a new Turkish Cypriot community leader com-mitted to a federal settlement—thus ending forty years of domination by the secessionist Rauf Denktash—2005 was a fallow year for efforts to re-unite the island. Attempts to find a federal solution ahead of the accession of the Repub-lic of Cyprus to the EU on 1 May 2004 had failed when Greek Cypriots over-

whelmingly rejected a settlement plan drafted by UN Secretary-General Kofi
Annan (see AR 2004, pp. 74-75). The Turkish Cypriots had accepted the plan,
despite opposition to it by President Denktash. Thus, after years of being cast
in the role of the rejectionist party in the thirty-one-year-old dispute, the Turkish Cypriots became the object of efforts by the international community to end
the economic isolation arising from the embargo imposed by the Greek Cypriots through the use of their international recognition as the legitimate government of the country.

On 29 April 2004, after the collapse of the settlement efforts, the EU adopted
measures designed to promote freedom of movement of people and goods across
the demilitarised zone (DMZ) and to provide €259 million in aid to the Turkish
Cypriots during the period 2004-06 to boost their flagging economy. The Greek
Cypriots endorsed the aid package but said that it would have to be mediated
through the legally recognised authorities, which the Turkish Cypriots rejected.
As a consequence, the €120 million EU budgetary line for 2005 lapsed with none
of that year's aid disbursed.

The European Commission recognised export documents produced by the
Turkish Cypriot Chamber of Commerce and appointed phytosanitary experts to
carry out controls on products shipped from the north. However, the Greek
Cypriots said that, while there could be trade across the DMZ, any international trade would have to be conducted through recognised ports. The Turkish Cypriots demanded full opening of the northern ports of Famagusta and
Kyrenia. As a compromise the Greek Cypriots suggested a transit centre for
Turkish Cypriot goods, jointly supervised by Greek Cypriots, Turkish Cypriots, and EU officials, either at Larnaca or Famagusta. The Turkish Cypriots
continued to insist on unconditional direct trade, which the Greek Cypriots
continued to refuse, arguing that it would imply a form of recognition of the
TRNC. Turkish Cypriot exports continued, therefore, to be trans-shipped via
Turkey. Because of various bureaucratic obstacles and a general reluctance of
each community to purchase goods from the other, domestic trade in 2005
amounted only to about C£1 million north-to-south and just C£127,000 in the
opposite direction.

Conversely there was an increase in the flow of persons across the DMZ as
Turkish Cypriots travelled south to work, collect pensions, seek medical treatment, and apply for passports; while Greek Cypriots travelled north to deal with
property and other business matters, and to undertake sentimental and religious
pilgrimages. The UN reported in December 2005 that there had been more than
9 million crossings since control posts opened in 2003.

The UN Secretary-General, in the wake of the rejection of his settlement
package, shelved his mission of good offices and did not re-appoint a special
adviser for Cyprus. In the light of the more relaxed situation regarding the
DMZ, the United Nations Peacekeeping Force (UNFICYP) was reduced
between January and April from 1,238 to 860 and its operational sites and
patrol bases cut between one-half and one-third. Its civilian police complement was expanded.

Legislative elections in the TRNC on 20 February gave 44.5 per cent of the vote and twenty-four seats in the fifty-seat assembly to the left-of-centre Republican Turkish Party (CTP), which had consistently promoted a federal settlement. A coalition government was formed in collaboration with the Democratic Party of Serdar Denktash, the President's son. In presidential elections held on 17 April, the CTP leader, Mehmet Ali Talat, secured a first round victory with a vote of 55.6 per cent. (As the presidential post was supposed to be above politics, the CTP elected a new party leader, Ferdi Sabit Soyer, who became Prime Minister.) The eighty-one-year-old Rauf Denktash who had acted as Turkish Cypriot community leader since 1965 and as President of the breakaway republic since 1983, did not stand for re-election following the acceptance by the Turkish Cypriots of the Annan Plan, which he had opposed. He said that he would continue to lead a campaign for recognition of the TRNC as an independent nation or as a province of Turkey.

In the wake of the TRNC elections there was a flurry of contacts with a view to possible recommencement of settlement negotiations. On 17 May, the Secretary-General had informal contacts in Moscow with the Greek Cypriot President Tassos Papadopoulos and the Turkish Prime Minister Recep Tayyip Erdogan and between 30 May and 7 June Sir Kieran Prendergast, Under-Secretary General for Political Affairs, undertook exploratory contacts on the island and in Athens and Ankara. His conclusion was that "the gap between the stated positions of the parties on substance appears to be wide, while confidence between them does not seem high. [. . .] Launching an intensive new process prematurely would be inadvisable." Annan had meetings in New York with Papadopoulos on 16 September and with Talat on 31 October but concluded, in his semi-annual report to the UN Security Council on 29 November, that "while calls have come from all concerned for the resumption of negotiations, it appears that the conditions surrounding such a resumption necessitate further clarifications."

Meanwhile a confrontation between Turkey and the EU over Cyprus nearly jeopardised that country's efforts to commence accession talks for community membership. The European Council set 3 October as the date for the start of talks, subject to the satisfaction of a number of conditions by the Turkish government, including the signature and application of an additional protocol extending its association agreement to the ten enlargement states (of which Cyprus was one). Turkey signed the protocol on 29 July, but coupled it with a unilateral declaration which said that it would not recognise Cyprus until such time as there was a federal settlement. It also said that it would continue to ban Cypriot ships and aircraft from its ports and airports. After prolonged diplomatic manoeuvring, the government of the Republic of Cyprus was persuaded to agree to commencement of negotiations in exchange for conditions under which Turkey would either fully extend its association agreement or face suspension of negotiation of certain chapters of the acquis communautaire until such time as it became compliant (see p. 72). The situation was to be reviewed in the course of 2006.

WESTERN AND SOUTHERN EUROPE

TURKEY

CAPITAL: Ankara   AREA: 775,000 sq km   POPULATION: 71,700,000
OFFICIAL LANGUAGE: Turkish   POLITICAL SYSTEM: multiparty republic
HEAD OF STATE: President Ahmet Necdet Sezer (since May '00)
RULING PARTY: Justice and Development Party (AKP) (since Nov '02)
HEAD OF GOVERNMENT: Recep Tayyip Erdogan (since March '03)
MAIN IGO MEMBERSHIPS (NON-UN): NATO, OSCE, OECD, CE, OIC, ECO, BSEC
CURRENCY: new lira (end-'05 £1=TL2.32020, US$1=TL1.35150)
GNI PER CAPITA: US$3,750, US$7,680 at PPP ('04)

NEGOTIATIONS on Turkey's accession to the European Union began formally in Luxembourg on 3 October. A demand by Austria that the document setting out the framework within which the negotiations were to be conducted should mention that these might lead to a privileged partnership rather than to full membership was withdrawn at the last moment. However, while membership remained the objective, Turkey was warned that success could not be guaranteed and that the talks would last at least ten years. Before this limited commitment could be achieved, Turkey extended to the ten new members that joined the EU on 1 May 2004 the provisions of its customs union with the original membership. One of these new members was the Republic of Cyprus, whose Greek Cypriot government did not control the northern third of the island which was ruled by a Turkish Cypriot administration, recognised by Turkey alone as the Turkish Republic of Northern Cyprus (TRNC). Turkey's decision to extend the customs union was accompanied by a declaration that it did not recognise the jurisdiction of the Republic of Cyprus over the whole island. The EU answered with a statement that the same provisions should be applied to all members and that it would decide by the end of 2006 whether Turkey had met its obligations under the extended customs union (see p. 71).

Both Turkey and Turkish Northern Cyprus (where the left-wing politician, Mehmet Ali Talat, who had campaigned in favour of the UN settlement plan rejected by the Greek Cypriots the previous year, increased his majority in parliamentary elections on 20 February and was elected President of the republic on 17 April, see p. 71) failed to get the negotiations restarted under UN auspices, and the Greek Cypriots continued to block the aid which the EU had promised the Turkish Cypriots.

The unresolved Cyprus problem was one reason why the emphasis in Turkey's relationship with the EU moved from the formal start of membership negotiations to efforts to avoid their suspension. Negotiations were also threatened by concern over freedom of expression in Turkey. On 1 June Turkey introduced a new penal code, as the finishing touch of its reforms to meet the standards of democratic governance required of candidates for EU membership. However, the government of Recep Tayyip Erdogan, leader of the ruling Justice and Development Party (AKP), disregarded warnings by Turkish journalists that, although more liberal in intention, the new code contained provisions which threatened freedom of expression. These concerns were heightened on 7 October when a Turkish Armenian journalist, Hrant Dink, was given a suspended prison sentence of six months for insulting "Turkishness". There was an international outcry when the same charge was brought against Turkey's best-known novelist, Orhan Pamuk. His trial opened on 16 December amid clashes between nationalist critics and liberal supporters of the author, and was immediately adjourned, as the magistrate ruled that the Minister of Justice, who had tried to distance himself from the affair, had to authorise the prosecution. As the year ended, the Minister had still to commit himself, and nationalist lawyers were trying to incite further proceedings against liberals, while the authorities were considering bringing contempt of court charges against critics of the judiciary. One high-profile case, which brought the government into conflict with the higher education board, concerned the detention of the rector of the university in Van accused of irregularities in purchases of equipment. The rector, Yucel Askin, who was known for his hostility to Islamists, was freed pending trial at the end of December, but Enver Arpali, the assistant secretary-general of the university, who was detained with him, committed suicide in prison.

Kurdish nationalist militants of the PKK (Kurdistan Workers Party) continued to infiltrate from northern Iraq, sending snipers and laying mines in the south east of the country where the security forces suffered a number of casualties. In November the authorities promised to investigate reports that a bomb attack on a known PKK supporter in the mountainous south-eastern province of Hakkari had been part of an undercover security operation by the Turkish gendarmerie. An offshoot of the PKK, operating under the name of Freedom Falcons of Kurdistan (TAK), targeted the tourist industry. The worst attack occurred on 16 July in the Aegean coastal resort of Kusadasi where a bomb planted in a minibus killed five, including a British and an Irish national. Turkish efforts to persuade the USA to take action against the PKK in Iraq yielded no concrete results. Nevertheless close relations were maintained with the US administration. Prime Minister Erdogan visited the USA three times, meeting President George W. Bush on 8 June; Secretary of State Condoleezza Rice was in Ankara in February; and in December the directors of the US security agencies, the Central Intelligence Agency (CIA) and the Federal Bureau of Investigation (FBI), went to Turkey, while the Turkish commander of land forces General Yasar Buyukanit held discussions in the US capital, Washington DC.

The prospect of EU membership emboldened Kurdish nationalist politicians in Turkey, who launched a new Democratic Society Party (DTP) in November. It took over from the Democratic People's Party (DEHAP), which dissolved itself on 20 November. The following month fifty-six mayors (including Osman Baydemir, mayor of Diyarbakir, the chief city of the Kurdish-inhabited region), most of whom had been elected on the DEHAP ticket, joined DTP. They then took the unprecedented step of asking the Danish authorities to resist Turkish government pressure to withdraw the licence of the Kurdish satellite television station, Roj-TV, on the grounds that it transmitted terrorist propaganda.

Prime Minister Erdogan's statement on 10 August that he recognised that Turkey faced a Kurdish problem and that he intended to solve it by democratic means was criticised by opposition parties. They accused the government of failing to protect national interests by yielding to EU pressure on rights for the Kurds, as well as on Cyprus. The campaign was led by the Republican People's Party (CHP), which used to be described as left-of-centre or social-democratic. The party re-elected to the leadership Deniz Baykal, seen increasingly as a Turkish nationalist politician. Nationalist influence was further strengthened when transfers from other parties allowed the Motherland Party (ANAP) to acquire twenty-two seats in the Grand National Assembly (the unicameral legislature). It elected a new leader, Erkan Mumcu, formerly a minister in Erdogan's government.

The economy grew by 5.5 per cent in the first nine months of the year. On 25 May a ceremony in Baku, the Azerbaijani capital, marked the completion of the Baku-Tbilisi-Ceyhan pipeline, built at a cost of some US$3 billion by a consortium led by the global energy group, BP. The shipment of Azeri oil through this new facility was expected to start in mid-2006. On 17 November another major project, the Blue Stream pipeline, which carried Russian natural gas directly to Turkey (and thus supplemented the pipeline which ran through Ukraine and the Balkans) was inaugurated at a ceremony in the Turkish Black Sea port of Samsun. The pipeline, which was laid by Italian engineers at a depth of up to 2,150 metres under the Black Sea, had an annual capacity of 3.7 billion cubic metres. Russia's President Vladimir Putin, who joined Erdogan and the Italian Prime Minister Silvio Berlusconi, at the ceremony, proposed that a parallel pipeline should be built to ship Russian oil through Turkey to world markets.

Foreign trade expanded: exports growing by over 16 per cent to US$66 billion and imports by 20 per cent to US$105 billion in the first eleven months of the year. Increased tourist revenue helped to offset the growing trade deficit: the number of foreign visitors increased by a fifth to over 20 million. They spent US$14.5 billion. Inflation (in terms of consumer prices) fell from 9.3 per cent to a record low level of 7.7 per cent year-on-year. The Istanbul stock exchange index rose from 25,000 to 40,000 points during the year. In December, news that the UK's Vodaphone company had paid over US$4.5 billion for control of Telsim, Turkey's second largest mobile telephone operator, enhanced market optimism. So too did the agreement reached in December with the IMF, which had been monitoring Turkey's stabilisation programme since the 2001 financial crisis (see AR 2001, pp. 111-12). The IMF declared itself satisfied with Turkey's progress, and specified that reform of the social security system should be the most important next step. However, the improvement in the economy had little effect on employment: with only half the population of working age participating in the labour market, some 10 per cent were unemployed, a proportion that rose to nearly 20 per cent among young people.

III CENTRAL AND EASTERN EUROPE

POLAND—BALTIC STATES—CZECH REPUBLIC—SLOVAKIA—HUNGARY—
ROMANIA—BULGARIA

POLAND

CAPITAL: Warsaw   AREA: 323,000 sq km   POPULATION: 38,200,000
OFFICIAL LANGUAGE: Polish   POLITICAL SYSTEM: multiparty republic
HEAD OF STATE: President Lech Kaczynski (PiS), (since Dec '05)
RULING PARTIES: Law and Justice (PiS) and Civic Platform (PO)
HEAD OF GOVERNMENT: Kazimierz Marcinkiewicz (PiS), Prime Minister (since Oct '05)
MAIN IGO MEMBERSHIPS (NON-UN): NATO, OSCE, CE, CEI, CEFTA, CBSS, OECD, Francophonie, EU
CURRENCY: zloty (end-'05 £1=Zl5.59220, US$1=Zl3.25740)
GNI PER CAPITA: US$6,090, US$12,640 at PPP ('04)

Two opposition centre-right parties—Law and Justice (PiS) and Civic Platform
(PO)—won a landslide in elections to both houses of the legislature on 25 September. Together they took 288 seats in the 460 seat Sejm (the lower house).
Their victory was followed in October by a run off election for the presidency in
which the populist Lech Kaczynski (PiS), with 54 per cent of the vote, defeated
his rival, Donald Tusk (PO), who had won the first round. However, the low
turnout in these contests—41 per cent and 51 per cent respectively—reflected
widespread disillusionment with politics.

Following the legislative elections, the leader of the PiS, the nationalist and conservative Jaroslaw Kaczynski, declined the post of Prime Minister on the grounds
that his identical twin, Lech, was running for the presidency in the October. Coalition talks with the more centrist and pro-European Union PO failed and eventually a Cabinet was constructed from Law and Justice legislators and independents
(the latter receiving eight out of the seventeen posts), with the premiership going
to Kazimierz Marcinkiewicz of the PiS.

The main loser was the Democratic Left Alliance (SLD). Despite polling 41
per cent in the previous (2001) elections, whilst in government it had been unable
to pass any legislation, including urgent budget reforms. Its entire leadership
resigned in May and the party slumped to a mere 11 per cent of the vote (fifty-five
seats) in the September election. The defeat reflected many corruption scandals,
and accusations that SLD members had profited from the post-communist privatisation of state resources.

The SLD had also failed to tackle unemployment, which at 17.6 per cent was
the highest in the EU. Only 52 per cent of those of working age had a job, many
of them in the hugely inefficient state bureaucracy. Strategically-placed groups,
such as miners, secured early pensions, despite fierce opposition from the independent Central Bank which pointed out that this would put Poland's budget
deficit far in excess of the limits required for the country to join the eurozone.
However, as the EU's biggest new entrant, and the USA's main ally in Eastern

Europe, Poland became the region's largest foreign investment destination (74 per cent of inward investment from the EU). Exports boomed, the current account was sound, and inflation remained low.

The elections also reflected a popular feeling that de-communisation was incomplete. The new President, Lech Kaczynski, condemned a "Bermuda quadrangle" of corrupt politicians, police agents, businessmen, and criminals who were holding Poland back. Such populist rhetoric was accompanied by a raft of right-wing social policies. He opposed abortion and gay rights, seeking a "moral renewal" and Christian values. He supported the death penalty, despite EU policy. A more pro-nationalist stance included seeking German payment of reparations for World War II damages.

On 18 February, the Institute of National Memory apologised for leakage via the Internet of a communist-era secret service file of agents, collaborators, and their victims. Its list of 240,000 names failed to distinguish agents from victims, thus leading to the fear that the innocent would be condemned by public opinion.

On 21 August, former President General (retd) Wojciech Jaruzelski, mainly remembered in Poland for his imposition of martial law to curb the Solidarity movement in 1981 (see AR 1981, pp. 116-18), apologised for his role in the five-power invasion of Czechoslovakia in August 1968 to crush the "Prague spring" reform movement (see AR 1968, pp. 212-21). On Czech television, the eighty-two-year-old stated that the decision had been "wrong" and "shameful".

Lech Walesa, the veteran trade unionist and post-communist President, on 31 August hosted a large gathering of world leaders to mark the 25th anniversary of the Gdansk agreement, at which Solidarity was born (see AR 1980, pp. 109-14; 505-10). The Presidents of Georgia and Ukraine were greeted with standing ovations as they declared that Solidarity's example should inspire democracy activists in Belarus to topple their own authoritarian President. Polish speakers called for a more muscular EU policy towards Russian and other post-Soviet regimes in regard to democracy and human rights.

Polish concern continued over the close relationship between the German and Russian governments. In particular, there was anxiety about potential "energy blackmail" signalled by the new North European Gas Pipeline due to cross from Russia through the Baltic Sea to Germany, thus bypassing Poland and Ukraine. Polish analysts saw the scheme as political rather than economic, enabling Russia to exert pressure by threatening to turn off supplies to Central Europe without jeopardising lucrative deliveries to Western Europe.

Poland's relations with its eastern neighbours continued the tensions of 2004, when Poland had joined the EU and backed Ukraine's pro-Western presidential candidate, Viktor Yushchenko, while Russia supported his pro-Russian opponent. These strains were extended to Belarus, whose autocratic leader, President Alyaksandr Lukashenka, began a crackdown on his country's 400,000-strong Polish ethnic minority. Fearing that this group could start a Ukrainian-style revolution, Belarusian police raided the headquarters of an organisation representing ethnic Poles in Belarus and arrested the body's two leaders. Following diplomatic expulsions from both Minsk and Warsaw, the USA expressed concern about "a continuing pattern of harassment against those seeking to peace-fully express their views". A radio station was set up in Poland to transmit to Belarus and former Solidarity activists helped Belarusian dissidents to set up printing presses. Polish universities admitted Belarusian students banned from universities at home.

Relations with Russia deteriorated still further after the mugging of three sons of a Russian diplomat in a Warsaw park on 31 July by a gang of Polish skinheads. In apparent retaliation, two Polish diplomats were assaulted outside the country's Moscow embassy on 11 August; a Polish journalist and embassy secretary were also attacked.

The main domestic preoccupation was the death of the first Polish Pope, John Paul II (see p. 433; for obituary see p. 546). A week of national mourning was held for the man whose triumphant first return pilgrimage to Poland in June 1979 was widely seen as inspiring Solidarity (see AR 1979, pp. 110-11).

ESTONIA—LATVIA—LITHUANIA

Estonia

CAPITAL: Tallinn   AREA: 45,000 sq km   POPULATION: 1,345,000
OFFICIAL LANGUAGE: Estonian   OFFICIAL SYSTEM: multiparty republic
HEAD OF STATE: President Arnold Rüütel (since Sept '01)
RULING PARTIES: coalition of the Estonian Reform Party (ER), the Estonian People's Union (ERL), and the Estonian Centre Party (EK) (since April '05)
HEAD OF GOVERNMENT: Andrus Ansip (ER), Prime Minister (since April '05)
MAIN IGO MEMBERSHIPS (NON-UN): OSCE, CE, PFP, BC, CBSS, EU, NATO
CURRENCY: kroon (end-'05 £1=K22.7723, US$1=K13.2648)
GNI PER CAPITA: US$7,010, US$13,190 at PPP ('04)

Latvia

CAPITAL: Riga   AREA: 65,000 sq km   POPULATION: 2,300,000
OFFICIAL LANGUAGE: Latvian   POLITICAL SYSTEM: multiparty republic
HEAD OF STATE: President Vaira Vike-Freiberga (since July '99)
RULING PARTIES: coalition of the People's Party (TP), New Era (JL), the Union of Greens and Farmers (ZZS), and the Latvia First Party (LPP)
HEAD OF GOVERNMENT: Aigars Kalvitis (TP), Prime Minister (since Dec '04)
MAIN IGO MEMBERSHIPS (NON-UN): OSCE, CE, PFP, BC, CBSS, EU, NATO
CURRENCY: lats (end-'05 £1=L1.01310, US$1=L0.59010)
GNI PER CAPITA: US$5,460, US$11850 at PPP ('04)

Lithuania

CAPITAL: Vilnius   AREA: 65,000 sq km   POPULATION: 3,400,000
OFFICIAL LANGUAGE: Lithuanian   POLITICAL SYSTEM: multiparty republic
HEAD OF STATE: President Valdas Adamkus (since July '04)
RULING PARTIES: coalition of the Lithuanian Social Democratic Party (LSDP), New Union-Social Liberals (NS-SL), Labour Party (DP), and the Farmers and New Democracy Union (VNDPS) (since Dec '04)
HEAD OF GOVERNMENT: Algirdas Brazauskas (LSDP), Prime Minister (since July '01)
MAIN IGO MEMBERSHIPS (NON-UN): OSCE, CE, PFP, BC, CBSS, Francophonie, EU, NATO
CURRENCY: litas (end-'05 £1=L5.02520, US$1=L2.92720)
GNI PER CAPITA: US$5,740, US$12,610 at PPP ('04)

THE Baltic states of ESTONIA, LATVIA and LITHUANIA had experienced an amazing year in 2004, achieving membership of both the European Union and NATO. The year 2005 could hardly be as dramatic. Nevertheless, it proved eventful for the three states in both the domestic and international contexts. Domestically, there were new governments in ESTONIA and LITHUANIA, as well as constant volatility in the ruling coalition in LATVIA. Internationally, the three states illustrated their delicate stance between East and West. ESTONIA and LATVIA both attempted to ratify border agreements with the Russian Federation, yet both failed. In May Latvia's President attended the 60th anniversary of the Soviet defeat of Nazi Germany, only for the Estonian and Lithuanian heads of state to refuse their invitations. Nevertheless, all three Presidents met US President George W. Bush, who visited LATVIA in May. Finally, all three states maintained troops in Iraq, although the end of 2005 saw increased calls for their withdrawal.

The beginning of 2005 saw the arrival of a new government in LITHUANIA, led by Prime Minister Algirdas Brazaukas. The centre-left ruling coalition consisted of four political groupings: the Social Democrats (LSDP), the New Union-Social Liberals, the Labour Party (DP), and the Farmers and New Democracy Union. Throughout the year, the Lithuanian government was on shaky ground. The Economics Minister, Viktor Uspaskich, was one of many sources of instability. The Russian-born millionaire had created the populist DP, which significantly overlapped with the Social Democrats and the Social Liberals in terms of policies and voters. In June 2005, President Valdas Adamkus urged Uspaskich to resign after the Economics Minister and the Vilnius mayor, Arturas Zuokas, of the opposition Liberal and Centrist Union, accused each other of corruption. However, after an ethics commission ruled that Uspaskich had not kept public and private interests separate, particularly in areas of business in Moscow, the Economics Minister resigned. Nevertheless, the ruling coalition continued even after the departure of the DP leader (Uspaskich). By November, however, Uspaskich attempted to bring down the government by urging the coalition to remove Brazaukas as Prime Minister. Brazaukas's party, the LSDP, responded by declaring that it would pull out of any coalition if the Prime Minister were deposed. Thus, despite a rocky start and end to 2005, the Lithuanian ruling coalition remained intact.

The same could not be said of ESTONIA. At the beginning of the year, the ruling coalition, headed by Prime Minister Juhan Parts, consisted of three political groupings: Res Publica (Parts's party), the Reform Party, and the People's Union faction. In February 2005, a police investigation into the mishandling of classified documents in the Estonian Foreign Ministry led to Parts sacking Foreign Minister Kristina Ojuland. Although Ojuland's Reform Party (ER) was able to nominate her successor, the party was displeased with the Prime Minister, and ER leader Andrus Ansip stated that the coalition would only endure if Prime Minister Parts resigned. After a change of heart, however, the two parties came to an agreement to go on as before. Less than a month later, the boot was on the other foot for Res Publica when the Estonian Parliament approved a no-confidence vote in Res Publica's Justice Minister, Ken-Marti Vaher, in March. Parts promptly resigned in protest, marking something of an end to the party's meteoric rise to power. The new coalition consisted of the Reform Party and People's Union as before, but now with the Centre Party. Reform Party head Ansip became the new Prime Minister. This arrangement remained in place, despite two setbacks: the first in August with a failed no-confidence vote against Education Minister Mailis Reps of the Centre Party, and the second in September with the resignation of Defence Minister Jaak Joeruut of the Reform Party, following the "T-shirt" affair, when people associated with his ministry were seen wearing T-shirts at a soccer match bearing the names of former Communist Party members (including the President, Prime Minister, and Joeruut himself), with the slogan "commies into the oven!". Despite Res Publica's exclusion from the ruling coalition, it still retained significant influence at the municipal level in co-operation with coalition member, the Centre Party.

While LATVIA saw a relatively stable year for its ruling coalition following a turbulent 2004, it too suffered from the competition of two dominant centre-right parties—the People's Party and New Era—which, along with the centrist Latvia First Party (LPP), made up the ruling coalition. The government suffered two senior resignations in 2005. The first casualty was Interior Minister Eriks Jekabsons, of the LPP, who resigned in October after a dispute over the status of Russian billionaire Boris Berezovsky who had visited Latvia and had been declared persona non grata by the Latvian National Security Council. The LPP replaced Jekabsons with Dzintars Jaundzeikars as Interior Minister. In December, the more significant resignation of Defence Minister Einars Repse came after an investigation into property deals and investments. Former head of the Bank of Latvia, founder of the New Era party, former Prime Minister, and outgoing Defence Minister, Repse had been a controversial figure since entering politics in 2002. While at one time it was believed that New Era was nothing more than a front for Repse, the party had proven itself to be more substantial since the collapse of the Indulis Emsis government in 2004. One final notable resignation was that of Latvia's first post-Soviet Foreign Minister, Janis Jurkans, who had been a lone moderate voice on the centre-left spectrum of Latvian politics.

As members of the EU and NATO, the Baltic states' role in the Baltic region and within Europe more widely assumed greater prominence in 2005. ESTONIA and LATVIA both started and ended the year with no formal border with the Russian Federation, despite attempts in both cases to ratify the agreements. In the Soviet period, both states had ceded to Soviet Russia territorial areas contiguous with Russia's Pskov oblast: the Petseri region and the western bank of the Narva River—formerly part of inter-war Estonia—and the Abrene region—formerly part of inter-war Latvia. While the border between the two northern Baltic states and Russia was generally recognised, formal border treaties between them remained unratified. The breakdown in talks came about when the Baltic governments each added a resolution to their respective treaties, in both cases recognising the loss of territory following involuntary inclusion into the Soviet Union. The Russian government took these resolutions to mean a claim on Russian territory and refused to ratify the treaties in their current state, although they set the border exactly where the Russian side wished it to be. Despite significant pressure from EU governments at the EU-Russia summit in June, the EU ended the year lacking an official border with Russia in the northern Baltic region.

Baltic-Russian relations were also in the headlines for two other significant events. First, on 9 May Russia celebrated the 60th anniversary of victory in World War II. Like other world leaders, the Estonian, Latvian and Lithuanian heads of state were invited to attend the ceremonies in Moscow. President Vaira Vike-Freiberga of LATVIA promptly accepted the invitation. After slow deliberation, her counterparts from ESTONIA and LITHUANIA stated that they would not attend the celebrations, since the defeat of Nazi Germany had led to "occupation" for the Baltic states. The US government expressed its appreciation for the delicate position of Vike-Freiberga with a presidential visit to Riga, the Latvian capital, prior to the Moscow ceremony.

Secondly, September saw the crash of a Russian SU-27 fighter aircraft in LITHUANIA as it was on its way to Russia's Kaliningrad oblast. Coincidentally, on the same day, seven Russian military aircraft violated ESTONIAN airspace on their way to Kaliningrad. For the Baltic states and the surrounding region, these events raised two important issues. NATO monitored the airspace of the Baltic states, as members of that organisation, and the crash and airspace violations raised concerns about NATO's ability to defend the Baltic states. Furthermore, the events led to calls for the demilitarisation of Kaliningrad oblast, surrounded as it was by NATO member-states. The Russian government, however, refused to countenance such a prospect.

The issue of the Russian-speaking minorities in the Baltic states seemed to become somewhat less fraught in 2005. The year saw the Council of Europe close its monitoring office in LATVIA following the ratification of the framework convention for the protection of national minorities. In 2004, Latvian education reforms came into force, prompting considerable protest amongst some sections of the Russian-speaking community. The 2005 school year started without so much as a placard. Rather than Russian minorities in the Baltic states, the focus instead was on Baltic ethnic minorities further afield. ESTONIA paid considerable attention to Finno-Ugric groups in Russia, particularly the Mari-El. Likewise, the Latvian Foreign Ministry reached out to those Latvians still living in Russia. Finally, like Poland, LITHUANIA was particularly conscious of its ethnic minority in Belarus.

CZECH REPUBLIC

CAPITAL: Prague   AREA: 79,000 sq km   POPULATION: 10,200,000
OFFICIAL LANGUAGE: Czech   POLITICAL SYSTEM: multiparty republic
HEAD OF STATE: President Václav Klaus (ODS) (since Feb '03)
RULING PARTIES: Czech Social Democratic Party (CSSD), Christian Democratic Union-Czech
   People's Party (KDU-CSL), and the Freedom Union-Democratic Union (US-DEU)
HEAD OF GOVERNMENT: Jiri Paroubek (CSSD), Prime Minister (since April '05)
MAIN IGO MEMBERSHIPS (NON-UN): NATO, OSCE, CE, CEI, CEFTA, OECD, Francophonie, EU
CURRENCY: koruna (end-'05 £1=Kor42.2729, US$1=Kor24.6238)
GNI PER CAPITA: US$9,150, US$18,400 at PPP ('04)

FOR the Czech Republic, 2005 was a year of political comebacks and an unexpectedly strong economy. Having taken over as Prime Minister in August 2004, Stanislav Gross was struck by scandal in January 2005 in connection with the uncertain provenance of property held by him and his wife, Sarka Gross. Gross's defenders argued that the scandal's emergence was part of a political campaign designed to weaken his position prior to the Social Democrats' party congress, to be held on 25-27 March. While Gross aimed to turn the Czech Social Democratic Party (CSSD) into a modern, centrist party, his only competitor for the CSSD chairmanship was Labour and Social Affairs Minister Zdenek Skromach, who wanted to see the party shift to the left. Gross was elected chairman, even though it was clear before the congress that one of the CSSD's two junior partners, the Christian Democrats (KDU-CSL), would be likely to leave a Gross-led Cabinet. Under Gross's leadership, public support for the CSSD sank to less than 10 per cent, and it became increasingly apparent that the opposition Civic Democrats (ODS) would form a government with the KDU-CSL after the next legislative elections in June 2006.

In a parliamentary vote of confidence on 1 April, the KDU-CSL joined the ODS in voting against the Gross Cabinet, which survived only thanks to the abstention of deputies representing the opposition Communists. Just as the country appeared to be on the verge of early elections, the CSSD managed to make a fresh deal with the KDU-CSL and its other junior partner, the Freedom Union (US-DEU), by putting forward a new candidate for the post of Prime Minister. Even this occurred only after considerable fumbling, however, as the CSSD's initial choice to replace Gross—the Czech Republic's ambassador to the EU, Jan Kohout—failed to gain sufficient support from within the party. Finally, Gross resigned and was replaced as Prime Minister on 25 April by Jiri Paroubek, with only a few minor changes in the government's composition. Gross decided to leave politics altogether in September after his name was raised in connection with a privatisation scandal concerning the Unipetrol petrochemicals giant.

A relative political unknown who had previously served as Local Development Minister, Paroubek demonstrated surprising agility in political manoeuvring upon his accession to the premiership, having convinced his party's junior coalition partners to remain in the Cabinet, forged agreement on a new policy statement, and persuaded left-wing CSSD rebels to vote in favour of the new government. Paroubek's government won a vote of confidence on 13 May, receiving the support of all 101 of the parliamentary deputies who represented the CSSD and its two junior partners. Thus, the government maintained its razor-thin majority in the 200-member Chamber of Deputies (the lower house of the bicameral Parliament). After Paroubek assumed the post of Prime Minister, his popularity grew rapidly, and he also helped the party to improve its standing, bringing it to within a few percentage points of the ODS.

In the latter part of 2005, Czech politics became increasingly focused on the 2006 parliamentary elections. Under Paroubek, the CSSD shifted back toward the Left, and in the last months of the year the party angered the KDU-CSL by joining forces with the opposition Communists to approve several key bills. Desperate to raise public support before the elections, the CSSD was reluctant to approve any major economic reforms and instead backed several measures to increase public spending. In December, the Parliament finally approved much-delayed increases in regulated rents; however, these would not take effect until after the elections, scheduled as they were to stretch over a four-year period beginning in January 2007.

The Czech economy performed much better than expected in 2005. Many indicators reached their best levels since the mid-1990s, demonstrating the benefits of the Czech Republic's membership in the European Union. GDP reached its highest growth rate since 1995, while the country's balance of trade recorded the first surplus since 1993. Moreover, the Czech Republic attracted record inflows of direct foreign investment, partly thanks to the privatisation of several key firms, including Cesky Telecom (which was sold to Telefónica of Spain) and Unipetrol (sold to PKN Orlen of Poland). The inflow of foreign investment helped to bring down unemployment rates after the record highs of 2004: the Ministry of Labour and Social Affairs put the average jobless rate at 9 per cent in 2005, down from 9.2 per cent the previous year. Consumers also benefited from record low interest rates, with the Czech National Bank's base rate set at just 1.75 per cent in April-October, before rising back to 2 per cent. Despite low interest rates, the Czech koruna strengthened by 6.6 per cent against the euro in 2005. Despite surging energy prices, average annual inflation reached just 1.9 per cent in 2005, down from 2.8 per cent during the previous year. The country's fiscal results were also considerably better than expected, with the state budget deficit falling to just 1.9 per cent of GDP, as strong economic growth helped to boost revenue.

In regard to foreign affairs, the situation was rather quiet in 2005, aside from occasional outbursts over the question of the Sudeten Germans (ethnic Germans expelled from Czechoslovakia after World War II). In the summer, Paroubek took a brave stance in calling upon Czechs to acknowledge the existence of a democratic resistance movement among Sudeten Germans during World War II and proposing that ethnic German anti-fascists be compensated, at least in a symbolic way, for the loss of their property during the expulsions. In regard to the EU, the failure of the referendums in France and the Netherlands on the EU constitution saved the Czech Republic from potential embarrassment (see pp. 40; 48). Even before those votes, the Czech Republic was seen as one of the few new EU member states where the constitution's approval was uncertain. The ruling parties would have found it impossible to gain a majority in the Parliament in favour of the EU constitution, given the opposition of both the ODS and the Communists. Prospects for a successful referendum were also questionable.

SLOVAKIA

CAPITAL: Bratislava   AREA: 49,000 sq km   POPULATION: 5,400,000
OFFICIAL LANGUAGE: Slovak   POLITICAL SYSTEM: multiparty republic
HEAD OF STATE: President Ivan Gasparovic (since June '04)
RULING PARTIES: Slovak Democratic and Christian Union (SDKU), Hungarian Coalition Party
   (SMK), and Christian Democratic Movement (KDH) form ruling coalition
HEAD OF GOVERNMENT: Mikulas Dzurinda (SDKU), Prime Minister (since Oct '98)
MAIN IGO MEMBERSHIPS (NON-UN): OSCE, CE, PFP, CEI, CEFTA, OECD, EU, NATO
CURRENCY: Slovak koruna (end-'05 £1=K55.0734, US$1=K32.0800)
GNI PER CAPITA: US$6,480, US$14,370 at PPP ('04)

THE political situation in Slovakia was somewhat shaky in 2005, but the country continued to record economic and foreign policy success. Within the four-party ruling coalition, relations were especially tense between the Alliance of the New Citizen (ANO) and the Christian Democratic Movement (KDH). In May, personal conflicts between the top two officials at the Education Ministry—Minister Martin Fronc of the KDH and state secretary Frantisek Toth of ANO—contributed to the failure of an education reform bill. ANO rejected the legislation, marking the first time that the government was disunited over an important reform matter. Later that month, Toth took over the post of Culture Minister, replacing ANO's Rudolf Chmel.

Political tensions heightened again in August, when the KDH demanded ANO leader Pavol Rusko's dismissal as Economy Minister because of a financial scandal. After failing to heed Prime Minister Mikulas Dzurinda's call to resign voluntarily, Rusko was dismissed on 24 August, and he subsequently withdrew ANO from the ruling coalition. Nonetheless, a majority of ANO parliamentary deputies, led by former journalist Lubomir Lintner, opted to continue supporting Dzurinda's administration and forged an agreement with the three remaining ruling coalition partners: the KDH, Dzurinda's Slovak Democratic and Christian Union (SDKU), and the Hungarian Coalition Party (SMK). Lintner's group was thus able to keep ANO's two remaining ministers in office and to name a replacement to head the Economy Ministry, with Jirko Malcharek taking that post in October.

Dzurinda had been running a minority government since late 2003, but the coalition continued to function, thanks to the support of independents. With Rusko's departure, however, the government experienced its worst crisis since taking office in 2002, as some independents were initially reluctant to back the Cabinet. In mid-September, the opposition refused to attend the Narodna Rada (the 150-seat unicameral legislature) for several days, and the necessary quorum of seventy-six deputies was not reached, contributing to speculation that early legislative elections would be held. After more than a week of delay, the Narodna Rada finally started operating on 21 September, with seventy-seven deputies present. This followed the surprising switch of two deputies from the opposition Movement for a Democratic Slovakia (HZDS) to Lintner's ANO group, accompanied by allegations that they had been "bought." In an apparent effort to clean up the government's image, Dzurinda backed the resignation of Labour and Social Affairs Minister Ludovit Kanik in October, based on questionable financial dealings. Kanik was replaced by the respected sociologist, Iveta Radicova, who became the first woman in the Dzurinda Cabinet. Although questions were also raised regarding the finances of Agriculture Minister Zsolt Simon, he remained in his post, with full support from the SMK.

With most of the key reforms already in place, the most important piece of legislation requiring approval following the crisis was the 2006 state budget, which served as a key test of the government's sustainability. The budget was approved with surprising ease on 13 December, gaining the support of seventy-nine votes in the Narodna Rada.

Regional elections in November offered some indication of the level of support for the various parties. As was the case in the June 2004 elections to the European Parliament, the elections to Slovakia's eight regional legislatures were characterised by very low turnout and surprisingly good results for the ruling parties. In the second-round run-off to elect regional chairmen, however, the opposition managed to win all eight posts, with only around 11 per cent of the electorate participating.

The SDKU opposed early elections in 2005 in the belief that the party would have better chances of success the longer it stayed in power, particularly given the expectations of strong economic results in 2006. In 2005 Slovakia continued to record rapid GDP growth, based on strengthening gross fixed investment and household demand. Private consumption was boosted by a reduction in inflation, a strong recovery of real wages, and declining unemployment rates. On the fiscal front, the country appeared to be in good shape to meet its goal of adopting the euro by 2009, and the state budget deficit was well below target in 2005, at just 2.3 per cent of GDP. Slovakia's accession to the EU's exchange rate mechanism (ERM-II) waiting room in late November put the country well ahead of its central European neighbours in regard to eurozone membership.

In regard to foreign policy, Slovakia hosted a summit between US President George W. Bush and his Russian counterpart Vladimir Putin in February, marking the first visit of a sitting US President to Slovakia. In May, Slovakia approved the European constitution through a vote in the Narodna Rada, making it the seventh EU member state to ratify the document. In October, Slovakia was elected for the first time ever as a non-permanent member of the UN Security Council, with its term beginning in January 2006.

HUNGARY

CAPITAL: Budapest   AREA: 93,000 sq km   POPULATION: 10,100,000
OFFICIAL LANGUAGE: Hungarian   POLITICAL SYSTEM: multiparty republic
HEAD OF STATE: President Laszlo Solyom (since Aug '05)
RULING PARTIES: coalition of Hungarian Socialist Party (MSzP) with Alliance of Free Democrats-
    the Hungarian Liberal Party (SzDSz)
HEAD OF GOVERNMENT: Ferenc Gyurcsany (MSzP), Prime Minister (since Sept '04)
MAIN IGO MEMBERSHIPS (NON-UN): NATO, OSCE, CE, CEFTA, CEI, PFP, OECD, EU
CURRENCY: forint (end-'05 £1=Ft367.423, US$1=Ft214.022)
GNI PER CAPITA: US$8,270, US$15,620 at PPP ('04)

FOLLOWING a year in which Hungary joined the European Union, 2005 was a time of modest achievements. The economy grew healthily but at the same time the IMF and OECD warned of trouble ahead unless the government made significant policy changes. Relations with neighbouring countries grew warmer and the National Assembly (unicameral legislature) elected the country's third President since the end of communism in Hungary in 1989. However, domestic politics became more polarised in the run up to elections expected in 2006.

Hungary's economic growth rate fell during 2005 to below 4 per cent, down from 4.6 per cent in 2004. The IMF said that the country had, "moved from being a 'star' performer to one of the slower growing economies among the new EU member states", although growth was still significantly better than the EU average. The OECD warned of risks to the country's fiscal sustainability.

In January, EU Finance Ministers ruled that the Hungarian government had failed to take the action required of it when the EU initiated an "excessive deficit procedure" in July 2004. Hungary's Finance Minister, Tibor Draskovics, was sacked in April and replaced by János Veres. The situation became worse when the EU's statistical office, Eurostat, ruled as unacceptable two major government accounting adjustments. The government had wanted to include money from the planned sale of motorways to a state-owned company, and push the payment of the "13th month" bonus to public sector workers into the following fiscal year. With these measures ruled out, the government budget deficit ballooned from an expected 3.6 per cent to 6.1 per cent, more than double the EU's official limit. All of this put in doubt Hungary's plans to join the eurozone in 2010.

Nonetheless the country's income per head continued to rise, as did its exports. Hungary remained an attractive place for foreign investment: the South Korean tyre-maker, Hankook, announced plans to build a €500 million plant south of Budapest; and the British airports operator, BAA, paid €1.8 billion for a 75 per cent stake in the capital's Ferihegy airport, the country's biggest ever privatisation. Hungary's national airline, Malev, on the other hand, remained in state hands despite expectations at the beginning of the year that it was due to be sold.

Hungarian politics remained highly divisive with the governing Hungarian Socialist Party (MSZP) and Prime Minister Ferenc Gyurcsány engaging in a series of bitter debates with the opposition Hungarian Civic Alliance (FIDESZ), led by Viktor Orbán. Many of these debates remain rooted in Hungary's 20th century history with politicians regularly accusing each other of being "nationalists" or "communists". Elections were due in 2006, the 50th anniversary of the Hungarian uprising against Soviet rule, so that most analysts expected the political atmosphere to become even more polarised.

The presidency, however, remained a non-partisan post. On 7 June the National Assembly elected the former chief justice of the Constitutional Court, László Sólyom, as President. He had been proposed by an environmental non-governmental organisation, Védegylet, and nominated by FIDESZ in opposition to the government's candidate, Katalin Szili, the Speaker of Parliament. Sólyom won by just three votes in the final ballot because the junior party in the governing coalition, the Alliance of Free Democrats (SZDSZ), refused to support Szili, arguing that the President should not be a member of the ruling party. Sólyom was inaugurated on 5 August in a low key ceremony.

Hungarian farmers celebrated their first year of EU membership with three weeks of angry demonstrations in front of the National Assembly in protest against overdue payments of agricultural subsidies. On 25 April the Prime Minister sacked the Agriculture Minister, Imre Nemeth, and replaced him with Jozsef Graf, a veteran Socialist Party MP, saying that Agriculture needed a minister who operated more like a manager than a politician to sort out the mess.

On 17 January Gyurcsány announced that his government would hold an annual joint meeting with its Romanian counterpart in order to help its neighbour join the EU. The first such meeting took place on 20 October in the Romanian capital, Bucharest. It marked a significant improvement in relations between two countries which had frequently argued over the rights of the large Hungarian minority in Romania and other issues. Relations with Serbia, which also had a significant Hungarian minority, improved during 2005, after a year in which the Hungarian government accused Serbia of tolerating "atrocities". However, in June, Hungary's Foreign Minister, Ferenc Somogyi, made representations to the Serbian authorities following allegations of attacks on ethnic Hungarians in the northern province of Vojvodina.

Relations with Saudi Arabia, however, plummeted after the Prime Minister made what he intended to be a light-hearted remark about the country's football team following a match against Hungary. Speaking at a private party in February, he said that the Hungarian players had shown great courage against a team of Arab terrorists. Gyurcsány apologised but Saudi Arabia recalled its ambassador until May.

In January the country marked the 60th anniversary of the liberation of the Budapest ghetto with events to remember the half-million Hungarian Jews killed in the Nazi Holocaust. In March the US government agreed to pay US$25 million in compensation for Hungarian Jewish property seized by US Army personnel in 1944.

In a first for central Europe, the Hungarian authorities launched an association for police officers from the Roma minority in December and a recruitment drive to increase the number of Roma officers. However, there was bad news for another minority community: in April the human rights committee of the National Assembly refused to recognise around 2,500 people as being descendents of the Huns of Attila, the Central Asian tribes which conquered most of Europe in the fifth century. Hungary had thirteen recognised minorities, each of which was entitled to state support for schools and cultural institutions.

ROMANIA

CAPITAL: Bucharest   AREA: 238,000 sq km   POPULATION: 21,900,000
OFFICIAL LANGUAGE: Romanian   POLITICAL SYSTEM: multiparty republic
HEAD OF STATE: President Traian Basescu (DA), since Dec '04
RULING PARTIES: coalition of the Justice and Truth Alliance (DA: the National Liberal Party (PNL)
and the Democratic Party (PD)), the Democratic Union of Hungarians in Romania (UDMR),
and the Conservative Party (PC), (since Dec '04)
HEAD OF GOVERNMENT: Calin Popescu-Tariceanu (PNL), Prime Minister (since Dec '04)
MAIN IGO MEMBERSHIPS (NON-UN): OSCE, CE, CEI, PFP, CEFTA, BSEC, Francophonie, NATO
CURRENCY: new leu (end-'05 £1=NL5.36250, US$1=NL3.12370)
GNI PER CAPITA: US$2,920, US$8,190 at PPP ('04)

THIS was a year of contrasts and contradictions for Romania, exemplified by two weeks of political drama in July when Prime Minister Călin Popescu-Tăriceanu announced that he was about to resign, only to rescind his decision the day after he had been expected to step down. Romania made steady progress towards membership of the EU; yet there were still lingering doubts about whether it had met the EU's criteria for joining, as envisaged, in January 2007. Meanwhile Tăriceanu's centrist coalition government continued to enjoy considerable popularity, notwithstanding the frequent criticisms aimed at it by the Prime Minister's political ally, the equally popular President Traian Băsescu. Continuing economic growth, fuelled by a consumer boom, helped create something of a "feel-good" factor.

The year, and the work of the new government, began with a bang when a system of flat-rate income tax and corporation profit tax was introduced on 1 January. The impact of the new tax, set at the low rate of 16 per cent, was enormous. Most Romanians had more money to spend, and did so with relish; compliance with the payment of taxes improved; but there were growing indications that the huge cuts in the tax rate would have to be recouped from somewhere else.

The initial impact of the flat-rate tax system was to demonstrate that the new administration meant business. Thereafter, political developments were shaped by tensions between the President and his Prime Minister as well as between the two main coalition partners, Băsescu's Democratic Party (PD) and Tăriceanu's National Liberal Party (PNL).

Băsescu started calling for early elections almost as soon as the government, in whose formation he had played an instrumental role, had taken office. By urging a fresh vote while the new administration was enjoying its "honeymoon" period with the electorate, the President hoped to secure a stable majority for the governing coalition after the inconclusive results of the elections held in late 2004 (see AR 2004, pp. 91-92). He argued that the best guarantee of fulfilling the election promises of the Truth and Justice Alliance (DA)—the electoral partnership of the PD and the PNL—was a strong government. Prime Minister Tăriceanu disagreed. He was concerned that another protracted period of electioneering might slow down Romania's reforms and delay its accession to the EU. Besides, the two junior partners in the coalition—the Democratic Union of Hungarians in Romania and the Conservative Party (the renamed Romanian

Humanist Party)—were resolutely opposed to early elections which they feared
would lead, at the very least, to a weakening of their influence.

The matter came to a head in early July. After the Constitutional Court
rejected a package of seventeen laws on judicial reform that were required for
EU membership, Tăriceanu announced that his government would resign on 18
July to prepare the ground for early elections. However, following a visit to
Brussels, where European Commission officials had already repeatedly indicated that fresh elections would slow down Romania's integration with the EU,
the Prime Minister rescinded his decision on 19 July. Tăriceanu argued that the
government needed to focus all its attention on repairing the damage caused by
severe flooding which had made thousands of people homeless. In any case, by
then the Constitutional Court had approved the package of laws, amended by
Parliament (the bicameral legislature).

Tăriceanu's "u-turn" provoked further strains in his relations with Băsescu. The
President turned up the volume of his criticism, at times sounding a more effective critic of his own government than the opposition Social Democratic Party
(PSD) which was still recovering from its unexpected electoral defeats. In April
PSD activists delivered their own shock when former Romanian President Ion Ili-
escu's return—at the age of seventy-five—to his party's leadership was defeated
at the PSD's congress. Instead of voting for the veteran politician, who had dominated Romania's political life since the fall of the communist dictatorship in
1989, delegates opted for ex-Foreign Minister Mircea Geoană in the hope that he
would revitalise their party.

Changes in personnel were also in evidence on the government side where the
Prime Minister reshuffled five posts in a bid to steady the administration and preserve the delicate balance between the Prime Minister and the President as well as
between their respective parties, the strongly pro-business PNL and the more
social democratic PD.

Romania passed a milestone in its integration with the EU when it signed (along
with Bulgaria, see p. 90) its accession treaty on 25 April. The European Commission's annual progress report in October repeated some of the familiar complaints about Romania's main shortcomings: further action was needed to combat
corruption, exercise greater discipline over the use of EU assistance, reduce pollution by industry, and improve food hygiene standards.

More severe criticism of Romania's policies came from the IMF which in late
October broke off talks on extending a precautionary stand-by facility that was
due to expire in mid-2006. The IMF's disapproval was directed primarily against
the tax cuts. It warned that unless value-added tax were increased, the cuts would
endanger both fiscal stability and the government's anti-inflation policy. Whatever the long-term dangers highlighted by the IMF, during the year the economy
continued to perform well. GDP grew by a respectable 4.2 per cent; the annual
inflation rate at 8 per cent was down by 1 per cent on the previous year; and unemployment was largely unchanged at just over 6 per cent.

In its foreign relations, Romania made substantial progress in fostering closer
links not just with the all-important EU, with also with the USA. It cemented this

alliance during a visit to Bucharest in December by US Secretary of State Condoleezza Rice, when the two countries signed an agreement to make four Romanian military bases available to the USA. Meanwhile, Romanian officials rejected allegations made in November by Human Rights Watch, a US-based campaigning group, that Romania (along with Poland) may have hosted secret detention facilities for the interrogation of suspected international terrorists captured by US security forces.

Apart from the disastrous floods in the spring and summer, Romania was also badly hit by the arrival of avian influenza (bird 'flu) in October. The H5N1 strain was detected in the Danube delta on the Black Sea. Thousands of wildfowl and poultry were destroyed as a precautionary measure: there were no human victims.

BULGARIA

CAPITAL: Sofia   AREA: 111,000 sq km   POPULATION: 7,800,000
OFFICIAL LANGUAGE: Bulgarian   POLITICAL SYSTEM: multiparty republic
HEAD OF STATE: President Georgi Purvanov (since Nov '01)
RULING PARTIES: coalition of the Bulgarian Socialist Party (BSP), the National Movement Simeon II (NDSV), and the Turkish Movement for Rights and Freedoms (DPS)
HEAD OF GOVERNMENT: Sergei Stanishev (BSP), Prime Minister (since Aug '05)
MAIN IGO MEMBERSHIPS (NON-UN): OSCE, CE, PFP, CEI, CEFTA, BSEC, Francophonie, NATO
CURRENCY: lev (end-'05 £1=L2.84700, US$1=L1.65840)
GNI PER CAPITA: US$2,740, US$7,870 at PPP ('04)

THIS was an electoral year for Bulgaria, which saw yet another change of government. Elections to the 240-seat Narodno Sabranie (National Assembly, the unicameral legislature) took place in June but it took fifty-two days to form a Cabinet, at a time when Bulgaria was struggling with summer floods and a very demanding and tight EU schedule of reforms. In August, Bulgaria's Socialist Party (BSP), which had gained 30.95 per cent of the vote (eighty-two seats), finally signed a coalition deal with the centre-right National Movement Simeon II (NDSV) of outgoing Prime Minister Simeon Saxecoburggotski, thereby ending seven weeks of deadlock. (The NDSV had won 19.88 per cent of the vote and fifty-three seats in the elections). The BSP, the successor to the Communist Party, had won the elections in 1990 and 1994 but lost power on both occasions after major economic crises. Under Sergei Stanishev, the party had become more enthusiastic about joining NATO and a keen supporter of entry into the EU.

Stanishev was appointed Prime Minister with the support of the NDSV and the liberal Movement for Rights and Freedoms (DPS), which represented Bulgaria's 800,000 Muslims, mainly ethnic Turks. The DPS, led by long-serving chairman Akhmed Dogan, had played a balancing role in the Narodno Sabranie for fifteen years, participating in every government since 1989. It had taken thirty-four seats in the elections.

A new group in the Narodno Sabranie was the radical nationalist entity called Ataka, which won 8 per cent of the vote (twenty-one seats) on a reactionary platform opposing the integration of Turkish and Roma minorities.

In addition to electoral turbulence, Bulgaria suffered from summer storms and torrential rains which led to severe flooding and widespread destruction. During three months, the bad weather affected two million people, claiming the lives of twenty while 10,000 lost their homes. So acute was the sense of emergency that the army was called in to help with some of the rebuilding work.

In April, Bulgaria and Romania signed EU accession treaties, paving the way for them to join the EU in January 2007. The treaties contained a safeguard clause delaying entry for a year if either country failed to meet EU standards. In its October annual report, the European Commission warned the two countries that they must fight corruption and speed up reforms in order to join the EU on schedule. Bulgaria, in particular was advised to tackle organised crime, human trafficking, its weak judicial system, and the protection of intellectual and industrial property rights. The Commission gave Bulgaria and Romania six months to deal with such matters of urgency and committed itself to take a decision by April or May 2006 on when to accept them as member-states.

There were several significant economic deals during the year. Telekom Austria bought Bulgaria's biggest mobile phone operator, Mobiltel, for €1.6 billion, making this the largest ever foreign acquisition by an Austrian company. Telecommunication companies had become a highly popular market for buyers in Bulgaria's improving economy and in view of impending EU membership. Furthermore, Bulgaria agreed a project with Russia and Greece to build a trans-Balkan 285 km oil pipeline from the Black Sea port of Burgas to the northern Greek town of Alexandroupolis on the Aegean. The aim of the pipeline was to allow Russian crude oil exports to sidestep the congested Bosphorus Strait. Finally, the Bulgarian government approved the construction of the country's second nuclear power plant, at Belene, on the shore of the river Danube. The Kozloduy nuclear power station, also on the shore of the Danube, already supplied more than 40 per cent of the country's electricity. However, two of the Kozloduy plant's six reactors had already shut down and two more would have to do so before Bulgaria joined the EU.

The year ended with the withdrawal of Bulgaria's troops from Iraq. The 400-strong contingent returned by 31 December, having lost thirteen soldiers and six civilians. The Narodno Sabranie had voted in May to pull out Bulgaria's troops by the end of the year, in response to strong public opposition to the country's involvement in the war.

ALBANIA—BOSNIA & HERZEGOVINA—CROATIA—MACEDONIA—
SLOVENIA—SERBIA & MONTENEGRO

ALBANIA

CAPITAL: Tirana   AREA: 29,000 sq km   POPULATION: 3,200,000
OFFICIAL LANGUAGE: Albanian   POLITICAL SYSTEM: multiparty republic
HEAD OF STATE: President Gen. (retd) Alfred Moisiu (since June '02)
RULING PARTY: Democratic Party of Albania (PDS) leads five-party coalition (since Sept '05)
HEAD OF GOVERNMENT: Sali Berisha (PDS), Prime Minister (since Sept '05)
MAIN IGO MEMBERSHIPS (NON-UN): OSCE, PFP, CE, CEI, BSEC, OIC, Francophonie
CURRENCY: lek (end-'05 £1=AL179.074, US$1=AL104.310)
GNI PER CAPITA: US$2,080, US$5,070 at PPP ('04)

THIS was a year of national elections in Albania and the transfer of power to a new Prime Minister, Sali Berisha, who was fighting his political opponent, Prime Minister Fatos Nano, for the sixth time in Albania's post-communist era. In September, after two months of political wrangling, former President Sali Berisha, leader of the right-of-centre Democratic Party of Albania (PDS), was officially declared the victor of July's general election. Allegations of voting irregularities had delayed the final result. International observers monitored the elections and their judgment weighed heavily upon the decision of the EU in November to conclude the negotiations for a stabilisation and association agreement with Albania, with a view to signing the agreement in 2006. The verdict was that while voting was mainly peaceful, with a turnout of over 50 per cent, the overall process "only partially" complied with international standards.

The Albanian electorate opted for change after eight years of socialist government because of internal splits within the Socialist Party (PPS), which had tarnished the party's image, and because of perceived widespread corruption. Berisha, who had served as President for six years during the 1990s, promised to crack down on corruption, human trafficking, and organised crime. His new government was a coalition of five parties, led by the PDS, with control of eighty-one of the 140 seats in the Assembly of Albania (the unicameral legislature). Berisha's first action was to reduce the number of ministries from nineteen to fourteen, and his first promises included the speeding up of reforms needed for EU and NATO integration, the fight against corruption, ending mass poverty, and help for small businesses.

Having lost the election—the PPS won fourty-two seats—Nano, announced in September that he was resigning as party chairman. At an extraordinary congress in October the PPS elected the mayor of Tirana, Edi Rama, to replace Nano.

Albania was among the poorest countries in Europe; official unemployment stood at 15 per cent although most analysts agreed that it was more than double this figure. Corruption and a weak judicial system were the two main impediments to foreign funds. The economy was sustained principally by remittances from Albanians working abroad: around 750,000 Albanians worked in Greece and another 250,000 in Italy. Funds sent back by these two groups alone were estimated to amount to about US$1 billion annually, equivalent to about half the national budget.

The country still suffered from very poor infrastructure. In November power cuts left most Albanians without electricity for eighteen hours a day because of low water levels at hydropower stations. According to some analysts, Albania's electricity network was on the brink of collapse, with water supplies in the hydropower plants reaching the minimum level. The most recent hydroelectric plant had been built some thirty years previously and there had been little investment in the network since.

The new government cancelled a deal to sell the state-owned telephone company, Albtelecom, to a Turkish consortium, claiming that the arrangement (approved by the former government) contained serious legal errors. Albtelecom had a monopoly of fixed-line telephones in Albania, although other companies operated in the mobile phone sector.

On the EU-Albanian front, news was more encouraging. The European Commission told Albania in November that talks on the stabilisation and association agreement could be concluded in the coming months, giving greater impetus to the process of Albania's integration into the EU.

BOSNIA & HERZEGOVINA

CONSTITUENT REPUBLICS: Federation of Bosnia & Herzegovina (FBiH) and Republika Srpska (RS, Serb Rebublic)
CAPITAL: Sarajevo   AREA: 51,129 sq km   POPULATION: 3,800,000
OFFICIAL LANGUAGE: Serbo-Croat   POLITICAL SYSTEM: multiparty republic
HEAD OF STATE: Ivo Miro Jovic (HDZ) (Croat) (chairman since June '05, elected May '05); Mirko Sarovic (SDS) (Serb) (elected Oct '02); Sulejman Tihic (SDA) (Bosniak) (elected Oct '02)
PRESIDENTS OF REPUBLICS: Niko Lozancic (HDZ), (FBiH, since Jan '03); Dragan Cavic (SDP), (RS, since Nov '02)
PRIME MINISTERS: Adnan Terzic (SDA) (Republic of Bosnia & Herzegovina, since Dec '02); Ahmet Hadzipasic (FBiH, since Feb '03); Pero Bukejlovic (SDS) (RS, since Jan '05)
MAIN IGO MEMBERSHIPS (NON-UN): OSCE, CEI
CURRENCY: marka (end-'05 £1=M2.84660, US$1=M1.65810)
GNI PER CAPITA: US$2,040, US$7,430 at PPP ('04)

THE year marked the tenth anniversary of the Dayton accords (see AR 1995, pp. 126-27; 559-62) that had ended a three year war (1992-95) which had cost 250,000 lives, created 1.2 million refugees, and caused enormous physical destruction. Ten years on, progress had been achieved in some areas: much of the war damage had been repaired through a systematic reconstruction effort; the country was operating internationally as a single state—albeit with substantial domestic autonomy for its two entities, the Serb Republic (Republika Srpska, RS) and the Croat-Muslim Federation of Bosnia & Herzegovina (FbiH)—and conducting free and fair elections; and a large number of refugees had returned or regained their properties. Yet much remained to be done in a country ethnically divided, with a poor economy, a weak political process, and a disaffected population.

Over recent years, the international administrators had focused on reforms that would strengthen the central Bosnian state in order to improve government and the economy and make it possible for the country to join international organisations. As a result some reforms were introduced regarding a state judicial system, a single customs service, a single intelligence service, and a single defence structure. In 2005, Bosnia sent its first national troops to Iraq in the form of a unit made up of thirty-six soldiers from all three main ethnic groups: Muslims, Serbs, and Croats. As High Representative of the international community in Bosnia & Herzegovina, Lord Paddy Ashdown concentrated on efforts to construct a single state with central institutions to replace the existing complex system of overlapping and rival authorities. During 2005, Ashdown pursued, among other tasks, the abolition of the country's two ethnically-divided police forces and the creation of a single national police structure, which was one of the conditions set by the EU for embarking upon negotiations for a stabilisation and association agreement with Bosnia & Herzegovina. The task proved Herculean because of strong resistance by the political authorities in Republika Srpska. Another new state-level multi-ethnic organisation was set up to tackle the issue of missing persons from the Bosnian war. Ten years after the war it was estimated that between 15,000 and 20,000 people were still unaccounted for.

At a more intergovernmental level, the governments of Bosnia & Herzegovina, Croatia, and Serbia & Montenegro agreed to draw up action plans that would be combined into a single document with the aim of resolving the refugee issue by the end of 2006. The agreement, signed by the three governments in Sarajevo in January 2005, was one of the most important tripartite deals since the Dayton accords. The issue of property restitution had been one of the post-war successes, achieved as a result of pressure from Bosnia's High Representatives, ensuring the population's right to resume possession of their pre-war homes. Some 95 per cent of such properties had been reclaimed although in most cases these had been subsequently sold rather than reinhabited by their original owners.

Following the example already set in Serbia, a war crimes court opened in Bosnia in March. It came under the authority of the Bosnian judiciary, but was to be administered by a panel of international judges and prosecutors for five years. In May, the UN's International Criminal Tribunal for the Former Yugoslavia (ICTY) in The Hague sent the first case to the new court. Radovan Stankovic, a Bosnian Serb accused of the rape of Muslim women in the eastern Bosnian town of Foca, was the ICTY's first referral to a national jurisdiction. The transfer of cases of middle- and lower-level suspects by the ICTY was part of its strategy to accelerate and terminate its work by 2010. Serbia had already tried a number of its own cases involving Serbs, but not yet dealt with a case handed on by The Hague tribunal.

In November, EU Foreign Ministers agreed to start negotiations for a stabilisation and association agreement with Bosnia & Herzegovina, as a result of progress reported in the country and as an incentive for further internal reforms. However, it was made clear that the speed of the talks would depend on the pace of domestic reforms and full co-operation with the ICTY. In addition, the EU continued to maintain around 6,000 peacekeeping troops in Bosnia, known as EUFOR and constituting the EU's largest military operation. The troops had been in place since 2004, when NATO had handed over its peacekeeping duties in Bosnia & Herzegovina to the EU.

Ten years after the end of the war, many Bosnians believed that the political process needed to move on and that the constitution imposed under the Dayton accords had reached its limits. Dayton had helped to build peace, but had failed to construct a common state. The High Representative, through pressure and, at times, authoritarian rule, had imposed most of the changes in Bosnia. To mark the tenth anniversary of the Dayton accords, the three members of the Bosnian presidency went to the USA to commemorate the event and, more importantly, to discuss plans for a new constitution. The new High Representative, who would take over from Ashdown from February 2006, Christian Schwarz-Schilling, was expected to create a functional common Bosnian state with a view to handing over power to local politicians.

CROATIA

CAPITAL: Zagreb   AREA: 57,000 sq km   POPULATION: 4,500,000
OFFICIAL LANGUAGE: Croatian   POLITICAL SYSTEM: multiparty republic
HEAD OF STATE: President Stipe Mesic (HNS)(since Feb '00)
RULING PARTIES: Croatian Democratic Union (HDZ) in coalition with the Croatian Social Liberal
   Party (HSLS) and the Democratic Centre (DC)
PRIME MINISTER: Ivo Sanader (HDZ), (since Dec '03)
MAIN IGO MEMBERSHIPS (NON-UN): OSCE, CE, CEI, PFP
CURRENCY: kuna (end-'05 £1=K10.7279, US$1=K6.24890)
GNI PER CAPITA: US$6,590, US$11,670 at PPP ('04)

THERE were two key developments during the year in Croatia: the start of accession talks with the EU in October, and the much anticipated arrest of the third most wanted criminal suspect of the International Criminal Tribunal for the Former Yugoslavia (ICTY) (after the former Bosnian Serb political and military leaders, Radovan Karadzic and Ratko Mladic), Croatian General Ante Gotovina, who was detained in Spain in December, after four years on the run.

Gotovina had been indicted in 2001 on war crimes charges connected with the August 1995 Croatian offensive against Serbs from the self-declared republic of Krajina in Croatia. About 200,000 Serbs were expelled from the region during the offensive, known as "Operation Storm" (see AR 1995, p. 121), and Gotovina was alleged to have failed to prevent the deliberate murder of some 150 Serbs. The indictment also accused him of co-ordinating a campaign of pillage and looting throughout operations in ethnically Serb areas of the region. Following his arrest, his supporters staged protests in Zagreb and other cities: Ante Gotovina was regarded by some of his compatriots as a national hero, given that during the course of less than a week in August 1995 "Operation Storm" had ended more than four years of Serb control in an area that accounted for about one-quarter of Croatia's territory. Subsequently, the Croatian government had been criticised by the UN and the Organisation for Security and Co-operation in Europe (OSCE) for failing to do enough to facilitate the return of those refugees who wanted to go back to Croatia. Many refugees had sold their homes and taken citizenship in Serbia & Montenegro instead. In August, thousands of Croats in the town of Knin celebrated the tenth anniversary of another Croatian offensive; yet in a conciliatory gesture, Croatian President Stipe Mesic asked on behalf of his country for forgiveness from those who had been wronged.

While most people were seeking a resolution to modern war crimes, others continued to be haunted by older ones. In April, survivors of the Jasenovac death camp gathered in the place that sixty years previously had been the scene of some of the worst atrocities of World War II. The Jasenovac camp—known as "the Auschwitz of the Balkans"—was run by the Croatian Fascist Ustasha—a Nazi puppet regime—and its victims were Serbs, Jews, Roma, and Croats. Most estimates calculated the numbers killed at around 100,000, although Serbs talked of 700,000 deaths.

EU-Croatian relations during 2005 went through ups and downs. Initially, the start of accession talks in March were postponed; negotiations eventually began seven months later. The EU deferred Croatian entry talks on the eve of their starting date because it judged that the Croatian government was still failing to do enough to track down the fugitive General Gotovina. The postponement of accession negotiations put pressure on the centre-right government of Prime Minister Ivo Sanader to take more substantive measures to deal with those suspected of providing a support network for the General. However, it also alienated Croatian public opinion, and support for the process of integration into the EU fell dramatically during the summer. In an unexpected turn, the EU decided to begin membership talks with Croatia on 3 October after the UN's chief war crimes prosecutor judged that the Croatian government was fully co-operating with the ICTY. Croatia thus joined Turkey for the start of accession talks with the EU, since the decision to open talks with Croatia was the factor that led Croatia's ally, Austria, to lift its objections to opening accession negotiations with Turkey (see p. 72).

MACEDONIA

CAPITAL: Skopje   AREA: 26,000 sq km   POPULATION: 2,100,000
OFFICIAL LANGUAGE: Macedonian   POLITICAL SYSTEM: multiparty republic
HEAD OF STATE: President Branko Crvenkovski (since May '04)
RULING PARTIES: coalition of Social Democratic Alliance for Macedonia (SDSM), Party for
    Democratic Integration (BDI), and Liberal Democratic Party (LDP)
HEAD OF GOVERNMENT: Vlado Buchkovski (SDSM), Prime Minister (since Dec '04)
MAIN IGO MEMBERSHIPS (NON-UN): OSCE, PFP, CE, CEI, Francophonie
CURRENCY: Macedonian denar (end-'05 £1=D88.8067, US$1=D51.7296)
GNI PER CAPITA: US$2,350, US$6,480 at PPP ('04)

IN March, the country organised its first municipal elections since new local boundaries were drawn in August 2004 which gave greater autonomy to ethnic Albanians in areas where they predominated (see AR 2004, p. 100). While the elections took place in a peaceful atmosphere, international observers pointed out a number of irregularities and instances of intimidation. In July, the Sobranje (the unicameral legislature) passed a further law giving Albanians the right to fly the Albanian flag in districts where they constituted the majority. Since 2001, the Sobranje had adopted fifteen constitutional amendments and seventy new or revised laws, as required by the Ohrid agreement signed in August 2001 which ended an eight-month conflict between government forces and armed ethnic Albanian groups (see AR 2001, p. 139). These laws aimed at strengthening the rights of the ethnic Albanian minority by giving local communities greater control over local policing, their language, education, and the use of national symbols. The full implementation of the Ohrid agreement was a major precondition for Macedonia's membership of the EU and NATO.

Ethnic tensions and the implementation of the Ohrid agreement were not the only headache for the Macedonian government. The population was more concerned with the poor state of the economy, very high unemployment of around 35 per cent, average monthly salaries of little more than US$200, and the extensive grey economy. Although some modest economic growth was recorded in 2005, considerable impediments remained, including a lack of transparency in economic decision-making, deficient regulation, corruption, and a weak judicial system. Foreign direct investment also remained limited at around 2 per cent of GDP because of the absence of large privatisations, an unfavourable business climate, and the problems in enforcing property rights.

In March, Macedonia's former Interior Minister, Ljube Boskovski, surrendered to the International Criminal Tribunal for the Former Yugoslavia (ICTY) in The Hague and pleaded not guilty. Boskovski was accused of crimes committed by security forces during the 2001 conflict between the government and ethnic Albanian rebels. He was indicted along with his bodyguard and another senior police officer. As a fiery hardline politician during the 2001 clashes, Boskovski was very popular with the press and the people. Yet he fell from grace in 2004 when he fled to Croatia (he held dual citizenship and owned a hotel there), charged with the deaths of seven immigrants at the hands of the Macedonian police.

The dispute over the name of the country continued to trouble relations with Greece, which continued to argue that the use of the name "Macedonia" implied territorial pretensions towards the region of northern Greece that bore the same name. In September, UN special representative Matthew Nimitz presented a proposal that the country be called by its constitutional name (the Republic of Macedonia) by those countries that had already recognised it as such. In bilateral relations with Greece, however, the name would be Republika Makedonija—Skopje. For international use the country should keep its chosen name, but transcribe it as Republika Makedonija until 2008, after which it could use the name Republic of Macedonia. Some observers argued that the Nimitz compromise bore the clear imprint of US views on the dispute. At a time of deep divisions within the EU, Macedonia had backed the US-led invasion of Iraq and sent troops to support the coalition forces. It had also supported the US position in the controversy with the EU over the International Criminal Court (ICC). As a reward, in November 2004 the US government had abandoned its former neutrality over the nomenclature dispute and recognised Macedonia under its constitutional name, the Republic of Macedonia (see AR 2004, p. 100). The fears that Greece might bloc Macedonia's candidacy in the EU were averted in the European Council when it was agreed that the EU would use "Former Republic of Macedonia" rather than the country's constitutional name (see p. 69).

The year closed with the European Council decision in December to grant Macedonia a formal candidate status, based on the European Commission's recommendation.

SLOVENIA

CAPITAL: Ljubljana   AREA: 20,000 sq km   POPULATION: 2,000,000
OFFICIAL LANGUAGE: Slovene   POLITICAL SYSTEM: multiparty republic
HEAD OF STATE: President Janez Drnovsek (LDS) (since Dec '02)
RULING PARTIES: coalition of the Slovenian Democratic Party (SDS), New Slovenia (Nsi), the
   Slovene People's Party (SLS), and the Democratic Party of Pensioners of Slovenia (DeSUS)
   (since Dec '04)
PRIME MINISTER: Janez Jansa (SDS) (since Dec '04)
MAIN IGO MEMBERSHIPS (NON-UN): OSCE, CE, PFP, CEI, CEFTA, Francophonie, EU, NATO
CURRENCY: tolar (end-'05 £1=T348.689, US$1=T203.110)
GNI PER CAPITA: US$14,810, US$20,730 at PPP ('04)

As a full member of the European Union since 2004, Slovenia was the third EU
member state to vote in favour of the EU constitution. In February the National
Assembly (the lower chamber in Slovenia's legislature) ratified the constitution
with an overwhelming majority. However, the pattern of ratification was not followed when the referendums in France and the Netherlands in June rejected the
proposed constitution, thereby halting its progress and creating uncertainty over
its future (see pp. 40; 48; 368-70).

In June, Slovenian Foreign Minister Dimitrij Rupel and the Foreign Minister
of Croatia, Kolinda Grabar-Kitarovic, signed a joint declaration on avoiding
border incidents between two countries. The signing took place during an inter-
government meeting, the first held at this level in fourteen years. The document
was described as a building block in efforts to establish a political framework
between Croatia and Slovenia. The delegations also signed a readmission
accord; as well as bilateral protocols on double taxation avoidance and co-operation in the customs sector, culture, and education. The Prime Ministers of the
two countries agreed to hold regular consultations to settle outstanding issues
and improve bilateral ties. Such issues included border questions, the settlement
of the long-running dispute over the former Ljubljanska Banka's debt to Croatian depositors, and the status of the Krsko nuclear power plant. Separately,
Slovenia, Croatia, and Italy signed a trilateral co-operation agreement on environmental protection and joint actions in case of ecological emergencies in the
northern Adriatic Sea.

In November, President Janez Drnovsek stirred up diplomatic waters and
upset Slovenia's relationship with Serbia by calling for independence for the
international protectorate of Kosovo. The government of Slovenia appeared to
have been caught by surprise by the statement. Drnovsek's proposal angered
Serbian officials, who cancelled arrangements for the Slovene President's visit
to Serbia. Unperturbed by the diplomatic row, Drnovsek visited Kosovo and
met its President, Ibrahim Rugova, and officials from the UN mission there,
UNMIK. The Slovenian government sought to distance itself from the President and his actions.

SERBIA & MONTENEGRO

CONSTITUENT REPUBLICS: Montenegro (13,812 sq km), Serbia (88,316 sq km)
CAPITAL: Belgrade   AREA: 102,128 sq km   POPULATION: 8,200,000
OFFICIAL LANGUAGE: Serbo-Croat   POLITICAL SYSTEM: joint state
HEAD OF STATE: President Svetozar Marovic (DPS) (since March '03)
RULING PARTIES: the Democratic Party of Serbia (DSS), the G17 Plus (G17+), and the Serb
    Renewal Movement/New Serbia (SPO-NS) form coalition in Serbia; Democratic Party of
    Socialists (DPS) and Social Democrats (SDP) form governing coalition in Montenegro
PRESIDENTS OF REPUBLICS: Boris Tadic (President of Serbia, since July '04); Filip Vujanovic
    (President of Montenegro, since June '03); Ibrahim Rugova (DLK) (President of Kosovo,
    since March '02)
PRIME MINISTERS: Vojislav Kostunica (DSS) (Serbia) (since March '04); Milo Djukanovic (DPS)
    (Montenegro) (since Jan '03); Bajram Kosumi (AAK) (Kosovo) (since March '05)
MAIN IGO MEMBERSHIPS (NON-UN): OSCE (suspended), CE, CEI, EBRD
CURRENCY: dinar (end-'05 £1=D124.464, US$1=D72.4997)
GNI PER CAPITA: US$2,620 ('04, excl Kosovo)

IN 2005, the two republics of the state of Serbia & Montenegro continued their uneasy co-existence. Early in the year Montenegrin leaders suggested to their Serbian counterparts an end to the union and the establishment of two independent republics. As expected, the Serbian Prime Minister, Vojislav Kostunica, rejected this proposal as a breach of the agreement setting up the joint state which had been signed in 2003 under EU auspices (see AR 2003, p. 121). The state union's constitutional charter of 4 February 2003 permitted the two parties to begin independence procedures as early as February 2006, but neither side could propose complete separation before that time. Montenegro's government had repeatedly signalled that it was intending to hold a referendum on independence soon after that date.

Internal Serbian party politics continued to be divided, first by the rivalry between the Democratic Party (DS), led by the Serbian President Boris Tadic, and the Democratic Party of Serbia (DSS), led by Prime Minister Kostunica; secondly, by the participation in the minority coalition government of the Socialist Party of former Yugoslav President and war crimes indictee Slobodan Milosevic; and, thirdly, by the extreme nationalist Serbian Radical Party, the largest single party in the Serbian legislature. On the economy, the Serbian government continued with reforms as prescribed from abroad based on external support, market-economy measures, and integration into international financial institutions. Serbia continued to attract foreign direct investment and raised money by privatising state assets.

In the autumn, the Defence Minister of Serbia & Montenegro, Prvoslav Davinic, resigned amid scandal over his authorisation of the purchase of a large consignment of military equipment from a private contractor. The Minister was replaced by General (retd) Zoran Stankovic, who had links to war crimes fugitive, former Bosnian Serb commander Ratko Mladic. Stankovic's appointment prompted speculation regarding Mladic's possible surrender to the UN International Criminal Tribunal for the Former Yugoslavia (ICTY) in The Hague. In December, Serbia & Montenegro also appointed a new commander of the armed forces, General Dragan Puskas, as part of a wider attempt to reform the country's military and move closer to NATO. Since the fall of Milosevic in October 2000, there had been attempts to modernise the Serbian military, but progress was slowed by a continuing reluctance on the part of the authorities to hand over suspects to the ICTY.

Co-operation with the ICTY had been a particularly controversial issue in Serbia, affecting the country's relations with the West on the one hand, and causing domestic distress and political infighting on the other. Despite severe pressure on Serbia from the international community and The Hague Tribunal's chief prosecutor Carla del Ponte to comply with the demands of the ICTY, Prime Minister Kostunica had been reluctant to order any arrests for fear that they would destabilise his minority government. Kostunica, a moderate nationalist, regarded the ICTY with scepticism and as biased against Serbia. The USA and the EU, for their part, intensified their pressure on the country to co-operate with the ICTY. The USA repeated its threat to cut foreign aid, and the EU warned that it would freeze the association and stabilisation process and issue a negative progress evaluation. Inside Kostunica's minority government coalition, the technocratic G17+ party, headed by Deputy Prime Minister Miroljub Labus and Finance Minister Mladjan Dinkic, made it clear that it would withdraw unless there was a favourable EU feasibility study for the stabilisation and association process. During the first months of 2005, therefore, Serbia adopted a major policy change on co-operation with the ICTY and the government exerted pressure on the highest-profile indictees to turn themselves in, offering the incentive of financial support to their families. In February, the first fruits of this new policy became evident when General Vladimir Lazarevic surrendered to the Tribunal. By the end of the month, two more generals had surrendered, and these were followed by other indictees including General Sreten Lukic and General Nebojsa Pavkovic.

The Hague Tribunal itself was under pressure to complete all trial activities by 2008 as part of the UN Security Council's completion strategies for the ICTY (and for the International Criminal Tribunal for Rwanda). Yet this schedule had been hampered by the failure to apprehend all indictees (especially the most wanted ones, like Ratko Mladic or the Bosnian Serb leader Radovan Karadzic), by doubts about the readiness of some judicial institutions in the former Yugoslav countries to take over cases from The Hague, and by the ICTY's own financial problems.

Relations between Serbia & Montenegro and the EU progressed significantly with the start of stabilisation and association agreement talks in October 2005, a preliminary step on the road to EU membership. Within a single stabilisation and association framework, the EU would continue to conduct separate talks with Serbia and with Montenegro, based on the twin-track approach adopted in 2004. These separate talks could then be transformed into two separate agreements, should the Montenegrins decide on independence. However, the successful conclusion of these talks and the signing of an agreement depended largely on full co-operation and compliance with the ICTY.

In November, the ICTY cleared two former Kosovo Albanian rebel commanders of war crimes' charges relating to the conflict with Serb forces in 1998, and found a third man guilty. Haradin Bala became the first Kosovo Albanian to be convicted by the Tribunal and was sentenced to thirteen years in jail for the mis-

treatment and murder of Serb civilian prisoners and their alleged Albanian collaborators. Three more Kosovo Albanians were indicted in 2005, including the
Prime Minister, former guerrilla commander Ramush Haradinaj. (He had
resigned as Prime Minister on 8 March before surrendering to the ICTY.) The
capture of Haradinaj in February was greeted with protest and dismay among
Kosovo Albanians, most of whom considered him a national hero. The guerrilla
leader turned Prime Minister, who had commanded the Kosovo Liberation Army
(KLA), was seen as one of the few leaders who had been able to stand up to the
Serbs during the war. He was charged on thirty-seven counts of war crimes and
crimes against humanity, including persecution, murder, and rape: atrocities committed against Serb, Roma, and ethic Albanian alleged collaborators during the
1998-99 Kosovo conflict. Former student activist Bajram Kosumi was elected as
Prime Minister of Kosovo's interim government on 23 March on the promise that
he would continue Haradinaj's policies, focusing on developing the economy, pursuing Kosovo's independence, and meeting human rights and minority rights
benchmarks set by the international community.

In October, the UN Security Council gave the green light for negotiations to
resolve the status of Kosovo. Secretary-General Kofi Annan made this recommendation to the Security Council following a report on the progress of the
province. The report proposed that talks should be launched in 2006 despite several shortcomings in the economy (high unemployment and widespread poverty),
the rule of law (fragile police and judiciary and inability to handle organised
crime, corruption, and inter-ethnic crime), and ethnic relations within society
(inter-ethnic crimes and violence often going unreported).

It was agreed that negotiations would be conducted through shuttle diplomacy in an effort to reach an agreement within a year. The task of mediation
was assigned to the former Finnish President Martti Ahtisaari, who had helped
to broker a ceasefire between NATO and Serbia in 1999. Negotiations were
expected to result in some form of independence for Kosovo, with a continuing role for foreign peacekeepers to prevent further outbreaks of violence
between Kosovo's ethnic Albanian majority and its remaining Serbs. In addition, the EU would play a key role in the period after the status of Kosovo was
decided, by taking over policing from the UN, sending prosecutors, judges, and
prison staff to strengthen the rule of law, and substantially increasing aid to
help cut unemployment. Talks would be based on a minimum set of commonly
agreed principles including: (i) no partition of Kosovo; (ii) no return to the situation obtaining before March 1999 under which Kosovo's autonomy was
denied by Serbia; (iii) no union of Kosovo with neighbouring states; and (iv)
the protection of minorities.

Nevertheless, by the end of 2005 the views of the two sides remained dia-
metrically opposed: Kosovo Albanians were seeking full independence; Serbs
were claiming "more than autonomy, less than independence", and were seeking to retain sovereignty over Kosovo, a single seat at the UN as Serbia & Montenegro, and control of the external borders. Even the more moderate President
of Serbia, Boris Tadic, had declared earlier in February, during a visit to the

province, that he would never accept an independent Kosovo. The Serbian government was particularly worried over the fate of the remaining 200,000 Serbs in Kosovo, who lived in very hazardous conditions, about half of them in enclaves protected by NATO troops in a population some 2 million strong, 90 per cent of whom were ethnic Albanians.

RUSSIA, WESTERN CIS AND THE CAUCASUS

RUSSIA

CAPITAL: Moscow   AREA: 17,075,000 sq km   POPULATION: 142,800,000
OFFICIAL LANGUAGE: Russian   POLITICAL SYSTEM: multiparty republic
HEAD OF STATE: President Vladimir Putin (since May '00)
RULING PARTY: United Russia party
PRIME MINISTER: Mikhail Fradkov (since March '04)
MAIN IGO MEMBERSHIPS (NON-UN): CIS, APEC, OSCE, G-8, CE, PFP, CBSS, BSEC, AC
CURRENCY: rouble (end-'05 £1=R49.3418, US$1=R28.7414)
GNI PER CAPITA: US$3,410, US$9,620 at PPP ('04)

RUSSIA ended 2005 poised to assume for the first time the presidency of the G-8 group of the world's most industrialised democracies in 2006. It was a significant coup for Russia's President, Vladimir Putin, in that it underlined Russia's improved international standing, which was mainly dependent upon its economic potential (particularly as a supplier of energy) and its nuclear status. However, there was criticism from those who saw Russia as careless of the democratic standards which supposedly marked out G-8 members. That Putin's Russia would not admit such international pressure, however, was made absolutely explicit in the President's state of the nation address on 25 April to a joint session of the Federal Assembly (the bicameral Russian legislature, consisting of the upper Federation Council and the lower State Duma). Putin laid out a vision of Russia's uniqueness, extending even to the "civilising mission of the Russian nation on the Eurasian continent". For Russia, he said, the ideal of democracy was to be tempered by the need for security: "democratic procedures should not develop at the expense of law and order, or stability which has been so hard to achieve, or the steady pursuit of the economic course we have taken." The implicit contrast was between the supposed stability of Putin's Russia and the chaos of the immediate post-Soviet years under his predecessor as President, Boris Yeltsin. In a passage that attracted widespread attention abroad, Putin described the collapse of the Soviet Union (in 1991) as "a major geopolitical catastrophe of the century", which had brought impoverishment to the Russian population and national disintegration to the country. This nostalgia for the Soviet Union was also a theme of the ceremonies marking the 60th anniversary of the end of World War II in Europe, which were attended in Moscow on 9 May by more than fifty world leaders.

Looking back to the Soviet era, then, the Russian presidency in 2005 projected a more powerful role for the state in managing society, energy policy, and Russia's federal structure. At the same time, the presidency failed to address fundamental problems which posed the threat of future instability, particularly in the north Caucasus and within the economy.

POLITICS. Political developments in 2005 were shaped by the prospect of post-Putin Russia. The President would finish his second consecutive term of office in 2008, and was constitutionally prohibited from seeking a further term. Speculation about his successor was thus a constant theme. In November, Putin promoted two close allies, both of whom were possible successors: Defence Minister Sergei Ivanov became, concurrently, Deputy Prime Minister, whilst head of the presidential administration Dmitry Medvedev was named as First Deputy Prime Minister. One potential opposition challenger for the presidency, however, Mikhail Kasyanov, found himself in July facing criminal investigation for abuse of office over a property deal concluded in 2004 before he was dismissed as Prime Minister. Over the year, Kasyanov continued to speak out against the undermining of democracy in Russia, but it was not certain that he would emerge unscathed from the criminal enquiry against him.

Before the presidential elections, polling for the State Duma would be held in December 2007. The legislation drafted in 2004 altering the rules for these elections (see AR 2004, p. 107) became law in July 2005. It was likely to give the State Duma an even more pro-government hue, since it favoured large parties, such as the pro-presidential United Russia, and penalised smaller opposition groups. Upsets were still possible, of course, but the political establishment had other ways of dealing with these, as the elections in December to the Moscow city duma (legislature) demonstrated. On a turnout of about 35 per cent, United Russia took twenty-eight of the thirty-five seats, with the Communist Party of the Russian Federation (KPRF), which still commanded a fairly stable electorate, second with four seats (17 per cent of the vote). However, the party that had been expected to take votes from United Russia, the nationalist Rodina (Motherland), was barred from standing after a court ruling that it had screened a racist television advertisement. Rodina claimed that the authorities had manipulated the scandal in order to exclude it from the ballot.

Whilst they were able to suppress challenges from individuals and political parties, the Russian authorities were most concerned by the threat of a popular rebellion—possibly assisted by foreign groups—such as had occurred during Ukraine's "orange revolution" of 2004. To this end, controversial legislation was adopted in December which restricted the activities of non-governmental organisations (NGOs), particularly those which were branches of foreign NGOs or which received foreign funding. Putin commented in November that "the ongoing financing of political activity in Russia from overseas should be closely supervised". The President later responded to international condemnation of the legislation by ordering some of its most draconian clauses to be scrapped (although some thought that this softening had been stage-managed), but charities, think tanks, and pressure groups faced being closed down in 2006 if they infringed new regulations on their modes of financing and registration with the Russian authorities.

Further restrictions of democracy were seen as the legislation enacted in December 2004 came into force abolishing elections for the leaders of Russia's constituent regions. The first presidential nominations to these posts in most cases reappointed the incumbent. However, new governors were named in ten regions (out of thirty-two appointments in 2005). The new appointees tended to have little connection with the region to which they were nominated, suggesting that the presidency was attempting to reassert central control over Russia's regions. The year also saw the first merger of regions into larger units, again suggesting a recentralisation of government. A union between the small Komi-Permyak autonomous okrug and the surrounding Perm krai was completed on 1 December, thereby reducing the number of Russia's constituent regions and republics (the "subjects of the federation") to eighty-eight. Additionally, successful referendums were held in 2005 to start the process of merging the Taimyr and Evenki okrugs with the surrounding Krasnoyarsk krai, and of merging the Koryak autonomous okrug into Kamchatka oblast.

Overall, these developments looked like a reversal of the public activism which had shaped the perestroika era of the late 1980s. Perestroika also receded with the deaths in 2005 of two major figures from those years: journalist Yegor Yakovlev; and politician and intellectual Aleksandr Yakovlev (no relation), who had been known as the "godfather of perestroika" (for obituary see p. 552).

THE ECONOMY. Russia's economy continued to be awash with oil revenues. Critics warned that Russia could face the challenges of "Dutch disease" (a syndrome named after the economic difficulties experienced in the 1960s by the Netherlands after the discovery of North Sea oil). "Dutch disease" would mean that dollar revenues from exported energy would force up the value of the local currency, thus making imports cheaper but exports more expensive on the world market and, potentially, leading to the deindustrialisation of the economy. An IMF mission reported in December that Russia's economic growth was becoming imbalanced because of low investment and rising consumption, and that inflation, rouble appreciation, and rising imports could in future contribute to the problems. GDP growth in 2005 was projected to be some 6 per cent.

The high oil revenues did allow Russia to make early repayments on debts to the IMF and the Paris Club of sovereign creditors. In February, Russia repaid outstanding debt to the IMF of SDR (special drawing rights) 2.19 billion (from a loan agreed in March 1996); and in August it made early repayment of US$15 billion in debt to the Paris Club, reducing the outstanding debt from US$43 billion to US$28 billion. The early repayments were possible because of the healthy oil stabilisation fund, into which oil revenues from sales at a price above US$27 per barrel were poured. At the end of 2005, the fund was estimated to contain about US$50 billion.

The consolidation of Russia's energy sector in state hands, which had been seen in 2004 with the breakup of the oil company Yukos, continued (see AR 2003, pp. 128-29; 2004, pp. 109-10). In September, the state-controlled energy giant, Gazprom, acquired a controlling share in Sibneft—the fifth-largest oil company in Russia—from oligarch Roman Abramovich. Having apparently adopted a different survival strategy from that of Yukos's founder Mikhail Khodorkovsky, who in May was finally sentenced to nine years' imprisonment for fraud and tax evasion at the end of a lengthy trial, Abramovich opted to sell the state his oil holdings and agree to be renominated as governor of Chukotka oblast.

One of the worst problems affecting Russia was that of endemic corruption. In October, Transparency International, the international NGO dedicated to combatting corruption, reported that on its annual corruption perceptions index Russia had fallen to joint 126th place (out of 158), from joint 90th place in 2004. A Russian study of corruption released in July by the think tank and polling organisation, INDEM, reported a tenfold increase in the amount paid to officials in bribes since its previous survey in 2001. Similarly, in June the Organisation for Economic Co-operation and Development (OECD) issued a report describing Russia as "a weak state with strong bureaucrats" which was experiencing a "drift towards more interventionist, less rule-governed state behaviour".

The government announced a new social investment programme in September. Healthcare, education, agriculture, and housing were to benefit from extra funds from the budget surplus, which was projected in the draft 2006 budget at R776 billion. The need to increase social spending was impressed upon the government in January and February when the usually quiescent population staged nationwide demonstrations in protest against the replacement of benefits in kind—such as free or subsidised transport, housing, utilities, and healthcare—with cash payments. Pensioners were particularly affected. However, with promises to increase spending on benefits and the reintroduction of subsidised transport in some regions, the protests soon subsided.

TERRORISM. The year brought no improvement in the situation in the north Caucasus. Indeed, the separatist leadership in Chechnya was radicalised in 2005 following the killing by Russian forces in March of Chechnya's popularly elected president (not recognised by Russia), Aslan Maskhadov. Maskhadov, who was allegedly killed in error during an attempt to capture him, had offered negotiations in February to resolve the conflict, having ordered separatist forces to embark upon a ceasefire. However, although he was a moderating influence upon the Chechen separatist movement, Maskhadov had not exerted complete control over it, and when his replacement, Abdul-Khalim Sadulayev, in August named Shamil Basayev as Deputy Prime Minister, it was anticipated that the conflict would escalate. Basayev was the commander responsible for organising some of the most serious recent attacks upon Russian civilians, including the school siege at Beslan, North Ossetia, in 2004 (see AR 2004, pp. 108-09).

On 13 October, attacks by rebels in Nalchik, the capital of the north Caucasus republic of Kabardino-Balkaria, showed that the Chechen conflict had indeed widened. Sadulayev had announced in May that commanders had been appointed for all sectors of the "Caucasus front". The attacks on fifteen targets in Nalchik, including the airport and security agencies' headquarters, were allegedly co-ordinated by Basayev, and in the two hours' fighting thirty-three federal troops, twelve civilians, and ninety-one insurgents had been killed, according to official figures. Reports in the Russian media suggested that radical Islam was growing stronger in the north Caucasus because of economic degradation and heavy-handed policing by the authorities. The Nalchik débâcle also showed that Russian security forces lacked co-ordination: the attacks had occurred despite the presence of extra federal forces in the area after information about the impending operation had been leaked.

BELARUS—UKRAINE—MOLDOVA

Belarus

CAPITAL: Minsk   AREA: 208,000 sq km   POPULATION: 9,800,000
OFFICIAL LANGUAGES: Belarusian & Russian   POLITICAL SYSTEM: multiparty republic
HEAD OF STATE AND GOVERNMENT: President Alyaksandr Lukashenka (since July '94)
RULING PARTY: Non-party supporters of President Lukashenka
PRIME MINISTER: Syarhey Sidorski (since Dec '03)
MAIN IGO MEMBERSHIPS (NON-UN): CIS, OSCE, PFP, CEI, NAM
CURRENCY: Belarusian rouble (end-'05 £1=BR3,697.88, US$1=BR2,154.00)
GNI PER CAPITA: US$2,120, US$6,900 at PPP ('04)

Ukraine

CAPITAL: Kyiv (Kiev)   AREA: 604,000 sq km   POPULATION: 48,000,000
OFFICIAL LANGUAGE: Ukrainian   POLITICAL SYSTEM: multiparty republic
HEAD OF STATE: President Viktor Yushchenko (since Jan '05)
RULING PARTY: Our Ukraine (NU)
HEAD OF GOVERNMENT: Yury Yekhanurov, Prime Minister (since Sept '05)
MAIN IGO MEMBERSHIPS (NON-UN): CIS, OSCE, CE, PFP, BSEC, CEI
CURRENCY: hryvna (end-'05 £1=H8.66700, US$1=H5.04850)
GNI PER CAPITA: US$1,260, US$6,250 at PPP ('04)

Moldova

CAPITAL: Chisinau (Kishinev)   AREA: 34,000 sq km   POPULATION: 4,200,000
OFFICIAL LANGUAGE: Moldovan   POLITICAL SYSTEM: multiparty republic
HEAD OF STATE AND GOVERNMENT: President Vladimir Voronin (since April '01)
RULING PARTY: Communist Party of Moldova (PCM)
PRIME MINISTER: Prime Minister Vasile Tarlev (since April '01)
MAIN IGO MEMBERSHIPS (NON-UN): CIS, OSCE, CE, PFP, BSEC, CEI, Francophonie
CURRENCY: leu (end-'05 £1=ML22.0174, US$1=ML12.8250)
GNI PER CAPITA: US$710 (excl data for Transdniestr republic), US$1,930 at PPP ('04)

IN BELARUS, President Alyaksandr Lukashenka continued his repression of the opposition, blithely disregarding the repeated calls from the West—the USA in particular—for change in "Europe's last dictatorship". The phrase was uttered by US Secretary of State Condoleezza Rice and the US President George W. Bush on their visits to Europe in April and May, apparently in the hope that the 2006 presidential elections in Belarus would see a popularly-driven and peaceful change of government along the lines of those in other former Soviet states: the "rose revolution" in Georgia of 2003 and the "orange revolution" in Ukraine of 2004. However, Lukashenka appeared determined to disregard this pressure, warning in January that "there will be no rose, orange, or banana revolutions in our country".

Pressure from the USA was largely ineffective, given that the Belarusian government retained the support of Russia. This was made explicit in December when Lukashenka had a meeting with Russian President Vladimir Putin, arranged at very short notice. The outcome of the meeting was confirmation that Russia would continue to supply gas at heavily subsidised prices to its neighbour, a stance in sharp contrast to Russia's announcement in November that it planned to at least double (and in Ukraine's case quadruple) gas prices for its other former Soviet neighbours, including Georgia, Armenia, Moldova, and the three Baltic states.

Eastern European countries, particularly Poland, also called in August for the export of peaceful revolution to Belarus, but it seemed unlikely that they could exert much leverage, given that Western Europe remained heavily dependent upon Russian gas supplies. The advancing project between Russia and Germany to construct a North European Gas Pipeline from Russia to Germany under the Baltic Sea—thus bypassing Poland and Ukraine—was a crucial factor that hindered the evolution of a common EU policy in support of democratisation in Belarus (see pp. 76-77).

Nevertheless, the Belarusian opposition did, in 2005, coalesce around a common candidate for the 2006 presidential elections. In October, a rally of opposition forces selected Alyaksandr Milinkevich—a physicist and civil society activist—to stand against Lukashenka, who in 2004 had arranged a referendum lifting the constitutional limit on the number of terms a president could serve, raising the possibility of his remaining President for life (see AR 2004, pp. 111-12). Still, it was doubtful whether Milinkevich and the opposition would be able to withstand the electoral machine of the government. An early sign that the elections were unlikely to be conducted fairly was the vote by the House of Representatives (the lower chamber of the bicameral Belarusian legislature) in December to schedule them for 19 March 2006, four months earlier than stipulated in the Belarusian constitution. With the security forces exerting continual pressure on the democratic opposition's media outlets and regularly arresting democratic activists on the slightest pretext, the likelihood of Lukashenka's being unseated either in the ballot or by peaceful protest seemed slim.

In UKRAINE the year brought a jolting return to "normality" after the euphoria of 2004's "orange revolution", in which the liberal government of Viktor Yushchenko had replaced the corrupt cronyism of former President Leonid Kuchma and his allies (see AR 2004, pp. 113-15). By early autumn however, political rivalries tore apart the unity of the "orange" forces, and Yushchenko on 8 September dismissed his former ally, Prime Minister Yuliya Tymoshenko—known as the "orange princess"—and her entire Cabinet, claiming that infighting had paralysed the government. The Tymoshenko government, appointed in January, saw bitter mutual accusations of corruption surface between Tymoshenko and her allies on the one hand, and, on the other, the group that had formed around another leader of the "orange" forces, Petro Poroshenko, a close ally of

Yushchenko and secretary of the National Security and Defence Council who had been passed over for the premiership in Tymoshenko's favour.

In an apparent attempt to calm passions, Yushchenko on 9 September nominated Yury Yekhanurov, governor of Dnipropetrovsk oblast (region), as the new Prime Minister, and by the end of September had managed to form a government dominated by members of the ruling People's Union-Our Ukraine (NSNU) party and apolitical technocrats. However, in order to gain the endorsement of the Verkhovna Rada (Ukraine's unicameral legisalture) for his nominee Yekhanurov, Yushchenko had been forced to enter into a deal with his former rival for the presidency, Viktor Yanukovych, summarised as a ten-point "memorandum of understanding". This document attracted widespread criticism as a betrayal of the "orange revolution". Among its provisions were guarantees of good faith on Yushchenko's part, such as a promise to conduct the 2006 legislative elections without government interference, and a pledge to respect the constitutional reforms to transfer some presidential powers to the legislature, which had been agreed during the 2004 presidential election dispute. Yushchenko's supporters felt that such promises were degrading in that they implied the possibility that the President might engage in such illegitimate actions. Most damaging, however, were the promises in the "memorandum" to draft new legislation which would grant immunity from prosecution to local level elected officials. Such legislation, said critics, would, in effect, grant an amnesty to all those officials who had engaged in falsifying the results of the initial round of the 2004 presidential election. The concession was felt by many to be a betrayal of the people who had demonstrated peacefully in the "orange revolution" to overturn those falsified election results and bring Yushchenko to power.

The President's image was fruther damaged by revelations over the summer of the lavish lifestyle being led by his son, nineteen-year-old Andrei Yushchenko. President Yushchenko was forced to apologise to journalists, after accusing one of them of "behaving like a hitman" for revealing Andrei's excesses.

If he lost much kudos at home during the year, abroad Yushchenko was the face of Ukraine's new role as the beacon of peaceful transformation of autocratic regimes. Visiting the USA in April, Yushchenko addressed a joint session of Congress (the bicameral legislature) where lawmakers waved orange scarves in homage. In a state visit to the UK in October, Yushchenko became the first recipient of the new Chatham House prize awarded by the UK's Royal Institute for International Affairs (a research institute, also known as Chatham House) for the individual deemed to have "made the most significant contribution to the improvement of international relations in the previous year". There was progress in the key policy aims of the Yushchenko administration to integrate Ukraine into international structures. By the end of 2005, the USA and the EU had both granted the country market economy status; the goal of World Trade Organisation (WTO) membership was thought likely to be achieved in 2006; and the prospect of an invitation from NATO for Ukraine to join its membership action plan was moving closer.

Ukraine's further progress towards Euro-Atlantic integration would depend upon the conduct and result of the legislative elections to be held in March 2006. These elections were all the more important given that from 2006 Ukraine would begin shifting power away from the presidency and towards the legislature. However, at the end of the year it was still uncertain whether the "orange" forces grouped around Yushchenko in the People's Union-Our Ukraine NSNU bloc and around Tymoshenko in the Yuliya Tymoshenko bloc would be able to reunite. Although she had declared, upon being dismissed as Prime Minister, that she was moving into opposition to Yushchenko, Tymoshenko appeared to reverse this position in November when she welcomed proposals from the NSNU to join forces for the elections. The move to unite had been prompted by opinion polls suggesting that the Party of Regions of their rival Viktor Yanukovych was potentially more popular than either of the "orange" forces around Yushchenko or Tymoshenko.

Ukraine was widely praised in 2005 for having dealt with some of the corruption endemic during the Kuchma era. One of Yushchenko's key campaign pledges was fulfilled in October with the reprivatisation of the Kryvorizhstal steel works, sold at auction to the international Mittal Steel consortium for US$4.8 billion, some six times what had been paid for it in 2004, when it had been sold by the state to a consortium of businessmen closely linked to Kuchma and including his son-in-law, Viktor Pinchuk. The Yekhanurov government pledged after the sale that there would be no more "reprivatisations", in an attempt to reassure foreign investors who had been made nervous by Tymoshenko's eagerness to reverse the sales of numerous other former state concerns.

The gains of the "orange revolution", analysts generally agreed, far outweighed its negative aspects. Despite problems of confused government under Yushchenko and the split in the "orange" ranks, Ukraine benefitted from the vibrancy of civic society, efforts to combat corruption, and an increase in media freedoms. Economic growth slowed in 2005 to 3 per cent, from a peak of 12 per cent in 2004; but, according to an IMF assessment concluded in November, Ukraine's medium-term outlook was "highly favourable, provided the right policies are put into place". Reforms to complete the transition to a market economy were necessary, concluded the IMF, in order to "unleash the economy's significant untapped potential". However, in addition to the political uncertainty stirred up by the impending elections, a complicating factor at the end of 2005 was the threatening gas crisis prompted by a demand from Russia for a fourfold increase in the price of the gas supplied to Ukraine.

Elections in MOLDOVA in March saw the ruling Communist Party of Moldova, the PCM, returned to power, although with a reduced majority; in April PCM leader President Vladimir Voronin was elected to a second term in office by the Parlamentul (the unicameral legislature). However, this apparent continuity in government masked a shift in the PCM's policy away from reliance upon Russia and—at least ostensibly—towards the more pro-Western stance adopted by governments in Georgia and Ukraine. Moldova's opposition parties, the centrist

Democratic Moldova Bloc (BDM) and the centre-right Christian Democratic Popular Party (PPCD), both complained that the PCM's policy shift had stolen support from them; although the PCM's reduced majority appeared to indicate that its more pro-Western electoral platform in the 2005 elections had actually cost it support amongst its left-wing electorate.

The 6 March elections to the Parlamentul resulted in 45.98 per cent of the vote going to the PCM, with the BDM gaining 28.53 per cent, and the PPCD 9.07 per cent. Turnout was 64.09 per cent of registered voters. The results translated into fifty-six seats for the PCM, thirty-four for the BDM, and eleven for the PPCD in the 101 seat Parlamentul. (The PCM had held seventy-one seats in the previous legislature). Having gained more than the essential fifty-five seat threshold, the PCM was able to form a government, which it did on 19 April, retaining many members of the previous Cabinet, including the Prime Minister, Vasile Tarlev. On 4 April the Parlamentul confirmed Voronin in power, with seventy-five votes out of seventy-eight cast that day. Voronin, in his inauguration speech, praised the Georgian and Ukrainian "rose" and "orange" revolutions which had moved those countries away from Russia's sphere of influence, and pledged to pursue membership of the EU for Moldova, as well as promising economic modernisation and an improved standard of living, and reintegration with the separatist Transdniester region.

A new plan to resolve the issue of the self-proclaimed Transdniester republic—an area of eastern Moldova which had declared independence in 1990—was proposed in April by the Ukrainian President Viktor Yushchenko. It envisaged widening the negotiations to include the EU and USA in the framework of powers already involved (Russia, Ukraine, and the Organisation for Security and Co-operation in Europe (OSCE)). In principle, the plan included the reintegration of Transndiester within Moldova, but with "special status", as well as international monitoring of the Transdniester section of the Moldova-Ukraine border. The Moldovan side added as a condition of accepting the plan the withdrawal of some 1,500 Russian troops stationed in Transdniester: these had been due to withdraw by the end of 2003 under an agreement negotiated with the OSCE in 1999, but, as the OSCE noted at its December conference, no movement to withdraw the troops had occurred in 2005. A related development was the inauguration in October of an EU border assistance mission, under which fifty EU customs officers would patrol the Moldovan-Ukrainian border in an effort to clamp down on the smuggling of goods between Transdniester and Ukraine. Moldova alleged that the Transdniester authorities were able to sustain the region's self-proclaimed independence through smuggling, thereby diverting revenue which should have gone to Moldova.

On 11 December, the Transdniester region staged elections to its Supreme Soviet (legislature); these were not recognised as legitimate by the OSCE or the Moldovan government.

Amendments to Moldova's constitution were adopted in August, abolishing the death penalty. No executions had been carried out, and no capital sentences passed, since 1991. The amendments brought Moldova into line with international conventions on human rights.

ARMENIA—GEORGIA—AZERBAIJAN

Armenia

CAPITAL: Yerevan   AREA: 30,000 sq km   POPULATION: 3,000,000
OFFICIAL LANGUAGE: Armenian   POLITICAL SYSTEM: multiparty republic
HEAD OF STATE: President Robert Kocharian (since Feb '98)
RULING PARTIES: Republican Party of Armenia (NHK) heads coalition with Country of Law (OY)
    party and Armenian Revolutionary Federation (Dashnak/HHD)
PRIME MINISTER: Andranik Markarian (since May '00)
MAIN IGO MEMBERSHIPS (NON-UN): CIS, OSCE, PFP, BSEC, CE, CEI
CURRENCY: dram (end-'05 £1=D775.113, US$1=D451.500)
GNI PER CAPITA: US$1,120, US$4,270 at PPP ('04)

Georgia

CAPITAL: Tbilisi   AREA: 70,000 sq km   POPULATION: 4,500,000
OFFICIAL LANGUAGE: Georgian   POLITICAL SYSTEM: multiparty republic
HEAD OF STATE: President Mikheil Saakashvili (since Jan '04)
RULING PARTY: National Movement-Democratic Front (since March '04)
PRIME MINISTER: Zurab Noghaideli (since Feb '05)
MAIN IGO MEMBERSHIPS (NON-UN): CIS, CE, OSCE, PFP, BSEC
CURRENCY: lari (end-'05 £1=L3.05810, US$1=L1.78130)
GNI PER CAPITA: US$1,040, US$2,930 at PPP ('04, based on regression)

Azerbaijan

CAPITAL: Baku   AREA: 87,000 sq km   POPULATION: 8,300,000
OFFICIAL LANGUAGE: Azeri   POLITICAL SYSTEM: multiparty republic
HEAD OF STATE: President Ilham Aliyev (since Oct '03)
RULING PARTY: New Azerbaijan Party (YAP)
PRIME MINISTER: Artur Rasizade
MAIN IGO MEMBERSHIPS (NON-UN): CIS, OSCE, PFP, BSEC, OIC, ECO, CE
CURRENCY: manat (end-'05 £1=M7,908.21, US$1=M4,606.50)
GNI PER CAPITA: US$950, US$3,830 at PPP ('04)

POLITICAL developments in all three south Caucasus states in 2005 called into question the depth of their respective leaders' commitment to reform and democratisation. While some progress was registered in the search for a solution to the Nagorno-Karabakh conflict, Georgian politicians' belligerent posturing effectively neutralised President Mikheil Saakashvili's repeated peace initiatives towards the breakaway republic of South Ossetia.

The National Assembly (the unicameral legislature) of ARMENIA on 11 May approved a package of draft amendments to the constitution intended to curtail the powers of the president and augment those of the legislature, expand basic freedoms, and formalise dual citizenship. These changes were later amended under pressure from the Council of Europe's Venice Commission (the advisory European Commission for Democracy through Law). The legislature endorsed the final draft in August-September, and opposition deputies suspended their boycott of parliamentary proceedings (which they had begun in February 2004) and launched a public campaign to persuade the electorate not to participate in the nationwide referendum on the amendments on 27 November. Local observers estimated voter turnout in the referendum at between 14 and 20 per cent, but the authorities announced that more than 65 per cent of the country's 2.3 million eligible voters had participated, with more than 93 per cent voting in favour of the amendments. The approval of one-third of all eligible voters was required for the amendments to be adopted.

The opposition Artarutiun bloc claimed that the referendum had been rigged but failed to make good on repeated pledges to mobilise the population and force the government to resign. National Assembly Speaker Artur Baghdasarian, who was chairman of the Country of Law (OY) party, one of the two junior partners in the three-party governing coalition, also complained about the referendum and submitted evidence of voting irregularities to the Prosecutor General's office. Baghdasarian, who had publicly criticised Prime Minister Andranik Markarian in February and March, indicated that OY might quit the government in 2006.

US-born former Foreign Minister Raffi Hovannisian announced in December that he planned to run in the 2008 presidential election and later made public an open letter to President Robert Kocharian implicitly accusing him of rigging his own re-election and of ordering political murders.

In AZERBAIJAN, over 2,000 candidates representing twenty-six parties and blocs registered to participate in the elections to the Milli Mejlis (unicameral legislature) on 6 November, but some 450-500 of these were later disqualified or withdrew. The most important election alliances were New Politics (Yeni Siyaset) uniting former senior officials, including exiled former President Ayaz Mutalibov; plus Etibar Mamedov's Azerbaijan National Independence Party; and Liberty (Azadlyq), which united the Musavat party, the Democratic Party of Azerbaijan (ADP), and the progressive wing of the divided Azerbaijan Popular Front Party.

On 11 May and 25 October, President Ilham Aliyev issued decrees instructing government officials to take all necessary measures to ensure that polling was free and fair; in late June the Milli Mejlis approved forty-three amendments proposed by Aliyev to the existing election law. These did not, however, meet the opposition's demand for equal representation on election commissions at all levels, and Azadlyq staged a series of demonstrations in Baku in September and October, some swiftly dispersed by police, to demand further guarantees that the elections would be fair.

The final election returns gave the ruling New Azerbaijan Party over fifty of the 125 Milli Mejlis seats, a tally questioned by the opposition which, like international monitors, alleged widespread falsification. Nominally independent candidates, most of them aligned with the authorities, won forty-two seats; Azadlyq, seven; and New Politics two; but only a handful of opposition candidates representing smaller parties took up their seats. Azadlyq convened demonstrations in Baku on 13, 19 and 26 November calling for the annulment of the poll results and fresh elections. Police used violence to break up the 26 November demonstration, injuring dozens of participants in the process, and then prevented a further protest on 18 December. Repeat elections were scheduled for 13 May 2006 in ten constituencies.

The Azerbaijani police cracked down twice on alleged subversion: in early July they arrested Ruslan Bashirli, leader of the opposition youth organisation Yeni Fikir, and charged him with having accepted money from Armenian intelligence services to destabilise the political situation. In early October former Milli Mejlis Speaker and ADP chairman Rasul Guliev announced his intention of returning from the USA, where he had lived in exile since 1996, to Baku; but after being temporarily detained by the Ukrainian authorities on 17 October—when his plane landed to refuel in Simferopol—he abandoned the attempt. Azerbaijani police subsequently arrested Economic Development Minister Farkhad Aliev (no relation to the President), Health Minister Ali Insanov, and several other senior officials on suspicion of conspiring with Guliev to overthrow the country's leadership.

Elmar Huseynov, editor of the outspoken opposition journal *Monitor*, was gunned down on 2 March outside his apartment; as of the end of the year his murderers had not been found.

The Prime Minister of GEORGIA, Zurab Zhvania, was found dead with a friend in a Tbilisi apartment on 3 February in circumstances that remained unclear as of the end of the year (see p. 553). Georgian police and US Federal Bureau of Investigation (FBI) experts gave the cause of death as asphyxiation by a faulty gas heater, but Zhvania's brother told journalists that he suspected foul play. President Mikheil Saakashvili named Finance Minister Zurab Noghaideli to succeed Zhvania but left the composition of the Cabinet largely unchanged. In October, Noghaideli acceded to a parliamentary ultimatum to dismiss French-born Foreign Minister Salome Zourabichvili, whom deputies accused of protectionism, nepotism, and high-handed behaviour. Zourabichvili subsequently convened a meeting of her political sympathisers and pledged to form a political movement. On 19 October Gela Bezhuashvili, a trained lawyer and career diplomat who served in 2004 as Defence Minister and then as National Security Council secretary, was named to succeed Zourabichvili as Foreign Minister.

Four Georgian opposition parties aligned to select a single candidate to oppose the ruling National Movement in four of five by-elections on 1 October, but in each case the National Movement candidate won. Later in October, the Conservative and Republican Party parliament factions merged to create a new faction, the Democratic Front. The parliamentary opposition forced the suspension of debate on a declaration of national accord and on controversial amendments to the criminal and criminal-procedural codes, including one empowering police to "shoot to kill."

Sergei Bagapsh won the 12 January repeat presidential election in the unrecognized republic of Abkhazia (in Georgia) with over 90 per cent of the vote, but subsequently faced repeated criticism from the opposition Forum of National Unity of Abkhazia which was formed in March. Efforts by the UN to resolve the Abkhaz-Georgian conflict made minimal progress.

In January, July and late October, President Saakashvili unveiled successive initiatives to resolve the conflict with South Ossetia which the USA and the Organisation for Security and Co-operation in Europe (OSCE) endorsed, but Georgia's Defence Minister, Irakli Okruashvili, continued to threaten military action. A mortar attack on the South Ossetian capital, Tskhinvali, on 20 September drew sharp criticism from both Russia and South Ossetia. After talks in Ljubljana, Slovenia, under the OSCE aegis in early December failed to bring the two sides closer to a compromise, South Ossetian President Eduard Kokoity countered with an alternative peace plan, but the two sides failed to make further progress during talks in Moscow on 27-28 December.

The foreign ministers of ARMENIA and AZERBAIJAN met international mediators from the OSCE's Minsk group for settling the Nagorno-Karabakh conflict on five occasions to discuss approaches to resolving the dispute. The two countries' Presidents likewise met in May and August, and in December the Minsk group expressed optimism that a breakthrough was possible in 2006.

Russia and GEORGIA finally reached agreement on 30 May on a timeframe for the closure of Russia's two remaining military bases in Georgia, but Russia's perceived continuing support for Abkhazia and South Ossetia impelled the Georgian legislature to demand the withdrawal of Russian peacekeeping forces deployed in those two conflict zones and their replacement by international troops. Russia's announcement in December of the imminent doubling of the price of natural gas supplied to ARMENIA, AZERBAIJAN, and GEORGIA risked further straining its relations with those countries in 2006.

US President George W. Bush visited GEORGIA in May, pledging support for the new leadership which had come to power in the November 2003 "rose revolution". Vladimir Arutiunian, who hurled a hand grenade in the direction of Bush and Saakashvili as they addressed crowds in Tbilisi on 10 May, was apprehended by police in late July and went on trial in late November on charges of attempted murder and terrorism.

All three south Caucasus states continued talks with the EU on their formal inclusion in its "new neighbours" programme. NATO endorsed individual partnership action plans submitted by ARMENIA and GEORGIA.

AZERBAIJAN registered record economic growth of 25.2 per cent during the first eleven months of 2005. Construction of the Baku-Tbilisi-Ceyhan oil export pipeline was completed in late April, and the first Caspian oil was pumped into the pipeline in May (see p. 74). ARMENIA notched up economic growth of 12.2 per cent during January-October and concluded a new three-year loan agreement with the IMF in May. In GEORGIA, annual GDP growth was 8.5 per cent.

IV THE AMERICAS AND THE CARIBBEAN

UNITED STATES OF AMERICA

CAPITAL: Washington, DC   AREA: 9,364,000 sq km   POPULATION: 293,500,000
OFFICIAL LANGUAGE: English   POLITICAL SYSTEM: multiparty republic
HEAD OF STATE AND GOVERNMENT: President George W. Bush, Republican, since Jan '01
RULING PARTY: Congress is controlled by the Republicans
MAIN IGO MEMBERSHIPS (NON-UN): NATO, OSCE, OECD, G-8, OAS, NAFTA, APEC, AC, CP, PC,
    ANZUS
CURRENCY: dollar (end-'05 £1=US$1.71680, €1=$1.17955)
GNI PER CAPITA: US$41,400, US$39,710 at PPP ('04)

A tumultuous year brought the USA continuing war abroad and catastrophic natural disaster at home. Conflict intensified and civilian and military casualties increased in Afghanistan and Iraq amid halting signs of political progress and peaceful reconstruction. Hurricane Katrina brought once-in-a-century devastation to the nation's Gulf Coast, taking at least 1,300 lives, destroying billions of dollars worth of property, and desolating—perhaps beyond restoration—large parts of one of the nation's great cities. Continuing war and natural cataclysm stretched the resources and challenged the resolve of governments, particularly the federal government, to respond in ways befitting the might and will of the world's only superpower. The limited success of those responses generated great public concern over the course of the year. A significant focus of that concern was the administration of George Walker Bush. By the year's end, the President—whose election success of the previous year had rested so much on the public's faith in his ability to lead—found that leadership increasingly questioned from the storm-blasted bayous of Louisiana to the bomb-blasted streets of Baghdad.

POLITICS. President George W. Bush began the year confidently, eager to spend the political "capital" that he spoke of having won in his 2004 re-election. He had some success in advancing a legislative agenda intended to "keep America the economic leader of the world". Bush's January State of the Union address outlined his desire to reform the tax code, protect "entrepreneurs" from "junk lawsuits", provide further aid to education, make healthcare more affordable, and develop a "comprehensive energy strategy". Elements of the President's legislative priorities became law during the year. In February, Bush signed the Class Action Fairness Act, aimed at diminishing the nation's "lawsuit culture". In August, the Energy Policy Act became law. Sought by Bush since early in his presidency, the bill passed both House and Senate (the lower and upper house of the bicameral Congress, the federal legislature) by large majorities. Critics to right and left claimed that it did so only because controversial proposals—such as opening the Arctic National Wildlife Refuge to oil exploration—were dropped and numerous "pork-barrel" projects (funding of benefit to particular interest groups) added. The same month Bush signed the mammoth US$286.4 billion Transportation Equity Act. Designed to "bring up this transportation system into the 21st century" according to the President, to its many critics the bill represented a monument to old-style political venality. The bill's supporters emphasised the need to repair and expand transport networks, as well as the thousands of jobs that would be created. Critics pointed to over 6,300 "earmarks"—or special projects—inserted into the bill, with minimal oversight, at the request of individual members of Congress. Many of the projects, such as a multi-million dollar bridge to a tiny Alaskan community, would otherwise have been unlikely to receive funding. Few members seemed able to resist the opportunity to bring money and jobs to their state or district. These projects added an estimated US$24 billion to the bill. Whatever the political benefits for individual members in their home districts, the gargantuan excess of the transport bill only added to the public scorn for Congress as a whole.

Bush's ambition was evident in his determination to reform the social security system. Recognising the federal pension scheme as "a symbol of the trust between generations" and "a great moral success", Bush began his second term insisting that without "wise and effective reform" it was heading for bankruptcy. One controversial proposal was the introduction of "voluntary personal retirement accounts" which would allow individuals to invest a portion of their social security taxes into a personal retirement account, the proceeds of which would supplement their social security income. A country-wide tour to promote his plan proved largely unsuccessful. Democrats and senior citizen advocacy groups dismissed claims for the system's impending bankruptcy as scaremongering and plans for even partial "privatisation" as reckless. Supporters of reform dismissed such talk as itself reckless scaremongering, but many Republicans also proved unwilling to support reform of the social security system.

Illegal immigration, especially across the Mexican-US border, was another issue close to the President's heart that prompted strong disagreement, including within his own party. Bush supported replacing an "outdated" immigration policy "unsuited to the needs of our economy and to the values of our country" with one that neither penalised "hardworking people who want only to provide for their families" nor prevented businesses from hiring "willing workers" able "to fill jobs Americans will not take". Bush's insistence that new procedures would keep out "drug dealers and terrorists" failed to placate those who demanded radical measures to restore the integrity of the nation's borders. In April, an anti-illegal immigration group called the "Minutemen Project", after Revolutionary War militias, began patrolling the Mexican-US border (see p. 113). Claiming to be a "neighbourhood watch" for the nation, reporting but not confronting suspected illegal crossers, the group was criticised, by Bush and the American Civil Liberties Union among others, as "vigilantes". Other politicians, such as Congressman Tom Tancredo (Republican, Colorado), were supportive, and many more shared their view of the problem if not their chosen remedy. Thus the "Minutemen" symbolised the gulf between President Bush and the majority of citizens for whom the nation's "broken borders" represented a threat to its economy, culture, and security.

From social security to border security, complex domestic issues generated heated disagreement in the country, and both between and within political parties.

Second-term presidents, with no further elections to contest, have usually found it more difficult to rally support from those who do have to face re-election. In Bush's case, the growing willingness of usually reliable allies to oppose his policies—and so early in his second term—was particularly striking, given his administration's first-term successes in maintaining partisan loyalty and discipline.

Disagreement among usually strong allies was on display during the selection of nominees to fill two Supreme Court vacancies that opened in the summer. On 1 July Associate Justice Sandra Day O'Connor announced her intention to retire on the naming of her successor. Appointed by President Ronald Reagan in 1981, O'Connor was the first woman to serve on the Supreme Court. Although O'Connor herself rejected the term, over her tenure she had come to be seen as the Court's "swing vote", leaning to the left in various abortion cases while tending to the right on affirmative action and providing the decisive vote in *Bush v. Gore*, a decision that effectively ensured that George W. Bush would win the 2000 presidential election (see AR 2000, pp. 146-47).

For the first vacancy on the nation's highest court since 1994, President Bush nominated judge John G. Roberts Jr. of the US Court of Appeals for the District of Columbia. The fifty-year-old Roberts had established a career as a top appellate attorney, often arguing before the Supreme Court, and as a deputy solicitor general in the (1989-1993) administration of President George H. W. Bush (the current President's father). Before the nomination process could proceed, however, a second vacancy was created when the sixteenth Chief Justice of the US Supreme Court, William Hubbs Rehnquist, died on 3 September. Appointed as an associate justice in 1972 and promoted to Chief Justice by Ronald Reagan, Rehnquist was a hero to conservatives for his decades-long role in moving the Supreme Court rightwards (for obituary see pp. 547-48). Rehnquist had been ill with thyroid cancer. President Bush nominated Roberts to replace Rehnquist. The Senate held nomination hearings in September at which Roberts proved knowledgeable in constitutional law and assured in the art of taking quite some time to say not very much. Republicans hailed him as a great legal mind of his time. Many Democrats disliked Roberts's conservatism while acknowledging his sterling qualifications for the position. On 22 September the Senate judiciary committee voted thirteen to five for Roberts's nomination, with three of eight Democrats supporting him. A week later, the Senate voted seventy-eight to twenty-two in favour of the man who had once clerked for Rehnquist becoming his successor.

That a conservative replaced a conservative helped smooth Roberts's path. As attention returned to President Bush's choice to replace the Court's "moderate swing vote", Democrats insisted on like-for-like. Convinced that this was the historic, court-changing, moment towards which they had been working for decades, conservatives insisted on a judicial heavyweight of proven conservative opinions. Partisans and pundits of all stripes joined in predicting a fierce battle over the nomination. On 3 October they joined in expressing surprise at Bush's nomination of Counsel to the President Harriet Ellan Miers. The selection provoked consternation among most conservatives who questioned why the President had picked a nominee with no judicial experience and indeterminate judicial philosophy when so many first-rate conservative judges were ready to serve. Miers's strong record of legal and political activity in Texas did little to placate conservative critics who were left, in the words of leading conservative pundit William Kristol, "disappointed, depressed and demoralised" by the choice.

The administration's clumsy attempts to assure supporters that Miers was sound on conservative issues, and its over-confident insistence that the President's judgement could and should be trusted, left most conservatives unimpressed. The President and his advisers underestimated how strongly conservatives would view the selection of Miers not merely as a mistake but as a betrayal. Democrats and liberals mostly stayed silent as the fight on the Right enveloped the beleaguered Miers. With few defenders and some Republican senators signalling an unwillingness to support her, the President accepted Miers's withdrawal. The Miers nomination looked clumsy compared to the smoothness of Roberts's selection and of his chaperoning through the nomination process. It looked especially so in the longer context of the Bush administration's exceptional past successes in marshalling the nation's heterogeneous Right behind its policies. On 31 October, Bush nominated US Circuit Court of Appeals judge Samuel Alito, whose name had been on every conservative's "list" of acceptable nominees.

The Miers fiasco appeared to many observers as symptomatic of deeper problems afflicting an administration increasingly high-handed and out of touch, even towards its own supporters. This dangerous political combination was also on display in what had come to be called the Plame Affair. In July 2003 newspaper columnist Robert Novak—citing two unnamed senior administration officials as his sources—revealed that Valerie Plame was a covert agent for the CIA, the Central Intelligence Agency. Plame was the wife of retired ambassador Joseph Wilson, an outspoken critic of the administration's decision to invade Iraq. Amidst outrage within the CIA and amongst the administration's political opponents at the possibly deliberate exposure of a covert agent (potentially a federal crime), the Justice Department initiated an investigation in September 2003. It appointed as special prosecutor Patrick Fitzgerald, a US attorney in Chicago known as an assiduous and fair investigator. Fitzgerald empanelled a grand jury (to decide whether criminal charges should be brought) which, by the summer of 2005, had heard from numerous witnesses, among them former Secretary of State Colin Powell and Vice-President Richard (Dick) Cheney.

By July most attention focused on the testimony of two prominent White House advisers—Karl Rove, chief adviser to the President, and I. Lewis "Scooter" Libby, Dick Cheney's chief-of-staff—and two journalists: Matthew Cooper of *Time* and Judith Miller of the *New York Times*. Cooper and Miller initially refused to testify, claiming the right to protect confidential sources. In the autumn, their legal arguments rejected by the courts, Cooper and Miller both testified before the grand jury, having received assurances that their sources had no objection. Miller did so only after spending eighty-five days in jail for contempt of court. As it emerged that Cooper and Miller had testified to discussing Plame with Rove and Libby respectively, the political world buzzed with speculation that the administration officials would be indicted. On 28 October Libby was indicted on five charges, including obstruction of justice and perjury. Rove, who appeared before the grand jury four times, was not indicted although sources close to the investigation insisted that he was not yet in the clear. The Plame affair became a popular emblem for what Bush's critics (and increasingly his friends) saw as his unhealthy reliance on a few advisers, his administration's intolerance of opponents, and its ruthlessness towards them. To critics of the President's national security policy, and particularly of his conduct of the Iraq war, the attack on Plame and Wilson spoke most loudly of Bush's rejection of any criticism of the reasons for going to war or the conduct of the occupation and reconstruction of Iraq.

NATIONAL SECURITY. The Iraq war, the continuing US presence in Afghanistan and the conduct of the "global war on terror" remained central to US policy abroad and to political debate at home. Administration policy continued to be shaped by a vision of the USA's global role that combined longstanding notions of US exceptionalism with the more recent imperative of homeland defence in a time of terrorism. The oft-stated presidential commitment to spread freedom—"God's gift to the world"—coalesced with security considerations and strategic necessity to create a situation in which, as Bush explained in his second inaugural address, "we are led, by events and common sense, to one conclusion: the survival of liberty in our land increasingly depends on the success of liberty in other lands. The best hope for peace in our world is the expansion of freedom in all the world."

The year began with mixed news for those who believed that the invasion of Iraq would facilitate the expansion of freedom in the Middle East. On 12 January came official word that the search for weapons of mass destruction in Iraq had ended. Many insurgents remained, the most notorious of whom—Abu Misab Zarqawi—remained beyond the reach of the US forces and their Iraqi allies. Insurgents continued their policy of targeting both Iraqis associated with the government and coalition troops. The heavy toll of civilian and military casualties provided the background to elections for a 275-seat transitional national assembly and eighteen provincial assemblies, scheduled for 30 January. In the face of appeals, even from supporters of the election within the Iraqi government, that the election be postponed until the security situation improved, President Bush insisted that the election would be "a turning point in the history of Iraq, a milestone in the advance of freedom, and a crucial advance in the war on terror". Election day brought a wave of attacks across the country, including a rocket attack on the US embassy which killed two. Yet Bush appeared to be vindicated when around 8.5 million Iraqis defied intimidation and violence to go to the polls. A turnout of about 57 per cent—close to that of the 2004 US elections—led even critics of the administration to acknowledge that the election had been a greater success than many had thought possible (see pp. 185-88).

This tangled interplay between the political and the military, between signs of peaceful change and continuing violent conflict, characterised events throughout the year. It also shaped the tempo and tenor of domestic debate on the war. As the election count was completed in mid-February, violent anti-coalition and anti-government attacks remained ubiquitous in Iraq, ranging from small assaults to massive car bombs such as one in February which killed over 100 Iraqis looking for work as police officers in the town of Hilla. Fears grew that Sunni alienation, reflected in their very limited participation in the election, would not be mitigated by Shi'ite and Kurdish promises to include representative Sunnis in negotiations over the new constitution. Yet Sunni engagement in the process, albeit often in opposition to developments which they believed contrary to their interests, increased over time. Far more Sunnis were among the 63 per cent of Iraqis who participated in the October referendum on the proposed new constitution, many voting against it. The respectable turnout strengthened claims that the invasion and subsequent occupation was paving the way for a freer Iraq. December elections for a new Iraqi legislature again brought millions to the polls, including many Sunnis, offering a further sign to some of democratic hope. Violence did not abate, however. October saw the death of eighty more US troops, taking the total number of US dead past 2,000. Sixty-eight US troops died in December, a little below the monthly average for the year, bringing the total number of US fatalities since the war began to 2,180.

The domestic focus on US casualties (over 16,000 had also been wounded) was intensified by the efforts of Cindy Sheehan, a Californian whose son, Army Specialist Casey Sheehan, had been killed during a fire-fight near Baghdad in early April of 2004. After President Bush rejected her request for a meeting, Sheehan established a camp near the vacationing President's ranch in Crawford, Texas. The camp proved a media magnet and Sheehan became the high-profile embodiment of an enlivened anti-war movement previously struggling for the mainstream media's attention. Bush responded to accusations that he did not grasp the human cost of the war in an August speech before an audience of veterans of foreign wars. Citing the precise number of US dead in Iraq and Afghanistan, Bush declared that the USA would "finish the task that they gave their lives for", specifically, the expansion of freedom abroad and the strengthening of security at home. It followed, in Bush's view, that withdrawal would undermine the mission and devalue the sacrifice of those who had already given their lives.

As casualties rose, opinion polls registered the public's increasing rejection of the President's argument. By the autumn, only one-third of people polled thought that the nation was safer as a result of the war, while over one-half favoured US troops being withdrawn immediately or as soon as possible, even if that was before Iraq had become a stable democracy, this itself being a goal that increasing numbers of people considered beyond reach. As public support for war declined, politicians' willingness to criticise it increased. In November, Pennsylvania Democratic Congressman John Murtha, an ex-marine, described the administration's conduct of the Iraq war as "a flawed policy wrapped in illusion" and argued that it was "time to bring the troops home". Murtha's personal history and pro-military political record ensured that his views would be taken seriously. Few political leaders were prepared to embrace Murtha's call for rapid withdrawal, but increasing numbers did challenge the administration's conduct of the war. More now agreed with Murtha's conclusion that "the presence of US troops in Iraq" was a barrier to peaceful progress, as it had become a "catalyst" for much of the violence.

With support for the Iraq war declining and the Plame affair fuelling claims that the administration would do anything to silence criticism of its reasons for invading Iraq, leading Democrats felt emboldened to return to the question of why the USA had gone to war. Senators such as John Kerry (Democrat, Massachusetts), who had voted for the resolution authorising force in October 2002, now charged that they—and the nation—had been misled by the administration's manipulation of evidence. For much of the year, opinion polls showed declining public support for the conflict as well as growing scepticism regarding the stated reasons for going to war.

The expansion of freedom in Afghanistan remained a work in progress. In May, President Bush and his Afghan counterpart, Hamid Karzai, agreed to a strategic partnership to encourage democracy, fight extremism, and attack the opium industry. Karzai's government continued to face severe problems in extending its control to large portions of the country. Elections, initially scheduled for June 2004, were eventually held in September 2005, with about 50 per cent of eligible voters turning out to vote for almost 6,000 candidates (see pp. 264-65). Four years after the Taliban's overthrow, an estimated 19,000 US troops remained in Afghanistan. Those forces, and their coalition and Afghan allies, faced increasing attacks as the Taliban showed signs of reconstituting itself as a serious fighting force. In June sixteen navy SEALs and special operations troops died when enemy fire brought down the Chinook helicopter carrying them to the rescue of fellow fighters, three of whom also died in an engagement with Taliban forces in the mountains near the Pakistani border. The troops killed in June were among the ninety-nine US servicemen who died on active duty in Afghanistan in 2005, almost double the death toll for 2004.

The year brought changes both to national security personnel and to the structure of the homeland security apparatus. In January Condoleezza Rice was confirmed as Colin Powell's replacement as Secretary of State, the nation's top diplomatic post. In February Michael Chertoff, a former prosecutor and judge, replaced Tom Ridge as Secretary of the Department of Homeland Security. In April, John Negroponte, previously ambassador to Iraq, became the USA's first Director of National Intelligence. The creation of this position—with authority over the federal government's many intelligence-gathering efforts and its intelligence budget—had been a central recommendation of the 2004 report of the September 11 Commission (see AR 2004, pp. 125; 498-512).

The means employed to gather intelligence—particularly the interrogation of prisoners and the use of electronic surveillance—generated intense domestic debate. In January and September respectively, Army Reservist Charles Graner and Private Lynndie England—the two most visible participants in the Abu Ghraib prisoner abuse scandal—received prison sentences. In May, Army Reserve Brigadier General Janis Karpinski, the commanding officer at Abu Ghraib, was found guilty of dereliction of duty and demoted to the rank of colonel. The disciplining of a senior officer was evidence for some that the system would not tolerate such aberrant behaviour, regardless of which ranks were involved. That Karpinski was the only senior officer found to have any culpability for the abuse was evidence for others of the inadequacy of the investigation. Fears persisted that systemic abuse of prisoners existed from Afghanistan to Guantánamo Bay (the US prison in Cuba). Senator John McCain (Republican, Arizona) campaigned for much of the year for legislation that would ban the "cruel, inhuman, or degrading" treatment of prisoners under US control anywhere in the world. McCain, arguing that torture was both unproductive and un-American, gained significant cross-party support, including from leaders in his own party such as Senator John Warner of Virginia. Opponents maintained that in a new kind of war, with terrorist attack an omnipresent danger, the USA could not afford to be bound by traditional standards and limits. McCain's campaign was given impetus by a November article in the *Washington Post* claiming that the CIA was operating secret camps in third countries in Europe as well as Afghanistan and Thailand in which suspected terrorists were being imprisoned and interrogated. Secretary of State Rice spent much of her December visit to Europe insisting that the USA did not torture prisoners nor did it hand them over to other countries to torture them on its behalf. On 15 December, after months of attempting to dilute its wording and impact, Bush appeared with McCain to endorse the inclusion of the latter's anti-torture provision in a forthcoming defence bill (see p. 431).

The following day a *New York Times* article on the government's electronic eavesdropping on US citizens prompted debate regarding the legitimate limits of surveillance in a time of war. The *Times* had delayed publication for a year at the administration's request. The newspaper reported that the government had been operating wiretaps without warrants, including of the communications of US citizens, apparently in contravention of the 1978 Foreign Intelligence Surveillance Act (FISA) and despite a provision in FISA that would have allowed the government to seek warrants after the fact in cases of emergency. Defenders of the surveillance argued that FISA did not fit all the cases involved and, more broadly still, that the President needed wide powers to act in a time of war. The controversy reignited debates that had arisen at various times in the year, especially around efforts to extend the Patriot Act, some of the provisions of which raised concerns among civil libertarians from all points on the political spectrum. The anniversary of 11 September (2001) passed with no further terrorist attack on "the homeland", implicit evidence at least that security practices and structures had been improved since the attacks.

HURRICANE KATRINA. The developing Homeland Security apparatus faced its greatest test in response to a natural, rather than terrorist-inspired, catastrophe. By common agreement, it failed that test. Hurricane Katrina struck Florida on 25 August as a category 1 storm, causing significant damage and taking eleven lives before moving out into the Gulf of Mexico, gaining strength, and turning northward towards the Gulf Coast. On 27 August President Bush declared a federal state of emergency for Louisiana and for Mississippi and Alabama the following day. As Katrina strengthened to a category 5 storm—the strongest rating—the next day, governors Kathleen Blanco of Louisiana and Haley Barbour of Mississippi declared states of emergency. Ray Nagin, mayor of New Orleans, issued a voluntary—then a mandatory—evacuation order. Hundreds of thousands of vehicles inched inland on packed highways as similar orders were issued along the coast.

Katrina came ashore as a category 4 storm, early in the morning of Monday 29 August. Storm surges of fifteen feet, and often higher, battered coastal communities east of the Mississippi River. The storm all but obliterated towns such as Waveland and Bay Saint Louis, Mississippi. Tens of thousands of homes in the parishes surrounding New Orleans lay under water. Even as early reports told of New Orleans having been spared the worst, the waters of Lake Pontchartrain were flowing over and through some of the city's levees. By day's end on 30 August, 80 per cent of the city lay under water. As many as 100,000 residents remained in the city, unwilling or unable to leave. Some were relatively safe in the drier parts of town while others squeezed into attics or perched on rooftops. Some were abandoned in homes and hospitals, while others were forced into "shelters of last resort" such as the Louisiana Superdome and the city's Convention Centre where conditions would quickly deteriorate in the absence of power, sanitation, and sufficient food and water. As the storm passed, and relief efforts began, thousands of square miles of the US south had been seriously damaged and hundreds of thousands of its residents faced desperate circumstances, from homes destroyed to family members missing or dead.

Those charged with leading the relief and recovery efforts faced a monumental task. Many individuals, and groups such as the Coast Guard, worked tirelessly to rescue thousands from flood waters and devastated homes. Nevertheless, an astonished—and increasingly angry—public watched as day after long day the consequences of natural catastrophe were compounded by the incompetent, indecisive, and uncoordinated nature of the response to it. The public demanded to know why government reactions seemed so fitful and fragmented, especially when experts had been predicting for days the damage that such a hurricane could do to the levees of New Orleans and to the many communities along the coast.

No leaders or level of government escaped scrutiny and recrimination, but most attention focused on the federal government's response. On 29 August President Bush was quick to reassure "the folks there on the Gulf Coast" that "when the storm passes, the federal government has got assets and resources that we'll be deploying to help you". Yet days after Katrina struck, many rural communities remained without power or supplies and had seen no sign of relief workers. Violence and looting was on the increase in New Orleans (although not to the extent that many exaggerated accounts from politicians and reporters at the time suggested). The evacuation of thousands from the Superdome did not begin until Wednesday and was not completed until Sunday. Days into the disaster, Terry Ebbert, Louisiana head of the Federal Emergency Management Agency (FEMA), described his agency's response to this "national emergency" as a "national disgrace".

Particular individuals came under intense scrutiny. Michael Chertoff, given authority over FEMA in the new Homeland Security structure, at times appeared unaware either of the scale of the emergency or the problems with the federal reaction to it. On 31 August, Chertoff declared himself "extremely pleased with the response that every element of the federal government, all of our federal partners, have made to this terrible tragedy". Such praise jarred with the observations of those in the region or watching around the world, provoking one incredulous journalist into asking Chertoff if he watched television. FEMA director Michael Brown also faced severe criticism. People demanded to know why Brown responded so passively to one of the worst hurricanes to hit the nation in a century. On the day Katrina struck, Brown asked Chertoff for 1,000 relief personnel. While giving them forty-eight hours to arrive in the region, he asked rescue workers from other states not to go to the region unless requested to do so. Brown appeared to be out of touch with the scale of the disaster and out of his depth in dealing with it. Questions were raised as to why a person with almost no experience of disaster management had come to occupy the most important such job in the country. On 9 September Brown was replaced as head of the relief effort by Vice Admiral Thad W. Allen, Chief of Staff of the Coast Guard. On 12 September Brown resigned from FEMA.

The man who, as late as 2 September, told "Brownie" that he was "doing a heck of a job" also faced harsh criticism for his perceived lack of leadership in the early stages of the crisis. Vacationing at his Texas ranch as Katrina hit the Gulf Coast, President Bush went ahead with a scheduled visit to Arizona to promote his social security reform plan. As 80 per cent of a major US city disappeared under flood waters and hundreds of miles of coastline offered a continuous vista of devastation, the President found time to play a round of golf. Bush surveyed the damage on the Wednesday as he flew back to Washington DC, having cut short his vacation. The next day he requested US$10.5 billion from Congress to fund initial relief efforts. On Friday he made his first visit to the devastated area and met state and local leaders. Speaking in New Orleans, he promised not to forget the city. His tone, however—joking, for example, about his own past visits to the famed party city—struck many as inappropriate and indicative of Bush, like others in his administration, still not having grasped the gravity of the crisis.

Facing a social crisis and a political fiasco of its own making, the administration eventually developed a plan for disaster relief that was also intended to make clear that it did, indeed, understand the urgency of the situation. National Guard and federal troops gradually brought increasing order and supplies to New Orleans, while relief workers did eventually fan out through the region. Bush spoke again in New Orleans on 15 September. He promised to "do what it takes, [. . .] stay as long as it takes, to help citizens rebuild their communities and their lives". He assured "all who question the future of the Crescent City" that there was "no way to imagine America without New Orleans, and this great city will rise again".

Relief efforts were compounded by another major hurricane, Rita, which hit the Texas and Louisiana coastlines in late September, causing hundreds of thousands to leave the area (including some who had just fled Katrina), closing down much of the region's oil refining capacity, and generating severe flooding and damage in coastal areas of the western Gulf of Mexico. After an October visit to Louisiana and Mississippi, President Bush would not visit the region again before year's end. By then, many areas of New Orleans remained largely uninhabitable and reconstruction had barely begun in many towns along the coast. Tens of thousands of families remained scattered across the country in trailers, hotels, and the homes of family members and kind strangers. An increasing number now occupied their own new homes, had new jobs, and showed little inclination to return. Evidence mounted that the country would indeed have to start imagining what it would look like without the New Orleans it had long known.

Looking at Katrina's meaning for national security, many were discouraged by what the federal response implied about the preparedness of the new security apparatus developed over the preceding four years. "If we can't respond faster than this to an event we saw coming across the Gulf for days", asked former Speaker of the House of Representatives, Republican Newt Gingrich, "then why do we think we're prepared to respond to a nuclear or biological attack?" The President himself admitted that "Katrina exposed serious problems in our response capability at all levels of government", going on to say that "to the extent the federal government didn't fully do its job right, I take responsibility."

ECONOMY. Figures from the census bureau, released as New Orleans sank, revealed that the nation's poverty rate had increased in 2004 from 12.5 per cent to 12.7 per cent. A total of 37 million people lived below the poverty line (measured in 2004 as pre-tax income of US$9,827 for a one-person household) while median incomes for both men and women had fallen. The number of people without health insurance rose to almost 46 million. The President himself responded to concerns about economic, and racial, inequality in an address at the National Cathedral in Washington DC on 16 September. "The Gulf Coast must be rebuilt with an eye toward wiping out the persistent poverty and racial injustice plain to all in the suffering of the black and the poor in hurricane Katrina's wake", Bush declared. "As we clear away the debris of a hurricane, let us also clear away the legacy of inequality."

A week earlier, the President suspended the application in hurricane-hit regions of the Davis-Bacon Act, legislation requiring that federal projects paid workers the prevailing wage for the job in the area. Bush pointed to his authority to do so in a time and place of "national emergency". Supporters of the move argued that it would speed reconstruction and create more jobs. Opponents charged that it would reduce income in areas where prevailing wages—US$9 an hour for construction jobs in New Orleans, for example—were already low. Critics contrasted this step with the no-bid contracts for the Halliburton energy and construction company, without which any response to a national crisis was now seemingly incomplete, interpreting both as further examples of the administration's devotion to its friends and indifference to the public. Partly in response to such criticisms, the suspension of the Davis-Bacon Act was later lifted.

The year's parade of corporate criminals reinforced the notion of an economy in which the good of the public, or even the shareholder, was too often little more than an afterthought. In July, Bernard Ebbers, one-time head of the WorldCom telecommunications company, cried in court as he was sentenced to twenty-five years in prison for a variety of financial crimes estimated to have cost the company about US$11 billion and tens of thousands of employees their jobs. In September, L. Dennis Kozlowski and Mark Swartz, formerly chief executive officer and chief financial officer respectively of multinational corporation Tyco, were sentenced to prison terms of from eight and one-third to twenty-five and a half years, and ordered to pay fines and restitution for cheating their company out of over US$500 million.

The lords of the public sector did not escape scrutiny, as Katrina proved something of a catalyst for a debate on federal spending. The federal largesse that followed federal lethargy in responding to Katrina provoked demands that economies be made elsewhere. Leading Republicans like Senator Lindsey Graham of South Carolina called for the 2006 implementation of the Medicare Prescription Drug, Improvement, and Modernisation Act—intended to provide senior citizens with subsidised medicines—to be delayed. Others called for revisiting the massive transportation bill to cut some of the spending devoted to politicians' pet projects for their districts. These proposals met strong opposition from various interest groups and lobbyists as well as politicians in both parties.

Complaints about "runaway spending" were not new, but grew throughout the year as both the administration and Congress seemed complicit in ever-increasing spending, deficits, and debts. The President's US$2.57 trillion budget, sent to Congress in February, did little to allay fiscal fears on both Right and Left. Proposed cuts to various programmes such as farm subsidies, education, and even healthcare for military veterans were insufficient for some and wrongly targeted in the view of others. Many Democrats, joined by a few Republicans, argued against renewing tax-cuts that favoured the wealthy. At Senate hearings in April, Alan Greenspan, chairman of the Federal Reserve (the US central bank), argued that the federal budget deficit was on an "unsustainable path" which, unless reversed, would eventually "cause the economy to stagnate or worse". Greenspan called for Congress to take action, which he accepted might have to include some tax increases. President Bush's claim that "restraining the spending appetite of the federal government" was a priority rang increasingly hollow to concerned taxpayers and fiscal conservatives. Although he had often threatened to do so, Bush had yet to exercise his veto power after almost five years in office. By year's end, with the costs of war and reconstruction at home and abroad still rising, the national debt stood at close to US$8.2 trillion. Interest payments on the debt cost in the region of US$900 million per day.

FOREIGN AFFAIRS. That foreign creditors held over half the federal debt offered striking evidence for the inextricable connections between economic and political life at home and trade and diplomacy abroad. The USA's efforts to navigate its economic and diplomatic relations with other countries were frequently characterised by the interplay between the stated aim of expanding free trade for the supposed benefit of all and the countervailing power of particular economic interests within both the USA and the nations it had to deal with.

Economic relations with China, one of the government's largest creditors, continued to be a central focus of US foreign policy. In July, China slightly relaxed its policy of tying the yuan's value to that of the US dollar, a policy that US exporters had long complained hurt their competitiveness in the Chinese market. The administration responded positively to the move, but critics, dismissing it as tokenism, emphasised China's continued disregard for copyright laws and the flood of inexpensive Chinese goods into the USA.

The question of who benefited from free trade surrounded the debate over the Central American Free Trade Agreement (CAFTA), which was narrowly approved in July by the House and Senate. Vigorous lobbying by the administration was needed to counter wide-ranging opposition from groups such as sugar industry lobbyists afraid of "cheap imports" and labour unions afraid of jobs being exported to "cheap labour" economies. Many Central and Latin Americans remained to be convinced that the agreement would benefit their countries. In a November visit to Argentina for the summit of the Americas, 10,000 protestors made clear their disagreement with Bush's free trade policies. The meeting itself brought no agreement on expanding free trade further throughout the hemisphere (see p. 156).

No region of the world was the focus of more intense discussion of free markets and fair dealing, global trade and local development, than Africa. African debt and development took centre stage at the G-8 summit of industrialised nations, held in Scotland in July. Before the summit, President Bush announced a series of aid packages for Africa, including, in June, a five-year, US$1.2 billion commitment to fight malaria. The summit ended with the assembled nations committing themselves to debt cancellation, the doubling of African aid by 2010 to US$50 billion a year, and the further opening of trade to and from the continent.

Also in July the World Trade Organisation (WTO) agreed with Brazil that the US$4 billion in federal supports received annually by US cotton growers unfairly undermined cotton growers in places such as Brazil and West Africa. Powerful domestic economic interests made it unlikely that Western governments would eliminate such barriers to genuinely free trade in the near future. Whatever its limits in practice or its potential for creating conflict, even among allies, expanding the realm of free trade remained an essential element of a US mission, as President Bush promised in his inaugural address, to spread freedom to "the darkest corners of the world".

When Bush spoke of "the darkest corners of the world" he likely had foremost in mind countries like Iran and North Korea. Various talks throughout the year made little progress towards reducing US concerns about the nuclear programmes of either of these states. A pattern of deadlock and resumption characterised the "six-party" talks between the USA, North Korea, South Korea, China, Japan, and Russia. Bilateral talks between North Korea and the USA— an approach previously resisted by the latter—also took place as part of these wider negotiations, but little progress had been made by year's end. The European countries of France, Germany, and the UK took the lead in negotiations with Iran about the development of its nuclear programme. Discussions proceeded under the shadow of US scepticism and the Europeans' own growing frustration with Iran's responses to their efforts. By the end of the year, these talks had made few concrete steps towards a resolution that would ease European and US fears of nuclear weapons' proliferation while accommodating Iran's stated aim of building a nuclear programme solely for the production of energy. US relations with established members of Asia's nuclear power club proved more amicable. In March, the administration approved the long-blocked sale of F-16 fighter jets to Pakistan. In July, the USA and India reached an agreement to allow the latter to develop its nuclear energy programme with both international assistance and inspection, while its nuclear weapons programme would remain beyond international inspection.

President Bush discussed nuclear proliferation with Russian President Vladimir Putin during a visit to Europe in February, the same month that North Korea officially acknowledged that it possessed nuclear armaments (see p. 318). The President's other overseas trips included visits in May to Russia, where he commemorated the 60th anniversary of Germany's defeat in World War II; and to Latvia, the Netherlands, and Georgia. In November, the President attended the Asia Pacific Economic Co-operation (APEC) leaders' meeting in South Korea, also visiting China, Japan, and Mongolia. The same month he visited Panama and Brazil, as well as Argentina for the summit of the Americas.

SOCIETY AND CULTURE. In April the President and First Lady Laura Bush attended Pope John Paul II's funeral in Rome (see p. 58), an event that received saturation coverage in the US media. The excessive and undiscriminating coverage of the new Pope's election (complete with "chimney-cam" windows in the corner of the nation's television screens) offered further evidence for the growing inclination of the USA's cultural producers and reporters to blur, rather than emphasise, the lines between the ephemeral realms of fame and celebrity and the life-and-death worlds of politics and power. The weekend before the G-8 summit, a free concert in Philadelphia—one of nine "Live 8" events around the world—called on numerous celebrities from the entertainment world to focus attention on the problem of global poverty by participating in a day-long festival of entertainment and exhortation. In December *Time* magazine named billionaire computer magnate Bill Gates and his wife Melinda Gates as their "persons of the year", an award they shared with philanthropic Irish musician Bono. In 2005 the couple's foundation gave over US$1 billion dollars to various causes, much of it to health projects such as the immunisation from common diseases of children in Africa, a continent where more than one million people died from malaria alone in 2005.

The many influential US figures who died in 2005 included culinary creators Gerry Thomas, who invented the TV dinner, and H. David Dalquist, who invented the Bundt pan; journalists Jack Anderson and Peter Jennings; writers Evan Hunter, Saul Bellow, and Hunter S. Thompson; playwright Arthur Miller and poet Robert

Creeley; and influential feminist thinkers Andrea Dworkin and Elizabeth Janeway. Singer Luther Vandross died, as did talk-show host Johnny Carson, screenwriter Ernest Lehman, actress Anne Bancroft, and legendary cabaret performer Hildegarde. Diplomat George Kennan, and politicians Eugene McCarthy and Shirley Chisholm—the first black woman elected to the House of Representatives—passed away. So too did entrepreneur John Johnson; architect Philip Johnson; basketball big man George Mikan; microbiologist Maurice Hilleman, creator of numerous life-saving vaccines; and soldier William Westmoreland, commander of US forces in Vietnam from 1964 to 1968 (see Obituaries).

Other deaths recalled battles past and wars continuing. Rose Mary Woods, secretary to President Richard Nixon and important figure in the Watergate scandal that led to Nixon's impeachment and resignation, died in an Ohio nursing home, aged eighty-seven. Peter Rodino, Democratic chairman of the House judiciary committee and leading figure at the impeachment hearings also died. The mysterious figure at the heart of the Watergate scandal revealed himself in May. W. Mark Felt, a senior FBI official at the time, admitted in *Vanity Fair* magazine that he had been "Deep Throat", the anonymous source whose inside information assisted *Washington Post* journalists Carl Bernstein and Bob Woodward in their investigation of the story (see AR 1973, pp. 62-74, 1974 pp. 72-83).

On 31 March, Terri Schiavo, a severely brain-damaged Florida woman, died after a long legal battle between her husband Michael Schiavo, who favoured her being allowed to die, and her parents Robert Schindler and Mary Schindler, who denied that their daughter was in a "persistent vegetative state" from which she would never recover. Schiavo's case became, for a while, the focus of ongoing cultural and political battles surrounding issues of freedom, privacy, and the sacredness of human life. After a complicated series of court cases challenging and defending the initial court decision that Terri Schiavo would have wanted to die, her feeding tubes were removed on 18 March. Schiavo died thirteen days later. Under intense pressure from religious and right-to-life groups, congressional Republicans passed last-minute legislation intended to prevent Schiavo being allowed to die. This effort sat badly with a majority of the public who saw it as neither principled nor legally justifiable but rather as the worst kind of political pandering.

The country was reminded of the violent side of the culture wars in April, when home-grown terrorist Eric Rudolph pleaded guilty and was sentenced to four consecutive life sentences for various bombings, including one that maimed an employee of a Birmingham, Alabama, abortion clinic in 1998, and another which killed one and injured more than 100 in Centennial Park, Atlanta, during the 1996 Olympic Games. Further evidence that the USA's history with terrorism long pre-dated September 2001 came in June, in the form of a Senate apology for past failures to enact anti-lynching legislation. From the 1880s to the 1940s over 4,700 people were lynched, more than two-thirds of them African American; an average of sixty-eight people per year. That reported lynchings had fallen to just a few per year by the 1940s was due in no small part to the civil rights movement that had been active throughout the century. An influential and iconic figure in that movement died in October. Often referred to as "the mother of the civil rights movement", Rosa Parks was more the grandchild of a movement that had been struggling for decades to achieve equal rights for African Americans and other minority groups. Parks was no less important for that, joining the movement at a crucial time and, by refusing to give up her seat on a Montgomery, Alabama, bus in 1955, becoming the catalyst for one of the movement's greatest successes: the Montgomery bus boycott (see p. 545).

In October, Rosa Parks lay in state in the Capitol Rotunda, the first woman and second African American accorded an honour previously bestowed on such luminaries of the national story as Abraham Lincoln, J. Edgar Hoover, John F. Kennedy, and Ronald Reagan. Journalists and commentators with a tenuous grasp of history and a limited vocabulary emphasised Parks's "humble" and "dignified" demeanour throughout her life. Parks herself had spoken of being "tired of giving in" at her history-making moment of resistance, a phrase that has always encompassed a world of meaning for the oppressed and forgotten. As Parks lay in state, the tired and troubled survivors of Hurricane Katrina— whether African American or not—were already fading from the public mind. The brief national soul-searching over present ills and inequities was almost over. The beached and battered waterfront casinos of the Gulf Coast, fitting symbols of the exuberant and fragile new US economy, were being reconstructed. Tomorrow would indeed be another day.

CANADA

CAPITAL: Ottawa   AREA: 9,971,000 sq km   POPULATION: 31,900,000
OFFICIAL LANGUAGES: English & French   POLITICAL SYSTEM: multiparty system in Commonwealth
HEAD OF STATE: Queen Elizabeth II (since Feb '52)
GOVERNOR-GENERAL: Michaëlle Jean (since Sept '05)
RULING PARTY: Liberal Party (since Oct '93)
HEAD OF GOVERNMENT: Paul Martin, Prime Minister (since Dec '03)
MAIN IGO MEMBERSHIPS (NON-UN): NATO, OECD, OSCE, G-7, OAS, NAFTA, APEC, CP, AC,
    CWTH, Francophonie
CURRENCY: Canadian dollar (end-'05 £1=C$2.00540, US$1=C$1.16820)
GNI PER CAPITA: US$28,390, US$30,660 at PPP ('04)

MINORITY government marked Canada's political life in 2005. Elected in June 2004, the Liberal Party, under new Prime Minister Paul Martin, began the year in a precarious position in the federal Parliament, holding 135 seats in the 308-seat House of Commons (the lower chamber). Against it were three opposition parties: the Conservatives with ninety-nine seats; the socialist New Democratic Party with nineteen seats; and the separatist Bloc Québécois with fifty-four seats, all from the province of Quebec. Having met a series of confidence tests throughout the year, the Martin government finally fell on 28 November in a vote of 171-133. The government immediately resigned and a general election was set for 23 January 2006.

The Liberal government's hold on power was threatened during the year by the fall-out from an ugly political scandal in Quebec. Following the near victory of a proposal for sovereignty in a Quebec referendum in 1995 (see AR 1995, pp. 162-65), the Liberal government, headed by Jean Chrétien, had mounted an advertising campaign to boost the national government's image within the largely French-speaking province. Sporting and community events across Quebec were sponsored through federal grants, the money being distributed by advertising agencies friendly to the Liberal Party. However, sums were paid to the agencies that bore little relationship to services provided, and government accounting practices were blatantly ignored. When Martin succeeded Chrétien as Prime Minister in December 1993, he appointed an enquiry under Quebec Superior Court judge John Gomery to look into the way in which the advertising campaign had been conducted. A series of hearings early in the year revealed misdemeanours and both Chrétien and Martin were called to testify. The latter, although Finance Minister under Chrétien, was exonerated since he had taken no part in the distribution of funds in Quebec. Chrétien was not so fortunate. His supervision of the programme was judged to be exceedingly lax, leading Gomery to assign to him responsibility for the maladministration of public funds. Other individuals were ordered to return funds or, in some cases, referred for criminal prosecution. The revelations were damaging to the Liberal Party, especially in Quebec. The separatist movement, which had appeared to be in decline, was dramatically revived as the separatist Bloc Québécois branded the affair an insult to the good name of Quebecers.

The re-emergence of separatism in Quebec was not the only provincial issue with which Martin had to deal. Newfoundland and Labrador, and its sister province of Nova Scotia, had long argued that they were denied their full share of revenue from off-shore oil and gas resources. The federal government clawed back some of these revenues to augment a fund set up to help poorer provinces. The two maritime provinces argued that, as disadvantaged regions, they should not have to contribute to the fund. Martin accepted their position and they were allowed to keep their offshore revenues whilst also benefiting from the fund.

Canada announced, on 13 April, long-awaited proposals to implement the 1997 Kyoto Protocol, designed to reduce greenhouse gas emissions. The federal government committed itself to spend C$10 billion over the next seven years to reduce emissions to 6 per cent below 1990 levels. This goal would be achieved by significant reductions in the use of fossil fuels and the purchase of emission credits.

An important piece of social legislation was passed by the Commons on 28 June. The definition of marriage was changed to encompass relations between couples of the same sex. Earlier, the Supreme Court and most of the higher courts in the provinces had approved the new definition, arguing that it was in conformity with the equality principle enshrined in Canada's charter of rights. Canada thus joined socially progressive countries such as the Netherlands and Belgium in enacting such legislation. Spain took the same step a few days after Canada (see p. 62).

A surprise announcement in August was that the next governor-general of Canada, to take office in September, would be a black immigrant from Haiti,

Michaëlle Jean, a talented television journalist, who had come to Canada as a child. She would represent Queen Elizabeth II, Canada's head of state. Thoroughly bilingual, the appointment of Jean was widely seen as symbolising Canada's transformation into a country in which multiculturalism was strongly entrenched.

The Canadian economy profited from high energy prices, coupled with a strong demand from the US market. GDP was expected to rise by 2.9 per cent during the year. Inflation remained in check, with the consumer price index standing at 2 per cent in November and the unemployment rate at 6.7 per cent.

The federal budget was presented by Finance Minister Ralph Goodale on 23 February. It revealed a massive planned increase in government expenditure over the five years between 2005 and 2010. Social goals, including an ambitious national childcare plan, lay at the heart of the budget. There was also money for strengthening the armed forces and for increasing development aid from its present 2.5 per cent of GDP to 3 percent over 2005-06. A larger share of the federal petrol tax would be transferred to the cities to support public transport. Notwithstanding such ambitious plans, Goodale predicted another balanced budget, the eighth in a row.

Nor was increased spending confined to the formal budget statement. On 26 April Martin entered into a deal with Jack Layton, the head of the New Democratic Party, to add another C\$4.6 billion to expenditure over the next two years. Layton demanded more money for social housing, the environment and foreign aid. To win the support of Layton's party, Martin agreed to the additional expenditure. Thus fortified, Martin placed his budget before the Commons on 19 May. A tied vote resulted, with 152 members supporting the government and 152 opposed. In this situation UK parliamentary practice required the elected Speaker to cast the deciding vote. He supported the government and the budget was duly passed, the first time this situation had occurred in Canadian history.

Canada and the USA, close military partners since World War II, experienced foreign policy differences. In 2003 Canada had refused to join the US intervention in Iraq; now Canada declined to participate in the missile defence shield for North America to be constructed by the USA. The issue had been a controversial one in Canada, but on 24 February the government announced that Canada did not see a compelling reason to participate in the scheme. A vigorous debate ensued in the Commons but the Martin government's stand was approved. There was uncertainty regarding the decision, however, since one year previously an amendment had been negotiated in the functions of the North American Aerospace Command. This allowed the Command—a bilateral agency—to communicate aerial surveillance information to the US authority responsible for the missile defence project.

Canada supported wider US objectives in the Middle East by participating in the NATO operation to bring stability to Afghanistan. Beginning in the late summer it moved a force, eventually to number 2,200 personnel, to Kandahar, a region where the Taliban was strongly entrenched.

The largest bilateral trade flow in the world passed across the Canadian-US border. Two disputes persisted at the beginning of the year: one to be settled and the second placed on the road to resolution. The first dispute involved closing the US border to Canadian cattle after a single case of bovine spongiform encephalopathy (BSE or "mad cow disease") was discovered in Alberta. Thorough testing of animals on each side of the border led the USA to lift the ban on 14 July.

Another dispute, going back to 2002, made progress. For three years the USA had imposed a 28 per cent duty on Canadian construction lumber entering the country. It claimed that the Canadian provinces, in the issuance of permits to cut timber, granted a subsidy to their lumber producers. A total of US$5 billion had been collected through the imposition of the duties. Under US law these funds were to be turned over to companies hurt by the alleged subsidy. Over the years, five rulings by North American Free Trade Association (NAFTA) panels had upheld the Canadian argument that its timber-cutting practices were fair and reasonable. On 10 August a three-member special appeal panel declared that there was no basis for the duties and ordered the USA to return the funds collected. The US government rejected the decision, insisting that Canada enter into negotiations to resolve the issue. This Canada refused to do, arguing that the USA must be prepared to accept the dispute resolution procedures of a trade agreement which it had sworn to uphold. At the end of the year the US Congress (the bicameral legislature) repealed the law permitting the proceeds from tariff duties to be awarded to interests hurt by trade disputes. Canadian lumber interests were cheered by the action, which seemed to offer a way forward to the resolution of the softwood lumber dispute.

MEXICO AND CENTRAL AMERICA

MEXICO—GUATEMALA—EL SALVADOR—HONDURAS—NICARAGUA— COSTA RICA—PANAMA

MEXICO

CAPITAL: Mexico City   AREA: 1,958,000 sq km   POPULATION: 103,800,000
OFFICIAL LANGUAGE: Spanish   POLITICAL SYSTEM: multiparty republic
HEAD OF STATE AND GOVERNMENT: President Vicente Fox Quesada (since Dec '00)
RULING PARTIES: National Action Party (PAN) holds presidency; Institutional Revolutionary Party
    (PRI) largest party in legislature
MAIN IGO MEMBERSHIPS (NON-UN): OAS, SELA, ALADI, ACS, APEC, NAFTA, OECD
CURRENCY: Mexican peso (end-'05 £1=MP18.2622, US$1=MP10.6377)
GNI PER CAPITA: US$6,770, US$9,590 at PPP ('04)

THE year was dominated by political manoeuvrings in the build up to the July 2006 presidential election, and by continuing discussions with the USA over border security and immigration. In the battle for the presidency, one of the leading candidates, Mexico City's mayor Andrés Manuel López Obrador, running for the left-wing Party of the Democratic Revolution (PRD), survived an attempt to force him out of the race. On 8 April, Mexico's Congress (the bicameral legislature) stripped López Obrador of his political immunity so that he could face prosecution over a minor land dispute. The move was seen as a purely political decision to weaken his presidential ambitions, organised as it was by the Institutional Revolutionary Party (PRI) and the National Action Party (PAN) of President Vincente Fox Quesada. The vote provoked international condemnation, as well as a large-scale demonstration in Mexico City which attracted hundreds of thousands of people. The protests paid off when Fox dismissed the chief federal prosecutor who had been in charge of the prosecution, which led in turn to the case being dropped. Soon afterwards, López Obrador resigned his position as mayor and began his campaign for the presidency.

Nevertheless, the resurgence of the Institutional Revolutionary Party (PRI) which had begun in 2004 was maintained. For example, on 3 July PRI candidate Enrique Peña won the important Mexico State gubernatorial election with more than 50 per cent of the vote. In late October, Roberto Madrazo emerged as the presidential nominee for the PRI, despite some opposition from within his party. In the same week the National Action Party (PAN) of President Fox chose Felipe Calderón, Mexico's former Energy Minister, as its candidate in the presidential elections (under the constitution, Fox was barred from running for a second term). However, Calderón's victory came at the expense of a candidate who had received the personal endorsement of Fox, indicating the latter's fading support amongst the PAN membership. One further, and potentially very important, development in the presidential race came in June with the first public appearance in five years of the Zapatista rebel group leader, subcomandante Insurgente Marcos (formerly known as Rafael Sebastián Guillén Vicente). Marcos's return was the prelude to an announcement at the end of the year that he was to undertake a nationwide tour to promote a new, non-violent political movement.

The other issue of particular importance related to security and immigration across the Mexico-US border. The two countries were once again unable to make progress on an immigration deal that would have given between 4 and 6 million Mexicans, residing illegally in the USA, guest-worker status. Rather, the focus was on preventing illegal immigration from Mexico to the USA. This spilled into unofficial action. For example, the "Minutemen Project"—a vigilante initiative organised by US citizens to "hunt down" illegal Mexican immigrants crossing the border—was established in April (see p. 115). The Mexican authorities reacted very negatively to the group's activities and later in the year successfully co-sponsored a UN resolution which urged governments to act against private individuals or groups undermining the government's border control functions.

The pressure for action in the USA to address the issue of illegal immigration led senior US politicians to propose a range of ideas. The most high profile of these came in November when President George W. Bush announced a series of immigration reform measures, including "constructing physical barriers to entry". The prioritising of this issue was a consequence of earlier Republican pressure in Congress (the bicameral US legislature) to build a "sea-to-sea" double fence along the entire Mexican-US border. Although Bush did not support the erection of a fence along the entire border, he called for the expansion of fencing in urban areas and the construction of new patrol roads elsewhere.

On 16 December, the US House of Representatives (the lower chamber of Congress) passed a bill based largely on the measures laid out by the President. The Mexican government in turn criticised the measures, objecting to the building of barriers along the border. However, despite tensions between Mexico and the USA over the issue of immigration, joint action was forthcoming in response to the escalating drug-related violence in border areas such as Nuevo Laredo. On 18 October Mexican chief federal prosecutor Daniel Cabeza de Vaca and US Attorney General Alberto Gonzales agreed to implement a number of measures to improve law enforcement along the border.

In other news, Mexico's Supreme Court in May upheld President Fox's right to veto the federal budget (although it later watered down the decision, allowing his veto to be overturned by a two-thirds majority in the Congress). The President had brought the case after the opposition-controlled Chamber of Deputies had refused to accept a number of his suggested changes to the 2005 budget (see AR 2004, p. 141). The ruling was thought likely to give Fox and future Presidents greater leverage in budgetary negotiations with Congress.

CENTRAL AMERICA

Guatemala

CAPITAL: Guatemala City   AREA: 109,000 sq km   POPULATION: 12,600,000
OFFICIAL LANGUAGE: Spanish   POLITICAL SYSTEM: multiparty republic
HEAD OF STATE AND GOVERNMENT: President Oscar Berger (GANA) (since Jan '04)
RULING PARTIES: Grand National Alliance (GANA), composed of the Movimiento Reformador and the Partido Solidaridad Nacional, in coalition with the National Union for Hope (UNE) and the National Advancement Party (PAN)
MAIN IGO MEMBERSHIPS (NON-UN): OAS, SELA, CACM, ACM, ACS, NAM
CURRENCY: quetzal (end-'05 £1=Q13.0344, US$1=Q7.59250)
GNI PER CAPITA: US$2,130, US$4,140 at PPP ('04, based on regression)

El Salvador

CAPITAL: San Salvador   AREA: 21,000 sq km   POPULATION: 6,700,000
OFFICIAL LANGUAGE: Spanish   POLITICAL SYSTEM: multiparty republic
HEAD OF STATE AND GOVERNMENT: President Antonio Elías (Tony) Saca (ARENA) (since June '04)
RULING PARTIES: National Republican Alliance (Arena) in coalition with the National Conciliation Party (PCN) (since March '03)
MAIN IGO MEMBERSHIPS (NON-UN): OAS, SELA, CACM, ACS
CURRENCY: Salvadorian colón (end-'05 £1=C15.0250, US$1=C8.75200)
GNI PER CAPITA: US$2,350, US$4,980 at PPP ('04, based on regression)

Honduras

CAPITAL: Tegucigalpa   AREA: 112,000 sq km   POPULATION: 7,100,000
OFFICIAL LANGUAGE: Spanish   POLITICAL SYSTEM: multiparty republic
HEAD OF STATE AND GOVERNMENT: President Ricardo Maduro (since Jan '02)
PRESIDENT ELECT: Manuel "Mel" Zelaya Rosales
RULING PARTY: National Party of Honduras (PNH)
MAIN IGO MEMBERSHIPS (NON-UN): OAS, SELA, CACM, ACS, NAM
CURRENCY: lempira (end-'05 £1=L32.4380, US$1=L18.8950)
GNI PER CAPITA: US$1,030, US$2,710 at PPP ('04, based on regression)

Nicaragua

CAPITAL: Managua   AREA: 130,000 sq km   POPULATION: 5,600,000
OFFICIAL LANGUAGE: Spanish   POLITICAL SYSTEM: multiparty republic
HEAD OF STATE AND GOVERNMENT: President Enrique Bolanos Geyer (since Jan '02)
RULING PARTY: Liberal Constitutionalist Party (PLC)
MAIN IGO MEMBERSHIPS (NON-UN): OAS, SELA, CACM, ACS, NAM
CURRENCY: gold córdoba (end-'05 £1=C28.2405, US$1=C16.4500)
GNI PER CAPITA: US$790, US$3,300 at PPP ('04)

Costa Rica

CAPITAL: San José   AREA: 51,000 sq km   POPULATION: 4,100,000
OFFICIAL LANGUAGE: Spanish   POLITICAL SYSTEM: multiparty republic
HEAD OF STATE AND GOVERNMENT: President Abel Pacheco de la Espriella (since May '02)
RULING PARTY: Social Christian Unity Party (PUSC)
MAIN IGO MEMBERSHIPS (NON-UN): OAS, SELA, CACM, ACS
CURRENCY: colón (end-'05 £1=C852.624, US$1=C496.650)
GNI PER CAPITA: US$4,670, US$9,530 at PPP ('04, based on regression)

Panama

CAPITAL: Panama City   AREA: 76,000 sq km   POPULATION: 3,000,000
OFFICIAL LANGUAGE: Spanish   POLITICAL SYSTEM: multiparty republic
HEAD OF STATE AND GOVERNMENT: President Martín Torrijos Espino (PRD) (since Sept '04)
RULING PARTIES: New Nation alliance (PN) composed of the Democratic Revolutionary Party
(PRD) and the Popular Party (PP)
MAIN IGO MEMBERSHIPS (NON-UN): OAS, SELA, NAM
CURRENCY: balboa (end-'05 £1=B1.71680, US$1=B1)
GNI PER CAPITA: US$4,450, US$6,870 at PPP ('04, based on regression)

THE President of GUATEMALA, Oscar Berger, won an important victory in Congress (the unicameral legislature) in March with the approval of the country's membership of the US-Central America Free Trade Agreement (US-CAFTA). However, the view of the public did not match that of the politicians. In over two weeks of protests following the vote, one person was killed and many more were injured. The demonstrators objected to the perceived inadequacies in the labour and agricultural provisions of the agreement. In an attempt to mollify opponents, Berger promised a number of measures to alleviate some of the negative effects of US-CAFTA.

The country's security and human rights situation continued to pose problems during the year. In April, the government was forced to introduce a security protection plan for those working in the judicial system, after one judge was murdered and a state prosecutor was shot. Both attacks occurred in the western province of San Marcos and were allegedly linked to drug and contraband trafficking. In July, the UN opened a human rights office in Guatemala, seven months after the withdrawal of the UN Verification Mission in Guatemala (MINUGUA), which had overseen the 1996 peace accords. The move reflected continuing international concern over abuses in the country. November saw the arrest in the USA of the head of Guatemala's anti-narcotics police unit, his deputy, and another officer, on charges of importing and distributing cocaine in the USA. In response the Guatemalan government agreed to overhaul its anti-drugs agency. Also in November, the escape of a number of prisoners from a top-security prison in the southern town of Escuintla led to the sacking of the country's Defence Minister.

A state of emergency was introduced on 5 October after hurricane Stan struck GUATEMALA. According to official statistics, 699 people died, another 844 remained unaccounted for, and almost 3.5 million lost their homes or livelihoods. Also, the coffee and tourism sectors were badly affected. In total it was estimated that Stan caused US$2.5 million of damage.

In EL SALVADOR President Antonio Elías "Tony" Saca of the centre-right Nationalist Republican Alliance (ARENA) retained popularity during his first year in office. Despite such support, one issue that remained of particular concern to the public was the high level of crime, and in May an anti-crime initiative was undertaken with a series of house-to-house searches. However, the measure garnered strong criticism, as it was similar to a tactic that had been used regularly by the military and the security forces during the civil war in the 1980s and early 1990s. Nevertheless, Saca's generally positive standing amongst the electorate helped to consolidate ARENA's leading position ahead of the 2006 legislative and municipal elections. Conversely, the deep divisions within the opposition leftist Farabundo Martí National Liberation Front (FMLN) impeded the party's chances of electoral success. In January, two FMLN deputies were expelled from the party after they voted with the government to support provisions within the 2005 budget. This meant that the FMLN lost its position as the largest party in the legislature. A further three legislators left the party in September. Furthermore, in June and September a total of 500 members of the FMLN resigned from the party after differences over its ideological direction and performance.

In other developments, the Congress approved the sending of a new contingent of troops to Iraq, the fifth mission since the US-led invasion in 2003. El Salvador was the only Latin American country with soldiers in Iraq.

Elections held in HONDURAS on 27 November ended in chaos with disputed results and claims of voting irregularities. The presidential candidate for the opposition Liberal Party (PL), Manuel "Mel" Zelaya Rosales, declared himself the winner after the first votes were counted, and the victory was then confirmed by the head of the supreme electoral tribunal, himself a Liberal Party member. However, the National Party (PN) refused to concede defeat, and outgoing President Ricardo Maduro, who was serving his last term, said that he would not step down. The counting of the remaining votes was then suspended. After interventions by the Organisation of American States and the US ambassador to Honduras, the process was resumed, but was again halted. The electoral authorities then announced that 300,000 ballots would be reviewed. With little confidence left in the electoral council, a new commission with all the main parties represented was created to carry out the review. During this time of uncertainty, supporters from both parties undertook large-scale protests, and a PN activist was shot dead. Eventually, ten days after the elections, the ruling PN's presidential candidate, Porfirio Lobo Sosa, conceded defeat. On a 46 per cent turnout Zelaya won 49.9 per cent to Lobo's 46.2 per cent. He was to be inaugurated on 26 January 2006. In elections for the National Congress the PL gained victory, although not an overall majority.

In NICARAGUA a process of national dialogue was established in January in an attempt to end the political stand off between President Enrique Bolaños Geyer and the unicameral National Assembly (legislature), which was dominated by the Constitutional Liberal Party (PLC)—the former party of the President—and the Sandinista National Liberation Front (FSLN). Agreement for the talks came soon after the Assembly had ratified a number of controversial changes to the constitution which weakened presidential power, in defiance of a ruling from the Central American Court of Justice. In February relations between the President and National Assembly worsened over the extent of the planned budget deficit, which in turn led to the IMF and Inter-American Development Bank suspending financial assistance to the country. The disagreements between the executive and the legislature led to the national dialogue being suspended at a time of growing civil unrest. The uncertainty worsened in early summer when the President tried to solve a growing energy crisis caused by unpaid bills and high international oil prices. He used emergency powers to push through increases in electricity tariffs, arguing that these were required to prevent major blackouts across the country. In response the Supreme Court, controlled by members of the PLC and FSLN, ruled that the new electricity charges were illegal and ordered the government to revoke them. Then, despite the best efforts of the Organisation of American States to ease political tensions, the PLC and FSLN created a commission to lift the President's immunity from prosecution and begin investigations into his alleged misuse of public funds during the 2001 election campaign.

However, towards the end of the year the warring parties stepped back from the brink. This may have been in part because of a visit to the country by US Deputy Secretary of State Robert Zoellick, who said that Nicaragua's "promising future" was in danger and warned against removing a democratically elected President from power. In October, an agreement was reached to suspend the application of the earlier constitutional reforms which had weakened presidential power, and the National Assembly shelved its attempt to lift President Bolaños's immunity from prosecution and the related investigation into alleged electoral fraud. Subsequently, in November all sides agreed to resume the national dialogue, and the Assembly then supported Bolaños in pushing through a number of legislative measures to reassure the IMF of Nicaragua's commitment to economic reform. Despite the progress achieved in overcoming the political crisis, however, high levels of mistrust remained.

The year in COSTA RICA was dominated by legislative conflict and presidential fragility. In early February President Abel Pacheco de la Espriella was taken to hospital complaining of heart pains, which his doctors said were the result of stress and overwork. In late January one of the two Deputy Presidents, Luis Fishman, resigned from his post, citing "personal reasons", while the President attempted the difficult task of passing a controversial tax reform package and securing legislative approval for the US-Central American Free Trade Agreement (US-CAFTA). The President demanded that the first measure had to be passed before the second would be considered. However, the smaller parties in the unicameral Legislative Assembly, which held the balance of power, opposed the tax measures and held up ratification of the US-CAFTA agreement. In response the President's Social Christian Unity Party (PUSC) pushed through a number of administrative changes to speed up the voting process. This tactical advantage for the President, however, was soon undermined by accusations that he had accepted a number of luxury gifts. These came on top of an ongoing enquiry into his alleged receipt of contributions from Taiwanese companies prior to the 2002 presidential election. In an attempt to regain the initiative, President Pacheco and the PUSC organised special sessions for the legislature which began on 1 December and included legislation on the fiscal reforms and US-CAFTA.

The newly elected President of PANAMA, Martín Torrijos Espino, took advantage of his "honeymoon" period and his party's legislative majority in February to pass a series of fiscal reforms designed to correct the country's large budget deficit. However, in April the government's commitment to fiscal discipline was tested when protests against high oil prices forced the authorities temporarily to reduce the duty on imported fuels. Then, in June, despite a general strike across some parts of the public sector and days of often violent unrest, the unicameral National Assembly approved legislation that restructured the country's social security system. However, public opposition to the reforms was so strong that President Torrijos was forced to gain legislative approval to suspend the changes soon afterwards. In an attempt to find a way out of the crisis, a period of national dialogue was established in July which continued for five months. During this time, the government was placed under additional pressure by further rises in the cost of imported fuels. In response, the authorities reduced the tax payable on diesel and ordered public sector offices to reduce energy consumption. The long-standing dispute over social security reform was seemingly resolved in November when the government and opposition groups agreed to a set of watered-down proposals.

THE CARIBBEAN

CUBA—JAMAICA—DOMINICAN REPUBLIC AND HAITI—WINDWARD & LEEWARD ISLANDS—BARBADOS—TRINIDAD & TOBAGO—THE BAHAMAS—GUYANA, BELIZE AND SURINAME—UK DEPENDENCIES—NETHERLANDS ANTILLES AND ARUBA— US DEPENDENCIES

CUBA, JAMAICA, DOMINICAN REPUBLIC AND HAITI

Cuba

CAPITAL: Havana   AREA: 115,000 sq km   POPULATION: 11,365,000
OFFICIAL LANGUAGE: Spanish   POLITICAL SYSTEM: one-party republic
HEAD OF STATE AND GOVERNMENT: President Fidel Castro Ruz (since Jan '59)
RULING PARTY: Cuban Communist Party (PCC)
MAIN IGO MEMBERSHIPS (NON-UN): OAS (suspended), ALADI, ACS, SELA, NAM
CURRENCY: Cuban peso (end-'05 £1=Cub1.71680, US$1=Cub1.0000)
GNI PER CAPITA: upper-middle income: US$826-US$3,255 ('04 est),

Jamaica

CAPITAL: Kingston   AREA: 11,000 sq km   POPULATION: 2,700,000
OFFICIAL LANGUAGE: English   POLITICAL SYSTEM: multiparty system in Commonwealth
HEAD OF STATE: Queen Elizabeth II
GOVERNOR-GENERAL: Sir Howard Cooke (since Aug '01)
RULING PARTY: People's National Party (PNP)
HEAD OF GOVERNMENT: Percival J. Patterson, Prime Minister (since March' 92)
MAIN IGO MEMBERSHIPS (NON-UN): OAS, SELA, ACS, Caricom, ACP, CWTH, NAM
CURRENCY: Jamaican dollar (end-'05 £1=J$110.670, US$1=J$64.4650)
GNI PER CAPITA: US$2,900, US$3,630 at PPP ('04)

Dominican Republic

CAPITAL: Santo Domingo   AREA: 49,000 sq km   POPULATION: 8,900,000
OFFICIAL LANGUAGE: Spanish   POLITICAL SYSTEM: multiparty republic
HEAD OF STATE AND GOVERNMENT: President Leonel Fernández Reyna (PLD) (since Aug '04)
RULING PARTY: Dominican Revolutionary Party (PRD)
MAIN IGO MEMBERSHIPS (NON-UN): OAS, SELA, ACS, ACP, NAM
CURRENCY: Dominican Republic peso (end-'05 £1=DP58.1551, US$1=33.8750)
GNI PER CAPITA: US$2,080, US$6,750 at PPP ('04, based on regression)

Haiti

CAPITAL: Port-au-Prince   AREA: 28,000 sq km   POPULATION: 8,600,000
OFFICIAL LANGUAGE: French   POLITICAL SYSTEM: multiparty republic
HEAD OF STATE: Interim President Boniface Alexandre (Chief Justice of the Supreme Court) (since Feb '04)
HEAD OF GOVERNMENT: Gerard Latortue, interim Prime Minister (since March '04)
MAIN IGO MEMBERSHIPS (NON-UN): OAS, SELA, Caricom, ACS, ACP, Francophonie
CURRENCY: gourde (end-'05 £1=G72.3611, US$1=G42.1500)
GNI PER CAPITA: US$390, US$1,680 at PPP ('04, based on regression)

ON 8 July, Hurricane Dennis hit CUBA leaving ten people dead and destroying thousands of houses. In total, more than 1.4 million people had to leave their homes, and President Fidel Castro Ruz estimated the damage caused at US$1 billion. In the aftermath of the hurricane, offers of aid from the USA and the EU were rejected, although assistance from "friendly" countries, such as Venezuela, was accepted. In November Castro launched a campaign against theft and corruption. Included within this was a crackdown on one of Cuba's last remaining commercial activities: agricultural markets. According to the Communist Party's provincial weekly newspaper, *Tribuna de Havana*, three dozen trucks of produce destined for farmers' markets were seized because growers were selling goods for personal profit before fulfilling state quotas. Towards the end of December Cuba announced GDP growth for 2005 of 11.8 per cent, the highest since the 1959 revolution. However, in 2005 Cuba applied a new method to calculate economic output, which took into account the quality of service provided in sectors such as education and public health, and reflected better the added value created. Despite the economy's apparent health, Cuba's agriculture sector was hit by the disclosure that the sugar industry had had its worst harvest since 1908, in large part caused by the country's continuing drought (see AR 2004, p. 149).

Internationally, on 8 November, a record number of countries backed a UN resolution calling on the USA to lift its economic embargo against Cuba. However, the organisation had no power to enforce its decision, and US envoy to the UN John Bolton called the vote "a complete exercise in irrelevancy". A more positive development came with deepening economic co-operation between Cuba and the People's Republic of China. Bilateral trade reached US$520 million in 2004, with Chinese investments in 2005 seen in a number of Cuba's most important sectors, including nickel and oil production, tourism and agriculture.

In JAMAICA the country's Ministry of Industry and Tourism predicted strong growth in airline and cruise ship tourism in 2005, coming after a record year for Jamaican tourism in 2004. That year, tourist arrivals increased by 4.8 per cent, with 1,326,918 foreign stopover visitors. The sector benefited from a weak US dollar, which increased price competitiveness, and continued terrorist risks elsewhere in the world. In other developments, Bruce Golding succeeded Edward Seaga as leader of the Jamaica Labour Party; a US report named Jamaica as a major illegal drug-producing state; and Prime Minister Percival J. Patterson undertook an official visit to the People's Republic of China in part to encourage China to invest in Jamaica's bauxite industry.

More than 1,650 murders were recorded during the year—an all-time record—which meant that the country surpassed South Africa and Colombia in having the world's highest murder rate.

For the DOMINICAN REPUBLIC the year was one of economic revival after the problems that beset the country during 2004 (see AR 2004, pp. 149-50). President Leonel Fernández successfully restructured the country's debt with the support of the IMF and gained legislative agreement for important fiscal and banking reforms. Despite tough measures that included a significant cut in the public sector workforce, tax increases, and spending reductions, Fernández retained his popularity.

In other developments, Fernández secured the country's entry into the US-Central America Free Trade Agreement, which secured vital foreign investment and trade with the USA. On 16 August, three Haitians were murdered in the Dominican Republic precipitating the recall of Haiti's most senior diplomat. The incident highlighted the rising tensions between the two neighbours as the Dominican Republic undertook a mass repatriation programme of Haitian immigrants.

Elections in HAITI were delayed until sometime in 2006. Originally scheduled for November 2005, presidential and legislative elections were postponed on three occasions and were finally scheduled for January and February 2006. However, in late December the elections were postponed for a fourth time. Poor organisation helped to delay the votes, with members of a high-level electoral supervision committee resigning in frustration over the absence of political support.

Also, the security situation remained difficult with armed rebel groups challenging the transitional government's authority in the provinces, while gangs took control of many urban areas. Attempts to stabilise the situation were hindered by an under-equipped and under-manned national police force, and a UN force, MINUSTAH, that found it difficult to take action in densely populated and lawless areas of the country. The overall security situation was not helped by the escape of almost 500 prisoners from the national prison in February, the alienation by the interim government of the civil and grassroots coalition, Group 184, and the continued strong and vocal support for the ousted President Jean-Bertrand Aristide (see AR 2004, p. 150). Two incidents in December highlighted the continued poor security situation in Haiti. On 24 December armed bandits killed a Jordanian UN soldier, while on 29 December two members of the Organisation of American States, and one of their spouses, were kidnapped.

WINDWARD AND LEEWARD ISLANDS

Antigua & Barbuda

CAPITAL: St John's   AREA: 440 sq km   POPULATION: 80,000
OFFICIAL LANGUAGE: English   POLITICAL SYSTEM: multiparty system in Commonwealth
HEAD OF STATE: Queen Elizabeth II
GOVERNOR-GENERAL: Sir James B. Carlisle (since June '93)
RULING PARTY: United Progressive Party (UPP)
HEAD OF GOVERNMENT: Baldwin Spencer, Prime Minister (since March '04)
MAIN IGO MEMBERSHIPS (NON-UN): OAS, OECS, Caricom, ACS, ACP, CWTH
CURRENCY: East Caribbean dollar (end-'05 £1=EC$4.63530, US$1=EC$2.7000)
GNI PER CAPITA: US$10,000, US$10,360 at PPP ('04)

Dominica

CAPITAL: Roseau   AREA: 48,400 sq km   POPULATION: 71,000
OFFICIAL LANGUAGE: English   POLITICAL SYSTEM: multiparty republic in Commonwealth
HEAD OF STATE: President Nicholas Liverpool (since Oct '03)
RULING PARTY: Dominica Labour Party (DLP)
HEAD OF GOVERNMENT: Roosevelt Skerrit, Prime Minister (since Jan '04)
MAIN IGO MEMBERSHIPS (NON-UN): OAS, ACS, OECS, Caricom, ACP, CWTH, Francophonie
CURRENCY: East Caribbean dollar (see above)
GNI PER CAPITA: US$3,650, US$5,250 at PPP ('04)

St Christopher (Kitts) & Nevis

CAPITAL: Basseterre   AREA: 260 sq km   POPULATION: 47,000
OFFICIAL LANGUAGE: English   POLITICAL SYSTEM: multiparty system in Commonwealth
HEAD OF STATE: Queen Elizabeth II
GOVERNOR-GENERAL: Sir Cuthbert Sebastian (since Jan '96)
RULING PARTY: St Kitts-Nevis Labour Party (SKNLP)
HEAD OF GOVERNMENT: Denzil Douglas, Prime Minister (since July '95)
MAIN IGO MEMBERSHIPS (NON-UN): OAS, ACS, Caricom, OECS, ACP, CWTH
CURRENCY: East Caribbean dollar (see above)
GNI PER CAPITA: US$7,600, US$11,190 at PPP ('04)

St Lucia

CAPITAL: Castries   AREA: 616 sq km   POPULATION: 164,000
OFFICIAL LANGUAGE: English   POLITICAL SYSTEM: multiparty system in Commonwealth
HEAD OF STATE: Queen Elizabeth II
GOVERNOR-GENERAL: Perlette Louisy (since Sept '97)
RULING PARTY: St Lucia Labour Party (SLP)
HEAD OF GOVERNMENT: Kenny D. Anthony, Prime Minister (since May '97)
MAIN IGO MEMBERSHIPS (NON-UN): OAS, ACS, OECS, Caricom, ACP, CWTH, NAM, Francophonie
CURRENCY: East Caribbean dollar (see above)
GNI PER CAPITA: US$4,310, US$5,560 at PPP ('04)

St Vincent & the Grenadines

CAPITAL: Kingstown   AREA: 390 sq km   POPULATION: 108,000
OFFICIAL LANGUAGE: English   POLITICAL SYSTEM: multiparty system in Commonwealth
HEAD OF STATE: Queen Elizabeth II
GOVERNOR-GENERAL: Freddy Ballantyne (since Sept '02)
RULING PARTY: Unity Labour Party (ULP)
HEAD OF GOVERNMENT: Ralph Gonsalves, Prime Minister (since April '01)
MAIN IGO MEMBERSHIPS (NON-UN): OAS, ACS, OECS, Caricom, ACP, CWTH
CURRENCY: East Caribbean dollar (see above)
GNI PER CAPITA: US$3,650, US$6,250 at PPP ('04)

Grenada

CAPITAL: St George's   AREA: 344 sq km   POPULATION: 106,000
OFFICIAL LANGUAGE: English   POLITICAL SYSTEM: multiparty system in Commonwealth
HEAD OF STATE: Queen Elizabeth II
GOVERNOR-GENERAL: Sir Daniel Williams
RULING PARTY/IES: New National Party (NNP)
HEAD OF GOVERNMENT: Keith Mitchell, Prime Minister (since June '95)
MAIN IGO MEMBERSHIPS (NON-UN): OAS, SELA, ACS, Caricom, OECS, ACP, CWTH, NAM
CURRENCY: East Caribbean dollar (end-'05 £1=EC$4.63530, US$1=EC$2.7000)
GNI PER CAPITA: US$3,760, US$7,000 at PPP ('04)

TWO countries in the Windward and Leeward group held parliamentary elections during the year. A general election was held in DOMINICA in May, which saw Prime Minister Roosevelt Skerrit's Dominican Labour Party (DLP) defeat the opposition United Workers Party. The DLP won twelve out of the twenty-one seats contested. However, its former coalition partner, the Dominica Freedom Party (DFP), lost both its seats. The performance of the DFP was a setback for a party that had held power in Dominica from 1980 until 1995. In ST VINCENT & THE GRENADINES on 7 December, Prime Minister Ralph Gonsalves and his United Labour Party (ULP) were returned for a second term of office. The ULP won twelve seats in the House of Assembly (unicameral legislature), while the New Democratic Party won the remaining three. The outcome was identical to the 2001 election result.

A vote of a different kind came in ST LUCIA with former Prime Minister Sir John Compton winning the leadership of the United Workers Party (UWP). Compton, aged seventy-nine, won a convincing victory over incumbent Dr Vaughn Lewis, and so regained leadership of a party that he had founded over forty years previously. The contest was extremely acrimonious, and Lewis complained that Compton's comeback after a ten-year retirement was an opportunistic move, now that the UWP was ahead of the ruling St Lucia Labour Party in the polls. In DOMINICA another of the region's elder statespersons, Dame Mary Eugenia Charles, died in September at the age of eighty-six. She had led the DLP for many years, and became the Caribbean's first women Prime Minister in 1980 (see AR 1980, p. 94; for obituary see pp. 528-29).

Away from party politics, Hurricane Emily hit GRENADA in July, coming only eight months after Hurricane Ivan (see AR 2004, p. 152). Initial estimates put the cost of Emily at US$200 million, but the costs were compounded by the fact that the island was still recovering from the heavy impact of Ivan. Fortunately, Grenada's tourism sector survived Emily intact, but agriculture was seriously affected. ANTIGUA & BARBUDA won the second round of its World Trade Organisation dispute with the USA over Internet gambling. Having already won an earlier victory, Antigua & Barbuda also achieved a broadly favourable ruling on appeal. The ruling stated that the US government must grant Antiguan Internet gambling firms fair access to the US market. International relations were also important to ST KITTS & NEVIS during the year. On 27 September, Chen Shui-bian became the first President of Taiwan to visit St Kitts & Nevis since diplomatic ties were established between the two countries in 1983. The visit was part of a region-wide tour by the Taiwanese leader to consolidate his country's diplomatic links in the area. In recent years much of the Caribbean's diplomatic support had swung behind the People's Republic of China, and away from recognising Taiwanese statehood. However, for St Kitts & Nevis (as well as for St Vincent & the Grenadines) the relationship with Taiwan remained beneficial with significant Taiwanese investment and preferential treatment being proffered.

BARBADOS, TRINIDAD & TOBAGO, THE BAHAMAS

Barbados

CAPITAL: Bridgetown   AREA: 430 sq km   POPULATION: 272,000
OFFICIAL LANGUAGE: English   POLITICAL SYSTEM: multiparty system in Commonwealth
HEAD OF STATE: Queen Elizabeth II
GOVERNOR-GENERAL: Sir Clifford Husbands
RULING PARTY: Barbados Labour Party (BLP)
HEAD OF GOVERNMENT: Owen Arthur, Prime Minister (since Sept '94)
MAIN IGO MEMBERSHIPS (NON-UN): OAS, SELA, ACS, Caricom, ACP, CWTH, NAM
CURRENCY: Barbados dollar (end-'05 £1=Bd$3.43350, US$1=Bd$2.0000)
GNI PER CAPITA: US$9,270, US$15,060 at PPP ('04)

Trinidad & Tobago

CAPITAL: Port of Spain   AREA: 5,128 sq km   POPULATION: 1,323,000
OFFICIAL LANGUAGE: English   POLITICAL SYSTEM: multiparty republic in Commonwealth
HEAD OF STATE: President Max Richards (since Feb '03)
RULING PARTY: People's National Movement (PNM) (since Oct '02)
HEAD OF GOVERNMENT: Patrick Manning (PNM), Prime Minister (since Dec '01)
MAIN IGO MEMBERSHIPS (NON-UN): OAS, SELA, ACS, Caricom, ACP, CWTH, NAM
CURRENCY: Trinidad & Tobago dollar (end-'05 £1=TT$10.7767, US$1=TT$6.27740)
GNI PER CAPITA: US$8,580, US$11,180 at PPP ('04)

The Bahamas

CAPITAL: Nassau   AREA: 14,000 sq km   POPULATION: 320,000
OFFICIAL LANGUAGE: English   POLITICAL SYSTEM: multiparty system in Commonwealth
HEAD OF STATE: Queen Elizabeth II
GOVERNOR-GENERAL: Sir Orville Turnquest
RULING PARTY: Progressive Liberal Party (PLP)
HEAD OF GOVERNMENT: Perry Christie, Prime Minister (since May '02)
MAIN IGO MEMBERSHIPS (NON-UN): OAS, SELA, ACS, Caricom, ACP, CWTH
CURRENCY: Bahamian dollar (end-'05 £1=B$1.71680, US$1=B$1)
GNI PER CAPITA: US$14,920, US$16,140 at PPP ('04)

ON 30 March, the only adult penal institution in BARBADOS, Glendairy prison, erupted in violence, leading to the deaths of two prisoners, and to several other prisoners and some warders being seriously injured. Several fires were also started, which caused widespread damage to the prison. The situation became so serious that the authorities were forced to evacuate the facility and redistribute 1,000 prisoners to three alternative sites. The government also sought and gained the support of the Regional Security System (the East Caribbean police and military mutual assistance force) to provide the additional manpower needed to secure the temporary holding facilities.

The energy sector in TRINIDAD & TOBAGO grew by 10.5 per cent in 2004, according to data from the Caribbean Development Bank, mainly due to the performance of the exploration and production, refining, and petrochemicals subsectors. Overall, GDP growth amounted to 6.7 per cent in 2004, and the economy was expected to match that figure in 2005. Although the economy was performing well, consumer confidence fell during the year as a consequence of rising crime levels. By September there had been 260 murders, more than in all of 2004. More particularly, there were a number of bomb attacks during the latter part of the year in the capital, Port of Spain. The attacks began on 11 July, and continued until 14 October when a fifth bomb exploded. A total of thirty people were injured in the five attacks. In an unrelated development Yasin Abu Bakr of the radical Islamic group Jamaat-al-Muslimeen was arrested on 8 November, and formally charged with inciting members of his mosque to demand money and property by force.

In March, the government of THE BAHAMAS granted a fifty-year lease on the island's decommissioned US missile base to Gold Rock Creek Enterprises Ltd, the developers of the US$100 million Bahamas Film Studio Project. Less good news for the country came in July when two Austrian tourists were murdered in their hotel room. The local tourist industry feared that the incident would undermine strong visitor growth, which amounted to 8.9 per cent in 2004. Further, on 19 December, a seaplane crash off Miami in the USA led to the deaths of eleven Bahamian passengers from the island of Bimini, whose total population was only 1,600.

GUYANA, BELIZE, AND SURINAME

Guyana

CAPITAL: Georgetown   AREA: 215,000 sq km   POPULATION: 772,000
OFFICIAL LANGUAGE: English   POLITICAL SYSTEM: multiparty republic
HEAD OF STATE: President Bharrat Jagdeo (since Aug '99)
RULING PARTY: People's Progressive Party-Civic (PPP-C)
PRIME MINISTER: Samuel Hinds (since Dec '97)
MAIN IGO MEMBERSHIPS (NON-UN): OAS, SELA, AP, ACS, Caricom, ACP, CWTH, NAM
CURRENCY: Guyanese dollar (end-'05 £1=G$326.183, US$1=G$190.000)
GNI PER CAPITA: US$990, US$4,110 at PPP ('04, based on regression)

Belize

CAPITAL: Belmopan   AREA: 23,000 sq km   POPULATION: 283,000
OFFICIAL LANGUAGE: English   POLITICAL SYSTEM: multiparty system in Commonwealth
HEAD OF STATE: Queen Elizabeth II
GOVERNOR-GENERAL: Sir Colville Young
RULING PARTY: People's United Party (PUP)
HEAD OF GOVERNMENT: Said Musa, Prime Minister (since Aug '98)
MAIN IGO MEMBERSHIPS (NON-UN): OAS, SELA, ACS, Caricom, ACP, CWTH, NAM
CURRENCY: Belize dollar (end-'05 £1=Bz$3.37770, US$1=Bz$1.96750)
GNI PER CAPITA: US$3,940, US$6,510 at PPP ('04)

Suriname

CAPITAL: Paramaribo   AREA: 163,000 sq km   POPULATION: 443,000
OFFICIAL LANGUAGE: Dutch   POLITICAL SYSTEM: multiparty republic
HEAD OF STATE: President Ronald Venetiaan (since Aug '00)
RULING PARTIES: New Front for Democracy (NF) coalition supported by the A-Combination (A-
    Com) coalition
HEAD OF GOVERNMENT: Vice-President Ram Sardjoe (since Aug '05)
MAIN IGO MEMBERSHIPS (NON-UN): OAS, SELA, AP, ACS, Caricom, ACP, OIC, NAM
CURRENCY: Surinam dollar (end-'03 £1=S$4.70390, US$1=S$2.74000)
GNI PER CAPITA: US$2,250 ('04), -

GUYANA suffered its worst flooding in more than one hundred years in January, when a record rainfall of more than 35 inches was recorded; five people died. Inadequate natural drainage systems left large areas of the low-lying and densely populated Atlantic coast under several feet of water. It was estimated that more than 200,000 people (35 per cent of the population) were affected by the floods, with two thirds of the capital, Georgetown, flooded. Poor sanitation led to serious public health problems, which resulted in twenty deaths; food reserves and livestock holdings were destroyed, and there was an increased incidence of crime. In response to the crisis, numerous international agencies provided assistance, including the UN, the World Health Organisation, and the World Food Programme.

In other developments, Minister of Home Affairs Ronald Gajraj resigned in April, despite being cleared by an independent tribunal of having links with the so-called "Phantom Death Squad" (see AR 2004, p. 155).

The year in BELIZE was dominated by serious industrial unrest. Problems began in late January when a two-day general strike crippled the country. The strike, called by the National Trade Union Congress of Belize, left schools and businesses closed and thousands of people without electricity, water, or telephone services. The Union had demanded that the government repeal new tax increases and implement full salary increases owed to public sector workers. Further, in April employees of Belize Telecommunications Ltd (BTL) went on strike, leaving Belize without communications for several days. The strike was in response to government plans to sell off BTL; employees were demanding a controlling stake in the firm. The strike precipitated more general anti-government protests that turned violent and led to one person being killed and over 100 arrests. Commenting on the unrest, Caribbean Community chairman Dr Ronald Venetiaan, President of Suriname, expressed deep concern about the situation and the effect that it would have on the Belizean economy.

In elections held in SURINAME on 25 May the ruling New Front (NF) coalition, led by President Dr Ronald Venetiaan, lost ten of its thirty-three seats in the fifty-one-seat National Assembly (the unicameral legislature). The National Democratic Party, under former President and military dictator Desi Bouterse, won fifteen seats, thereby more than doubling its representation. The remaining seats were taken by the People's Alliance for Prosperity, led by another ex-President, Jules Wijdenbosch. Because no party held a majority in the National Assembly, and also lacked the two-thirds majority needed to select a president, two rounds of voting proved inconclusive. As a consequence, the choice was passed to the country's 891-member People's Assembly, which comprised the national legislature plus district and provincial councils. In a vote taken on 3 August, incumbent President Venetiaan was re-elected to serve a second term.

UK OVERSEAS TERRITORIES

Anguilla

CAPITAL: The Valley   AREA: 96 sq km   POPULATION: 12,200 (est.)
OFFICIAL LANGUAGE: English   POLITICAL SYSTEM: semi-autonomous UK overseas territory
GOVERNOR-GENERAL: Alan Huckle (since May '04)
RULING PARTIES: Anguilla National Alliance (ANA) & Anguilla Democratic Party (ADP) form Anguilla United Front (AUF) coalition
HEAD OF GOVERNMENT: Osbourne Fleming (ANA), Chief Minister (since March '00)
MAIN IGO MEMBERSHIPS (NON-UN): Caricom (obs.)
CURRENCY: East Caribbean dollar (end-'05 £1=EC$4.63530, US$1=EC$2.7000)
GNI PER CAPITA: n/a

Bermuda

CAPITAL: Hamilton   AREA: 53 sq km   POPULATION: 64,000
OFFICIAL LANGUAGE: English   POLITICAL SYSTEM: semi-autonomous UK overseas territory
GOVERNOR-GENERAL: John Vereker
RULING PARTY: Progressive Labour Party (PLP)
HEAD OF GOVERNMENT: Alex Scott, Prime Minister (since July '03)
MAIN IGO MEMBERSHIPS (NON-UN): Caricom (obs.)
CURRENCY: Bermudian dollar (end-'05 £1=Bm$1.71680, US$1- Bm$1)
GNI PER CAPITA: high income: US$10,066 or more ('04 est), -

British Virgin Islands

CAPITAL: Road Town   AREA: 153 sq km   POPULATION: 21,300 (est.)
OFFICIAL LANGUAGE: English   POLITICAL SYSTEM: semi-autonomous UK overseas territory
GOVERNOR-GENERAL: Thomas Townley Macan (since Oct '02)
RULING PARTY: National Democratic Party (NDP)
HEAD OF GOVERNMENT: Orlando Smith, Chief Minister (since June '03)
MAIN IGO MEMBERSHIPS (NON-UN): OECS (assoc.), Caricom (assoc.)
CURRENCY: US dollar (end'05 £1=1.71680)
GNI PER CAPITA: n/a

Cayman Islands

CAPITAL: George Town, Grand Cayman   AREA: 259 sq km   POPULATION: 44,000
OFFICIAL LANGUAGE: English   POLITICAL SYSTEM: semi-autonomous UK overseas territory
GOVERNOR-GENERAL: Stuart Jack (since Nov '05)
RULING PARTY: People's Progressive Movement (PPM) (since May '05)
HEAD OF GOVERNMENT: Kurt Tibbetts (since May '05)
MAIN IGO MEMBERSHIPS (NON-UN): Caricom (obs.)
CURRENCY: Cayman Island dollar (end-'05 £1=CI$1.42180, US$1=CI$0.82820)
GNI PER CAPITA: high income: US$10,066 or more ('04 est)

Montserrat
CAPITAL: Plymouth   AREA: 102 sq km   POPULATION: 4,483 (est.)
OFFICIAL LANGUAGE: English   POLITICAL SYSTEM: semi-autonomous UK overseas territory
GOVERNOR-GENERAL: Deborah Barnes-Jones (since May '04)
HEAD OF GOVERNMENT: John Osborne, Chief Minister (since April '01)
MAIN IGO MEMBERSHIPS (NON-UN): OECS, Caricom, ACS
CURRENCY: East Caribbean dollar (see above)
GNI PER CAPITA: n/a

Turks & Caicos Islands
CAPITAL: Cockburn Town   AREA: 430 sq km   POPULATION: 20,200 ('01 Census est.)
OFFICIAL LANGUAGE: English   POLITICAL SYSTEM: semi-autonomous UK overseas territory
GOVERNOR-GENERAL: Richard Tauwhare (since July '05)
RULING PARTY: Progressive National Party (PNP)
HEAD OF GOVERNMENT: Michael Misick (PNP), Chief Minister (since Aug '03)
MAIN IGO MEMBERSHIPS (NON-UN): Caricom (assoc.)
CURRENCY: US dollar (end-'05 £1=1.71680)
GNI PER CAPITA: n/a

Two elections were held during the year. In ANGUILLA Chief Minister Osbourne Fleming and his Anguilla United Front (AUF) coalition were returned to power on 21 February. The AUF's victory was secured in part by the rise in the country's GDP of almost 14 per cent in 2004, Anguilla's strongest level of growth in two decades. Three months later, in the CAYMAN ISLANDS the opposition People's Progressive Movement (PPM), led by Kurt Tibbets, gained a clear election victory. The PPM won nine of the fifteen seats in the Legislative Assembly. The former ruling United Democratic Party, under the leadership of McKeeva Bush, won five seats, while the remaining seat went to an independent candidate. Crucial issues during the election campaign were the level of autonomy from the UK and the policy towards foreign residents.

Elsewhere, the issue of independence for BERMUDA remained a hot political topic (see AR 2004, p. 158). After a visit to Bermuda in late March, Julian Hunte, leader of the UN decolonisation committee, claimed that the island was uniquely prepared for independence. Hunte argued that Bermuda's well-developed economic and political systems and its high level of literacy meant that it was well positioned for full autonomy. Despite such comments, support for independence remained in a clear minority, although the numbers in favour of ending constitutional ties with the UK increased during the year.

In the BRITISH VIRGIN ISLANDS the thirteen-member Legislative Council passed the 2005 budget on 17 February. The budget maintained the fiscal discipline of the previous year, which had allowed the government to record its first surplus in the overall balance since 2001. The 2005 budget was agreed within the context of buoyant tourism and financial services sectors.

In MONTSERRAT the Princess Royal, Princess Anne, opened the new airport terminal building on 22 February, and on 11 July the first scheduled flight to the island took place, operated by Windward Islands Airways International

(Winair). Scheduled air services had ceased ten years previously, following the eruption of the Soufrière Hills volcano in July 1995 (see AR 1995, p. 197).

Meanwhile, the TURKS & CAICOS saw the appointment of a new British governor. The country's Chief Minister, Dr Michael Misick, welcomed Richard Tauwhare and called for progress towards the adoption of a new constitution, and more effective action in the area of national security.

NETHERLANDS ANTILLES AND ARUBA

Netherlands Antilles

CAPITAL: Willemstad (Curaçao)   AREA: 800 sq km   POPULATION: 222,000
OFFICIAL LANGUAGES: Dutch, Papiamento & English   POLITICAL SYSTEM: autonomous dependency
  of the Netherlands
GOVERNOR-GENERAL: Fritz Goedgedrag (since July '02)
RULING PARTY: Antillean Restructuring Party (PAR) heads coalition
HEAD OF GOVERNMENT: Etienne Ys, Prime Minister (since June '04)
CURRENCY: Neth. Antilles guilder (end-'05 £1=AG3.07300, US$1=AG1.79000)
GNI PER CAPITA: high income: US$10,066 or more ('04 est)

Aruba

CAPITAL: Oranjestad   AREA: 193 sq km   POPULATION: 99,000
OFFICIAL LANGUAGE: Dutch   POLITICAL SYSTEM: autonomous dependency of the Netherlands
GOVERNOR-GENERAL: Olindo Koolman
RULING PARTY: People's Electoral Movement (MEP)
HEAD OF GOVERNMENT: Nelson O. Oduber (MEP), Prime Minister (since Sept '01)
CURRENCY: Aruba guilder (end-'05 £1=AG3.07300, US$1=AG1.79000)
GNI PER CAPITA: high income: US$10,066 or more ('04 est), -

THE constitutional future of the NETHERLANDS ANTILLES was decided in early December when it was agreed that the union (the Kingdom of the Netherlands), involving five islands, should be dissolved and new forms of government introduced. Recent referendums held in four of the five islands had called for change: Curaçao and Sint Maarten voted for *status aparte* (already held by Aruba); while Bonaire and Saba preferred the status of Kingdom Islands, with stronger links to the Netherlands. The only dissenting island was Sint Eustatius, whose population voted in April 2005 to preserve the union. However, by the year's end, Sint Eustatius had agreed to the Netherlands Antilles' dissolution.

Under the new arrangements, Curaçao and Sint Maarten would become separate and autonomous members of the Kingdom of the Netherlands, while the three other territories would become Kingdom Islands, the exact status of which had yet to be decided. Under the reforms, the Netherlands also agreed to assist the islands to restructure their US$2.8 billion public debt.

The reputation of ARUBA suffered a set back during the year after the disappearance on the island of an eighteen-year-old high school graduate from Alabama in the USA. Natalee Holloway was seen last seen in public on 30 May, leaving a bar with three young men. The mother of the girl heavily criticised the subsequent investigation into her daughter's disappearance. The entire island hunted for the missing student. The Dutch military sent aircraft and personnel to help with the search; FBI agents became involved, so too a team of Texas-based search specialists. However, no trace of the young woman was found, and no one was formerly charged in the case. The negative coverage of the incident in the US media led to concerns that Aruba's important tourist sector would suffer.

US DEPENDENCIES

Puerto Rico
CAPITAL: San Juan   AREA: 9,103 sq km   POPULATION: 3,929,000
OFFICIAL LANGUAGES: Spanish & English   POLITICAL SYSTEM: multiparty system in US Commonwealth
GOVERNOR-GENERAL: Anibal Acevedo Vilá (PPD)
RULING PARTY: New Progressive Party (PNP)
CURRENCY: US dollar (end-'05 £1=1.71680)
GNI PER CAPITA: high income: US$10,066 or more ('04 est)

US Virgin Islands
CAPITAL: Charlotte Amalie   AREA: 342 sq km   POPULATION: 113,000
OFFICIAL LANGUAGE: English   POLITICAL SYSTEM: semi-autonomous overseas territory of the USA
GOVERNOR-GENERAL: Charles Turnbull (Democratic Party)
RULING PARTY: Democrats
CURRENCY: US dollar (end-'05 £1=1.71680)
GNI PER CAPITA: high income: US$10,066 or more ('04 est)

TENSIONS in PUERTO RICO were fuelled in September after fugitive Puerto Rican nationalist Filiberto Ojeda Rios was killed in an FBI shoot-out. Rios, leader of the *Macheteros* (or Cane Cutters) movement, had been on the run since he was convicted in absentia for the 1983 US$7 million armed robbery of a bank depot in Connecticut, USA. Rios's killing prompted a number of incidents, including the firing of shots at a guardhouse of the federal court building and bomb threats to US businesses and government buildings. Economic problems in the territory, including a growing fiscal crisis, also precipitated unrest towards the end of the year. A weeklong series of protests was held in early November. On 6 November, for example, the Federation of Teachers marched in protest at the growing number of public-sector redundancies and the government's refusal to negotiate wage increases for state employees.

Despite these economic problems the Puerto Rico Industrial Development Company noted that the Commonwealth was the world's largest international exporter of pharmaceutical products in 2003, with a 24.5 per cent share of the total. Furthermore, sixteen of the twenty best-selling pharmaceuticals in the USA were manufactured in Puerto Rico. Meanwhile, a report by Mercer human resource consulting company ranked the Puerto Rican capital, San Juan, jointly with Mexico's Monterrey, as the safest city in Latin America.

More than 250 people from throughout the US VIRGIN ISLANDS gathered on the islands of St John on 1 October for the Virgin Islands unity rally and peace march. Demonstrators were protesting over the perceived inaction by local and federal officials investigating a series of alleged "racially-motivated" hate crimes. In other developments, the territory's large petroleum refinery situated on St Croix benefited from high world oil prices. In 2004 the value of petroleum refined on the island grew by 40 per cent to reach US$6.7 billion.

SOUTH AMERICA

BRAZIL—ARGENTINA—PARAGUAY—URUGUAY—CHILE—PERU—BOLIVIA—
ECUADOR—COLOMBIA—VENEZUELA

BRAZIL

CAPITAL: Brasília   AREA: 8,547,000 sq km   POPULATION: 178,700,000
OFFICIAL LANGUAGE: Portuguese   POLITICAL SYSTEM: multiparty republic
HEAD OF STATE AND GOVERNMENT: President Luiz Inacio "Lula" da Silva (since Jan '03)
RULING PARTY: Workers' Party (PT) heads coalition
MAIN IGO MEMBERSHIPS (NON-UN): OAS, ALADI, SELA, Mercosur, AP, CPLP
CURRENCY: real (end-'05 £1=R4.00950, US$1=R2.33550)
GNI PER CAPITA: US$3,090, US$8,020 at PPP ('04)

As the year began, it was a near certainty that President Luiz Inácio ("Lula") da Silva would win a second term in office in presidential elections scheduled to be held in October 2006. By the end of the year, however, the political landscape in Brazil had changed significantly and it was unclear whether Lula would even seek re-election. The change to da Silva's position was caused by the eruption in June of a corruption scandal, in which his ruling Workers' Party (PT) was accused of bribing coalition partners in return for their support in Congress (the bicameral federal legislature), and of operating an illegal scheme to raise money for election campaigns. The allegations fractured the fragile coalition government and tarnished the image of the PT, which had won power in 2002 vowing to govern without corruption (see AR 2002, pp. 182-83). Once the scandal broke, it dominated political life in Brazil, leading to the launch of a string of Congressional inquiries, paralysing the government's legislative agenda, and prematurely ending several high-profile political careers. The affair was sufficiently notorious in Brazil to earn the label of *Mensalão*, or "monthly payment", scandal.

Although the origins of the scandal could be traced back to low-ranking public sector officials, the highest echelons of the political establishment became embroiled in allegations of wrongdoing as the year progressed. The significance of the accusations became clear on 14 June when Roberto Jefferson, the leader of the Brazilian Labour Party (PTB), accused senior PT officials of paying legislators in return for their support of government reforms in Congress. The PTB itself had been accused of bribing officials from state-owned companies. Jefferson resigned on 17 June, when the PTB announced that it would leave the coalition government. On 14 September, Jefferson's political career was ended when Congress voted to expel him from the legislature on the grounds that his party had accepted illegal bribes from the PT. His expulsion meant that he was automatically disqualified from holding political office in Brazil for eight years.

As the scandal developed, numerous witnesses testified before congressional inquiries, leading to more allegations of wrongdoing, including deals involving the appointment of allies to senior positions in state-owned companies in return for cash payments. President da Silva was not personally implicated but many of his closest allies were accused of direct involvement in the scandal, most notably Chief Minister of the Cabinet Jose Dirceu. Dirceu, who had been a founding member of the PT in 1980 and had helped the party to win power in 2002, resigned from government on 16 June, returning to Congress to refute the accusations made against the PT. However, a Congressional inquiry concluded on 1 September that Dirceu was the mastermind of the bribes-for-votes scheme, and legislators voted on 1 December to expel him from Congress on the grounds of unethical behaviour, meaning that he, too, was automatically disqualified from holding political office in Brazil for eight years. Similar proceedings were launched against sixteen other legislators, including six from the PT, many of whom resigned to avoid the possibility of expulsion from Congress. According to the findings of another Congressional inquiry, published in November, Dirceu had colluded with Marcos Valerio Fernandes de Souza, an advertising executive who had been given contracts by the government. It was alleged that Valerio had used public money to guarantee loans of at least US$17 million to the PT.

In a bid to shore-up Congressional support for the coalition government, President da Silva in July announced several ministerial changes, removing from office those who had been implicated in the allegations of wrongdoing. Also in July, four of the most senior officials from the PT, including its president José Genoíno, resigned or took a leave of absence from the party after they, too, were accused of malfeasance. Valdemar Costa Neto, president of the Liberal Party (PL, another coalition member), on 1 August joined the list of politicians to lose their jobs over the scandal. Costa Neto resigned from Congress after admitting corruption. During a speech that was broadcast live on television in August, President da Silva apologised to the nation and asked for the public's forgiveness, prompting some 20,000 people to march on the streets of Brasília to show their support for his leadership. A counter demonstration by an estimated 12,000 people also took place in August, in which protesters demanded da Silva's impeachment.

Another key figure to resign over allegations of corruption was the president of the Chamber of Deputies (the lower house), Severino Cavalcanti, of the conservative Brazilian Progressive Party (PPB). Cavalcanti resigned on 21 September after he was accused of receiving payments from a businessman in exchange for the extension of a contract to operate a restaurant in Congress. Cavalcanti's resignation led to a minor victory for President da Silva, after Aldo Rebelo, of the government-allied Communist Party of Brazil (PC do B), was elected to replace him. The election of Rebelo, who was the government's preferred candidate, was important because the Chamber of Deputies president had significant authority over the scope of Congressional inquiries into the bribery allegations. President da Silva scored another nominal triumph on 9 October when Ricardo José Ribeiro Berzoini was elected to replace Genoíno as PT president. Ribeiro Berzoini was a supporter of da Silva's leadership and his election was deemed likely to reduce some of the internal pressure, which had arisen from those factions of the PT that were disillusioned by the revelations of sleaze.

Although many observers predicted that the expulsion hearings would help to defuse the scandal, new allegations of wrongdoing continued to surface. These included the publication by *Veja*, a leading weekly magazine, of an article on 31 October which alleged that the PT had received up to US$3 million in illegal election campaign contributions from Cuba in 2002. The government and the Cuban authorities denied the claim, but the cost of the scandal to da Silva's image was high, a position that was verified in November when opinion polls published by the research institute CNT/Sensus indicated that his approval rating had dropped to an all-time low of 46.7 per cent. The dramatic fall in da Silva's popularity coincided with the publication in November of a report by another Congressional committee, which concluded that the allegations made against the PT were substantially true. One of da Silva's most influential and highly regarded colleagues, Finance Minister Antonio Palocci, was also forced to defend himself against allegations of misconduct when he appeared on 16 November at a hearing in the Senate (the upper house). Palocci denied allegations—made against him by a former colleague—that he had illegally received money from a company which had won local government contracts during his tenure as a city mayor in São Paulo state. Although Palocci received a robust public defence from President da Silva, the pressure on him was mounting as the year ended, partly because of the allegations made against him but also because of the country's lacklustre economic performance in 2005.

Economic growth was forecast to reach only 2.5 per cent over the year, having slowed markedly after a robust performance in 2004 of just under 5 per cent. The government also exceeded its target of containing inflation to a maximum of 5.1 per cent, when forecasts showed that it was likely to reach 5.7 per cent for the year. Brazil's high interest rates continued, although the country's Central Bank did, in December, reduce the rate to 18 per cent. The government made two announcements in December, which indicated that it wanted to achieve greater economic independence ahead of the presidential elections in 2006. Thanks to a strong fiscal performance, Brazil would repay ahead of schedule the US$2.6 billion which it owed to the Paris Club of sovereign creditor nations, thereby saving some US$100 million in interest payments. The country would also make early repayment of the US$15.5 billion which it owed to the IMF, saving a further US$900 million.

In other developments, scientists discovered that the Amazon rainforest was being destroyed twice as quickly as previously estimated. According to a study published on 21 October in the journal *Science*, the damage caused by selective logging—a process of illegally removing valuable individual trees and leaving surrounding trees in position, but damaged—had not been included in earlier calculations of rates of deforestation. The Green Party (PV) withdrew from the ruling coalition in May after the government revealed, on 18 May, that destruction of the Amazon rainforest had reached its second-fastest level ever during 2004. Also in May, the government rejected US$40 million of funding for HIV/AIDS prevention programmes from the US Agency for International Development (USAID) because it was unwilling to condemn prostitution, which was an obligation imposed upon Brazil as a condition of the US funding. Brazilian officials said that the US government's efforts to link foreign aid to pro-abstinence policies were based upon "biblical principles" rather than scientific evidence.

ARGENTINA

CAPITAL: Buenos Aires   AREA: 2,780,000 sq km   POPULATION: 38,200,000
OFFICIAL LANGUAGE: Spanish   POLITICAL SYSTEM: multiparty republic
HEAD OF STATE: President Néstor Kirchner (since May '03)
RULING PARTY: Justicialist Party (PJ)
HEAD OF GOVERNMENT: Alberto Fernandez (Chief of Cabinet) (since May '03)
MAIN IGO MEMBERSHIPS (NON-UN): OAS, SELA, ALADI, Mercosur
CURRENCY: peso (end-'05 £1=AP5.19530, US$1=AP3.02630)
GNI PER CAPITA: US$3,720, US$12,460 at PPP ('04)

IN Argentina, three key events during the year put President Néstor Kirchner on a path towards gaining greater control of the country's economy. The first, in June, brought to an end three-and-a-half-years of confrontation with the country's private creditors when the government concluded the restructuring of its nearly US$100 billion of debt. The deal to restructure the debt was made possible after 76.1 per cent of the country's private creditors accepted a government proposal—made in January—to swap the defaulted debt for new bonds, which were worth around 35 per cent of the value of the debt. The reduction in the value of the debt—known as a "haircut"—was one of the highest ever for a sovereign debt swap deal. Many private creditors refused to accept the offer, claiming that it failed to repay enough of what they were owed, and some took legal action against the government in a bid to prevent it from exchanging around US$7 billion of bonds. Although a US district court ruled on 29 March that the bonds in question should be frozen, this decision was overturned on appeal on 13 May, allowing the government to proceed with the debt swap.

The second event was Kirchner's announcement on 15 December that his government would repay its entire US$9.8 billion debt to the IMF by the end of 2005. Kirchner described the decision as the most important one that he had made since taking office in May 2003, pledging to be robust in his dealings with the IMF. According to media reports, the country's foreign reserves—held at Argentina's Central Bank—would fund the payment. Some financial analysts were sceptical about the decision to repay the debt, claiming that interest payments to the Central Bank would be higher than those charged by the Fund. A desire to achieve more economic independence was instrumental in the government's decision to repay the debt, but the move was also influenced by the fact that it would reduce any residual pressure to re-enter into negotiations with aggrieved private creditors.

The highly regarded and influential Economy Minister, Roberto Lavagna, was unexpectedly involved in the third event: his dismissal in November as part of a Cabinet reshuffle. Lavagna was sacked after he criticised Federal Planning and Public Investment Minister Julio de Vido—who was a close ally of Kirchner—for allegedly allowing contractors to overcharge the government for road-building contracts. The sacking of Lavagna was clearly not related to the country's economic performance, which resulted in growth of an estimated 8.2 per cent during the year, fuelled mainly by an increase in consumer demand and booming exports. Many analysts interpreted Lavagna's dismissal as part of a plan by President Kirchner to exercise his authority and advance leftist economic policies. Regardless of the specific motives behind the three events, the outcome certainly signalled that Argentina's economy had fully recovered following the country's economic collapse in 2001 (see AR 2001, pp. 204-07).

Felisa Miceli, the president of the state-owned National Bank of Argentina, was appointed as Lavagna's replacement; and the appointment of Nilda Garré as Defence Minister meant that women headed both the Economy and Defence Ministries for the first time in the country's history. The Cabinet reshuffle also included the appointment of Jorge Taiana as Foreign Minister. The reshuffle was prompted by mid-term legislative elections held on 23 October, in which three departing Cabinet ministers won seats in Congress (the bicameral federal legislature). The elections were perceived by observers as a referendum on Kirchner's leadership and an opportunity for him to strengthen his position within the ruling (Peronist) Justicialist Party (PJ), ahead of a possible re-election campaign in 2007.

In the elections, 127 seats in the 256-seat Chamber of Deputies (the lower house) and twenty-four seats in the seventy-two-seat Senate (the upper house) were contested. Kirchner's Front for Victory (FPV)—a faction of the PJ allied to the President—secured 39 per cent of the overall vote, while its rivals within the PJ won only 9.5 per cent, and the opposition Radical Civil Union (UCR) secured 15 per cent. The results increased the FPV's representation to fifty seats in the Chamber of Deputies, and fourteen seats in the Senate, giving it a majority in the upper house. Voter turnout was over 70 per cent. Gubernatorial elections in the province of Corrientes were held concurrently. In these, Arturo Colombi of the Radical Civil Union and Justicialist Party (JUCR) won 60.6 per cent of the vote, defeating Carlos Rubin of the Autonomist, Liberal, and New Party (ALN), who won 32.4 per cent.

The country also made progress in attempts to secure justice for two different sets of victims: those of the country's "dirty war" era in the 1970s and those of the country's worst ever terrorist attack. The Supreme Court in Buenos Aires on 14 June ruled that two amnesty laws enacted in 1986-87 were unconstitutional (see AR 2003, p. 195). The Full Stop Law of 1986 and the Due Obedience Law of 1987 had granted immunity from prosecution to most military officers for most crimes committed during the late 1970s. The legislation had been twice repealed by Congress, first in 1998 and then again in August 2003 to strengthen the 1998 repeal, which had not been retrospective. The ruling opened up the possibility of human rights abuse trials for former military officers. Lieutenant Commander Adolfo Francisco Scilingo Manzorro, a fifty-eight-year-old Argentinian former senior naval officer, was on 19 April sentenced to 640 years in prison, at the High Court in Madrid, Spain, for his role in the detention, torture, and assassination of thirty political prisoners during the country's "dirty war" era. Under Spanish law, Scilingo would serve a maximum of thirty years in prison. Jorge Luis Magnacco, a doctor who had helped to steal babies born to political prisoners during the "dirty war" era, was on 22 April sentenced to ten years in prison. Magnacco had falsified the birth certificate of a baby born to a political prisoner and then given the child up for adoption.

Meanwhile, investigations into Argentina's worst ever terrorist attack—the bombing in July 1994 of a Jewish community centre in Buenos Aires—led to Lebanon, where the Shi'ite Muslim movement, Hezbullah, on 11 November denied allegations that it had been involved. Investigators in Argentina and the US Federal Bureau of Investigation (FBI) said they had identified Ibrahim Hussein Berro, a twenty-one-year-old Lebanese citizen, as the suicide bomber of the offices of the Argentine Jewish Mutual Association (AMIA), after relatives of his, living in the USA, testified that he had been a member of Hezbullah. Five men were acquitted in September 2004 of charges relating to the bombing and there had been fierce criticism in Argentina of the investigation into the attack (see AR 2004, p. 165). President Kirchner issued a decree in July that acknowledged responsibility for governmental failures and vowed to bring to justice the perpetrators of the attack, which had killed eighty-five people and injured more than 200 others.

In other developments, more than 8,000 police officers were on duty during the fourth summit of the Americas, which was convened in the seaside resort of Mar del Plata, on 4-5 November. A counter-summit, involving thousands of citizens opposed to US-led free market economic policies, was held simultaneously. There were several violent clashes between the police and protesters after small groups of demonstrators threw Molotov cocktails, set fire to a bank, and burned US flags. At least twenty people were injured and some sixty-four others were arrested. It was thought that four home-made bombs, which exploded on 6 October at US-owned banks and a shop in Buenos Aires, had been designed as a protest against US President George W. Bush's attendance at the summit (see p. 126).

Also in Buenos Aires, thousands of people on 30 December commemorated the first anniversary of a fire at a nightclub in the capital, in which 194 people were killed (see AR 2004, p. 163). Many of the victims' families attended a remembrance service before convening outside President Kirchner's office to protest against what they called a corrupt scheme, in which safety inspection and police officers were alleged to have accepted money to ignore poor standards of safety. Buenos Aires city mayor Aníbal Ibarra, who was responsible for safety inspections in the capital, was suspended in October as part of an ongoing investigation into his responsibility for the tragedy, and some thirty other people, including the nightclub owner, faced murder-related charges. No trials had commenced as the year ended.

PARAGUAY—URUGUAY—CHILE—PERU—BOLIVIA—ECUADOR—COLOMBIA—VENEZUELA

Paraguay

CAPITAL: Asunción   AREA: 407,000 sq km   POPULATION: 5,800,000
OFFICIAL LANGUAGE: Spanish   POLITICAL SYSTEM: multiparty republic
HEAD OF STATE AND GOVERNMENT: President Nicanor Duarte Frutos (PC) (since Aug '03)
RULING PARTIES: Colorado Party (PC), supported by Authentic Radical Liberal Party (PLRA)
MAIN IGO MEMBERSHIPS (NON-UN): OAS, ALADI, SELA, Mercosur
CURRENCY: guarani (end-'05 £1=G10,472.2, US$1=G6,100.00)
GNI PER CAPITA: US$1,170, US$4,870 at PPP ('04, based on regression)

Uruguay

CAPITAL: Montevideo   AREA: 177,000 sq km   POPULATION: 3,400,000
OFFICIAL LANGUAGE: Spanish   POLITICAL SYSTEM: multiparty republic
HEAD OF STATE AND GOVERNMENT: President Tabaré Vázquez (EP-FA), since March '05
RULING PARTY: Progressive Encounter-Broad Front (EP-FA) controls legislature
MAIN IGO MEMBERSHIPS (NON-UN): OAS, ALADI, SELA, Mercosur, NAM
CURRENCY: peso Uruguay (end-'05 £1=UP40.6870, US$1=UP23.7000)
GNI PER CAPITA: US$3,950, US$9,070 at PPP ('04)

Chile

CAPITAL: Santiago   AREA: 757,000 sq km   POPULATION: 16,000,000
OFFICIAL LANGUAGE: Spanish   POLITICAL SYSTEM: multiparty republic
HEAD OF STATE AND GOVERNMENT: President Ricardo Lagos Escobar (since March '00)
RULING PARTIES: Concertación coalition composed of Party for Democracy (PPD), Socialist (PS),
    Christian Democratic (PDC), & Social Democratic Radical (PRSD) parties
MAIN IGO MEMBERSHIPS (NON-UN): OAS, ALADI, SELA, APEC, NAM, Mercosur
CURRENCY: Chilean peso (end-'05 £1=Ch879.062, US$1=Ch512.050)
GNI PER CAPITA: US$4,910, US$10,500 at PPP ('04)

Peru

CAPITAL: Lima   AREA: 1,285,000 sq km   POPULATION: 27,500,000
OFFICIAL LANGUAGES: Spanish, Quechua, Aymará   POLITICAL SYSTEM: multiparty republic
HEAD OF STATE AND GOVERNMENT: President Alejandro Toledo (since '01)
RULING PARTY: Perú Possible party
PRIME MINISTER: Pedro Pablo Kuczynski (since Aug '05)
MAIN IGO MEMBERSHIPS (NON-UN): OAS, APEC, ALADI, SELA, CA, AP, NAM
CURRENCY: new sol (end-'05 £1=S5.88930, US$1=S3.43050)
GNI PER CAPITA: US$2,360, US$5,370 at PPP ('04)

Bolivia

CAPITAL: La Paz and Sucre   AREA: 1,099,000 sq km   POPULATION: 9,000,000
OFFICIAL LANGUAGES: Spanish, Quechua, Aymará   POLITICAL SYSTEM: multiparty republic
HEAD OF STATE AND GOVERNMENT: President Eduardo Rodríguez (since June '05)
PRESIDENT ELECT: Evo Morales (MAS)
RULING PARTIES: Nationalist Revolutionary Movement (MNR) heads coalition with Civic Solidarity
    Union (UCS), Movement of the Revolutionary Left (MIR), Free Bolivia Movement (MBL),
    Democratic Nationalist Action (ADN), and Unity and Progress Movement (MUP)
MAIN IGO MEMBERSHIPS (NON-UN): OAS, ALADI, SELA, AG, CA, NAM, Mercosur
CURRENCY: boliviano (end-'05 £1=B13.7340, US$1=B8.0000)
GNI PER CAPITA: US$960, US$2,590 at PPP ('04)

Ecuador

CAPITAL: Quito   AREA: 284,000 sq km   POPULATION: 13,200,000
OFFICIAL LANGUAGE: Spanish   POLITICAL SYSTEM: multiparty republic
HEAD OF STATE AND GOVERNMENT: President Col Lucio Gutierrez (since Jan '03)
RULING PARTIES: Popular Socialist Party (PSP), Ecuadorian Roldosist Party (PRE)
MAIN IGO MEMBERSHIPS (NON-UN): OAS, ALADI, SELA, AG, CA, NAM
CURRENCY: US dollar (end-'05 £1=1.71680)
GNI PER CAPITA: US$2,180, US$3,690 at PPP ('04)

Colombia

CAPITAL: Santa Fe de Bogotá   AREA: 1,139,000 sq km   POPULATION: 45,300,000
OFFICIAL LANGUAGE: Spanish   POLITICAL SYSTEM: multiparty republic
HEAD OF STATE AND GOVERNMENT: President Alvaro Uribe Velez (since Aug. '02)
RULING PARTY: Government is supported by Liberal Party (PL)
MAIN IGO MEMBERSHIPS (NON-UN): OAS, ALADI, SELA, AG, CA, ACS, NAM
CURRENCY: Colombian peso (end-'05 £1=Col3,925.39, US$1=Col2,286.53)
GNI PER CAPITA: US$2,000, US$6,820 at PPP ('04, based on regression)

Venezuela

CAPITAL: Caracas   AREA: 912,000 sq km   POPULATION: 26,100,000
OFFICIAL LANGUAGE: Spanish   POLITICAL SYSTEM: multiparty republic
HEAD OF STATE AND GOVERNMENT: President Hugo Chávez Frias (since Feb '99)
RULING PARTY: Fifth Republic Movement (MVR)
MAIN IGO MEMBERSHIPS (NON-UN): OAS, ALADI, SELA, CA, ACS, OPEC, NAM
CURRENCY: bolívar (end-'05 £1=Bs4,439.66, US$1=Bs2,586.08)
GNI PER CAPITA: US$4,020, US$5,760 at PPP ('04)

POLITICAL DEVELOPMENTS. A near impotent opposition in VENEZUELA meant that an increased majority in the National Assembly (the unicameral legislature) for President Hugo Chávez Frias's Fifth Republic Movement (MVR), and other parties allied to him, was a likely outcome of parliamentary elections held on 4 December. The decision by five opposition parties to withdraw from the elections just days before the polling began meant that pro-Chávez parties not only increased their majority, but won all 167 seats. The opposition boycotted the election over concerns that the information from electronic voting machines and fingerprint scanners could, in theory, be matched to reveal the political affiliation of individual voters. Although the National Electoral Council (CNE) rejected the opposition's disquiet (and withdrew the use of fingerprint scanners), the international media had already seized upon the debate, and covered the election with the tone of controversy which it frequently associated with Venezuela's socialist leader. President Chávez angrily claimed that the US government had encouraged the boycott because opinion polls indicated that the opposition would be heavily defeated at the ballot box and therefore it suited US political objectives to create an impression of electoral malfeasance.

Chávez's anger towards the US administration was tempered on 18 December by the news from BOLIVIA that the Movement Towards Socialism (MAS) party leader, Evo Morales, had swept to a decisive and historic victory in presidential elections. Although Morales was widely tipped to win the presidency—helping to consolidate the region's sharp swing to the Left—it was the scale of the victory that surprised analysts, and even Morales himself. Winning some 54.1 per cent of the first round vote, Morales had secured the clearest mandate to govern in Bolivia since at least 1982, when democracy was restored to the region's poorest and least stable country. By winning more than half of the popular vote, Morales avoided the need for a second round vote, in which Congress (the bicameral federal legislature) would have been required, under the country's constitution, to choose between the first and second placed candidates. The conservative Jorge Fernando "Tuto" Quiroga Ramírez of the Democratic and Social Power (PODEMOS) party was Morales' closest rival, but Quiroga conceded defeat after polling 28.6 per cent of the vote. Morales was an Aymara Indian and his victory marked the country's first ever election of an indigenous head of state. Support for Morales amongst the electorate was based upon his pledges to nationalise the country's natural gas industry, promote indigenous rights, and reduce the influence of US-backed policies, such as the eradication of coca. The inauguration of Morales as Bolivia's new President was due to take place in January 2006.

In CHILE, Michelle Bachelet Jeria—a former Defence Minister—somewhat surprisingly failed to win an absolute majority in presidential elections held on 11 December. Bachelet, of the Socialist Party of Chile (PSC)—a faction of the ruling Concertación coalition—secured 45.96 per cent of the vote, whilst her closest rival, Sebastián Piñera Echenique of the National Renewal Party (NR), won 25.41 per cent. The absence of an absolute majority meant that Bachelet and Piñera would contest a second round of voting, which was scheduled to take place on 15 January 2006, to determine which of them would succeed President Ricardo Lagos when his term in office ended on 11 March 2006. Joaquín Lavín Infante, of the Independent Democratic Union (UDI), trailed in third place, winning 23.23 per cent of the vote, whilst the radical leftist Tomas Hirsch Goldschmidt of the Communist Party of Chile (PCC) secured 5.4 per cent. Bachelet, who had been tortured and exiled during the country's former dictatorship (1973-90), had campaigned for a continuation of the liberal social programmes and free market economic policies implemented by Lagos, whose Concertación coalition was seeking its fourth consecutive term in office.

A constitutional court ruling in COLOMBIA in November allowed President Alvaro Uribe Velez to announce that he would seek an unprecedented second four-year-term in presidential elections scheduled for May 2006. In October the Court had ruled that a law allowing presidents to serve more than one term in office was constitutional, ratifying a vote to that effect in December 2004 by Congress (the bicameral legislature). The court's November ruling approved the legality of a second piece of legislation, the Electoral Guarantees Law, which had been designed to prevent incumbent presidents from abusing their powers by gaining an unfair electoral advantage. Opinion polls in Colombia indicated that President Uribe's approval rating stood at some 70 per cent as the year ended, suggesting that he was on course to win an absolute majority in 2006.

Tabaré Vázquez's victory in presidential elections held in URUGUAY in October 2004 (see AR 2004, p. 167) was followed by his inauguration on 1 March. In his inaugural address to Congress (the bicameral legislature), Vázquez pledged to govern for all Uruguayans and promised to uncover the truth about the disappearance of dissidents during the 1973-85 military dictatorship. Vázquez made his first formal policy announcement on 2 March: the implementation of a "social emergency plan" to help reduce poverty. He also signed a series of trade and energy supply agreements with President Chávez of VENEZUELA, including an agreement under which the Venezuelan state-run oil company, Petroleos de Venezuela (PDVSA), would open an office in the Uruguayan capital, Montevideo, and work in partnership with Uruguay's national energy company as part of a broader attempt to unify state oil companies in the region.

Whilst elections in 2005 demonstrated the region's flourishing democratic credentials, its long history of political instability frequently resurfaced. In ECUADOR, President Colonel Lucio Gutiérrez in April fell prey to the country's propensity to remove its leaders from office prematurely. In PERU, meanwhile, the country's worst political crisis since President Alejandro Toledo took office in 2001 was triggered when the entire Cabinet was forced to resign over the appointment of a minister who was loathed by colleagues [see below].

Mass public protests against President Gutiérrez in April in Quito, the capital of Ecuador, only ended when Congress (the unicameral legislature) controversially voted to remove him from office, claiming that he had abandoned his post. Vice President Alfredo Palacio was immediately installed as his replacement. The protests followed months of public disquiet over Gutiérrez's decision in December 2004 to dismiss the country's Supreme Court, alleging that its judges were biased against him. In a move that was widely condemned by advocates of democracy, Gutiérrez installed new judges, most of whom were his political allies. The protests against Gutiérrez were sparked by the Court's decision on 31 March to annul corruption charges against former President Abdala Bucaram Ortiz, allowing him to return to Ecuador on 2 April after eight years of exile in Panama. According to reports, Bucaram went into hiding in Peru (before once again seeking asylum in Panama) upon hearing the news of Gutiérrez's removal from office. Two people died and more than fifty others were injured during clashes between the police and protesters, prompting the military to withdraw its support for Gutiérrez and forcing the now deposed President to escape dramatically from the besieged presidential palace in a helicopter. Gutiérrez fled to Brazil, where he was granted asylum, but he later visited the USA (in June), Peru (in July), and Colombia (in August), before returning to Ecuador on 14 October. Upon his return to ECUADOR, the authorities swiftly executed a warrant, which had been issued in July, for his arrest on charges that he had attempted to destabilise the government by refusing to recognise President Palacio as his successor. As the year ended, Gutiérrez remained in custody, vowing to "carry out all legal and constitutional procedures to recover the power now illegally in the hands of the usurper".

The appointment of a new Supreme Court remained a dominant political issue in ECUADOR until 28 November when an independent four-member panel appointed a new Court comprising thirty-one new judges, after a selection process monitored by international observers. For the remainder of the year, President Palacio invested much of his political capital in attempts to call a referendum on convening a constituent assembly to rewrite the country's constitution. He was forced to abandon his plans in December when the Supreme Electoral Tribunal (TSE) rejected his proposal for a second time, claiming that his plans were unconstitutional. Congress had also been in dispute with Palacio over his referendum plans and threatened to impeach him unless he abandoned them. In a separate development, Interior Minister Mauricio Gándara was dismissed on 8 September amidst criticism that he had failed to act decisively when oil installations were sabotaged by protesters in August. The protests forced Petroecuador, the state oil company, temporarily to suspend crude oil output, the country's largest source of export income.

In PERU, the appointment on 11 August of Fernando Olivera Vega—a close political ally of President Toledo—as Foreign Minister caused sufficient consternation amongst the Cabinet that it led to the resignation of Prime Minister Carlos Ferrero Costa. Olivera was a controversial figure and unpopular in the Cabinet because of his known support for the cultivation of coca, which was used for traditional purposes but was also the raw ingredient in the production of cocaine. Ferrero and Olivera had publicly quarrelled over the cultivation of coca, creating an ongoing rift between the two men. According to Peru's constitution, the resignation of the Prime Minister meant that the entire Cabinet was forced to resign. The discord created by Olivera's appointment led to his resignation on 13 August, after just two days in office. The crisis was brought to an end on 16 August when President Toledo announced a new Cabinet, led by the former Economy Minister, Pablo Kuczynski, who was appointed as Prime Minister.

As the country's Cabinet crisis ended, the spectre of former President Alberto Keinya Fujimori's return to politics in PERU became a theoretical possibility when he collected a new Peruvian passport from the country's embassy in Japan on 14 September. Fujimori had fled to Japan in 2000 following a corruption and human rights abuse scandal that toppled his government (see AR 2000, p. 172). Although he was subsequently disqualified from holding public office in Peru until at least 2011, he arrived in CHILE, vowing to contest the Peruvian presidential elections in 2006, but was arrested by the Chilean authorities on 7 November after the Peruvian government learned of his whereabouts and requested his extradition As the year ended, Fujimori was still in detention in Chile, after that country's Supreme Court ruled on 15 November that he should remain in custody pending the outcome of the extradition battle. The Peruvian authorities on 23 December approved twelve charges of corruption and human rights abuses, which were expected to form the basis of an official request to the Chilean Foreign Ministry.

In other political developments, President Chávez's self-proclaimed "Bolivarian revolution" continued to unfold in VENEZUELA during the year, despite significant domestic and international opposition. A land tenure law enacted in 2001 led in January to a nationwide ninety-day review intended to determine the validity of land titles and the productivity of estates. According to the authorities, the review demonstrated that up to half of the land reviewed was idle or of questionable legal status, which later led to the state's seizure and redistribution of millions of hectares of land, providing the country's indigenous Indians and urban poor with an opportunity to climb out of poverty. Business leaders and other political opponents of Chávez claimed that the land seizures were unconstitutional and called upon the Supreme Court to intervene, but the President was undeterred and vowed in September to accelerate the pace of land reform. According to estimates, some 75 per cent of farmland in Venezuela was owned by less than 5 per cent of the population. Chávez dealt another blow to international investors of capital in Venezuela on 21 September, when he announced his plans to cancel foreign gold and diamond mining concessions and to stop issuing new ones to foreign companies. The announcement came just days after he had declared that he would create a national state-owned mining company modelled on the state-owned oil company, Petroleos de Venezuela (PDVSA).

Also in VENEZUELA, the former leader of the Venezuelan Workers' Confederation (CTV), Carlos Ortega, was on 13 December sentenced to fifteen years and eleven months in prison for fomenting civil rebellion. Ortega was captured by the police in Caracas in March, following his return to Venezuela from Costa Rica, where the authorities had withdrawn the political asylum status granted to him in 2003. (Ortega had fled to Costa Rica after the collapse of a general strike, which badly damaged Venezuela's economy. Ortega was a leading proponent of the strike, which was called as part of a broader attempt by the union leader to force Chávez to resign or to announce early elections, see AR 2003, pp. 208-10). In a separate development, the Supreme Court in Caracas on 11 March overturned its ruling of August 2002 that there was insufficient evidence to proceed with rebellion charges against four senior officers who had participated in the unsuccessful military coup against President Chávez in April 2002 (see AR 2002, pp. 198-99). The ruling meant that a case against the four officers—General Efrain Vasquez Velasco, Air Force General Pedro Pereira, Vice Admiral Hector Ramirez Perez, and Rear Admiral Daniel Comisso Urdaneta— could be prepared by the authorities.

HUMAN RIGHTS AND CORRUPTION DEVELOPMENTS. Numerous former leaders, their associates, and alleged accomplices were pursued by public prosecutors throughout the year, demonstrating a growing desire to bring to justice those who had abused power during the region's undemocratic past.

The former dictator of CHILE, General (retd) Augusto Pinochet Ugarte, in November spent his ninetieth birthday under house arrest and facing charges of human rights abuse and tax fraud. In December, he lost an appeal before the Supreme Court in Santiago, opening up the possibility of his facing charges for his alleged role in the disappearance and presumed murder in 1975 of six political opponents, in what was known as "operation Colombo". The panel of five judges, voting by a margin of three votes to two, rejected a defence argument that the former dictator was unfit to stand trial, overturning previous decisions. Charges were likely to be brought against Pinochet in connection with three further disappearances, also thought to be part of "operation Colombo". In September, Pinochet had been stripped of his immunity from prosecution in the case. The former dictator's house arrest in November was ordered when he was charged with tax fraud, forgery, and declaring false income statements to limit the amount of his taxable income. Ongoing investigations had revealed that Pinochet had amassed a personal fortune of some US$27 million, which was held in secret overseas bank accounts. In October, he was stripped of immunity from prosecution in this case also.

In November, General (retd) Manuel Contreras Sepúlveda, the former head of Chile's notorious secret police, the National Intelligence Directorate (DINA), was sentenced to three years in prison in connection with the murder in 1976 of Julia del Rosario Retamal Sepúlveda, a school teacher and political opponent of the Pinochet regime. Contreras, who was also sentenced in January to twelve years in prison for the abduction and presumed murder of a leftist activist in 1975, in May submitted a document to the Supreme Court which claimed to reveal the fate of 580 people who had "disappeared" during Pinochet's dictatorship. Within the thirty-two-page document, Contreras blamed Pinochet personally for many of the human rights violations that had occurred during the former dictator's rule. As part of investigations in the "operation Colombo" case, public prosecutors in November ordered Pinochet and Contreras to meet one another, to help investigators to establish who had controlled DINA. Both Pinochet and Contreras had denied responsibility for operational command of the former secret police.

Despite the advent of democracy in the region, there remained reminders of the way in which the authorities had once routinely dealt with civil protests. Thousands of citizens in CHILE on 11 September marked the 32nd anniversary of the military coup which had overthrown the democratically elected government of President Salvador Allende in 1973. During violent clashes between protesters and the police in Santiago, teenager Cristian Castillo Diaz was shot and killed by a stray bullet. Castillo's family blamed the police for his death. At least twenty-one police officers were injured and more than eighty protesters were arrested during the violence. A teenage boy was also killed in COLOMBIA on 10 November when police officers opened fire during an operation to remove indigenous Indians who had occupied a farm in the south-western province of Cauca. The farm was one of three occupied since October by some 10,000 indigenous Indians, who were protesting against the government's land redistribution programme.

Also in CHILE, the authorities took action against a colony in the south of the country, formerly known as Colonia Dignidad and later renamed Villa Baviera. The colony's leader, Paul Schaefer, an eighty-three-year-old German citizen who had fled to Argentina from Chile in 1997, was arrested in Buenos Aires on 10 March and deported to Chile days later, where he remained in detention as the year ended. Schaefer was wanted by the Chilean authorities on charges that he and a cult of German followers had helped DINA during the Pinochet era by allowing the colony to be used as a centre for the torture of political prisoners. He was also charged with involvement in the disappearance of two political activists. The police on 14 June seized a haul of weapons, which included submachine guns, rocket launchers, and anti-personnel mines, from two underground bunkers at the colony, after they had received intelligence notifying them of the arsenal's location. As part of the ongoing investigations into allegations that the colony had been used as a torture centre, the authorities on 26 August seized complete control of the colony and its assets, which included a school, a hospital, and several businesses within the 15,000 hectare estate.

The former President of BOLIVIA, Gonzálo Sánchez de Lozada, was in February charged with genocide; as the year ended he was detained pending a trial. Former Bolivian Defence and Interior Ministers Carlos Sanchez Berzain and Yerko Kukoc were also charged with genocide, while thirteen other former members of the Cabinet were charged as accomplices. The charges related to the deaths of at least sixty people in protests in 2003 against government plans to export natural gas (see AR 2003, pp. 202-04).

The removal from office of President Gutiérrez in ECUADOR also had implications for former President Gustavo Noboa Bejarano, who was placed under house arrest on 8 May just weeks after his return to the country from exile in the Dominican Republic, where he had fled in 2003 to escape corruption charges in Ecuador. The authorities in Costa Rica announced on 10 May that they had for the second time granted political asylum to Ecuador's disgraced former Vice President Alberto Dahik Garzoni, who had been accused of corruption in 1995. Both Dahik and Noboa had returned to Ecuador in April after the Supreme Court—packed with Gutiérrez's allies—annulled the charges brought against them. The charges were reinstated when President Palacio was installed as Gutiérrez's replacement.

The disgraced former head of the Peruvian National Intelligence Service (SIN), Vladimiro Montesinos, remained in custody at the end of the year, serving a fifteen year prison sentence for embezzlement, conspiracy, and corruption. In August, Montesinos was put on trial on a string of other charges, including human rights abuses and weapons trafficking. Public prosecutors in PERU alleged that Montesinos had led the notorious death squad, "Grupo Colina", thought to be responsible for the kidnapping and murder of suspected leftist rebels in the early 1990s as part of a campaign to destroy the Shining Path (Sendero Luminoso), a Maoist guerrilla movement. On 1 December, Montesinos was sentenced to a further four years in prison for taking bribes from a Chilean businessman in return for allowing him to build a food plant on a nature reserve outside Lima. Also in PERU, the former armed forces and army commander, General (retd) Nicolas de Bari Hermoza Rios, was sentenced on 16 May to eight years in prison after being convicted on charges of embezzlement which took place during the regime of former President Fujimori. Hermoza was already serving a prison sentence for other corruption convictions.

Successive governments in URUGUAY had never investigated the whereabouts of the remains of some 180 Uruguayans who were thought to have died during the period of the country's military rule (1973-85). In March, President Vázquez ordered the armed forces to identify possible burial sites and, as the year approached its end, government-appointed forensic experts excavated the remains of two people at separate locations near Montevideo. Evidence gathered at the sites suggested that both sets of remains belonged to people killed during the dictatorship.

DRUGS, CIVIL CONFLICT, AND TERRORISM. Despite a nominal breakthrough, the forty-one-year long civil conflict in COLOMBIA caused disappointment, condemnation, and devastation for President Uribe in 2005. The breakthrough came in November, after the leftist National Liberation Army (ELN) announced that it was prepared to engage in exploratory negotiations with the government over the terms of a possible peace process. ELN leaders and government negotiators on 21 December ended five days of talks in Cuba, where they agreed to reconvene in January 2006 to begin drafting an agenda for a formal peace process. The agreement with the ELN—the country's smallest illegal army—was a minor triumph for peace, but Uribe was dealt a devastating blow on 27 December by the Colombian Revolutionary Armed Forces (FARC), Colombia's largest leftist guerrilla organisation. Twenty-nine Colombian soldiers were killed and six others were injured during a battle with FARC guerrillas near the Macarena National Park, in the state of Meta. The soldiers had been overseeing the eradication of a coca plantation, when around 400 FARC rebels attacked them with mortars and heavy artillery. The death toll was the highest suffered by the military since President Uribe was elected in 2002, vowing to crush the insurgency with tough security policies. In response to the FARC attack, Uribe on 28 December vowed to eradicate all coca plantations in the area where the incident had occurred.

There was more disappointment for Uribe over his government's negotiations with the United Self Defence Forces of Colombia (AUC), a right-wing paramilitary organisation; and a new law passed in June to encourage AUC fighters to demobilise was universally condemned as being too lenient. Under the terms of a demobilisation agreement—the Santa Fe de Ralito (demilitarisation) agreement—signed in July 2003, the 20,000-strong AUC was due to surrender its weapons by 31 December 2005. However, only some 14,000 paramilitaries had demobilised by the end of the year and the government, in November, agreed to extend the deadline to 15 February 2006. The extension was part of a deal to persuade the AUC to resume demobilisation, which it had suspended in October in protest at a government decision on 30 September to imprison leading AUC commander Diego Adolfo Murillo Bejarano (also known as Adolfo Paz or Don Berna). The Chamber of Deputies (the lower house of the Colombian bicameral legislature) on 21 June had approved the controversial Justice and Peace bill, which set out a legal framework for the demobilisation of AUC fighters. The bill was controversial because it included a provision to limit to a maximum of eight years the prison sentences of demobilised fighters who agreed to co-operate with government investigations. The law included a provision for prosecutors to investigate fighters who surrendered their weapons and then charge those accused of serious crimes, such as war crimes or crimes against humanity. A delay in the publication of regulations setting out the detailed conditions under which investigators should pursue charges meant that almost all demobilised fighters were set free.

In PERU, the second retrial of Abimael Guzman, the founder of the Shining Path movement, opened in Lima on 26 September but had not been concluded by the end of the year. Public prosecutors alleged that Guzman had led a violent insurgency, which had included the massacre in 1983 of sixty-nine people in Lucana-marca. Although Guzman was convicted by a military court in 1992, the conviction was overturned after the Constitutional Court ruled in 2003 that anti-terrorism laws enacted by former President Fujimori were unconstitutional. A civilian retrial in 2004 collapsed after two senior judges resigned. Maritza Garrido Lecca, who had helped Guzman to evade capture by the Peruvian authorities, was on 4 October sentenced to twenty years in prison for links to Shining Path. According to government and security officials, Shining Path guerrillas were still operating in the country, although they had turned their attention away from Maoist politics and were now involved in the illegal drug trade. President Toledo on 22 December declared a state of emergency in the remote Huanuco region, after the government blamed Shining Path guerrillas for the death of eight police officers who were shot and killed during an ambush on a police vehicle on a routine patrol.

Also in PERU, some 154 men representing a nationalist organisation known as the Etnocacerista Movement on 4 January laid down their arms after a four-day siege of a police station in Andahuaylas, 440 km south-east of Lima. The siege was led by Major (retd) Antauro Humala, who had been briefly imprisoned and then pardoned for his part in an uprising led by his brother, Lieutenant Colonel Ollanta Humala Tasso, in 2000 against the former President Fujimori. In a separate development, Humala Tasso in December announced his intention to contest the Peruvian presidential elections scheduled for April 2006, telling his supporters that the country needed a nationalist energy policy to reclaim its sovereignty.

RELATIONS WITH THE USA. The left-wing forces that had, in recent years, scored notable electoral victories in South America—principally due to a strong public desire to reduce the influence of US-backed economic policies—appeared to give the US government a renewed sense of political interest in the region in 2005.

The election of Morales, a former leader of coca leaf farmers, was widely predicted to lead BOLIVIA into diplomatic tensions with the USA. Although Morales was opposed to drug trafficking, he had vowed to legalise the cultivation of coca for traditional purposes. The US administration was vehemently opposed to this and was committed to the unrealistic goal of eradicating coca cultivation. Morales's decision to visit President Fidel Castro Ruz's Cuba on his first overseas trip as president-elect on 30 December appeared to be his way of saying that he intended to strengthen further the integration of leftist politics within the region, in opposition to US-led free market policies.

The fiery and often theatrical relations between President Chávez of VENEZUELA and the US administration of President George W. Bush featured prominently, provoking near saturation media coverage throughout the year. Chávez's accusation in December that the US government had interfered in the Venezuelan parliamentary elections was symptomatic of the deep distrust and significant political chasm that had developed between the two countries. The tone for the year was set in February, when Chávez accused the US government of plotting to assassinate him and warned that Venezuelan oil exports to the USA would be stopped in the event of his premature death. US Christian activist and influential

Republican party supporter, Pat Robertson, on his television show in August added some credibility to Chavez's accusation by calling for the assassination of the Venezuelan leader, describing him as a "terrific danger" to the USA. Robertson added that Venezuela had become "a launching pad for communist infiltration and Islamic extremism", and claimed that the assassination of Chávez would be "a whole lot cheaper than starting a war". Robertson's remarks captured a sense of President Chávez's negative public image in the USA but also portrayed a non-chalant disregard for the consequences of war, which was an outlook that a sub-stantial proportion of the region's electorate associated with the ultra-conservative Right in the USA. Venezuela's Vice President, José Vicente Rangel, described Robertson's comments as "terrorist statements", claiming that they exposed the hypocrisy of the USA's "war on terror". The US government distanced itself from Robertson, saying that his comments were "inappropriate" but that they had been made in his capacity as a private citizen.

The US embassy announced on 22 April that VENEZUELA had suspended bilat-eral military exchanges between the two countries, established under an agree-ment made in 1951. Two days later, Chávez asked four US military instructors to leave Venezuela after they had allegedly publicly criticised the President. The ten-sion between the two countries was heightened by US suspicions that Venezuela was supporting FARC guerrillas in COLOMBIA, and by two deals signed by Venezuela to purchase arms and military equipment from Russia and Spain. The US government in September included Venezuela in a list of twenty countries deemed to have "failed to make progress in meeting their international counter-narcotics obligations". The Venezuelan authorities claimed that the decision was politically motivated, a position that was supported by the fact that the USA did not impose on VENEZUELA the economic sanctions normally applied to countries included in the list, such as a suspension of aid programmes. Instead, the USA confirmed that it would continue to fund selected programmes that supported democratic institutions in Venezuela, including opposition parties. The inflam-matory exchanges reached a peak in October when Chávez claimed to be in pos-session of intelligence reports proving that the US government was planning a military invasion of Venezuela, adding that he was preparing for that possibility. He warned that US aggression against Venezuela would result in soaring oil prices within the USA. Chávez had previously claimed on a number of occasions that the US government wanted to gain control of Venezuela's oil reserves but US offi-cials consistently dismissed his allegations. Despite the near constant friction, the year passed without a military confrontation between the two countries.

In contrast, Colombia's relations with the USA remained warm throughout the year, allowing the media to continue to describe President Uribe as the USA's closest ally in the region. US Secretary of State Condoleezza Rice on 1 August certified that COLOMBIA had met statutory criteria on "respect for human rights", which allowed the US government to release around US$70 million in foreign aid. The certification allowed the release of the last 12.5 per cent of foreign aid under the 2004 "plan Colombia" agreement and the first 12.5 per cent of foreign aid under the 2005 "plan Colombia" agreement. The certification was criticised by the London-based human rights organisation, Amnesty International, which had condemned the authorities in Colombia for failing to bring to justice the perpetrators of human rights abuses.

In ECUADOR, Foreign Minister Antonio Parra announced on 23 June that the government would not sign an agreement to protect US military personnel based in Ecuador from prosecution in the International Criminal Court (ICC), even if it meant a reduction in foreign aid from the US government. The US airforce had since 1999 operated a base in the port city of Manta, 400 km west of Quito, as part of an anti-drug-trafficking strategy. Meanwhile, legislators in PARAGUAY on 1 June agreed to the arrival of some 400 US military personnel in the country for joint training and humanitarian operations. The decision caused concern and speculation amongst governments in neighbouring countries, which feared that the USA intended to build a permanent military base in Paraguay, as was the case when it signed a similar agreement with Ecuador in 1999. The US and Paraguayan authorities dismissed the concerns and speculation, citing the long history of joint military and humanitarian exercises between the two countries. Unlike in Ecuador, the Senate (the upper house of the Paraguayan bicameral legislature) in May voted to grant US military personnel operating in the country immunity from prosecution in the ICC.

Officials in PERU and the USA announced on 7 December that a free trade agreement between the two countries had been struck. Under the terms of the agreement, tariffs and other barriers to goods and services would be eliminated, expanding trade between the two countries and allowing Peruvian exporters duty-free access to the US market.

REGIONAL RELATIONS. A diplomatic row between COLOMBIA and VENEZUELA that erupted on 14 January was defused by 1 February when the Colombian government declared that it would, in future, respect Venezuela's sovereignty. The origins of the rift dated back to December 2004 when Venezuelan army bounty hunters, who had been paid by the Colombian government, captured Rodrigo Granda (also known as Ricardo Gonzalez) in Caracas. The Colombian authorities originally claimed that Granda—the so-called "foreign minister" of FARC—was captured on Colombian soil but it was later revealed that he had been seized in Venezuela. President Chávez on 14 January suspended trade agreements between the two countries and recalled the Venezuelan ambassador to Caracas. President Uribe accused the Venezuelan authorities of harbouring Colombian "terrorists" and on 20 January sent information to Venezuela, which apparently included details of Colombian "terrorists" living over the border. The Venezuelan authorities sent a similar reciprocal list to Colombia on 21 January.

VENEZUELA was also involved in a diplomatic rift with Mexico, which occurred in November following the collapse of talks about plans for a regional free trade agreement. President Chávez and Mexican President Vicente Fox Quesada exchanged insults with one another after the fourth summit of the Americas, which was hosted by Argentina (see p. 156). Fox, who was a supporter of the proposed regional agreement, criticised Chávez for adopting a negative attitude towards the USA. Chávez responded by calling Fox a "puppy dog of the empire", which prompted Mexican officials to demand an apology and threaten the withdrawal of Mexico's ambassador from Caracas. The spat, which escalated on 14 November when both governments withdrew their ambassadors, was defused by the end of the month.

More than a century of tensions between PERU and CHILE resurfaced in November after the Peruvian Congress on 3 November voted unanimously to approve a bill that claimed sovereignty over 37,900 sq km of waters in the Pacific Ocean controlled by Chile. The authorities in Chile said that the new law was illegal because it violated treaties signed by the two countries in 1952 and 1954, and confirmed that Chile would continue to exercise sovereignty over the area, which contained valuable fish resources. Peru's territorial claim revived a dispute that had simmered between the two countries since Chile took swathes of Peruvian territory during the War of the Pacific (1879-83).

V MIDDLE EAST AND NORTH AFRICA

ISRAEL

CAPITAL: Jerusalem   AREA: 21,000 sq km   POPULATION: 6,800,000
OFFICIAL LANGUAGE: Hebrew   POLITICAL SYSTEM: multiparty republic
HEAD OF STATE: President Moshe Katzav (since July '00)
RULING PARTIES: Likud party in coalition with Labour and the United Torah Judaism party (since Jan '05)
HEAD OF GOVERNMENT: Ariel Sharon (Kadima), Prime Minister (since March '01)
CURRENCY: shekel (end-'05 £1=Sh7.90350, US$1=Sh4.60370)
GNI PER CAPITA: US $17,380, US$23,510 at PPP ('04)

THE year was dominated by Prime Minister Ariel Sharon's controversial plan for a unilateral Israeli withdrawal from the Gaza Strip which reached fruition in August despite concerted internal opposition. Sharon had first outlined details of the plan in early 2004 (see AR 2004, pp. 180-81) and, despite forceful opposition from settlers and their ultra-nationalist backers, and also from within the ranks of Sharon's own ruling Likud party, in June the Supreme Court removed the final legal obstacle to Israel's withdrawal from Gaza, which, along with the West Bank, had been under Israeli occupation since the Six-Day War of 1967. Sharon received widespread international praise for his action, but months of intense pressure left their mark and at the end of the year he was hospitalised after suffering a mild stroke.

The year had started with the formation of a new government, Sharon's previous coalition having collapsed in December 2004, when the 2005 budget failed to pass its first reading due to turmoil surrounding the Gaza disengagement plan (see AR 2004, p. 181). The new government was made up of Sharon's Likud party, Shimon Peres's Labour Party, and the ultra-orthodox United Torah Judaism party. The veteran Peres was appointed as the senior Vice Premier, with his own ministry.

Sharon's new government pressed ahead with the Gaza disengagement plan. The Knesset (the unicameral legislature) voted in mid-February to approve a US$900 million compensation package for Jewish settlers who would be uprooted from the Gaza Strip (and four West Bank settlements). In late March the Knesset rejected a proposal for a referendum on the disengagement plan, as proposed by Sharon's opponents in the Likud. Three prominent Cabinet ministers, led by Finance Minister (and Sharon arch-rival) Binyamin Netanyahu, voted for the referendum. Shortly afterwards Sharon overcame the last legislative obstacle to the withdrawal when the Knesset finally approved the 2005 budget. If Sharon had failed to win final approval for the budget by the end of March, his new government would have automatically fallen, thereby triggering an early general election.

Natan Sharansky, the former Soviet Jewish dissident who had emigrated to Israel in 1986, resigned as Minister without Portfolio responsible for Jerusalem, Social and Diaspora Affairs in early May in protest at the Gaza disengagement plan. Sharansky said that he believed that disengagement would create a "terrible rift" in the nation and described the plan as "a tragic mistake that will exacerbate the conflict with the Palestinians, increase terrorism and dim the prospects of a forging a genuine peace". Despite such opposition, in June the Supreme Court ruled that the disengagement plan was constitutional, thereby removing the last legal obstacle to Israel's withdrawal. Groups of settlers seeking to block any withdrawal from occupied land had filed twelve petitions calling for disengagement legislation to be invalidated or significantly rewritten on the grounds that it violated their human rights. The Court accepted that evacuation impinged upon the settlers' "human dignity", but said that their removal had been mandated legally by the Knesset and "appropriate compensation" had been ensured by law.

Netanyahu resigned as Finance Minister on 7 August, minutes before the Cabinet gave its final approval for the first evacuation of settlements in the Gaza Strip. Netanyahu said that it was an "irresponsible move" that would harm Israel's security. The evacuation operation began in earnest on 15 August (the official deadline for Israeli civilians to leave Gaza) when thousands of Israeli police officers and soldiers moved to surround the Gaza settlements. Over the following week the security forces managed to evacuate all twenty-one settlements in Gaza (with a population of 8,518 inhabitants) and four settlements in the West Bank (with 674 residents, a tiny percentage of the 250,000 settlers in the entire West Bank and the further 200,000 in Israeli-annexed East Jerusalem). Although there were frequent clashes and a number of settlers were injured, there was little serious violence and the operation ended in Gaza on 22 August and the West Bank on 23 August. Once the settlers had been removed, bulldozers and mechanical diggers began destroying settler homes in Gaza. The decision to destroy some 2,000 homes had been taken unilaterally by Israel, but in co-ordination with the Palestine National Authority (PNA). Upon the completion of the withdrawal, Sharon received a congratulatory telephone call from Palestinian President Mahmoud Abbas on his "brave and historic" decision to dismantle the settlements after thirty-eight years of occupation. On 12 September the Israeli army completed the withdrawal of soldiers from the interior of the occupied Gaza Strip, handing control of the territory to the PNA. After Israel's final withdrawal, thousands of Palestinians entered the empty settlements and began stripping the buildings bare of wire and fencing. They also started to demolish synagogues left standing under an Israeli government decision.

Israel's withdrawal from Gaza had a swift and positive impact on the country's foreign relations. Citing the withdrawal as the impetus for an improvement in relations, Pakistan held its first high-level diplomatic talks with Israel in early September. The meeting between Israeli Foreign Minister Silvan Shalom and his counterpart from Pakistan, Mian Kurshid Mahmood Kasuri, took place in the Turkish city of Istanbul, Turkey being one of the few Muslim countries to have full diplomatic relations with Israel. However, officials in Pakistan were keen to point out that the meeting was not a prelude to the formal recognition of

Israel. There were also reports in September and October which hinted at a general thaw in relations between Israel and some Gulf states, including Qatar, Kuwait, Bahrain, and the United Arab Emirates.

Sharon suffered a serious political setback in early November when he lost a vote in the Knesset on the appointment of two Likud loyalists to the Cabinet. Shortly afterwards Amir Peretz, leader of the Histadrut trade union confederation, defeated Shimon Peres in an internal ballot for the post of chairman of the Labour Party. Peretz's surprise victory threw Israel's shaky ruling coalition into turmoil as the new Labour leader promised to end the party's governing alliance with Likud. Faced with this loss of his legislative majority, Sharon agreed to call an early general election in March 2006 and then, in a dramatic move which caught both his supporters and opponents by surprise, on 21 November he announced his resignation from the Likud, the party he had helped found in 1973, and his intention to form a new centrist party, Kadima (Forward), with which to contest the forthcoming general election. Sharon said that Likud in its present form was "unable to lead Israel to its national goals". At least fourteen Likud members of the Knesset, including four ministers, immediately announced their support for Sharon's new party, as did Peres. In mid-December Defence Minister Lieutenant-General (retd) Shaul Mofaz also joined Kadima, whilst the Likud elected Netanyahu as its leader. The battle lines were drawn for the forthcoming election. Kadima was ahead in the opinion polls but new uncertainties surfaced on 18 December when the aging and overweight Sharon suffered a minor stroke, thus raising doubts about the future of his fledgling party.

Whilst Israel's withdrawal from the Gaza Strip overshadowed almost all other events during the year, there were a number of other important developments. In March a government-commissioned report concluded that illegal Jewish settlement outposts had been developed and expanded in the West Bank with the connivance of government departments. In April, President Vladimir Putin of Russia made an historic visit to Israel; and Ezer Weizman, the military commander and politician who had served as President of Israel from 1993 to 2000, died at the age of eighty (for obituary see p. 551). Stanley Fischer, the former IMF first deputy managing director, became the eighth governor of the Bank of Israel, the central bank, in May. Jonathan Jay Pollard, who was serving a life sentence in the USA having been found guilty in 1987 of spying for Israel (see AR 1987, p. 194), lost an appeal against his sentence in July. Israel's Supreme Court in September ordered the government to consider a drastic change to part of the route of its controversial 600 kilometre security barrier, while upholding its right to construct the barrier inside the West Bank (for map see AR 2003, p. 216). Omri Sharon, the son of Prime Minister Sharon, in November pleaded guilty at his trial on charges involving financial contributions to his father's 1999 campaign for leadership of Likud.

PALESTINE—EGYPT—JORDAN—SYRIA—LEBANON—IRAQ

PALESTINE

ADMINISTRATIVE CAPITAL: Ramallah   INTENDED CAPITAL: East Jerusalem   AREA: 5,970 sq km for
     West Bank territories and 365 sq km for Gaza   POPULATION: 3,800,000
OFFICIAL LANGUAGE: Arabic   POLITICAL SYSTEM: multiparty republic under partial Israeli occupation
HEAD OF STATE AND GOVERNMENT: President Mahmoud Abbas (since Jan '05)
RULING PARTY: Fatah (since Jan '05)
PRIME MINISTER: Ahmed Qurie
CURRENCY: Jordanian dinar and Israeli shekel (end-'05 £1=JD1.21630, US$1=JD0.70840;
     £1=Sh7.90350, US$1=Sh4.60370)
GNI PER CAPITA: US $1,120 ('04)

IN elections held in the Palestinian territories on 9 January Mahmoud Abbas was
elected as President of the Palestine National Authority (PNA), winning over 62
per cent of the vote. Abbas, the chairman of the PLO (Palestine Liberation Organisation) executive, had stood as the candidate of Fatah, the PLO's most powerful
faction. He replaced Ruhi Fattuh, Speaker of the Palestine Legislative Council
(PLC—the Palestinian legislature), who had been made acting President following the death of Yassir Arafat in November 2004 (see AR 2004, pp. 182-84). The
closest challenger to Abbas, with almost 20 per cent of the vote, was Mustafa
Barghuthi, an independent human rights activist and a critic of the PNA. He was
a distant relative of the imprisoned Fatah leader Marwan Barghuthi, who in mid-
December 2004 had withdrawn from the presidential contest. The elections were
boycotted by the Islamist organisations Hamas and Islamic Jihad on the grounds
that involvement would recognise the legitimacy of the 1993 Oslo peace accords
between Israel and the PLO.

Abbas's reputation as a moderating influence within the PNA meant that there
was a palpable sense of relief in the West at his widely anticipated victory. US
President George W. Bush hailed the election as an "historic day for the Palestinian people" and an essential step towards an independent Palestinian state. Bush,
who had severed all US contact with Arafat, said that he would welcome a visit
from Abbas.

Israeli Prime Minister Ariel Sharon telephoned Abbas to congratulate him on
his election victory. The short telephone conversation broke a freeze of almost
four years between Israeli leaders and the highest level of the Palestinian leadership. However, in a pattern that would repeat itself throughout the year, contact
between the two sides was broken off after only a few days following a Palestinian attack on the Karni terminal—the main cargo crossing point in the Gaza
Strip— in which six Israelis were killed. After failing to secure a ceasefire agreement from Hamas, the main Palestinian Islamist faction, Abbas responded by
deploying Palestinian security forces in frontline areas of the Gaza Strip. Sharon
reacted to the deployment by lifting a ban on security contact with Abbas, thereby
allowing Israeli and Palestinian security officials to co-ordinate their responses to
militant action in the Gaza Strip. In late January Israel ordered its troops to stop
all offensive operations in the Gaza Strip and to scale them back sharply in the

West Bank. The army was also ordered to stop assassinating Palestinian militants unless they presented an immediate threat to Israeli lives; to lift an unspecified number of roadblocks in the West Bank; and to re-open all three crossings from Israel into the Gaza Strip. Sharon issued a statement in which he said that the "conditions are now ripe to allow us and the Palestinians to reach a historic breakthrough". In early February Israel agreed to release 900 Palestinian prisoners and to pull back troops gradually from West Bank towns.

Abbas and Sharon held their first summit meeting in the Egyptian Red Sea resort of Sharm el-Sheikh on 8 February. The meeting was also attended by President Hosni Mubarak of Egypt and King Abdullah II of Jordan. At the end of the meeting, Abbas told reporters that he and Sharon had "jointly agreed to cease all acts of violence against Israelis and Palestinians everywhere". Sharon, in a separate statement, said that he and Abbas had "agreed that all Palestinians will stop all acts of violence against all Israelis everywhere, and in parallel, Israel will cease all its military activity against all Palestinians everywhere".

During the following days a number of "confidence building" policies and measures were implemented by both sides. Israel outlined additional steps to ease travel restrictions on Palestinians and released 500 of the 900 prisoners it had listed earlier in the month. For his part, President Abbas engineered the appointment of a new reformist Cabinet, composed mainly of technocrats. Prime Minister Ahmed Qurie and Minister of External Affairs Nabil Shaath were among the few who survived a radical pruning of "old guard" Arafat loyalists. Abbas also began the daunting task of reforming the byzantine Palestinian security apparatus, a key demand of Israel and the USA. Three security chiefs were dismissed, followed by a further ten in April, as part of an attempt to consolidate more than a dozen disparate and sometimes rival forces into a unified command. Abbas also held meetings with leaders of Hamas and Islamic Jihad, who reportedly agreed to continue an informal "cooling down period".

That period came to a sudden and violent end on 25 February when a suicide bomber blew himself up in a queue of young Israelis outside a night club in central Tel Aviv, killing five and wounding many others. It was the first Palestinian suicide attack since Arafat's death in November 2004. The attack was claimed by Islamic Jihad, but Israeli officials spoke of Syrian involvement. Sharon issued a routine warning to the Palestinians, telling the leadership to take "vigorous action against terrorism", or face a military response. Despite the bombing, however, Israel continued with its police of restraint and in mid-March Israeli troops transferred security control to the Palestinians in Jericho, the one West Bank town that had been almost entirely free of violence in recent years. It was the first area to be returned to PNA control since Israel reoccupied the West Bank in 2002. Shortly afterwards, Israel also handed over control of the town of Tulkarm, which was walled off from Israel by the controversial West Bank security barrier.

After a three-day meeting in Egypt with President Abbas, thirteen Palestinian factions, including Hamas and Islamic Jihad, issued a statement on 17 March accepting a conditional ceasefire. The militants' statement used the Arabic term for "calm" (*tahdia*) rather than those meaning "truce" or "ceasefire" and said that the agreement would expire at the end of 2005 if their demands, including military withdrawals and prisoner releases, were not met. The *tahdia* was first tested in early April when the Israeli army shot dead three Palestinian teenagers in the Rafah refugee camp in the Gaza Strip. Hamas and Islamic Jihad said that they were "reconsidering" their commitment to the *tahdia*, but refrained from immediate retaliation. A matter of days after the Rafah killings, Sharon met George W. Bush at the US President's ranch in Crawford, Texas. After the talks, Bush delivered an unusually stern public warning to Sharon against plans to expand Jewish settlements in the West Bank. Bush was reported to have voiced specific objections against a scheme to expand the West Bank settlement of Maale Adumin, which would prevent an eventual Palestinian state from having a foothold in any part of Arab East Jerusalem. However, Bush softened his public rebuke by reaffirming his promise of April 2004 (see AR 2004, pp. 185-86) that Israel would not be compelled to stage a full withdrawal to the pre-1967 borders in any final settlement with the Palestinians, and would be able to retain some West Bank settlements.

In late May Abbas finally arrived in the US capital for talks with Bush, who immediately pledged US$50 million in direct aid to the PNA to develop the Gaza Strip after Israel's planned withdrawal in August (see p. 171). After the meeting, Bush renewed his administration's commitment to an independent Palestinian state and described Abbas as a "man of courage", saying that he had great faith in his personal character and his platform of peace. Fresh from his visit to the USA, Abbas held a second summit meeting with Sharon at the latter's official residence in Jerusalem on 21 June. The meeting was routine: the two leaders discussed issues relating to Israel's planned withdrawal from the Gaza Strip and Sharon renewed calls for the PNA to curb militants and take action on the "terrorist issue."

The peace process suffered a further setback on 12 July when a Palestinian suicide bomber blew himself up at the Hasharon shopping mall in the Israeli resort town of Netanya, killing two women and two teenage girls. The attack was claimed by Islamic Jihad. Israeli officials said that it would not disrupt the planned Israeli withdrawal from the Gaza Strip, which had been set for mid-August. Although some sections of Islamic Jihad had abided by the period of *tahdia* agreed by the main Palestinian factions, other members in the West Bank, around Tulkarm and Jenin, had continued to carry out suicide bomb attacks. Shortly after the bombing in Netanya, Sharon ordered "a relentless attack" on the leadership of Islamic Jihad, whilst Israeli troops re-entered Tulkarm. The uneasy Israeli-Palestinian truce came under further pressure in mid-July when Israel launched a wave of air-strikes on targets in Gaza in response to Hamas rocket attacks from positions in northern Gaza which resulted in the death of an Israeli woman in the settlement of Nativ Haasara. Israel massed thousands of troops along the border of the Gaza Strip and warned that it would invade unless the PNA acted to prevent such attacks. US Secretary of State Condoleezza Rice made a hastily-arranged visit to the region in an effort to help defuse tension.

The relative calm that accompanied the Israel evacuation of the Gaza Strip in mid-August ended late in the month when Israeli troops raided a refugee camp near Tulkarm, killing five suspected militants. On 12 September the Israeli army completed the evacuation of Jewish settlers and soldiers from the interior of the occupied Gaza Strip, handing control of the territory to the PNA. President Abbas said that the next step after the Israeli withdrawal from Gaza was to establish a Palestinian state. Tension again increased in late September after a Palestinian truck carrying rockets exploded during a Hamas "victory" parade in Jabaliya refugee camp in Gaza, leaving twenty-one people dead and eighty wounded, most of them civilians. Israel denied any involvement in the incident, but Hamas fighters responded by launching mortar attacks into the southern Israeli border town of Sderot, injuring five Israelis. Israel moved tanks and artillery batteries to Gaza's eastern and northern borders, began mass arrests of Hamas and Islamic Jihad militants in the West Bank—especially around Ramallah—and resumed its controversial policy of targeted assassinations. Israeli helicopter gunships circling Gaza used missiles to kill four Hamas militants and an Islamic Jihad leader, Mohammed Khalil. In early October Palestinian police fought running gun battles with Hamas militants in Gaza City. The fighting erupted when Abbas ordered a ban on public displays of weapons, in response to Israeli and US pressure to rein in militants.

Palestinian gunmen killed three Israeli civilians and wounded at least five others in mid-October in two drive-by shootings in the West Bank. Responsibility for both attacks was claimed by the Fatah-affiliated al-Aqsa Martyrs' Brigade. Israel responded by imposing new travel restrictions on Palestinians in the West Bank and suspending contact with the PNA. In late October Israeli soldiers shot and killed Louay Sa'adi, one of the most wanted Islamic Jihad military commanders, and Majed Ashkar, his lieutenant, in Tulkarm. Islamic Jihad's retaliation was swift: a suicide bomber hit a busy market in the northern Israeli coastal town of Hadera, killing five Israelis. An Israeli helicopter then carried out a retaliatory airstrike on a car carrying two senior Islamic Jihad activists in Gaza's Jabaliya refugee camp. Eight Palestinians died in the attack.

President Abbas visited the USA again in late October for a second round of talks at the White House with President Bush, who said that Israel's withdrawal from Gaza provided a "magnificent opportunity" to make progress towards peace. However, Bush put the onus on the Palestinians to act first "by confronting the threat that armed gangs pose to a genuinely democratic Palestine". Earlier in the month, Israel and the PNA had postponed a planned summit meeting between Abbas and Prime Minister Sharon. Although the postponement did not appear to signal a significant rift between the sides, Palestinian officials said that Abbas was unwilling to embark on talks without a guarantee of positive results. In particular, the Palestinians had wanted Israel to agree to the re-opening of Gaza's southern crossing into Egypt at Rafah, closed by Israel prior to its withdrawal from Gaza.

US Secretary of State Rice visited the region in mid-November and managed to broker an Israeli-Palestinian agreement regulating the borders of the Gaza Strip. The deal provided for the re-opening of the Rafah passenger crossing point into Egypt, overseen by UN monitors. Israel also agreed to increase the number of trucks allowed through the Karni crossing point. The movement of Palestinians from Gaza to the West Bank would also be eased, with Israeli-escorted passenger bus convoys to begin in mid-December. However, plans to begin the convoys were shelved by the Israelis after Islamic Jihad carried out another suicide bomb attack on the Hasharon shopping mall in Netanya in early December, killing five Israelis. Predictably, Israel responded with a targeted assassination in Gaza, using a helicopter to kill Mahmoud el-Arquan, the head of the sniper unit of the Gaza-based Popular Resistance Committees. Equally predictably, Palestinian militants fired volleys of home-produced Qassam rockets into Israel. In late December the Israeli military issued a communiqué announcing the establishment of a "buffer zone" in the northern Gaza Strip and warning Palestinians that they were liable to be shot and killed if they ventured into it.

Towards the end of the year much attention was focused on the forthcoming elections to the PLC scheduled for 25 January, 2006. It was widely agreed that the elections would be a tough test for President Abbas and his ruling Fatah faction. Fatah had been weakened by serious internal divisions after the so-called "young guard" had, in mid-December, announced its own party list, Al-Mustaqbal ("the Future"). The Al-Mustaqbal list included a number of younger prominent Fatah members who had emerged during the first Intifada (uprising) in the late 1980s, including imprisoned leader Marwan Barghuthi; Mohammed Dahlan, the former head of Palestinian preventive security in the Gaza Strip and the current Civil Affairs Minister; and Jibril Rajoub, the former head of Palestinian preventive security in the West Bank.

Moreover, for the first time Fatah would be challenged by Hamas, which had made extraordinary gains in recent local elections, where voters had refused to back Fatah candidates tainted by allegations of corruption. With Hamas officially deemed to be a terrorist organisation by the US and many other Western governments, there was considerable nervousness about what would happen should it win elections.

EGYPT

CAPITAL: Cairo AREA: 1,001,000 sq km POPULATION: 68,700,000
OFFICIAL LANGUAGE: Arabic POLITICAL SYSTEM: multiparty republic
HEAD OF STATE: President Mohammed Hosni Mubarak (since '81)
RULING PARTY: National Democratic Party (NDP)
PRIME MINISTER: Ahmad Mahmud Mohammed Nazif (since July '04)
MAIN IGO MEMBERSHIPS (NON-UN): AL, OAPEC, AU, COMESA, OIC, NAM, Francophonie
CURRENCY: Egyptian pound (end-'05 £1=E£9.85210, US$1=E£5.73870)
GNI PER CAPITA: US$1,310, US$4,120 at PPP ('04)

PRESIDENT Hosni Mubarak set the political agenda for 2005 by calling for an amendment to the constitution to allow for Egypt's first contested presidential election, before the expiry of his fourth term in office. This initiative came amid mounting pressure from the USA on Middle Eastern leaders to take measures to open up their political systems and foster the development of democratic institutions.

Mubarak announced his plan for a constitutional amendment in a speech in his home province of Menoufiya, in the Nile delta, on 26 February. He said that he had asked the People's Assembly (the legislature) to amend article 76 of the constitution to allow more than one candidate to stand in elections in order "to open a new era of reform". The existing system, under which Mubarak had secured four presidential mandates since 1982, entailed a vote in the People's Assembly, with the successful nominee being approved by a plebiscite. Mubarak's initiative came amid a small but vocal campaign by the "Kifaya" movement for him to stand down and allow for free elections.

The People's Assembly on 9 March duly passed a bill to amend the constitution to allow for a contested election, and the details of how the exercise should proceed were drawn up by a special committee and put to a national referendum on 25 May. In the meantime, Kifaya and other opposition forces, notably the banned Muslim Brotherhood, staged a series of demonstrations protesting against the restrictive nature of these proposals. In order to stand in the presidential election, a candidate needed to secure the support of 250 elected politicians, a difficult task given the dominance of the ruling National Democratic Party (NDP) over most institutions in Egypt. Despite these criticisms, and several violent confrontations between protestors and police, the referendum passed easily, with 83 per cent voting in favour, and a turnout of 54 per cent according to the official count.

Egypt also experienced a number of incidents involving armed militants, but there did not appear to be any connection between these attacks and the political confrontations. On 30 April a twenty-seven-year-old Egyptian killed himself and injured four tourists and three Egyptians in central Cairo in an apparently botched attack. Hours later the bomber's fiancée and sister fired ineffectually at a passing tour bus before killing themselves. Then, in the early morning of 23 July, a series of bombs ripped through Egypt's premier coastal resort of Sharm el-Sheikh, killing at least eighty-eight people, the vast majority of whom were Egyptians. The government said that there were links between these attacks and the Taba bombings, which had killed thirty-four people in October 2004 (see AR 2004, p. 190). Both attacks were large-scale, involved three simultaneous explosions, and were sophisticated in their execution and planning. According to the authorities, the Taba attacks were the responsibility of a group of disaffected Bedouin from north Sinai, led by a minibus driver whose family had left Gaza after the 1967 Arab-Israeli war.

Mubarak declared at the end of July that he would accept the NDP's nomination for the presidential election, which took place on 7 September. He won 88.5 per cent of the vote, with Ayman Nour, the leader of the recently formed al-Ghad Party, finishing a distant second with 7.6 per cent and Noaman Gomaa, leader of the New Wafd Party, third with 2.7 per cent. None of the remaining seven candidates won more than 0.5 per cent of votes cast. The shortcomings of this exercise in partial democracy were evident in the low turnout of only 23 per cent of the electorate. Mubarak was sworn in on 27 September.

In November and December elections were held for the People's Assembly over three rounds, each round including run-off polls in the event of no absolute majority being achieved. The state-run media initially proclaimed these elections to be the most free and most fair in Egypt's history, on account of the space provided to the opposition parties to present their arguments and owing to the latitude given to the banned Muslim Brotherhood (MB) to campaign on behalf of its candidates. However, after the first round and its run-offs were completed by mid-November, the main government newspaper, *Al-Ahram*, acknowledged that there had been widespread irregularities, including intimidation and vote-buying by pro-government candidates. The MB made a strong showing in this round, setting the scene for increasingly fractious encounters in the final two rounds. By the time the elections came to an end on 7 December, more than ten people had been killed in clashes related to the voting. The MB ended up with eighty-eight of the 444 elected seats (a further ten were selected by the President), its largest-ever tally. The NDP won 145 seats from its official list, but its total tally was inflated to 311 after 166 independents joined the ruling party's ranks: the heavy presence of these independents, most of whom were long-standing NDP members, was a telling reflection of the lack of discipline in the party. The legal opposition parties made a dismal showing, with only nine seats. Twelve seats were to be subject to re-run elections, and the remainder went to genuine independents.

After the election, Mubarak reappointed Ahmed Nazif as Prime Minister, and he carried out a limited reshuffle of the Cabinet, removing several veteran ministers and replacing them with new figures, many of them drawn from the business community. Nazif himself had been first appointed in July 2004, after serving as Minister of Communications and Information Technology. His first government had notable success in reviving the economy and restoring business confidence after a prolonged period of sluggish growth and low investment. Egypt recorded a current-account surplus of more than US$2.9 billion in the 2004-05 fiscal year (1 July-30 June), and inflows of foreign direct investment (FDI) were officially estimated at US$3.9 billion. The FDI figure was considerably higher than the modest tally in previous years (US$407 million in 2003-04) partly because of the inclusion of investments related to the oil sector (previously omitted). However, the total for non-oil FDI was still a much-improved US$1.3 billion. FDI flows in the second half of the calendar year were also boosted by a number of large privatisation deals, including the sale of the state's stakes in two leading joint-venture banks. Real GDP growth in 2004-05 was 4.9 per cent, compared with 4.1 per cent the previous fiscal year.

JORDAN

CAPITAL: Amman   AREA: 89,000 sq km   POPULATION: 5,400,000
OFFICIAL LANGUAGE: Arabic   POLITICAL SYSTEM: multiparty monarchy
HEAD OF STATE AND GOVERNMENT: King Abdullah ibn al-Husain (since Feb '99)
PRIME MINISTER: Marouf Bakhet (since Nov '05)
MAIN IGO MEMBERSHIPS (NON-UN): AL, OIC, NAM
CURRENCY: Jordanian dinar (end-'05 £1=JD1.21630, US$1=JD0.70840)
GNI PER CAPITA: US$2,140, US$4,640 at PPP ('04)

JORDAN underwent a politically turbulent year in 2005, with two changes of government and, in November, a major terrorist incident, involving suicide bomb attacks on three hotels in the capital, Amman.

The first clear sign of dissension within the political establishment came in February with the resignation of the Planning and International Co-operation Minister, Bassem Awadallah, a close confidant of King Abdullah II. His decision reflected disagreements within the government over control of spending programmes financed by foreign aid. The image of the government suffered further during March as a result of two incidents affecting relations with other Arab states. The first involved reports that a Jordanian had been responsible for a suicide bomb attack which resulted in the death of 125 people in the mainly Shi'ite Iraqi city of Hilla (see p. 189). The Foreign Minister, Hani Mulki, reacted to anti-Jordanian protests in Iraq by recalling Jordan's senior diplomat in Baghdad. This caused embarrassment for the King, who was obliged to smooth matters over with the Iraqi government. Mulki was again in the firing line when he aroused the ire of Saudi Arabia by presenting an Arab-Israeli peace plan ahead of the Arab League summit conference in Algiers at the end of March (see p. 383). This initiative was strongly opposed by a number of Arab states, and the King made little effort to conceal his annoyance with the way in which his Foreign Minister had handled the matter. On 5 April, the government of Prime Minister Faisal al-Fayez resigned, and the King appointed Adnan Badran, an academic from a prominent Jordanian political family, to head a new government. Badran quickly ran into trouble when the House of Representatives (the lower chamber of the bicameral legislature) rejected his choice of Bassem Awadallah as Finance Minister. The matter was resolved on 18 June when Awadallah announced that he would step down. Badran announced a revised Cabinet list on 1 July, putting Adel Kudah, the former head of the privatisation unit, in charge of the Finance Ministry. The new line-up also saw the return of Marwan al-Muasher, one of Jordan's most influential political figures, who was appointed Deputy Prime Minister.

The Badran government was in turn replaced two weeks after the Amman bombings on 9 November, which left sixty people dead, most of them Jordanians. A statement was issued by the Iraqi branch of the Islamist militant movement, al-Qaida, saying that it had carried out the attack because of Jordan's role in supporting US operations in Iraq. The man appointed to head the new government was Marouf Bakheet, Jordan's ambassador to Israel, who had retired from the army in 1999, having reached the rank of major-general, after twenty-five years' service. Immediately after the Amman bombings he was recalled to Jordan to take charge of the national security council, attached to the Royal Court, and was then appointed Prime Minister. The King said that the new government should seek to advance political reforms within the framework of a National Agenda. The publication of this document was delayed because of the November bombings, but it was believed to include proposals for new laws on political parties and the conduct of elections.

SYRIA

CAPITAL: Damascus   AREA: 185,000 sq km   POPULATION: 17,800,000
OFFICIAL LANGUAGE: Arabic   POLITICAL SYSTEM: multiparty republic
HEAD OF STATE AND GOVERNMENT: President Bashar al-Assad (since July '00)
RULING PARTIES: Ba'ath Arab Socialist Party and six allies in the National Progressive Front
PRIME MINISTER: Mohammed Naji al-Atri (since Sept '03)
MAIN IGO MEMBERSHIPS (NON-UN): AL, OAPEC, OIC, NAM
CURRENCY: Syrian pound (end-'05 £1=S£89.6315, US$1=S£52.2100)
GNI PER CAPITA: US$1,190, US$3,550 at PPP ('04)

THE reverberations of the assassination of Lebanon's former Prime Minister, Rafik al-Hariri, in the Lebanese capital, Beirut, on 14 February dominated Syrian political life in 2005 (see pp. 182-83; for obituary see p. 524). The Syrian regime was immediately blamed for the assassination by Lebanese supporters of Hariri because of the control that Syria exerted over security in Lebanon and because of the well-documented antagonism between Syrian President Bashar al-Assad and the late Lebanese leader. Following large anti-Syrian demonstrations in Beirut in March, Assad decided that he had no option but to withdraw his forces from Lebanon, as required by UN Security Council resolution 1559 (2004). The last Syrian soldier left Lebanese soil at the end of April, thereby ending an era which had begun in 1976 when Syrian troops first intervened in the Lebanese civil war (see AR 1976, pp. 186-91). In the meantime, on 7 April, the UN Security Council resolved to set up a commission to investigate the Hariri assassination.

As international pressure on Syria mounted, with respect to the insurgency in neighbouring Iraq as well as in response to events in Lebanon, the main domestic issue was the congress of the ruling Ba'ath party, the first such meeting since 2000. The congress, which was held on 6-9 June, resulted in a number of prominent old-guard figures being voted off the party's regional command, including Abdel-Halim Khaddam, who at the same time relinquished his position as Vice-President, and Mustafa Tlas, a former Defence Minister. The congress also debated proposals on political reforms, without reaching any firm conclusions; and approved a reorientation of the Syrian economy from a socialist to a "social market" system. This trend was reinforced immediately after the congress when Abdullah al-Dardari, a leading proponent of market-based reforms, was appointed Deputy Prime Minister for Economic Affairs. Al-Dardari was the head of a unit that drew up a five-year plan, to take effect from 2006, based on stimulating high levels of growth through mainly private investment. In the interests of transparency, he allowed for the first time the full report from a confidential IMF consultation on the Syrian economy to be published, in October.

Reform, whether economic or political, was overshadowed in the second half of the year by the Hariri investigation. Detlev Mehlis, the head of the UN commission, issued his first report on 21 October (for text see pp. 490-92). It maintained that there was converging evidence that Lebanese and Syrian intelligence officials were responsible for the assassination. An unofficial earlier version of the report that was released to the press—purportedly in error—included the names of several senior Syrian regime figures in a witness statement on alleged meetings to discuss the Beirut operations. The UN Security Council passed a resolution on 31 October demanding full co-operation from Syria in the next phase of the investigation. On 12 October, before publication of the Mehlis report, the Syrian Interior Minister, Ghazi Kenaan, who had been chief of Syrian military intelligence in Lebanon between 1982 and 2002, was found dead in his office, apparently having committed suicide. Kenaan had earlier told a Lebanese journalist of his dismay at allegations made in a Beirut television programme that he had fostered gross corruption during his period in Lebanon.

After extensive negotiations, Mehlis interviewed five Syrian officials in Vienna in early December as suspects in the case. He issued a second report on 12 December, which reaffirmed the conclusion that Syrian intelligence agents were implicated, but which also called for more time to complete the investigation. At the end of the year, the Assad regime received a further blow when Abdel-Halim Khaddam gave a series of interviews to the Arab and European media stating his conviction that the Syrian intelligence services had killed Hariri.

LEBANON

CAPITAL: Beirut   AREA: 10,000 sq km   POPULATION: 4,600,000
OFFICIAL LANGUAGE: Arabic   POLITICAL SYSTEM: multiparty republic
HEAD OF STATE AND GOVERNMENT: President Emile Lahoud (since Nov '98)
PRIME MINISTER: Prime Minister Fouad Siniora (since July '05)
MAIN IGO MEMBERSHIPS (NON-UN): AL, OIC, NAM, Francophonie
CURRENCY: Lebanese pound (end-'05 £1=L£2,581.99, US$1=L£1,504.00)
GNI PER CAPITA: US$4,980, US$5,380 at PPP ('04)

THE assassination of former Prime Minister Rafik al-Hariri in a massive car-bomb explosion in the capital, Beirut, on 14 February was a turning point in Lebanon's modern history. Hariri had played a central role in Lebanon's political and economic reconstruction after the era of conflict between 1975 and 1989 and was one of the leading statesmen of the Middle East. His killing was an event that was bound to elicit a powerful political response, both in Lebanon and in the international arena. Suspicion immediately fell on Syria, whose security services were deeply involved in most aspects of Lebanese politics. The Syrian regime had put heavy pressure on Hariri in August 2004, when he was Prime Minister, to back an extension of the term of Lebanese President Emile Lahoud. Hariri obliged, clearly against his will, and subsequently tendered his resignation (see AR 2004, p. 193). This led to the passage of UN Security Council resolution 1559 (2004), calling for free elections, the withdrawal of foreign forces and the disarming of Hezbullah, Lebanon's largest Shi'ite Muslim party.

Hariri's assassination was followed by a series of anti-Syrian demonstrations in Beirut, the largest of which took place on 8 March, marking the creation of a broad political front of Christian, Sunni Muslim, and Druze parties. In an effort to show that not all Lebanese were opposed to Syria, Hezbullah staged a counter-demonstration on 14 March. However, the Syrian government acknowledged that it had no option but to pull out its forces, in compliance with resolution 1559, or else face serious retribution from the UN Security Council. The last Syrian forces left Lebanon by the end of April (see p. 181).

In the meantime, a UN commission started investigating the Hariri assassination. At the end of August, acting on the recommendation of Detlev Mehlis, the commission's head, Lebanese police arrested four of Lebanon's most senior security officials and charged them with being involved in the Hariri killing. Mehlis stated in a report issued on 21 October that converging evidence pointed to Lebanese and Syrian intelligence agencies being responsible for the assassination (for text see pp. 490-92). As the investigation proceeded there were a number of car-bomb attacks on prominent Lebanese figures, most of them known for their opposition to Syria. On 2 June Samir Kassir, a renowned journalist, died in one of these attacks; later in the year, on 12 December, his managing editor at *Al-Nahar* newspaper, Gebran Tueni, who was also a member of the National Assembly (unicameral legislature), was killed by a roadside bomb.

The departure of Syrian forces was followed by legislative elections in May and June. A Sunni-Christian-Druze bloc headed by Saad al-Hariri, son of the late Prime Minister, took seventy-two of the 128 seats. In second place was the Shi'ite alliance of Hezbullah and Amal, with thirty-five seats. The remaining twenty-one seats went to the Free and Patriotic Movement of Michel Aoun, a former army commander who had recently returned to Lebanon after fifteen years in Syrian-imposed exile. On 19 July Fouad Siniora, a former Finance Minister and close confidant of Rafik al-Hariri, became Prime Minister. He remained in office for the rest of the year, although the effectiveness of his government was compromised by the tensions arising from the ongoing investigation into the Hariri case.

IRAQ

CAPITAL: Baghdad   AREA: 438,000 sq km   POPULATION: 25,261,000
OFFICIAL LANGUAGE: Arabic   POLITICAL SYSTEM: transitional government under military occupation
HEAD OF STATE: President Jalal Talabani (since April '05)
HEAD OF GOVERNMENT: Ibrahim al-Jaafari, Prime Minister (since April '05)
MAIN IGO MEMBERSHIPS (NON-UN): AL, OPEC, OAPEC, OIC, NAM
CURRENCY: New Iraqi dinar (end-'05 £1=NID2,522.94, US$1=NID1,469.60)
GNI PER CAPITA: lower-middle income: US$826-US$3,255 ('04 est)

In late November US President George W. Bush laid out a strategy for "complete victory" in Iraq under which US forces would increasingly concentrate on the threat posed by international terrorism in the country and hand over to the Iraqi security forces operations against indigenous insurgents. The President did not indicate when Iraqi security forces would be capable of containing the domestic insurgency and did not offer a date for the ultimate withdrawal of US forces from the country, claiming that such "artificial timetables" would serve only to embolden the insurgents. The growing prominence of the theme of "Iraqification"—a rhetorical shift likened by some to President Richard Nixon's ill-fated declaration of "Vietnamisation" in the late 1960s—reflected Bush's record low approval ratings and indicated that Republican legislators, facing mid-term elections in 2006, were becoming increasingly concerned by the quagmire in Iraq and the casualty rate amongst US personnel (see pp. 118-20). In late October the US military death toll in Iraq climbed past 2,000, a fraction of the 56,000 lost in the Vietnam War, but almost certainly many more than had been envisaged by Bush when he delivered his victory speech aboard the *USS Abraham Lincoln* in May 2003 (see AR 2003 pp. 240; 551-53). Throughout 2005 the UK government of Prime Minister Tony Blair remained staunch in its support of the USA's policy in Iraq. Other members of the coalition, facing growing domestic opposition to the war, began to distance themselves. Portugal, Moldova, the Netherlands, Bulgaria, and Ukraine all withdrew their troops from Iraq during the year, while others promised reductions in 2006. At the close of the year troops from the following countries remained in Iraq: USA (155,000), UK (8,500), South Korea (3,500), Italy (2,900), Poland (1,500), Australia (1,370), Romania (860), Georgia (850), Japan (550), and Denmark (530).

Iraq itself remained an extraordinary patchwork with conditions varying greatly in different parts of the country. The Kurdish-controlled north was generally peaceful and prosperous, while people in the capital, Baghdad, and the central provinces of the "Sunni triangle" lived in perpetual fear of suicide bombers, kidnappers, Iraqi security forces, and coalition troops. In the face of growing attacks by the Sunni Arabs (led, at least symbolically, by the Jordanian-born, Afghan-trained Islamist Abu Misab Zarqawi, head of the al-Qaida Organisation for Holy War in Iraq), the USA relied increasingly on the two main Iraqi communities, so that the country slowly came under the control of a Kurdish-Shi'ite alliance whose authority was reaffirmed in legislative elections held in December. The increasingly marginalised Sunni community engaged reluctantly in the political process, but the great majority of Iraqis voted along ethnic or religious lines, ensuring that the country was turning from a strong, unitary state into a fractured confederation.

LEGISLATIVE ELECTIONS AND POLITICAL DEVELOPMENTS. Elections were held on 30 January to elect a 275-member transitional National Assembly to replace the interim legislature selected by the National Conference in August 2004 (see AR 2004, p. 196). Voters also elected governing councils for Iraq's eighteen provinces (see map on p. 187), whilst those living in the northern Kurdish-controlled areas elected deputies to the autonomous regional legislature, the Iraqi Kurdistan National Assembly. The elections ended the Sunni Muslim dominance of Iraq and marked a dramatic assertion of Shi'ite Muslim power after decades of oppression. Furthermore, it heralded a shift in the balance of power in the Middle East, raising the prospect of a "Shi'ite crescent" that would run from Iran through Iraq to Lebanon via Syria, whose Alawite leadership formed a branch of Shi'ite Islam. The Shi'ites, long repressed under the Ottomans, the British, and then the pro-Western dictators of the region, emerged as a new and potent political force.

The main Shi'ite Muslim coalition, the United Iraqi Alliance, won more than 48 per cent of the vote and 140 of the 275 Assembly seats, thereby providing it with a narrow majority within the new Assembly. A Kurdish coalition, the Kurdistan Alliance List, benefiting from a high turnout in the Kurdish north, won almost 26 per cent of the vote and seventy-five seats. The Sunni Muslim minority, who had controlled Iraq under the regime of ousted President Saddam Hussein, emerged as the biggest losers in the election. The Iraqi List of interim Prime Minister Ayad Allawi, which had courted Sunni support, won less than 14 per cent of the vote and only forty seats. National turnout was recorded at just over 58 per cent, but in some Sunni-dominated areas, where the insurgency was at its fiercest, voting had been almost non-existent. Sunni insurgents launched a record number of attacks on election day—260 compared with a daily average of between sixty and seventy—but failed to disrupt the vote in Shi'ite and Kurdish areas.

The new transitional National Assembly convened on 16 March in a vast convention centre in the heavily protected "Green Zone" in the centre of Baghdad. The Assembly took its first step towards forming a government in early April with the election of Hajem al-Hassani, a moderate Sunni Arab, as Speaker, and Hussein al-Shahristani (a Shi'ite Muslim) and Aref Taifour (a Kurd) as his deputies. Further progress was made a few days later with the election of Jalal Talabani, leader of the Patriotic Union of Kurdistan (PUK) and one of the longest serving figures in contemporary Iraqi Kurdish politics, to the largely ceremonial post of President. The outgoing interim President, Ghazi Mashal Ajil al-Yawer (a Sunni Muslim tribal leader from northern Iraq), and the outgoing Finance Minister, Adel Abdul Mahdi (a member of the Shi'ite Supreme Council for the Islamic Revolution in Iraq), were elected as Vice Presidents. President Talabani and his two deputies (together comprising the three-member presidential council) appointed Ibrahim al-Jaafari, Vice President in the interim government formed in June 2004 (see AR 2004, pp. 194-95) and leader of the (Shi'ite) Da'wa Party, as Prime Minister and invited him to form a new government. Al-Jaafari's appointment as Prime Minister—the country's most powerful position—further symbolised the rise to power of the majority Shi'ites after decades of brutal oppression under Saddam's Sunni-dominated regime. Al-Jaafari was seen as a moderate Islamist, who favoured a strong role for Muslim teachings.

After much political wrangling, al-Jaafari's new Cabinet took office in early May. Shi'ite Muslims were given seventeen posts and the Kurds nine. In what was seen as an attempt to undermine the Sunni-led insurgency, al-Jaafari awarded eight Cabinet posts to Sunni Arabs, although only six were filled. The new Cabinet was notable for the return to prominence of Ahmed Chalabi, the secular Shi'ite leader of the Iraqi National Congress (INC)—the umbrella opposition group to Saddam—who was appointed as a Deputy Prime Minister. Once the favoured ally of the US neo-conservatives who had planned and executed the US invasion of Iraq, Chalabi had fallen out of favour with the US government over claims that he had provided inaccurate pre-war intelligence and had passed US secrets to Iran.

With the new government in place, attention focused on the difficult issue of drafting of a new constitution that was agreeable to all factions. The Sunnis were opposed to a draft drawn up by the Shi'ites and the Kurds, largely because it allowed for the creation of autonomous federal regions and the prospect of Sunni marginalisation in Iraq's oil-free central regions. (The Kurds, however, had also expressed concerns that constitutional provisions for the role of Islam in determining the legal system might allow for rule by conservative Shi'ite religious law.) A 15 August deadline for approval of a final draft of the constitution passed without agreement and Sunnis dropped out of the negotiations and began mobilising voters to reject any draft put before them in a referendum. A draft constitution was finally read to the National Assembly on 28 August, but no vote was taken. Crucially, article 114 of the draft stated that "the regions comprise one province or more, and two regions or more have the right to join into one region", suggesting that any of Iraq's eighteen provinces (or governorates) could band together and that Kurdish and Shi'ite semi-autonomous regions would therefore be constitutionally viable (for text see pp. 501-20).

The referendum on the new constitution went ahead as planned on 15 October. The constitution was approved, but only by the narrowest of margins. Although nationwide almost 79 per cent of voters approved, it was overwhelmingly rejected in the two main Sunni Arab provinces (Anbar and Salahuddin). However, in the mixed province of Ninevah only 55 per cent voted against the constitution, 11 per cent short of the two-thirds majority in three provinces required to block ratification. Reports indicated that Ninevah's large and well-organised Kurdish population had turned out in force to bolster the "yes" vote. Elsewhere, the vote was largely split along sectarian lines, with a massive "yes" vote throughout the Shi'ite south and Kurdish north. Sunni Arabs turned out in large numbers to vote against the constitution, a reversal of their behaviour in the January elections which they had largely boycotted.

The next step in the political process took place on 15 December with the election of a new, plenipotentiary legislature to replace the interim National Assembly

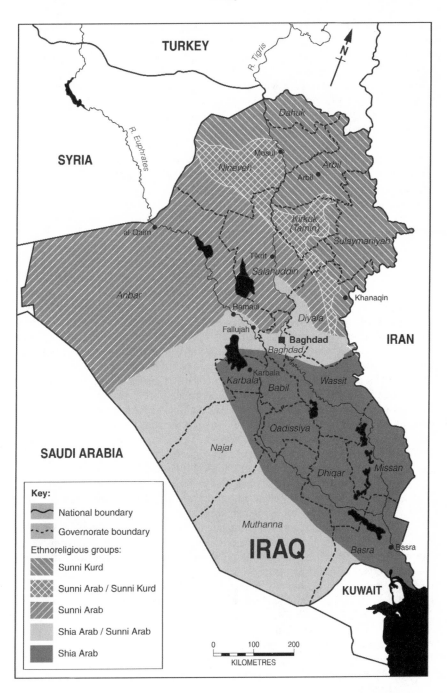

elected in January. As envisaged in the new constitution, the 275-member Council of Representatives was elected for a four-year term. Provisional results indicated that the religious Shi'ite Muslim alliance and the Kurdish alliance had won at least 150 seats. The main Sunni Arab alliance ended its boycott of the electoral process, but appeared to have won only thirty-five seats, prompting allegations by Sunni politicians of electoral malpractice and calls for fresh elections to be held. A massive security operation by the Iraqi army—supported by US forces—meant that there were few insurgent attacks on election day.

THE INSURGENCY. The growing strength and resilience of the Iraqi insurgency during 2005 meant that US and Iraqi forces struggled to contain it; defeating it seemed a very distant prospect. Originally, the insurgents had targeted coalition forces, but during 2005 attacks were directed increasingly at the police and defence forces of the new Iraqi government. The country's deep ethnic and sectarian divisions provided a major dynamic of the insurgency. The most intense Sunni insurgent activity took place in the cities and countryside along the Euphrates River from the Syrian border town of al-Qaim through Ramadi and Fallujah to Baghdad, and also along the Tigris River from Baghdad north to Tikrit. There was also heavy guerrilla activity in the so-called "triangle of death" south of Baghdad. Insurgents maintained a key supply line stretching from Syria through al-Qaim and along the Euphrates to Baghdad and central Iraq, the Iraqi equivalent of the "Ho Chi Minh trail" in Vietnam. Throughout the year, US and Iraqi forces carried out numerous operations designed to destroy or disrupt insurgent "ratlines". The insurgents controlled most of the cities and towns of Anbar province, including Ramadi, the capital. Al-Qaim, the key point on the insurgent infiltration route from Syria, was also under rebel control. Baghdad was one of the most contested regions of the country. Suicide attacks and car bombs were almost daily occurrences in the city, and the roads out of Baghdad were regarded as some of the most dangerous in the world.

The insurgency was composed of at least a dozen major guerrilla organisations, all subdivided into countless smaller cells. Whilst the exact composition of the insurgency was difficult to determine, analysts divided it into several main ideological strands, some of which were believed to overlap. These included Abu Misab Zarqawi and other foreign Islamist fighters, united by Sunni Wahhabi doctrine; indigenous Sunni Islamists; remnants of Saddam's Ba'ath Party; and nationalists and communists. In addition, there were bands of criminal insurgents operating as "hired guns". Mention of some of the more significant insurgent actions during the year is given below.

Throughout January Sunni insurgents carried out daily attacks aimed at disrupting the National Assembly elections. In the first week of the year at least fifty national guardsmen were killed in a series of attacks in Baghdad, Balad, Tikrit and elsewhere, whilst insurgents also shot and killed Ali al-Haidari, Baghdad's provincial governor. In late January the US military suffered its gravest one-day losses of the war as thirty-one marines died in the crash of a transport helicopter in the desert in western Iraq and six other soldiers died in combat.

In the immediate aftermath of the 30 January elections Iraq remained relatively calm. However, the lull soon ended and a series of suicide attacks and car bombings in and around Baghdad on 18 February killed at least thirty-six people and wounded fifty-eight others. An attack in the mainly Shi'ite city of Hilla, 100 kilometres south of Baghdad, on 28 February killed at least 125 people and left 130 others wounded when a suicide bomber drove an explosive-laden truck into a crowd of police and army recruits. A suicide bomber blew himself up on 10 March inside a Shi'ite mosque in the northern city of Mosul, killing at least fifty people and wounding more than 100 others. A Sunni Muslim militant group, the Soldiers of the Prophet's Companions, claimed responsibility for the attack, stating that it was defending the Sunni faith against the "flood tide of the Shi'ites who are invading Muslim countries".

Insurgents launched large attacks on 2 April when fighters carried out a co-ordinated series of assaults on Abu Ghraib prison, west of Baghdad, with car bombs, rocket-propelled grenades, mortars, and small-arms fire. In late April gunmen shot dead Lame'a Abed Khadawi, an Iraqi female member of the transitional National Assembly. Khadawi was the first Assembly member to be killed. A wave of insurgent attacks across Iraq between 28 April and 1 May resulted in the deaths of at least 105 Iraqis and eleven US soldiers. Groups loyal to Abu Misab Zarqawi claimed responsibility for many of these. A large number of the incidents were suicide missions, reportedly carried out by young men from Saudi Arabia, Yemen, and other Arab countries. A suicide bomber struck the northern Kurdish city of Arbil on 4 May, killing as many as sixty men who had been queuing outside the offices of the Kurdistan Democratic Party (KDP), which doubled as a police recruitment centre. The attack was claimed by the Ansar al-Sunna militant group. At least fifty-eight people were killed and forty-four wounded two days later when a suicide attacker exploded a car bomb near a vegetable market in the mainly Shi'ite Muslim town of Suwayra, 50 kilometres south-east of Baghdad.

The guerrilla war intensified throughout June, with US and Iraqi troops carrying out a series of anti-insurgency sweeps, while the insurgents continued to stage car and suicide bomb attacks in Baghdad and elsewhere. Although the insurgents increasingly targeted members of the Iraqi security forces, US forces continued to take casualties. A relative lull in insurgent attacks was broken on 10 July when suicide bombers killed at least forty people in four separate attacks. In the deadliest blast, a man wearing an explosive vest detonated himself in a crowd of about 400 army applicants at the gate of Muthanna military airfield in Baghdad. A suicide bombing at a petrol station next to a Shi'ite mosque in Musayyib, a mixed Sunni-Shi'ite town 70 kilometres south of Baghdad, on 16 July killed more than ninety-eight people and wounded 150 others.

On 1-2 August a total of twenty-one US marines was killed in three separate attacks near Haditha, in the Euphrates valley. At least forty-three people were killed and seventy-six wounded when a series of car bombs exploded on 17 August at the crowded Nadha bus station in central Baghdad. As many as 1,000 people were killed in Baghdad on 31 August when a stampede broke out on the Imams' Bridge over the Tigris River, which was crowded with Shi'ites commemorating the death of a Shi'ite holy figure at a nearby shrine. Although the police said that there had been no attack on the bridge, tensions had been running high after a volley of mortar shells killed seven people inside the enclosure of the shrine. The dead—mostly women and children—were either suffocated or drowned in the Tigris.

Suicide car bomb attacks in Baghdad and other towns and cities killed hundreds of Iraqis during September. The attacks by Sunni Arab insurgents on Shi'ite Muslim targets escalated in the run up to the constitutional referendum on 15 October. Another notable feature of the security situation during September was an increase in violence and tension in the largely Shi'ite south, where UK forces had hitherto co-existed relatively peacefully with the Shi'ite community. In one of the bloodiest and most sustained attacks since the 2003 invasion, up to a dozen insurgent bombings and shootings saw around 160 people killed and 500 wounded in Baghdad on 14 September. The attacks came after Zarqawi had sworn to avenge a recent US-Iraqi offensive against Tal Afar. In an audio message released on an Islamist website, Zarqawi said that al-Qaida was declaring "all out war on the Rafidha [a pejorative word for Shi'ites] wherever they are in Iraq". In the deadliest incident, a suicide bomber pulled up near a crowd of poor day labourers waiting for work by a public square in the predominantly Shi'ite north Baghdad neighbourhood of Khadimiya. The attacker called the crowd over to his truck with offers of work, then detonated the vehicle killing at least 114 people and wounding 160 others.

The violence took a new turn on 28 September when insurgents deployed a female suicide bomber who killed six men lining up to enlist in the Iraqi army in Tal Afar. Although female suicide bombers had been used by the Tamil Tigers in Sri Lanka, the Palestinians, and the Chechens, none had struck since the start of the Iraqi insurgency.

Three suicide bombers detonated car bombs almost simultaneously in Balad on 29 September, killing at least ninety-nine people and wounding more than 124. A suicide bombing outside a Shi'ite mosque in Hilla on 5 October killed at least twenty-five people and wounded ninety more. Many of the dead and the wounded had arrived for the funeral of a man killed in an earlier blast; others had gathered to pray on the first day of the Muslim holy month of Ramadan. The US military announced on 31 October the deaths of seven US servicemen in Iraq, making October the bloodiest month for US forces since January. The attacks—in Yusifiya, south of Baghdad, and near Balad—brought the number of US troops killed in October to ninety-two, the highest monthly total since January, when 107 troops had been killed.

Two suicide bombers killed at least seventy-seven people and destroyed two Shi'ite mosques in the north-eastern town of Khanaqin, close to the border with Iran, on 18 November. The bombers walked into the mosques when they were full for Friday noon prayers. Ten US marines were killed and eleven wounded in a roadside bomb attack carried out on 1 December on the outskirts of Fallujah. Two suicide bombers walked into Baghdad's police academy on 6 December and blew themselves up, killing at least forty-three officers and cadets and wounding seventy-three more.

KIDNAPPINGS AND EXECUTIONS OF FOREIGN HOSTAGES. Kidnappings continued on an almost daily basis throughout 2005. The majority of those kidnapped were Iraqis, including women and children abducted by what appeared to be common criminals seeking ransoms. Other Iraqis were abducted for political reasons, while some were simply abducted and murdered in revenge killings that raised the spectre of sectarian war between the Sunnis and the Shi'ites. Foreigners were also kidnapped as an attempt by insurgents to intimidate, as well as influence the media's coverage of the situation in Iraq. In most cases, the hostage takers demanded that troops from the hostage's home country be withdrawn from Iraq.

Florence Aubenas, a French journalist working for the French newspaper *Libération*, disappeared in Baghdad in early January and was assumed to have been kidnapped. She was freed in June in circumstances which appeared to have been kept deliberately vague by the French authorities, who nonetheless rejected suggestions that a ransom had been paid.

A videotape issued in late January showed a US hostage, Roy Hallums, pleading for his life. Hallums, who worked for the Saudi Trading and Construction Company supplying food to the Iraqi army, had been seized during an attack on his office in Baghdad in November 2004 along with four others. Three of the captives—a Nepalese and two Iraqis—were released and a fourth, Filipino Robert Tarongoy, was freed in June. Hallums was eventually rescued by US troops in an isolated farm house 25 kilometres south of Baghdad in early September.

Giuliana Sgrena, an Italian journalist with the Rome-based newspaper *Il Manifesto*, was seized in Baghdad in early February. A statement issued on an Islamist website by the Jihad Organisation said that her fate depended on Italy withdrawing its troops from Iraq. Sgrena was eventually freed in early March. However, her release prompted a serious diplomatic crisis between the Italian and US governments when a car carrying her to Baghdad airport was fired upon by US troops. Sgrena was injured and Nicola Calipari, an Italian secret service agent who had overseen negotiations to secure her release, was killed, apparently while trying to protect her from the gunfire. US officials claimed that the car had been speeding towards a checkpoint and had ignored warning signals from a patrol. The Italian authorities maintained that the shooting began without warning and that the car had been travelling at a normal speed (see p. 46).

Three Romanian journalists—Marie Jeanne Ion, Sorin Dumitru Miscoci, and Ovidiu Ohanesian—were kidnapped in Baghdad's Mansour district in late March. Almost a month later the Qatar-based al-Jazeera satellite television station broadcast a videotape in which a militant group threatened to kill the three unless Romanian troops pulled out of Iraq within four days. However, the three were freed, unharmed, in late May. Jeffrey Ake, a US contract worker, was kidnapped in Baghdad in mid-April. In a videotape broadcast a few days later Ake urged the US administration to open a dialogue with the Iraqi resistance to save his life. Nothing more was heard of him.

Douglas Wood, a sixty-three-year-old Australian engineer, was kidnapped by the Shura Council of the Mujahideen of Iraq in late April. A videotape released shortly afterwards showed Wood pleading for the US, Australian, and UK governments to withdraw their forces from Iraq. Wood was freed by Iraqi and US troops in June from a house in Baghdad, together with an Iraqi contractor kidnapped on a different occasion. The Ansar al-Sunna militant group announced in early May that it had ambushed a foreign security convoy in western Iraq and had captured a Japanese man, Akihiko Saito. The group said that Saito, a former paratrooper and veteran of the French Foreign Legion, had been "seriously injured" and later reports said that he had died.

Ihab al-Sharif, the Egyptian chargé d'affaires in Iraq, was kidnapped in Baghdad in early July, marking the most prominent abduction of a foreign Arab official. Zarqawi claimed responsibility for the kidnapping and said that al-Sharif had been killed after being found guilty of apostasy because Egypt had "allied itself to the Jews and Christians". His body was not recovered. Also in early July, gunmen attacked the senior Bahraini and Pakistani diplomats in separate attacks as they drove through Baghdad. The highest ranking Algerian diplomat in Iraq, Ali Billaroussi, and his colleague, Azzedine Belkadi, were kidnapped in Baghdad in late July. A few days later Zarqawi's group claimed that both diplomats had been killed because Algeria "is governing against God's law". In a statement issued in early November, the same group said that it had sentenced to death two Moroccan embassy employees kidnapped in Baghdad.

Four aid workers and peace activists—UK national Norman Kember (aged seventy-four); US national Tom Fox; and Canadians James Loney and Harmeet Singh Sooden—were abducted in Baghdad in late November. The four worked for the aid group Christian Peacemaker Teams. A video delivered to al-Jazeera showed the four sitting on the floor beneath the banner of a previously unknown group, the Swords of Righteousness Brigade. On the tape, the kidnappers accused their captives of being "spies of the occupying forces". In subsequent videotapes released in early December, the group threatened to kill the hostages unless the US and UK governments released all Iraqis held in detention centres in Iraq.

Susanne Osthoff, a prominent German archaeologist and aid worker, was kidnapped in Baghdad in late November. The kidnappers threatened to kill her unless the German government stopped co-operating with the US-backed Iraqi administration. Germany was currently training members of the new Iraqi army in bases outside the country. Osthoff, a Muslim convert who spoke fluent Arabic and had lived in Iraq for a number of years, was the first German to be kidnapped in Iraq. She was released unharmed in mid-December.

Gunmen abducted a Frenchman, Bernard Planche, in the Mansour district of Baghdad in early December. At the end of the month the Dubai-based television channel, al Arabiya, broadcast a videotape of Planche seated in front of armed militants. In the tape, a group called the Surveillance for the Sake of Iraq Brigade threatened to kill Planche unless France ended its "illegitimate presence" in Iraq. Ronald Schulz, a US security consultant, was kidnapped by the Islamic Army in Iraq in early December. The group threatened to kill Schulz unless all Iraqi prisoners were freed within forty-eight hours. After the deadline passed the group posted a massage on an Islamist website saying that Schulz had been executed.

TRIAL OF SADDAM HUSSEIN. The trial of former President Saddam Hussein, who had been captured by US troops in December 2003 (see AR 2003, p. 247), opened in a heavily-guarded courthouse in Baghdad on 19 October. In the first instance, Saddam and seven of his former Ba'athist associates were charged with crimes against humanity for ordering the execution of at least 143 people in the mainly Shi'ite village of Dujail, 55 kilometres north of Baghdad, in the aftermath of a July 1982 attempt on Saddam's life. Judge Rizgar Mohammed Amin, who headed a five-member panel, told Saddam and the seven other former officials that they were charged with "murder, forced expulsion, imprisonment, failure to comply with international law, and torture". All eight pleaded not guilty and the trial was adjourned until late November.

The other seven defendants were: Barzan Ibrahim Hasan al-Tikriti (former presidential adviser and half-brother of Saddam, arrested in April 2003); Taha Yasin Ramadan al-Jizrawi (former Vice President, arrested in August 2003); Awad Hamad al-Bandr al-Saadun (a former chief judge in the Revolutionary Court); Abdullah Kadam Roweed al-Musheikhi (a former senior member of the then-ruling Ba'ath Party from Dujail); Mizher Abdullah Kadam Roweed al-Musheikhi (Abdullah Kadam Roweed's son and another former senior Ba'athist); Ali Dayim Ali (a Ba'ath official from Dujail); and Mohammed Azawi Ali (a Ba'ath official from Dujail).

Gunmen kidnapped Sadoun Saif al-Janabi, the legal counsel for al-Bandr, in the Shaab district of east Baghdad in mid-October. Janabi's body was later found dumped near a Baghdad mosque. A second defence lawyer, Adel al-Zubeidi, representing Ramadan, was killed in an ambush in Baghdad in early November. Iraqi police announced in late November that they had foiled a plan to assassinate Raad Juhee, the chief investigative judge in the trial.

The trial re-opened on 28 November, but was adjourned after a few hours after Ramadan refused to allow the court to appoint a replacement for his assassinated representative. During the short hearing, former US attorney Ramsey Clark and former Qatari Justice Minister Najib al-Nauimi were formally inducted as advisers to Saddam's defence team. The trial re-opened on 5 December and the first courtroom witness testified to the Dujail massacre. Ahmed Hassan Mohammed al-Dujaili, a teenager at the time of the alleged killings, told the court that the security forces had rounded up hundreds of villagers and then proceeded to kill people with a human meat grinder and to subject others to physical and mental torture. The evidence provided a graphic reminder of how brutal Saddam's regime had been. But as the year ended there was evidence that for some Iraqis the chaos and uncertainty of the present was creating an increasing nostalgia for the certainties and security of the past.

SAUDI ARABIA—YEMEN—ARAB STATES OF THE GULF

SAUDI ARABIA

CAPITAL: Riyadh   AREA: 2,150,000 sq km   POPULATION: 23,200,000
OFFICIAL LANGUAGE: Arabic   POLITICAL SYSTEM: non-party monarchy
HEAD OF STATE AND GOVERNMENT: King Abdullah ibn Abdul Aziz (since Aug '05), also Prime Minister
HEIR APPARENT: Crown Prince Sultan ibn Abdul Aziz (since Aug '05), also Deputy Prime Minister
MAIN IGO MEMBERSHIPS (NON-UN): AL, OPEC, OAPEC, GCC, OIC, NAM
CURRENCY: Saudi riyal (end-'05 £1=SR6.43840, US$1=SR3.75040)
GNI PER CAPITA: US$10,430, US$14,010 at PPP ('04, based on regression)

AFTER the highly-charged atmosphere of 2003-04, when the kingdom was confronted by a wave of Jihadist militancy that threatened to unravel the delicately balanced Saudi social contract, the House of Saud was able to reflect with some satisfaction on the way it restored a measure of stability, and instituted changes, to the
body politic in 2005. The series of terrorist attacks that had targeted the expatriate
business community over 2004 subsided as the belated Saudi security response
finally quelled the insurgency's ardour. The death of King Fahd ibn Abdul Aziz on
1 August, ten years after he was incapacitated by a serious stroke (see pp. 537-38),
allowed for the smooth succession of his half-brother, Crown Prince Abdullah ibn
Abdul Aziz , who injected renewed momentum behind reform efforts.
    More importantly, the Saudi political class started to realise the urgent need
for pressing ahead with a raft of political, social, and economic reforms if the
instability that had marked previous years was to be avoided. The three rounds
of municipal elections in the spring proved to be the first experiment in democracy in the country's eighty-year history, leading to the election of half the country's municipal councillors and establishing, for the first time, the principle that
citizens should have the right to decide who would represent them. Though
turnout was generally low and Western-style liberal candidates fared predictably
poorly, the local polls were widely seen as a success in a country unused to competitive electioneering.
    Abdullah's accession proved the catalyst for a wave of political change. Having
bided his time as the kingdom's *de facto* ruler for the past decade (though without
the full authority of a monarch), the new King began his reign with familiar gusto.
His first act set the tone, pardoning a number of dissidents who had only a few
months previously been convicted of "undermining the authority of the state".
Subsequent reshuffles of personnel in the highest echelons of the House of Saud
were crafted to ensure that under King Abdullah the government would be in a
much stronger position to reshape the kingdom's arcane structures than ever it was
while Fahd was king.
    The release of the three intellectuals imprisoned at the behest of the powerful
conservative Interior Minister, Prince Naif ibn Abdul Aziz, in May 2004 was a significant pointer to the shift in power effected since Abdullah's succession. Just
three months earlier, the three men—Matrouk al-Faleh, Abdullah al-Hamid, and
Ali al-Damaini—had been sentenced to jail terms of up to nine years for calling
for the establishment of a constitutional monarchy. In a calculated snub to Naif,

the Interior Minister was also compelled publicly to announce their release. The gesture had more than symbolic significance. Abdullah's decision to grant amnesties to the men suggested that the conservatives' stock response to dissent—throwing people in jail—would no longer pass muster.

The clipping of Naif's wings confirmed Abdullah's tightening grip on the levers of power. Abdullah had been preparing for succession as Fahd's health deteriorated over the first half of the year, shoring up his authority with the removal of Prince Bandar bin Sultan, the influential Saudi ambassador to the USA, and his replacement by the reformist former ambassador to the UK, Prince Turki al-Faisal. In recognition of his strong international contacts and close ties to US President George W. Bush, Bandar—the son of the new Crown Prince Sultan ibn Abdul Aziz—was named as secretary general of the newly formed National Security Council. With a remit to inject new ideas into security policy—previously the fiefdom of Naif—the Council further bolstered Abdullah's reformist ambitions.

The changes in Saudi Arabia percolated from the top down. The Wahhabi establishment suffered a reverse in fortunes in 2005, having reasserted itself in the wake of the terrorist campaigns of 2003-04. With reformist signals coming from the top, the Saudi press dared to take on other totems of the conservative clerical establishment. The new spirit of openness evident across large sections of Saudi media saw the activities of the controversial religious police (Mutawa) subject to unprecedented criticism. Newspaper articles now routinely covered incidents of Mutawa harassment of ordinary Saudis. The government, for its part, broached sensitive issues such as reform of the education curriculum, a subject close to Abdullah's heart. New efforts were made to rein in the influence of extremist clerics, whether in school, university or mosque.

Abdullah, who was now able to invest the office of King with real meaning after ten years in which Fahd's illness had prevented decisive leadership, anchored the Saudi reform effort with the promulgation of his "national dialogue" events. These public sessions—criticised in some quarters as little more than public relations stunts—brought together a range of intellectuals, women, clerics, Shi'ites, and liberals, and were designed to ensure that the House of Saud could influence the direction of public debate about the kingdom's future. For example, they provided a forum for the regime to find new ways of accommodating its traditional position as a "defender of the faith"—in this case the Wahhabi strand of Islam that became much maligned as the foster parent of extremist Islam as practised by the followers of Osama bin Laden—with a more pluralist role, which would allow the questioning of traditional religious and social orthodoxies.

Saudi Arabia's accession to the World Trade Organisation on 11 December heralded a new focus on trade liberalisation and reform of the country's investment regime. This, too, was expected to make its impact felt on the social character of Saudi Arabia, with attendant commitments to reform the judiciary and the country's wider commercial culture.

The period of introspection enforced by the outbreak of Jihadist militancy in 2003, and the climate after the 11 September 2001 attacks on the USA, looked to be coming to an end. Where US policy towards Saudi Arabia in the dark days of 2003-04 had been driven by a perception that the stability of the House of Saud (and of Saudi oil exports) were best served by propping up the regime, it became evident in 2005 that the US administration now saw the Saudi government as capable of playing a positive role on the diplomatic stage. The USA started to focus on the contribution that Saudi Arabia could provide in choking off growing Iranian influence in Iraq. However, the Saudi government was a reluctant conduit for US interests in Iraq and remained out of the fray as Iraq's security situation deteriorated further, being more concerned about preventing terrorist contagion from that country infecting its own society. Elsewhere, however, Saudi Arabia betrayed an increasing willingness to undertake diplomatic initiatives. Saudi officials played a decisive role as interlocutors in the Syria-Lebanon crisis (see pp. 181-83): as one of the few Arab states able to influence the Syrian government, the Saudi leadership strove to reinforce the need for Syria's good behaviour against its former client state. On the other hand, Saudi Arabia remained reluctant to bring its diplomatic clout to bear on the Israeli-Palestinian conflict, where its contacts were weaker and historical links less visible.

YEMEN

CAPITAL: Sana'a   AREA: 528,000 sq km   POPULATION: 19,800,000
OFFICIAL LANGUAGE: Arabic   POLITICAL SYSTEM: multiparty republic
HEAD OF STATE AND GOVERNMENT: President (Field Marshal) Ali Abdullah Saleh (since May '90)
RULING PARTY: General People's Congress (GPC)
PRIME MINISTER: Abd al-Qadir Abd al-Rahman Bajammal (since April '01)
MAIN IGO MEMBERSHIPS (NON-UN): AL, OIC, NAM
CURRENCY: Yemeni rial (end-'05 £1=YR334.612, US$1=YR194.910)
GNI PER CAPITA: US$570, US$820 at PPP ('04)

THE government continued to face down a variety of security threats in 2005, including those mounted by militants associated with Osama bin Laden's al-Qaida network, along with other assorted Salafists, Ba'athists, Zaydi, and tribal elements. The prevalence of the threat—with many branches of the state having been penetrated by militant Salafists and Ba'athists, the latter a legacy of the close historical ties with the Iraq of ousted President Saddam Hussein—forced Yemen's President Ali Abdullah Saleh to announce a major reorganisation of the state security organisations in 2005. The Jihadist presence appeared particularly strong inside the Yemeni security service, the Political Security Organisation, which officials accused of having allowed a number of militants to escape captivity.

Saleh's anti-terrorism strategy was accelerated, with a crackdown on militant strongholds and the astute deployment of government largesse. However, an uprising in the spring by the Zaydis—a branch of Shi'ite Islam—tested the authorities' capacity to quell the various rebel activities. Zaydi militants suffered hundreds of fatalities as the security forces challenged them in their mountain retreats in March and April. President Saleh pointed the finger of blame at outside forces, notably Iran, as fomenting and funding the Zaydi insurgency. This appeared far-fetched, however, for the roots of the conflict lay in long-standing anti-government feeling among Zaydi Yemenis. The resurgence of violence in March followed the killing by government forces of three Zaydi fighters at an arms market. Unrest continued throughout the year, with twelve policemen killed by Zaydi militants in an ambush near the northern town of Saada on 29 October.

Saleh's announcement in July that he would step down as President in 2006 prompted renewed concerns about the country's continued stability. The news was particularly worrying for the US administration of President George W. Bush, which remained heavily reliant on Saleh's ability to hold the country together. Within Saleh's ruling General People's Congress (GPC), his resignation announcement—something of a peculiarity by regional standards—sparked a wave of introspection as the lack of an obvious suitable replacement became apparent. Much speculation focused on the potential for getting a military figure to stand as President, in the hope that the exertion of military might would help keep the country united and stable.

Yemen's ties with the USA remained strong throughout the year as the Bush administration continued to view Saleh as a key ally in the "war on terror" and essential to efforts to quell al-Qaida activity in the south Arabian region. But there were also signs of US frustration at the prevalence of corruption in the Yemeni government and at the lack of democratic change under Saleh's rule. US diplomats let it be known that there would be more funds available to Yemen if it proved capable of engaging in political reform.

ARAB STATES OF THE GULF

United Arab Emirates (UAE)

CONSTITUENT REPUBLICS: Abu Dhabi, Dubai, Sharjah, Ras al-Khaimah, Fujairah, Umm al-Qaiwin, Ajman
CAPITAL: Abu Dhabi   AREA: 77,000 sq km   POPULATION: 4,284,000
OFFICIAL LANGUAGE: Arabic   POLITICAL SYSTEM: non-party republic, comprising federation of monarchies
HEAD OF STATE AND GOVERNMENT: Shaikh Khalifa Bin Zayed al-Nahyan (Ruler of Abu Dhabi), President of UAE (since Nov '04)
PRIME MINISTER: Shaikh Maktoum bin Rashid al-Maktoum (Ruler of Dubai), Vice-President and Prime Minister of UAE (since Nov '90)
MAIN IGO MEMBERSHIPS (NON-UN): AL, OPEC, OAPEC, GCC, OIC, NAM
CURRENCY: UAE dirham (end-'05 £1=Dh6.30560, US$1=Dh3.67300)
GNI PER CAPITA: high income: US$10,066 or more ('04 est), US$21,000 at PPP (est)

Kuwait

CAPITAL: Kuwait   AREA: 18,000 sq km   POPULATION: 2,500,000
OFFICIAL LANGUAGE: Arabic   POLITICAL SYSTEM: non-party monarchy
HEAD OF STATE: Sheikh Jabir al-Ahmad al-Jabir al-Sabah (since Dec '77)
PRESIDENT ELECT: Crown Prince Sheikh Saad al-Abdullah al-Salim al-Sabah
PRIME MINISTER: Sheikh Sabah al-Amad al-Jabir al Sabah (since July '03)
MAIN IGO MEMBERSHIPS (NON-UN): AL, OPEC, OAPEC, GCC, OIC, NAM
CURRENCY: Kuwaiti dinar (end-'05 £1=KwD0.50120, US$1=KwD0.29200)
GNI PER CAPITA: US$17,970, US$19,510 at PPP (est based on regression)

Oman

CAPITAL: Muscat   AREA: 300,000 sq km   POPULATION: 2,700,000
OFFICIAL LANGUAGE: Arabic   POLITICAL SYSTEM: non-party monarchy
HEAD OF STATE AND GOVERNMENT: Sultan Qaboos bin Said al-Saeed (since July '70)
MAIN IGO MEMBERSHIPS (NON-UN): AL, GCC, OIC, NAM
CURRENCY: rial Omani (end-'05 £1=RO0.66100, US$1=RO0.38500)
GNI PER CAPITA: US$7,890, US$13,250 at PPP (est)

Qatar

CAPITAL: Doha   AREA: 11,400 sq km   POPULATION: 637,000
OFFICIAL LANGUAGE: Arabic   POLITICAL SYSTEM: non-party monarchy
HEAD OF STATE AND GOVERNMENT: Sheikh Hamad bin Khalifa al-Thani (since June '95)
HEIR APPARENT: Crown Prince Shaikh Tamin Bin Hamad al-Thani (since Aug '03)
MAIN IGO MEMBERSHIPS (NON-UN): AL, OPEC, OAPEC, GCC, OIC, NAM
CURRENCY: Qatar riyal (end-'05 £1=QR6.24990, US$1=QR3.64050)
GNI PER CAPITA: high income: US$10,066 or more ('04 est)

Bahrain

CAPITAL: Manama   AREA: 685 sq km   POPULATION: 725,000
OFFICIAL LANGUAGE: Arabic   POLITICAL SYSTEM: constitutional monarchy
HEAD OF STATE: Sheikh Hamad bin Isa al-Khalifa (since March '99)
HEAD OF GOVERNMENT: Sheikh Khalifa bin Sulman al-Khalifa, Prime Minister (since Jan '70)
MAIN IGO MEMBERSHIPS (NON-UN): AL, OAPEC, GCC, OIC, NAM
CURRENCY: dinar (end-'05 £1=BD0.64710, US$1=BD0.37700)
GNI PER CAPITA: US$12,410, US$18,070 at PPP (est)

HAVING taken over as President of the UNITED ARAB EMIRATES (UAE) and ruler of Abu Dhabi in November 2004, Shaikh Khalifa Bin Zayed al-Nahyan injected significant changes into the federation's political system in his first full year in office. The initial fruits of reform came in December, when the President announced plans for the first elections to the Federal National Council (FNC), the UAE's consultative chamber. However, the reform announced by Shaikh Khalifa disappointed many UAE citizens who had hoped for a more ambitious experiment in democracy. Under the plans, a selected council of notables, likely to comprise 2,000 men from across the seven-member federation, would select half of the FNC's twenty members.

More encouraging was the response to the elections to the Abu Dhabi Chamber of Commerce and Industry (ADCCI) on 5 December. Women both stood for and voted in the election to the ADCCI board, which was expected to provide an effective platform for reform of the UAE business climate. Two non-UAE nationals were also elected to the board. This election, the first genuinely democratic ballot in the country's history, was seen as a marker for future political reform.

Shaikh Khalifa also shifted the country's external relationships, pressing Saudi Arabia on the contentious issue of their shared border. The *UAE Yearbook 2006*, an official publication brought out at the end of the year, included for the first time the 25-kilometre Khor al-Udeid strip of land between Abu Dhabi and QATAR as territory belonging to the UAE, despite a 1974 border treaty that had ceded the area to Saudi Arabia. Confirming the UAE's growing confidence in its relations with the Saudi government, Khalifa made the border issue, which also covered the question of a major oil field that spanned both Saudi and UAE territory—a central plank of his leadership whereas his predecessor, Shaikh Zayed Bin Sultan al-Nahyan, had been happy to let it rest undisturbed.

Succession issues came to the fore in KUWAIT. Rifts within the al-Sabah ruling family emerged in the wake of calls by the head of the National Guard, Shaikh Salem Bin Ali Bin Salem al-Sabah, for reforms to redress "flaws" in the constitution. Ministers were accused of acting unilaterally, confirming the growing tensions between the rival al-Salem and al-Jaber wings of the ruling family. The continued ill-health of Crown Prince Shaikh Saad al-Abdullah al-Salem al-Sabah weakened the al-Salems within the hierarchy. Meanwhile, strife within Kuwait's unicameral legislature, the National Assembly, prevented movement on a key range of reforms, particularly the major oil field expansions scheme, Project Kuwait, which Assembly members opposed for allowing foreign control of Kuwaiti hydrocarbon reserves.

Political reform reared its head in some of the other Gulf states. In QATAR, a new constitution came into force in June, providing for enhanced civil liberties, including a free press, and with freedom of assembly enshrined in law. Though political parties remained outlawed, the emir, Shaikh Hamad Bin Khalifa al-Thani, hinted that this would be redressed in future legislation. Under the new constitution, two-thirds of the forty-five-member Majlis al-Shura would be elected by universal adult suffrage.

A terrorist attack in QATAR on 20 March underlined the vulnerability of the Gulf states to Jihadist militant activity. One UK national was killed and twenty others injured when a suicide bomber struck at the Doha Players theatre outside the capital, near a British school. However, the incident was seen as an isolated event and the authorities maintained a strong grip on the security situation. No further attacks took place during the remainder of 2005.

Unrest also infected BAHRAIN, where social issues gained greater prominence. Unemployment, a major problem afflicting Bahrain's growing Shi'ite population, proved the catalyst for three days of clashes in December between stone-throwing protesters and government forces. The outbreak of violence followed a series of mostly peaceful demonstrations earlier in the year highlighting the unemployment issue. In the aftermath of the violent protests, which were sparked by police actions preventing protestors from gathering outside the Royal Court, the government attempted to calm tensions by meeting human rights campaigners, in a sign of its intention to prevent new outbreaks of violence.

Tensions in BAHRAIN were also heightened after the government passed a controversial law banning the formation of political associations based on class, sect, profession or geographical area, as well as their receipt of foreign financial donations. The existing, mainly Shi'ite, opposition groups were unlikely to be affected by the law and decided to register as recognised political groups by a November deadline. This was thought likely to herald an increasing participation in the political process by groups like al-Wefaq and the National Democratic Action Society, which had previously boycotted the government's attempts to establish democratic institutions. Jihadist militancy remained only a distant threat in Bahrain, despite the continued presence of the US Sixth Fleet off its shores.

In OMAN, the normally placid political scene was disrupted by the arrest and conviction in May of a number of Ibadi rebels, who were charged with conspiring to overthrow the government. Most Omanis were followers of Ibadi Islam, but the rebels were accused of plotting to establish an Ibadi imamate and overthrow Sultan Qaboos bin Said al-Saeed, with further rumours suggesting a planned attack on the Muscat cultural festival in January. After the trial, Qaboos granted the rebels an amnesty, a gesture confirming the Sultan's consensual style of leadership. A wider insurgency failed to materialise, although hundreds of demonstrators did take to the streets in May to protest against the handing down of guilty verdicts. Political reform efforts in the sultanate were notable by their absence, and political parties remained banned, although Qaboos did take measures to introduce a culture of civic rights with the implementation of a civil status decree. Concerns about the succession to Qaboos continued, in the wake of the Sultan's refusal to name an heir.

SUDAN—LIBYA—TUNISIA—ALGERIA—MOROCCO—WESTERN SAHARA

SUDAN

CAPITAL: Khartoum   AREA: 2,500,000 sq km   POPULATION: 34,400,000
OFFICIAL LANGUAGE: Arabic   POLITICAL SYSTEM: multiparty republic
HEAD OF STATE AND GOVERNMENT: President (Gen.) Omar Hasan Ahmed al-Bashir (since Oct '93),
    previously Chairman of Revolutionary Command Council (since June '89)
RULING PARTIES: government of national unity including the National Congress Party (NCP) and
    the Sudan People's Liberation Movement (SPLM) (since Sept '05)
MAIN IGO MEMBERSHIPS (NON-UN): AL, AU, COMESA, OIC, ACP, NAM
CURRENCY: Sudan dinar (end '04 £1=SD395.788, US$1=SD230.545)
GNI PER CAPITA: US$530, US$1,870 at PPP ('04)

THE civil war between the government of Sudan and the rebel Sudan People's Liberation Movement (SPLM)—whose military wing was the Sudan People's Liberation Army (SPLA)—ended on 9 January when Lieutenant-General John Garang, the SPLA leader, and Ali Osman Taha, Sudan's First Vice President, signed a comprehensive peace agreement (CPA) in Nairobi, Kenya, in the presence of Sudan's President Omar Hasan Ahmed al-Bashir, eleven other African heads of state, and the outgoing US Secretary of State, General (retd) Colin Powell. The agreement brought to an end twenty-one years of war in southern Sudan between the Islamist government in Khartoum and the SPLM/A rebels, who wanted greater autonomy for the oil-rich, mainly Christian and animist, south of the country. The CPA, comprising eight protocols, which had been negotiated over a period since July 2002 (see AR 2002, p. 234), provided for a six-month "pre-interim" period, followed by six years' transition (beginning in July), during which the ten southern states would have an autonomous government, with national elections to be held before the end of the third year. Finally, in 2011, the southern states would hold a referendum on independence.

In July an interim constitution was ratified and on 9 July Garang was sworn in as Sudan's new First Vice-President with much optimism and jubilation for creating a "New Sudan" in which the southerners assumed their rightful share of power and resources. But the euphoria turned into rioting when Garang was killed on 30 July in a helicopter crash on the Ugandan-Sudanese border whilst returning from a meeting in Uganda with President Yoweri Museveni. The riots left 130 people dead and many injured. Although conspiracy theories abounded, the crash appeared to have been an accident resulting from bad weather and poor visibility. (For Garang's obituary see p. 533.)

Garang's deputy, Lieutenant-General Salva Kiir Mayardit, was sworn in as First Vice President of Sudan on 11 August, and president of the government of the autonomous region of Southern Sudan. In accordance with the CPA's provisions, Southern Sudan's first Cabinet was appointed in October, after an Interim Legislative Council (legislature) had been created in the region's capital, Juba. The Council comprised 110 members from the SPLM, twenty-five from Sudan's ruling National Congress Party (NCP) and twenty-six from other southern politi-

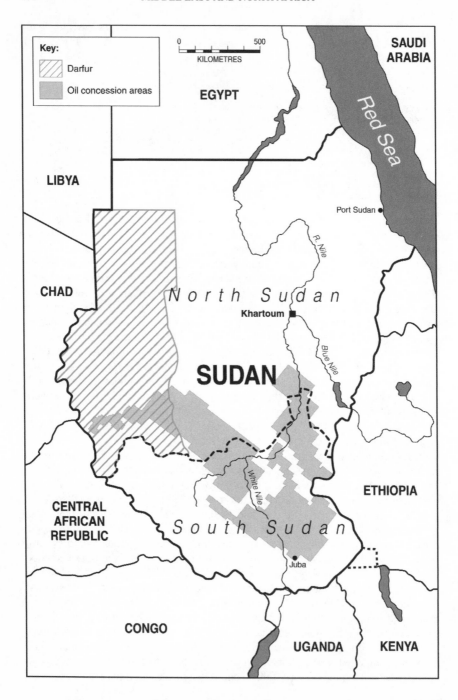

cal forces. Southerners who were living in exile or internally displaced began to return, but financial resources were needed urgently to provide for them. Donor countries met in Oslo, Norway, in April and pledged $US4.5 billion over three years to support the reconstruction of the south and the voluntary repatriation of refugees. The UN established a new peacekeeping force, UNMIS (UN Mission in the Sudan), which would monitor the ceasefire in the south.

The CPA also provided for the creation of an interim government of national unity. This was finally formed in September, with the forty-seven posts shared between the northern ruling NCP (52 per cent), the southern SPLM (28 per cent), northern opposition parties (14 per cent), and the southern opposition (6 per cent). Of the twenty-nine ministries, sixteen went to the NCP, nine to the SPLM, and the remainder to the smaller opposition parties. The key Energy Ministry remained under NCP control.

Relations with Chad gradually deteriorated over the year. In December Chad's President Idriss Déby accused the Sudanese government of supporting Chadian rebels and it was reported in October that seventy-five people had been killed in an attack by the pro-Sudanese government militia, the Janjawid, on a village inside Chad. In August Ugandan troops attacked a unit from the Ugandan rebel group, the Lord's Resistance Army (LRA), inside Sudan, killing twenty of them. In September members of the LRA ambushed a school bus in Lako, southern Sudan, and killed fourteen people. At the end of December at least twenty-seven Sudanese refugees were killed in protests near the UN office in the Egyptian capital, Cairo, demanding to be resettled in a third country. Egypt did not legally recognise the presence of Sudanese refugees and provided them with no welfare services.

The conflict in Darfur, western Sudan, with its devastating consequences to the local people and to the stability of Chad, continued, accompanied by serious violations of human rights and international humanitarian law (see AR 2004, pp. 214-15). In September, Jan Egeland, the UN under-secretary-general for humanitarian affairs and emergency relief co-ordinator, warned that unless the violence ceased, his organisation would not be able to provide assistance for the 2.5 million people afflicted by the conflict.

In April the USA granted formal recognition to the International Criminal Court (ICC) by abstaining, rather than voting against, in UN Security Council resolution (1593) to bring individuals who had committed crimes in Darfur before the ICC tribunal in The Hague (see p. 423). A UN enquiry identified fifty-one Sudanese from among army officers, officials, tribal leaders, and rebels who should be tried by the ICC. No names were disclosed, however. The government of Sudan rejected the resolution and said that it would conduct its own enquiry. Juan Mendez, the UN Secretary-General's special adviser for the prevention of genocide, stated in October that Sudanese officials were taking only "cosmetic steps" to prevent human rights abuses in Darfur. However, despite international efforts to strengthen the arms embargo, increased funds for the African Union peacekeeping force, and progress with the ongoing negotiations in Abuja, Nigeria, there was no end to the violence.

China became the dominant economic partner of the Sudanese government, particularly in the oil sector. Oil revenues in 2005 were expected to exceed US$1 billion and the IMF predicted that Sudan's economy would grow by 8.3 per cent in 2005, rising to 13.4 per cent in 2006. India emerged as a major partner in commercial ventures, and its ICSA power company secured a US$140 million contract from Sudan's National Electricity Corporation to set up a power transmission line network. India's International Corporation for Petroleum and Natural Gas also signed a contract worth US$194 million for a 741-kilometre-long oil pipeline to export petroleum products from the Gaili refinery, north of Khartoum, to Port Sudan.

LIBYA

CAPITAL: Tripoli　AREA: 1,760,000 sq km　POPULATION: 5,674,000
OFFICIAL LANGUAGE: Arabic　POLITICAL SYSTEM: one-party republic
HEAD OF STATE: Col Moamar Kadhafi, "Leader of the Revolution" (since '69)
HEAD OF GOVERNMENT: Shukri Mohammed Ghanim, Secretary General of General People's
　Committee (since June '03)
MAIN IGO MEMBERSHIPS (NON-UN): AL, OPEC, OAPEC, AMU, AU, OIC, NAM
CURRENCY: Libyan dinar (end-'05 £1=LD2.30320, US$1=LD1.34160)
GNI PER CAPITA: US$4,450 ('04),

IN late August, Moamar Kadhafi received Senator Richard Lugar, chairman of the Senate foreign relations committee, at the head of a high level US delegation. Shortly afterwards Seif al-Islam Kadhafi, the leader's son, declared that full diplomatic relations would be established with the USA "in the next few days" with representation upgraded to ambassadorial level, and predicted that Libya would be removed from the US list of states supporting terrorism before the end of the year. The US State Department, however, was more cautious and indicated that there were still many questions to be settled.

In mid-October a memorandum of understanding was signed in Tripoli between the UK and Libya to allow the Home Office to deport Libyan nationals held in the UK on suspicion of supporting terrorism back to Libya. The memorandum included a written assurance from Libya that deportees would be treated in a humane manner in accordance with internationally accepted standards. The human rights group Amnesty International stated that as torture and suspicious deaths in custody were still being reported in Libya, it was dangerously misguided to assume that the agreement would be respected.

On 25 December the Libyan Supreme Court ordered a retrial of the five Bulgarian nurses and Palestinian doctor condemned to death in 2004 for infecting Libyan children with the HIV virus (see AR 2004, p. 217). Bulgaria and Libya announced that they would set up a charity fund for the families of the infected children and resume talks about compensation payments in January 2006. The Bulgarian President welcomed the reversal of the death sentences but predicted that the release of the nurses would have a very high price. Earlier, Bulgaria's former Foreign Minister stated that Libya had suggested exchanging the nurses for Lockerbie detainee, Abd al-Baset al-Megrahi, but that he (the minister) had rejected any such deal.

In early March the Libyan leader again expressed his opposition to the introduction of political parties and called for an increase in the size of the security forces in order "to defend the country and protect the dignity of the people". In late June Libya's weak and divided opposition groups in exile met for the first time in London. They agreed to unite and called for regime change through peaceful means. In an interview with the Qatar-based satellite television station al-Jazeera at the beginning of August, the leader of the opposition Libyan Muslim Brotherhood admitted that his movement had had intermittent contacts with the Libyan authorities since 1999 through Libya's representative at the UN, but denied that the Brotherhood's decision not to attend the London conference was linked to commitments made during these talks. He insisted that the movement had chosen not to participate because it had its own peaceful programme based on dialogue with the regime.

Meanwhile, in a long speech on the future of the country, Seif al-Islam Kadhafi announced that plans were being drawn up to release imprisoned members of the Muslim Brotherhood. He also stated that as a result of recent dialogue some imprisoned members of extremist Islamist groups had turned away from violence and their situation would be reviewed. An initiative would be announced to compensate Libyans whose financial assets and properties had been confiscated during the socialist era, including those who had left the country. The Kadhafi Foundation was making efforts to bring about the voluntary return of all Libyan expatriates, and some 787 had already returned. He also called for the reopening of files on Libyans executed or liquidated following illegal tribunals, and for their relatives to receive compensation. Decrees and laws were being prepared to encourage the emergence of a free press and independent radio stations he suggested. In early October, however, it was reported that the Supreme Court would have the final decision on the imprisoned members of the Muslim Brotherhood amidst rumours of strong opposition to the proposed reforms, and in December Shukri Mohammed Ghanim, Secretary General of the General People's Committee, insisted that Libya's political system already allowed for people's participation. Any significant political change seemed unlikely.

After speculation that he might boycott the meeting, Kadhafi attended the Arab League summit in Algiers in late March but the long awaited heads of state summit of the Arab Maghreb Union, scheduled to take place in Tripoli at the end of May, was postponed indefinitely after King Mohammed VI of Morocco announced that he would not attend (see pp. 210; 384-85). The African Union's fifth annual heads of state summit was held in Sirte in July and ended with appeals for a substantial increase in aid from the West, despite comments by the Libyan leader that they should not beg for money from rich states.

The government reiterated its commitment to economic liberalisation, but little progress was made in implementing the ambitious privatisation programme. There was, however, a high level of participation in two new rounds of bids for oil exploration and production licensing in January and October, when US, European and Asian companies were awarded permits.

TUNISIA

CAPITAL: Tunis   AREA: 164,000 sq km   POPULATION: 10,000,000
OFFICIAL LANGUAGE: Arabic   POLITICAL SYSTEM: multiparty republic
HEAD OF STATE AND GOVERNMENT: President (Gen.) Zine el-Abidine Ben Ali (since Nov '87)
RULING PARTY: Constitutional Democratic Rally (RCD)
PRIME MINISTER: Mohammed Ghannouchi (since Nov '99)
MAIN IGO MEMBERSHIPS (NON-UN): AL, AMU, ICO, AU, OIC, NAM, Francophonie
CURRENCY: Tunisian dinar (end-'05 £1=TD2.34200, US$1=TD1.36420)
GNI PER CAPITA: US$2,630, US$7,310 at PPP ('04)

THE ruling Rassemblement constitutionnel démocratique (RCD) again secured a landslide victory in local elections held in May, winning 94 per cent of the 4,366 seats on municipal councils according to official sources; turnout was 83 per cent. The party faced no opposition in 199 of the 264 municipalities and won 80 per cent of the vote in the remaining sixty-five. Four opposition parties managed to win a total of 262 seats (the Mouvement des démocrates socialistes taking almost half). The Democratic Coalition for Citizenship (including the Parti démocratique progressiste (PDP), Ettajdid, and the Forum démocratique pour le travail et les libertés), which had withdrawn from the elections accusing the government of resorting to threats to prevent its candidates standing in key towns, condemned the results. The government insisted that the candidates had been excluded because they failed to comply with the rules. President Zine el-Abidine Ben Ali later announced that those opposition parties that had won seats on municipal councils would qualify for representation on regional councils.

Indirect elections for the newly created upper house, the Chamber of Councillors, were held in July, with the ruling RCD winning seventy-one of the eighty-five elected seats. The fourteen seats reserved for the unions remained vacant as the Union générale tunisienne du travail refused to participate, stating that it wanted to select its own representatives instead of having candidates chosen by an electoral college dominated by the RCD. The remaining forty-one seats were appointed by the President and included the leader of Tunisia's Jewish community.

In September a Tunis court banned the Ligue tunisienne des droits de l'homme (LTDH) from holding its annual conference after several members close to the ruling RCD instigated legal action against the LTDH leadership for allegedly violating the organisation's internal statutes. The president, Mokhtar Trifi, accused the authorities of a deliberate attack on an organisation which had become "the only centre of resistance against a despotic government", a view echoed by international human rights organisations.

Tunisia hosted the second world summit on the information society in November amidst heavy security. Attended by delegates from 176 countries, it was the largest meeting ever organised under UN auspices (see pp. 408-09). For the Ben Ali regime, it was intended to showcase Tunisia as a modern country which had mastered information technologies. Critics pointed out that in fact it highlighted the other face: a police state that tolerated no criticism, imprisoned its opponents, flouted human rights, muzzled the press, and routinely blocked access to Internet sites used by dissidents. A month before the summit, eight leading political opponents staged a hunger strike calling for more freedom and the release of some 500 political prisoners; they continued their protest until the summit closed. A few days before the summit opened, a French journalist was viciously attacked in the centre of Tunis after reporting on violent clashes between the police and supporters of the hunger strikers; a Belgian camera crew had their camera seized and the film confiscated. Robert Meynard, secretary-general of Reporters sans frontières, was refused entry to the country to attend the summit, and efforts by representatives of civil society to organise an alternative summit were thwarted by the authorities. When the Swiss Federal President declared that it was unacceptable that governments represented at the meeting jailed citizens for using the Internet to criticise the authorities, state television ceased broadcasting until he had finished his speech. Amnesty International called for a UN enquiry.

Political opponents accused the West, especially France, of "passive complicity", insisting that behind the grand declarations urging political reforms and respect for human rights they allowed Ben Ali to act with total impunity because his regime was seen as a bulwark against radical Islamism. Ben Ali was condemned by opposition parties and human rights groups for inviting Israeli Prime Minister Ariel Sharon to the summit. In the end, Israel was represented by its Foreign Minister, Silvan Shalom, accompanied by a large delegation. Protestors chanting anti-Israeli slogans denounced the visit as an attempt to normalise relations with the Jewish state.

In December the IMF estimated economic growth at 5 per cent during 2005, despite high oil prices, the dismantling of the WTO multi-fibre agreement, and a slowdown of demand in Europe, Tunisia's major export market. It was confident that the country's large trade deficit would be offset by strong revenue from tourism.

ALGERIA

CAPITAL: Algiers   AREA: 2,382,000 sq km   POPULATION: 32,400,000
OFFICIAL LANGUAGE: Arabic   POLITICAL SYSTEM: multiparty republic
HEAD OF STATE AND GOVERNMENT: President Abdelaziz Bouteflika (since April '99)
RULING PARTIES: National Liberation Front (FLN) heads coalition which also includes National
     Democratic Rally (RND), and Movement for a Peaceful Society (MSP)
PRIME MINISTER: Ahmed Ouyahia (since May '03)
MAIN IGO MEMBERSHIPS (NON-UN): AL, OPEC, OAPEC, AMU, AU, OIC, NAM
CURRENCY: dinar (end-'05 £1=AD125.340, US$1=AD73.0100)
GNI PER CAPITA: US$2,280, US$6,260 at PPP ('04, based on regression)

IN August President Abdelaziz Bouteflika announced details of his "charter for peace and national reconciliation". After a vigorous campaign throughout the country to promote the project, it was put to a referendum on 29 September. According to official sources, it was approved by 97.36 per cent of voters with a turnout of 79.6 per cent, a figure challenged by the opposition as "inconceivable". Under the terms of the charter, members of armed Islamist groups who surrendered voluntarily to the authorities would be pardoned together with those already condemned, imprisoned, or wanted for acts of terrorism, with the exception of those implicated in collective massacres, rapes, or bomb attacks on public places. The security forces were exonerated from serious human rights abuses, notably on the issue of the thousands who "disappeared" during the 1990s, and all allegations of a deliberate state policy of disappearances were rejected. Indeed, there was fulsome praise for the security services. The families of the disappeared (whom the charter called "victims of the national tragedy") would be eligible for compensation. The Front islamique du salut (FIS) was held responsible for the tragic events of the 1990s and forbidden from ever resuming its political activities.

The referendum was strongly opposed by some political parties, notably the Front des forces socialistes (FFS) and the Rassemblement pour la culture et la démocratie (RCD), as well as by human rights organisations and support groups for the families of the disappeared. They called for a boycott and accused the authorities of denying them access to the state media and of intimidation during their campaigning against the referendum. Opponents insisted there should be no pardon without truth and justice and that no one should benefit from impunity. The President was accused of using the referendum as a plebiscite to reinforce his power and as a prelude to constitutional amendments that would allow him to stand for a third term in 2009.

Sporadic violence continued, resulting in some fifty deaths each month, mostly attributed to the Groupe salafiste pour la prédication et le combat (GSPC), the last of the armed Islamist groups still active after the security forces had announced in January that they had dismantled the Groupe islamique armé and arrested its leaders. In the run up to the referendum the GSPC stepped up its attacks and issued a communiqué rejecting the President's peace offer and reiterating its commitment to follow jihad ("holy war") until the establishment of an Islamic state. The Algerian authorities insisted that the GSPC was linked to al-Qaida and had made an alliance with Abu Misab Zarqawi's group in Iraq, a claim supported by French intelligence but disputed by some specialists. In July the GSPC had praised the kidnapping and execution of two Algerian diplomats in Iraq by Zarqawi's group (see p. 192). GSPC cells also remained active on Algeria's southern borders and in Europe, with France singled out as "enemy number one".

In the troubled Berber-speaking Kabylia region, voters boycotted the referendum in large numbers and turnout was the lowest in the country, only 11 per cent in the two main cities, Tizi Ouzou and Bejaia. In early January talks between the pro-dialogue wing of the citizens' movement, the Coordination des aarchs, dairas et communes (CADC), and Prime Minister Ahmed Ouyahia had resumed and agreement was reached to implement the El-Kseur platform, including making Tamazight an official language, "within the framework of the constitution and the laws of the country". Shortly before the referendum Bouteflika visited the region but made no reference to reconciliation between Kabylia and the central authorities. Four days later, the President insisted that Arabic would remain the country's only official language, contradicting the agreement made by his Prime Minister.

In local elections in Kabylia on 24 November the FFS and its fraternal rival the RCD won over half of all seats on municipal and provincial councils but the parties of the presidential alliance, the Front de libération nationale (FLN) and the Rassemblement national démocratique (RND), improved on their performance and seemed likely to benefit from the deep divisions between their opponents (the FFS, RCD and CADC). No single party secured a majority of seats on most councils, requiring tactical alliances to ensure that they could function properly.

Bouteflika returned to Algiers on 31 December after an absence of five weeks in Paris for an operation on a bleeding stomach ulcer. Official secrecy had surrounded his precise medical condition.

Relations with France became strained after the French National Assembly (the lower legislative chamber) passed a law in February which included an article emphasising the positive role of the French presence in Algeria. Bouteflika denounced the law as an act of "mental blindness" and even compared the actions of the French colonial authorities with those of the Nazis. As a result of the dispute, the historic treaty of friendship between the two countries, which should have been signed by the end of the year, remained blocked.

The controversial new hydrocarbons law was finally passed in March. In November the Finance Minister defended his decision to base the annual budget for 2006 on an oil price of US$19 per barrel even though the actual price was US$60. He revealed that since 2000 some US$30 billion had been transferred to a stabilisation fund of which US$13 billion had been used to repay debt.

MOROCCO

CAPITAL: Rabat   AREA: 447,000 sq km   POPULATION: 30,600,000
OFFICIAL LANGUAGE: Arabic   POLITICAL SYSTEM: multiparty monarchy
HEAD OF STATE AND GOVERNMENT: King Mohammed VI (since July '99)
RULING PARTY: Socialist Union of Popular Forces (USFP) heads broad coalition
PRIME MINISTER: Driss Jettou (non-party), since Oct '02
MAIN IGO MEMBERSHIPS (NON-UN): AL, AMU, OIC, NAM, Francophonie
CURRENCY: dirham (end-'05 £1=D15.9141, US$1=D9.26990)
GNI PER CAPITA: US$1,520, US$4,100 at PPP ('04)

IN a speech to the nation in May, King Mohammed VI announced a national initiative for human development to fight poverty, marginalisation and exclusion, declaring that any exploitation of social misery for political purposes, especially to encourage extremism, was morally unacceptable.

In June a court of appeal upheld a sentence forbidding outspoken critic Ali Lmrabet from working as a journalist for ten years after he had challenged official orthodoxy on the Sahrawi (Western Saharan) refugees, and in July Nadia Yassine, spokesperson for the leading Islamist association, al Adl was-'l Ihsan, was put on trial for insulting the monarchy after she expressed her preference for a republican regime. In December the Minister of Justice announced that he had set up a unit to monitor the press. Several journalists faced charges for defamation and very heavy fines after reporting on sensitive subjects.

In October the Chamber of Representatives (the lower house of the bicameral legislature) approved the bill regulating political parties (see AR 2004, p. 224), which set more stringent rules concerning democratic practices and transparent financial management. In a speech at the opening of Parliament, the King had stated that the new legislation would strengthen political parties and facilitate the construction of a democratic society. He called on the political parties to incorporate new elites and initiate new generations into the principles of democratic participation. By contrast, critics insisted that the bill was designed to limit the right of association and to strengthen central control over political life. A number of parties were involved in mergers as a result of the legislation.

The Equity and Reconciliation Commission (IER), inaugurated in January 2004 to investigate serious human rights abuses committed between 1960 and 1999 (see AR 2004, p. 224), presented its final report to the King at the end of November. The IER had examined 16,861 individual dossiers and some 9,280 victims had received compensation. Investigators had discovered the graves of 663 political opponents who had disappeared and died in illegal detention centres. The report recommended that the state should offer its apologies to the 20,000 victims, ensure that no one responsible for human rights abuses benefited from impunity, and attempt to establish the truth in cases that remained outstanding. The King expressed his resolve to "turn the page on these dark years". The New York based Human Rights Watch regretted that the IER was only a consultative body and that no state institution was obliged to implement or even seriously consider its recommendations. It urged that torturers, who were not named in the report, be brought to justice. In December the French judge investigating the disappearance of opposition politician Mehdi Ben Barka, in 1965, stated that the Moroccan authorities continued to obstruct his enquiries.

During the year the King pardoned 285 Islamists condemned under anti-terrorist legislation, including 164 members of Salafiya Jihadiya, and commuted the death penalty imposed on another twenty-four Islamists. These gestures caused surprise and some disquiet. In November police arrested seventeen Islamists suspected of planning terrorist attacks against US and Israeli interests in Morocco and against the Parliament in Rabat. Eleven members of another group suspected of organising terrorist acts were arrested in Casablanca in December.

In January King Juan Carlos of Spain made an official visit to Morocco, the first by a Spanish monarch since 1979. Bilateral relations continued to be dominated by the Western Sahara dispute and the problem of illegal immigration. In September and early October hundreds of illegal immigrants from sub-Saharan Africa made repeated attempts to enter the Spanish enclaves of Ceuta and Melilla, and several were killed and many wounded as Spanish and Moroccan security forces tried to repel them (see pp. 61-62). Morocco subsequently repatriated several thousand illegal immigrants by plane to their countries of origin, and continued to deny accusations that it had abandoned hundreds in the desert near the borders with Algeria and Mauritania, without food or water.

King Mohammed attended the Arab League summit in Algiers in March, his first visit to Algeria since his accession, and held a private meeting with President Abdelaziz Bouteflika. Morocco welcomed Algeria's decision in April to abolish visa requirements for Moroccan visitors, but hopes of a thaw in relations proved premature. In May the King refused to attend the Arab Maghreb Union summit after Bouteflika reaffirmed Algeria's support for Polisario (see pp. 384-85), and in June a visit by the Algerian Prime Minister was cancelled at Morocco's request.

In October two Moroccan civilians employed at the Moroccan embassy in Baghdad were kidnapped and sentenced to death by Abu Misab Zarqawi's group (see p. 192). In December the authorities denied allegations in the local press that the US Central Intelligence Agency had transferred terrorist suspects to secret detention centres in Morocco where they were tortured.

WESTERN SAHARA

CAPITAL: Al Aaiún   AREA: 284,000 sq km   POPULATION: 244,900
STATUS: regarded by Morocco as under its sovereignty, whereas independent Sahrawi Arab
   Democratic Republic (SADR) was declared by Polisario Front in 1976
MAIN IGO MEMBERSHIPS (NON-UN): AU

AT the end of April the UN Security Council agreed a six-month extension of the mandate of the Mission for the Referendum in Western Sahara (MINURSO) and called on Morocco and Polisario to co-operate with the UN to end the continuing impasse. In mid-August Polisario released the remaining 404 Moroccan prisoners of war in an operation supervised by Senator Richard Lugar, chairman of the Senate foreign relations committee, at the request of US President George W. Bush. Lugar called on Morocco and Algeria to seize this positive development to create a climate conducive to resolving the dispute. By mid October, however, when the UN Secretary-General's new personal envoy Peter van Walsum made his first visit to the region, he concluded that the position of the key players was "quasi-irreconcilable".

At the end of May a large pro-independence demonstration in Al Aaiún led to violent clashes between protestors and Moroccan security forces which quickly spread to other towns. These were the most serious disturbances in the territory since the riots in October 1999. Independent sources accused the Moroccan security forces of using disproportionate force during the demonstration after protestors had burnt the Moroccan flag and thrown stones at the police, and of aggravating the situation by pursuing protestors into private houses. The protests continued and by late October there were reports of daily clashes between youths and the police. In one such incident a young Sahrawi died after being beaten by the police. Polisario declared that he was the first martyr in a peaceful *"intifada"* (the name given to the Palestinian resistance to Israeli occupation) against Moroccan occupation and called for urgent UN intervention to protect Sahrawi citizens.

Several foreign delegations on fact-finding missions were refused entry to the territory, and international human rights organisations expressed growing concern about the deteriorating situation, imprisonment of local human rights activists, and torture of detainees.

Reporting to the UN Security Council in late October, the Secretary-General acknowledged the continuing deadlock between the parties over how to achieve "a mutually acceptable solution that would enable the people of the Western Sahara to exercise their right of self-determination". Nevertheless, he called for a further six-month extension of MINURSO's mandate to April 2006, a recommendation adopted unanimously by the Security Council. The extension was supposed to allow van Walsum to hold further talks with the parties, but it was unclear what these could actually achieve.

At the beginning of November, in an address to mark the 30th anniversary of the "green march", King Mohammed VI declared that Morocco refused to renounce any part of its Saharan territories and reiterated his wish to seek a negotiated political solution that would grant autonomy to these provinces within the framework of Moroccan sovereignty. The Royal Consultative Council for Saharan Affairs would be reorganised to include not only local notables, but also new elites and associations active in civil society, especially the young and women. The King also called for greater efforts to lift the siege imposed on "our citizens confined to the camps around Tindouf [. . .] their future is in a democratic and united Morocco". Algeria and Polisario continued to insist on the Sahrawis right to self-determination but international support for the Baker plan (see AR 2003, p. 266) was ebbing away. The USA, France, and Spain, in particular, appeared to favour Morocco's autonomy proposals in order to close a troublesome dossier and protect the stability of one of the West's key allies.

In May the Sahrawi Arab Democratic Republic (SADR) invited international oil companies to bid for exploration licences for twelve blocks offshore the Western Sahara. UK companies were the only bidders. In October the SADR warned Kerr-McGee and partners, licensed by the Moroccan government, not to drill offshore the disputed territory because it could not guarantee the safety of their staff.

VI EQUATORIAL AFRICA

HORN OF AFRICA—KENYA—TANZANIA—UGANDA

ETHIOPIA—ERITREA—SOMALIA—DJIBOUTI

Ethiopia

CAPITAL: Addis Ababa   AREA: 1,104,000 sq km   POPULATION: 70,000,000
OFFICIAL LANGUAGE: Amharic   POLITICAL SYSTEM: multiparty republic
HEAD OF STATE: President Girma Woldegiorgis (since Oct '01)
RULING PARTY: Ethiopian People's Revolutionary Democratic Front (ERPDF)
HEAD OF GOVERNMENT: Meles Zenawi, Prime Minister (since Aug '95)
MAIN IGO MEMBERSHIPS (NON-UN): AU, COMESA, ACP, NAM
CURRENCY: birr (end-'05 £1=Br14.9780, US$1=Br8.72460)
GNI PER CAPITA: US$110, US$810 at PPP ('04, based on regression)

Eritrea

CAPITAL: Asmara   AREA: 118,000 sq km   POPULATION: 4,500,000
OFFICIAL LANGUAGES: Arabic & Tigrinyam   POLITICAL SYSTEM: transitional government
HEAD OF STATE AND GOVERNMENT: President Isayas Afewerki (since May '93)
RULING PARTY: People's Front for Democracy and Justice (PFDJ)
MAIN IGO MEMBERSHIPS (NON-UN): AU, COMESA, ACP, NAM
CURRENCY: nakfa (end-'05 £1=N23.1761, US$13.5000)
GNI PER CAPITA: US$180, US$1,050 at PPP ('04, based on regression)

Somalia

CAPITAL: Mogadishu   AREA: 638,000 sq km   POPULATION: 9,938,000
OFFICIAL LANGUAGES: Somali & Arabic   POLITICAL SYSTEM: transitional government
HEAD OF STATE AND GOVERNMENT: President Colonel Ahmed Abdullahi Yusuf (since Oct '04)
PRIME MINISTER: Prime Minister Ali Mohammed Gedi (since Nov '04)
MAIN IGO MEMBERSHIPS (NON-UN): AL, AU, ACP, OIC, NAM
CURRENCY: Somalia shilling (end-'05 £1=Ssh2,849.80, US$1=Ssh1,660.00)
GNI PER CAPITA: low income: US$825 or less ('04 est)

Djibouti

CAPITAL: Djibouti   AREA: 23,000 sq km   POPULATION: 716,000
OFFICIAL LANGUAGES: Arabic & French   POLITICAL SYSTEM: multiparty republic
HEAD OF STATE AND GOVERNMENT: President Ismail Omar Guelleh (since April '99)
RULING PARTIES: Union for a Presidential Majority (UMP) (since Jan '03)
PRIME MINISTER: Dilleita Mohamed Dilleita (since March '01)
MAIN IGO MEMBERSHIPS (NON-UN): AL, AU, COMESA, ACP, OIC, Francophonie, NAM
CURRENCY: Djibouti franc (end-'05 £1=DFr299.573, US$1=DFr174.500)
GNI PER CAPITA: US$1,030, US$2,270 at PPP ('04, based on regression)

In ETHIOPIA elections took place in mid-May to the bicameral legislature, comprising the lower house, the 548-seat Council of People's Representatives, and the 110-seat upper house, the Council of the Federation. Initial results indicated that the ruling Ethiopian People's Revolutionary Democratic Front (EPRDF) had won over 300 seats in the Council of People's Representatives (down from 467 in the previous election), but the main opposition alliance, the Coalition for Unity and Democracy (CUD), claimed that there had been massive irregularities in the voting. The CUD charge was lent support by the New York-based Human Rights Watch which had issued a pre-election report alleging that systematic political repression had prevented people from participating freely in the campaign.

At least twenty-six people were killed and more than 100 wounded when security forces fired into crowds of protesting students in the capital, Addis Ababa, in early June. The shootings followed two days of student protests and weeks of rising tensions over the conduct of the elections. The government blamed the CUD for the violence, but the CUD insisted that the student protests had been spontaneous. The killings were the worst in Addis Ababa since April 2001 when the security forces had killed over forty people following a wave of student protests (see AR 2001, p. 258).

Final elections results had still not been released by the National Electoral Board of Ethiopia (NEBE) in late August when the EU's election observer mission released its own report which said that key elements of the May vote had failed to meet international standards. It reported widespread abuses, including the arrest of opposition party members. Prime Minister Meles Zenawi responded angrily, describing the EU mission as "a farce" and the report as "garbage". In early September the NEBE announced the final election results which showed that the EPRDF had won 327 seats against 109 for the CUD. The chairman of the latter, Hailu Shawel, announced that the party intended to boycott the new Council of People's Representatives and called for the immediate resignation of the Meles government. However, in October the new legislature re-elected Meles for a further five-year term as Prime Minister and a new Cabinet was formed. A number of high-profile ministers were removed, apparently to allow them to dedicate themselves to bolstering the EPRDF. Five of the new ministers were members of the Oromo ethnic community, Ethiopia's largest, with approximately 30 million people. Seven were from the Amhara community, the second largest ethnic group. Three members, including Meles himself, were Tigrayan, who constituted some 6 per cent of the population and had spearheaded the seventeen-year guerrilla war against the former Dergue regime of Colonel Mengistu Haile Mariam.

Fresh violence erupted in Addis Ababa in early November. Over forty people were killed during anti-government protests organised by the CUD. Prime Minister Meles charged the CUD leadership with trying to "overthrow the duly constituted government" and warned that treason charges could be forthcoming. In December it was reported that Western donors, appalled by the government's brutal treatment of the CUD, were planning to withhold direct budgetary support to the Meles government.

Concern grew during the year that ERITREA and ETHIOPIA were on course for a second bloody border war: the first, in 1998-2000, had cost some 70,000 lives. In April, after a series of clashes in the far west of the two countries' border, close to neighbouring Sudan, Eritrean President Isayas Afewerki said that the inevitability of war with Ethiopia was "a firm conclusion that we have reached". This conclusion, Isayas explained, was based on "our assessment that Ethiopia harbours expansionist ambitions and will act on them".

In early October ERITREA announced that it would no longer allow the UN Mission in Ethiopia and Eritrea (UNMEE) to use helicopters on the Eritrean side of the temporary security zone (TSZ) separating the two countries. The move rendered the UN mission blind to alleged troop concentrations and movements in the disputed border region and raised further concerns that fresh conflict was brewing. In late November the UN Security Council adopted resolution 1640 (2005) which expressed "grave concern" at Eritrea's decision to restrict the movement of UN peacekeepers. Eritrea responded in early December by ordering the expulsion from its territory of all European, US, Canadian and Russian peacekeepers (about ninety of the 230 UNMEE staff in Eritrea). The Eritreans were further aggrieved in mid-December when the Eritrea-Ethiopia claims commission at the Permanent Court of Arbitration in The Hague, the Netherlands, ruled that Eritrea had started the 1998-2000 border war by invading the town of Badme. Ethiopia was found liable for abusing civilians and looting or destroying property in subsequent military actions and during its occupation of Eritrean territory, but nonetheless said that it intended to seek "hundreds of millions of dollars" in compensation.

On the domestic front, Ali Sayyid Abdullah, the Eritrean Foreign Minister, died of a heart attack in August. Mohammed Omer was appointed as acting Foreign Minister.

Efforts to foster peace and begin the process of nation-building in SOMALIA by relocating the seat of government from Kenya to Somalia itself failed conspicuously. A year which began with a sense of optimism ended in the usual cycle of violence between foreign-backed warlords. The rising influence of al-Qaida-inspired Islamist militia activity added a new dimension to the chaos.

President Colonel Ahmed Abdullahi Yusuf and Prime Minister Ali Mohammed Gedi returned home to Somalia in late February for the first time since their government had been formed in neighbouring Kenya in late 2004 (see AR 2004, p. 230). Thousands of people took to the streets of the capital, Mogadishu, to welcome them on their brief visit, which was designed to examine the possibility of relocating their government from Kenya to Mogadishu. Almost inevitably, the plan to relocate began to break down in mid-March when the transitional legislature sitting in the Kenyan capital, Nairobi, voted to block Yusuf and Gedi's intention to allow the deployment in Somalia of peacekeeping troops from the country's three front-line neighbours: Djibouti, Ethiopia, and Kenya. Instead, the legislators wanted to deploy peacekeepers only from Uganda and Sudan, the two non-front line members of the regional Inter-Governmental Authority on Development (IGAD), which had played a major role in the long-drawn-out peace process. The legislative session, held in Nairobi's Grand Regency Hotel, descended into an all-out brawl, with opposing legislators physically attacking each other. Gedi escaped unhurt after he was rushed out of the hotel by security guards.

Gedi made another brief visit to Mogadishu in early May where he addressed hundreds of his supporters in one of the city's football stadiums; moments after he left the stadium, a bomb exploded killing at least fifteen people and wounding around forty others. The attack served to strengthen the judgment of Gedi and Yusuf that Mogadishu remained unsafe and that no government could function in the city until it was pacified through the deployment of a front-line state peacekeeping force. However, against the wishes of Gedi and Yusuf, the Speaker of the transitional legislature, Sharif Hasan Shaikh Aden, and around thirty other members of the assembly, arrived in Mogadishu in mid-May with the stated intention of establishing the transitional legislature in the city. Aden said that a drive to demobilise the city's rival factions and militias was well under way and that security was improving. A number of powerful faction leaders, including Mohammed Qanyare Afrah (Minister of National Security), Muse Sudi Yalahow (Minister of Trade), Usman Hasan Ali Ato (Minister of Public Works and Housing) and Umar Mohammed Mahmud (Minister of Religious Affairs and Endowments), all offered their support to Aden's plan to relocate the legislature to Mogadishu.

The dispute over where to locate the transitional government deepened in late May when heavy fighting broke out in Baidoa, one of the alternative sites favoured by Yusuf and Gedi. At least nineteen people died and a further twenty-eight were injured. Baidoa was controlled by a faction led by Mohamed Ibrahim Habsade, a member of the legislature who opposed its location in the city. His forces were reportedly attacked by Ethiopian-backed militias who supported President Yusuf. In mid-June Prime Minister Gedi and his supporters within the transitional legislature and Cabinet moved out of Kenya and began establishing a base in the town of Jowhar, some 90 kilometres north of the Somali capital, Mogadishu. With Gedi in Jowhar, Yusuf and Speaker Aden travelled to Sana'a, the capital of Yemen, for talks aimed at resolving the crisis over the location of the government. The talks failed, Aden returned to Mogadishu, but Yusuf remained in Sana'a to try and win some military assistance from Yemen. Yusuf eventually relocated to Jowhar in July. Prime Minister Gedi made another visit to Mogadishu in early November and only narrowly survived an assassination attempt when his convoy hit a landmine and was attacked by grenades. Gedi was unharmed, but at least three of his bodyguards were reportedly killed.

In the north, the self-declared Republic of Somaliland held legislative elections in September, the first since Somaliland had seceded from Somalia in 1991 (see AR 1991, pp. 250-51). Elections were held to the eighty-two-member House of Representatives and President Dahir Riyale Kahin's National Democratic Alliance (UDUB) emerged with the largest number of seats, thirty-three, compared with twenty-eight for the main opposition party, Solidarity (Kulmiye), and twenty-one for the Justice and Restoration (UCID). Kulmiye and the UCID later announced that they had agreed to co-operate in the new legislature.

In September police in Hargeisa, the capital of Somaliland, arrested seven people accused of being members of an al-Qaida cell. President Kahin said that the men were mostly Somalis and had been trained at a camp outside Mogadishu.

Ismael Omar Guelleh was re-elected unopposed as President of DJIBOUTI in April. Guelleh stood as a candidate of the pro-government coalition, the Union pour la majorité presidentielle (UMP), which had also won legislative elections held in January 2003 (see AR 2003, p. 272). Opposition parties boycotted the presidential poll and, despite official turn-out figures close to 80 per cent, they claimed that few people had bothered to vote for Guelleh. In May the President reappointed Dilleita Mohamed Dilleita as Prime Minister. Dilleita's new Cabinet included a number of new appointees including Ali Farah Assoweh (Economy, Finance and Planning in charge of Privatisation) and Mohamed Dini Farah (Employment and Solidarity).

As the base for the combined joint task force-Horn of Africa (CJTF-HOA), Djibouti continued to play a major role in the USA's efforts to pursue its "war on terror" in the Horn of Africa. In May US marines with the CJTF-HOA launched one of their most visible hunts for Islamist militants in Somalia

KENYA

CAPITAL: Nairobi   AREA: 580,000 sq km   POPULATION: 32,400,000
OFFICIAL LANGUAGES: Kiswahili & English   POLITICAL SYSTEM: multiparty republic in Commonwealth
HEAD OF STATE AND GOVERNMENT: Mwai Kibaki (NARC) (since Dec '02)
RULING PARTY: National Rainbow Coalition (NARC) (since Dec '02)
MAIN IGO MEMBERSHIPS (NON-UN): AU, COMESA, ACP, CWTH, NAM
CURRENCY: Kenya shilling (end '05 £1=Ks124.379, US$1=Ks72.4500)
GNI PER CAPITA: US$460, US$1,050 at PPP ('04)

VOLATILE politics resulted from the struggle over the new "Wako" constitution, which was adopted by the National Assembly (the unicameral legislature) in July. President Mwai Kibaki was accused of reneging on his pre-election undertaking to cede some power to a Prime Minister, expected to be Raila Odinga, the Luo leader of the Liberal Democratic Party (LDC), which was a member of the ruling National Rainbow Coalition (NARC). When Kibaki, whose core support came from part of the Kikuyu ethnic group—the so-called "Mount Kenya mafia"— refused to compromise, evidently bent on retaining power, seven Cabinet ministers, including Odinga, rebelled. With the orange as their symbol, they mounted a well-planned campaign to secure a "no" vote in the referendum to be held on 2 November. The government was reported to have spent Ks2 billion on a lacklustre campaign to win support for a "yes" vote, which was characterised by the banana symbol. The campaign sharpened ethnic divisions and split the Kenya African National Union (KANU), the former ruling party, into two rival camps.

Though the campaign was marred by some violence, polling day itself was relatively peaceful. The result—3,579,241 votes (58.1 per cent) were cast against the constitution and 2, 578,831 (41.9 per cent) for it—was widely seen as a protest vote against Kibaki's leadership. He accepted this humiliating defeat, but reacted by dismissing his entire Cabinet. He then squandered the opportunity to give the government a fresh look and reappointed many former ministers in a bid to hold together his fragile coalition. He excluded nearly all those who had opposed him over the constitutional issue and also dropped Chris Murungaru, a close ally and former Minister of Transport, who was alleged to be involved in shady procurement deals which were under investigation. The political situation remained fluid with everything to play for: the President was suffering from ill-health, ethnic tensions had increased, the National Assembly was prorogued until March 2006, and the shape of the new constitution remained to be determined.

According to Edward Clay, the UK high commissioner, corruption was still rampant, characterised by the "massive looting" of public funds. In February John Githongo, the highly respected official appointed in January 2003 to root out corruption, resigned and sought refuge in London. In December he pledged to return to Kenya and present a detailed dossier of his findings to the National Assembly's public accounts committee. Plans by members of the National Assembly to award themselves heavy bonuses provoked angry reactions on the part of church, business, and trade union leaders, and in the press. Pledges to tackle corruption had been announced in the budget in June, but were regarded sceptically since little was done to clear up outstanding cases.

In March the World Trade Organisation (WTO) held a three-day conference in Mombasa, with the focus on services. Kenya Airways announced a significant increase in profits and the start of scheduled flights to China. A South African consortium, Rift Valley Railways, won the right to run the Kenyan and Ugandan railways for the next twenty-five years (a decision to offer joint management of the railways for tender having been taken in 2003).

Kenya's June budget stressed the need to increase economic growth—it reached 4.3 per cent in 2004-05—in order to alleviate poverty. Measures to reduce the latter included the abolition of VAT on kerosene and milk, and easing the tax burden on the low-paid by raising the tax threshold. Health spending was to be stepped up—only 17 per cent of those needing anti-retroviral drugs against HIV/AIDS were being treated. Civil servants were to receive extra pay, with schoolteachers the main beneficiaries.

TANZANIA

CAPITAL: Dodoma   AREA: 945,000 sq km   POPULATION: 36,600,000
OFFICIAL LANGUAGES: Kiswahili & English   POLITICAL SYSTEM: multiparty republic in Commonwealth
HEAD OF STATE AND GOVERNMENT: President Jakaya Kikwete (CCM) (since Dec '05)
RULING PARTY: Chama Cha Mapinduzi (CCM)
PRESIDENT OF ZANZIBAR: Amani Abeid Karume (since Oct '00)
PRIME MINISTER: Edward Lowassa (since Dec '05)
MAIN IGO MEMBERSHIPS (NON-UN): AU, SADC, ACP, CWTH, NAM
CURRENCY: Tanzanian shilling (end-'05 £1=Tsh1,998.30, US$1=Tsh1,164.00)
GNI PER CAPITA: US$330 (mainland Tanzania only), US$660 at PPP ('04)

PRESIDENTIAL and legislative elections—delayed because of the death of a vice-presidential candidate—were held on 14 December. The presidential candidate of the ruling Chama cha Mapinduzi (CCM)—Foreign Minister Jakaya Kikwete—secured some 80 per cent of the votes; Ibrahim Lipumba, leader of the Civic United Front (CUF), his main challenger, and the eight other candidates shared the remainder. Kikwete pledged to use his huge legislative majority—the CCM won 206 of the 232 elected seats—to maintain the economic and social gains made by President Benjamin Mkapa, who stepped down having served two terms but remained as CCM chairman. The new President's priorities were to attract outside investment, exploit the country's rich mineral resources, and improve infrastructure, the weakness of which impeded the development of the agricultural sector upon which 80 per cent of the population depended.

While the voting on the mainland was peaceful, in semi-autonomous Zanzibar it was marred by violence; nine people were killed in Pemba. The presidential election in Zanzibar attracted six candidates, but as in the 1995 and 2000 polls, the main contest was between the CCM and CUF candidates: Amani Abeid Karume, the incumbent, and Seif Sharif Hamad, the CUF secretary-general. Karume was returned to power but the CUF maintained that the contest had been rigged.

Basil Mramba, the Finance Minister, said that despite the high growth rate of 6.7 per cent, the government would depend on foreign aid for 41 per cent of its spending in the forthcoming year. More than half the budget would go to implement the government's strategy for economic growth and reducing poverty. In January the UK government relieved Tanzania, which was classified as a "heavily indebted poor country", from paying 10 per cent of its debt to the World Bank over the next ten years. The money saved would be spent on increasing the number of children in secondary education, which stood at less than 10 per cent. In May the government cancelled its World Bank-funded water privatisation contract with BIWATER, a UK-based company, on the grounds that the water supply to Dar es Salaam had deteriorated rather than improved; BIWATER threatened legal action. This raised doubts about the wisdom of carrying out the next phase of privatisation, involving other utilities.

UGANDA

CAPITAL: Kampala   AREA: 241,000 sq km   POPULATION: 25,900,000
OFFICIAL LANGUAGE: English   POLITICAL SYSTEM: multiparty republic in Commonwealth
HEAD OF STATE AND GOVERNMENT: President Yoweri Museveni (since Jan '86)
RULING PARTY: National Resistance Movement (NRM) heads broad-based coalition
PRIME MINISTER: Apolo Nsibambi (since April '99)
MAIN IGO MEMBERSHIPS (NON-UN): AU, COMESA, ACP, CWTH, OIC, NAM
CURRENCY: new Uganda shilling (end-'05 £1=Ush3,122.77, US$1=Ush1,819.00)
GNI PER CAPITA: US$270, US$1,520 at PPP ('04, based on regression)

POLITICAL events threatened economic stability during the year. In February the unicameral Parliament approved a motion by 221 votes to eighteen, with three abstentions, to hold a referendum to determine whether Uganda should return to a multi-party system. On 28 July, 92.44 per cent of nearly 4 million people voted in favour, thus formally ending the no-party "movement" system which President Yoweri Museveni had introduced upon taking power in 1986 (see AR 1986, pp. 227-28).

Legislators amended the constitution to extend the two-year period that a president could serve and Museveni announced that he would seek re-election in March 2006. Tension mounted further when, in late October, Kizza Besigye, chairman of the Forum for Democratic Change, returned from exile in South Africa to present himself again as a presidential candidate: he had been easily defeated by Museveni in 2001 (see AR 2001, p. 264). His arrest and detention in November on charges of treason and rape were widely regarded as politically motivated and sparked riots in Kampala; his supporters were roughly treated by pro-government militias. A regime hitherto praised for its enlightened policies was condemned by human rights organisations, the domestic and overseas press, and the donor community. A December poll in a pro-government news-paper put Besigye ahead of Museveni in the urban areas and at the turn of the year a high court judge ruled that he had been illegally detained and freed him on bail, thereby enabling him to resume his election campaign.

The government withdrew its troops from the Democratic Republic of Congo (DRC) in May, but was reported to be using militias to protect its commercial interests in the mineral-rich Ituri district. In December the International Court of Justice (ICJ) at The Hague ordered Uganda to pay reparations for its unlaw-ful intervention and five-year occupation of the region (see pp. 418-19). Pro-tracted peace talks with the Lord's Resistance Army (LRA) proved abortive and the LRA continued its destructive raids into northern Uganda. In October the ICJ issued arrest warrants against Joseph Kony, the LRA rebel leader, his deputy, and three commanders.

The supposedly "pro-poor" budget increased excise duty on petrol and diesel, imposed higher licence fees on cars and motor cycles, and raised VAT from 17 to 18 per cent. There were also tax cuts—for example, on second-hand clothing and medicine—and a 29 per cent increase in funding for agriculture, which had been badly hit by drought. Donors were expected to contribute some 40 per cent of government expenditure.

The government, which had pioneered the fight against HIV/AIDS in Africa (see AR 1986, pp. 229-30; 1987, p. 244), was accused of obstructing the distribu-tion of condoms and of becoming over-dependent on the policies of sexual absti-nence and marital fidelity favoured by Janet Museveni, the First Lady. Homo-sexuality remained a crime punishable by life imprisonment.

Former President Milton Obote died in exile in October (for obituary see pp. 543-44).

NIGERIA—GHANA—SIERRA LEONE—THE GAMBIA—LIBERIA

NIGERIA

CAPITAL: Abuja   AREA: 924,000 sq km   POPULATION: 139,800,000
OFFICIAL LANGUAGE: English   POLITICAL SYSTEM: multiparty republic in Commonwealth
HEAD OF STATE AND GOVERNMENT: President (Gen. retd) Olusegun Obasanjo (since May '99)
RULING PARTY: People's Democratic Party (PDP)
MAIN IGO MEMBERSHIPS (NON-UN): AU, ECOWAS, OPEC, ACP, OIC, NAM, CWTH
CURRENCY: naira (end-'05 £1=N223.821, US$1=N130.375)
GNI PER CAPITA: US$390, US$930 at PPP ('04, based on regression)

NIGERIA enjoyed a relatively quiet political year while its President, Olusegun Obasanjo, earned enhanced respect as an ambassador for Africa, especially at the G-8 summit at the beginning of July.

Good governance and the fight against corruption were political priorities. The report of the human rights violations investigation committee (the Oputa panel) was made public in January: its principal conclusion was that three former military rulers had been responsible for extra-judicial killings during their periods in power. The panel had been established in 1999 by President Obasanjo. However, the sensitive nature of the findings relating to former military rulers had persuaded the government to suppress the report for two years until it was brought to light by the Nigeria Democratic Movement, a non-governmental organisation based in Washington DC, which published the report on its website. It made specific accusations against three former military rulers: General Muhammed Buhari (1983-85), General Ibrahim Babangida (1985-93), and General Abdulsalam Abubaker (1998), and recommended that they should be barred from holding public office.

The fight against corruption made headlines through the year. In January the inspector general of police, Tafa Balogun, took early retirement following an official investigation into allegations of money laundering. The economic and financial crimes commission (EFCC) investigation revealed money laundering involving more than N1 billion of treasury bills traced to eleven separate accounts controlled by Balogun. He was charged on seventy counts in April. In a separate case (also in January) Rear Admiral Samuel Kolawole and Rear Admiral Francis Agbiti were dismissed from the navy after a court-martial found them guilty of helping steal a tanker full of oil. On 22 March the President dismissed his Minister of Education, Fabian Osuji, for paying the president of the Senate (the upper house of the bicameral legislature) and other senators N55 million in bribes to increase the education budget. The scandal came to light a week after both houses of the legislature had presented the President with a revised budget for 2005 in excess of his proposals of October 2004 (see AR 2004, p. 238). Chief Adolphus Wabra, the president of the Senate, then resigned. In April the President dismissed another minister, Mobolaji Osomo, responsible for Housing and Urban Development, for repeatedly disobeying a presidential directive concerning the sale of government properties in Lagos to prominent individuals such as ministers, state governors, and family members of the President's wife. Obasanjo cancelled the sales and ordered a transparent bid process. On 15 September in London Diepseye

Alamieyeseigha, the governor of Bayelsa state in the Delta region, was arrested on theft and money laundering charges (UK£1 million in cash was seized from his London home).

Ngozi Okonjo-Iweala, Nigeria's female Finance Minister, received death threats and made many enemies as a result of her efforts to battle corruption. One of her first major victories was the discovery that there were 5,000 more names on the civil service payroll than people turning up to work. She had spent twenty years working in the World Bank when in 1999 Obasanjo asked her to return to Nigeria and help "clean house", a task which she pursued with notable courage.

On 11 January police in Germany arrested Abba Abacha, the son of the late dictator General Sani Abacha, on a Swiss extradition order relating to charges of money laundering, fraud, and abuse of administrative duties. In February the Swiss Supreme Court removed the final obstacle to the repayment to Nigeria of funds which had been deposited by President Abacha, and rejected an appeal by his family. The court ruled that the greater part of US$505 million of Abacha funds frozen in Swiss banks was "clearly of criminal origin" and that US$458 million could be returned to Nigeria at once. A further US$40 million would remain frozen in Switzerland while US$7 million was deemed "only probably of criminal origin" and would be transferred to an escrow (third party) account in Nigeria. The US$505 million total represented just under a quarter of the estimated US$2.2 billion that Abacha had deposited abroad during his dictatorship. Meanwhile, Abba Abacha was extradited to Switzerland and formally charged with money laundering. The first instalment of the laundered money (US$290 million) was returned to Nigeria in September.

Oil revenues in 2004 came to US$25 billion yet after thirty-five years of significant oil wealth almost 60 per cent of Nigerians were still living on less than US$1 a day. The promise of debt relief that emerged from the G-8 summit in July (see pp. 20-21) appeared less generous and more fraught by the end of the year. The much vaunted debt forgiveness deal for Nigeria, involving US$30 billion, required the country to repay US$12 billion of debt between October 2005 and March 2006 in order to get the remaining US$18 billion cancelled. Gordon Brown, the UK Chancellor of the Exchequer, described this as a small proportion of Nigeria's debt, when in fact it represented 40 per cent (twice the proportion required of Iraq in 2004). Brown claimed that Nigeria could afford this because of its oil revenue.

On 22 September 100 armed fighters from the separatist Niger Delta People's Volunteer Force (NDVF) stormed the Idama oil platform belonging to Chevron Oil in the Niger Delta to demand the immediate release of their leader, Alhaji Mujahid Dokuba-Asari, the self-styled "Lord of the Creek", who had been arrested and charged with treason. The platform was closed down. The NDVF threatened to continue violence throughout the Delta region until Dokuba-Asari was freed (see AR 2004, p. 237).

In October Nigeria's First Lady, Stella Obasanjo, died of post-operative complications having undergone fat-reducing cosmetic surgery in Spain.

In December Professor Dora Akunyili ("Doctor Dora"), the director general of the national agency for food and drug administration and control in Nigeria, received the international service human rights award for her public awareness campaign and clampdown on corruption which had led to an 80 per cent fall in the level of fake drugs being distributed in Nigeria. The World Health Organisation calculated that 10 per cent of drugs worldwide were fake: when Dr Dora took on the job in 2001 an estimated 80 per cent of drugs in Nigeria were fake, with sometimes deadly implications for those who were treated with them.

GHANA—SIERRA LEONE—THE GAMBIA—LIBERIA

Ghana

CAPITAL: Accra   AREA: 239,000 sq km   POPULATION: 21,100,000
OFFICIAL LANGUAGE: English   POLITICAL SYSTEM: multiparty republic in Commonwealth
HEAD OF STATE AND GOVERNMENT: President John Agyekum Kufuor (since Jan '01)
RULING PARTY: New Patriotic Party (NPP)
MAIN IGO MEMBERSHIPS (NON-UN): AU, ECOWAS, ACP, CWTH, NAM
CURRENCY: cedi (end-'05 £1=C15,622.4, US$1=C9,100.00)
GNI PER CAPITA: US$380, US$2,280 at PPP ('04, based on regression)

Sierra Leone

CAPITAL: Freetown   AREA: 72,000 sq km   POPULATION: 5,400,000
OFFICIAL LANGUAGE: English   POLITICAL SYSTEM: multiparty republic in Commonwealth
HEAD OF STATE AND GOVERNMENT: President Ahmad Tejan Kabbah (since March '96)
RULING PARTY: Sierra Leone People's Party (SLPP)
MAIN IGO MEMBERSHIPS (NON-UN): AU, ECOWAS, OIC, ACP, CWTH, NAM
CURRENCY: leone (end-'05 £1=Le5,034.40, US$1=Le2,932.51)
GNI PER CAPITA: US$200, US$790 at PPP ('04)

The Gambia

CAPITAL: Banjul   AREA: 11,300 sq km   POPULATION: 1,449,000
OFFICIAL LANGUAGE: English   POLITICAL SYSTEM: multiparty republic in Commonwealth
HEAD OF STATE AND GOVERNMENT: President (Col) Yahya Jammeh (since Sept '96), previously
    Chairman of Armed Forces Provisional Revolutionary Council (from July '94)
RULING PARTY: Alliance for Patriotic Reorientation and Construction (APRC)
MAIN IGO MEMBERSHIPS (NON-UN): AU, ECOWAS, ACP, CWTH, OIC, NAM
CURRENCY: dalasi (end-'05 £1=D49.2709, US$1=D28.7000)
GNI PER CAPITA: US$290, US$1,900 at PPP ('04, based on regression)

Liberia

CAPITAL: Monrovia   AREA: 97,750 sq km   POPULATION: 3,449,000
OFFICIAL LANGUAGE: English   POLITICAL SYSTEM: multiparty republic
HEAD OF STATE AND GOVERNMENT: Gyude Bryant, Chairman of interim administration (since Oct '03)
RULING PARTY: Congress for Democratic Change (CDC)
MAIN IGO MEMBERSHIPS (NON-UN): AU, ECOWAS, ACP, NAM
CURRENCY: Liberian dollar (end-'05 £1=L$90.9878, US$1=L$53.0000)
GNI PER CAPITA: US$110 ('04)

IN March GHANA celebrated forty-eight years of independence and appeared to have settled into a genuinely democratic mould under the New Patriotic Party whose leader, John Kufuor, had won a second term as President in December 2004. On 11 January Kufuor selected his new thirty-four member Cabinet, which included eleven new appointments. The President remitted the remainder of jail sentences passed on two former ministers of the opposition National Democratic Congress (NDC) in power from 1992 to 2000: these were Kwame Peprah (Finance) and Victor Selormey (his deputy) who had been jailed for four and eight years respectively for causing financial loss to the state.

There was an impressive improvement in the economy during the year, with GDP growth for 2006 forecast at 6 per cent. The cocoa and gold sectors—Ghana's most important commodities—showed particularly good results. An upbeat President Kufuor, on a visit to the UK at the beginning of November, claimed that inflation had been reduced from 50 to 14 per cent. The 2005 budget was presented by the government as oriented towards growth and job creation. However, in February the price of petrol was raised by 50 per cent from US$2 to US$3 per litre, reflecting global market conditions. The huge price rise had an adverse impact on the economy and especially hurt ordinary people whose transport costs rose dramatically. Whilst on the macro level the economy was stronger in 2005 than it had been five years earlier when Kufuor came to power, the stronger areas had not benefited the poorest people, and many rural inhabitants continued to live on US$1 a day.

Ghana claimed to be West Africa's most stable country. Therefore it was deeply concerned by unrest in neighbouring countries and the influx into Ghana of refugees who were seen as both a potential burden on the economy and a security risk. In April refugees from Darfur, on the other side of the continent, arrived in Ghana amidst widespread anger with the security services which appeared at a loss to know how they had entered the country. Later, rebels from the New Forces movement in neighbouring Côte d'Ivoire arrived in Ghana and once again the security services were criticised. Following the presidential elections of 24 April in neighbouring Togo there was a significant influx of refugees into Ghana. There was further alarm after a UN report revealed how rebel fighters from the wars in Liberia and Sierra Leone had been recruited by dissidents to create problems in other countries in the region. It was debatable as to whether these refugees posed a genuine threat to Ghana, but the anxiety reflected a growing global concern about migration and security issues. However, cross-border movement pre-dated colonial times, and was also permitted under the protocols of the Economic Community of West African States (ECOWAS), to which Ghana belonged.

After three years of peace, Sierra Leone began to put the war behind it. On a visit to London in March, the Vice President, Solomon Berewa, spoke with optimism of the future. The country was enjoying GDP growth of 6-7 per cent and had experienced single digit inflation over two years. These achievements, he said, owed much to massive international support from the UN, ECOWAS, and especially the UK, which had provided financial support for military, judicial and social reforms as well as budgetary support.

Further signs of the post-war recovery included the reopening in April of the Sierra Leone rutile (titanium dioxide) mines after ten years. These used to be the country's largest employer, the biggest taxpayer to government, and contributed 50 per cent of foreign exchange earnings. The government decided to levy only a 3 per cent tax on the diamond industry, which produced revenue of US$120 million in 2004; it rejected calls for a higher tax on the grounds that this would encourage smuggling. The government also decided to allow dual citizenship for members of Sierra Leone's diaspora to encourage its members to return or otherwise contribute to the country's development.

The Special Court which had been established in 2002 to judge war crimes committed during the civil war of 1991-2001 announced on 1 March that its chief prosecutor, David Crane, was to resign for family reasons as of July. In May the Court announced that it had elected Raja Fernando of Sri Lanka as its new president. He would replace Emmanuel Ayoola.

On 30 June the UN Security Council unanimously passed resolution 1610 (2005) to extend the peacekeeping mandate of the UN Mission in Sierra Leone (UNAMSIL) for a final six months until 31 December. UNAMSIL had been established in October 1999 and its mandate had last been extended in September 2004. The resolution envisaged a continued UN presence in the country to support the Sierra Leone government after the withdrawal of UNAMSIL at the end of the year. The UN Integrated Office in Sierra Leone (UNIOSIL) would be established for an initial twelve months from 1 January 2006. UNIOSIL's tasks would be to develop a national plan for human rights and establish a human rights commission; to help the National Electoral Commission conduct elections in 2007; to strengthen the Sierra Leone security sector; to co-ordinate with UN missions and regional organisations in West Africa in dealing with "cross border challenges" such as the illicit movement of small arms, human trafficking and smuggling; and to co-ordinate activities with the Special Court (war crimes tribunal).

However, the government faced a major problem in the capital, Freetown. Before the civil war it had had a population of 250,000 but this had grown to over a million as a result of the huge influx of refugees during the fighting. These were returning only slowly to their places of origin and so the capital remained crowded, with many living in poor conditions.

According to the constitution President Kabbah would step down in 2007 and two rival contenders for the presidency declared themselves during the year. These were the Vice President, Solomon Berewa, and Charles Margai, the nephew of Sierra Leone's first Prime Minister Sir Milton Margai.

In February THE GAMBIA celebrated forty years of independence, which it had achieved without struggle and without adopting any obvious political ideology. If independence had been easy, however, the subsequent effort to gain economic viability had been a struggle. Under President Colonel Yahya Jammeh, who had seized power in a 1994 military coup, the economic emphasis had been to develop private sector growth. Thus, in 2005 the Gambia was one of the few African countries on the World Bank's fast track initiative programme. After a difficult period in 2001-02, the economy made a strong recovery; during 2003 and 2004 GDP grew by 8.8 per cent and 8.6 per cent respectively. Even so, average per capita income amounted to a mere at US$290. Agriculture remained the key to the economy with 75 per cent of the labour force engaged in the sector, which contributed 25-30 per cent of GDP and generated about 40 per cent of export earnings. However, the agriculture sector faced severe problems such as inadequate investment, a declining labour supply, institutional bottlenecks, and inadequate rural infrastructure and market access. The economy remained heavily dependent upon aid but while donor flows accounted for 18 per cent of general revenue in 2004, they were estimated at only 7 per cent for 2005. The Gambia, with a debt ratio of 189 per cent of GDP hoped to meet its World Bank and IMF-determined heavily indebted poor countries (HIPC) completion point during the year.

In April, as part of his fight against corruption, President Jammeh announced the establishment of a public accountability and anti-corruption unit (PAACU) to combat corruption in the public service. The government also placed fresh emphasis upon education and health. The budget allocated 22 per cent of revenue to education, and gross enrolment in primary schools reached 91 per cent of eligible children. In the health sector the government established various agencies to improve nutrition and fight disease, including HIV/AIDS.

With presidential elections due in 2006, five opposition parties established the National Alliance for Democracy and Development (NADD) in order to present a credible challenge to Jammeh.

The climax of the year in Liberia was the October-November election battle for the presidency between the football star George Weah and the economist-politician Ellen Johnson-Sirleaf, but for most of the year the government and country were still trying to sort out the legacies of the civil war. The measure of the task was demonstrated by statistics which showed that at the end of the civil war in 2003 the economy had shrunk by 31 per cent, debts stood at US$3 billion, the unemployment rate was 80 per cent, and the national budget had shrunk to US$80 million from US$300 million prior to the war.

On 14 March the National Transitional Legislative Assembly (NTLA) voted unanimously to suspend the Speaker, George Dweh, and his deputy, Eddington Varmah, indefinitely, following an investigation into their administrative and financial malpractices. There was mounting popular support for strong action against corruption. Subsequently, the NTLA elected George Korkor and David Gballah as acting Speaker and acting Deputy Speaker respectively.

On 14 April the UN Security Council, in accordance with resolution 1521 (2003), decided to add five names to the international travel restrictions imposed by that resolution. These were George Dweh (the recently suspended Speaker), General Sumo Dennis, General Kia Farley, General Sampson Gwen, and General D. Benjamin Taylor Jr. On 21 June the UN Security Council adopted resolution 1607 (2005) to renew sanctions on diamonds until 21 December. Sanctions on timber, arms, and travel had been renewed for twelve months in December 2004. On 19 September, under resolution 1626 (2005) the Security Council extended the mandate of the UN Mission in Liberia (UNMIL) until 31 March 2006, and authorised a temporary increase in UN military personnel to a total of 15,520, to ensure that the UN support provided for the Special Court for Sierra Leone (the war crimes tribunal) did not reduce UNMIL's capabilities in Liberia.

By 11 October when George Weah, who was not yet forty, stood as one of twenty-two candidates for the presidency, huge excitement had been generated on behalf of the footballer who was a national hero. His main rival, Ellen Johnson-Sirleaf, by contrast, was a woman of sixty-six who had wide international experience working for Citibank, the UN, and the World Bank. On 10 October, the last day before polling, an estimated 100,000 people took to the streets in support of Weah, though more sober Liberians wanted Sirleaf. The elections were the first since the end of fourteen years of bloody civil war and witnessed a big turnout of voters. The results of the first round of voting gave Weah 30 per cent of the vote and Sirleaf 19.6 per cent. A run-off was set for 8 November, when, with 90 per cent of the votes counted, Sirleaf gained 59.1 per cent, and Weah 40.9 per cent. The run-off was given a clean bill of health by international observers who acted as monitors although supporters of Weah claimed that vote-rigging had taken place. Ellen Johnson-Sirleaf thus became Africa's first female President. She was due to assume her duties on 16 January 2006.

WEST AFRICAN FRANCOPHONE STATES—CENTRAL AFRICAN FRANC ZONE

SENEGAL—MAURITANIA—MALI—GUINEA—CÔTE D'IVOIRE— BURKINA FASO—TOGO—BENIN—NIGER

Senegal

CAPITAL: Dakar   AREA: 197,000 sq km   POPULATION: 10,500,000
OFFICIAL LANGUAGE: French   POLITICAL SYSTEM: multiparty republic
HEAD OF STATE AND GOVERNMENT: President Abdoulaye Wade (since April '00)
RULING PARTY: Front for Changeover (FAL) coalition
PRIME MINISTER: Macky Sall (since April '04)
MAIN IGO MEMBERSHIPS (NON-UN): AU, ECOWAS, UEMOA, ACP, OIC, NAM, Francophonie
CURRENCY: CFA franc (end-'05 £1=CFAFr954.700, US$1=CFAFr556.110)
GNI PER CAPITA: US$670, US$1,720 at PPP ('04, based on regression)

Mauritania

CAPITAL: Nouakchott   AREA: 1,026,000 sq km   POPULATION: 2,900,000
OFFICIAL LANGUAGES: French & Arabic   POLITICAL SYSTEM: multiparty republic
HEAD OF STATE AND GOVERNMENT: Colonel Ely Ould Mohamed Vall (since Aug '05)
RULING PARTY: Mauritanian Military Council for Justice and Democracy (MCJD) (military junta) (since August '05)
PRIME MINISTER: Sidi Mohamed Ould Boubacar (since August '05)
MAIN IGO MEMBERSHIPS (NON-UN): AU, UEMOA, AMU, AL, ACP, OIC, NAM, Francophonie
CURRENCY: ouguiya (end-'05 £1=O465.755, US$1=O271.300)
GNI PER CAPITA: US$420, US$2,050 at PPP ('04, based on regression)

Mali

CAPITAL: Bamako   AREA: 1,240,000 sq km   POPULATION: 11,900,000
OFFICIAL LANGUAGE: French   POLITICAL SYSTEM: multiparty republic
HEAD OF STATE AND GOVERNMENT: President Gen. (retd) Amadou Toumani Touré (since June '02)
RULING PARTY: Alliance for Democracy in Mali (ADEMA) is main party in presidential majority
PRIME MINISTER: Prime Minister Ousmane Issoufi Maiga (since April '04)
MAIN IGO MEMBERSHIPS (NON-UN): AU, ECOWAS, UEMOA, AL, ACP, OIC, NAM, Francophonie
CURRENCY: CFA franc (see above)
GNI PER CAPITA: US$360, US$980 at PPP ('04)

Guinea

CAPITAL: Conakry   AREA: 246,000 sq km   POPULATION: 8,100,000
OFFICIAL LANGUAGE: French   POLITICAL SYSTEM: multiparty republic
HEAD OF STATE AND GOVERNMENT: President (Gen.) Lansana Conté (since Dec '93); previously
    Chairman of Military Committee for National Recovery (from April '84)
RULING PARTY: Party of Unity and Progress (PUP)
PRIME MINISTER: Cellou Dalein Diallo (since Dec '04)
MAIN IGO MEMBERSHIPS (NON-UN): AU, ECOWAS, ACP, OIC, NAM, Francophonie
CURRENCY: Guinean franc (end-'05 £1=GFr7,390.62, US$1=GFr4,305.00)
GNI PER CAPITA: US$460, US$2,130 at PPP ('04)

Côte d'Ivoire

CAPITAL: Abidjan   AREA: 322,000 sq km   POPULATION: 17,100,000
OFFICIAL LANGUAGE: French   POLITICAL SYSTEM: transitional government under international super-
    vision
HEAD OF STATE AND GOVERNMENT: President Laurent Gbagbo (since Oct '00)
RULING PARTIES: Ivoirian Popular Front government controls south; rebel New Forces control north
PRIME MINISTER: Charles Konan Banny, (since Dec '05)
MAIN IGO MEMBERSHIPS (NON-UN): AU, ECOWAS, UEMOA, ACP, OIC, NAM, Francophonie
CURRENCY: CFA franc (see above)
GNI PER CAPITA: US$770, US$1,390 at PPP ('04)

Burkina Faso

CAPITAL: Ouagadougou   AREA: 274,000 sq km   POPULATION: 12,400,000
OFFICIAL LANGUAGE: French   POLITICAL SYSTEM: multiparty republic
HEAD OF STATE AND GOVERNMENT: President (Capt.) Blaise Compaoré (CDP) (since Dec '91); previ-
    ously Chairman of Popular Front (from Oct '87)
RULING PARTY: Congress for Democracy and Progress (CDP)
PRIME MINISTER: Paramanga Ernest Yoli (since Nov '00)
MAIN IGO MEMBERSHIPS (NON-UN): AU, ECOWAS, UEMOA, ACP, OIC, NAM, Francophonie
CURRENCY: CFA franc (see above)
GNI PER CAPITA: US$360, US$1,220 at PPP ('04, based on regression)

Togo

CAPITAL: Lomé   AREA: 57,000 sq km   POPULATION: 5,000,000
OFFICIAL LANGUAGES: French, Kabiye & Ewem   POLITICAL SYSTEM: multiparty republic
HEAD OF STATE AND GOVERNMENT: President Faure Gnassingbé (RPT) (since May '05)
RULING PARTY: Rally of the Togolese People (RPT)
PRIME MINISTER: Prime Minister Edem Kodjo (CPP) (since June '05)
MAIN IGO MEMBERSHIPS (NON-UN): AU, ECOWAS, ACP, OIC, NAM, Francophonie
CURRENCY: CFA franc (see above)
GNI PER CAPITA: US$380, US$1,690 at PPP ('04, based on regression)

Benin

CAPITAL: Porto Novo AREA: 113,000 sq km POPULATION: 6,900,000
OFFICIAL LANGUAGE: French POLITICAL SYSTEM: multiparty republic
HEAD OF STATE AND GOVERNMENT: President Mathieu Kérékou (since March '96)
RULING PARTY: Union for the Benin of the Future (UBF)
MAIN IGO MEMBERSHIPS (NON-UN): AU, ECOWAS, UEMOA, ACP, OIC, NAM, Francophonie
CURRENCY: CFA franc (see above)
GNI PER CAPITA: US$530, US$1,120 at PPP ('04)

Niger

CAPITAL: Niamey AREA: 1,267,000 sq km POPULATION: 12,100,000
OFFICIAL LANGUAGE: French POLITICAL SYSTEM: multiparty republic
HEAD OF STATE AND GOVERNMENT: President Mamadou Tandja (since Dec '99)
RULING PARTY: National Movement for a Society of Development (MNSD)
PRIME MINISTER: Prime Minister Hama Amadou (since Jan '00)
MAIN IGO MEMBERSHIPS (NON-UN): AU, ECOWAS, UEMOA, ACP, OIC, NAM, Francophonie
CURRENCY: CFA franc (see above)
GNI PER CAPITA: US$230, US$830 at PPP ('04, based on regression)

The year in SENEGAL saw the political position of President Abdoulaye Wade eroded, in a far cry from the early years of his presidency. Reverberations from the 2004 dismissal and arrest of former Prime Minister Idrissa Seck (see AR 2004, p. 245) continued to be felt. In July Seck's trial began on charges of embezzlement, before a special court reserved for criminal allegations against government officials. Reportedly, he said during a December court appearance: "Everything I did, Wade was in the know, and it was he who told me to do it".

There was increasing anger on the part of all the opposition parties, few of which remained in what had once been a broad coalition government, at the prospect of delaying the legislative elections. These had been scheduled for May 2006, but Wade announced that it would be cheaper to hold them at the same time as presidential elections due in March 2007. The National Assembly legislated to that effect in December, which led to a massive rally of all twenty-four opposition parties to launch a "*tout sauf Wade*" (everyone but Wade) campaign. Nevertheless, the President, aged seventy-nine, was apparently determined to stand for another seven-year term.

Problems for Wade also arose at the beginning of the year from his pardon and amnesty for the killers in 1993 of Maître Boubacar Sèye, the vice-president of the constitutional council. A book published in Paris by a prominent critic of the regime, Abdou Latif Coulibaly, implicated the President in the crime.

The dominant event in MAURITANIA was the coup d'état of 3 August, when President Maaouyia Ould Taya was in Saudi Arabia for the funeral of King Fahd. Ould Taya had been in power for twenty-one years, but his regime had become increasingly unstable and unpopular. The coup was bloodless and apparently welcomed by much of the population.

A ruling Military Council for Justice and Democracy (CMJD) was led by Colonel Ely Ould Mohammed Vall, the country's police chief, and comprised sixteen colonels and a naval commander. The announcement of the coup, several hours after the seizure of key buildings in the capital, Nouakchott, said: "The military and security forces have unanimously decided to put an end to the totalitarian practices of regime from which our people have suffered so much in the last years." The new council pledged to "establish favourable conditions for an open and transparent democratic system" adding it did not intend to stay in power for more than two years.

Opposition parties, while welcoming the coup, expressed the hope that the new rulers' promises would be implemented. The African Union (AU), the EU, and the USA all condemned the coup, but after an AU mission visited the country the organisation reversed its position—on the grounds that there was popular support for the coup—and instead appealed for elections to be held soon. Israel condemned the coup, although the new regime said that it would continue diplomatic relations (controversially opened by Taya's government) with the Jewish state in order not to "alienate Western opinion". The officers in the CMJD were said to have strong Arab nationalist opinions.

The CMJD appointed a new Prime Minister, Sidi Mohammed Ould Boubacar, who had already held the post in 1982-93 under the Taya regime, but had recently been in exile in France. In September an amnesty was announced for all political prisoners, including former military commander Saleh Ould Hanenna, sentenced to life imprisonment earlier in the year for a 2004 coup attempt. In the same trial, former President Mohammed Khouna Ould Haidallah, had been acquitted of treason (see AR 2004, p. 246).

It was a quiet year politically in MALI, although the economy was experiencing a period of continued growth. One of the world's poorest countries, Mali was one of the nations to benefit from debt relief as agreed at the July G-8 summit (see pp. 20-21). The President, Amadou Toumani Touré, at the end of the year hosted one of the largest international meetings that Mali had ever seen: the Africa-France summit (see pp. 363-64), using newly built conference facilities.

Government in GUINEA continued to be paralysed by the prolonged chronic illness of President Lansana Conté. Despite rampant inflation, a huge informal sector, rice riots, chaotic government, and deep poverty in a country of immense mineral wealth, the ailing diabetic President floundered on. At the beginning of the year Conté had survived an assassination attempt, when shots were fired at his motorcade. Despite rumours of an international plot, in February the popular Lieutenant Mamadouba "Toto" Camara was arrested and jailed for the attack.

In September, the country's mounting disorganisation led a coalition of the main opposition politicians, the Republican Front for Democratic Change, to appeal for the President to resign in order to prevent a feared slide into chaos, saying: "You have become a brake, an obstacle to Guinea's development. [. . .] You are sick, you must make the wise decision to leave now before others make it for you."

At the end of the year, however, municipal elections saw the ruling party, the Party for Unity and Progress (PUP), register a convincing victory in most constituencies, although the opposition alleged there were grave irregularities.

The year in CÔTE D'IVOIRE saw a continuation of "no peace, no war", which had prevailed since the outbreak of conflict and de facto partitioning of the country in September 2002. The beginning of the year was dominated by the mediation of South Africa's President Thabo Mbeki, appointed in November 2004 in view of the stalemated mediation of West Africans, the non-implementation of previous peace deals, and the increased tension around the anti-French campaign of that month (see AR 2004, pp. 248-49).

The Mbeki mediation got off the ground slowly, as the South Africans sought to be methodical, and were disconcerted by early statements from President Jacques Chirac of France that South Africans would have difficulty mastering the crisis because they did not understand "the soul and psychology of west Africans". The rebels in the North, who called themselves the "New Forces", were suspicious of the South Africans, who they felt were too close to President Laurent Gbagbo. The fact that both Gbagbo's Ivoirian Popular Front (FPI) and the ruling African National Congress of South Africa were together in the Socialist International reinforced that suspicion. After a period of prevarication and delay, all parties were invited to a meeting in Pretoria and signed a new peace deal essentially based on the 2003 Linas-Marcoussis accord engineered by the French, which had never been fully implemented (see AR 2003, p. 290).

The Pretoria accord contained the important innovation that President Gbagbo agreed that his principal opponent, Alassane Ouattara, could personally stand in the presidential elections, which it was reaffirmed could still take place before 30 October. The issue of Ivoirian nationality (known as *Ivoirité*), which had been a bone of contention since 1995 and had led to the ban on Ouattara in that year and in 2000 (on the grounds that he was more Burkinabe than Ivoirian, see AR 2000, p. 251), was still to be decided through legislation by the Gbagbo-controlled National Assembly.

France meanwhile had sought reinforced backing from the UN, in view of increased feelings of vulnerability after anti-French demonstrations. The Pretoria accord led to an extension of the mandate of the UN operation (ONUCI), supported by 6,000 UN troops, in addition to the separately administered 4,000 French troops of Operation Licorne, in place in the "zone of confidence" between north and south since October 2002.

Of equal importance to the breakthrough over Ouattara was a fresh agreement on the difficult issue of disarmament of the New Forces and their integration into the National Army. This was a key aim of Gbagbo and his party, and although a first military meeting took place, incidents in the west of Côte d'Ivoire, at Douékoué, in which northerners were massacred, damaged northern confidence and thus prevented progress. A further meeting in Pretoria in June attempted to re-launch the process, but this time a serious new obstacle emerged in the shape of half-hearted legislation on both *Ivoirité* and the elections, which aroused fresh suspicions in the North.

This new blockage exasperated the South Africans who felt that the legislation embodied a measured compromise, but they had underestimated the real fears of the North. Fresh frictions between populations worsened the situation, and statements by South African ministers caused New Forces' spokesmen to say that they no longer had confidence in the South African mediation. It thus became clear that no elections could take place by 30 October, as disarmament had not begun and an electoral commission had not been created.

Officially, the South Africans continued their role until the AU's security summit in Addis Ababa, Ethiopia, on 9 October, which recommended Gbagbo's continuation in office for another year, during which elections would have to be held. Most significantly, a new prime minister would be appointed to replace Seydou Diarra, who had been in power since Linas-Marcoussis and had been stymied systematically by Gbagbo and the FPI. At this point the AU chairman, President Olusegun Obasanjo of Nigeria, re-entered the fray and, jointly with Mbeki, helped facilitate the choice of a prime minister. This took a whole month. Eventually, at the Africa-France summit in Togo in early December, the two Presidents joined with President Chirac of France in announcing the name of Charles Konan Banny, for the previous fifteen years the chairman of the West African Central Bank (BCEAO). One of the main obstacles to his nomination had been former President Konan Bedié, a fellow Baoulé (and hence a possible political competitor), who only gave his assent when Banny promised he would not stand in the presidential elections. Although a southerner, Banny had a close relationship with Ouattara, his predecessor at the BCEAO.

Banny took a month to form a government, with all parties represented, and rapidly found that his background as a banker and technocrat had not prepared him for the jungle of Ivoirian politics. He faced objections from the FPI and the Gbagbo clan, who were alarmed that they had lost the key portfolios of Finance and Defence to non-political appointees. They were also concerned at reports that Banny, in co-operation with the international community, planned to engineer the dissolution of the FPI-dominated National Assembly, a move that he believed necessary to ensure that the planned elections were free and fair.

In Burkina Faso the authoritarian grip of President Blaise Compaoré, in power for eighteen years, showed no sign of relenting. This was apparent in the manner in which he engineered his re-election on 13 November in the country's first contested multi-party race. He defeated a field of twelve opponents, in the face of bitter opposition criticisms, assisted by the opposition's inability to field a single candidate.

The result announced by the Independent National Election Commission gave the President 80.3 per cent of the vote, with his nearest rival, Benewende Stanislas Sankara, obtaining 4.94 per cent. Some opposition candidates alleged fraud, but observers from "tame" organisations like La Francophonie said that the election had been fair. The President's campaign manager estimated that the cost of the campaign had been about US$1.8 million.

Togo in 2005 was plunged into political turmoil by the death on 5 February of the country's dictator, President Gnassingbé Eyadéma, who had ruled for thirty-eight uninterrupted years (for obituary see p. 531). Two days later, at the instigation of leading members of the military, his thirty-nine-year-old son Faure Gnass-ingbé was installed as President, although the constitution stipulated that the president of the National Assembly (the unicameral legislature), Foumbara Natchaba, should assume the office for sixty days prior to elections. Natchaba, on an aircraft returning from Paris, was diverted to neighbouring Benin, where he was kept in seclusion whilst the legislature obediently amended the constitution to legitimise Faure Gnassingbé's succession. Natchaba, although in the camp of the presidential party, was considered too strong-willed a character to protect the Gnassingbé family's interests.

The international reaction, especially in West Africa, was much stronger than Togo's ruling ethno-military clique had anticipated. The move was condemned by the chairman of ECOWAS, President Tandja of Niger, and AU chairman President Obasanjo of Nigeria, while the president of the AU commission, former Malian President Alpha Oumar Konaré, openly described the events as a "coup d'état", saying that no AU member should recognise the new regime until democracy was restored. ECOWAS leaders met in emergency session, imposed an arms embargo, and suspended Togo's membership.

Equally influential were strong international condemnations, notably from the USA and the EU, which resumed the aid embargo that had begun to be relaxed late in 2004 (see AR 2004, pp. 249-50). Even France, which had been one of the late President's principal supporters, felt obliged to distance itself. There was also a mass demonstration against the new regime in the capital, Lomé, on 19 February.

Two days after assuming office, after visiting the Presidents of Libya and Gabon, Faure Gnassingbé announced he was stepping down and returning the country to constitutional rule. However, it was not Speaker Natchaba, but his deputy, Abass Bonfoh, who was installed as the acting head of state, charged with the organisation of elections. Notwithstanding the firm stand of African states against usurpation of power, it was soon apparent that there was still everything to play for, as the new attachment to constitutional observance meant that Togo's main opposition leader, Gilchrist Olympio, would once again be excluded from the election on the grounds of residency qualifications. The government proceeded to call elections for 23 April; the sanctions imposed in Africa were lifted and recognition restored.

Olympio's party, the Union of Forces for Change (UFC), chose as its "surrogate" candidate the septuagenarian Emmanuel Bob Akitani, who had already discharged this function in 2003 when Olympio had likewise been excluded (see AR 2003, pp. 291-92). The campaign was difficult, with outbreaks of violence, and opposition media harassment, and the UFC's computers were all destroyed on election eve. Under the circumstances the UFC did well to secure 38 per cent of the vote, against the 60 per cent won by Faure Gnassingbé, who was duly declared President amidst a host of opposition protests. ECOWAS observers deemed the election free and fair, despite obvious irregularities such as the fact that all telephone communications, except those of the military, were cut from the eve of the election to the announcement of the result.

A post-election demonstration was ferociously repressed, with possibly hundreds of demonstrators killed. In the aftermath of the election some 30,000 refugees fled to neighbouring Ghana and Benin, although a government-sponsored inquiry into the violence blamed the deaths on the opposition. Attempts by Nigeria's President to mediate between Gnassingbé and Olympio with the aim of creating a government of national unity foundered, and President Gnassingbé was obliged to turn to a tame opposition leader, Edem Kodjo, who had played the role before, as Prime Minister.

Although the new President promised reforms in his father's system of government in such areas as the judiciary and the media, his real intentions remained unclear. Although some old guard were cleared from the army, the Gnassingbé family—through the President, and his brother Kpatcha Gnassingbé, the Minister of Defence—appeared to be tightening its grip on security while preaching moderation and openness. Since the French had provided endorsement, as well as ECOWAS neighbours, the most important arbiter now seemed to be the EU, which still insisted on its twenty-two conditions for democracy, few of which had been implemented by the end of year.

The Republic of BENIN in 2005 saw the twilight of the long rule of President Mathieu Kérékou, who had first came to power as a young coup-making colonel in 1972. Now over seventy, and not in good health—although still capable in 1996 and 2001 of winning elections conducted in an atmosphere that was relatively free and fair—he finally let it be known in the course of the year that he would not be standing again in the elections scheduled for March 2006.

Towards the end of the year, however, he began to warn that it might not be possible to hold the elections on the allotted date because of lack of government funds. It was not clear if this was due to genuine bankruptcy, or merely a desire to extract more funding from a not entirely generous international community

NIGER once again found itself the focus of unwelcome international attention because of the ravages of regular cyclical drought, which hit especially cruelly in 2005. With a particular irony, the news broke internationally just after the "Live-8" concerts at the time of the G-8 summit had brought some of Africa's problems to the attention of the world audience. President Mamadou Tandja felt obliged to criticise the publicity because he believed that agencies (and even the UN) were using Niger's misfortune to pump up their fundraising efforts.

The year had a promising beginning, as Tandja had been re-elected for a second term late in 2004, and then became ECOWAS chairman in January. He was embroiled in mediation in the Ivoirian crisis (see above), which—as others had already discovered—was a frustrating exercise. It was hard for him to play a neutral role, as Nigeriens were lumped together with all the Sahelians, including those from the north of Côte d'Ivoire, as "foreigners".

CAMEROON—CHAD—GABON—CONGO—CENTRAL AFRICAN REPUBLIC—EQUATORIAL GUINEA

Cameroon

CAPITAL: Yaoundé   AREA: 475,000 sq km   POPULATION: 16,400,000
OFFICIAL LANGUAGES: French & English   POLITICAL SYSTEM: multiparty republic in Commonwealth
HEAD OF STATE AND GOVERNMENT: President Paul Biya (since Nov '82)
RULING PARTY: Cameroon People's Democratic Movement (CPDM)
PRIME MINISTER: Ephraim Inoni (since Dec '04)
MAIN IGO MEMBERSHIPS (NON-UN): AU, CEEAC, ACP, OIC, CWTH, NAM, Francophonie
CURRENCY: CFA franc (end-'05 £1=CFAFr954.700, US$1=CFAFr556.110)
GNI PER CAPITA: US$800, US$2,090 at PPP ('04)

Chad

CAPITAL: Ndjaména   AREA: 1,284,000 sq km   POPULATION: 8,800,000
OFFICIAL LANGUAGES: French & Arabic   POLITICAL SYSTEM: multiparty republic
HEAD OF STATE AND GOVERNMENT: President (Col) Idriss Déby (since Dec '90)
RULING PARTIES: Patriotic Salvation Movement (MPS), Union for Renewal and Democracy (URD)
   & National Union for Development and Renewal (UNDR)
PRIME MINISTER: Pascal Yoadimnadji (since Feb '05)
MAIN IGO MEMBERSHIPS (NON-UN): AU, CEEAC, ACP, OIC, NAM, Francophonie
CURRENCY: CFA franc (see above)
GNI PER CAPITA: US$260, US$1,420 at PPP ('04)

Gabon

CAPITAL: Libreville   AREA: 268,000 sq km   POPULATION: 1,374,000
OFFICIAL LANGUAGE: French   POLITICAL SYSTEM: multiparty republic
HEAD OF STATE AND GOVERNMENT: President Omar Bongo (PDG) (since March '67)
RULING PARTY: Gabonese Democratic Party (PDG)
PRIME MINISTER: Jean-François Ntoutoume-Emane (since Feb '99)
MAIN IGO MEMBERSHIPS (NON-UN): AU, CEEAC, ACP, OIC, NAM, Francophonie
CURRENCY: CFA franc (see above)
GNI PER CAPITA: US$3,940, US$5,600 at PPP ('04)

Congo

CAPITAL: Brazzaville   AREA: 342,000 sq km   POPULATION: 3,900,000
OFFICIAL LANGUAGE: French   POLITICAL SYSTEM: multiparty republic
HEAD OF STATE AND GOVERNMENT: President Denis Sassou-Nguesso (since Oct '97)
RULING PARTIES: Congolese Labour Party (PCT) heads United Democratic Forces alliance
MAIN IGO MEMBERSHIPS (NON-UN): CEEAC, ACP, NAM, Francophonie
CURRENCY: CFA franc (see above)
GNI PER CAPITA: US$770, US$750 at PPP ('04)

Central African Republic

CAPITAL: Bangui   AREA: 623,000 sq km   POPULATION: 3,900,000
OFFICIAL LANGUAGE: French   POLITICAL SYSTEM: transitional government
HEAD OF STATE AND GOVERNMENT: President Gen. François Bozizé (since March '03)
RULING PARTIES: National Convergence "Kwa Na Kwa" (KNK) coalition
PRIME MINISTER: Elie Dote (since June '05)
MAIN IGO MEMBERSHIPS (NON-UN): AU, CEEAC, ACP, OIC, NAM, Francophonie
CURRENCY: CFA franc (see above)
GNI PER CAPITA: US$310, US$1,110 at PPP ('04, based on regression)

Equatorial Guinea

CAPITAL: Malabo   AREA: 28,000 sq km   POPULATION: 506,000
OFFICIAL LANGUAGES: Spanish & French   POLITICAL SYSTEM: multiparty republic
HEAD OF STATE AND GOVERNMENT: President (Brig.-Gen.) Teodoro Obiang Nguema Mbasogo (since
    Aug '79)
RULING PARTY: Equatorial Guinea Democratic Party (PDGE)
PRIME MINISTER: Miguel Abia Biteo Borico (since June '04)
MAIN IGO MEMBERSHIPS (NON-UN): AU, CEEAC, ACP, NAM, Francophonie
CURRENCY: CFA franc (see above)
GNI PER CAPITA: US$3,256-10,065 ('04 est), US$7,400 at PPP ('04)

The year in CAMEROON fell between elections, so there was a greater tendency to concentrate on the economy. Relations with the donor community seemed in better shape than previously, when the IMF had been severely critical of aspects of governance. The government's three year economic programme received cautious approval, and Cameroon hoped that it might be on course for debt alleviation in 2006.

It was another difficult year for CHAD, as President Idris Déby struggled with an increasingly problematic military situation, as well as increased dissidence within his own army. The side-effects of the Darfur rebellion in neighbouring Sudan continued to be felt, both in the form of cross-border attacks by the Janjawid militias, and the fact that Déby's own ethnic group— the Zaghawa, who dominated the Chadian army—straddled the border (see p 203; AR 2004, p. 253).

In September there was another coup plot, and in December one of Déby's closest collaborators, his nephew and former head of presidential administration Tom Erdimi, with a group of dissident officers, called on the army to overthrow the President. This was followed by a serious attack over the border on the oasis of Adré by a group of rebels, who were reinforced by a number of deserters from the Chadian army. At the end of November Déby had already complained that Sudan was arming rebels with a view to destabilising Chad, and at the end of December he sought mediation from both Nigeria and Libya.

CENTRAL AFRICAN REPUBLIC saw a period of further consolidation for President François Bozizé, in power since a coup in 2003 (see AR 2003, pp. 295-96). After a number of delays, the long-promised presidential and legislative elections were held on 13 March, although the first round of voting was inconclusive. The incumbent, Bozizé, secured 43 per cent, while Martin Ziguélé, a former Prime Minister, won 27 per cent, and André Kolinga, President in the 1980s, obtained 13 per cent. The second round run-off on 22 May gave Bozizé 64.6 per cent and Zeguélé 35.4 per cent. Bozizé had described the election as "a novel event in the Central African Republic: a true democracy is being established".

In GABON the year was dominated by preparations for the presidential elections of November. Although President Omar Bongo Ondimba took the country through the motions of a democratic exercise, there was little doubt that he would be returned for another seven-year term of office, although he turned seventy in

December. In the election, he received 79.21 per cent of votes cast, with his near-est rival, Pierre Mamboundou, obtaining 13.57 per cent. Predictably, both Mam-boundou and the third-placed candidate, Zacharie Myboto, claimed that there had been massive fraud.

It was a difficult year for the Republic of CONGO, where, in spite of the strong-armed rule of President Denis Sassou Nguesso, signs of instability continued. In January a purge of the army was announced along with a sweeping reform of all the security services because of "anarchic recruitment". At the same time former rebel leader Frederic Bitsangou, who was connected to the notorious Ninja mili-tia, announced a disarmament of troops within his fiefdom, the "Pool" area around Brazzaville. However, in April a group of dissident Ninja attacked a UN convoy in the south. The Ninja question arose again later in the year, when the founder of the movement, former Prime Minister Bernard Kolélas, in exile since 2000, was allowed to return for the burial of his wife. Fervour at his return led to violence in the suburbs of the capital. In December he was granted a full amnesty.

Also in April, it was announced that the government had foiled a coup plot by a group of officers arrested for arms thefts at the gendarmerie armoury. A number of further arrests of soldiers had been made in the capital and in Pointe Noire, and in July a major trial of a group of senior army officers in what was called the "Brazzaville Beach affair", exposed by human rights groups, began. They were accused of killing 335 refugees returning from Democratic Republic of the Congo (DRC) in 1999. The charges included genocide, crimes against humanity, and murder, but the trial rapidly ran into procedural difficulties, and a month later ended with all of the accused being acquitted. The court found that they were not "individually responsible" for the killings.

EQUATORIAL GUINEA continued to experience vertiginous growth rates, as well as apparent continued ease in ignoring the appeals from opposition parties and international human rights organisations against the continued stranglehold of the Nguema clan which had dominated the country's politics since independ-ence in 1968.

The year began with the conclusion of the "Mark Thatcher affair", the bizarre conspiracy between opposition leader Severo Moto and a group of South African-based mercenaries to overthrow the Equato-Guinean government. In January, after a plea-bargaining with the South African authorities, Sir Mark Thatcher (son of the former British Prime Minister) pleaded guilty to helping to fund the coup plotters by chartering a helicopter. Thatcher, who had been jailed in Zimbabwe, paid a UK£265,000 fine and left the country. Plotters remained in prison in both Zimbabwe and in Equatorial Guinea, although in March the Zimbabwe High Court cut their sentences, and the six-man Armenian air crew of the helicopter were released in Malabo in June. The government in Malabo tried to mend fences with the UK government (which had admitted that it had known something was in the offing) by appointing a senior party official to be ambassador in London. In September, however, the Equato-Guinean government lost the claim for damages that it had brought in London against some of the mercenaries and their celebrity financiers, making it an affair from which only lawyers benefited.

Before the end of the year it was reported that oil revenues had risen to US$4.2 million per day, and were likely to be swelled further by revenues from gas deposits. It was expected that state coffers should benefit to the tune of US$2 billion in 2006. However, the UN's human development index recorded the country as slipping further into poverty, since few of the extra funds were being spent productively.

GUINEA-BISSAU—CAPE VERDE—SÃO TOMÉ & PRÍNCIPE

Guinea-Bissau

CAPITAL: Bissau   AREA: 36,000 sq km   POPULATION: 1,533,000
OFFICIAL LANGUAGE: Portuguese   POLITICAL SYSTEM: transitional government
HEAD OF STATE AND GOVERNMENT: President João Bernardo "Nino" Vieira (since Oct '05)
RULING PARTIES: Forum of Convergence for Development coalition
PRIME MINISTER: Aristides Gomes (PAIGC) (since Nov '05)
MAIN IGO MEMBERSHIPS (NON-UN): AU, ECOWAS, UEMOA, ACP, OIC, NAM, CPLP, Francophonie
CURRENCY: CFA franc (end-'05 £1=CFAFr954.700, US$1=CFAFr556.110)
GNI PER CAPITA: US$160, US$690 at PPP ('04)

Cape Verde

CAPITAL: Praia   AREA: 4,000 sq km   POPULATION: 481,000
OFFICIAL LANGUAGE: Portuguese   POLITICAL SYSTEM: multiparty republic
HEAD OF STATE: President Pedro Pires (since March '01)
RULING PARTY: African Party for the Independence of Cape Verde (PAICV)
HEAD OF GOVERNMENT: José Maria Pereira Neves, Prime Minister (since Feb '01)
MAIN IGO MEMBERSHIPS (NON-UN): AU, ECOWAS, ACP, NAM, CPLP, Francophonie
CURRENCY: CV escudo (end-'05 £1=CVEsc160.516, US$1=CvEsc93.5000)
GNI PER CAPITA: US$1,770, US$5,650 at PPP ('04, based on regression)

São Tomé & Príncipe

CAPITAL: São Tomé   AREA: 965 sq km   POPULATION: 161,000
OFFICIAL LANGUAGE: Portuguese   POLITICAL SYSTEM: multiparty republic
HEAD OF STATE AND GOVERNMENT: President Fradique de Menezes (since Sept. '01)
RULING PARTIES: Movement for the Liberation of São Tomé and Príncipe (MLSTP) leads coalition
PRIME MINISTER: Maria do Carmo Trovoada Pires de Carvalho Silveira (MLSTP) (since June '05)
MAIN IGO MEMBERSHIPS (NON-UN): AU, CEEAC, ACP, NAM, CPLP, Francophonie
CURRENCY: dobra (end-'05 £1=Db12,480.8, US$1=Db7,270.00)
GNI PER CAPITA: US$370 ('04)

GUINEA-BISSAU was still struggling for political stability in the aftermath of the civil war of 1998-99. An important step in the process was the holding of presidential elections, the first since the bloodless military coup against former President Kumba Yalla in 2003 (see AR 2003, p. 305). Though the election proceeded relatively peacefully, it led to new tensions.

After being cleared by the Supreme Court to stand in the election, Yalla announced that his overthrow had been illegitimate and that he remained President. Neither this nor his brief seizure of the presidential building ahead of the poll helped him secure victory in the first round of voting in June, in which he came third. In a second round, in July, victory went to João Bernardo "Nino" Vieira, a highly controversial figure who had came to power in a coup, then been deposed in the civil war. His victory was contested by the ruling party within the legislature, the original liberation movement, the African Party for the Independence of Guinea-Bissau and Cape Verde (PAIGC). Its leader, Prime Minister Carlos Gomes Junior, initially said that he would not recognise the new President. In September a group of PAIGC legislators defected to Vieira, after which the Forum of Convergence for Development, a loose opposition coalition, claimed a legislative majority. In October, after months of feuding, Vieira sacked Carlos Gomes and in November replaced him with Aristides Gomes, one of the defectors from the PAIGC. In the new government, five ministers were members of Yalla's Social Renovation Party (PRS) and the PAIGC was effectively excluded.

The government of Prime Minister José Maria Neves spent much time in 2005 trying to integrate CAPE VERDE into the European Union. Neves won support for the idea from leading politicians of the former colonial power, Portugal, and then visited a number of European countries in November to argue the case for a special partnership between Cape Verde and the EU. Neves mentioned as an eventual goal full EU membership for Cape Verde, with euros replacing escudos as the country's currency.

The completion in 2005 of a new international airport close to the capital was expected further to boost tourism, which had grown by 25 per cent per year since 2000. Meanwhile, in July the US government's millennium challenge corporation approved aid of US$110 million to Cape Verde over five years to support poverty reduction and economic growth.

By the end of 2005 the government of the twin-island state of SÃO TOMÉ & PRÍNCIPE had not received the promised initial bonanza from oil. The government, dependent on the US$5 million earned from cocoa exports and some US$25 million of foreign aid, remained strapped for cash. The signing of production contracts for five offshore oil exploration licences in the joint development zone (JDZ) shared with Nigeria was supposed to have triggered the payment of some US$55 million to São Tomé, but this was jeopardised by the award of the most promising two offshore blocks to the Texas-based, but Nigerian-controlled, oil company Environmental Remediation Holding Corporation (ERHC), which had no experience of oil exploration and few financial resources. Both the country's attorney general and the Movement for the Liberation of São Tomé and Príncipe (MLSTP, the foremost party within the coalition government) were highly critical of the award to ERHC. Over this issue and his inability to deal with a civil service strike over the non-payment of salaries, Prime Minister Damião Vaz d'Almeida resigned on 2 June.

President Fradique de Menezes admitted that the terms negotiated by ERHC meant that São Tomé would forfeit some of the front-end bonuses that had been expected, but he would not approve a review of the licenses. As relations between the President and the MLSTP deteriorated, the latter called for the presidential and legislative elections scheduled for 2006 to be brought forward, but Menezes refused. As the year ended, it was revealed that the Foreign Minister, Ovideo Pequeño, a close ally of Menezes, had spent nearly US$500,000 of aid from Morocco on equipment for the presidency and the Foreign Ministry. Key foreign donors warned that they would not disburse further funds if aid was used in this way. With the government cash-starved, the police and the rapid reaction security force trained in Angola threatened to take to the streets to protest against the non-payment of salaries and poor working conditions.

Realising that oil would be no quick fix for the poverty in which over half the population lived, the government—now led by Maria do Carmo Silveira—in December asked donors for US$169 million to finance the first three years of a plan to lift 50,000 people out of poverty and improve the country's infrastructure. US$60 million was pledged, but it remained to be seen how successfully the plan could be implemented, even if the country's external debt—one of the highest per capita in the world—were cancelled.

VII CENTRAL AND SOUTHERN AFRICA

DEMOCRATIC REPUBLIC OF CONGO—BURUNDI AND RWANDA—
MOZAMBIQUE—ANGOLA

DEMOCRATIC REPUBLIC OF CONGO

CAPITAL: Kinshasa   AREA: 2,345,000 sq km   POPULATION: 54,800,000
OFFICIAL LANGUAGE: French   POLITICAL SYSTEM: transitional government
HEAD OF STATE AND GOVERNMENT: President Maj.-Gen. Joseph Kabila (since Jan '01)
RULING PARTIES: coalition including government forces and members of rebel groups
MAIN IGO MEMBERSHIPS (NON-UN): AU, SADC, COMESA, CEEAC, ACP, Francophonie, NAM
CURRENCY: Congo franc (end-'05 £1=CFr755.372, US$1=CFr440.000)
GNI PER CAPITA: US$120, US$680 at PPP ('04, based on regression)

ON 18 and 19 December, the holding of the referendum on the constitution completed the first stage of the long-awaited electoral process in the transitional period after the DRC's civil war. The often-delayed referendum—a major logistical achievement with 24 million registered voters—took place peacefully at over 40,000 polling stations. Moderate levels of participation were reported, and initial results indicated that "yes" votes had reached high levels, especially in the east, and that even in Kinshasa approval ranked marginally higher than rejection. Civic groups and opposition parties criticised a lack of voter education, with some calling for a boycott, although the authorities said that 500,000 copies of the text had been distributed. Constitutional provisions included limiting presidential terms to a maximum of two, doubling the number of provinces (with considerable fiscal independence from the centre), and the granting of citizenship to anybody resident in the country at independence in 1960. There was strong international pressure for a "yes" vote from members of the International Committee in Support of the Transition in the DRC, under the aegis of the UN.

Bickering between political groupings threatened to destabilise the transition, however. In January South Africa's President Thabo Mbeki had intervened to dissuade Jean-Pierre Bemba, leader of the Mouvement pour la Libération du Congo (MLC), from pulling out of the fragile transitional government, after an official of the country's independent electoral commission announced that elections might be delayed by six months. Subsequently, several people were killed in riots in Kinshasa. Parties participating in the transitional structures tended to sympathise with deadline extensions, while those outside remained opposed. As voter registration advanced, calls by the Union pour la démocratie et le progrès social (UDPS) for demonstrations in late June were not backed by religious or student leaders, although clashes with police led to deaths in Kinshasa, Tshikapa, and Mbuji-Mayi.

The government failed to control inflation or to hold the value of the franc steady. Twelve-month inflation rose to 26 per cent in May and the franc depreciated from CF391 to CF515 to the dollar between June 2004 and April, although it recovered slightly to CF450 in mid-June. In February, an IMF mission recommended continued support despite the failure to achieve monetary and debt targets. Recognising that corruption as well as mismanagement remained issues, the presidency launched an anti-corruption operation dubbed "clean hands" in October, and four officials were arrested for embezzlement. A report published in November estimated that over US$30 million of tax revenue had been stolen between 2001 and 2005.

The ongoing crisis in eastern Congo, where UN and government troops faced off against different militia groups, was the most intractable of the problems facing the government, and remained entangled with political problems in Uganda and Rwanda (see AR 2004, p. 259). The Rwandan government insisted on the right to fight rebels from the Forces démocratiques pour la libération du Rwanda in both North and South Kivu regions. According to MONUC (the UN force), there were about 8,000 Rwandan fighters still in the DRC, most of them not *Interahamwe* (the Hutu militia responsible for the 1994 Rwandan genocide). Relations with Uganda worsened late in the year after incursions by the Lord's Resistance Army (LRA) into Congolese territory. A UN report published in February accused Uganda of violating the UN arms embargo by continuing to ship armaments to militias in the north-eastern Ituri region, and in December an International Court of Justice judgement ordered Uganda to pay compensation to the DRC, in the order of billions of dollars, for destabilising eastern Congo (see pp. 220; 418-19).

Renewed fighting broke out in the war-torn Ituri district in January, between the predominantly Hema Union des patriotes congolais (UPC) and the Lendu Front nationaliste intégrationiste (FNI) (see AR 2004, p. 258), displacing thousands of people, and necessitating further relief operations by UN agencies and non-governmental organisations. At the same time, UN forces continued to work to persuade fighters to disarm and demobilise, with mixed success. By the end of the year the security situation had improved significantly, partly as a result of the deployment of government and UN troops in the gold mining areas of Kilo and Mongwalu. In November, around a thousand militia fighters surrendered, although some subsequently escaped, and in December a militia leader accused of massacring UN peacekeepers in February was arrested, sending a strong signal to other rebels.

Some of the 4.5 million Congolese displaced by the violence began to return, with a trickle of people returning to Equateur province in early January. As fighting subsided, refugees began to come back from Tanzania, the Republic of Congo, and the Central African Republic, in many cases by boat or motorised canoe along the Congo and Obangi rivers, or across Lake Tanganyika. Fresh outbreaks of fighting, especially in eastern DRC, continued to provoke smaller waves of displaced persons, who gradually returned as things quietened down.

Efforts to improve regional co-operation bore fruit in February when Rwandan and DRC officers met in Bukavu in South Kivu, to find ways of clearing up security issues. The Tripartite Plus One Joint Commission wrote to the UN Security Council in October asking that MONUC be mandated to use force to disarm foreign militias in the DRC. In November a Security Council mission visited the DRC as well as Rwanda and Uganda and criticised delays in the transition, as well as calling for stronger regional support for the process and for co-operation on regional security.

Human rights activist Pascal Kabungulu Kibembi was assassinated at his home in Bukavu on 31 July by three armed men, part of a pattern of human rights violations throughout the year, especially in zones of conflict. In March, the New York-based Human Rights Watch called for reform of the justice system to facilitate the prosecution of perpetrators of sexual abuse, and in October a legal precedent was set when former soldiers from the MLC were court-martialled for rape in Equateur province. UN troops continued to contribute to sexual violence and rape against local women during the year (see AR 2004, pp. 260; 368). In early February, UN Secretary-General Kofi Annan announced a ban on UN troop fraternisation with locals, in reaction to a report on rape and abuse. Six Moroccan soldiers were arrested soon afterwards, and a commander dismissed. In September, the Nigerian government withdrew its police contingent after similar accusations.

BURUNDI AND RWANDA

Burundi

CAPITAL: Bujumbura   AREA: 28,000 sq km   POPULATION: 7,300,000
OFFICIAL LANGUAGES: French & Kirundi   POLITICAL SYSTEM: multiparty republic
HEAD OF STATE AND GOVERNMENT: President Pierre Nkurunziza (CNDD-FDD) (since Aug '05)
RULING PARTY: National Council for the Defence of Democracy-National Forces for the Defence of Democracy (CNDD-FDD) (since July '05)
MAIN IGO MEMBERSHIPS (NON-UN): AU, COMESA, CEEAC, ACP, NAM, Francophonie
CURRENCY: Burundi franc (end-'05 £1=BrF1,673.83, US$1=BrF975.000)
GNI PER CAPITA: US$90, US$660 at PPP ('04, based on regression)

Rwanda

CAPITAL: Kigali   AREA: 26,000 sq km   POPULATION: 8,400,000
OFFICIAL LANGUAGES: French, Kinyarwanda & English   POLITICAL SYSTEM: multiparty republic
HEAD OF STATE AND GOVERNMENT: President Paul Kagame (RPF) (since April '00)
RULING PARTIES: Rwandan Patriotic Front (RPF) heads five party coalition
PRIME MINISTER: Bernard Mazuka (since April '00)
MAIN IGO MEMBERSHIPS (NON-UN): AU, COMESA, CEEAC, ACP, NAM, Francophonie
CURRENCY: Rwanda franc (end-'05 £1=RFr924.470, US$1=RFr538.500)
GNI PER CAPITA: US$220, US$1,300 at PPP ('04, based on regression)

IN BURUNDI conditions remained troubled despite major political advances in the transition to democracy, with popular expectations high following the completion of the complex election process in September. The main problems were poverty, ethnic rivalry, and ongoing fighting in the west of this densely populated country. The situation was complicated by the long drawn-out return of large numbers of refugees, with 400,000 people still awaiting repatriation by October.

The successful democratic local elections on 3 June were followed by legislative elections a month later. These resulted in the peaceful accession to power of the former rebel group, National Council for the Defence of Democracy-National Forces for the Defence of Democracy (CNDD-FDD), under the new power-sharing constitution which had been overwhelmingly approved in a referendum in February. Pierre Nkurunziza of the CNDD-FDD was subsequently elected Burundi's first post-transition President at a joint session of the National Assembly and the Senate (the two chambers of the bicameral legislature). The final step in the process consisted of elections for village (*colline*) heads, which were held in September. Nkurunziza, following the constitution, named one Tutsi and one Hutu as Vice-Presidents, and appointed a cross-party twenty-member Cabinet with a 60:40 ratio of Hutus to Tutsis. One of the vice-presidential posts and seven of the ministerial portfolios were held by women, including Foreign Affairs, Justice, and Commerce and Industry; the Speaker of the National Assembly was also female.

The new Cabinet held its first meeting on 9 September, prioritising peace, security, corruption, and regional co-operation as key issues. President Nkurunziza and his ministers then began a series of visits to the provinces to evaluate local conditions firsthand. One of the most popular measures taken by the new government was the abolition of school fees, announced by Nkurunziza on 26 August. However, the step led, predictably, to a significant increase in primary school enrolments in September, with half a million primary school pupils registered and class sizes in some areas rising to 150.

The road to this outcome had by no means been smooth, as violence continued to simmer throughout the year. The Hutu rebel group, the Forces nationales de libération (FNL), led by Agathon Rwasa (see AR 2004, p. 262), remained a serious threat. Early in the year the FNL mounted armed actions near the capital, Bujumbura, in one incident killing the provincial governor of Bubanza in an ambush. Despite desertions later in the year, the rebels had not laid down their arms by December, continuing to attack both soldiers and civilians in the western provinces. Nonetheless, there was significant overall progress in disarmament and reintegration, with nearly 18,000 former combatants demobilised by mid-October. In December the United Nations Operation in Burundi (ONUB) started to pull out, with the withdrawal of the Mozambican contingent.

Food security in rural areas remained a concern. Famine was declared in January in the two northern provinces of Kirundo and Muyinga, with some deaths reported after a poor harvest. International agencies identified poor weather conditions in 2003 and 2004 as key factors lowering yields of maize and beans. Staple foods doubled in price from the levels of August 2004, and the total food deficit for 2005 was over 300,000 metric tons. In northern and central provinces families sold livestock and began migrating to look for food or work. The 2005 coffee harvest was also poor compared with previous years, after the sector had been liberalised by decree on 14 January. Despite these difficulties, the World Bank announced in August that Burundi had met the conditions for the effective cancellation of US$1.5 billion in debt servicing. Burundi was the 28th country to qualify for enhanced debt relief under the Heavily Indebted Poor Countries (HIPC) initiative.

By contrast, the aftermath of the 1994 genocide still dominated affairs in RWANDA in 2005. Trials of *genocidaires* continued through the UN-mandated

International Criminal Tribunal for Rwanda (the ICTR) and the controversial traditional courts, while the problem of exiled Rwandan militias in the eastern Democratic Republic of Congo remained unresolved. In March, trials of suspects accused of "category two" crimes began in over 700 Gacaca jurisdictions (traditional courts refurbished to relieve pressure on the judicial system). These courts, seen as overly politicised, provoked the flight into Burundi of 8,000 Hutu early in the year, many of whom were then expelled in July. In August, 36,000 people accused of genocide-related offences were released, but the authorities cautioned that they would still have to face trial. Ibuka, an organisation of genocide survivors, expressed outrage. Several hundred former detainees later began serving Gacaca sentences, performing community service. In December, the Gacaca administration reported that the number of local leaders implicated in genocide cases had ballooned since March from under 700 to nearly 30,000.

The ICTR, which was based in Arusha, Tanzania, tried to accelerate the processing of major cases before its mandate ended in 2008. Prosecutor Hassan Jallow announced in January that seventeen dossiers were complete, and the ICTR began handing over dossiers on suspects who were still at large to the Rwandan government. In March the ICTR opened a fourth court room and moved to abolish cumbersome group trials. In September, an appeals court upheld a life sentence for Jean de Dieu Kamuhanda, a former government minister. Important suspects who were arrested or surrendered during the year included Joseph Serugendo of Radio Télévision Libre des Mille Collines. The former Commerce Minister, Juvenal Uwilingiyimana, who had been indicted by the ICTR, was found dead in Brussels, Belgium, in December, an apparent suicide.

Rebels across the border in eastern Democratic Republic of Congo posed an ongoing threat (see p. 242). In March, the Forces démocratiques pour la libération du Rwanda (FDLR) offered to disarm, but President Paul Kagame refused to negotiate preconditions and insisted that some FDLR members would be tried for genocide. By July, militia groups in the DRC were coming under pressure from UN troops, and a deadline was set for complete disarmament by 30 September. But the divided FDLR still insisted on preconditions, and immediate hopes for a settlement were dashed after its leader, Emmanuel Hakizimana, signed an opposition ultimatum in November, while a UN Security Council delegation was visiting the region,.

Meanwhile, Rwandan refugees trickled home: in February a group of 500 returned from Uganda under the auspices of the UN High Commissioner for Refugees (UNHCR), and more returned in October. Rwanda was itself host to over 50,000 refugees from the DRC and Burundi, according to UNHCR estimates.

Relations with the DRC and Uganda remained poor, and the Rwandan government's diplomatic isolation was not eased by the democratisation of Burundi. A UN Security Council mission visited the region in November, with one of its objectives the cooling of tension with the DRC.

In April the World Bank and the IMF announced that Rwanda had qualified for debt relief by achieving macro-economic stability, and the country continued to receive a steady flow of development aid from the international community.

MOZAMBIQUE

CAPITAL: Maputo   AREA: 802,000 sq km   POPULATION: 19,100,000
OFFICIAL LANGUAGE: Portuguese   POLITICAL SYSTEM: multiparty republic in Commonwealth
HEAD OF STATE AND GOVERNMENT: President Armando Emilio Guebuza (Frelimo) (since Feb '05)
RULING PARTY: Front for the Liberation of Mozambique (Frelimo)
PRIME MINISTER: Luisa Diogo (since Feb '04)
MAIN IGO MEMBERSHIPS (NON-UN): AU, SADC, ACP, CWTH, OIC, NAM, CPLP
CURRENCY: metical (end-'05 £1=M40,644.1, US$1=M23,675.0)
GNI PER CAPITA: US$250, US$1,160 at PPP ('04, based on regression)

As the country's first new administration for nearly two decades was sworn in early in February amid promises to shake things up, Mozambique's main problems remained HIV/AIDS, chronic drought, and the absence of food security in rural areas. Liberation war veteran and wealthy businessman Armando Guebuza of the Frelimo Party took over as President from Joaquim Chissano, also of Frelimo, who had held the post without interruption since the death of Samora Machel in an air crash in late 1986 (see AR 1986, p. 249). In his inaugural speech, Guebuza promised to wage an "unrelenting fight" against poverty, crime, corruption, and bureaucratic incompetence. His first Cabinet appointments introduced many fresh faces, with six former provincial governors among the new appointees, while retaining technocrat Luisa Días Diogo as Prime Minister. The new administration made several immediate and highly-publicised moves to deliver change, cutting back on government privileges such as subsidised access to cars, petrol, and mobile phones. At the same time, an efficiency and discipline drive was launched to ensure that meetings started on time, and that officials were at their desks during working hours. In May, a government plan to build a luxury holiday home for ex-President Chissano was dramatically reduced in scale. In the first half of the year, President Guebuza visited all of Mozambique's provinces, and at a three-day meeting of the Council of Ministers in July to report on his trip, demanded "more action, dedication, and commitment" from members of his Cabinet.

The main opposition party, Renamo, which had won ninety seats to Frelimo's 160 in the December 2004 elections to the Assembly of the Republic, the unicameral legislature (see AR 2004, pp. 264-65), challenged the results in a disorganised fashion in an appeal to the Constitutional Council in January, alleging fraud. However, the challenge was submitted days past the deadline, and on different grounds from an earlier objection, and was, therefore, thrown out on technical grounds. Nevertheless, whilst on 20 January the Constitutional Council validated the election results, it also expressed anxiety over organisational aspects and lack of transparency in the conduct of the elections, concerns echoed by the Carter Centre in Atlanta, Georgia, USA, which had monitored the ballot. In March, partly as a result of these criticisms, the Assembly moved to establish an ad hoc commission to revise the electoral law.

Relations between the government and Renamo remained strained throughout the year. In April, opposition deputies walked out of the Assembly en masse during a budget debate, and in August a Renamo spokesman angrily accused the government of "recruiting" former guerrillas for a "strategy of destabilisation", in an apparent reference to their integration into the police force. The most serious incident took place in September, when several people were killed in clashes between Renamo supporters and police in Mocimboa da Praia, in the northern province of Cabo Delgado, over the results of municipal elections several months earlier.

In June, the government appealed for 70,000 metric tonnes of food aid for seven of the country's ten provinces, mainly in the central and southern regions, while about half a million Mozambicans faced severe food shortages. By October, the number of people in need had risen to 800,000, as 40 per cent of the maize harvest was lost and maize prices doubled. According to a mission from the UN's Food and Agriculture Organisation and World Food Programme which visited the country in April and May, traditional methods for dealing with scarcity in drought-prone areas had been undermined by the impact of HIV/AIDS, acute malnutrition, and the fragility of community networks.

The HIV/AIDS budget for the year was US$5 million, while estimated adult prevalence rose from 14.9 per cent in 2004 to 15.6 per cent, with the highest rates in Maputo, Beira, Nampula, and Tete.

On the economic front, the trend towards reliance on large projects for export earnings continued. In November, at the end of his first official visit to Portugal, the former colonial power, President Guebuza signed a surprise agreement opening the way for the transfer of the Cahora Bassa hydro-electric scheme to Mozambican ownership. In an apparent goodwill gesture, Portugal agreed to accept payment of only US$950 million against a claimed debt of US$2.3 billion.

At the end of the year, the second trial of Aníbal "Anibalzinho" dos Santos began in Maputo under stringent security. Anibalzinho, accused of the murder of investigative journalist Carlos Cardoso in November 2000, had twice escaped from jail and fled the country, in 2002 and 2004 (see AR 2003, p. 307).

ANGOLA

CAPITAL: Luanda   AREA: 1,247,000 sq km   POPULATION: 14,000,000
OFFICIAL LANGUAGE: Portuguese   POLITICAL SYSTEM: multiparty republic
HEAD OF STATE AND GOVERNMENT: President José Eduardo dos Santos (since Sept '79)
RULING PARTY: Popular Movement for the Liberation of Angola-Workers' Party (MPLA) heads nominal coalition
PRIME MINISTER: Fernando da Piedade Dias dos Santos (since Dec '02)
MAIN IGO MEMBERSHIPS (NON-UN): AU, COMESA, SADC, CEEAC, ACP, NAM, CPLP
CURRENCY: readj kwanza (end-'05 £1=Kw138.671, US$1=Kw80.7755)
GNI PER CAPITA: US$1,030, US$2,030 at PPP ('04, based on regression)

THREE years after the end of the three decades of war, Angola had become sub-Saharan Africa's second largest oil producer after Nigeria and benefited from soaring oil prices. Production was running at over 1 million barrels per day, and was expected to reach 2 million barrels within two years (see AR 2004, p. 266). Diamonds worth US$1 billion were sold, and Endiama, the state diamond company, predicted a fivefold increase within five years.

With the Angolan economy one of the fastest-growing in the world, and the country at peace, the post-war reconstruction gathered pace. Numerous large-scale infrastructure projects were approved, including a new airport outside the capital, the upgrading of the main ports, and new highways from Lobito to Benguela and north from Luanda. China was the largest foreign partner in reconstruction, and the second-largest importer of Angolan oil, after the USA.

On the negative side, many in the northern province of Cabinda, where the oil was produced, continued to harbour hopes of secession, and there were continued reports of human rights violations perpetrated there by the state security forces. The demobilisation process had still not been completed, and although most of the refugees from neighbouring countries had returned, many found adjusting to life back in Angola difficult. Most serious of all, corruption and lack of fiscal transparency and accountability remained endemic, both in the economy and in the reconstruction process. The result was that only a small elite benefited from the vast new wealth. Most Angolans remained extremely poor and state social spending remained very limited. With life-threatening diseases still rampant in many areas, Angola was ranked 160 out of 177 countries on the UN Human Development Index. Despite a general improvement in agricultural production, it was estimated that in south-eastern Kuando Kubango province—a stronghold of the main opposition party, UNITA—half of the population did not have access to adequate food. When the World Food Programme announced in late 2005 that, with donor contributions dropping, it would not have sufficient money to continue general food distribution in Angola after March 2006, some predicted a humanitarian disaster in the south. There and in the east, an estimated 10 million landmines also remained to be cleared. Their presence hampered reconstruction work and inhibited the opening of national parks in the south to tourists. Tourism was more practical on the long, undeveloped Atlantic coastline, and a number of new hotels were planned for the beachfront at Luanda, away from the squalid slums in which the majority of the 5 million residents of the capital lived.

UNITA suspected that the government was dragging its feet over holding a general election, though the government insisted that one would take place in 2006. In August a national electoral commission of eleven members was approved by the National Assembly (unicameral legislature). No date was set for the poll, however, and the task of registering over 7 million eligible voters went very slowly, especially in the rural areas and former war zones. Though UNITA remained within the power-sharing arrangement that had helped to stabilise the political scene in the aftermath of the war, without the means to return to war it was powerless to prevent the ruling party getting its way. It remained to be seen, therefore, whether the election would take place in 2006 and under what conditions. Few expected the MPLA to lose control, but the opposition Social Renewal Party (PRS) in the diamond-producing east was thought likely to increase its representation in the National Assembly.

In November the ruling elite lavishly celebrated thirty years of Angolan independence, seemingly forgetting the half million or more people who had died in the post-independence civil war. Other Angolans thought there was more to celebrate when the country's football team qualified for the world cup finals in Germany in 2006.

ZAMBIA—MALAWI—ZIMBABWE—BLNS STATES

ZAMBIA

CAPITAL: Lusaka   AREA: 753,000 sq km   POPULATION: 10,500,000
OFFICIAL LANGUAGE: English   POLITICAL SYSTEM: multiparty republic in Commonwealth
HEAD OF STATE AND GOVERNMENT: President Levy Patrick Mwanawasa (since Jan '02)
RULING PARTY: Movement for Multi-Party Democracy (MMD)
MAIN IGO MEMBERSHIPS (NON-UN): AU, COMESA, SADC, ACP, CWTH, NAM
CURRENCY: Zambian kwacha (end-'05 £1=Kw5,862.72, US$1=Kw3,415.00)
GNI PER CAPITA: US$450, US$890 at PPP ('04)

THE high global copper price, thanks to rising demand from China and elsewhere, was good news for Zambia as copper was its main export earner and a major employer. Copper production rose by about 100,000 tons in 2005 despite a strike at the largest mine, Konkola, in July over wages, and was expected to reach 750,000 tons in 2007. Copper was exported by rail to Dar es Salaam in Tanzania and Durban in South Africa, and plans were unveiled to link Zambia via Benguela railway, rebuilt with Chinese input, to the port of Lobito in Angola.

While the copper belt in the north and the capital enjoyed new levels of prosperity, the rural south was hard-hit by a lack of rain. In November President Levy Mwanawasa declared a national food crisis and appealed for international assistance. A 15 per cent duty on imported maize was scrapped in a bid to encourage commercial imports, most of which came from South Africa, and the government removed a requirement that imported maize be tested for genetically modified organisms. At the end of the year, it was estimated that more than a million people needed food aid.

With tourists not going to Zimbabwe because of the Mugabe regime, southern Zambia did benefit from a significant increase in tourism, especially Livingstone, the capital of the south, and the nearby Victoria Falls. More significantly, Zambia benefited from the debt cancellations agreed by the Paris Club of international creditors in May and then the G-8. Money saved on debt repayments was to be spent on health and education. Zambia felt confident enough to ask to be reviewed under the African peer review mechanism of the African Union and the New Partnership for Africa's Development (NEPAD).

During the year over 17,000 refugees from Angola who had been living in Zambia for many years returned home. The Zambian government's attempt to prosecute the former President, Frederick Chiluba, and other former government officials, in a UK court came to naught, but Chiluba still faced charges of corruption and the theft of US$23.3 million of state monies.

The main political issue in 2005 was whether or not a new constitution would be put in place before the presidential and legislative elections due in 2006. A draft constitution was prepared by the constitution review commission, appointed in 2003, but opposition groups called for a new constitution to be drawn up by a constituent assembly. Mwanawasa said there was neither time nor money for this to be done before the 2006 election. The Oasis Forum—a body comprising the Law Association of Zambia and the main churches—organised demonstrations in many parts of the country—including over 10,000 people in Lusaka, the capital—in an attempt to force the President to back down.

Mwanawasa meanwhile won support within his divided ruling Movement for Multiparty Democracy (MMD) to run for a second term in the 2006 election. Some in the party still supported Chiluba and disliked Mwanawasa's anti-corruption campaign. Before the party's congress, the popular Austin Chewe—a potential challenger to Mwanawasa—was expelled for campaign irregularities, and many others were suspended in line with the President's policy of zero tolerance on corruption. A former Vice President, Nevers Mumba, until May the main challenger to Mwanawasa, was expelled after he claimed that Mwanawasa was bribing delegates to vote for him. The party rejected the allegations as groundless. The MMD suffered another blow when its national chairman, Chitalu Sampa, resigned and joined a new grouping—the Party for Unity, Democracy and Development (PUDD)—of which he then became chairman.

MALAWI

CAPITAL: Lilongwe   AREA: 118,000 sq km   POPULATION: 11,200,000
OFFICIAL LANGUAGE: English   POLITICAL SYSTEM: multiparty republic in Commonwealth
HEAD OF STATE AND GOVERNMENT: President Bingu wa Mutharika (DPP), since May '04
RULING PARTY: United Democratic Front (UDF)
MAIN IGO MEMBERSHIPS (NON-UN): AU, COMESA, SADC, ACP, CWTH, NAM
CURRENCY: Malawi kwacha (end-'05 £1=Kw210.388, US$1=Kw122.550)
GNI PER CAPITA: US$170, US$620 at PPP ('04)

WHILE Malawi was wracked by political crisis, its population grew poorer. Three-quarters of the country's 11 million people survived on less than one US dollar per day. In early October it was estimated that one-third of the population faced starvation as a consequence of the worst harvest in a decade combined with the ravages of HIV/AIDS. The official estimate was that 1 million people were infected with HIV, and fewer than 50,000 were taking anti-retroviral drugs. With the south especially badly affected by drought, the UN appealed for massive aid. The World Bank called for a comprehensive rural development strategy for the longer-term, claiming that if proper irrigation were put in place, future droughts would no longer produce massive food shortages.

President Bingu wa Mutharika remained at daggers drawn with his predecessor, Bakili Muluzi, leader of the United Democratic Party (UDF). Having broken with the UDF, Mutharika formed his own party, the Democratic Progressive Party (DPP). Muluzi and the UDF—now an opposition party in the National Assembly (the legislature)—proposed that Mutharika should be impeached for violating the constitution. Opponents of Mutharika accused him of having misused public funds for a variety of purposes, including the launch of the DPP. Mutharika tried to rein in government spending and tackle corruption, especially in the police force; he also agreed to higher pay for civil servants. Despite this, the government was able to cut overall spending, for which it won praise from the IMF and for which it hoped to be rewarded with debt cancellation.

Many threats and accusations were made among the political elite. After Gwanda Chakuamba—a leading opposition figure who had joined the DPP and been made Minister of Agriculture—was dismissed and then detained for questioning over allegations that he had bought a luxury car with World Bank funds, he joined Mutharika's opponents in calling for his impeachment.

In June, with the impeachment motion before the National Assembly and the country's budget not approved, international donors voiced their concern that the fierce political battle was interfering with efforts to deal with the food crisis. The government then reluctantly agreed to the opposition's proposal for fertiliser subsidies to farmers, but the cost involved meant that the idea of a universal fertiliser subsidy programme was dropped and a limited number of subsistence producers were given access to fertilisers at half the commercial price. By the end of the year, with better rains and thanks to the roll-out of the fertiliser programme, it seemed likely that the maize crop in 2006 would greatly exceed the 1.3 million tons produced in 2005. Meanwhile, the DPP increased its support in by-elections, at the expense of the UDF, and the largest opposition party became the Malawi Congress Party, headed by John Tembo.

ZIMBABWE

CAPITAL: Harare   AREA: 391,000 sq km   POPULATION: 13,200,000
OFFICIAL LANGUAGE: English   POLITICAL SYSTEM: multiparty republic in Commonwealth
HEAD OF STATE AND GOVERNMENT: President Robert Mugabe (since Dec '87); previously Prime
     Minister (from April '80)
RULING PARTY: Zimbabwe African National Union-Patriotic Front (ZANU-PF)
MAIN IGO MEMBERSHIPS (NON-UN): AU, COMESA, SADC, ACP, NAM
CURRENCY: Zimbabwe dollar (end-'05 £1=Z$145,216, US$1=Z$84,587.6)
GNI PER CAPITA: low income: US$825 or less ('04 est), US$2,180 at PPP ('03)

IN the run-up to the general election held on 31 March, Zimbabwe experienced markedly reduced levels of intimidation and violence compared with the 2000 elections (see AR 2000, pp. 272-73) and the presidential poll of 2002 (see AR 2002, pp. 288-90). But through its exclusive control of polling stations and the count, the governing Zimbabwe African National Union-Patriotic Front party (ZANU-PF) of President Robert Mugabe assured its own victory. Recycling a flawed and out-of-date voters' roll, the ruling party awarded itself an estimated 1 million phantom votes to distribute as it wished. Given the exclusion of opposition observers from polling stations, and threats to remove food aid from rural constituencies that returned a candidate from the opposition Movement for Democratic Change (MDC), there was little confidence that the outcome would reflect the will of the people.

The results, processed through the "national election logistics centre", gave the ruling party seventy-eight seats, with the MDC reduced from fifty-seven in the previous Parliament to forty-one. One seat, in the Midlands constituency of Tsholotsho, was won by Jonathan Moyo, the former Information Minister who had been dismissed in 2004 by Mugabe (see AR 2004, p. 271), who stood as an independent. With the President entitled to appoint thirty seats to the 150-member

Parliament, ZANU-PF emerged with the two-thirds majority needed to amend the constitution. The MDC had been defeated in some of its safest seats, and pointed to serious voting irregularities in twenty-one constituencies. "We didn't expect it to be so glaring", declared a party official. The triumphant eighty-one-year-old Mugabe announced he would go on until his century.

Within days of the election the official observer mission of the Southern African Development Community (SADC) declared the contest free and fair, though a minority report subsequently challenged this view. The view of the independent Zimbabwe electoral support network, which had deployed observers at two-thirds of the 8,000 polling stations, said that despite the apparent calm, Zimbabwe's voters had been "gripped by terror".

The shattered hopes of an optimistic MDC increased pressure on its leader, Morgan Tsvangirai. His call for a fresh election "under a completely different constitutional dispensation" went unheeded, as did Bulawayo's Archbishop Pius Ncube's appeal—perhaps mindful of Ukraine's "orange revolution" four months previously (see AR 2004, pp. 113-15)—for the people to take peacefully to the streets.

In a country in which democratic processes were routinely ignored, the mandate for constitutional change hardly mattered. Mugabe announced plans to create a second legislative chamber (the Senate); to confiscate the passports of government critics; and to nationalise Zimbabwe's land in an attempt to forestall restitution claims from displaced white farmers. A dispute over the Senate election of 27 November soon split the demoralised MDC. After three rigged elections, Tsvangirai vetoed participation in another sham poll. His deputy, Gibson Sibanda, and other leading party members, opted to continue the challenge. In a very public and increasingly bitter quarrel during the final months of the year, the MDC appeared to have destroyed itself and with it the only real challenge to Mugabe. In the event the MDC won seven seats in the sixty-six-seat Senate, mostly in Matabeleland, in a contest with a 19.4 per cent voter turnout.

If Mugabe had eliminated opposition at home, it remained vociferous abroad. In January a UN report identified Zimbabwe, Burma (Myanmar) and North Korea as the worst-governed countries in the world. Condoleezza Rice, the US Secretary of State, named it in a list of six "outposts of tyranny" (together with Cuba, Burma, North Korea, Iran, and Belarus). The USA and the EU renewed travel bans on leading ZANU-PF legislators and officials. In February *The Zimbabwean*—a newspaper aimed at the 3 million Zimbabweans living abroad—was launched in the UK. The masthead identified it as "a voice for the voiceless".

By far the strongest international criticism was provoked by the government's campaign of forced eviction and slum clearance in urban areas, named "operation murambatsvina", or "drive out trash". From 19 May army battalions and riot police demolished shanty towns in Harare, Bulawayo, and other urban centres, coercing thousands of citizens into inadequate transit centres. The President justified the initiative as a strategy to rid cities of squalor and crime and resettle the disadvantaged. The opposition saw it as a means to punish urban voters who had repeatedly rejected ZANU-PF at the polls, exiling them to rural areas where their vote would be neutralised. A report commissioned by UN Secretary-General Kofi Annan, and published days before the G-8 summit, strongly criticised the clearance programme, describing it as a grave humanitarian crisis.

Gideon Gono, the governor of the Reserve Bank of Zimbabwe, struggled to maintain a semblance of operational efficiency and fiscal plausibility within a regime which had deteriorated into a cluster of antagonistic and competitive cadres. Gono's policies had reduced inflation from the record level of 620 per cent in 2004 to under 130 per cent by March 2005. But increasing electricity and fuel costs pushed inflation to 260 per cent in August, and to 586 per cent at the end of the year. By May the Zimbabwean dollar had declined 35 per cent against the US dollar, and in mid-August it slipped a further 23 per cent. On the black market one US dollar bought 90,000 Zimbabwean dollars, the price of two loaves of bread.

Threatened with Zimbabwe's expulsion from the IMF over defaulted interest payments, Mugabe travelled cap-in-hand to China and then to South Africa in August. Neither country proved willing to bale him out. The following month Zimbabwe unexpectedly repaid US$150 million to the IMF, reportedly having raided the foreign exchange accounts of private companies. The World Bank described Zimbabwe's parlous economic position as unprecedented in a country which was not at war.

By the end of the year fuel was unobtainable outside the black market, and the national airline was temporarily grounded. Rubbish accumulated in the streets as refuse collections were suspended. Frequent power cuts damaged businesses, while the water supply, even when available, was declared unfit to drink. Some 700,000 displaced Zimbabweans remained homeless, while Mugabe fulminated against the iniquities of the Western powers.

BOTSWANA—LESOTHO—NAMIBIA—SWAZILAND

Botswana

CAPITAL: Gaborone   AREA: 582,000 sq km   POPULATION: 1,725,000
OFFICIAL LANGUAGES: English and Setswana   POLITICAL SYSTEM: multiparty republic in Commonwealth
HEAD OF STATE AND GOVERNMENT: President Festus Mogae (since March '98)
RULING PARTY: Botswana Democratic Party (BDP)
MAIN IGO MEMBERSHIPS (NON-UN): AU, SADC, SACU, ACP, CWTH, NAM
CURRENCY: pula (end-'05 £1=P9.45370, US$1=P5.50661)
GNI PER CAPITA: US$4,340, US$8,920 at PPP ('04)

Lesotho

CAPITAL: Maseru   AREA: 30,000 sq km   POPULATION: 1,809,000
OFFICIAL LANGUAGES: English & Sesotho   POLITICAL SYSTEM: multiparty monarchy in Commonwealth
HEAD OF STATE: King Letsie III (since Jan '96)
RULING PARTY: Lesotho Congress for Democracy (LCD)
HEAD OF GOVERNMENT: Bethuel Pakalitha Mosisili, Prime Minister (since June '98)
MAIN IGO MEMBERSHIPS (NON-UN): AU, SADC, SACU, ACP, CWTH, NAM
CURRENCY: maloti (end-'05 £1=M10.8885, US$1=M6.34250)
GNI PER CAPITA: US$740, US$3,210 at PPP ('04)

Namibia

CAPITAL: Windhoek   AREA: 824,000 sq km   POPULATION: 2,000,000
OFFICIAL LANGUAGES: Afrikaans & English   POLITICAL SYSTEM: multiparty republic in Commonwealth
HEAD OF STATE: President Hifikepunye Pohamba (SWAPO), since March '05
RULING PARTY: South West Africa People's Organisation (SWAPO)
HEAD OF GOVERNMENT: Nahas Angula, Prime Minister (since March '05)
MAIN IGO MEMBERSHIPS (NON-UN): AU, SADC, COMESA, SACU, ACP, CWTH, NAM
CURRENCY: Namibian dollar and South African Rand (end-'05 £1=N$10.8885, US$1=N$6.34250)
GNI PER CAPITA: US$2,370, US$6,960 at PPP ('04, based on regression)

Swaziland

CAPITAL: Mbabane   AREA: 17,350 sq km   POPULATION: 1,120,000
OFFICIAL LANGUAGES: English & Siswati   POLITICAL SYSTEM: non-party monarchy in Commonwealth
HEAD OF STATE: King Mswati III (since '86)
HEAD OF GOVERNMENT: Absalom Themba Dlamini, Prime Minister (since Nov '03)
MAIN IGO MEMBERSHIPS (NON-UN): AU, SADC, SACU, ACP, CWTH, NAM
CURRENCY: lilangeni/pl. emalangeni (end-'05 £1=E10.8885, US$1=E6.34250)
GNI PER CAPITA: US$1,660, US$4,970 at PPP ('04)

THE year reflected once again the large socio-economic challenges that Botswana, Lesotho, Namibia, and Swaziland faced relating to the difficulties of economic diversification, competition from China in textiles, and another cycle of drought. The high prevalence of HIV/AIDS and the costly anti-retroviral campaigns rolled out by all four governments inhibited the efficiency of their economies.

BOTSWANA, long-heralded as an example of a well-functioning democracy, expelled an Australian-born University of Botswana political science lecturer, Professor Kenneth Good, following an article he had written lambasting President Festus Mogae's decision to handpick Vice-President Lieutenant-General

Ian Khama as his successor. Good noted that there had been long-standing concerns over Khama's management style when he was head of the army: he had bypassed the government's tendering processes by allegedly awarding bids to family members. The government's action, endorsed by the courts, raised concerns about the extent of freedom of speech.

Real GDP growth was 5.7 per cent in 2004 but economic analysts estimated that the figure would drop in 2005 to between 3 and 4 per cent. The Paris-based Risques Internationaux rated Botswana "as the best African risk", but noted that the country was grappling with reduced economic growth rates and continuing problems of achieving desired diversification outside the buoyant mineral sector. A major constraint to diversification was the overvalued currency. In May a crawling peg exchange rate mechanism was introduced to prevent the pula from being "misaligned".

Botswana was the world's top diamond producer by value and was voted the world's safest place for mining investment by Australia's world risk survey of global mining. It also opened its first gold mine in February. Mupane, developed by Australian mining company Gallery Gold, planned to produce 100,000 ounces a year, with a minimum lifespan of five years. Mupane's opening came just days after Botswana announced a new mineral investment strategy, the objective of which was to encourage investment in non-diamond sectors.

There was a decline in agricultural production which was blamed on the government's monopoly in the beef and ostrich industries, and the failures of the state-run Botswana meat commission (BMC). Government control of the BMC was largely responsible for the uncompetitiveness of the cattle market, which had led to several livestock farmers opting to invest in other sectors. According to the Central Statistics Office, the national cattle herd declined from 3 million in the late 1980s to around 1.7 million in 2005. During 2005 Botswana drew up a contingency plan for controlling and eventually eradicating foot and mouth disease (FMD), so that it could meet the beef export preconditions set by the EU. The cattle industry was Botswana's second-largest foreign currency earner, after diamonds, but the FMD outbreaks in 2002-03 froze beef exports to emerging markets as well as to the EU, its largest customer.

HIV/AIDS remained a significant problem with an overall national prevalence rate for the virus of 17 per cent, rising as high as 40 per cent among thirty to thirty-five year-olds. The government continued to mount a vigorous public education campaign, and launched free anti-retroviral treatment and a nationwide "prevention of mother-to-child transmission" programme.

Tensions between Botswana and Zimbabwe continued as the political and economic situation in the latter deteriorated further. Border controls were increased and the construction of a 500 kilometre electric fence, patrolled by security forces, was accelerated. It was aimed at reducing the influx of illegal migrants and livestock smuggling. FMD had been introduced into Botswana from Zimbabwe in 2002.

In May LESOTHO held its first ever nationwide local government elections. (In 2004 it had held a successful national election—see AR 2004, p. 274.) The ruling

Lesotho Congress for Democracy (LCD) won most of the seats (one-third of which were reserved for women) but turnout was only around 30 per cent.

As with other countries in the region, Lesotho entered its fourth year of drought. Of a population of just under 2 million people, almost 50 per cent lived in poverty and a lack of funding made food aid distribution difficult. The Southern Africa Development Community (SADC)'s vulnerability assessment committee put the number of people in need of aid at 548,000. Limited resources compelled the World Food Programme to suspend its operations in Lesotho in May.

In order to achieve the UN's millennium development goals of halving poverty by 2015, Lesotho would need an annual economic growth of 7.5 per cent. In 2004 real GDP growth slowed to about 2 per cent, from over 3 per cent in the previous two years. This had been primarily due to "the impact of adverse shocks affecting manufacturing and agriculture", according to the IMF.

The expiry of the World Trade Organisation's multi-fibre agreement at the beginning of 2005, which lifted the quota on Chinese-made garments and thus brought into the global market a flood of cheap products, led to the closure of several textile mills. Although Lesotho still received duty-free access to the US market under the Africa Growth and Opportunity Act (AGOA), it found it difficult to compete against the low wages and economies of scale of China and India. Lesotho's industry was also adversely affected by the pegging of its currency to the South African rand, which strengthened against the US dollar.

HIV prevalence among pregnant women in Lesotho was exceptionally high, although there were indications that it could be stabilising. Mean HIV prevalence was 27 per cent, slightly lower than the 29 per cent measured in 2003.

Following elections in NAMIBIA in 2004 a new President, Hifikepunye Pohamba, was inaugurated on 21 March. This was the first transfer of power since Namibia's independence in 1990 (see AR 1990, pp. 295-96) although Pohamba was largely seen as Sam Nujoma's handpicked successor, a view strengthened by Pohamba's decision to retain thirty-two members of Nujoma's Cabinet. In December Parliament passed a controversial bill that accorded Nujoma "founding father" status.

A recount of votes cast in Namibia's national elections in 2004 (see AR 2004, p. 275) confirmed the ruling party's landslide victory. Four opposition parties had jointly applied to the Namibian High Court in April to have the November 2004 elections declared null and void, with the request that the poll be rerun. A recount was ordered but it merely confirmed SWAPO's victory.

One of the themes of President Pohamba's inaugural speech was that there would be "zero tolerance for waste and corruption". The first concrete salvo against corruption was made in August when the deputy minister of works, transport and communication, Paulus Kapia, was forced to resign, following a High Court liquidation inquiry into how a US$5.7 million investment in his company, Avid Investment Corporation, went missing.

Namibia's annual GDP growth rate for 2004 was estimated to be 4.8 per cent. According to the IMF, however, Namibia's national debt had ballooned from N$143 million at independence in 1990 to N$12 billion in 2005. The expiry on 1 January 2005 of quota restrictions on clothing and textile imports from China and India to US and EU markets had an adverse effect on the textile industry. The Rhino Garments factory, a subsidiary of the Malaysian company, Ramatex Textiles, had to close at the end of March, with the loss of 1,600 jobs. The Namibian government had promoted Ramatex as an important part of its export diversification strategy.

The discovery of two apartheid-era mass graves in November at a former military base near the border with Angola reopened questions about Namibia's recent history and the debate about whether it should establish a truth and reconciliation commission along the lines of that in South Africa. SWAPO ruled this out, however, saying that it was committed to a policy of reconciliation.

The prevalence rate for HIV/AIDS infection in Namibia was estimated at 22.3 per cent. The government had begun anti-retroviral treatment in August 2003 and by June 2005 there were 17,000 people receiving treatment. The government planned to allocate "at least 2 per cent of the national budget" for HIV/AIDS-related activities. During the year, an additional budget of N$65 million was approved by Parliament to help cover the rising costs of providing antiretroviral treatment for government employees infected by HIV/AIDS.

Just over 2,000 Namibian refugees from the Dukwe camp in north-eastern Botswana returned to Namibia after an agreement between Namibia, Botswana and the UN High Commissioner for Refugees was signed in April. The refugees had fled Namibia in 1998 during a wave of violence caused by secessionist fighting on the border with Angola (see AR 1998, p. 307).

SWAZILAND agreed a draft constitution in June which was signed into law the following month by King Mswati III and was due to come into effect in January 2006. Under its terms, the King would continue to appoint the Prime Minister and Cabinet, principal secretaries, chiefs, and high court judges, and could also dissolve Parliament. One third of parliamentary seats were to be reserved for women, but it remained unclear whether political parties would be permitted. Private property was secured but the King could abrogate all rights granted to the Swazi people by the constitution if he considered them to be in conflict with the public interest.

Opposition groups rejected the final document on the grounds that it had been unduly influenced by the King. This opposition saw a series of bombings against government buildings, and in December thirteen members of the Swaziland Youth Congress (SWAYOCO)—a wing of the banned People's United Democratic Movement (PUDEMO)—were charged with high treason in connection with the campaign.

A by-election in October saw a member of a banned political party win a seat in Swaziland's Parliament for the first time in thirty-three years. He was a member of the outlawed Ngwane National Liberatory Congress (NNLC), but because electoral laws did not permit political groupings to participate, he had stood as an independent.

Economically, Swaziland faced a particularly difficult year, following real GDP growth of only 2.1 per cent in 2004, compared with a population growth rate of

2.9 per cent. During 2005, unemployment continued to be very high (45 per cent), while about two-thirds of the population lived in poverty.

The cornerstone of the government's goal to reduce poverty and create jobs was increasing foreign direct investment. However, this was constrained by the amount of "red tape" facing potential investors, and also by a new law that gave Swazis the power to challenge foreign ownership of small and medium businesses, where such enterprises might otherwise be run by Swazis.

Agriculture and the textile sector suffered setbacks in 2005. Although seven out of ten Swazis derived their livelihood from agriculture, agriculture had declined from 10.6 per cent of GDP in 1999 to 8.6 per cent in 2004-05. In April the EU banned imports of Swazi beef products after Swaziland failed to produce the necessary documentation needed to track the origin of slaughtered cattle. Furthermore, the Swazi government succumbed to pressure from cattle owners and indefinitely suspended a law requiring all animals to be branded for identification.

Swaziland also experienced its fourth year of drought. A parliamentary report on the food shortage noted that there were some 265,000 vulnerable people in need of food aid in the latter half of 2005.

Agricultural setbacks were mirrored in the textile sector, where companies closed and employment fell from 31,000 in June 2004 to 15,000 by December 2005. The decline was the result of the end of the WTO's multi-fibre agreement (see above) and the delay earlier in the approving of AGOA II by the US Congress. These difficulties were also compounded by the strength of the Swazi currency against the US dollar. The lilangeni was pegged to the South African rand, which had appreciated substantially against the dollar during 2005.

Swaziland's HIV/AIDS prevalence rate continued to rise. A study of pregnant women released in April showed that in 2005 the rate among women was 42.6 per cent. The total population had an HIV prevalence rate of approximately 20 per cent. The country had begun roll-out of anti-retroviral drugs at seventeen distribution points, but had experienced shortages.

SOUTH AFRICA

CAPITAL: Pretoria   AREA: 1,221,000 sq km   POPULATION: 45,600,000
OFFICIAL LANGUAGE: Afrikaans, English & nine African languages   POLITICAL SYSTEM: multiparty
   republic in Commonwealth
HEAD OF STATE AND GOVERNMENT: President Thabo Mbeki (since June '99)
RULING PARTY: African National Congress (ANC)
MAIN IGO MEMBERSHIPS (NON-UN): AU, SADC, SACU, CWTH, NAM
CURRENCY: rand (end-'05 £1=R10.8885, US$1=R6.34250)
GNI PER CAPITA: US$3,630, US$10,960 at PPP ('04, based on regression)

DURING 2005 South Africa increased its multilateral involvement in the rest of Africa. Its economy performed well, but questions arose about the government's commitment to tackle corruption and strengthen democratic institutions.

As part of the ongoing controversy over the South African government's arms procurement deal, Schabir Schaik—a businessman and financial adviser to Deputy President Jacob Zuma—was found guilty of corruption and fraud. Judge

Hilary Squires found that there was a "generally corrupt relationship" between Schaik and Zuma and that the latter had intervened on behalf of Shaik's business interests on at least four occasions. Following Squires's ruling, President Thabo Mbeki dismissed Zuma, a move which earned Mbeki kudos both domestically and internationally and which was seen as indicative of a firm anti-corruption stance at the highest levels of government. Zuma was subsequently charged by the National Prosecuting Authority. He was replaced as Deputy President by Phumzile Mlambo-Ngcuka.

Zuma's woes were compounded in December, when he was formally charged with rape. The alleged victim, a thirty-one-year-old HIV/AIDS activist, claimed that she had been assaulted at Zuma's home in November. Zuma denied the allegation, but he suspended his participation in leading structures of the ruling African National Congress (ANC) after the charge was laid against him.

Zuma's dismissal caused political divisions: the Congress of South African Trade Unions (COSATU) and the South African Communist Party (SACP)—both members of the ANC-led tripartite alliance—came out in his support. Furthermore, the ANC's national executive committee stated that he would remain as deputy president of the party. Zuma benefited from the growing perception that Mbeki was out of touch with the needs of ordinary South Africans and that his government's pursuit of macroeconomic stability through neo-liberal economic policies was to blame for the continued high unemployment.

The growing frustration among ordinary people over the failure of all tiers of government efficiently to deliver services—contrasted with the large remuneration packages and alleged corruption of many senior officials in local government—was reflected in the numerous demonstrations (some violent) which were held throughout the country. Insufficient skilled managerial and technical staff, together with corruption, were key factors in the failure. But although Mbeki repeatedly emphasised the need to root out corruption at all levels, the government's approach was inconsistent. In the "oilgate" scandal, it was alleged that PetroSA, a South African parastatal company, had paid R15 million to oil supplier Imvume Management, of which R11 million was donated to the ANC ahead of the general election in 2004. The weekly *Mail & Guardian* newspaper was gagged by a court when it tried to print further disclosures in the case and the public protector ruled that he could not investigate the matter further as he had no authority to look into the affairs of private bodies. By contrast, some progress was made in the "travelgate" scandal, where a number of legislators had abused their parliamentary travel vouchers, working together with travel agencies.

The economy remained buoyant, growing by 5 per cent in the second quarter, boosted by a consumer and commodities boom (part of which was the result of the huge demand from China). However, the strengthening of the rand against the US dollar and the euro had a negative impact on the country's competitiveness and hence on its exports. Unemployment remained high: 26 per cent of South Africans were actively seeking jobs in 2005. Of those employed, one in four South Africans—and two-thirds of the workers engaged in informal, domestic, and agricultural work—continued to earn less than US$150 per month.

President Mbeki placed Mlambo-Ngcuka in charge of the accelerated and shared growth initiative (ASGI), a programme designed to tackle the problem of unemployment and raise the country's economic growth rate above 6 per cent per year. In a report approved by the Cabinet, Mlambo-Ngcuka's team identified six constraints to growth: currency volatility, infrastructural bottlenecks, the regulatory burden on business, weak service delivery, the skills shortage, and import parity pricing. Linked to this was the government's infrastructural upgrading programme begun earlier in the year, which would see R320 billion invested in infrastructure over a five-year period.

South Africa became a net exporter of capital and was the biggest foreign direct investor in Africa in 2005. An IMF report lauded the success of the social, monetary, and fiscal policies implemented, but recommended a relaxation of labour protection mechanisms to help boost employment.

The UNAIDS global AIDS epidemic update report, released in November, found that of the 25.8 million people worldwide living with HIV, 6 million were in South Africa. However, only 15 per cent of people in need of anti-retroviral treatment there had access to the drugs. In addition, of about 33,000 pregnant women who were HIV-positive, only 18,857 received protective treatment. By contrast, in Uganda, Zambia, and Zimbabwe, almost all the women tested positive were reported to have received treatment.

In the foreign policy realm, South Africa continued to play an important role in mediating conflicts on the continent. During 2005 it was active in Côte d'Ivoire and in the Sudan, as well as in Burundi and the Democratic Republic of Congo, where it had had a much longer involvement, including troop deployments. In Côte d'Ivoire, in particular, President Mbeki became personally involved in the mediation between President Laurent Gbagbo and the northern rebels (see pp. 231-32). However, the limits of committed mediation when the parties were not ready for compromise were very evident during 2005. While the political situation in Côte d'Ivoire had improved somewhat by the end of the year, there were times during the process when South Africa came close to abandoning its efforts. In the Darfur region of Sudan, South Africa deployed troops in 2005, as part of the first African Union peacekeeping mission (see p. 203).

South Africa had over 140,000 asylum seekers from Zimbabwe, Côte d'Ivoire, and the Great Lakes region, according to Human Rights Watch, which also found in a report published in November 2005 that, while South Africa had adequate refugee laws on paper, asylum seekers did not enjoy any protection in practice.

VIII SOUTH ASIA AND INDIAN OCEAN

IRAN—AFGHANISTAN—CENTRAL ASIAN STATES

IRAN

CAPITAL: Tehran   AREA: 1,633,000 sq km   POPULATION: 66,900,000
OFFICIAL LANGUAGES: Farsi (Persian)   POLITICAL SYSTEM: multiparty republic, under religious
   leadership
SPIRITUAL GUIDE: Ayatollah Seyed Ali Khamenei (since June '89)
HEAD OF STATE: President Mahmoud Ahmadinejad (since Aug '05)
MAIN IGO MEMBERSHIPS (NON-UN): OPEC, ECO, CP, OIC, NAM
CURRENCY: Iranian rial (end-'05 £1=IR15,607.8, US$1=IR9,091.50)
GNP PER CAPITA: US$2,300, US$7,550 at PPP ('04)

THE year was dominated by two issues, each of which suggested that Iran was moving further under the control of Islamic hardliners and away from the West. In June the outgoing reformist President, Seyyed Mohammad Khatami, was replaced by the ultra-conservative Mahmoud Ahmadinejad. Also, during the course of the year, Iran showed no signs of being willing to accede to the West's demands that it cease the development of its nuclear programme.

The presidential elections were the most unpredictable in the Islamic republic's twenty-six-year history. In May the conservative-dominated constitutional watchdog, the Council of Guardians, dashed the hopes of reformists by disqualifying all but six of the 1,014 candidates for the presidency. The first round of voting, on 17 June, failed to produce an outright winner, thereby necessitating a run-off, on 24 June, in which Mahmoud Ahmadinejad, an extreme conservative, defeated Ali Akbar Hashemi Rafsanjani by 7 million votes. All of the losing candidates raised questions of ballot-rigging, and there were allegations that the office of Supreme Leader Ayatollah Khamenei had intervened in favour of Ahmadinejad. The success of Mahmoud Ahmadinejad surprised many Iranians, since he was considered to be extremely doctrinaire and ideologically close to the revolutionary Islamic credo of Ayatollah Ruhollah Khomeini.

Ahmadinejad had a political career forged by the 1979 Islamic revolution. He had volunteered for the *basij* (military youth brigades) in 1980 and was promoted to be a commander of the revolutionary guards logistics division. He was politically motivated and was eventually given the governor-generalship of Maku and Khoy (in eastern Iran) and acted as advisor to the leadership in Kurdistan. He took advantage of his release from military duties to take a doctorate in engineering in 1987. After a period of comparative obscurity he became governor general of the new Ardebil ostan (province) in 1997. Elevation to mayor of Tehran in the local government elections of 2003 gave him access to the senior echelons of the Islamic regime and some exposure to the public. He was accepted by the electorate as a clean-handed Muslim who could address the many problems faced by the country, including corruption in official quarters, the lack of employment opportunities, and inertia in the domestic economy.

The new President overtly endorsed the principles laid down by Ayatollah Khomeini, but also developed his own vision of an imminent return of the Twelfth Imam (who went into occultation in the ninth century), and claimed to experience divine support. His motivation was drawn from his fundamentalist Islamic convictions, as demonstrated by his conservatism in social affairs, his support for welfare subsidies before economic growth, and his aggressive dislike of Western culture.

Ahmadinejad's hardline policies on the imposition of Islamic and revolutionary values at home and confrontation with the Western world abroad shook market confidence. The Iranian commercial classes and foreign investors took a negative view of the changes imposed following the election. A radical purge of the establishment was undertaken, including the replacement of Cabinet ministers, managers of state-owned banks, and leading diplomats. The Majlis (elected assembly), although itself having a conservative majority, rejected four of the new President's Cabinet appointments, including his choice of Oil Minister, on the grounds that they lacked sufficient ministerial experience.

Iranian foreign policy was dominated by the country's development of its nuclear industry, which was viewed with suspicion in the West as being designed to facilitate the eventual manufacture of nuclear weapons. Despite Iranian claims that the programme was aimed solely at the peaceful generation of electricity, the issue caused conflict between the Islamic regime and the International Atomic Energy Agency (IAEA), the USA, and the EU, the latter being represented by a troika of three European countries—France, Germany, and the UK—which were negotiating on its behalf. Iran had agreed in November 2004 to suspend nuclear enrichment as part of a deal negotiated with the troika whereby the EU resumed trade talks with Iran more than eighteen months after these had been frozen amid concerns over the nuclear issue.

The US government took a harder line towards Iran than did the EU, insisting that the Iranians' nuclear ambitions had to be curbed and refusing to rule out military action to achieve this end. (This threat was widely viewed as lacking credibility given the USA's military commitment in what increasingly appeared to be an unwinnable war in Iraq, see pp. 118-20; 188-90.) Although the USA was in favour of reporting the country to the UN Security Council for being in breach of the Nuclear Non-Proliferation Treaty (NPT), on 11 March US Secretary of State Condoleezza Rice backed the EU's diplomatic approach. In return, the EU agreed to take the nuclear issue to the Security Council if negotiations failed. The talks continued, although no breakthrough was achieved.

The situation changed when Mahmoud Ahmadinejad took office on 3 August. At the beginning of the month Iran announced that it was to resume the conversion of raw uranium into gas—a preliminary stage of uranium enrichment—at its Isfahan nuclear facility. The seals which had been put in place by the IAEA inspectors were broken on 10 August and negotiations with the EU troika were suspended amid dire warnings of the consequences if Iran were to proceed further down the road of unilateral action. Defiantly addressing the UN General Assembly on 17 September, President Ahmadinejad insisted on Iran's "inalienable right" to develop a peaceful nuclear energy programme and stated that the pursuit of nuclear weapons was contrary to the country's religious principles. On 24 September the IAEA board of governors approved a resolution allowing for Iran to be reported to the UN Security Council if the impasse was not resolved, a move which the Iranian Foreign Ministry denounced as "illegal and illogical".

Relations between Iran and the West worsened when, on 26 October, President Ahmadinejad made a speech in Tehran which described Israel as a "disgraceful blot" and reiterated a demand first made by Ayatollah Khomeini that the Jewish state be "wiped off the face of the world". The remarks caused outrage which was fuelled by further statements from Ahmadinejad in December, including a televised speech on 14 December in which he described the Holocaust as "a myth" which had been used by Europeans to create a Jewish state in the heart of the Islamic world, and said that the Jews should be moved to land in "Europe, the United States, Canada or Alaska".

Nevertheless, the year ended on a slightly more positive note when the IAEA board of governors met in Vienna on 24 November and decided against referring Iran to the UN Security Council, and the EU troika invited Iran to resume negotiations on a plan to transfer uranium enrichment to Russia. This compromise offered a glimmer of hope and in late December officials from Iran and the EU troika met for direct talks, the first to have been held since August. It was also agreed that Iran would hold direct talks with Russia on the creation of a joint Iranian-Russian company to enrich uranium in Russia, under Russian supervision.

Progress was made in re-establishing links with China and India, but Iran remained at odds with neighbouring Arab states over issues such as sovereignty over three islands in the Persian Gulf—Great Tumb, Little Tumb, and Abu Musa—whilst Turkey had commercial disputes with Iran. Pakistan and Afghanistan were aligned towards the USA and reluctant to welcome Iranian diplomatic advances.

The economy was quick to absorb persistently high oil revenues, but these were used mainly to fund the import of foreign goods and services, above all, consumer items. Oil revenues exceeded budget expectations at an actual US$46 billion from an output that ran at 3,950 barrels per day by December 2005. Even so, a budget deficit of US$11 billion was likely, caused by high outgoings to subsidise food, medicines, and fuel. State corporations failed to meet their forecast savings of US$4 billion. Economic growth was estimated at approximately 6 per cent in real terms in 2005, lifting Iranian GDP to US$242.2 billion, although this was largely generated by the oil sector. Inflation was estimated by the Central Bank at 15 per cent in the twelve months to September, with other sources suggesting that it exceeded 20 per cent.

AFGHANISTAN

CAPITAL: Kabul   AREA: 650,000 sq km   POPULATION: 28,766,000 ('03)
OFFICIAL LANGUAGES: Pushtu, Dari (Persian)   POLITICAL SYSTEM: multiparty republic
HEAD OF STATE AND GOVERNMENT: President Hamid Karzai (since Dec '04)
MAIN IGO MEMBERSHIPS (NON-UN): ECO, CP, OIC, NAM
CURRENCY: afgani (end-'05 £1=Af73.8203, US$1=Af43.0000)
GNI PER CAPITA: low income: US$825 or less ('04 est.)

AFGHANISTAN finally held its first democratic legislative elections since 1969 on 18 September, following several delays for reasons of security and administration. The landmark national and local elections, which produced a turnout of just over 50 per cent, were deemed "free, fair, and transparent" by an EU parliamentary delegation. However, other observers later became concerned that the vote had been marred by intimidation and fraud. Many of the approximately 300 female candidates reported that they had been subject to death threats and that their campaign posters had been defaced. Emma Bonino, head of the EU election observation mission, warned that the ballot would fail to produce a sustainable democratic political culture, and revealed that violence had prevented her team from monitoring the poll in five of the country's southern provinces.

When provisional results for the 249-member House of the People (the lower house of the new bicameral legislature, the National Assembly) were announced in October, it emerged that at least half of the seats had been won by conservative Islamic figures and former fighters, including former Taliban commanders. A further fifty seats were taken by independents, and eleven by former communists. Women secured sixty-eight seats, resulting in a higher percentage of female representation than in many Western legislatures. Many analysts predicted that the new legislature would be a deeply divided and confrontational body, comprising non-aligned individuals rather than established parties.

The country's new legislature eventually convened in December for its inaugural session. Opposition leader Yunus Qanuni, who had finished second to President Hamid Karzai in the presidential elections of September 2004, was elected Speaker of the National Assembly and chairman of the lower house.

Notwithstanding the political process, the security situation in Afghanistan remained grave. The year began with an assassination attempt on the powerful warlord (and unsuccessful presidential candidate) General Rashid Dostam, who survived an attack by a suicide bomber at a mosque in his northern stronghold of Sheberghan on 20 January. A Taliban spokesman claimed responsibility, stating that it was revenge for Dostam's collaboration with US forces and his killing of captured Taliban fighters in 2001.

The US military freed eighty-one Afghan prisoners on 16 January as part of a reconciliation programme under which most suspected Taliban members held in custody were to be released. A number of prisoners claimed that they had been badly treated or tortured by US forces, and most denied any links with the Taliban. Hundreds of prisoners held in military custody by the USA at Guantánamo Bay in Cuba and elsewhere were due to be repatriated, following a joint announcement on 4 August that the USA and Afghanistan had agreed on a gradual transfer of detainees to the custody of the Afghan government. In September a US military court handed down minimal sentences to four US soldiers convicted of the abuse of two Afghan prisoners who had died in custody. The servicemen were the first serving in Afghanistan to be convicted for such abuses. A leaked investigative report in May had revealed the extent of senior US military officials' involvement in systematic abuse of detainees. The accounts of "a culture of abuse" were hugely damaging to the US administration and prompted the UN to demand an independent enquiry by local human rights investigators (see also p. 121).

In February NATO Defence Ministers announced an expansion of the alliance's peacekeeping role into the west of the country, committing NATO to control of US-led operations and command of all Western troops. September saw the UN Security Council agree to extend the mandate of the International Security Assistance Force (ISAF) for a further twelve months from 13 October, while UK Defence Secretary John Reid announced on 14 November that the UK faced a "prolonged" engagement in Afghanistan following its assumption of control of ISAF in May 2006 for nine months. The expanded role for UK troops—to fill the gap left by a US withdrawal—would see them move out of the relative safety of Kabul into the Taliban stronghold of the turbulent Helmand province in the south. British MPs later warned that with the escalation of troop numbers the UK risked becoming mired in a long-term commitment to a country facing growing insurgency. The US administration would withdraw around 4,000 troops—most of its contingent—in the south early in 2006. On 8 December NATO Foreign Ministers agreed to increase the alliance's contingent of troops, which would expand the peacekeeping force by up to 6,000 (to around 16,000 troops) during 2006.

The killing of a UK development worker and kidnapping of an Italian aid worker marked the end of a lull in violence against foreigners. Stephen MacQueen, a World Bank expert working in consultation with the Afghan administration, was shot dead by unidentified gunmen in Kabul on 7 March. Clementina Cantoni, who helped Afghan widows in her work with Care International, was abducted from her vehicle in the capital on 16 May. She was released unharmed on 9 June.

The US military suffered high fatalities in helicopter crashes during the year, with three large Chinook troop-carrying aircraft coming down in April, June, and September, resulting in the deaths of thirty-six soldiers in total (see p. 120). A further helicopter crash resulted in the death of seventeen Spanish troops belonging to ISAF in August (see p. 60). A US air strike, intended to target what the military called a terrorist compound, killed seventeen Afghan civilians on 2 July in a village in Kunar province. The strike was part of a disastrous mission to rescue a four-strong group of Navy SEALs who had called for help after coming under attack. The troubled operation, which included the Chinook crash in June, proved the most costly for the USA since the removal of the Taliban in 2001.

KAZAKHSTAN—TURKMENISTAN—UZBEKISTAN—KYRGYZSTAN—TAJIKISTAN

Kazakhstan

CAPITAL: Astana   AREA: 2,717,000 sq km   POPULATION: 15,000,000
OFFICIAL LANGUAGES: Kazakh & Russian   POLITICAL SYSTEM: multiparty republic
HEAD OF STATE AND GOVERNMENT: President Nursultan Nazarbayev (since Feb '90)
RULING PARTY: Fatherland Party (Otan)
PRIME MINISTER: Daniyal Akhmetov (since June '03)
MAIN IGO MEMBERSHIPS (NON-UN): CIS, PFP, OSCE, OIC, ECO
CURRENCY: tenge (end-'05 £1=T229.487, US$1=T133.675)
GNI PER CAPITA: US$2,260, US$6,980 at PPP ('04)

Turkmenistan

CAPITAL: Ashgabat   AREA: 488,000 sq km   POPULATION: 4,900,000
OFFICIAL LANGUAGE: Turkmen   POLITICAL SYSTEM: multiparty republic
HEAD OF STATE AND GOVERNMENT: President (Gen.) Saparmurat Niyazov (since Jan '90)
RULING PARTY: Democratic Party of Turkmenistan (DPT)
MAIN IGO MEMBERSHIPS (NON-UN): CIS, PFP, OSCE, OIC, ECO, NAM
CURRENCY: Turkmen manat (end-'05 £1=M8,837.83, US$1=M5,148.00)
GNI PER CAPITA: US$1,340, US$6,910 at PPP ('04)

Uzbekistan

CAPITAL: Tashkent   AREA: 447,000 sq km   POPULATION: 25,900,000
OFFICIAL LANGUAGE: Uzbek   POLITICAL SYSTEM: multiparty republic
HEAD OF STATE AND GOVERNMENT: President Islam Karimov (since March '90)
RULING PARTY: People's Democratic Party (PDP)
PRIME MINISTER: Shavkat Mirziyoev (since Dec '03)
MAIN IGO MEMBERSHIPS (NON-UN): CIS, PFP, OSCE, OIC, ECO, NAM
CURRENCY: sum (end-'05 £1=S2,025.77, US$1=S1,180.00)
GNI PER CAPITA: US$460, US$1,860 at PPP ('04)

Kyrgyzstan

CAPITAL: Bishkek   AREA: 199,000 sq km   POPULATION: 5,100,000
OFFICIAL LANGUAGES: Kyrgyz & Russian   POLITICAL SYSTEM: multiparty republic
HEAD OF STATE AND GOVERNMENT: President Kurmanbek Bakiev (since March '05)
RULING PARTY: Democratic Movement of Kyrgyzstan heads coalition
PRIME MINISTER: Feliks Kulov (since Sept '05)
MAIN IGO MEMBERSHIPS (NON-UN): CIS, PFP, OSCE, OIC, ECO
CURRENCY: som (end-'05 £1=S70.9036, US$1=S41.3011)
GNI PER CAPITA: US$400, US$1,840 at PPP ('04)

Tajikistan

CAPITAL: Dushanbe   AREA: 143,000 sq km   POPULATION: 6,400,000
OFFICIAL LANGUAGE: Tajik   POLITICAL SYSTEM: multiparty republic
HEAD OF STATE AND GOVERNMENT: President Imamoli Rahmonov (since Nov '92)
RULING PARTY: People's Democratic Party of Tajikistan
PRIME MINISTER: Akil Akilov (since Dec '99)
MAIN IGO MEMBERSHIPS (NON-UN): CIS, OSCE, OIC, ECO, PFP
CURRENCY: somoni (end-'04 £1=5.3469, US$1=2.7850)
GNI PER CAPITA: US$280, US$1,150 at PPP ('04)

POLITICAL DEVELOPMENTS. KYRGYZSTAN experienced considerable turbulence in 2005. Elections to the newly established unicameral Supreme Assembly (the legislature) were held on 27 February. The following day, demonstrations erupted throughout the country in protest at alleged vote-rigging in favour of pro-government candidates. Tensions remained high for several weeks, particularly in southern Kyrgyzstan. On 20 March, demonstrators in the southern city of Jalabad stormed government buildings; once inside, they began smashing furniture and burning property. Four days later, the unrest spread to the capital, Bishkek. Thousands of people, wearing pink and yellow emblems to signify the "tulip revolution" (reminiscent of the orange banners displayed by protesters in Ukraine in 2004), took to the streets and forced President Askar Akayev and his government to resign. The crowds then went on a wild spree of rioting and looting. The total cost of the damage was estimated at over US$24 million. At least three people were killed and several hundred injured.

A degree of order was re-established when Kurmanbek Bakiev, leader of the main opposition party and himself a former Prime Minister, was appointed interim head of state, pending presidential elections. Another opposition leader, Feliks Kulov, was freed from prison where he was serving a ten-year sentence for alleged abuse of office, and given charge of the security forces. Meanwhile, Akayev fled the country. Bakiev formed an interim government, dominated, as expected, by opposition figures. The Kyrgyz Supreme Court annulled the results of the February-March elections and ruled that the old legislature would retain its mandate until fresh elections could be held.

Cracks in the opposition ranks surfaced in April, when Kulov announced that he would run for President. It was feared that the rivalry between Bakiev, a southerner, and Kulov, a northerner, would result in a dangerous regional split. However, Kulov withdrew his candidacy following the violence in UZBEKISTAN (see below) and fears that the unrest would spread across the border. Instead, he received an assurance that if Bakiev won, he (Kulov) would be given the post of Prime Minister. On 10 July Bakiev gained a landslide victory, receiving almost 90 percent of the vote. Kulov was duly appointed Prime Minister. Yet relations between the two men remained fragile. The situation was further complicated in the autumn, when the nexus between political power and criminal networks was highlighted by a series of violent incidents that included the murder of two MPs and prison riots that were allegedly motivated by political links. Some opposition groups accused Kulov of complicity in these actions. In October, the capital witnessed large rallies for and against the Prime Minister. President Bakiev, too, was mired in allegations of corruption and nepotism. Thus, by the end of the year the euphoria of the "tulip revolution" had largely given way to disillusionment and disappointment.

UZBEKISTAN experienced even greater turmoil. The central episode was the violence that erupted in Andijan, a town in the east of the country, on 13 May. This was triggered by two simultaneous occurrences. Whether or not they were connected remained unclear. One was a large, peaceful demonstration in support of a group of twenty-three men on trial for membership of the Akromiya, an illegal, allegedly extremist, Islamist organisation named after its founder, Akrom Yoldashev. The other was an armed insurgency mounted by unknown combatants. The insurgents attacked government buildings, including military-police stations, the local prison, and the central administrative office; they also took hostages, set fire to civilian cars, and caused major damage to the theatre and cinema in the central square. Uzbek security troops responded with force and in the ensuing attacks an unknown number of people—including civilians, insurgents, policemen, government officials, and medical staff—was killed. Estimates of the death toll ranged from under 200 to over 1,500.

In the aftermath of the violence, several hundred people fled across the border into KYRGYZSTAN. The great majority (approximately 400) of the refugees consisted of young men. For the Kyrgyz government, this posed a real security threat since southern Kyrgyzstan (adjacent to Uzbekistan) had a history of insurgencies and Islamic radicalism; moreover, it was permeated by drug trafficking and other forms of contraband trade. Thus, the uncontrolled influx of hundreds of unknown individuals—some perhaps armed—was a matter of grave concern to the Kyrgyz authorities. However, after initial reluctance they agreed to give them temporary asylum. At the end of July, under the auspices of the UN High Commissioner for Refugees (UNHCR), 439 of the refugees were airlifted to Romania.

Human rights activists and journalists insisted that the Uzbek government had brutally attacked innocent demonstrators and deliberately massacred large numbers of people. International organisations and many Western governments accepted this account, and called for an international commission to investigate the incident. The Uzbek authorities believed that some Western agencies (governmental or non-governmental) had known about the insurgency in advance, and had proffered support and encouragement; consequently, they would not countenance Western involvement in the investigation. Over the following months they arrested numerous suspects. The defendants went on trial at the end of September; all were found guilty and received long prison sentences.

In TAJIKISTAN, by contrast, the situation was relatively stable. Elections to the Assembly of Representatives (the lower chamber of the bicameral legislature) were held on 27 February, with run-offs on 13 March. The pro-presidential People's Democratic Party won almost 75 per cent of the vote; the Communist Party and the Islamic Rebirth Party made a weak showing, while the other opposition parties failed to pass the 5 per cent minimum threshold. Some foreign observers, including the head of the observer mission from the Organisation for Security and Co-operation in Europe (OSCE), noted that the elections "did not meet the key obligations and standards of the OSCE and the international community", but acknowledged that there had been positive factors such as the participation of a broad spectrum of political parties. Importantly, there had been no violence. Elections to the National Assembly (the upper chamber) took place on 24-25 March. As expected, all of the new senators were supporters of the President. The main outcome of these elections was to enable President Rahmonov to tighten his hold on the levers of power, since both houses of the legislature were now controlled by his supporters.

In KAZAKHSTAN, too, there was an election. In August, the authorities made a snap announcement that the presidential election scheduled for 2006 would be held on 4 December 2005. This caught the opposition parties off guard and left them with very little time to organise their campaigns. Nevertheless, five candidates did register as contestants. The incumbent, President Nursultan Nazarbayev, was generally regarded as the most likely winner, although some observers considered Zharmakhan Tuyakbay, the candidate standing on behalf of the opposition alliance "For a Fair Kazakhstan", to be a serious contender. The Nazarbayev campaign emphasised an impressive record of achievements and held out a vision of future progress and prosperity. His pronouncements, made in prestigious venues, received nationwide publicity. Opposition candidates, meanwhile, complained of harassment and obstruction. The independent media experienced intimidation and persecution, including the illegal seizure of print runs and the forced closure of newspapers.

As anticipated, Nazarbayev was re-elected for another seven-year term. There was, as always, criticism of the electoral proceedings both from domestic commentators and from some foreign monitors, including the OSCE observer mission. Yet no one seriously doubted that Nazarbayev would have won, no matter how stringently the election had been conducted. What was somewhat unexpected was the size of his majority, amounting to over 90 per cent of the vote. This massive show of confidence was partly prompted by the fear that the disturbances in neighbouring KYRGYZSTAN and UZBEKISTAN might be repeated in KAZAKHSTAN if an inexperienced leader came to power.

In TURKMENISTAN there was little perceptible change. Legislative elections, in which 131 candidates competed for places in the fifty-seat Mejlis, were held in December 2004, with run-offs in January 2005. According to official sources, 77 per cent of the electorate turned out to vote, a markedly lower proportion than in the elections in December 1999, when a turn-out of 99.6 per cent was recorded. No foreign observers were allowed to monitor the proceedings. In March President Saparmurat Niyazov proposed that contested presidential elections should be held in 2009, but after desultory debate during the year the matter was shelved in favour of maintaining the status quo.

INTERNATIONAL AND REGIONAL RELATIONS. After the disturbances in KYRGYZSTAN and UZBEKISTAN, one of the chief concerns of the international community was the future of the military bases of the Western coalition forces (primarily of the USA) in these countries. Opened in autumn 2001, the bases provided logistical support for the military campaign in Afghanistan (see AR 2001, p. 331; map, p. 325). The US deployment in KYRGYZSTAN included some 800 air force troops, tanker aircraft, and military transport aircraft. In February, a request to allow AWACS reconnaissance aircraft to be based on Kyrgyz territory was rejected by the then government. The new government reiterated this position, but allegations that permission had been given covertly surfaced throughout the year. The new Kyrgyz leadership appeared uncertain as to how to manage the situation. Immediately after his election as President, Bakiev seemed to want the USA to set a deadline for terminating its military presence. This conformed to the position adopted by the Shanghai Co-operation Organisation (see below). When US Defence Secretary Donald Rumsfeld visited Bishkek in late July, however, the official response was that Kyrgyzstan accepted the need for the continued US presence. Nevertheless, the Kyrgyz government did broach questions of financial recompense for the lease of the base and for environmental damage. After months of negotiation, in January 2006 the USA agreed to increase annual rent payments from under US$50 million to US$200 million.

The authorities in UZBEKISTAN were also concerned about the ongoing US presence on their territory. Some eighteen months previously they had requested clarification regarding the USA's use of the Qarshi-Khonobod base. However, no definitive answer was received, and in July 2005 Uzbekistan formally demanded that US personnel vacate the facility within six months. The USA responded that it would indeed leave the base, but claimed that this action was being taken in protest at the Uzbek government's handling of the Andijan incident. The German base at Termez, also part of the Western coalition, was not affected by these disputes and continued to function as previously.

The Russian air base at Kant, KYRGYZSTAN, which had been established in 2003, formed part of the strategic deployment of the Commonwealth of Independent States' (CIS) Collective Security Treaty Organisation (other members at this time included KAZAKHSTAN and TAJIKISTAN, but not UZBEKISTAN). In 2005 Russia announced plans for capital investment in the infrastructure in and around the base, with the aim of strengthening the capabilities of the CIS collective rapid reaction forces in the Central Asian region. President Bakiev welcomed this project, stressing the importance of the base for enhancing both national and regional security. It was also emphasised that the base would help the local economy (unlike the US base, which was often criticised for making too little contribution to the life of the host community).

In the bilateral sphere, the most notable developments were the strengthening of the relationship between KAZAKHSTAN and its two large neighbours, Russia and China. In July China and Kazakhstan announced plans to establish a strategic partnership. Trade and economic co-operation between the two countries were expanding rapidly. In October, in the face of strong international competition, the China National Petroleum Corporation (CNPC) clinched the purchase of the Canadian oil company PetroKazakhstan. The deal, which cost US$4.18 billion, was the largest foreign purchase made to date by a Chinese company. PetroKazakhstan's assets included twelve oil fields and exploration licences in six areas of Kazakhstan, as well as the Shymkent refinery. The company's total annual production exceeded 7 million tonnes of crude oil. In December, the inauguration of the new 1,000-kilometre oil pipeline from Atasu in central Kazakhstan to Alashankou in western China was a landmark event, significantly increasing and diversifying Kazakhstan's export potential. Future phases of this project would extend the pipeline to Kazakhstan's oil-rich Caspian littoral.

During the year a number of important agreements were also concluded with Russia, several of which related to the energy sector. In July came the announcement of a deal between Kazakh Kazmunaygaz and Russian Rosneft for the joint development of the giant Kurmangazy oil field (recoverable reserves conservatively estimated at 980 million tonnes) in the Caspian Sea. It was envisaged that some US$23 billion would be invested in the project over a period of fifty-five years, the first ten years to be devoted to exploration, the remaining period to extraction. It was expected that the Kazakh budget would receive income of over US$30 billion from the deal. Another major development was the signing of an agreement on the creation of a joint power-generation venture. This, President Nazarbayev pointed out, would make possible the creation of "a single energy system for Russia and Kazakhstan".

Good relations were further cemented by the Kazakh legislature's ratification, on 23 November, of the Kazakh-Russian state border treaty. Separate agreements were to be concluded later to address specific issues relating to the 7,500-kilometre border, such as the development of mineral resources, environmental protection, and the management of biological and water resources. Both parties to the treaty enthusiastically greeted it as an important step towards closer integration, with the ultimate goal of creating a "single economic space" (an embryonic project for a common market encompassing Russia, Belarus, Kazakhstan, and Ukraine).

A further move towards the creation of an "inner core" of CIS member states was the announcement, made in St Petersburg, Russia, in September, that the Central Asian Co-operation Organisation (CACO, comprising Russia, KAZAKHSTAN, UZBEKISTAN, TAJIKISTAN, and KYRGYZSTAN) was to merge with the Eurasian Economic Community (EEC) (Russia, Belarus, KAZAKHSTAN, KYRGYZSTAN, and TAJIKISTAN). This bombshell development highlighted Russia's increased authority and influence in the region. It would undoubtedly lead to closer economic, and political, co-ordination between the member states. Of particular note was the decision of UZBEKISTAN to join the merged organisation, since the Uzbek government had previously been highly critical of the Eurasian Economic Community and Russia's role within it.

Despite the emergence of a more closely knit structure, Kazakhstan, Kyrgyzstan, Tajikistan and Uzbekistan still favoured retaining the Commonwealth of Independent States as an overarching organisation. In August the Presidents of these states joined seven other heads of CIS member states for a summit meeting in Kazan, Russia; on the agenda was co-operation in various fields as well as reform of CIS institutions. TURKMENISTAN, however, announced that it was relinquishing full membership and would henceforth be an associate member.

There were also important developments in another regional organisation, the Shanghai Co-operation Organisation (SCO). The heads of member states (Russia, China, KYRGYZSTAN, KAZAKHSTAN, TAJIKISTAN and UZBEKISTAN) attended the annual summit meeting in Astana in July. The resulting joint declaration outlined common positions on a number of political, economic and security issues. The point which attracted most international attention, however, was the carefully worded request that "members of the anti-terrorist coalition set a final timeline for their temporary use of [. . .] infrastructure and stay of their military contingents on the territories of the SCO member states". In Western capitals this was viewed as a direct challenge to the US presence in the region. It undoubtedly emboldened some of the Central Asian states to voice concerns that had previously been suppressed (see above). The July summit also saw the accession of India, Iran, and Pakistan as observer members. This lent additional weight to the organisation, which seemed set to play a more active role in the region (see p. 354).

INDIA—PAKISTAN—BANGLADESH—SRI LANKA— NEPAL—BHUTAN

India

CAPITAL: New Delhi   AREA: 3,288,000 sq km   POPULATION: 1,079,700,000
OFFICIAL LANGUAGES: Hindi & English   POLITICAL SYSTEM: multiparty republic in Commonwealth
HEAD OF STATE: President A.P.J. Abdul Kalam (since July '02)
RULING PARTIES: Congress (I)-led United Progressive Alliance (UPA) coalition (since May '04)
HEAD OF GOVERNMENT: Manmohan Singh (INC), Prime Minister (since May '04)
MAIN IGO MEMBERSHIPS (NON-UN): SAARC, CP, CWTH, NAM
CURRENCY: Indian rupee (end-'05 £1=Rs77.2709, US$1=Rs45.0100)
GNI PER CAPITA: US$620, US$3,100 at PPP ('04, based on regression)

Pakistan

CAPITAL: Islamabad   AREA: 796,000 sq km   POPULATION: 152,100,000
OFFICIAL LANGUAGE: Urdu   POLITICAL SYSTEM: military regime with elected legislature in Commonwealth
HEAD OF STATE AND GOVERNMENT: President (Gen.) Pervez Musharraf (since June '01), formerly Chief Executive Officer of National Security Council (since Oct '99)
RULING PARTIES: coalition led by Pakistan Muslim League—Quaid-i-Azam (PML-Q)
PRIME MINISTER: Shaukat Aziz (PML—QA) (since August '04)
MAIN IGO MEMBERSHIPS (NON-UN): OIC, SAARC, ECO, CP, NAM, CWTH (suspended)
CURRENCY: Pakistan rupee (end-'05 £1=PRs102.644, US$1=PRs59.7900)
GNI PER CAPITA: US$600, US$2,160 at PPP ('04)

Bangladesh

CAPITAL: Dhaka   AREA: 144,000 sq km   POPULATION: 140,500,000
OFFICIAL LANGUAGE: Bengali   POLITICAL SYSTEM: multiparty republic in Commonwealth
HEAD OF STATE: President Iajuddin Ahmed (since Sept '02)
RULING PARTIES: Bangladesh Nationalist Party (BNP)-led coalition
HEAD OF GOVERNMENT: Khaleda Zia, Prime Minister (since Nov '01)
MAIN IGO MEMBERSHIPS (NON-UN): SAARC, CP, OIC, CWTH, NAM
CURRENCY: taka (end-'05 £1=Tk113.692, US$1=Tk66.2250)
GNI PER CAPITA: US$440, US$1,980 at PPP ('04)

Sri Lanka

CAPITAL: Colombo   AREA: 66,000 sq km   POPULATION: 19,400,000
OFFICIAL LANGUAGES: Sinhala, Tamil, English   POLITICAL SYSTEM: multiparty republic in Commonwealth
HEAD OF STATE: President Mahinda Rajapakse (SLFP) (since Nov '05)
RULING PARTIES: Sri Lanka Freedom Party (SLFP) heads United People's Freedom Alliance (UPFA) coalition (since April '04)
HEAD OF GOVERNMENT: Ratnasiri Wickremanayake, Prime Minister (since Nov '05)
MAIN IGO MEMBERSHIPS (NON-UN): SAARC, CP, CWTH, NAM
CURRENCY: Sri Lankan rupee (end-'05 £1=SRs175.289, US$1=SRs102.105)
GNI PER CAPITA: US$1,010, US$4,000 at PPP ('04)

Nepal

CAPITAL: Kathmandu   AREA: 147,000 sq km   POPULATION: 25,200,000
OFFICIAL LANGUAGE: Nepali   POLITICAL SYSTEM: non-party monarchy
HEAD OF STATE: King Gyanendra (since June '01)
MAIN IGO MEMBERSHIPS (NON-UN): SAARC, CP, NAM
CURRENCY: Nepalese rupee (end-'05 £1=NRs123.633, US$1=NRs72.0160)
GNI PER CAPITA: US$260, US$1,470 at PPP ('04)

Bhutan

CAPITAL: Thimphu   AREA: 46,500 sq km   POPULATION: 896,000
OFFICIAL LANGUAGES: Dzongkha, Lhotsan & English   POLITICAL SYSTEM: non-party monarchy
HEAD OF STATE: Dragon King Jigme Singye Wangchuk (since '72)
HEAD OF GOVERNMENT: Prime Minister (rotates among cabinet) Lyonpo Sangay Ngedup (since Sept '05)
MAIN IGO MEMBERSHIPS (NON-UN): SAARC, CP, NAM
CURRENCY: ngultrum (end '04 £1=Nu77.2709, US$1=Nu45.0100)
GNI PER CAPITA: US$760 ('04)

INDIA continued to consolidate its new position in 2005 as an emerging major force in Asian and in world affairs. Its Congress-led government completed the year without major political challenges. In the region as a whole there were no major changes in domestic or international alignments, with the exception of the electoral defeat of the government of SRI LANKA. Political violence was a recurrent problem in many parts of the region, and Sri Lanka and NEPAL in particular struggled to cope with longstanding insurgencies. Economic growth was in line with the trends of recent years, averaging 6-7 per cent, although all countries of the region to a greater or lesser degree suffered from high oil prices. In October PAKISTAN, and to a lesser extent INDIA, suffered an earthquake that left nearly 100,000 people dead and millions homeless in the Himalayan regions.

POLITICAL DEVELOPMENTS. In INDIA, 2005 was a year of consolidation and steady progress for the Congress-led government of Dr Manmohan Singh and the other parties grouped together in the United Progressive Alliance (UPA). Favourable trends in the economy enabled the government to press ahead with various pro-poor elements of its election manifesto and the UPA's common minimum programme, in particular the national rural employment guarantee scheme. In August a bill was passed giving legislative shape to a scheme which would provide 100 days' employment per year to each rural household, and implementation began towards the end of the year, although only in selected areas at first. State elections in February in the north Indian state of Haryana saw a landslide victory for Congress. The Congress ally, the Samajwadi Party, which controlled Uttar Pradesh—the country's largest state and often a battleground for Indian politics—saw little challenge to its position.

Manmohan Singh's position as Prime Minister seemed secure, although his own political base remained very limited and he depended entirely on the endorsement and support of Sonia Gandhi, the Congress president and widow of Rajiv Gandhi, and her family. There were rumours of strains in their relationship but little concrete evidence of serious problems. Other than the resignation of the Foreign Minister (see below), no changes took place in the Cabinet.

The left-wing elements which supported the government, although not as formal members of the UPA—notably the Communist Party of India Marxist, which continued to control the important state of West Bengal—were unhappy with the apparent pro-Western tilt by the government, but not to the extent of threatening the coalition's survival. They focused particularly on the agreement with the USA on India's nuclear status (see below), even though in many respects this gave India what it wanted and was seen by many commentators as a major step in India's emergence on the world stage.

Bihar, a key north Indian state, saw political upheaval during the year. Initially controlled by a coalition partner of Congress, the Rashtriya Janata Dal (RJD), the state saw no party or alliance gain a clear majority following elections in February. The governor then controversially decided to dissolve the assembly and impose central rule: the dissolution was subsequently declared unlawful by the Supreme Court. Fresh elections in November saw the victory of the National Democratic Alliance, in which the Bharatiya Janata Party (BJP) was an important partner. The new state chief minister, Nitish Kumar, represented the interests of low status caste groups who had felt that the previous government had not done enough for them. However, although the RJD had lost power in Bihar, its principal leader, the populist Lalu Prasad Yadav, remained a prominent member of the central government as Minister for Railways. Similar political problems were seen in the state of Jharkhand (earlier a part of Bihar), where a UPA partner, the Jharkhand Mukti Morcha, came to power in elections in February after alleged improper interference by the governor of the state. The party's leader, Shibu Soren, was a controversial figure who had been forced in 2004 to resign from the national government; after major street protests by the opposition he was forced to resign as chief minister of Jharkhand. His replacement, Arjun Munda, came from the BJP.

At the end of the year there was a generational change of leadership in the BJP. The former Prime Minister, Atal Behari Vajpayee, announced that he was retiring, while his successor as party leader, Lal Krishan Advani, who had faced internal criticism for apparently conciliatory remarks towards Pakistan during a visit there in May, also stood down. The new leader was Rajnath Singh, a former chief minister of Uttar Pradesh, perceived as being in good standing with the Hindu nationalist RSS (Rashtriya Swayamsevak Sangh—a founder of the BJP) but a low key figure relatively little known outside his home state. One of the BJP's most high profile figures, Uma Bharti, who was associated with its most anti-Muslim and nationalistic elements, was expelled at the end of the year for her vehement attacks on the party leadership. The Shiv Sena, a close ally of the BJP in Maharashtra in the past and with a powerful presence in Mumbai, continued to implode, with one of its senior leaders, Narain Rane, defecting to Congress in July, together with many of his supporters.

In December eleven MPs from several different parties, including both Congress and the BJP, were expelled from the Indian Parliament after having been filmed accepting bribes. Although similar "sting" operations had led to ministerial resignations in the 1990s, this was the first time that action had been taken against such a large group. In the same month the Foreign Minister, K. Natwar Singh, was forced to resign after being implicated in the Iraq "oil-for-food" scandal. The longstanding cases arising from the Bofors arms sales in the 1980s, in which it was alleged that the Gandhi family had been implicated, were however dismissed by the Delhi High Court during the course of the year.

In parallel to his government's ongoing dialogue with Pakistan, the Indian Prime Minister held talks with representatives of the Hurriyet Conference, the principal political organisation for Kashmiris who rejected the state's constitutional status as part of India. The government permitted Hurriyet leaders to visit both Pakistan-administered Kashmir and Pakistan to hold talks. As part of an earlier agreement with its electoral ally, the People's Democratic Party, the Congress itself took the leadership of the government in Jammu and Kashmir during the year.

India suffered from several terrorist attacks during the year. In July an attack by a Muslim group on the disputed site at Ayodhya, which had caused so much conflict in the early 1990s, was foiled, but bombs in Delhi in October caused many casualties, and in December there was an attack on a prominent educational institution in the southern city of Bangalore. A small Kashmiri group claimed responsibility for the Delhi attacks. Maoist guerrilla groups were also active, as they had been for many years, in isolated pockets, especially in the southern state of Andhra Pradesh where at least 250 people were killed in incidents during the year.

There were no significant changes at the federal level in PAKISTAN. The Prime Minister, Shaukat Aziz, remained in control, although always dependent on the support of the President. The government party, the Pakistan Muslim League, suffered significant internal divisions, which affected both Punjab and Sindh, but the opposition was unable to capitalise on them. Nawaz Sharif and Benazir Bhutto, the leaders of the two mainstream opposition political parties, remained abroad throughout the year. Talks took place between them but without major results. There was speculation that the Pakistan People's Party (PPP) might do a deal with the government, offering to support it in return for the cancellation of corruption charges against PPP leader Benazir Bhutto. There was similar discussion of the possibility of an accommodation with the Nawaz Sharif family, and Nawaz Sharif was granted a passport to allow him to travel beyond Saudi Arabia, where he had been exiled since 1999, but no concrete steps followed, and the government appeared to prefer a policy of inducing individual members of the opposition parties to defect to the PML. This was particularly noticed in the Punjab.

Local elections, the second since the military coup of 1999, took place in August and September, amidst widespread allegations that the polls were manipulated in various ways to ensure the victory of pro-government candidates. Although theoretically held on a non-party basis, the allegiances of the candidates were openly advertised. The most important change as a result of the elections was in Karachi, the country's principal city, where the locally dominant Muttahida Quami Movement (MQM), which had boycotted the previous polls in 2002, was successful.

The Muttahida Majlis-e-Amal (MMA)—the alliance of religious parties—remained in power in North-West Frontier Province (and in coalition with the PML in Balochistan also). However, its attempt to introduce the Hasba bill, which would have authorised the official enforcement of Islamic practices, was struck down by the Supreme Court in August. The members of the MMA were divided on whether to co-operate with the federal government. After considerable internal dissension, the pragmatic view prevailed, and the North-West Frontier Province chief minister was authorised to attend meetings of the National Security Council.

Province-centre relations were a major theme of Pakistan politics during the year. The three smaller provinces of Sindh, North-West Frontier Province, and Balochistan had long resented what they perceived as the unfair dominance of the Punjab. One major issue was whether or not to construct another large dam to meet Pakistan's water problems, and if so where. One particular project, at Kalabagh in Punjab, had been a bone of contention since shortly after independence. President General Pervez Musharraf tried hard during 2005 to generate a consensus in favour of its construction, but without success. Also of concern were the protracted efforts to secure agreement on the division of revenue between the capital, Islamabad, and the provinces and, in turn, on the formula for distribution between the provinces. However, attempts during 2005 to find an acceptable formula were unsuccessful. On the last day of the year, the Pakistan Cabinet decided, on the one hand, to go ahead with the Kalabagh dam even without a full consensus, and on the other to revive the Council of Common Interests, an institution that brought together federal and provincial leaders and which had not met for some years.

In Balochistan, where since independence there had been successive revolts against the authority of the state, a succession of armed attacks on government property and personnel, including key natural gas installations, took place during the year. The government responded to these with considerable force. At the end of the year military action was launched in the area around Kohlu, dominated by the Marri tribe. Blamed by the government on vested interests among the region's traditional tribal leadership, the episodes also reflected the feeling among some groups that outsiders were taking almost all the rewards of economic development in the province. A bomb explosion in Karachi at the end of the year was attributed to Baloch separatist elements. The government had appointed a Senate committee in 2004 to develop ideas to address Baloch grievances, and this made a number of recommendations during the course of 2005, which at the end of the year had yet to be implemented.

Throughout the year the government also had to cope with what amounted to an insurgency in Waziristan, one of the tribal areas along the border with Afghanistan where formal government presence had always been very limited. Taliban and elements supporting al-Qaida had based themselves there and had obtained substantial local support. Government actions alternated between force and negotiation, but the situation was unresolved at the end of the year. The USA, naturally, was anxious to see the government secure its hold on the region.

A number of social issues continued to make the headlines both nationally and internationally. Sectarian violence between Shi'ite and Sunni groups continued throughout the year in the mountainous area of Gilgit, and Christian and Ahmadi groups faced sporadic attacks. Several high profile rape cases were reported; in response to questions from reporters in September, while in the USA, President Musharraf appeared to downplay their importance.

In BANGLADESH, as for some years, the political scene was dominated by a stand-off between the two main parties, the Bangladesh Nationalist Party (BNP), currently in power, and the Awami League. The rivalry was itself a reflection of personal animosity between the party leaders. The Awami League seized every opportunity to launch demonstrations and strikes on issues ranging from price rises to the government's failure to curb the bombing campaign (see below). These events were often accompanied by violent clashes between police and demonstrators. The collective impact on the country and the economy was considerable. In January a prominent Awami League leader, A.M.S. Kibria, was killed by a grenade explosion at a political rally. The police arrested a number of members of the BNP, although at the end of the year the case was still pending. In April a court sentenced twenty-two individuals to death for their involvement in a similar case the previous year (the sentences themselves being subject to confirmation by the High Court). Most of those convicted also belonged to the BNP or its allies.

The year in Bangladesh was also marked by a rise in Islamic militancy. On 17 August there was a co-ordinated series of bomb blasts across the country. Several hundred small devices were set off during a short space of time by the Jamaat-ul-Mujahideen, a militant organisation that had been growing in size during the past few years, and whose leader, Asadullah Al Galib, had been arrested in February. Following the August attacks, there were several more bombs in different cities, including attacks on the courts, which caused a number of deaths and injuries. In February and in October the principal militant groups blamed by the government for the attacks were formally banned. Throughout the year Islamist groups waged a campaign against a heterodox Muslim group, the Ahmadis, and this led on occasion to violent clashes.

In October Bangladesh, for the fifth year in a row, received the unenviable distinction of being ranked by Transparency International (the international organisation dedicated to combating corruption) as the world's most corrupt state.

Scheduled presidential elections were held in SRI LANKA in November. Mahinda Rajapakse from the Sri Lanka Freedom Party (SLFP), who had been Prime Minister under the previous President, won the election, defeating another former Prime Minister, Ranil Wickremasinghe, from the other main party, the United National Party, by a narrow margin. He did so with the support on the one hand of the Jathika Hela Urumaya (JHU), representing some sections of the Buddhist clergy, and on the other the Janatha Vimukhti Peramuna (JVP), a Marxist party which was at the same time fiercely pro-Sinhalese. The Liberation Tigers of Tamil Eelam (LTTE) enforced a boycott in the Tamil areas of the island, which effectively led to the defeat of UNP candidate Wickremasinghe. The new President chose Ratnasiri Wickremanayake as the new Prime Minister.

President Rajapakse was generally regarded as a hardliner on the question of negotiating with the Tamil minority, and continued to insist on a unitary framework for the state, but he did not rule out a continuation of peace talks under the auspices of Norway. On the military front, however, the truce with the LTTE that had been in force since 2002, and under which the LTTE had enjoyed complete control of large parts of the north of the country, began to unravel towards the end of the year, with a series of attacks on military targets. On 12 August the Foreign Minister Lakshman Kadirgamar was assassinated, although the identity of his attacker remained unclear and the LTTE disclaimed responsibility.

Politics in NEPAL continued to be dominated on the one hand by the Maoist insurgency that had led to many deaths in the past few years, and on the other by tussles between the King and mainstream political parties over their respective powers. At the beginning of February King Gyanendra dismissed the elected government of Sher Bahadur Deuba and declared a state of emergency on the grounds that Deuba had failed adequately to deal with the Maoist insurgency. In July Deuba was jailed for two years on corruption charges. However, the level of Maoist activity continued unabated during the year. In September, the Maoist group declared a unilateral ceasefire for three months, later extended to four. During the course of this, they held talks with the principal political parties and issued a joint call for the establishment of a constituent assembly, a demand immediately rejected by the King and his ministers. However, the fact of the agreement between Maoists and political parties, which appeared to open the possibility of a ceremonial monarchy with only limited constitutional powers, was a major development in a situation which had appeared to be deadlocked.

In BHUTAN the gradual measures by the King to introduce a party-based democratic system continued with the further public discussion of a draft constitution. At the end of the year the King announced that once national elections under the new constitution had been held in 2008 he intended to abdicate in favour of his son.

NATURAL DISASTERS. Sri Lanka and the south-eastern coasts of India, along with the islands in the Bay of Bengal, had been badly hit by the tsunami disaster at the end of 2004, and Sri Lanka in particular continued to be affected by the massive and ongoing tasks of reconstruction (see map, p. 296). While some foreign assistance arrived, it was well below the total need.

India suffered further in July when Mumbai experienced 26 inches of rain in twenty-four hours, an unprecedented event which led to extensive flooding in the city and surrounding parts of Maharashtra. Over 1,000 deaths resulted and many millions lost their homes.

On 8 October, the Pakistan-controlled section of Kashmir (Azad Kashmir), adjacent areas of the North-West Frontier Province, and to a lesser extent the areas on the Indian side of the line of control were devastated by a major earthquake measuring 7.6 on the Richter scale. On the Pakistan side, deaths were estimated to be at least 73,000, with many more injured and millions made homeless. As the disaster happened in the morning, many schools and colleges collapsed on top of their students. The cities of Muzaffarabad and Balakot were particularly badly hit. The Pakistan army (which had itself suffered significant numbers of casualties) took primary responsibility for managing the immediate response. Despite a spontaneous outpouring of effort by all sections of society, the most remote settlements remained cut off for weeks, and for some time there was a sense of confusion and lack of direction. Foreign assistance also began to arrive from many different countries, with, for example, US and NATO troops from Afghanistan helping with some logistical issues and a large team of Cuban doctors and nurses providing medical assistance. Teams from Turkey, Indonesia, and elsewhere also participated.

On 19 November, an international donors conference was held in Islamabad, attended by the UN Secretary-General and other world leaders. Over US$5 billion was pledged, a figure which was higher than expected, although much of it was in the form of soft loans. Concerns were openly expressed by donors about the risk of money being siphoned off, and the Pakistan government went out of its way to meet demands for independent audit. Within Pakistan, questions were asked about the ineffectiveness of building controls in earthquake-prone areas, and the need to learn from other countries in this respect.

The earthquake disaster led to some co-operation between INDIA and PAKISTAN, although political considerations limited its extent. Crossing points were opened on the line of control in Kashmir to allow relief goods to cross, but India's offer of helicopters was declined on the grounds that Indian air force pilots were unacceptable on Pakistani territory. The offer of help from NATO was accepted, but the opposition used it as a stick to beat the government.

As with the earlier tsunami relief effort, INDIA was able to deal with the needs of the affected individuals on its side of the line of control without requiring foreign assistance.

ECONOMIC DEVELOPMENTS. The economy in INDIA performed steadily during the year, achieving a growth rate of approximately 7 per cent, with low inflation and high foreign exchange reserves. Foreign investment, both direct and portfolio, reached record levels, indicating growing international confidence, and the stock markets also reached unprecedented heights. However, high oil prices contributed to a widening trade deficit. The fiscal deficit also remained high, given the political constraints to widening the tax base. In June India's largest private business firm, Reliance, was split between the two sons of its founder, Dhirubhai Ambani, who had been feuding over control after his death. The expiry of the World Trade Organisation's multi-fibre agreement at the end of 2004 provided new opportunities for Indian exports both to the USA and the EU, although at the same time India itself received significantly increased volumes of textiles from China.

In an attempt to tackle rural poverty, still at very high levels despite the growth in the manufacturing and service sectors in the past few years, the government introduced a series of poverty reduction schemes, notably the national rural employment guarantee scheme (see above). The budget, presented in February, also attempted to find ways to ameliorate poverty levels through substantial increases in spending on health, education, and rural infrastructure. Under pressure from left-wing supporters of the coalition, notably the two communist parties, the government announced in August that it was not going to sell off profitable state enterprises. India was an active participant in the WTO negotiations in Hong Kong, although it was unable, along with other developing country participants, to achieve all its aims in the field of agriculture (see pp. 356-57). India's successes in the services sector in the last few years put it on the other side of the negotiating table from many other developing countries.

The PAKISTAN economy continued to perform well during the year as a whole, although the growth rate of 8.4 per cent reached in the financial year 2004-05 could not be sustained, principally because of lower cotton production and the continued high price of oil. GDP growth for the calendar year 2005 was estimated at approximately 7 per cent, while inflation rose to around 9 per cent. The earthquake devastation had only a marginal effect on the economy. The privatisation programme of the government saw the completion of the sale of two major units, the inefficient and loss-making power producer KESC, and the profitable but underperforming telecommunications provider PTCL. The latter sale, to the UAE-based Etisalat, nearly collapsed at the last moment, and the government was forced to offer the buyer more generous payment terms. A major stock market crash in March, attributed to speculation within a narrowly based market, also indicated some of the weaknesses that had yet to be overcome. Foreign investment at less than US$1 billion remained very low. Domestic savings rates also remained stubbornly low, as did the ratio of tax to GDP, which actually fell during the year to 10.1 per cent. A widening trade gap during the year was another major cause for concern.

Growth in BANGLADESH continued on a fairly steady path during the year, although the ending of the quota system for textile exports to Europe and elsewhere, which had provided a protected environment for Bangladesh, put considerable pressure on export earnings in the face of competition from China and elsewhere. High oil prices were a major issue and in September the government introduced a five-day week (with a longer working day) in order to save energy.

SRI LANKA was badly hit by the immediate aftermath of the 2004 tsunami, and also by the stalemate over negotiations between the government and the Tamil Tigers, but overall growth managed to reach an estimated 5.5 per cent. The tourist sector, critical for foreign exchange earnings, remained depressed during the year.

REGIONAL RELATIONS. After the optimism of the past couple of years, 2005 was a year of consolidation and reflection on future directions in relations between INDIA and PAKISTAN. Many visits, official and unofficial, were exchanged between the two countries. In April Pakistan's President Musharraf visited Delhi, a meeting which was seen as much more successful than his earlier summit meeting in India in 2001 (see AR 2001, p. 334). The Indian Foreign

Minister visited Islamabad in October. The Indian Prime Minister, Manmohan Singh, also met President Musharraf in New York at the time of the UN General Assembly. However, no substantive breakthrough was made on any of the major issues between the two countries, and to some extent the atmosphere seemed to cool. On the core issue of the status of Jammu and Kashmir, the Indian government maintained its stance that no change to the constitutional status of the state could be made, and that, therefore, the various ideas put forward by President Musharraf for greater internal self-government for the state could not be accepted. India also repeated its claims that elements in Pakistan were continuing to sponsor terrorist acts. The October bomb explosions in Delhi (see p. 275) hindered but did not completely derail relations. However, after lengthy negotiations it was decided that a bus service would be started across the line of control to make it easier for Kashmiris to visit family and friends. The service commenced in April, although on a small scale.

One longstanding issue, which was intertwined with the territorial dispute in Kashmir, was the question of control of water. India's construction of a dam at Baglihar on the Chenab river, which, although on its side of the line of control, affected water that eventually flowed to Pakistan, had been a contentious issue for some years, and at the beginning of 2005 Pakistan exercised its rights under the Indus Waters Treaty of 1960 to refer the matter to an independent arbitrator appointed by the World Bank. A dam on the Kishenganga river, which was predicted to have a major negative impact on the river as it flowed through the territory on the Pakistan side (where it was known as the Neelum) was also the subject of dispute.

INTERNATIONAL RELATIONS. A landmark agreement was reached in July between INDIA and the USA during a visit to Washington, DC by the Indian Prime Minister. The state visit was the culmination of the US decision to decouple its relations with India from the rest of South Asia—Pakistan in particular—and to see India as a strategic partner for the future. In essence, in return for India's agreeing to put its civilian nuclear facilities under international safeguards, the USA agreed to supply sensitive nuclear technology and to persuade its fellow members of the Nuclear Suppliers Group to do likewise. This move effectively released India from the sanctions imposed after its 1998 nuclear tests (see AR 1998, pp. 327-28), and as such the agreement came under intense scrutiny both within the USA and internationally. By the end of the year the agreement had still to be confirmed by the US Congress (bicameral legislature). The US decision appeared to have been driven primarily by a desire to build up India as a counter-balance to China, although it was not prepared to support India's campaign for a permanent seat on the UN Security Council. At the end of June, the USA also signed a wide-ranging ten-year agreement with India on defence issues, including joint weapons production and transfer of technology.

A major consequence of the new relationship was the decision by India to support the USA at the UN and the International Atomic Energy Agency over Iran's nuclear plans (see pp. 262-63). India declined to submit to US pressure, however, to withdraw from ambitious plans for a natural gas pipeline from Iran to India, passing through Pakistan.

Despite the agreements between India and the USA, which led to the cancellation of a planned visit to Washington, DC by Prime Minister Shaukat Aziz in August, PAKISTAN and the USA continued to co-operate in many areas, including the military. Pakistan was rewarded by a final resolution of the long-standing dispute over the supply of F-16 aircraft (although the actual purchase was delayed in order to release funds for earthquake relief). A number of high-level visits were made, including by Secretary of State Condoleezza Rice in March and Vice-President Dick Cheney in December. President Musharraf visited the USA in September. However, many in the USA held the view that some elements in the Pakistan army and intelligence agencies continued to support the Taliban resistance in Afghanistan and along the Pakistan border.

While INDIA had been developing relations with Israel ever since the early 1980s, PAKISTAN had traditionally adopted a policy of total non-cooperation. In September, however, the Pakistani Foreign Minister held an informal meeting in the Turkish capital, Istanbul, with his Israeli counterpart. This appeared to be a means of testing the water, although the general reaction in Pakistan was very negative.

China's relationship with INDIA continued to mature during the year, although it contained elements both of co-operation and rivalry. In a symbolic breakthrough, China withdrew its territorial claim to the Indian territory of Sikkim, while India had effectively recognised Chinese sovereignty over Tibet in 2003 (see AR 2003, p. 340). The Chinese Prime Minister, Wen Jiabao, visited both India and PAKISTAN in April, signing agreements with both countries. In the case of Pakistan an agreement was reached for the co-production of military aircraft.

Pakistan's Prime Minister Shaukat Aziz visited the Afghan capital Kabul in July to reassure the Afghan government that PAKISTAN was doing all it could to restrict the use of Pakistan territory by Afghan militants, although it was evident that the Afghan government felt that not enough had been done in practice. Manmohan Singh visited Kabul the following month, the first such visit by an Indian Prime Minister since 1976. INDIA had worked hard ever since the fall of the Taliban regime to strengthen its previously weak position in Afghanistan, and the visit was a major milestone in the development of a new relationship.

After two postponements, the second of them in February, a summit meeting of South Asian Association for Regional Co-operation (SAARC) leaders took place in Dhaka, BANGLADESH, in November (see p. 390). The business transacted was largely routine, including the adoption of the Dhaka Declaration on action against poverty and terrorism. It was decided to admit Afghanistan as the eighth member of SAARC, and also to accept Japan and China as observers. Both India and Pakistan attended the July meeting of the Shanghai Co-operation Organisation as observers (see pp. 271-72).

INDIA continued its campaign for a permanent seat on the UN Security Council, but made little significant progress during 2005.

INDIAN OCEAN STATES

Seychelles

CAPITAL: Victoria   AREA: 454 sq km   POPULATION: 85,000
OFFICIAL LANGUAGES: Seychellois, English & French   POLITICAL SYSTEM: multiparty republic in Commonwealth
HEAD OF STATE AND GOVERNMENT: President James Michel (since April '04)
RULING PARTY: Seychelles People's Progressive Front (SPPF)
MAIN IGO MEMBERSHIPS (NON-UN): AU (suspended), COMESA, OIC, IOC, ACP, CWTH, Francophonie, NAM
CURRENCY: Seychelles rupee (end-'05 £1=SRs9.47760, US$1=SRs5.52060)
GNI PER CAPITA: US$8,090, US$15,590 at PPP ('04)

Mauritius

CAPITAL: Port Louis   AREA: 2,040 sq km   POPULATION: 1,234,000
OFFICIAL LANGUAGE: English   POLITICAL SYSTEM: multiparty republic in Commonwealth
HEAD OF STATE: President Sir Anerood Jugnauth (since Oct '03)
RULING PARTIES: Social Alliance (AS), comprising the Mauritius Labour Party (MLP), Mauritian Party of Xavier Duval (PMXD), Mauritian Socialist Militant Movement (MMSM), Republican Movement (MR), and the Greens-Fraternal Organisation (VERTS-OF)
HEAD OF GOVERNMENT: Navin Ramgoolam (MLP), Prime Minister (since July '05)
MAIN IGO MEMBERSHIPS (NON-UN): AU, COMESA, SADC, ACP, IOC, CWTH, Francophonie, NAM
CURRENCY: Mauritian rupee (end-'05 £1=MRs52.4982, US$1=MRs30.5800)
GNI PER CAPITA: US$4,640, US$11,870 at PPP ('04)

Comoros

CAPITAL: Moroni   AREA: 1,860 sq km   POPULATION: 614,000
OFFICIAL LANGUAGES: Arabic & French   POLITICAL SYSTEM: multiparty federal republic
HEAD OF STATE: Col Assoumani Azali (since April '99); Anjouan President, Mohamed Bacar; Grande Comore President, Abdou Soule Elbak; Moheli President, Mohamed Said Fazul
MAIN IGO MEMBERSHIPS (NON-UN): AU, COMESA, ACP, AL, OIC, Francophonie, NAM
CURRENCY: franc (end-'05 £1=CFr716.024, US$1=CFr417.081)
GNI PER CAPITA: US$530, US$1,840 at PPP ('04, based on regression)

Madagascar

CAPITAL: Antananarivo   AREA: 587,000 sq km   POPULATION: 17,300,000
OFFICIAL LANGUAGES: Malagasy & French   POLITICAL SYSTEM: multiparty republic
HEAD OF STATE: President Marc Ravalomanana (since May '02)
RULING PARTY: I Love Madagascar Party (TIM)
HEAD OF GOVERNMENT: Jacques Sylla, Prime Minister (since May '02)
MAIN IGO MEMBERSHIPS (NON-UN): AU, COMESA, SADC, OIC, ACP, IOC, Francophonie, NAM
CURRENCY: ariary (end-'05 £1=MGA3,708.18, US$1=MGA2,160.00)
GNI PER CAPITA: US$300, US$830 at PPP ('04)

Maldives

CAPITAL: Malé   AREA: 300 sq km   POPULATION: 300,000
OFFICIAL LANGUAGE: Divehi   POLITICAL SYSTEM: non-party republic in Commonwealth
HEAD OF STATE AND GOVERNMENT: President Maumoon Abdul Gayoom (since Nov '78)
MAIN IGO MEMBERSHIPS (NON-UN): SAARC, CP, OIC, CWTH, NAM
CURRENCY: rufiya (end-'05 £1=R21.9745, US$1=R12.8000)
GNI PER CAPITA: US$2,510 ('04)

ALTHOUGH Albert René had relinquished the presidency of SEYCHELLES to James Michel in April 2004 (see AR 2004, pp. 303-04), he retained considerable influence over the government. René was re-elected as chairman of the ruling Seychelles People's Progressive Front (SPPF) in May and expanded the party's central committee, giving rise to accusations that it, rather than the Cabinet, was the effective government of the country. Michel, who lacked the popular appeal of either René or Wavel Ramkalawan, the opposition leader, appeared to be too weak politically to implement economic reforms.

James Mancham retired as leader of the moribund Democratic Party (DP) and was succeeded by Nichol Gabriel who moved the party closer to Wavel Ramkalawan's Seychelles National Party (SNP). Aware that the next elections were likely to be very closely contested, Michel held talks with the SNP to try to improve relations.

The IMF pressed the Seychelles to devalue its currency and increase economic liberalisation but both were resisted by the government. However, under pressure from the IMF, the 2005 budget promised greater progress with privatisation and there were strong hints that the all-powerful Seychelles Marketing Board (SMB)—the chief instrument of the Seychelles socialist economy—might be partly privatised.

In a realignment of its foreign relations, the Seychelles withdrew from membership of the Southern African Development Community (SADC) and remained suspended from voting rights in the African Union because of a dispute over its unpaid contributions. It remained, however, an active member of bodies directly concerned with Indian Ocean questions .

The Seychelles felt the effects of the 2004 tsunami (for map see p. 296). There were three deaths and the islands suffered flooding and damage to infrastructure. More significant was the loss of tourist revenue which damaged an already stagnant sector. Tourism accounted for 26 per cent of the islands' income and two-thirds of foreign exchange earnings. A tuna fishing agreement, signed with the EU, became effective in 2005. Forty trawlers were licensed to operate, with the annual catch increased from 46,000 tonnes to 55,000 tonnes. Fisheries accounted for 40 per cent of the islands' income and employed 14 per cent of the workforce.

Prime Minister Paul Bérenger had been confidently expected to win the July general election in MAURITIUS. In the event, the contest was won, with an 81.5 per cent turn out, by the opposition coalition, the Social Alliance (AS). Bérenger resigned and the leader of the Labour Party (a member of AS), Navin Ramgoolam, became Prime Minister. The former ruling Mauritian Militant Movement/Mauritian Socialist Movement (MMM/MSM) coalition won only twenty-two of the sixty seats and the President's son, Pravind Jugnauth, lost his seat. Tension immediately arose between the new Prime Minister and President Sir Aneerood Jugnauth, and there were suggestions that the latter, who belonged to the defeated MMM, should resign.

In October the AS won a landslide victory in the municipal elections, winning 122 out of 126 seats contested. One consequence of this was the dissolution of the MMM/MSM coalition. The AS immediately introduced free bus travel for the old, the disabled, and students and set out a programme which focused on investment in education and communications and on the reduction of unemployment and the budget deficit. There was continuing concern that Mauritius remained a major tax haven with 10,500 overseas companies registered, 90 per cent of them South African.

In June an accelerated action plan for the sugar industry was agreed. This provided for a 10 per cent reduction in the amount of land growing sugar, and for the production of ethanol as a petrol substitute. Sugar factories were to be powered by organic waste. The EU delayed implementing a cut in the support price for sugar.

In February the Union President of THE COMOROS, Assoumani Azali, made an official visit to France, the first by a Comorian President since independence in 1975. He was seeking increases in France's aid to the islands and was advised by the French to abandon his aspiration to seek another term as President. The political stalemate between Azali and the Presidents of the individual islands continued but the expectation grew that Assoumani would cede the presidency to a representative from the island of Anjouan as determined by the constitution.

In a move to unite political opinion in the islands, committees were set up in each island to consider the question of bringing Mayotte (a French collectivité territoriale) into the Comorian federation. The main concern remained the depressed state of the economy which was unlikely to improve while the constitutional impasse remained unresolved. Civil unrest in January saw further protests by health and education workers who had not been paid, and in September there were riots against a 40 per cent rise in the price of fuel, which left one person dead. In Anjouan demonstrations against the local rule of island President Mohamed Bacar led to two deaths, the imposition of a curfew, and the suspension of independent radio broadcasts.

In April there was an eruption of the Karthala volcano on the island of Grande Comore, which resulted in the temporary departure of 10,000 people and a severe water shortage.

With eyes focused on the presidential elections in 2007, politicians in MADAGASCAR turned away from the divisive events of 2002, which had installed Marc Ravalomanana in power (see AR 2002, pp. 330-31). The opposition AVI (Judged by Your Work), led by Norbert Ratsirahonana, strengthened its local government base. Albert Zafy, founder of CRN (the Committee for National Reconciliation), launched the Club of 17 and Group of 5 to highlight ethnic opposition in the country to the dominance of Merina politicians in the capital. Meanwhile in February, Pierrot Rajaonarivelo, general-secretary of the Association for the Rebirth of Madagascar (Arema), had his conviction for rebellion quashed and announced that he would run for President, bringing his party back into the political mainstream.

The position of TIM, the ruling party, became more unstable. Although Ravalomanana continued to build friendships with local power brokers, his Deputy

Prime Minister, Zaza Ramandimbiarison, resigned in March after which the post was dispensed with. Meanwhile, Prime Minister Jacques Sylla lost his post as secretary-general of TIM.

Madagascar continued its economic recovery following the collapse of 2002 and the cyclone damage of 2004. The IMF approved the continuation of the poverty reduction programme, which officially ended in March. Madagascar fulfilled the criteria for aid under the heavily indebted poor countries (HIPC) scheme, after which the USA and Japan wrote off all of the debt owed to them by Madagascar. Inflation, which had peaked at 27 per cent in 2004, was expected to fall to 5 per cent while GDP would grow to 6.5 per cent. Bidding for oil concessions from the USA, China, and Norway was encouraged. Madagascar formally joined the Southern African Development Community (SADC) in August.

In January a new national currency was introduced. The ariary—the name of the pre-colonial currency—formally replaced the Malagasy franc.

Elections for the Majlis, the unicameral legislature of the MALDIVES, were held on 22 January, having been postponed from December 2004 because of the Indian Ocean tsunami. All candidates were officially independents. However, under increasing international pressure for democratic reform, the Majlis in June voted unanimously for a constitutional amendment allowing the legalisation of political parties and licences for private broadcasting stations. Four political parties subsequently registered: Adhaalath (Justice) Party (AP), Gayoom's Maldivian People's Party (DRP), the Islamic Democratic Party (IDP), and the main opposition party, the Maldivian Democratic Party (MDP), led by Mohammed Nasheed.

Demonstrations on 12 August in the capital, Malé, led to a series of arrests including that of Nasheed who was charged with terrorism and crimes against the state. After this the political and security situation steadily declined. The MDP, with branches on all the inhabited islands, kept up the pressure through meetings and demonstrations.

IX SOUTH-EAST AND EAST ASIA

SOUTH-EAST ASIAN STATES

BURMA (MYANMAR)—THAILAND—MALAYSIA—BRUNEI— SINGAPORE—VIETNAM—CAMBODIA—LAOS

Burma (Myanmar)

CAPITAL: Yangon (Rangoon); administrative capital Pyinmana   AREA: 677,000 sq km
POPULATION: 49,910,000
OFFICIAL LANGUAGE: Burmese   POLITICAL SYSTEM: military regime
HEAD OF STATE AND GOVERNMENT: Gen. Than Shwe, Chairman of State Peace and Development
    Council (since April '92)
PRIME MINISTER: Lt-Gen. Soe Win (since Oct '04)
MAIN IGO MEMBERSHIPS (NON-UN): ASEAN, CP, NAM
CURRENCY: kyat (end-'05 £1=K11.0216, US$1=K6.42000)
GNI PER CAPITA: low income: US$825 or less ('04, based on regression)

Thailand

CAPITAL: Bangkok   AREA: 513,000 sq km   POPULATION: 62,400,000
OFFICIAL LANGUAGE: Thai   POLITICAL SYSTEM: multiparty monarchy
HEAD OF STATE: King Bhumibol Adulyadej (Rama IX), since June '46
RULING PARTY: Thai Rak Thai (TRT) party
HEAD OF GOVERNMENT: Thaksin Shinawatra, Prime Minister (since Feb '01)
MAIN IGO MEMBERSHIPS (NON-UN): ASEAN, CP, APEC, NAM
CURRENCY: baht (end-'05 £1=Bt70.3868, US$1=Bt41.0000)
GNI PER CAPITA: US$2,540, US$8,020 at PPP ('04)

Malaysia

CAPITAL: Kuala Lumpur   AREA: 330,000 sq km   POPULATION: 25,200,000
OFFICIAL LANGUAGE: Bahasa Malaysia   POLITICAL SYSTEM: multiparty monarchy in
    Commonwealth
HEAD OF STATE: King Syed Sirajuddin Syed Putra Jamalullail, Sultan of Perlis (since April '02)
RULING PARTY: National Front (BN) coalition
HEAD OF GOVERNMENT: Abdullah Ahmad Badawi, Prime Minister (since Oct '03)
MAIN IGO MEMBERSHIPS (NON-UN): ASEAN, APEC, CP, OIC, CWTH, NAM
CURRENCY: ringgit Malaysia (end-'05 £1=RM6.48850, US$1=RM3.77950)
GNI PER CAPITA: US$4,650, US$9,630 at PPP ('04)

Brunei

CAPITAL: Bandar Seri Bagawan   AREA: 5,765 sq km   POPULATION: 361,000
OFFICIAL LANGUAGES: Malay & English   POLITICAL SYSTEM: sultanate in Commonwealth
HEAD OF STATE AND GOVERNMENT: Sultan Sir Hassanal Bolkiah (since '67)
MAIN IGO MEMBERSHIPS (NON-UN): ASEAN, APEC, OIC, CWTH, NAM
CURRENCY: Brunei dollar (end-'05 £1=Br$2.85460, US$1=Br$1.66280)
GNI PER CAPITA: high income: US$10,066 or more ('04 est)

Singapore

CAPITAL: Singapore   AREA: 1,000 sq km   POPULATION: 4,300,000
OFFICIAL LANGUAGES: Malay, Chinese, Tamil & English   POLITICAL SYSTEM: multiparty republic in
    Commonwealth
HEAD OF STATE: President S.R. Nathan (since Sept '99)
RULING PARTY: People's Action Party (PAP)
HEAD OF GOVERNMENT: Lee Hsien Loong, Prime Minister (since August '04)
MAIN IGO MEMBERSHIPS (NON-UN): ASEAN, APEC, CP, CWTH, NAM
CURRENCY: Singapore dollar (end-'05 £1=S$2.85460, US$1=S$1.66280)
GNI PER CAPITA: US$24,220, US$26,590 at PPP ('04)

Vietnam

CAPITAL: Hanoi   AREA: 332,000 sq km   POPULATION: 82,200,000
OFFICIAL LANGUAGES: Vietnamese   POLITICAL SYSTEM: one-party republic
HEAD OF STATE: President Tran Duc Luong (since Sept '97)
RULING PARTY: Communist Party of Vietnam (CPV)
PARTY LEADER: Nong Duc Manh, CPV secretary general (since April '01)
HEAD OF GOVERNMENT: Phan Van Khai, Prime Minister (since Sept '97)
MAIN IGO MEMBERSHIPS (NON-UN): ASEAN, APEC, NAM, Francophonie
CURRENCY: dong (end-'05 £1=Vnd27,320.4, US$1=Vnd15,914.0)
GNP PER CAPITA: US$550, US$2,700 at PPP ('04)

Cambodia

CAPITAL: Phnom Penh   AREA: 181,000 sq km   POPULATION: 13,600,000
OFFICIAL LANGUAGE: Khmer   POLITICAL SYSTEM: multiparty monarchy
HEAD OF STATE: King Norodom Sihamoni (elected Oct '04)
RULING PARTIES: Coalition of the Cambodian People's Party (CPP) and the United National Front
    for an Independent Neutral, Peaceful, and Co-operative Cambodia (Funcinpec) (since June '04)
HEAD OF GOVERNMENT: Hun Sen, Prime Minister (since July '97)
MAIN IGO MEMBERSHIPS (NON-UN): ASEAN, CP, Francophonie, NAM
CURRENCY: riel (end-'05 £1=R6,867.00, US$1=R4,000.00)
GNI PER CAPITA: US$320, US$2,180 at PPP ('04, based on regression)

Laos

CAPITAL: Vientiane   AREA: 237,000 sq km   POPULATION: 5,800,000
OFFICIAL LANGUAGE: Laotian   POLITICAL SYSTEM: one-party republic
HEAD OF STATE: President (Gen.) Khamtay Siphandon (since Feb '98)
RULING PARTY: Lao People's Revolutionary Party (LPRP)
HEAD OF GOVERNMENT: Boungnang Volachit, Prime Minister (since March '01)
MAIN IGO MEMBERSHIPS (NON-UN): ASEAN, CP, Francophonie, NAM
CURRENCY: new kip (end-'05 £1=K17,854.2, US$1=10,400.0)
GNI PER CAPITA: US$390, US$1,850 at PPP ('04)

THE effects of the tsunami that struck several countries in the region in December 2004 continued to be felt, with efforts made to identify the dead, to locate the missing, and to rebuild shattered communities (see map, p. 296). International humanitarian relief was made available for immediate assistance to survivors and long-term reconstruction efforts were begun. On 26 December, a year after the tsunami, commemorative ceremonies were held in many areas, including in THAILAND, where the tsunami had killed more than 5,000 people and left a further 2,000 missing. A tsunami "early warning system" for the Indian Ocean was expected to be in place by mid-2006, complementing a system already in service in the Pacific Ocean region.

The Paris Club of creditor nations offered in January to freeze debts owed to them by tsunami-hit countries, including both Thailand (US$59.2 billion) and MALAYSIA (US$48.6 billion). Some lobby groups, including the UK-based aid agency Oxfam, urged the Paris Club to write off the debt altogether, rather than merely defer payments

Another regional disaster threatened as warnings grew of a possible world-wide pandemic arising from avian influenza ("bird flu"). Outbreaks of the disease led to the slaughter of hundreds of thousands, perhaps millions, of chickens and other poultry. The disease continued to spread beyond Asia, with some transmission to humans, but thus far on only a small scale, with a reported forty-two deaths and ninety-three cases of human infection in VIETNAM, fourteen deaths and twenty-two cases in Thailand, and four deaths and a further four cases in CAMBODIA. Vietnam imposed a temporary ban on the import of poultry and poultry products from neighbouring countries in January. The country appealed for assistance in stockpiling drugs against the disease. Vietnam was also inoculating hundreds of millions of chickens and ducks against the disease, using vaccines developed in the Netherlands and China.

Besides these reminders of a shared fate, strides were also taken towards greater regional co-operation and a stronger sense of community, with the first East Asia summit being held in Kuala Lumpur, Malaysia, in December (see p. 389). The summit brought together the ten ASEAN (Association of South-East Asian Nations) member states as well as China, Japan, and South Korea, joined, for the first time, by India, Australia, and New Zealand. Australia's participation attracted particularly sharp criticism from former Malaysian Prime Minister Mahathir Mohamad, who characterised the country as an outsider. As a condition of their participation, Australia and New Zealand signed the ASEAN Treaty of Amity and Cooperation (1976) prior to their attendance, a requirement quickly agreed to by New Zealand, but resisted by Australia, which considered that doing so might impede its ability to deal with terrorist threats emanating from Asian countries. In signing the Treaty, Australia stated that in any case it had no plans to attack any Asian countries, although it refused to disavow a regional pre-emptive strike option if warranted by security concerns. New Zealand's Foreign Affairs Minister said that acceptance of the treaty would not inhibit the country from speaking out on human rights issues in South-East Asia.

Unlike the Asia-Pacific Economic Co-operation forum (APEC), the East Asian community gathering excluded the USA. The summit produced a draft charter enshrining human rights and democracy as central values for a community that would be "outward-looking", seeking "to strengthen global norms and universally recognised values".

A sense of community—of shared interests, values, and concerns—was also in evidence as South-East Asian nations displayed misgivings over developments in BURMA (MYANMAR). Members of the legislatures of several ASEAN countries urged their governments to be more active in encouraging democratic reform in Burma, notwithstanding the ASEAN "tradition" of non-interference in each other's domestic affairs. Burma had given assurances when admitted to ASEAN in 1997 that it would move ahead with a programme of political reform: these commitments had in no way been consummated (see AR 1997, pp. 326-27; 430). The legislators' terms for Burma's succession to the ASEAN chairmanship in 2006 were few but significant: to free opposition leader Aung San Suu Kyi and all other political prisoners immediately and unconditionally; and to reconstitute the National Convention to draw up a new constitution, ensuring full participation by the opposition National League for Democracy (NLD) and by the country's ethnic minorities (see AR 2004, p. 310). Some ASEAN legislators called for Burma to be expelled altogether from the organisation, unless it freed Aung San Suu Kyi and other political prisoners. This came as the regime announced that it was extending her period of home detention for a further twelve months. She had last been freed in May 2003 (see AR 2003, p. 355).

In March a Malaysian Cabinet Minister stated that his country would be asking BURMA to stand down as chair of the 2006 ASEAN ministerial meeting, a change from the non-interventionist position previously adopted by MALAYSIA towards Burma. Similar misgivings about Burma's taking up an ASEAN leadership role were also expressed by the government of SINGAPORE. In July the Burmese government agreed to defer its opportunity to serve as chairman of ASEAN for 2006-07 during a meeting of ASEAN Foreign Ministers in Vientiane, LAOS (see p. 389).

Prior to the December East Asia summit, the 2005 ASEAN chairman, Malaysian Prime Minister Abdullah Badawi, called on Burma to "release [. . .] those placed under detention". This statement represented a significant departure from ASEAN's general policy of non-intervention in members' affairs, reflecting the group's loss of patience with Burma, its embarrassment over the country, and its growing exasperation with its resistance to peaceful change. The Malaysian Foreign Minister, Syed Hamid Albar, urged genuine progress to be made, a reference to previous statements and gestures from the Burmese regime that ultimately amounted to very little.

In September the Prime Minister of THAILAND, meeting US President George W. Bush in Washington, DC, expressed "concern" over the situation in BURMA and agreed to work together to promote national reconciliation in that country. Former Czech President Vaclav Havel and Nobel Peace Prize winner Archbishop Desmond Tutu supported calls for UN Security Council action on Burma. At the APEC summit in South Korea in November, the US President characterised Burma as an "outpost of tyranny", identifying the country as one that had "not taken even the first steps towards freedom", with abuses by the military including "rape, torture, execution and forced relocation". US Secretary of State Condoleezza Rice called for ASEAN "engagement" to be "serious" about the country's "appalling human rights situation".

In December torture techniques used by Burma's security services against the regime's opponents were revealed in a report based on the testimony of thirty-five former political prisoners. The report, compiled by a Burmese exile group, was released to coincide with a UN Security Council discussion on the issue, although no concrete steps were taken.

Within BURMA the most dramatic development, and in some ways the most inexplicable, was the government's determination to relocate the administrative capital from Rangoon, on the coast, inland to Pyinmana, nearly 400 kilometres to the north. The main highway to Pyinmana was being expanded and the town itself was to be restructured. This occurred despite the regime's announcement in January of plans to replace what were described as dangerous buildings in Rangoon as part of an effort to transform the then capital into a modern city. Explanations for the move ranged widely, from reports that it reflected the views of General Than Shwe's personal astrologer to suggestions that the change was brought about by concerns over a possible invasion by the USA. What was not in dispute was that the new capital was in no way ready for its elevated responsibilities. Civil servants were given little notice as they were ordered to transfer to an area that was not much more than a collection of straw huts and rice paddies. Burmese wishing to resign rather than relocate to the new capital were forbidden to do so. The more centrally located site was declared a military zone, denied to foreigners. However, foreign embassies were also expected to move to Pyinmana, notwithstanding the absence of essential services. There were claims that the new capital was being built at least in part by forced labour.

Calls for a new constitution, rather than a new capital, continued to make little headway. On 17 February the National Convention, charged with the responsibility of constitutional revision, was reconvened after a seven-month break. The convention was boycotted by the NLD, however, following the military's refusal to release its leader from house arrest. Some governments, including that of the USA and some ASEAN members, criticised the convention as lacking legitimacy because of the boycott by opposition and ethnic groups.

While the state-controlled media stated that armed ethnic groups observing a ceasefire would be allowed to attend, prior to the meeting the military government arrested leading ethnic Shan political figures, including Hkun Htun Oo and Sai Nyunt Lwin, the chairman and secretary of the Shan Nationalities League for Democracy, the second largest vote winner in the aborted 1990 election. The League's support for a "genuine federal union" was denounced by the government as an effort to secede from the country to form a separate, independent Shan state.

In July the former Prime Minister and head of the Military Intelligence Bureau, General Khin Nyunt, and his two sons, were tried at Rangoon's Insein prison, where they were found guilty of bribery and corruption. Other members of the former Prime Minister's military intelligence operation were also convicted on corruption charges (see AR 2004, p. 309). About the regime's overall character there seemed little doubt, with the respected watchdog group, Transparency International, issuing a report which ranked Burma as the world's third most corrupt country.

Armed conflict also remaining an ongoing feature of Burmese political life. The Karen National Union (KNU) claimed in January that recent attacks by Burma's army showed that the regime failed to take the ceasefire seriously. (A ceasefire had been agreed in January 2004 between the Karen leader General Bo Mya and the then Prime Minister General Khin Nyunt.) Hundreds of Karen villagers in Burma fled to Thailand to escape the fighting, which occurred when Burmese army forces attacked a KNU military camp in a Thai border area.

In March a bomb was detonated on a bus in eastern Rangoon, while another was found and defused in the bus terminal. A bomb also exploded in a backpackers' hotel in the capital. Responsibility for that attack was claimed by a group called the Vigorous Burmese Student Warriors—denounced by the government as a terrorist organisation—which said that the attack was intended to halt the National Convention. In April a bomb exploded in a market in Mandalay, killing four people and injuring fourteen. At least eleven people were killed and more than 160 injured in bomb blasts in Rangoon in May. The attacks came at a time when a Thai trade fair was being held in the capital. Subsequently THAILAND sent a C-130 military transport to bring home 122 Thais participating in the trade fair. Three Thai nationals were injured in the attack, which the Burmese government blamed on ethnic armed groups (each of which denied responsibility). There was speculation that the bombings may have been the work of former Military Intelligence members, unhappy with the October 2004 sacking of Military Intelligence chief General Khin Nyunt. Another bomb exploded in Rangoon in October.

The conflict within Burma intermittently spilled over into neighbouring countries. In one incident police in MALAYSIA arrested more than 150 Burmese demonstrators in front of the Burmese embassy in Kuala Lumpur, where they were protesting at human rights abuses and calling for a change of government.

The peculiarities of Burmese political life were unmatched elsewhere in the region. In neighbouring THAILAND—a country where the military had been involved in politics in the past—legislative elections held on schedule, on 6 February, further consolidated the country's democratic transition, with Prime Minister Thaksin Shinawatra winning an impressive victory. The ruling Thai Rak Thai ("Thais Love Thais") (TRT) party of the billionaire Prime Minister achieved the most one-sided election result in the country's history. It had been the Prime Minister's goal to win 400 of the 500 seats in the House of Representatives (the lower chamber of the bicameral legislature). He very nearly achieved it. The TRT had won 200 constituency seats and forty-eight party-list seats in the 2001 election (see AR 2001, p. 353), and subsequently it had boosted its strength through mergers with smaller parties. The 2005 election was contested by twenty-three parties, but only the TRT fielded a candidate in each of the 400 constituencies. The leading opposition group, the Democrat Party, had candidates in 395, while the other main contenders included the Mahachon (People's Party) (with 302 candidates), Chart Thai (Thai Nation Party) with 265, and the New Aspiration Party, with 114 candidates. The election system gave voters two votes, one for a local candidate and the other for a political party. The 100 remaining seats were divided proportionally among the parties, with at least 5 per cent support needed to qualify for party-list seats.

In the elections, the TRT won 376 seats (up from 248); the Democrats won ninety-seven (down from 128). Only two other parties won any seats: Chart Thai, with twenty-five; and Mahachon, which won two seats. By contrast, the previous election had given Chart Thai forty-one seats, New Aspiration thirty-one, and Chart Pattana (National Development) twenty-nine. While the TRT victory was largely a vote of respect for Prime Minister Thaksin's leadership, it also reflected the weakness of the opposition, a desire for stability, and support for the government's economic policies, which included lavish spending programmes. In Thailand's south, where violence continued to cause loss of life, the Democrats won fifty-two of the fifty-four seats. In the rest of the country, the TRT was dominant. The results emphasised a regional division in Thai politics, while at the same time moving the country closer to a two-party system, one dominated, however, at least for the moment, by the Prime Minister's party.

The results gave Thaksin the opportunity (which he took) to dispense with his coalition partner, Chart Thai, and to govern alone. The Thai Foreign Minister, Surakiart Sathirathai, gave up the position, becoming Deputy Prime Minister. In the aftermath of the election the Thai Prime Minister launched the country's third "war on drugs", with Thaksin stating that "as long as I am still the Prime Minister I will not allow narcotic drugs to return". Following corruption scandals the Thai government was reshuffled in August. In October the TRT lost four provincial by-elections, defeats which prompted the Prime Minister to state that regions failing to vote for his party would receive less government funding.

The Thai government remained a partner and ally of the USA, contributing troops to the coalition forces in Afghanistan and Iraq. Thailand's own "war on terrorism" worsened, however, as in April the Muslim separatist attacks spread north, with a triple bomb attack on an airport, hotel, and supermarket which killed two people and wounded sixty. The separatist violence in the Muslim south proved intractable; the number of dead in the second half of 2005 was nearly double that of the first half. Despite the presence of 30,000 troops and police in the region, shootings, bombings, and arson attacks on civilian and military targets continued, with the government blaming local criminal organisations, drug dealers, and Islamic religious teachers for the violence. More than 500 people were killed in the Muslim-dominated provinces of Yala, Pattani, and Narathiwat, and in neighbouring Songkhla province, during 2005. In July the Thai Cabinet empowered the Prime Minister to counter the insurgency. In October Thailand's first Muslim army commander took command. Inspecting the site where Islamic militants had shot dead five soldiers, he cautioned troops against placing too much trust in the local population. Martial law was imposed on two districts of Songkhla province in November, following army claims that the areas were being used to stockpile weapons for the insurgency.

The Miss Universe contest held in Thailand in May represented a partial effort to promote tourism, which had declined in the aftermath of the tsunami. There were concerns about other consequences of the pageant, after photos of bikini-clad contestants at an ancient Buddhist temple site in Bangkok appeared in Thai newspapers, upsetting religious and cultural leaders.

Thailand's consolidation of democratic institutions was not mimicked in BRUNEI despite the reconvening (after a twenty-year hiatus) of Brunei's Legislative Council by Sultan Hassanal Bolkiah, and the 2004 amendments to the Brunei constitution providing for the Legislative Council to be a partially elected body (see AR 2004, p. 312). The elections had yet to be held. In May the Sultan removed four Cabinet Ministers—including a conservative Islamist Minister of Education—in a major reshuffle of his government. The changes brought corporate figures and civil servants into the government and reflected an effort to project an image of the oil-rich country as a moderate Islamic state. Among the appointments were the first-ever non-Muslim Cabinet Minister, Lim Jock Seng, an ethnic Chinese, who had previously been permanent secretary in the Foreign Ministry.

In MALAYSIA, Prime Minister Badawi continued to provide an example of a more open, consultative style of government, less combative than that of his predecessor, Mahathir Mohamad. Badawi also served as chairman of the fifty-seven-member Organisation of the Islamic Conference.

The Prime Minister's more moderate approach was reflected in improved ties between SINGAPORE and MALAYSIA. Badawi and Singapore's Prime Minister Lee Hsien Loong agreed in January to end a dispute over Singapore's land reclamation efforts in the Straits of Johor, which separated the two countries. Malaysia had previously taken the dispute to the International Tribunal on the Law of the Sea. However, Malaysia announced its intention to proceed with a causeway across the straits, a project that remained an outstanding issue between the two countries.

In March a warship returned to SINGAPORE from the Persian Gulf, ending the country's military contribution to coalition forces in Iraq. The ship had been dispatched to the Gulf with a crew of 180 in late November 2004 for three months, with a mission to protect the waters around key oil terminals, provide logistics support for coalition vessels and helicopters, and to conduct patrols and boarding operations. Singapore also deployed several hundred soldiers in Indonesia's Aceh province to assist with post-tsunami relief efforts. The country's largest-ever overseas deployment, the soldiers returned to Singapore on 22 January. Brunei's armed forces also participated in a relief exercise in Aceh following the tsunami, while security officials from both BRUNEI and MALAYSIA joined Libya in monitoring a ceasefire between the Moro Islamic Liberation Front and the Philippines government.

In April SINGAPORE approved a proposal to legalise casino gambling, opening the way for two multi-billion dollar casino resorts to be built, thereby potentially transforming the country's conservative image. More serious "image" problems surrounded the implementation of the country's capital punishment regime. There were protests over the hanging of a twenty-five-year-old Australian (of Vietnamese origin), Nguyen Tuong Van, on 2 December, who had been caught with 396 grammes of heroin and convicted of drug trafficking. The Australian government, which opposed the death penalty, made repeated but unsuccessful representations to Singapore to commute the sentence. However, calls for trade sanctions, including steps against Singapore Airlines, were dismissed by Australian Prime Minister John Howard. Singapore's significant investments in BURMA—a country believed by US and other drug agencies to be the second largest source of heroin after Afghanistan—complicated its moral stance against drug trafficking.

Law enforcement in MALAYSIA also became a focus of international attention when, in late November, an abuse scandal broke out, with police and immigration officials accused of engaging in strip searches of young Chinese women. Evidence included a video of a female police officer ordering a naked Chinese woman to do squat exercises, the video having been taken on a mobile phone without the officer's knowledge. The images drew protests from China, supporting claims that Chinese were being treated in a discriminatory manner by Malaysian authorities. In May Malaysia launched a major operation against illegal immigrants. "Operation firm" involved more than 20,000 soldiers, police officers, and immigration officials. Cash rewards were also promised to volunteers for every illegal worker whom they apprehended or for any Malaysian they found harbouring one. It was estimated that there were about 1.6 million illegal workers in the country, about 15 per cent of the workforce. The volunteers were given the right to carry guns and search properties without warrants.

Formal relations between the USA and VIETNAM continued to improve. Vietnam's Prime Minister Phan Van Khai visited Washington, DC in June, the highest ranking Vietnamese official to do so since the Vietnam War. President Bush and Prime Minister Phan signed an agreement which was designed both to prohibit government officials from forcing people to renounce their faith and to assist congregations to open houses of worship. The agreement followed the State Department's designation of Vietnam as a country "of particular concern" because of "ongoing and egregious violations of religious freedom".

Other human rights issues in the region involved government policies towards ethnic minorities. In January, VIETNAM, CAMBODIA and the UN High Commissioner for Refugees (UNHCR) met in the Vietnamese capital, Hanoi, to discuss the presence of ethnic minorities in Cambodia, following allegations from human rights groups about mass arrests, torture, and the increasing persecution of Christian Montagnards by Vietnam. Cambodia agreed not to host refugee camps along its border with Vietnam or to assist the entry of Montagnards into the country. Vietnam, Cambodia and the UNHCR agreed to resettle or repatriate 700 ethnic minority Vietnamese currently in Cambodia, with some members of the Montagnard minority being repatriated to Vietnam if they chose to return there and others being permitted to migrate to a third country if they wished. There were also concerns about the treatment of ethnic minorities in LAOS, including Hmong refugees returned to that country by Thai authorities in November.

The Cambodian Prime Minister, Hun Sen, responded in January to World Bank threats to freeze millions of dollars in assistance until a US$2.8 million loan was repaid. The World Bank had fifteen active projects in CAMBODIA, ranging from electrification to biodiversity programmes. The funds in question, allegedly misappropriated, were part of a project to assist with the demobilisation of part of Cambodia's military. Under the circumstances, Cambodia agreed to repay the funds. The government was more resolute with opposition leader Sam Rainsy, who was convicted in absentia of defaming both Prime Minister Hun Sen and National Assembly president Prince Norodom Ranariddh. Sentenced to imprisonment for eighteen months, the opposition leader had taken the precaution of fleeing to France earlier in the year. His lawyer announced that his client would be seeking a royal pardon.

Seeking to close a violent chapter in Cambodia's history, the UN announced in August that Michelle Lee of China, previously in charge of administrative support services for the UN genocide tribunal for Rwanda, would co-ordinate efforts to help the Cambodian government put surviving leaders of the Khmer Rouge on trial for genocide.

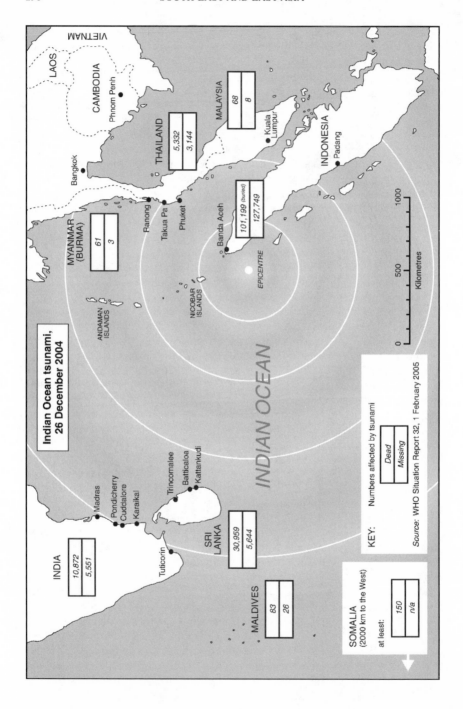

Indian Ocean tsunami, 26 December 2004

VIETNAM

LAOS

CAMBODIA
Phnom Penh

THAILAND
5,332
3,144

MALAYSIA
68
8

Kuala Lumpur

INDONESIA
Padang

Bangkok

Ranong
Takua Pa
Phuket

MYANMAR (BURMA)
61
3

Banda Aceh
101,199 (buried)
127,749
EPICENTRE

NICOBAR ISLANDS

ANDAMAN ISLANDS

1000
500
0
Kilometres

INDIAN OCEAN

Madras
Pondicherry
Cuddalore
Karaikal

Trincomalee
Batticaloa
Kattankudi

INDIA
10,872
5,551

Tuticorin

SRI LANKA
30,959
5,644

MALDIVES
83
26

KEY: Numbers affected by tsunami

Dead
Missing

Source: WHO Situation Report 32, 1 February 2005

SOMALIA
(2000 km to the West)
at least:

150
n/a

INDONESIA—EAST TIMOR—PHILIPPINES

Indonesia

CAPITAL: Jakarta   AREA: 1,905,000 sq km   POPULATION: 217,600,000
OFFICIAL LANGUAGE: Bahasa Indonesia   POLITICAL SYSTEM: multiparty republic
HEAD OF STATE AND GOVERNMENT: President General (retd) Susilo Bambang Yudhoyono (since Oct
   '04)
RULING PARTIES: Nationhood Coalition comprising the PDI-P and Golkar
MAIN IGO MEMBERSHIPS (NON-UN): ASEAN, APEC, CP, OIC, OPEC, NAM
CURRENCY: rupiah (end-'05 £1=Rp16,892.8, US$1=Rp9,840.00)
GNI PER CAPITA: US$1,140, US$3,460 at PPP ('04)

East Timor

CAPITAL: Dili   AREA: 153,870 sq km   POPULATION: 925,000
OFFICIAL LANGUAGES: Portuguese, Tetum and Bahasa Indonesian   POLITICAL SYSTEM: Transitional
   government overseen by UNTAET
HEAD OF STATE: President Jose Alexandre (Xanana) Gusmão (since April '02)
HEAD OF GOVERNMENT: Mari Alkatari
MAIN IGO MEMBERSHIPS (NON-UN): NAM, G-77, CPLP
CURRENCY: US dollar (end-'05 £1=1.71680)
GNI PER CAPITA: US$550 ('04)

Philippines

CAPITAL: Manila   AREA: 300,000 sq km   POPULATION: 83,000,000
OFFICIAL LANGUAGE: Filipino   POLITICAL SYSTEM: multiparty republic
HEAD OF STATE AND GOVERNMENT: President Gloria Macapagal-Arroyo (since Jan '01)
RULING PARTIES: Lakas ng EDSA-National Union of Christian Democrats (Lakas-NUCD)
MAIN IGO MEMBERSHIPS (NON-UN): ASEAN, APEC, CP, NAM
CURRENCY: Philippine peso (end-'05 £1=PP91.0478, US$1=PP53.0350)
GNI PER CAPITA: US$1,170, US$4,890 at PPP ('04)

AT the beginning of 2005 Indonesia was confronted by the massive task of reconstruction following the underwater earthquake and tsunami which overwhelmed the Aceh region of Sumatra in the last days of the previous year (see map, p. 296). By February the best calculations suggested that the catastrophe had caused 124,000 deaths with about 114,000 people still unaccounted for. In March, while local and international agencies were at full stretch in the first phase of emergency reconstruction, another earthquake erupted in the waters off western Sumatra. Though this did not generate a tidal wave, it did devastate a number of island communities, killing about 2,000 people. This disaster, which at any other time would have dominated national and world attention, passed almost unnoticed in the wake of what had gone before. By the end of the year reconstruction and rehabilitation in the tsunami-affected areas had progressed remarkably well, given the extent of the calamity.

Paradoxically, the natural disaster contributed indirectly to positive developments in one of the most challenging of Indonesia's manifold regional and religious conflicts. By the end of the year the long-standing and hitherto intractable separatist conflict between the Indonesian government and the Free Aceh Movement (GAM) seemed close to final settlement. The signs immediately following the tsunami had not been encouraging. Although GAM had offered an interim ceasefire amidst the devastation, the Indonesian army did not reciprocate (and, indeed, was accused of interfering with aid flows in order to reward and punish local communities for their stance in the conflict). Movement was underway beyond the region itself, however. In Finland (conveniently adjacent to the main base of the exiled GAM leadership in Sweden) proximity talks were being facilitated by Finland's former Prime Minister and veteran peace-broker Martti Ahtisaari (see p. 52). Several rounds of talks took place throughout the first half of the year with gradual movement reported as they progressed. The crucial breakthrough came in July when the Indonesian President, Susilo Bambang Yudhoyono, gave way on one of GAM's key demands: that it should be allowed to operate as a solely regional political party. This contravened a constitutional regulation that all Indonesian parties must be nationally based, a rule designed to prevent the realisation of Indonesia's permanent political nightmare of regional fragmentation across the national archipelago. In return, GAM agreed to abandon its demand for full independence, demobilise and disarm its 3,000-strong guerrilla force, and convert itself into a political movement committed to a political rather than military process. The elections associated with this were to be overseen by monitors from the EU and the Association of South-East Asian Nations (ASEAN).

Developments in Aceh were keenly observed in other parts of Indonesia which had been subject to long-standing separatist conflicts. Violence continued throughout 2005 in Papua (previously Irian Jaya, Indonesia's portion of the island of New Guinea). Here the Free Papua Movement (OPM) had for decades conducted a sporadic but continuous campaign against the Indonesian state. If successful, the Aceh settlement was thought to offer a model for meaningful regional autonomy which could provide a compromise between the strict, centralised system that had always characterised the Indonesian state, and full separation on the East Timor pattern.

In addition to political separatism Indonesia continued to suffer from inter-religious conflicts. The situation remained relatively calm in the previous epicentre of Muslim-Christian violence, the island of Ambon. But there was significant trouble on Sulawesi. In May more than twenty people died in a bomb attack on a Christian town in the centre of the province. Then, nearby in October, a group of Christian schoolgirls was attacked and three beheaded. It was widely assumed that this was an atrocity calculated to trigger a resumption of the large-scale intercommunal violence of a few years previously. In the event, calls for calm by the leaders of both religious communities, and the rapid deployment of extra police, seemed to defuse the crisis in the short term.

Radical Islamism continued to cause major domestic and international dilemmas in 2005. In March Abu Bakar Bashir, widely seen as the spiritual leader of the Islamist group, Jemaah Islamiah (JI), active throughout South-East Asia, was convicted of conspiracy in the preparation of the Bali bombings of October 2002 (see AR 2002, p. 340). Cleared of direct involvement, however, he received only a thirty-month prison sentence, the leniency of which led to some friction with Australia (whose nationals had been the principal victims of the attack) and the USA. The situation was not improved a few months later when, as part of an independence day general amnesty, even this sentence was reduced. In October, almost exactly on the third anniversary of the original attack, suicide bombers struck again in Bali, killing more than twenty (this time predominantly Indonesians). In the aftermath, a mob beset the main prison in the provincial capital, Denpassar, demanding the immediate execution of those convicted for the 2002 attacks (who had, in fact, already been transferred out of the province).

The judicial response to terrorism was more robust in September when a guilty verdict on a suspect charged with planning the bombing of the Australian embassy a year previously led to a death sentence (see AR 2004, p. 318). The one possibly positive sign during the year was evidence of a split in JI, with a dissident faction opposing the bombing campaign—with its inevitable local casualties—as counterproductive to the establishment of a wider support base.

Over the year the administration of President Yudhoyono, which took office in the latter part of the previous year, performed adequately rather than spectacularly well, which was perhaps reasonable given the range and depth of the political and economic problems inherited from its predecessor. In February Yudhoyono replaced the heads of the three wings of the armed forces in an attempt to consolidate civilian control over the military. It was a task eased by the fact that he was himself a former general but, significantly perhaps, he stopped short of removing the overall commander of Indonesia's armed forces (TNI). The "remilitarisation" of the TNI did, however, advance on another front with the dissolution of most of its network of commercial ventures. This rather odd excrescence of the military role had developed under the regime of President Suharto (1967-98) and had become one of the many loci of Indonesia's institutionalised corruption.

Signs at the beginning of the year that the new administration was determined to tackle head-on this legacy of corruption weakened as 2005 progressed. In April, in its first high profile case, the recently created commission for the eradication of corruption (KPK) had delivered a ten-year jail term and large fine to the former governor of Aceh province, Abdullah Puteh, for the diversion of public funds. The momentum was not maintained, however, and subsequent cases followed the more familiar pattern of confusion and compromise.

Although relations with the key Western allies were strained somewhat by a perceived lack of determination on the Indonesian front of the "war on terror", President Yudhoyono did have a successful state visit to the USA at the end of May. At the end of this, the US government announced the relaxation of an arms embargo originally imposed because of Indonesia's actions in East Timor. Relations with the unapologetically assertive government of John Howard in Australia were brittle throughout the year. Resentment at Indonesia's supposed shortcomings in confronting Islamist violence was exacerbated in May by the twenty-year jail term passed on a young Australian woman for drug smuggling. Less partisan observers, however, noted that the legal process had been conducted entirely properly and that the sentence was entirely in line with Indonesian law.

During 2005 the Philippines grappled with the long-standing and apparently intractable problems of armed separatism (recently complicated by an international Islamist dimension) and political instability and scandal.

The year began with a potentially menacing development in the continuing war between the Manila government and Islamic separatism. Fighting began in the southern island province of Mindanao when the army launched an attack on the Moro Islamic Liberation Front (MILF). Although the MILF was supposed to be maintaining a ceasefire, the government accused it of planning an alliance with the region-wide Islamist movement, Jemaah Islamiah (JI), widely blamed for much of the recent violence in nearby Indonesia (see above). Then, in February, a separate spate of violence began between the military and the older, and supposedly more moderate, Moro National Liberation Front (MNLF) from which more radical elements had originally broken to form the MILF. This outbreak involved heavy fighting on the island of Jolo in the south-western province of Sulu. The cause of the fighting was reportedly similar to that in Mindanao: the development of an alliance between an older separatist movement and a newer, more religiously oriented, Islamism. In this case a faction of the MNLF was alleged to have combined with the ultra-violent and ruthless Abu Sayyaf (AS) group. The true extent of these alliances (if they existed at all) was difficult to assess. Like much in the Philippines, it was probable that all was not as claimed by the government. Tarring older movements with the brush of contemporary terrorism was a useful means of demonising long-standing adversaries in an unresolved conflict and justifying the resumption of the military option. But if such a coalescence of forces was indeed taking place, it would constitute a major threat to a central government beset by a raft of military and political difficulties.

The Abu Sayyaf group dominated the news again in March when, following an alleged mass break-out attempt from a Manila prison, about thirty of its members—including a significant proportion of its leadership—were killed. Once again, the narrative of events was provided by the government. But there was little enthusiasm, either in the Philippines or abroad, to subject it to close examination. The AS, once a locally-based gang much involved in straightforward criminality, had mutated over recent years to epitomise the Islamist threat to the Philippine state.

National politics, which in the Philippines could rarely be accused of lacking in colour, were dominated in 2005 by the extent of President Gloria Macapagal-Arroyo's hold on office. Widely seen as a breath of business-like, incorrupt fresh air when she displaced her louche predecessor, José Estrada, from office in 2001 (see AR 2001, p. 360), her image had become increasingly tarnished over her period in power. In June she faced accusations of electoral fraud during the campaign which had returned her to office the previous year. Forced to admit irregular contacts with an Electoral Commission official, she nevertheless denied attempting to influence the conduct of the poll. More detailed accusations followed, however, and the opposition within the legislature began impeachment proceedings. In the event, her supporters in the two houses of the bicameral legislature were able to block the process. But Arroyo's position was already weak. Clear success in economic management, supposedly her strong suit, had so far eluded her. Moreover, her perceived closeness to the USA did not play well in a society always sensitive to any whiff of "neo-colonialism".

The suggestion that she was also just as much part of the old, graft-ridden political class as any of her predecessors was hugely damaging. Commonly in times of constitutional uncertainty in the Philippines, eyes turned nervously towards the role of the military, and 2005 was no exception. In May many of the non-commissioned officers who had been involved in the military "demonstrations" (or "attempted coup", depending upon interpretation) in 2003 (see AR 2003, p. 365) received lenient sentences at courts martial. This was followed by an apparent coup threat by former general and Defence Secretary Fortunato Abat. In less febrile times statements from such a relatively marginal figure would have been largely disregarded, but in the climate of mid-2005 it was taken more seriously and various prominent names—including those of former Presidents Estrada and Fidel Ramos—were stirred into the soup of speculation.

Amidst these swirling currents and counter-currents Arroyo continued with her project of shifting the structure of government from the presidential system embodied in the 1987 constitution to a more "European" parliamentary one. To this end a "citizens' consultative committee" was established to begin the process of gauging—and shaping—public opinion.

June brought the death of Cardinal Jaime Sin, one of the dominating figures of Philippine public life, and certainly one of the most respected (for obituary see pp. 549-50). The seventy-eight-year-old cleric had been in the front line of the "people power" demonstrations that had overthrown the Marcos regime in 1986 (see AR 1986, pp. 297-98) and had been prominent in the similar, though less dramatic, process which saw the overthrow of José Estrada and cleared the way for the accession of President Arroyo.

The year saw a much needed improvement in relations between EAST TIMOR and Indonesia. In March, East Timor's President Xanana Gusmão visited Jakarta where, with Indonesian President Susilo Bambang Yudhoyono, he signed into being a joint truth and friendship commission which was to investigate the violence in late 1999 preceding East Timor's independence (see AR 1999, pp. 347-48). While the gesture had considerable symbolic importance, more sceptical observers noted Indonesia's continuing reluctance either to punish those within its jurisdiction responsible for the violence or to co-operate with the UN in bringing them before an international court. However, the following month the Indonesian head of state was in East Timor where he made a well-judged and well-received visit to the Santa Cruz cemetery, scene of the 1991 massacre of hundreds of Timorese demonstrators by Indonesian soldiers. At a more practical level, the two Presidents signed an agreement definitively demarcating the border between East Timor and the Indonesian province of West Timor which had been the scene of sporadic trouble since 1999.

In April the UN Security Council agreed to maintain the UN's support mission, UNMISET, within East Timor. Secretary-General Kofi Annan argued that it was still necessary despite the strong progress made since independence. The new mandate involved a considerable reduction in the peacekeeping component of the operation, reflecting the improving security situation in the country and on its border with Indonesia.

EAST ASIAN STATES

PEOPLE'S REPUBLIC OF CHINA—HONG KONG—TAIWAN

People's Republic of China
CAPITAL: Beijing   AREA: 9,597,000 sq km   POPULATION: 1,296,500,000
OFFICIAL LANGUAGE: Chinese   POLITICAL SYSTEM: one-party republic
HEAD OF STATE: President Hu Jintao (since March '03)
RULING PARTY: Chinese Communist Party (CCP)
PARTY LEADER: Hu Jintao (since Nov '02)
CCP POLITBURO STANDING COMMITTEE: Hu Jintao, Wu Bangguo, Wen Jiabao, Jia Qinglin, Zeng
    Qinghong, Huang Ju, Wu Guanzheng, Li Changchun, Luo Gan
CCP CENTRAL COMMITTEE SECRETARIAT: Zeng Qinghong, Liu Yunshan, Zhou Yongkang, He
    Guoqiang, Wang Gang, Xu Caihou, He Yong
CENTRAL MILITARY COMMISSION: Hu Jintao, chairman (since March '04)
PRIME MINISTER: Wen Jiabao (since March '03)
MAIN IGO MEMBERSHIPS (NON-UN): APEC
CURRENCY: renminbi (RMB) denominated in yuan (end-'05 £1=Y13.8545, US$1=Y8.07020)
GNP PER CAPITA: US$1,290, US$5,530 at PPP ('04, based on bilateral comparison with USA)

Hong Kong Special Administrative Region
CAPITAL: Victoria   AREA: 1,000 sq km   POPULATION: 6,800,000
STATUS: Special Administrative Region of People's Republic of China (since 1 July 1997)
CHIEF EXECUTIVE: Donald Tsang Yam-Kuen (since June '05)
ADMINISTRATIVE SECRETARY: Rafael Hui (since June '05)
MAIN IGO MEMBERSHIPS (NON-UN): APEC
CURRENCY: Hong Kong dollar (end-'05 £1=HK$13.3109, US$1=HK$7.75350)
GNP PER CAPITA: US$26,810, US$31,510 at PPP ('04)

Taiwan
CAPITAL: Taipei   AREA: 35,981 sq km   POPULATION: 22,894,384 (July 2005 est.)
OFFICIAL LANGUAGE: Chinese   POLITICAL SYSTEM: multiparty republic
HEAD OF STATE AND GOVERNMENT: President Chen Shui-bian (DPP) (since May '00)
RULING PARTY: Democratic Progressive Party (DPP)
PRIME MINISTER: Frank Hsieh (since Jan '05)
MAIN IGO MEMBERSHIPS: APEC; Taiwan is not a member of UN or associated IGOs
CURRENCY: New Taiwan dollar (end-'05 £1=NT$56.3832, US$1=NT$32.8430)
GNI PER CAPITA: US$26,700 ('05 est)

IN the People's Republic of CHINA, sustained economic growth (estimated at around 9 per cent) and political stability amongst the central leadership were the hallmarks of the year; but rural unrest, a serious pollution incident, ongoing issues over disease control, and a deteriorating political relationship with Japan were major concerns. The "fourth generation" leadership remained in firm control, although widespread anti-Japanese demonstrations in the spring, and growing violent unrest over land issues in the countryside, showed that the Chinese Communist Party (CCP) did not have absolute control over the population at large.

The environmental consequences of China's rapid economic development were made starkly apparent in November following a chemical spill in the north east of the country. An explosion in a chemical factory near the city of Jilin saw around 100 tonnes of benzene (a known carcinogen) released into the Songhua river.

Local officials initially attempted to downplay the incident, but as its seriousness became clear the central government instigated a major pollution control initiative. Nonetheless all water supplies to Harbin, the provincial capital of Heilongjiang province, with a population of 3.4 million (9.5 million in the greater Harbin area), were stopped for four days. The movement of the 80 kilometre-long benzene slick downriver generated significant national and international coverage. The spill also threatened a major international incident as it approached Russia's Khabarovsk oblast (region) in late December. Although the chemicals were sufficiently dispersed by the time they left China to reduce the danger, China's Prime Minister Wen Jiabao formally apologised to Russia. The political repercussions of the spill saw the director of the state environmental protection administration (SEPA), Xie Zhenhua, resign on 2 December and Yu Li, the head of the state-owned petrochemical plant which had leaked the chemicals, was dismissed on 5 December. Wang Wei, the deputy mayor of Jilin, who had initially denied any danger from the spill, was reported to have committed suicide on 6 December. The spill came after a report released by SEPA in April claimed that all seven of China's major rivers and twenty-five of its twenty-seven principal lakes were polluted, some of them seriously.

The CCP's desire to control information was seen in the pressure exerted on traditional print media and on electronic media. In August the Culture Ministry announced a freeze on new foreign broadcasters being allowed to operate in China, and tighter controls on international broadcasters already operating within the country. Several high-profile cases of government co-operation with Western software and Internet companies suggested that the Chinese government was using its economic leverage to help re-establish, maintain, or extend its control over information. The Internet service provider, Yahoo, was widely criticised in the USA and Europe for helping to identify an activist who had posted anti-government material on a website, and Google, the company that had devised the world's most popular Internet search engine, was also reported to have developed a special search facility for its Chinese version which excluded terms and phrases deemed problematic by the Chinese authorities. Microsoft was also criticised for apparently agreeing to restrictions on search terms used in its software developed for the Chinese market. In the print media, Yang Bing, the editor of the controversial *Beijing News*, was dismissed, reportedly for encouraging critical commentary of corruption. His removal led to a strike by other journalists at the paper. The issue of censorship was reported to be generating significant tensions within the senior leadership.

2005 was the final year of the tenth five year plan and was marked by an assessment of changes made over the period 2001-05 and discussion over future plans for the economy. The fifth plenary session of the 16th Central Committee of the CCP in October approved the eleventh five year plan for the period 2006-11, but little detail of its content was released. Official discussions on the direction of economic development and overall management of the economy made increasing reference to the concept of "scientific development", a theoretical formulation closely associated with President Hu Jintao. "Scientific development" would, the

Party suggested, address the contradictions within current economic development, tackle inequalities, place the people at its centre, and promote harmony in society. China's rapid economic expansion was increasing the country's dependence on imported oil and, partly in response to this and partly in response to environmental concerns, the government announced that it would build forty nuclear power generation units by 2020, as well as doubling its reliance on renewable energy sources by the same year.

A relaxation in the fixed exchange rate of the renminbi (RMB) with the US dollar was announced in July. Officials announced that the currency would in future be pegged to a basket of (undisclosed) foreign currencies, and that the state would maintain strong influence over the RMB's value to prevent speculation in the currency. The move was widely welcomed by foreign governments, but many still complained that the RMB remained seriously undervalued. Foreign exchange reserves in December stood at US$818.9 billion, second only to those of Japan, and were expected to surpass Japan's reserves in 2006. China's ongoing large trade surpluses continued to generate tensions with key partners, especially in Europe and North America, but some of these were eased when trade agreements over textiles were signed with the EU (September) and the USA (November), following the expiry of the World Trade Organisation (WTO) textile quota system earlier in the year. The new agreements established a series of quotas on Chinese exports to these key markets.

The national bureau of statistics reported a fall in the number of rural residents living in "abject poverty" (less than 668 yuan per capita), to 26.1 million, and a fall in those classified as on low incomes (924 yuan) from 56.17 to 49.77 million. However, a report released in November by the Organisation for Economic Co-operation and Development (OECD) suggested that in order to maintain parity with urban income levels, the rural population would need to decline by tens, even hundreds, of millions. Rural unrest remained significant throughout the year, to such an extent that it attracted international media coverage. The government also announced a new strategy to develop the central region (Anhui, Henan, Hubei, Hunan, Jiangxi, and Shanxi) to address the ongoing problems of uneven development across China. The strategy would aim to complement the existing "open up the west" initiative which had seen significant extra investment into China's poorest regions.

Both domestic poultry and wildfowl continued to suffer in 2005 from isolated outbreaks of the H5N1 virus of avian influenza ("bird flu"), and a number of significant culls of poultry took place in addition to a mass inoculation campaign of poultry. Six human cases of the disease were reported. Government efforts to tackle the disease demonstrated a significant shift and improvement over earlier efforts, suggesting that lessons had been learned following the outbreak of severe acute respiratory syndrome (SARS) in 2003 (see AR 2003, p. 371; 2004, p. 323). World Health Organisation officials praised the efforts of the Chinese government, although some foreign observers and media groups maintained that the CCP's campaign of mass inoculation of all poultry would be ineffective or counter-productive.

China's biggest foreign policy concern was over relations with Japan. In March the CCP strongly criticised a rephrasing of the Japanese government's position on the Taiwan Strait. The CCP argued that Japan had broken with precedent in saying that any use of force in the Taiwan Strait would threaten Japan, and it demanded clarification of Japan's position. In April, the Chinese Foreign Ministry strongly criticised the Japanese government for approving new school textbooks which the Chinese side argued were "rife with historical distortion and misrepresentation". Four days later some of the largest urban demonstrations since the student reform movement of 1989 took place in cities across China. Some violent incidents occurred, with rocks being thrown at the Japanese embassy and some Japanese-owned commercial operations being damaged. Later in April the Chinese Foreign Minister, Li Zhaoxing, met his Japanese counterpart, Nobutaka Machimura, in Beijing. Machimura complained about the damage to Japanese property and the Chinese side responded with complaints about issues such as the textbook revisions, Japanese Prime Minister Junichiro Koizumi's repeated visits to the Yasukuni Shrine in Tokyo (which commemorated Japan's war dead, including convicted war criminals), and the ongoing disagreements over exploitation of maritime resources in disputed areas. President Hu and Prime Minister Koizumi met at the Asia-Africa Summit in Jakarta, Indonesia, at the end of April, and Hu called on Japan to reflect on history and to adhere to the previously agreed position on the question of TAIWAN. However these and a series of other ministerial meetings failed to make significant progress in improving relations. The situation deteriorated at the end of the year when Koizumi made his fifth visit to the controversial Yasukuni Shrine. As a consequence, both the Chinese and South Korean governments refused to meet their Japanese counterparts at further summit conferences later in the year. The persisting sensitivity of historical issues was again demonstrated in July by the discovery of a chemical warfare plant left behind by the Japanese occupation of north east China during the Sino-Japanese war (1937-45).

China's political relations with the USA remained healthy, although there were significant frictions over economic matters, and long-term problems related to China's growing political and military significance. In April the Chinese government protested against a US decision to investigate a range of Chinese textile products, complaining that doing so violated WTO legal provisions. The visit of US Secretary of Defence Donald Rusmfeld in early November was marked by a disagreement over the size and significance of Chinese military spending, whereas the visit by President George W. Bush as part of a wider tour of Asia later the same month focused on economic issues, especially the value of the Chinese currency and issues of intellectual property rights.

Relations with Russia remained strong, despite the chemical spill incident in November (see above). President Hu visited Moscow in May to attend the commemoration of the 60th anniversary of the end of World War II in Europe. Hu met Russian President Vladimir Putin for discussions regarding agreements over their common border and economic, military, and energy co-operation. The developing relationship with Russia was underscored by further top level meetings in the summer and by the first ever joint military exercises between the two sides which took place in August, involving an estimated 100,000 troops.

China continued to play a major role in the Korean peninsula, promoting the six-party talks and offering to broker agreements between the USA and North Korea over the latter's nuclear policy (see pp. 318-19). Prime Minister Wen made an important tour of South Asia, visiting Pakistan, Bangladesh, Sri Lanka, and India. In India he met Prime Minister Manmohan Singh and a number of issues were discussed, including increasing economic co-operation and trade and resolving the ongoing dispute over their common border. The visit resulted in a number of agreements, and both sides reported satisfactory progress on the border issue. Hu visited the UK, Germany, and Spain in November, with trade issues dominating the agenda. The European visit followed a setback to China's long-term strategy of ending the EU arms embargo imposed in 1989, when the German government announced in June that it was not prepared to lift the embargo without US support.

The Chinese government's frustration and anger at the political authorities in TAIWAN remained palpable. In April the CCP passed the "anti-secession law" which provided a legal framework for its policy of using force should Taiwan attempt to declare independence. The law was roundly criticised in Taiwan and by some foreign commentators. However, it did not mark a radical departure in China's policy, being fundamentally a reformulation of a long-standing position. Distrust of Taiwanese President Chen Shui-bian remained high, but there were significant visits to China by Lien Chan, chairman of Taiwan's opposition Kuomintang (KMT) (see below).

In January it was reported that Zhao Ziyang, the former Prime Minister, had died at the age of eighty-five. Zhao was a key figure in the economic reform agenda instigated by Deng Xiaoping, and had argued that political and legal reform was necessary in addition to rapid economic development. He was best remembered for having supported the demonstrators during the 1989 student-led reform movement in Tiananmen Square (see AR 1989, p. 338; for obituary see p. 553). His decision to depart from the agreed position on the students destroyed his political career and he spent the remainder of his life under house arrest in Beijing. Although there were no formal attempts to rehabilitate Zhao, the fact that several senior CCP figures were reported to have attended his funeral suggested that the senior leadership, at least in private, maintained some respect for Zhao and his views. In an event which may have been related, October saw the first official memorial ceremony for Zhao's mentor, Hu Yaobang, which was attended by President Hu Jintao and Prime Minister Wen Jiabao. Hu's death had triggered the student-led reform movement in 1989.

Two of the most important political figures from the turbulent years of the Cultural Revolution also died in 2005: former "Gang of Four" members Zhang Chunqiao and Yao Wenyuan. Zhang, who died in May, was the powerful head of official propaganda during the Cultural Revolution, and was officially labelled the "prime culprit of the Gang of Four" at their trial in 1981. Yao, who died in

December, was a literary critic whose writings were taken as the signal which started the Cultural Revolution in 1966 (see pp. 552-53).

The resignation of Chief Executive Tung Chee-hwa and ongoing debates about political reform dominated events in the HONG KONG Special Administrative Region. The economy was healthy, with government figures suggesting a growth rate in excess of 8 per cent.

In March, Chief Executive Tung Chee-hwa announced his retirement, citing health problems, although his growing unpopularity in Hong Kong and concern over his capabilities on the part of the CCP leadership in mainland China were widely reported to have been major contributory factors. Tung's retirement followed several months of speculation over his future, which had peaked in February when it was announced that he had been appointed to China's top political advisory body, the Chinese People's Political Consultative Conference (CPPCC). He was replaced by his deputy, Donald Tsang, for an interim period of not more than six months, until a new election could be organised by the Election Committee which represented Hong Kong's functional constituencies. The Hong Kong government asked for a revision of the law, in order to restrict the new Chief Executive to serving only the two remaining years of Tung's term and then face re-election for a five year period. This was granted by the National People's Congress (legislature) in mainland China in April. The move was criticised, however, as it circumvented Hong Kong's Court of Final Appeal, the body empowered to interpret Hong Kong's basic law.

Tsang was selected unopposed in June to succeed Tung, and was sworn in on 24 June. Tsang stated that he intend to make the administration more representative, but he was confronted with a similar problem to that which had beset his predecessor: how to please those in Hong Kong who were calling for more democracy, whilst not upsetting his ultimate political masters in the mainland government. Tsang had risen to prominence in Hong Kong when it was a British colony and was widely respected for his financial acumen and skill at handling the media.

In October Tsang announced the expansion of the Executive Council (Cabinet) to thirty, by adding eight ex-officio members, in a move regarded as increasing the Council's representative character. Important political reforms were also proposed, including doubling the Election Committee from 800 to 1,600, and increasing the size of the Legislative Council (LegCo, the unicameral legislature) by ten seats (to seventy), with five of them being directly elected. Tsang suffered a significant setback in December when the LegCo failed to endorse the proposed changes. Earlier in December opposition parties and civil and workers groups organised a march to call for greater democratic reform, and specifically for the direct election of the chief executive. Reports varied on the size of the march: organisers claimed in excess of 250,000 people took part, while police estimates suggested 63,000. Hong Kong's basic law did contain provisions for the direct election of the chief executive, but protestors were demanding a clear timetable for this.

The two main pro-mainland parties in Hong Kong—the Democratic Alliance for the Betterment of Hong Kong (DAB), and the Hong Kong Progressive Alliance (PA)—announced in February that they were to merge, taking the DAB's name. The PA had lost all of its four seats in the LegCo in the 2004 elections; the DAB had twelve seats.

In TAIWAN, President Chen Shui-bian suffered a number of political reverses over the course of the year, and heavy defeats for his Democratic Progressive Party (DPP) candidates in local elections in December. While economic growth remained solid, Chen's government was badly damaged by corruption scandals and a reinvigorated Kuomintang (KMT) opposition party, under the new leadership of Ma Ying-jeou. Tensions across the Taiwan Strait with mainland CHINA remained high. Chen adopted an increasingly antagonistic approach towards the Chinese government, whilst the KMT opposition promoted closer political ties; the Chinese leadership's decision to enact an anti-secession law, meanwhile, generated considerable concern and ill-feeling among pro-independence groups in Taiwan. Steady economic growth (estimated at 3.6 per cent) was driven, in large part, by growing dependence on the Chinese market, despite increased government efforts to encourage Taiwanese business to diversify.

In January, the mayor of the southern city of Kaohsiung, Frank Hsieh, replaced Yu Shyi-kun as Prime Minister. Yu had resigned after the DPP's Pan Green alliance (the DPP and the Taiwan Solidarity Union) had lost the December 2004 elections (see AR 2004, p. 328). Su Tseng-chang took over as DPP chairman from President Chen, who had resigned from the post in recognition of the DPP's poor performance in the elections. However the new DPP-led government soon ran into trouble, as Hsieh was dogged by corruption allegations from his time as mayor of Kaohsiung, and in September the opposition KMT refused to co-operate on legislative business until a full enquiry had been established. Subsequently, two senior presidential advisors, Chen Che-nan and Chen Min-hsien, resigned in October because of a judicial investigation into their alleged involvement in a profiteering scandal. The DPP had previously benefited significantly from its anti-corruption stance, but opinion polls indicated that the Taiwanese population now regarded it as no less corrupt than the opposition KMT.

At the very end of the year, the DPP suffered further severe setbacks in local elections on 3 December. On a voter turnout of over 66 per cent, the KMT won 408 (of 901) council seats, 173 (of 319) township-mayor contests, and fourteen (of twenty-three) county-mayor contests, with 50.96 per cent of the vote. The DPP won 192 council seats, thirty-five township-mayor contests, and six county-mayor contests, with 41.95 per cent of the vote. In the aftermath of the election DPP chairman Su Tseng-chang resigned, but Frank Hsieh's offer of resignation was declined by President Chan for the sake of political stability. As widely expected, however, Hsieh did in fact step down in January 2006.

The first direct flights between mainland CHINA and TAIWAN since 1949, which were arranged over the Chinese new year holiday in February, did not herald a significant improvement in the cross-Strait relationship. The tense situation became worse in March following the decision by the CCP in mainland China to introduce a legal framework for its long-standing opposition to Taiwanese independence—and its readiness to use force to prevent it—in the form of the "anti-secession law" (see above). The government of Taiwan and those opposed to reunification were highly critical of the new law which generated unease and disquiet in Taiwan. A government-supported rally saw several hundred thousand people in Taipei protest against the law.

By contrast, the KMT sought to improve relations across the Taiwan Strait. In April and May a party delegation, led by chairman Lien Chan, became the first official KMT group to visit mainland China since 1949. Lien met President Hu Jintao in Beijing and called for peaceful dialogue and the improvement of relations across the Strait; he visited a number of important memorial sites in Nanjing and Guangzhou. The visit was strongly criticised by the ruling DPP, who accused the KMT of attempting to "sell out" Taiwan to its powerful neighbour. One particular issue of contention was an offer by the mainland government to lend Taiwan two giant pandas. Pro-independence groups bitterly opposed this gesture, and much public discussion followed over the political, economic, and symbolic dimensions of "panda diplomacy".

In August the KMT swore in a new leader, Ma Ying-jeou, who had been elected by the party with a strong mandate in July. It was the first time that a KMT leader had been directly elected by the party membership. Ma, the well-regarded mayor of Taipei, called for better relations across the Strait and for direct air and sea links with the Chinese mainland, but he was also critical of the political system and human rights conditions which prevailed in China. Ma was almost certain to be the KMT's candidate in the 2008 presidential elections.

President Chen's own agenda for Taiwan was signalled clearly by a repeated call for comprehensive revision of its constitution. The constitutional reform issue was especially contentious because Chen's critics in Taiwan, as well as the government in mainland China, regarded it as part of a wider agenda to push Taiwan towards formal independence from China. To this end elections were held in May for a 300-seat ad hoc National Assembly, which would debate the proposed constitutional reforms. The results gave the DPP 127 seats, and the KMT—which supported the reforms—117 seats. The DPP's ally, the Taiwan Solidarity Union, which opposed the reforms, won twenty-one seats. However turnout was under 24 per cent.

The Assembly ratified a number of constitutional reforms adopted by the legislature in 2004, including reducing the size of the elected Legislative Yuan (unicameral legislature) from 225 to 113 seats, replacing the current multi-member constituencies with single-member districts, extending the term of the Legislative Yuan from three years to four, and abolishing the National Assembly, with its powers to impeach the president being transferred to the legislature, and constitutional reform matters to be decided by a 75 per cent approval in the legislature followed by a national referendum.

The constitutional reform issue added strains to Taiwan's relationship with the USA, with figures in the US administration cautioning Taiwan not to take any

actions which might alter the delicate political balance in the Taiwan Strait. Relations with Japan reflected the complex position that Japan occupied in the opinion of many Taiwanese. In April Shu Chin-chiang, leader of the pro-independence Taiwan Solidarity Union, visited the controversial Yasukuni Shrine in Tokyo
to pray for the some 30,000 Taiwanese interred there who had died fighting for
Japan in World War II. A counter-demonstration condemning the shrine was
organised by independent lawmaker Kao Chin Su-mei.

Taiwan's precarious diplomatic position suffered setbacks when diplomatic
relations were severed with Grenada (January) and Senegal (October), leaving
Taiwan being formally recognised by only twenty-five countries.

JAPAN

CAPITAL: Tokyo   AREA: 378,000 sq km   POPULATION: 127,800,000
OFFICIAL LANGUAGE: Japanese   POLITICAL SYSTEM: multiparty monarchy
HEAD OF STATE: Emperor Tsugu no Miya Akihito (since Jan '89)
RULING PARTIES: Liberal Democratic Party (LDP) in coalition with the New Komeito party
HEAD OF GOVERNMENT: Junichiro Koizumi, Prime Minister (since April '01)
MAIN IGO MEMBERSHIPS (NON-UN): APEC, CP, OECD, G-8
CURRENCY: yen (end-'05 £1=Y202.628, US$1=Y118.030)
GNI PER CAPITA: US$37,180, US$30,040 at PPP ('04)

PRIME Minister Junichiro Koizumi suffered mixed fortunes during 2005. On the
one hand. he raised Japan's international profile through numerous foreign trips;
oversaw an improvement in the economy as it emerged slowly from its eight-year
battle with deflation; and won a general election decisively. On the other, he
antagonised his near neighbours, China and South Korea, and found himself isolated in the east Asian region.

Throughout the year political debate centred on proposals for the privatisation
of Japan's postal services, for which Koizumi had campaigned since coming to
power in 2001. The proposals envisaged channelling the capital accumulated in
branches of the "postal empire"—especially postal savings and life insurance—
into the private sector. Little progress on reform had been made, however,
because of opposition within sections of Koizumi's own Liberal Democratic Party
(LDP) and entrenched interests like those of local postmasters. Koizumi had
pushed a set of proposals through Cabinet in September 2004 (see AR 2004, p.
331), and eventually, in April, the Cabinet placed six watered-down bills before
the Diet (the bicameral legislature) which passed the House of Representatives
(the lower house) by the narrow margin of 233 to 228. Some thirty-seven legislators from the LDP voted against, fourteen abstained, and senior figures within
the party resigned. The bills were, however, defeated in the House of Councillors
(the upper house) by 125 to 108, because of defections by LDP members.
Koizumi reacted vigorously, and dangerously, by calling a general election for 11
September on the issue of reform, particularly postal privatisation. In the event,
the LDP and its coalition partner, the smaller New Komeito party, achieved a landslide victory by winning 296 and 31 seats respectively, giving them a two-thirds
majority in the 480-seat chamber. Koizumi was vindicated by the result though

he had had to resort to unorthodox tactics to secure his majority, recruiting "assassin" candidates to stand against rebels from the LDP who had opposed postal reform and whom Koizumi had disowned. The opposition Democratic Party of Japan (DPJ), which had had some success in the Tokyo metropolitan assembly elections in July, suffered serious losses, holding on to only 113 of its 175 seats. Its leader, Katsuya Okada, resigned immediately.

After the endorsement by the electorate of his reform programme, Koizumi successfully steered his postal bills through both chambers of the Diet. As a result, the various branches in Japan Post would be split from 2007 into separate companies under an over-arching holding company to be, at the outset, wholly owned by the government.

Upon his re-election as Prime Minister in October, Koizumi reiterated his intention to stand down in a year's time as president of the LDP and, therefore, as Prime Minister. In the meantime, however, Koizumi presided over a new LDP which had been reshaped by the expulsion of those who had voted against postal privatisation. Koizumi also reshuffled his Cabinet radically, making a large number of new appointments. One of the underlying purposes of this was to give his potential successors an opportunity for ministerial experience over the course of the next year. Heizo Takenaka, an independent, who had been the architect of Koizumi's reforms in previous Cabinets, was created Minister of Internal Affairs and Minister of State with special responsibility for postal privatisation.

It was, therefore, with a mood of euphoria that the LDP celebrated the 50th anniversary of its formation in November 1955 (see AR 1955, pp. 307-08). Under his reform programme Koizumi was gradually reorienting the party's policies, particularly with regard to the issue of self-defence and the amendment of the 1947 pacifist constitution which had been foisted upon Japan in the aftermath of its defeat in the Pacific War. Within the party, the recommended revisions were debated and approved. In respect to the controversial Clause 9, which dealt with the maintenance of security forces, the recommendation was to retain the phrase about "renouncing war as an instrument of state policy" but to allow military forces to exist for the purpose of national defence and participation in UN operations overseas. However, these constitutional issues were politically sensitive and highly divisive, and it would take time to reach consensus with opposition parties in order to achieve their approval in the Diet.

In international relations, the year began with the aftermath of the December 2004 tsunami in South-East Asia (see map p. 296). Japan hosted a major UN conference in Kobe on disaster relief, and offered generous assistance in establishing an early warning system in the Indian Ocean area. Japan was also an active donor towards relief efforts for the Pakistan earthquakes in September-October (see pp. 278-79), and increased the volume of its overseas direct aid during the year.

Relations with the Koreas remained difficult throughout the year. The nuclear danger from North Korea was a major consideration, especially after North Korea announced in February that it possessed nuclear weapons (see p. 318). The fourth round of the six-party talks took place in September and North Korea agreed in principle to dismantle its nuclear weapons programme in return for aid; but this agreement unravelled almost immediately. Japan was also unsuccessful in getting support from China and South Korea over the question of returning family members of Japanese abductees in North Korea (see AR 2004, p. 331). Talks on the issue were resumed on 9 November but broke down after three days without any progress. The South Korea-Japan summit in June revealed much hostile feeling on various issues, including a territorial dispute over the uninhabited islets known as Tokdo by the Koreans and Takeshima by the Japanese. This lack of goodwill hindered any co-ordinated approach to the question of North Korea's nuclear weapons programme.

There were also serious issues in contention with China. It was true that the volume of Sino-Japanese trade had reached the same level as that between Japan and the USA; that cultural and educational ties between the two countries had never been stronger; and that Japanese investment in China was increasing by leaps and bounds. But on the negative side there was rivalry over oil supplies and disagreement over claims to the Senkaku Islands to the southwest of Okinawa, which were thought to be a possible source of much-needed oil for both countries.

Japan's history in the region was also a source of contention with both China and South Korea. In the spring a new junior high school history textbook, which had been approved by the screeners, was adopted by the Education Ministry. The government did not show undue concern because the book was only taken up by eighteen of some 11,000 schools. But China and South Korea protested, claiming that the book played down Japan's wartime role and "omitted to mention Japan's war crimes" (see pp. 305; 316). For two weeks in April multitudes of Chinese demonstrated in various cities, attacking the Japanese embassy in Beijing, the consulate-general in Shanghai, company offices, and Japanese restaurants. While refusing to give Japan any apology, the Chinese authorities were genuinely alarmed and took measures to restrain popular feelings, posting paramilitary units to guard Japanese properties. The two sides agreed to set up a joint committee to study historical issues as part of a reconciliation between the two countries. But in May, China's Deputy Prime Minister Wu Yi, who was visiting Japan to discuss improving relations, suddenly cut short her trip, rather publicly cancelling her meeting with the Prime Minister. Koizumi personally came under criticism by China on account of his past visits to the Yasukuni shrine in Tokyo where some war criminals were honoured among the nation's war-dead. He did not visit the shrine in August on the 60th anniversary of the end of World War II; but prominent members of his Cabinet did.

On 19 November Koizumi paid a visit to the Yasukuni shrine on a private, unofficial basis. This action led to China and South Korea snubbing him at the Asia-Pacific Economic Co-operation (APEC) meeting at Pusan, South Korea, which followed (see p. 390); and a planned summit conference of the three regional powers was postponed indefinitely. As the year ended, Sino-Japanese relations were in an unhappy state as the new Foreign Minister, Taro Aso, drew attention publicly to the widespread Japanese perception of China as a regional military threat.

Amid all this political excitement, Japan prepared to present its case for obtaining a permanent seat on the UN Security Council when that body was expanded in the course of reforms which were under consideration. Japan had lobbied for this for some years and hoped that, by going forward alongside Brazil, Germany, and India, it would stand a chance of election at the UN General Assembly in September (see p. 334). But Japan's case met with strenuous opposition from China and the proposal was withdrawn.

In the autumn Japan received brief visits from two world leaders. On 15 November US President George W. Bush spent time in Japan during the course of visits to China, South Korea, and Mongolia; the major outcome was Japan's withdrawal of its two-year ban on the import of US beef. The following week Russia's President Vladimir Putin visited Japan accompanied by a delegation of over 100 senior executives who were anxious to focus on Russia's desire for economic cooperation. Putin welcomed continuing Japanese investment in north-east Siberia, one of Russia's oil-rich regions. However, it remained unclear whether the planned east-bound energy pipeline from Siberia would terminate on the Sea of Japan coast, as Japan wished, rather than divert to China. There was no breakthrough on the Northern Territories (Kurile Islands) issue, but Putin signed a bilateral pact on counter-terrorism.

The contingent of 550 soldiers of Japan's Self-Defence Forces (SDF) continued to be posted at Samawah in southern Iraq. They were a peace-keeping unit employed on reconstruction and non-combatant humanitarian duties under the protection of UK, and later in the year of Australian, troops. Although Samawah was relatively peaceful, there were some casualties among the troops. A Japanese civilian contractor in Iraq was kidnapped in May and later died (see p. 192). On 14 December Koizumi extended the period that SDF troops would serve beyond the original December deadline but, in spite of Iraqi requests that Japan should not withdraw, spoke of a contemplated pullout without being specific about dates.

Domestically, a major event was the Aichi International Exhibition which opened in March, with its emphasis on science and technology. In the previous month an international airport serving the populous Nagoya area was opened in preparation for the exhibition. It was the first international airport in Japan to be built largely with private sector funding. By the time the exhibition closed at the end of September, it had attracted some 22 million visitors, exceeding initial expectations substantially.

Japan suffered a major railway crash at Amagasaki, Hyogo prefecture, on 25 April, causing 107 deaths and hundreds of injuries. A commuter train was derailed, allegedly because the driver was speeding to make up time on his schedule. The chairman of West Japan Railways resigned as a gesture to the bereaved.

Two developments affected the fortunes of the imperial family. On 15 November the Emperor's daughter, Princess Sayako Nori no Miya, married a commoner and gave up rights of succession within the royal family, though it was confirmed that she would retain her royal status. On a more general issue, an advisory panel which met throughout the year to consider revisions neces-

sary in the Imperial Household Law reported in November in favour of allowing females to succeed to the throne, contrary to the practice followed in the last
few centuries. If adopted, this would pave the way for Princess Aiko, the only
daughter of the Crown Prince, to succeed to the throne, a move which had widespread public support. No male heir had been born into the imperial family for
forty years, making it difficult to maintain the tradition of a male-only line of
succession. Koizumi announced that he would present a bill to the Diet in 2006
to implement the recommendations of the advisory panel; but the issue generated heated debate between modernisers and traditionalists.

SOUTH AND NORTH KOREA

South Korea

CAPITAL: Seoul   AREA: 99,000 sq km   POPULATION: 48,100,000
OFFICIAL LANGUAGE: Korean   POLITICAL SYSTEM: multiparty republic
HEAD OF STATE AND GOVERNMENT: President Roh Moo Hyun (since Feb '03)
RULING PARTY: Uri Party (since April '04)
PRIME MINISTER: Prime Minister Lee Hai Chan (Uri) (since June '04)
MAIN IGO MEMBERSHIPS (NON-UN): APEC, CP, OECD
CURRENCY: won (end-'05 £1=W1,735.38, US$1=W1,010.85)
GNI PER CAPITA: US$13,980, US$20,400 at PPP ('04)

North Korea

CAPITAL: Pyongyang   AREA: 123,370 sq km   POPULATION: 22,745,000
OFFICIAL LANGUAGES: Korean   POLITICAL SYSTEM: one-party republic
HEAD OF STATE: Kim Il Sung, Eternal President, died 1994
RULING PARTY: Korean Workers' Party (KWP)
PARTY LEADER: Kim Jong Il, KWP general secretary (since Oct '97)
PRIME MINISTER: Pak Pong Ju (since Sept '03)
MAIN IGO MEMBERSHIPS (NON-UN): NAM
CURRENCY: won (end-'05 £1=W1,545.08, US$1=W900.000)
GNP PER CAPITA: low income: US$825 or less ('04 est)

HAVING successfully overcome an impeachment attempt, and with an unexpectedly good showing for his supporters in the April 2004 elections to the
National Assembly (unicameral legislature), the Republic of Korea's (ROK—
SOUTH KOREA) President Roh Moo Hyun, looked forward to a less fraught
year. His presidency had another two years to run. The Uri Party ("Our
Party"), created to back him, enjoyed a majority that would make possible the
passing of his radical legislative programme, and he had shown himself capable internationally. With the continued enthusiasm for Korean popular culture
and with the emergence of a world-class scientist in the field of stem cell
research, South Korea looked ready to make even more of an international
impact. Problems still remained, especially in relation to the Democratic
People's Republic of Korea (DPRK—NORTH KOREA), and the apparent divergence between South Korean and US policies, but even in that field 2004 had
ended on a reasonably high note. There were clearly some tricky issues
ahead, including relations with Japan, but 2005 had been declared the year of

Korean-Japanese friendship, and both countries had promised to do all they could to make this a success.

In the event, 2005 proved to be a mixed year. There were some reforms. March saw the end of the family registration system, criticised by the UN human rights commission and long regarded as reinforcing male domination. Work began on modifications to the prosecution service, to reduce the power of prosecutors and increase the protection of defenders. The President encouraged an unprecedented degree of public participation in a decision on choosing a site for the disposal of low-level nuclear waste. An attempt began to tackle property speculation, a major factor in corruption. Although the constitutional court in 2004 thwarted plans to create a new capital to replace Seoul, Roh pushed ahead with the creation of an administrative city designed to take many government offices. More radical reforms, however, including those relating to the national security law, failed to make progress.

In by-elections in May, the UP fared badly and lost control of the National Assembly. The party's problems increased when it lost two further by-elections in the autumn. It also did badly in local elections and by the end of the year its popularity had fallen to below 20 per cent in opinion polls. At the same time, the leader of the main opposition Grand National Party (GNP), Park Geun Hye, the daughter of former President Park Chung Hee, regained some of her earlier popularity. Although the UP remained the largest single group in the Assembly, with 144 seats compared with the GNP's 127, the difficulty of getting legislation passed led Roh to suggest the formation of a coalition government. If this happened, he would consider giving up some powers, or even, in an echo of his earliest days in office, resigning the presidency altogether (see AR 2003, p. 382). The coalition proposal met with objections from all political quarters. Nothing daunted, Roh raised the issue again at the end of the year, with a similarly negative response. The National Assembly saw a return to violent exchanges between opposing members, with representatives exchanging blows on occasions.

Admissions by the National Intelligence Service (NIS) of an extensive programme of the wiretapping of political and economic leaders carried out under Roh's predecessors had wide repercussions. By November, two former NIS heads during Kim Dae Jung's presidency (1997-2002) were indicted on charges of illegal wiretapping. A former deputy director killed himself while under investigation. Not only the NIS was affected. Conversations taped at the time of the 1997 presidential elections, between Hong Seok Hyun—then the publisher of the *JongAng Ilbo* newspaper and later ambassador to the USA—and the vice president of the Samsung group, revealed plans to pay large sums of money to Lee Hoi Chan, the GNP candidate whom Kim Dae Jung defeated. Hong resigned, and eventually returned home to a prosecution investigation. Other corruption issues involved Russian oil, where large amounts of government money appeared to have gone missing.

Much of this had been the standard stuff of Korean politics for years. More devastating were allegations that the pioneer of stem cell research, Hwang Woo Suk, had engaged in unethical practices and had falsified his research results. Hwang claimed that in 2004 he had cloned the first human embryo, and in May 2005 that he had created stem cell lines from individuals. His work on animal cloning, culminating in August 2005 with a cloned Afghan hound, received international acclaim. South Koreans were delighted with the world-class researcher who had raised their country's international profile. The government honoured Hwang and provided substantial funds for his research. However, doubts arose over both his methods and results, and by the end of the year he was disgraced. In January 2006, Hwang admitted errors, but blamed his staff. Elsewhere, such an event might have been shrugged off, but such high hopes were fixed on Hwang that his fall was traumatic (see p. 405).

The economy provided better news. In November, the biennial IMF mission noted that an economic recovery was underway, although it was still weak in some areas. GDP was estimated at US$727 billion. GDP growth for the year had been forecast at 3.7 per cent, but a strong performance in the last quarter pushed it up to 4 per cent. Per capita income reached US$16,000, up from US$14,162 in 2004. Inflation remained low, at around 2 per cent, while the won continued its steady appreciation against the US dollar. Unemployment, at 3.7 per cent, remained low, but younger people were disproportionately affected. For the first time ever, South Korea's trade passed the US$500 billion level, making it the world's twelfth largest trading nation; it had been a mere $100 billion in 1998. China continued to be its main trading partner, with bilateral trade amounting to some $100 billion. Japan, the USA, and Saudi Arabia were the other leading trade partners.

In a mid-year review of his presidency, Roh claimed that he had successfully managed relations with Japan and the USA. Others were less sure. The year of Korean-Japanese friendship got off to a bad start. Documents relating to the 1965 normalisation treaty between the two countries fed into an ongoing debate about alleged pro-Japanese positions taken by the late President Park Chung Hee. In August, a private organisation published details of alleged senior collaborators, including Park and senior figures in the academic and media worlds. These claims played back into current domestic politics, since the descendants of many of those listed were still active. The longstanding Tokto (Korean)/Takeshima (Japanese) dispute about islands in the East Sea flared up periodically. In March, the Japanese ambassador asserted publicly that the islands were Japanese territory, sparking off riots outside his embassy. The dispute simmered on throughout the year. Japanese Prime Minister Junichiro Koizumi's visits to the Yasukuni shrine (a memorial to Japan's war dead, including convicted war criminals) added to the tension, as did the continued question of how Japanese history textbooks portrayed the past, and remarks from Japanese politicians about the benefits of colonial rule. Roh and Koizumi discussed these matters at a meeting in Seoul in June, and at the Asia-Pacific Economic Co-operation (APEC) meeting in Pusan in November, without resolving them (see pp. 312; 390).

Anti-US feeling seemed to subside somewhat. Although the two sides successfully discussed issues such as free trade, the relocation of the US embassy, and redeployment of US forces, as in previous years, it was the issue of how to handle NORTH KOREA that dominated relations. The South Koreans pressed the North on nuclear issues, but in other ways indicated that the North was no longer the threat it had been. In January, the Defence Ministry stopped listing North Korea as the country's main enemy. President Roh and US President George W. Bush met on several occasions, and there were many other high level exchanges between the two countries. All these meetings stressed that the two allies continued to work closely together on the North Korean issue, but the reality seemed different. South Korea argued that engagement was working. The USA appeared to differ. US statements castigated North Korea not only over the nuclear issue, but also over other matters, including human rights, conventional force reductions, and the alleged counterfeiting of US$100 bills. These issues seemed designed to undermine the China-sponsored six party talks on nuclear issues (see below). Alexander Vershbow, a former US ambassador to Russia, who became US ambassador to South Korea in the summer, added to the tension, regularly denouncing North Korea as a criminal regime. South Korea, while accepting that such issues were important, clearly did not share the US preoccupations, and many resented Vershbow's apparent disdain for his host government.

In other foreign policy fields, South Korea enjoyed a good year. Timely assistance to natural disasters, such as the Asian tsunami and the Pakistan earthquake, was well received. South Korean troops remained in Iraq. Relations with China were helped by growing economic links and by common opposition to Japan on issues such as school textbooks and the Yasukuni shrine. The debate over the status of the ancient kingdom of Koguryo, prominent in 2004, receded into a debate between scholars rather than between governments. The APEC meeting in Pusan in November, the largest such meeting ever held in South Korea, was judged a success.

Domestic developments in NORTH KOREA attracted relatively little international attention. There was speculation about moves to appoint a possible successor to Kim Jong Il, now in his early sixties, but there were no conclusive signs that this had occurred. Human rights remained an issue. In March, a Japanese television company aired what it claimed was footage of public executions in a city on the Sino-North Korean border. In April, the EU and Japan collaborated in a motion condemning North Korea before the UN human rights commission, a move attacked by North Korea as evidence of hostile intent. International food aid continued. However, during the course of the year, North Korea made it clear that it no longer wanted food aid supplied via the World Food Programme (WFP), which should be replaced by developmental aid. The WFP warned that large numbers of the young and old were still very vulnerable, but North Korea was adamant. North Korea also demanded that all resident non-governmental organisations (NGOs) leave the country by the end of the year. The official reason was that improved harvests meant that food aid was no longer needed. In fact, North Korea had always needed outside food supplies and food aid from China and South Korea was still accepted. Such aid involved no monitoring, however, an arrangement which the North Koreans clearly preferred. The withdrawal of the NGOs would probably make little real difference, given the large amounts of assistance from these other sources, but their departure symbolically indicated a cutting of outside links. The government announced that the sale of cereals in markets would be banned, and that the public distribution system, which had never completely closed down, would once again be used to supply cereals.

International attention was focused on the nuclear issue, though there was little progress. Six party talks (involving the two Koreas, Japan, China, Russia, and the USA) were suspended in June 2004, possibly while North Korea awaited the outcome of the US presidential election. The result dashed hopes of a change in US policy, and North Korea adopted a tough stand on the nuclear issue. Early in the year, it announced that it would not again participate in the six party talks, and that it possessed nuclear weapons. There was scepticism in South Korea about the latter claim. However, perhaps under pressure from China, North Korea announced in July that it would take part in further talks, and meetings subsequently began in Beijing. An apparent breakthrough came in September. In return for diplomatic recognition, the lifting of economic sanctions, the normalisation of relations with the USA, and the provision "at an appropriate time" of a light water reactor (LWR), North Korea would scrap its nuclear weapons, end all existing nuclear programmes, return to the Non-Proliferation Treaty and allow International Atomic Energy Authority (IAEA) inspectors back into the country. However, any euphoria about the agreement ended almost as soon as it was announced. North Korea said that it should be provided with a LWR before it met the requirements set out. The USA, for its part, said that there could be no question of a LWR for North Korea until its nuclear programme was completely and verifiably dismantled. At the same time, the US government intensified pressure on North Korea over other issues of concern. Despite efforts from the other participants, by the end of the year there had been no progress on a resumption of discussions on the nuclear issue. South Korea, in particular, unsuccessfully urged the USA to negotiate with North Korea. Meanwhile, the Korean Peninsula Energy Development Organisation (KEDO) closed down, thus effectively ending the 1994 US-North Korean agreed framework.

In contrast, North-South relations steadily developed. The total number of South Koreans visiting the North reached 87,000, compared with 26,000 in 2004. In addition, nearly 300,000 visited the Diamond Mountains on North Korea's east coast. For the first time, tourists could visit other areas, including Pyongyang. On the northern side of the demilitarised zone (DMZ)—the de facto border between the two Koreas since 1953—the Kaesong industrial zone grew in importance. Buses crossed the DMZ daily, telephone links were working, and goods from the zone found a ready market in South Korea. The city of Kaesong, once capital of a unified Korea until replaced by Seoul, became another tourist destination. Family reunions continued too, with some reunions conducted by video links. A North Korean delegation in Seoul to mark Liberation Day on 15 August made unprecedented visits to the National Assembly and to the National Cemetery. Bilateral trade passed the US$1 billion mark for the first time. More and more South Koreans, especially younger people, stated that they did not fear an invasion by North Korea.

China dominated North Korea's other international relations. Despite specula-tion that China was becoming tired of North Korean intransigence, aid and trade continued to increase. Chinese investment, US$50 million in 2004, was expected to reach US$85-90 million in 2005. Chinese trade, at US$1.5 billion, accounted for nearly 50 per cent of the North's entire trade. Most tourists to North Korea came from China. The latter's President, Hu Jintao, visited the North in October, and Kim Jong Il would travel to China in January 2006.

With Japan, the issue of abductees remained to the fore. The North rejected Japanese demands for further information but at the end of the year the two sides agreed to set up working groups on the nuclear issue, abductions, and the nor-malisation process. No rapid progress, however, was to be expected. Like the South, North Korea protested over issues such as the Tokto dispute, Yasukuni visits, and school textbooks.

MONGOLIA

CAPITAL: Ulan Bator   AREA: 1,564,116 sq km   POPULATION: 2,500,000
OFFICIAL LANGUAGES: Halh (Khalkha) Mongolia   POLITICAL SYSTEM: multiparty republic
HEAD OF STATE: President Nambaryn Enkhbayar (MAHN) (since June '05)
RULING PARTIES: Mongolian People's Revolutionary Party (MAHN) (since June '04)
HEAD OF GOVERNMENT: Prime Minister Tsakhiagiyn Elbegdorj (EO-A) (since August '04)
MAIN IGO MEMBERSHIPS (NON-UN): NAM, EBRD
CURRENCY: tugrik (end-'05 £1=T2,096.15, US$1=T1,221.00)
GNI PER CAPITA: US$590, US$2,020 at PPP ('04)

THE Mongolian Great Hural (MGH, the unicameral legislature) remained dead-locked following the indecisive elections of 2004 (see AR 2004, pp. 338-39). The power-sharing arrangement of a "Grand Coalition" under Prime Minister Tsakhi-agiyn Elbegdorj proved unable to develop a coherent approach to the problems of rising prices and unemployment. The coalition government was composed of equal numbers of ministers from the Mongolian People's Revolutionary Party (MAHN) and the three-party Motherland-Democracy (EO-A) coalition. How-ever, in February Minister of Defence Badarch Erdenebat and Minister of Profes-sional Inspection Affairs Ichinkhorloogiin Erdenebaatar—both of the Mother-land-Mongolian New Democratic Socialist Party (EO-MAShSN)—were dis-missed. The EO-MAShSN had in January withdrawn from the EO-A coalition, thereby threatening the future of the "Grand Coalition" government.

In March and April demonstrations numbering several thousand people were staged in protest over corruption and the poor state of the economy. Presidential elections were held on 22 May as scheduled, and saw the MGH Speaker, Nam-baryn Enkhbayar, of the MAHN, secure 53.4 per cent of the vote, on a turnout of 74.9 per cent. Second place went to Mendsayhany Enkhsaikhan of the Mongo-lian Democratic Party, with 19.7 per cent. Bazarsad Jargalsaikhan of the Repub-lican Party won 13.9 per cent, and Badarch Erdenebat of the Motherland Party polled 11.4 per cent.

Despite the clear election result, the situation in the Great Hural remained tense. In July the MAHN unilaterally declared an end to the "Grand Coalition" and announced that it was taking full governmental control. It did agree to allow serving Prime Minister Elbegdorj of the Democratic Party, a member of the former EO-A coalition, to remain in power until August 2006 when, under the terms of the 2004 deal between the MAHN and EO-A which had brought the "Grand Coalition" into being, he was scheduled to be replaced by Deputy Prime Minister Chultemiyn Ulaan (see AR 2004, p. 338).

November was dominated by the high profile visit of George W. Bush, the first to Mongolia by a serving US President. Bush's brief visit had three aims: to reward Mongolia for its 160-troop contribution to the US-led occupying forces in Iraq, to recognise the relative success of democratic and economic reform in the country, and to underscore Mongolia's potential strategic importance, given its geographic position between China and Russia.

X AUSTRALASIA AND THE PACIFIC

AUSTRALIA

CAPITAL: Canberra   AREA: 7,741,000 sq km   POPULATION: 20,100,000
OFFICIAL LANGUAGE: English   POLITICAL SYSTEM: multiparty system in Commonwealth
HEAD OF STATE: Queen Elizabeth II (since Feb '52)
GOVERNOR-GENERAL: Maj.-Gen. Michael Jeffery (since August '03)
RULING PARTIES: Liberal-National coalition
HEAD OF GOVERNMENT: John Howard, Prime Minister (since March '96)
MAIN IGO MEMBERSHIPS (NON-UN): APEC, PC, PIF, CP, ANZUS, OECD, CWTH
CURRENCY: Australian dollar (end-'05 £1=A$2.34030, US$1=A$1.36314)
GNI PER CAPITA: US$26,900, US$29,200 at PPP ('04)

THE Australian economy remained sound with low inflation and unemployment and continuing strong demand for mineral exports, especially to China. Drought conditions continued over large areas but were partly relieved by spring rains later in the year. Overall, though, the year was one of the hottest on record and ended with very high temperatures and bushfires.

The year saw few major political changes, with the Liberal-National coalition, led by John Howard, ruling at the federal level. The government enjoyed a majority in the House of Representatives (the lower chamber of the bicameral legislature) and in the Senate (the upper house) from mid-year, enabling it to push through a wide range of new measures on security, welfare and industrial relations. There was considerable pressure on the government to reduce taxes because of the large budget surplus, but this was resisted by Treasurer Peter Costello.

At state government level, the six states and two territories remained under the control of the Australian Labor Party (ALP), which was returned in elections in Western Australia and the Northern Territory in February and June respectively. The Northern Territory returned ten women to its legislative assembly—40 per cent of the total, a proportion believed to be among the highest in the world— amongst whom were chief minister Clare Martin and five Aboriginal members.

The leadership of the ALP changed following the federal election defeat of 2004 (see AR 2004, pp. 340-41). Mark Latham resigned in January, publishing his highly controversial diaries in September in which he described his party as a lost cause. He was replaced by the previous leader, Kim Beazley. By the end of the year the ALP had moved ahead in the polls but Beazley lagged far behind Howard as the preferred Prime Minister. The ALP premier of New South Wales, Bob Carr, retired in July after ten years in office.

There were no terrorist incidents in Australia but arrests of suspects continued and new legislation greatly extended the powers to arrest, search and detain. The measures were agreed between the commonwealth and states in November and accepted by the ALP opposition. They included limited detention without trial, restrictions on legal representation, the electronic tagging of suspects, penalties for belonging to a terrorist organisation, for advocating terrorism and for inciting hatred between ethnic groups. Increased budgetary and staffing allocations were made to security organisations, of which the most important— the Australian Security and Intelligence Organisation—gained new powers along with the Australian Federal Police. Islamic organisations gave their support to these measures while expressing concern about the possible impact on their communities.

Obtaining a majority in the Senate at mid-year, the government proceeded with several major measures which might otherwise have been frustrated. Most important and controversial was the virtual dismantling of the industrial arbitration system which had governed wages and working conditions for ninety years in varying forms. Strongly opposed by the trade unions and the ALP, the new law would reduce the power of the unions, move away from legally binding to individually negotiated wages and conditions, limit unlawful dismissal provisions, and create a national system which would largely replace those maintained by the states. Large demonstrations against the legislation were organised by the unions in Melbourne and several other cities. Union membership had dropped to well below one quarter of the workforce, but there was some general concern about the impact of the new law on overtime, holidays, and dismissals. Some of the ALP-governed states threatened to challenge the constitutionality of these changes in the High Court. The changes were publicised by a massive and expensive government advertising campaign which, however, appeared to have a negative effect on public opinion.

Australia's modest contribution to the US-led occupation of Iraq was maintained, despite a growing public scepticism towards the end of the year. John Howard took a very active role in foreign affairs. He visited the USA in July and September; Indonesia in January; China and Japan in April; and the UK in July. Special visits were arranged to Banda Aceh (in Indonesia) in January (in the aftermath of the Indian Ocean tsunami); to Australian troops in Iraq in July; and to Afghanistan in November. After some negotiation, Australia was invited to the first East Asia summit in Malaysia in December but failed to be accepted as a full partner in this new initiative. It was argued by Malaysia and some other participants that Australia was not an Asian country, a position endorsed by John Howard but not regarded by him as necessarily justifying exclusion (see pp. 289; 389). Police and military assistance continued for some Pacific island states, including Papua New Guinea (see p. 324) and the Solomons, and closer relations were developed with Indonesia to counter terrorism and unauthorised immigration.

The asylum seeker issue almost disappeared (see AR 2003, p. 390). No shiploads of asylum seekers arrived and those who remained on Nauru were allowed to settle in Australia on temporary protection visas (see p. 332). Immigration policy moved further towards accepting skilled settlers, including the growing numbers of those on temporary visas. The UK returned to its traditional position as the largest single source of immigrants, followed by New Zealand. The immigration department was severely criticised for its careless treatment of two wrongfully detained Australian nationals, and more generally for its organisational culture. Its leading officials were replaced in October. Refugee settlement services were largely transferred to private companies in October, causing concern among voluntary organisations and the Labor opposition. Most of the refugees accepted under the planned programme were from Africa, especially Sudan.

In December the first serious race riot in modern Australian history broke out in the beachside suburb of Cronulla, in Sydney, the capital of New South Wales. A crowd of about 5,000 attacked a small minority whom they believed to be Lebanese Muslims, in the culmination of several incidents on the popular beach, including an attack allegedly committed by Arab youths on two lifeguards. Gangs of young ethnic Lebanese made reprisal attacks against cars and other property. Public figures expressed their horror and were quick to claim that Australians were not racists. Tensions subsided over the Christmas break. The riot revealed not only underlying hostility between communities, but the intervention of small, specifically racist, organisations. Increased police powers were rapidly voted through the New South Wales parliament. These measures were subsequently used to control a riot by Aborigines in the provincial town of Dubbo on New Year's eve.

Aboriginal affairs remained of concern, with the new nominated national indigenous council considering several government initiatives. These included proposals to allow the private ownership of Aboriginal land, an extension of work incentives to replace the welfare system, and supporting payments for improvements in school attendance and services in remote communities. These marked a shift from the practices created under the previous ALP national government in the 1990s. Some of these policies were endorsed by emerging Aboriginal leaders, such as Noel Pearson and Warren Mundine, who were more influential on the Australian government than those who had previously led the elected Aboriginal and Torres Strait Islander Commission, effectively abolished in 2004 with the reallocation of its budget to other welfare providers (see AR 2004, p. 343).

Among those who died during the year were Australia's richest man, media and casino owner Kerry Packer (for obituary see p. 544); former Queensland premier Sir Joh Bjelke-Petersen (ninety-three); former community relations commissioner Al Grassby (seventy-eight); editor and social critic Donald Horne (eighty-three); and High Court judge Sir Ronald Wilson (eighty-two).

Makybe Diva achieved the record of winning the Melbourne Cup horse race in November for the third consecutive time, and Australia lost the cricket Ashes to England in September (see pp. 470-71). Among international visitors the most popular was Crown Princess Mary of Denmark, who was Australian by birth.

PAPUA NEW GUINEA

CAPITAL: Port Moresby   AREA: 463,000 sq km   POPULATION: 5,600,000
OFFICIAL LANGUAGES: Pidgin, Motu & English   POLITICAL SYSTEM: multiparty system in
Commonwealth
HEAD OF STATE: Queen Elizabeth II
GOVERNOR-GENERAL: Sir Paulias Matane (since May '04)
RULING PARTY: National Alliance Party (NAP)
HEAD OF GOVERNMENT: Sir Michael Somare (NAP), Prime Minister (since August '02)
MAIN IGO MEMBERSHIPS (NON-UN): APEC, CP, PC, PIF, ACP, CWTH, NAM
CURRENCY: kina (end-'05 £1=K5.20200, US$1=K3.03010)
GNI PER CAPITA: US$580, US$2,300 at PPP ('04, based on regression)

PAPUA New Guinea (PNG) politics remained as byzantine in their complexity and ruthlessness as ever during 2005. Successive Cabinet reshuffles and departmental reorganisations served to keep Prime Minister Michael Somare in office but, as always, the political energy devoted to the permanent power struggle that was Papua New Guinea public life was lost to the ever more desperate needs of social and economic development.

At a number of points throughout the year, the veteran—and always calculating—nationalist Michael Somare sought to underpin his position by playing the anti-Australian card. Never a vote loser, this tactic was aided and abetted by its target in 2005. The Australian centre-right government's brand of "plain-speaking" or "neo-colonial arrogance" (depending upon one's political preference) provided the perfect conditions for the confection of outrage in PNG's political class. In April a row broke out when security staff at Australia's Brisbane airport insisted that the PNG Prime Minister should be searched along with other passengers. Diplomatic protests were flatly rejected by Australia, and PNG's attempts to press the point by withdrawing from bilateral talks on aid merely exposed the weakness of its position.

In August the Australian Foreign Minister Alexander Downer visited Port Moresby in an attempt to revive the enhanced co-operation programme (ECP) which had stalled when the PNG Supreme Court ruled in May that the operational role of Australian police in the country was unconstitutional. A compromise was reached by which a reduced contingent of Australian specialist police would be assigned to headquarters duties rather than, as previously, deployed on the streets (see AR 2004, p. 344). Despite the agreement, however, Somare denounced Australia's supposed urge to control the Pacific region and revealed his own poor relationship with Downer.

At the beginning of the year the new constitution for Bougainville—the island which had fought a bitter war of secession against the central government between 1989 and 1997—was finally put in place after successive delays. In May elections were held for its thirty-nine-seat Legislative Assembly.

Early in the campaign for this, the near-mythical Francis Ona, the original leader of the Bougainville rebellion, made a dramatic appearance in Arawa, the provincial centre, the fist time he had been sighted for about sixteen years. Ona had declined to participate in the long process which had finally brought peace to Bougainville, though he had not actively resisted it. His emergence from the jungle, surrounded by armed supporters, at this crucial point caused considerable concern to those involved in the settlement. In the event, he had no impact on the electoral process which resulted in the victory of the party of Joseph Kabui who, though himself a veteran independence fighter and associate of Ona, had been prominent in the peace settlement. Then, in July, Ona's death was announced, reportedly from natural causes, although the timing and circumstances inevitably gave rise to tangle of conspiracy theories. Whatever the truth of his demise, it provided an oddly appropriate punctuation mark in the narrative of Bougainville's return to normality.

NEW ZEALAND—PACIFIC ISLAND STATES

NEW ZEALAND

CAPITAL: Wellington   AREA: 271,000 sq km   POPULATION: 4,100,000
OFFICIAL LANGUAGE: English   POLITICAL SYSTEM: multiparty system in Commonwealth
HEAD OF STATE: Queen Elizabeth II (since Feb '52)
GOVERNOR-GENERAL: Dame Silvia Cartwright
RULING PARTIES: New Zealand Labour Party (NZLP)-led coalition
HEAD OF GOVERNMENT: Helen Clark, Prime Minister (since Dec '99)
MAIN IGO MEMBERSHIPS (NON-UN): ANZUS (suspended), APEC, PC, PIF, CP, OECD, CWTH
CURRENCY: New Zealand dollar (end-'05 £1=NZ$2.52070, US$1=NZ$1.46843)
GNI PER CAPITA: US$20,310, US$22,130 at PPP ('04)

PRIME Minister Helen Clark succeeded in narrowly winning another term in office in the parliamentary elections held on 17 September. It was an historic victory for the Prime Minister, as she became the first New Zealand Labour Party leader to lead the party to three consecutive election victories. Labour won fifty seats, a loss of two from three years earlier, while its chief rival, the National Party, won forty-eight, a significant increase from the twenty-seven seats which it had held prior to the election.

The 2005 result resembled the three previous elections held under the "mixed member proportional" electoral system introduced in 1996, as no party was able to win a majority of the 121 seats in Parliament (the unicameral legislature). Therefore, both Labour and National tried to construct coalitions which were capable of winning a parliamentary vote of confidence. Although Labour's coalition partner, the Progressive Party, won only one seat, Labour was also able to benefit from the support of the Greens (with six seats), United Future (three seats), and New Zealand First (with seven seats). This five-party arrangement narrowly averted a change of government, as National also worked to put together a five-party coalition, embracing the ACT Party (with two seats) and the newly formed Maori Party (with four seats), as well as United Future and New Zealand First.

The election outcome had its own distinctive features. Both the United Future leader, Peter Dunne, and the New Zealand First leader, Winston Peters, accepted ministerial appointments, but remained outside Cabinet, with the latter's position (as Foreign Minister) the more controversial, as it contrasted sharply with his statement during the campaign that he was not interested in acquiring any of "the baubles of office". There were also concerns that his views about immigrants and immigration, as well as possible terror threats from Muslims, might compromise his ability to represent New Zealand's interests overseas. Further complicating the new government's credibility were claims from the new Foreign Minister that he and his party were not part of the governing coalition. His initial travels outside New Zealand attracted questions from other governments and from the media, as they sought to understand how it could be possible for a Foreign Minister not to be part of the government he had been sent overseas to represent. Subsequently Peters justified his decision to accept the post of Foreign Minister, and to support Labour, as being in the interests of "stability".

The shape of the new government reflected the bitter election campaign which had preceded it. The National Party's strong showing was at least partially due to public acceptance of criticisms made by its leader, Don Brash, of the government's "political correctness", including allegedly overly favourable government policies towards Maori, the indigenous people of New Zealand. Brash disputed the idea of a "partnership" with Maori and called for the abolition of the special parliamentary seats for Maori (first introduced in 1867). At the same time, Maori dissatisfaction with the Labour-led coalition's policies led to the formation of the Maori Party and the loss by Labour to that party of four of the seven Maori constituencies.

Labour's re-election was thus a narrow one, despite a strong economy and low unemployment. To some extent its success in economic management worked against it, as strong budget surpluses led to expectations of tax reductions that went unfulfilled. The government's image was also damaged by controversy surrounding some of its more prominent members. One Cabinet minister—a former school teacher—faced allegations that he had mistreated pupils and had subsequently misled Parliament by denying the accusations, leading to a police investigation. In another case a former Minister gave an interview in which he disparaged the Prime Minister and other Cabinet members, including references to their sexual orientation. The Prime Minister's own behaviour also had an impact on the campaign. A civilian driver and several police officers were tried and convicted after taking the Prime Minister on a high-speed motorcade to the South Island airport of Christchurch in order to allow her to fly to the capital, Wellington, in the North Island, in time for a rugby match. The Prime Minister's claim to have been unaware of the speed of the motorcade defied credibility, while her refusal to take any responsibility for the incident or to assist the accused in their defence strengthened perceptions of arrogance.

National's campaign was undermined by suggestions that the party would weaken the country's anti-nuclear legislation. A Cabinet minister accused the party of receiving funding and policy advice from the USA, a claim denied not only by National but also by the US embassy. At the same time, New Zealand showed little interest in reviewing its relations with the USA, despite an invitation to do so from the departing US ambassador, who described the relationship between the two countries as "backward-looking and starved of trust, open dialogue and mutual respect". The election took place little more than a month after the death on 13 August of former Labour Prime Minister David Lange, who had been closely associated with New Zealand's anti-nuclear stance. Lange's autobiography, *My Life*, in which he was critical of his former Labour colleagues (including Clark), had been released shortly before his death (for obituary see p. 539).

The election campaign brought about some changes of policy. In June the government withdrew a controversial proposal that would have required farmers to grant the public access to land containing lakes and rivers. Offsetting National's promises of tax cuts, the Labour Party offered to cancel interest on loans to students in tertiary education. Concerns were growing about the loss overseas of university graduates, and in December the new Parliament voted to do away with the interest on student loans for those graduates who chose to remain in New Zealand. Similarly, reflecting the influence of National's attacks on "privileges" for Maori, nearly all political parties promised deadlines of one kind or another on the filing and settlement of Maori claims under the 1840 Treaty of Waitangi.

Away from the election, international involvements included the Prime Minister's attendance at a summit in Jakarta, Indonesia, in January, which brought together countries contributing to the relief and recovery effort in the aftermath of the tsunami of late December 2004. New Zealand also continued its contribution to the NATO-commanded international security assistance force (ISAF) in Afghanistan, the only non-NATO country (other than Afghanistan itself) to participate. In November a New Zealand Supreme Court judge, Sir Kenneth Keith, was elected to the International Court of Justice, becoming the first New Zealander to sit on the world court since its establishment in 1946.

There were several high-profile occasions for New Zealanders to celebrate in 2005. The country's national rugby team, the All Blacks, had a string of sensational victories at home and abroad (see p. 472). The rugby year was capped when Prime Minister Clark flew to Dublin in November to make a personal appearance before the international rugby board, an effort that culminated in the unexpected decision to award New Zealand the right to host the 2011 rugby world cup. New Zealand's cricketers were less open to persuasion, however, refusing to cancel their scheduled matches in Zimbabwe despite a parliamentary resolution urging that the tour be abandoned in the light of human rights violations by the regime of President Robert Mugabe.

Further strides were taken by New Zealand's film industry. Following the success of his *Lord of the Rings* trilogy, Wellington director Peter Jackson devoted himself to a remake of *King Kong*, which was released in December. Also released that month was *The Lion, The Witch and The Wardrobe*, filmed in New Zealand and the first of a planned seven movies based on the *Narnia* stories of the British author C.S. Lewis.

PACIFIC ISLAND STATES

Fiji
CAPITAL: Suva   AREA: 18,375 sq km   POPULATION: 848,000
OFFICIAL LANGUAGES: Fijian, Hindi & English   POLITICAL SYSTEM: multiparty republic in Commonwealth
HEAD OF STATE: President Ratu Josefa Iloilo (since July '00)
RULING PARTY: United Fiji Party (SDL)
HEAD OF GOVERNMENT: Laisenia Qarase (since July '00)
MAIN IGO MEMBERSHIPS (NON-UN): CWTH, PC, PIF, CP, ACP
CURRENCY: Fiji dollar (end-'05 £1=F$2.99580, US$1=F$1.74500)
GNI PER CAPITA: US$2,690, US$5,770 at PPP ('04 est)

Kiribati
CAPITAL: Tarawa   AREA: 1,000 sq km   POPULATION: 98,000
OFFICIAL LANGUAGES: English & Kiribati   POLITICAL SYSTEM: multiparty republic in Commonwealth
HEAD OF STATE AND GOVERNMENT: President Anote Tong (since July '03)
MAIN IGO MEMBERSHIPS (NON-UN): CWTH, PC, PIF, ACP
CURRENCY: Australian dollar (end-'05 £1=A$2.34030, US$1=A$1.36314)
GNI PER CAPITA: US$970 ('04)

Marshall Islands
CAPITAL: Dalap-Uliga-Darrit   AREA: 200 sq km   POPULATION: 60,000
OFFICIAL LANGUAGES: English & Marshallese   POLITICAL SYSTEM: multiparty republic in free association with USA
HEAD OF STATE AND GOVERNMENT: President Kessai Note (since Jan '00)
RULING PARTY: United Democratic Party (UDP)
MAIN IGO MEMBERSHIPS (NON-UN): PC, PIF
CURRENCY: US dollar (end-'05 £1=1.71680)
GNI PER CAPITA: US$2,370 ('04)

Federated States of Micronesia
CAPITAL: Palikir (Pohnpei)   AREA: 701 sq km   POPULATION: 127,000
OFFICIAL LANGUAGE: English   POLITICAL SYSTEM: multiparty republic in free association with USA
HEAD OF STATE AND GOVERNMENT: President Joseph Urusemal (since May '03)
MAIN IGO MEMBERSHIPS (NON-UN): PC, PIF
CURRENCY: US dollar (end-'05 £1=1.71680)
GNI PER CAPITA: US$1,990 ('04)

Nauru
CAPITAL: Domaneab   AREA: 21.4 sq km   POPULATION: 12,088 ('01 est.)
OFFICIAL LANGUAGES: Nauruan & English   POLITICAL SYSTEM: one-party republic, special member of the Commonwealth
HEAD OF STATE AND GOVERNMENT: President Ludwig Scotty (since June '04)
MAIN IGO MEMBERSHIPS (NON-UN): CWTH, PC, PIF
CURRENCY: Australian dollar (see Kiribati)
GNI PER CAPITA: n/a

Palau (Belau)
CAPITAL: Koror   AREA: 460 sq km   POPULATION: 20,000
OFFICIAL LANGUAGE: English   POLITICAL SYSTEM: multiparty republic in free association with USA
HEAD OF STATE AND GOVERNMENT: President Tommy Remengesau (since Nov '00)
MAIN IGO MEMBERSHIPS (NON-UN): PC, PIF
CURRENCY: US dollar (end-'05 £1=1.71680)
GNI PER CAPITA: US$6,870 ('04)

Samoa

CAPITAL: Apia   AREA: 2,842 sq km   POPULATION: 179,000
OFFICIAL LANGUAGES: English & Samoan   POLITICAL SYSTEM: multiparty monarchy in Commonwealth
HEAD OF STATE: Susuga Malietoa Tanumafili II (since Jan '62)
RULING PARTY: Human Rights Protection Party
HEAD OF GOVERNMENT: Tuila'epa Sa'ilele Malielegaoi, Prime Minister (since Nov '98)
MAIN IGO MEMBERSHIPS (NON-UN): CWTH, PC, PIF, ACP
CURRENCY: Tala (end-'04 £1=T5.1369, US$1=T2.6752)
GNI PER CAPITA: US$1,860, US$5,670 at PPP ('04, based on regression)

Solomon Islands

CAPITAL: Honiara   AREA: 28,000 sq km   POPULATION: 471,000
OFFICIAL LANGUAGE: English   POLITICAL SYSTEM: multiparty system in Commonwealth
HEAD OF STATE: Queen Elizabeth II
GOVERNOR-GENERAL: Nathaniel Waena (since July '04)
RULING PARTY: People's Alliance Party (PAP)
HEAD OF GOVERNMENT: Allan Kemakeza, Prime Minister (since Dec '01)
MAIN IGO MEMBERSHIPS (NON-UN): CWTH, PC, PIF, ACP
CURRENCY: Solomon Island dollar (end-'05 £1=SI$12.8684, US$1=SI$7.49064)
GNI PER CAPITA: US$550, US$1,760 at PPP ('04, based on regression)

Tonga

CAPITAL: Nuku'alofa   AREA: 750 sq km   POPULATION: 102,000
OFFICIAL LANGUAGES: Tongan & English   POLITICAL SYSTEM: non-party monarchy in Commonwealth
HEAD OF STATE: King Taufa'ahua Tupou IV (since Dec '65)
HEAD OF GOVERNMENT: 'Ulukalala Lavaka Ata, Prime Minister
MAIN IGO MEMBERSHIPS (NON-UN): CWTH, PC, PIF, ACP
CURRENCY: pa'anga (end-'05 £1=P3.53620, US$1=P2.05973)
GNI PER CAPITA: US$1,830, US$7,220 at PPP ('04, based on regression)

Tuvalu

CAPITAL: Fongafle   AREA: 26 sq km   POPULATION: 10,200
OFFICIAL LANGUAGE: English   POLITICAL SYSTEM: non-party monarchy, special member of the Commonwealth
HEAD OF STATE: Queen Elizabeth II (since Feb '52)
GOVERNOR-GENERAL: Faimalaga Luka (since Sept '03)
HEAD OF GOVERNMENT: Maati Toafa, Prime Minister (since Oct '04)
MAIN IGO MEMBERSHIPS (NON-UN): PC, PIF, ACP, CWTH
CURRENCY: Australian dollar (end-'05 £1=A$2.34030, US$1=A$1.36314)
GNI PER CAPITA: n/a

Vanuatu

CAPITAL: Port Vila   AREA: 12,000 sq km   POPULATION: 215,000
OFFICIAL LANGUAGES: English, French & Bislama   POLITICAL SYSTEM: multiparty republic in Commonwealth
HEAD OF STATE: President Kalkot Mataskelekele (since Aug '04)
RULING PARTIES: Union of Moderate Parties (UMP)-led coalition (since July '04)
HEAD OF GOVERNMENT: Ham Lini (NUP), Prime Minister (since Dec '04)
MAIN IGO MEMBERSHIPS (NON-UN): CWTH, PC, PIF, ACP, Francophonie
CURRENCY: vatu (end-'05 £1=V194.723, US$1=V113.425)
GNI PER CAPITA: US$1,340, US$2,790 at PPP ('04)

SEVERAL Pacific Island states made strides towards greater stability during 2005, while others experienced changes of regime of one kind or another. The New Zealand territory of TOKELAU agreed to take part in a UN-observed self-determination plebiscite in 2006. Legislative elections in NIUE saw the re-election of the Prime Minister, Young Vivian. The small island state was removed from the blacklist compiled by the Organisation for Economic Co-operation and Development (OECD) of countries with lax anti-money laundering procedures, following the closure of its offshore banking and business registration service. The COOK ISLANDS was also removed from the blacklist, as was NAURU.

In the SOLOMON ISLANDS the prosecutions of militants and rebels continued, as the multinational regional intervention force, RAMSI (Regional Assistance Mission to Solomon Islands), maintained its presence in the country. One of the most notorious rebel fighters, Harold Keke, was convicted in March of the murder of a Cabinet minister, Father Augustine Geve, in August 2002. Two Cabinet ministers were replaced in March as a result of corruption charges.

A political crisis that began in FRENCH POLYNESIA in 2004 (see AR 2004, p. 349) was at least momentarily resolved following by-elections held on 13 February for the thirty-seven Windward Island seats in the Territorial Assembly (legislature) representing the islands of Tahiti and Moorea. The election saw the multi-party pro-independence Union for Democracy bloc, led by Oscar Temaru, win nearly 47 per cent of the vote, as against 40 per cent for the pro-autonomy Tahoeraa Huiraatira party of French Polynesia's President, Gaston Flosse. The Union for Democracy group won a larger share than at the May 2004 elections, giving it twenty-five of the thirty-seven seats at stake. The result initially meant deadlock in the Assembly, with twenty-seven seats for Temaru, twenty-seven for Flosse, and three aligned to neither man. This was broken following post-election defections during a no-confidence vote on 18 February which the Flosse government lost. On 3 March Temaru was elected President of French Polynesia, by twenty-nine votes to twenty-six, with two blank ballots. Despite stating that "independence is not on the agenda", he travelled during 2005 to independence and self-government celebrations in other Pacific countries, articulating his support for sovereignty and self-determination for French Polynesia.

In another French Pacific territory, WALLIS AND FUTUNA, located north-east of Fiji, an attempt by reformers to remove the King of Wallis, Le Lavelua Tomasi Kulimoetoke, in power since 1959, was resisted as his supporters blockaded roads around the island. The conflict was sparked off when French authorities insisted on implementing a court ruling that the King's grandson serve an eighteen-month prison sentence for involuntary homicide after he had killed a man while driving under the influence of alcohol. The grandson was surrendered to French authorities and flown to a prison in NEW CALEDONIA.

There were also disturbances in TONGA, as a strike over pay grievances gathered momentum to become a challenge to the ruling elite and its grip on power. There had already been some signs of change, as elections in March had been preceded by an offer from the King to appoint two of the "commoner" (or

people's) members of Parliament to Cabinet positions. An additional two Cabinet appointments were also to be made from among the MPs representing the
country's "nobles". Following the election, at which each of the seven incumbent pro-democracy commoners' MPs were re-elected, two were appointed to
Cabinet posts, the first time that non-members of the nobles group had been
given ministerial appointments. A month later, one of the representatives, Dr
Feleti Sevele, was appointed acting Prime Minister in the absence of the Prime
Minister (one of the King's sons) overseas.

Both before and after the election there were protests, initially stemming from
the announcement of a planned rise in electricity charges. In June more than
10,000 people (more than 10 per cent of the country's population) took part in a
protest march in the capital, with some banners demanding democracy and calling on the King to surrender political power. A strike by public servants, subsequently joined by teachers, began in July. A leader of the strikes was Prince
Tu'ipelehake, a nephew of the King but a critic of the status quo, elected as a
nobles' representative in a by-election in July. The strike resisted several mediation efforts as well as a tearful plea from the King's daughter, Princess Salote
Pilolevu Tuita, for strikers to return to work and children to return to school. The
disturbances came as the King, in failing health, was spending much of his time
receiving medical treatment in Auckland, New Zealand. The strikes were accompanied by vandalism at several schools, arson attacks on government vehicles, and
the burning down of an unoccupied house in Tonga belonging to the King.
Demonstrations in Auckland—home to many expatriate Tongans—in front of the
King's residence there brought Tongan police to New Zealand to provide the King
with additional protection. The forty-seven-day strike ended when the government agreed to strikers' pay demands, which included salary increases of from 60
to 80 per cent, as well as the formation of a commission to review the constitution. In October the King agreed to his nephew's proposal for the establishment
of a parliamentary committee on political reform.

The stability of Fiji's political system also seemed fragile, as repercussions
from the 2000 coup continued to be felt. In April a Cabinet minister and a Senator were given eight-month prison sentences for their role in an army mutiny
during the coup. Following their imprisonment they were visited by the country's Prime Minister, who was also promoting the enactment of a bill designed
to achieve "reconciliation, tolerance and unity". Subsequently the two men
were released from prison (to do community work) after serving just ten days
of their sentence. The "reconciliation" bill was endorsed by indigenous Fijians
through their provincial councils and the country's great council of chiefs, but
attracted both domestic and international criticism. The US ambassador warned
that an amnesty would offer a precedent for future coups. The bill was also
opposed by the commander of Fiji's army, Voreqe Bainimarama, who expressed
strong opposition to any amnesty and stated that he refused to accept back into
the army any soldiers implicated in the mutiny.

In January a former Fiji soldier who had served two years in jail for his role
in the 2000 coup attempt was re-arrested for his part in an alleged plot to assas-

sinate the deposed Prime Minister, Mahendra Chaudhry. Fiji police reported that three other members of Chaudhry's opposition Fiji Labour Party (deposed in the coup) had also been targets. The continued arrests and prosecutions suggested that any reconciliation between disaffected communities was a long way off. Some of the difficulties in achieving "tolerance" and "unity" were manifestly apparent in a statement by former Prime Minister Sitiveni Rabuka (who had himself led two coups in 1987) that no one of Indian ancestry should hope to become Fiji's Prime Minister.

Elsewhere in the Pacific, too, contemporary values and traditional perspectives continued to mingle, with often unpredictable results. In SAMOA, tensions between the concept of constitutionally protected individual rights and communal norms emerged once more. Following a court ruling that village councils did not have the right to banish people from their village, a judge's home was burned down following a decision allowing a man to return to his village. Six Samoan chiefs were among those charged with arson. On another matter having to do with the defence of Samoan culture and its people, the Samoan Parliament banned the establishment of overseas adoption agencies in the country and also prohibited the adoption of Samoan children by foreign couples, except where there was a blood relationship.

Appeals to PITCAIRN's traditions were less compelling, as its Supreme Court (sitting in New Zealand) dismissed the claim that underage sex had been a "tradition" on the island since the English first set foot there in 1790 with their Tahitian brides. The appeal from men convicted of sexual offences on Pitcairn (see AR 2004, p. 352) was to be taken to the Privy Council, in London, which was to consider claims that it was not understood that English law was applicable on the island and that relevant British legislation had not been properly promulgated.

Pacific Island states continued to be involved in wider international disputes and developments. TONGA was admitted to the World Trade Organisation in December, despite concerns about the cost of compliance with WTO requirements. In May NAURU transferred its diplomatic allegiance to Taiwan, leading to the severing of diplomatic relations by mainland China. Taiwan also reinforced its diplomatic ties with KIRIBATI and TUVALU, making salary payments to workers from those two countries stranded on Nauru following that country's inability to find the funds (about US$3.5 million) to pay them.

Australia agreed in October to remove almost all of the asylum seekers it had been holding in its off-shore processing centre on NAURU. Over the past four years more than 1,200 people, mostly Iraqis and Afghans, had been held there (see p. 322). In December Nauru lost its air link to the outside world after an Australian court permitted the seizure of Air Nauru's sole remaining commercial aircraft, a Boeing 737, following Nauru's failure to meet its loan payments.

Nauru's precarious financial position also had an influence on its participation in international organisations. In June Nauru voted in favour of Japan's proposals for an expansion of its whaling activities. Financial aid from Japan was also affecting other Pacific Island states' attitudes. The vote by the SOLOMON ISLANDS' representative at the June meeting of the International Whaling Commission in South Korea proved particularly controversial. Instructed to abstain, the country's Minister for Fisheries and Marine Resources defied the Cabinet by voting in support of Japan, leading to his resignation. By contrast, in addition to supporting Japan's whaling proposals, PALAU declared its support for Japan's being made a permanent member of the UN Security Council.

In PAPUA, Indonesian rule continued to be contested. The government reaffirmed its plans to divide Papua into five provinces, a policy suspended following a November 2004 ruling against it by the country's constitutional court. Disturbances were associated with the raising of the separatist flag, and there were demonstrations on 1 December, the anniversary of the proclamation of an independent state of West Papua (1962). The Indonesian government established an appointed Papuan people's council in October, composed exclusively of Papuans, with limited authority over cultural matters. About 100 people protested at the swearing-in ceremony in Jayapura, the capital.

Pacific entities linked to the USA continued to be strongly affected by the war in Iraq. By October seven US soldiers from AMERICAN SAMOA had been killed in the war, giving the territory the distinction of having the USA's highest war death rate as a percentage of population. A soldier from Yap, in the FEDERATED STATES OF MICRONESIA (FSM), was also killed when a bomb hit his vehicle in February. Two other soldiers from Micronesia—one from the FSM, the other from the COMMONWEALTH OF THE NORTHERN MARIANA ISLANDS (CNMI)—were killed in Iraq in October. In late December an eleventh Micronesian soldier, from GUAM, died in the conflict.

An earlier war also continued to exert its hold on the Pacific. A June visit to Saipan, in the CNMI, by the Japanese Emperor and his wife revived memories of World War II, when Japan occupied the islands before being defeated there by US forces. Emperor Akihito—whose father, Hirohito, was Japan's Emperor during the war—paid respects at a memorial to Japan's war dead; at a memorial to Korean war dead; and at monuments to the thousands of US troops killed in the battles and to islanders killed on Saipan and neighbouring islands. The trip was the first that the Emperor had made to a World War II battlefield.

In the CNMI the November elections brought power to Benigno Fitial and his Covenant Party. Fitial was elected as the CNMI's governor, defeating three other candidates, including the Republican and Democratic nominees, and the Covenant Party won half of the twenty-two House of Representatives seats as well as two of the six Senate seats up for election. The largest number of Senate votes was received by Maria Pangelinan, who became the CNMI's first woman Senator.

The Pacific Islands Forum held its 36th summit in Papua New Guinea in October, formally adopting the Pacific plan on regional co-operation, first raised at the 2003 Forum meeting in New Zealand. Australia and New Zealand rejected proposals for freer movement of Pacific Island labour into their two countries, citing concerns about islanders staying on once their work permits had expired.

XI INTERNATIONAL ORGANISATIONS

UNITED NATIONS AND ITS AGENCIES

DATE OF FOUNDATION: 1945   HEADQUARTERS: New York, USA
OBJECTIVES: To promote international peace, security and co-operation on the basis of the equality of member-states, the right of self-determination of peoples and respect for human rights
MEMBERSHIP (END-'05): 191 sovereign states; those not in membership of the UN itself at end-2005 were the Holy See (Vatican) and Taiwan (Republic of China), although all except Taiwan were members of one or more UN specialised agency
SECRETARY GENERAL: Kofi Annan (Ghana)

THIS was a year of celebration: the 60th anniversary of the organisation and the award of the Nobel Peace Prize to the Director General and the International Atomic Energy Agency; a year of investigation: a detailed and compelling analysis of the mismanagement of the "oil for food" programme; a year of reform, in which the members sought to address the challenges of the 21st century by attempting to make the United Nations relevant, effective, and efficient; and a year in which, for the first time since 1963, an Israeli ambassador to the UN chaired a General Assembly meeting.

ELECTIONS AND APPOINTMENTS. The 59th Session of the General Assembly on 13 June elected Jan Eliasson of Sweden as the President of the 60th Session. On 10 October the General Assembly elected Congo, Ghana, Peru, Qatar, and Slovakia to serve for two years on the Security Council beginning on 1 January 2006. They replaced as non-permanent members Algeria, Benin, Brazil, the Philippines, and Romania.

THE GENERAL ASSEMBLY. The General Assembly met in a high level plenary session from 14 to 16 September, attended by a record number of heads of state and government. This "world summit" approved in the "outcome document" (General Assembly resolution 60/1) a range of reforms of varying potency—some would have immediate impact, some had to be negotiated by an agreed date, and some were future intentions—in the main areas of development, security, human rights, and institutional reform of the UN.

The Secretary General had produced a report in March entitled "In larger freedom" which proposed an agenda for the "world summit" designed to make the UN more efficient, effective, and relevant. Annan had put forward a carefully balanced set of reforms believing that, although member states would have different priorities, they would be prepared to yield in areas where they had reservations if serious attention were given to issues to which they attached high importance. Thus, for many states the overriding priority was development, while for others it was human rights, terrorism, management, and institutional reform.

The summit produced commitments from both developed and developing states to reduce hunger and poverty by 50 per cent in the next ten years, including an agreement to provide extra finance for fighting poverty, improving healthcare and education, and for development projects; the adoption of trade liberalisation policies; and a decision to consider additional measures to ensure long-term debt sustainability for both heavily indebted poor states and, where appropriate, other debt-bearing states that were not part of that initiative.

All governments also agreed for the first time that terrorism (although this remained undefined) in all its forms and manifestations would be condemned. There was agreement that a comprehensive convention against terrorism should be sought by the General Assembly within the session ending on 30 September 2006; that the Nuclear Terrorism Convention should come into force quickly; that all states should agree to and implement the twelve other anti-terrorist conventions; and that a strategy for the international community to fight terrorism should be explored.

The summit decided that a Peacebuilding Commission—an intergovernmental advisory body—should be created and become operational by 1 January 2006. Its purposes would be to propose integrated strategies to help states that were emerging (usually) from civil war, in order to prevent a relapse into internecine violence. This included providing advice to the political organs; helping to obtain finance for short, medium, and long term recovery; providing longer and deeper attention by the international community to post-conflict recovery; and developing best practice. The leaders also endorsed the creation of an initial operating capability for a standing police force for peacekeeping, and recommended further development of the proposals for enhanced rapidly deployable military capabilities to reinforce peacekeeping operations in crisis. There was agreement, too, that the Secretary General's capacity for mediation and good offices should be strengthened.

The summit made far reaching decisions in human rights. First, all member states clearly and unambiguously accepted that there was a collective international responsibility to protect populations from genocide, war crimes, ethnic cleansing, and crimes against humanity. They expressed their willingness to take timely and decisive collective action, through the Security Council, when peaceful means proved inadequate and national authorities were failing to protect their populations. This, however, did not guarantee that the Security Council would so act, particularly if the permanent members were divided; nor that an appropriate mandate, leadership, armed forces, finance and other necessary resources would be provided quickly and effectively. Secondly there was agreement to establish a Human Rights Council within a year to replace the discredited, politicised Human Rights Commission. The complex negotiations on the method of election to the Council to ensure that states which fragrantly violated human rights could not become members; on the size, the composition, and whether the Council should be a standing body in session for the whole year; and on the transition from Commission to Council were to be conducted by the General Assembly. Thirdly, the summit supported the action plan to strengthen the Office of the High Commissioner for Human Rights (UNHCR) and to double the budget that the Office received, from 1.8 per cent to 3.6 per cent of the regular budget over the next five years. Finally, the summit welcomed the establishment of a new democracy fund to provide more resources for states that were moving from authoritarian to democratic forms of government. The fund had already received voluntary contributions of US$42.5 million by 25 October.

The summit also took decisions on institutional and management reform. The Economic and Social Council was given new tasks, including annual ministerial reviews and assessments, the convening of a biennial development co-operation forum, a more effective response to emergencies, better co-ordination of activities within the UN system and its peacebuilding role. The leaders asked the Secretary General to undertake a number of important tasks: to review all mandates that were more than five years old in order to allow the obsolete to be replaced by new priorities; to review the rules on the management of the budget, finance, and human resources; to propose a redundancy scheme for staff in order to ensure that the organisation had an appropriate range of personnel; and to submit an independent external evaluation of the entire oversight system of the UN and the specialised agencies. The Secretary General also received support for the measures that he had already taken—partly in light of the "oil for food" report findings—to establish an ethics office, to protect "whistle blowers", to improve procurement practices, and to enhance transparency within the Secretariat.

For all of the successes of the summit there were some resounding failures. The Security Council was not reformed, although the "open ended working group" would convene yet again in early 2006 to seek progress; there was no agreement on nuclear non-proliferation and disarmament, and little progress on the circumstances in which states might legitimately use force in self defence.

THE GENERAL DEBATE AND THE IMPLEMENTATION OF SUMMIT DECISIONS. The debate was principally focused on how the General Assembly would implement the tasks that it had been delegated by the "outcome document". The Assembly achieved substantial progress. The Assembly and the Security Council on 20 December approved resolutions to establish a thirty-one member Peacebuilding Commission (as mandated by the summit), consisting of seven members of the Security Council (including the permanent members); seven members of the Economic and Social Council, giving particular consideration to those that had experienced post-conflict recovery; five out of the top ten contributors to UN budgets, including voluntary contributions to UN agencies and programmes and the peacebuilding fund; five out of the top ten providers of military and civil police personnel to UN peace-keeping missions; and seven additional members, elected by the General Assembly, to redress remaining geographical imbalances and to include states with experience of post-conflict recovery.

The Assembly also expanded and transformed the existing central humanitarian funding mechanism into the new central emergency response fund to meet the summit request to improve the timeliness and predictability of humanitarian funding. It adopted an optional protocol to the 1994 convention on the safety of UN and associated personnel, which originally covered peacekeeping operations. Legal protection was now extended to UN staff who were engaged in providing humanitarian, political, and development assistance in peacebuilding and emergency humanitarian assistance. Lastly the Assembly decided that a high level meeting should take place in May and June 2006, which would assess the degree to which the commitments in the 2001 declaration on HIV/AIDS had been achieved.

THE BUDGET. The Secretary General proposed a US$3.6 billion budget for 2006-07. This represented a real increase of 0.1 per cent, before the revised estimates that would arise from the summit "outcome document". Growth in priority areas was to be funded largely through the reallocation of resources. The budget continued a trend of significant investment in staff development and information technology, and maintained the UN capacity to handle specific special political missions. More than 3,000 obsolete, ineffective, or marginally useful areas of expenditure had been discontinued.

After prolonged "closed door" intensive negotiations to break a diplomatic deadlock that threatened to leave the UN without a budget, the General Assembly on 24 December finally approved a budget of US$3.79 billion for 2006-07. Exceptionally, this was a conditional budget: the Secretary General was limited to spending US$950 million in the first six months of 2006. He would then have to request the further funds that he might need. The Assembly indicated that it anticipated that total expenditure for 2006 would be about US$1.9 billion.

The Assembly also agreed to establish an independent audit advisory committee to assist the Assembly in its oversight role. The Assembly provided an interim budget for the capital master plan for the renovation of the UN headquarters in New York. To ease the perennial cash flow problems of the organisation, the Assembly created a working capital fund of US$100 million for 2006-07. The fund would be used for a range of purposes, including the financing of budgetary appropriations pending the receipt of contributions from members. Previously, these had been supported by the temporary cross-borrowing from peacekeeping funds; this had become difficult because the Assembly had restricted borrowing to the small amounts of money that remained in completed missions (see AR 2004, pp. 356-57).

THE "OIL FOR FOOD" PROGRAMME: The Volcker Report. On 7 September the Independent Inquiry Committee under the chairmanship of Paul A. Volcker presented its definite report on the management of the UN's "oil for food" programme for Iraq (for extracts see pp. 492-500). The committee recognised that the programme was the largest, most complex and most ambitious humanitarian relief programme in the history of the UN, that the administration of the programme had to take into account political, security, financial, and economic concerns; and that the Security Council, the secretariat, and nine UN agencies, with varying degrees of financial and operational independence, were involved.

It accepted that the programme, which was conceived as a means of reconciling comprehensive sanctions against the Iraqi regime with the need to meet the humanitarian concerns of the population, had some notable successes: its existence helped to support the international effort to prevent Saddam Hussein from obtaining weapons of mass destruction, and minimal standards of nutrition and health were maintained by the population. These successes were achieved despite the lack of essential direction from the Security Council, pressures from competing political factions in Iraq, and endemic corruption on the ground.

The Committee believed that there were five reasons for mismanagement. First the Security Council failed to provide an appropriate mandate for the programme and therefore neither the Security Council nor the Secretary General was clearly in charge. Secondly, the administrative structure and the personnel practices of the UN were unable to meet the extraordinary challenges of the "oil for food" programme. Thirdly, notable among the UN's structural faults was a grievous absence of effective auditing and management controls. Fourthly, where corruption did occur in the UN, it reflected both managerial weakness and the absence of a strong institutional ethic. Finally the "oil for food" programme highlighted the difficulties of effective co-operation among UN agencies.

The Volcker committee made four recommendations. The Security Council should clarify the purpose and criteria of each programme and the execution should be delegated to the secretariat and appropriate agencies, with clear lines of reporting responsibility. A chief operating officer post should be created; the incumbent would be responsible for planning and personnel policies which emphasised professional and administrative talent. A strong "independent oversight board" with sufficient staff and authority should be established to ensure that the internal control, auditing, and investigatory functions were appropriately financed and staffed. Lastly, in large programmes with a common source of funds but with multiple delivery agencies, both the Security Council and the Secretary General must demand effective co-ordination from the outset.

Annan stated in response to the report that its findings must be deeply embarrassing to all. The Committee had shone a harsh light into the most unsightly corners of the organisation. None of the member states, secretariat, agencies, funds, or programmes could be proud of what it found. He deeply regretted that he was not diligent or effective enough in pursuing an investigation after the fact, when he learned that a company that employed his son, Kojo Annan, had been awarded a contract under the programme. He was profoundly disappointed that there was evidence of corruption among a small number of UN staff. However, as the chief administrative officer, he was responsible for failings revealed in the implementation of the programme and in the functioning of the secretariat.

THE SECURITY COUNCIL. The Security Council held 200 formal meetings, adopted seventy-one resolutions and issued sixty-seven presidential statements. The veto was not used. The Council revived its use of monthly wrap-up meetings when, at the end of Brazil's presidency on 30 March, it discussed the African dimension in the work of the Council. The Council sent missions to Haiti (which was the first to any Latin American or Caribbean state) between 13 and 16 April and to central Africa from 4 to 11 November.

THEMATIC DEBATES. The Council held thematic debates on peace-building; the role of civil society in conflict prevention and peaceful settlement of disputes; civilians in armed conflict, in which the Council determined that a key objective of peacekeeping operations should be the establishment of a secure environment for vulnerable groups and populations; Africa's food crisis as a threat to international peace and security; the impact of small arms in fuelling conflict; women, peace, and security; HIV/AIDS; and collaboration with regional organisations, in which the Council invited these organisations to participate in the UN standby peacekeeping arrangements.

COUNTER-TERRORISM. The Council on 25 April welcomed the General Assembly's consensus adoption on 13 April of the International Convention for the Suppression of Acts of Nuclear Terrorism. The Security Council condemned the terrorist attacks in London (7 July); Sharm el-Sheikh (23 July); Iraq (4 August); Bali, Indonesia (4 October); New Delhi (31 October); and Amman (9 November); and the assassination of an Egyptian (8 July) and two Algerian diplomats (27 July) in Iraq. At a meeting on 14 September attended by heads of state and government, the Council condemned all acts of terrorism irrespective of their motivation, the incitement of such acts, and repudiated attempts at their justification. The Council also received regular briefings by the chairmen of the counter terrorism committee, the committee for sanctions against al-Qaida, Osama bin Laden, the Taliban and their associates, the committee on measures against individuals or groups involved with or associated with terrorism (resolution 1566), and the non proliferation of weapons of mass destruction committee.

CHILDREN AND ARMED CONFLICT. On 26 July, in resolution 1612, the Security Council requested the Secretary General to establish a mechanism for the systematic monitoring and reporting of child abuse in situations of armed conflict or of concern. The mechanism would monitor grave violations by all parties to armed conflict, both governments and their opponents, with specific emphasis upon the killing and maiming of children, recruiting or using child soldiers, attacks against schools or hospitals, rape or other sexual violence against children, denial of humanitarian access for children, and child abduction. The Council created a working group to receive and assess these reports and to suggest measures that the Council might take against repeat offenders.

AFGHANISTAN. The Council's principal concerns were ensuring that conditions were propitious for conducting legislative elections; the overall security situation; and how to combat the illegal drugs trade. The Council renewed the mandates of both the UN Assistance Mission and the International Security Force (ISAF).

DARFUR. The Security Council took action on three fronts to resolve the situation in Sudan's Darfur region. First, on 29 March in resolution 1591, which was adopted by twelve votes with three abstentions (Algeria, China, and Russia), the Council gave the parties to the conflict thirty days to fulfil the range of commitments which they had entered into; if they failed to do so a travel and asset freeze would be imposed on any person who impeded the peace process, violated human rights, or failed to meet the obligations accepted in previous resolutions. Secondly, on 31 March in resolution 1593, in which there were four abstentions

(Algeria, Brazil, China, and the USA) the Council decided to refer the situation in Darfur since July 2002 to the prosecutor of the International Criminal Court, following the findings of the international commission of inquiry on Darfur established under Security Council resolution 1564 (2004) (see pp. 203; 423; 480-89). The Secretary General provided the prosecutor with documents, including a sealed envelope containing a list of suspects which had been received from the chairman of the international enquiry. On 29 June the prosecutor told the Council that there were admissible cases; that since 1 June there had been an investigation to gather facts and evidence relating to the crimes alleged to have taken place, as well as the groups and the individuals responsible for them. Thirdly, the Council continued to support the African Union's political and diplomatic efforts to secure a political settlement and its peacekeeping role in Darfur.

ISRAEL AND PALESTINE. The Council continued to receive monthly briefings from senior secretariat officials and to hold meetings on the factors affecting the peace process. The Secretary General appointed a special envoy for Gaza disengagement and, at the request of the General Assembly, proposed a framework for a registry of damage caused by the Israeli barrier.

IRAQ. The Council monitored the political transition in Iraq including the assistance provided by the UN mission. Members were informed about, and commented upon, Iraq's progress towards democracy and the various initiatives to support its political and economic reconstruction. The Council extended for a further twelve months the UN Assistance Mission and the multinational force.

LEBANON. The killing of the former Lebanese Prime Minister Rafik al-Hariri on 14 February by terrorist action prompted two UN investigations. The first was to enable the Secretary General to report to the Security Council on the circumstances, causes, and consequences of the attack. It reported that the Lebanese investigation was flawed and lacked the capacity and commitment to reach a satisfactory and credible conclusion and that, therefore, an independent international investigation was needed. This conclusion was endorsed by the Council in resolution 1595 on 7 April. The Secretary General appointed German prosecutor Detlev Mehlis as the head of the investigation.

In his first report Mehlis stated that there was evidence of Syria's involvement in the assassination, and invited the Syrian authorities to help the commission fill the gaps in its report by carrying out their own investigation (for extracts see pp. 490-92). In resolution 1636 the Council on 31 October defined the crime as a terrorist act; stated that the involvement in it of any state would constitute a serious violation of that country's obligations to prevent and refrain from supporting terrorism; called for Syria to co-operate fully and unconditionally with the commission; demanded that the Syrian authorities clarify a number of questions that remained unresolved and detain Syrian officials or individuals that the commission considered as suspects; insisted that Syria must not interfere in Lebanese domestic affairs; and that any individual suspected by the commission or the government of Lebanon of involvement in the crime must be subject to travel restrictions and the freezing of assets. The commission was requested to report on progress by 15 December, including Syria's co-operation.

Mehlis reported to the Council on 13 December that while Lebanon had facilitated the commission's work in all possible ways, the commission's relationship with Syria had been marked by conflicting signals causing confusion and delay. He noted that at the present rate of Syrian co-operation the investigation might take another year or two. On 15 December the Council in resolution 1644 demanded that Syria respond unambiguously and immediately to the commission, and extended the mandate until 15 June 2006 with the possibility of a further extension.

PEACEKEEPING. There were a number of important developments in peacekeeping. Two missions were concluded and one new one established: a multifunctional, 10,000-strong mission in Sudan which it was anticipated would last for six years. Its mandate was to support the implementation of the comprehensive peace agreement of 9 January; facilitate the return of refugees and displaced people; provide de-mining assistance; contribute to international efforts to protect and promote human rights; and take the necessary action to protect UN personnel and civilians.

The UN Mission in Ethiopia and Eritrea, UNMEE, had restrictions imposed upon it by Eritrea, including the banning of all UN helicopter flights and a demand for the withdrawal of all peacekeeping staff from the USA, Canada, Europe, and Russia. The Secretariat and the Security Council attempted to have these decisions reversed.

Annan appointed six legal experts to study how UN personnel serving in peacekeeping missions who committed criminal acts in areas where there was no functioning judicial system could be held accountable. MINUSTAH (the UN Stabilisation Mission in Haiti) established a disciplinary panel in December to explore whether UN soldiers had used excessive force in the Sarthe/Cazeau area of Port-au-Prince and had conducted inappropriate body searches.

The Secretariat took a number of steps to eliminate sexual exploitation and abuse by peacekeeping personnel. A report had been prepared by Prince Zeid Ra'ad Zeid Al-Hussein, the permanent representative of Jordan, which candidly examined the problem and provided a clear framework for action by the Secretariat and member states. The Secretariat adopted a policy of investigation, prevention, and enforcement. By the end of October the Secretariat had investigated allegations against 221 peacekeeping personnel: eighty-eight troops, including six commanders, had been repatriated and ten civilians dismissed. Preventive measures included training on conduct for all peacekeepers. To enforce standards there were telephone hotlines and focal points in missions to receive allegations, and the publication of lists of premises and areas frequented by prostitutes which had been placed out of bounds to all personnel.

SANCTIONS. New or expanded sanctions (usually arms embargoes, and travel restrictions and asset freezes against named individuals) were imposed in Darfur, the Democratic Republic of Congo, and Côte d'Ivoire. An expert advisory panel was appointed for Darfur and the mandates of the panels for Congo, Côte d'Ivoire, Somalia, and Liberia were renewed. The "world summit" declared that the Security Council should improve the monitoring of the implementation and effects of

UNITED NATIONS PEACEKEEPING MISSIONS 2005

Mission	Established	Present Strength	Renewal Date
UNTSO: United Nations Truce Supervision Organisation	May 1948	150 military observers; 102 international civilians; 119 local civilians. Total personnel: 371. Fatalities: 41. Appropriations for 2005: $29.04 million (gross).	
UNMOGIP: United Nations Military Observer Group in India and Pakistan	January 1949	42 military observers; 21 international civilians; 47 local civilians. Total personnel: 110. Fatalities: 10. Appropriations for 2005: $8.37 million (gross).	
UNFICYP: United Nations Peacekeeping Force in Cyprus	March 1964	840 military; 68 civilian police; 38 international civilians; 111 local civilians. Total personnel: 1,057. Fatalities: 174. Approved budget July 05 to June 06: $46.51 million (gross) including voluntary contributions of one third from Cyprus and $6.5 million from Greece.	June 2006
UNDOF: United Nations Disengagement Observer Force	June 1974	1,047 military; 37 international civilians; 104 local civilians. Total personnel: 1,188. Fatalities: 41. Approved budget from July 05 to June 06: $43.71 million.	June 2006
UNIFIL: United Nations Interim Force in Lebanon	March 1978	1,994 military; 100 international civilians; 296 local civilians. Total personnel 2,390. Fatalities: 250. Approved budget from July 05 to June 06: $99.23 million.	January 2006

UNITED NATIONS PEACEKEEPING MISSIONS 2005 *continued*

Mission	Established	Present Strength	Renewal Date
MINURSO: United Nations Mission for the Referendum in Western Sahara	April 1991	28 troops; 195 military observers; 6 civilian police; 124 international civilians; 96 local civilians. Total personnel 449. Fatalities: 11. Approved budget July 2005 to June 2006: $47.95 million (gross).	April 2006
UNOMIG: United Nations Observer Mission in Georgia	August 1993	122 military observers; 11 civil police; 102 international civilians; 183 local civilians; 1 UN volunteer. Total personnel 419. Fatalities: 8. Approved budget July 2005 to June 2006 $ 36.38 million (gross).	January 2006
UNMIK: United Nations Interim Mission in Kosovo	June 1999	36 military observers; 2,188 civilian police; 642 international civilians; 2,413 local civilians; 203 UN volunteers. Total personnel: 5,482. Fatalities: 35. Approved budget July 2005 to June 2006: $252.55 million (gross).	Established for an initial period of 12 months; to continue unless the Security Council decides otherwise.
UNAMSIL: United Nations Mission in Sierra Leone	October 1999	944 troops; 69 military observers; 30 civilian police; 216 international civilians; 369 local civilians. 83 UN volunteers. Total personnel: 1,711. Fatalities: 165. Approved budget July 2005 to December 2005: $113.22 million (gross).	Mission concluded on 31 December 2005. (It was replaced by the United Nations Integrated Office in Sierra Leone which had an initial 12 month mandate until 31 December 2006.)

UNITED NATIONS PEACEKEEPING MISSIONS 2005 *continued*

Mission	Established	Present Strength	Renewal Date
MONUC: United Nations Organisation Mission in the Democratic Republic of the Congo	November 1999	15,051 troops; 724 military observers; 786 civilian police; 816 international civilians; 1,388 local civilians; 482 UN volunteers. Total personnel: 19,247. Fatalities: 66. Approved budget July 2005 to June 2006: 1,153.89 million (gross). Approved by the General Assembly on 8 December 2005.	September 2006
UNMEE: United Nations Mission in Ethiopia and Eritrea	July 2000	3,132 troops; 205 military observers; 191 international civilians; 235 local civilians. 74 United Nations volunteers. Total personnel: 3,837. Fatalities: 10. Approved budget July 2005 to June 2006: $185.99 million (gross).	March 2006
UNMIL: United Nations Mission in Liberia	September 2003	14,656 troops; 193 military observers; 1,088 civilian police; 558 international civilians; 840 local civilians; 433 UN volunteers. Total personnel: 17,768 Fatalities: 60 Approved budget July 2005 to June 2006: $760.57 million (gross).	March 2006
UNOCI: United Nations Mission in Côte d'Ivoire	April 2004	6,701 troops; 195 military observers; 674 civilian police; 350 international civilians; 418 local civilians. 203 UN volunteers. Total personnel: 8,541. Fatalities: 12. Approved budget July 2005 to June 2006: $438.17 million (gross).	January 2006
MINUSTAH: United Nations Stabilization Mission in Haiti	June 2004	7,265 military; 1,741 civilian police; 449 international civilians; 489 local civilians. 164 UN volunteers. Total personnel: 10,108. Fatalities 10. Approved budget July 2005 to June 2006: $541.30 million (gross).	June 2006

UNITED NATIONS PEACEKEEPING MISSIONS 2005 *continued*

Mission	Established	Present Strength	Renewal Date
ONUB: United Nations Operation in Burundi	June 2004	5,336 troops; 189 military observers; 87 civilian police; 325 international civilians; 385 local civilians. 144 United Nations volunteers. Total personnel: 6,466 Fatalities: 19 Approved budget July 2005 to June 2006: $307.69 million (gross).	July 2006
UNMIS: United Nations Mission in the Sudan	March 2005	Authorised strength: 10,000 military; 715 civilian police; 1,053 international civilians; 2,690 local civilians; 208 UN volunteers. Total personnel: 14,579. Actual strength: 3,638 troops; 362 military observers; 222 civilian police; 511 international civilians; 983 local civilians; 67 UN volunteers: Total personnel 5,783. Approved budget from July 2005 to June 2006 approved by the General Assembly on 8 December 2005: $969.47 (gross).	March 2006

NOTES.

Different categories of personnel serving in peacekeeping missions as of 30 November 2005:

Military troops, observers and civilian police, 70,015

International civilian, 4,582

Local civilian, 8,476

UN volunteers, 1,854

Contributing countries, 107

Total *number* of fatalities from all categories in peacekeeping operations since 1948 to 30 November 2005: 2,040

Finance:

Approved budgets for the period 1 July 2005 to 30 June 2006, about $5.03 billion

Estimated total costs from 1948 to 30 June 2006, about $41.04 billion

Outstanding contributions to peacekeeping on 31 October 2005, about $1.8 billion

UNTSO and UNMOGIP are funded from the UN regular biennial budget. The costs to the UN of the fourteen other current operations are financed from their own separate accounts on the basis of legal binding assessments on all member states.

Sources: UN background note 30 November 2005 and UN current peacekeeping operations website.

UNITED NATIONS POLITICAL AND PEACEBUILDING MISSIONS 2005

Mission	Established	Present Strength	Current Authorisation
UNPOS: United Nations Political Office for Somalia	April 1995	Representative of the Secretary-General and Head of UNPOS: Francois Lonseny Fall (Guinea). 5 international civilians; 3 local civilians.	31 December 2005
Office of the Special Representative of the Secretary-General for the Great Lakes Region	December 1997	Special Representative of the Secretary-General: Ibrahimi Fall (Senegal). 8 international civilians; 8 local civilians.	31 December 2005
UNOGBIS: United Nations Peace-building Support Office in Guinea-Bissau	March 1999	Representative of the Secretary-General and Head of UNOGBIS: Joao Bernardo Honwana (Mozambique). 11 international civilians; 2 military advisers; 1 civilian police adviser; 13 local civilians.	31 December 2005
UNSCO: Office of the United Nations Special Coordinator for the Middle East	October 1999	Special Co-ordinator for the Middle East Peace Process and Personal Representative of the Secretary-General to the Palestine Liberation Organisation and the Palestine National Authority: Alvaro de Soto (Peru). 27 international civilians; 24 local civilians.	31 December 2005
BONUCA: United Nations Peace-building Office in the Central African Republic	February 2000	Representative of the Secretary-General and Head of BONUC: Lamine Cisse (Senegal). 25 international civilians; 5 military advisers; 6 civilian police; 44 local civilians. 1 UN volunteer.	31 December 2005

UNITED NATIONS POLITICAL AND PEACEBUILDING MISSIONS 2005 *continued*

Mission	Established	Present Strength	Current Authorisation
UNTOP: United Nations Tajikistan Office of Peace-building	June 2000	Representative of the Secretary-General for Tajikistan: Vladimir Sotirov (Bulgaria). 10 international civilians; 1 civilian police adviser; 18 local civilians.	1 June 2006
Office of the Special Representative of the Secretary-General for West Africa	November 2001	Special Representative of the Secretary-General: Ahmedou Ould-Abdallah (Mauritania). 7 international civilians; 7 local civilians.	31 December 2005
UNAMA: United Nations Assistance Mission in Afghanistan	March 2002	Special Representative of the Secretary-General: Jean Arnault (France). 190 international civilians; 749 local civilians; 11 military observers; 6 civilian police; 42 UN volunteers.	26 March 2006
UNAMI: United Nations Assistance Mission for Iraq	August 2003	Special Representative of the Secretary-General for Iraq: Ashraf Jehangir Qazi (Pakistan). Authorised strength: 816-344 international civilians; 472 local civilians. Current strength (staff are based in Iraq, Jordan and Kuwait): 225 international civilians; 345 local civilians; 5 military advisers.	12 August 2006

UNITED NATIONS POLITICAL AND PEACEBUILDING MISSIONS 2005 *continued*

Mission	Established	Present Strength	Current Authorisation
UNOTIL: United Nations Office in Timor-Leste	21 May 2005	Special Representative of the Secretary General and Head of Office: Sukehiro Hasegawa (Japan). 158 international civilians; 281 local civilians; 15 military advisors; 56 civilian police; 36 UN volunteers.	21 May 2006

NOTES.

UNAMA, and UNOTIL, although political missions are directed and supported by the Department of Peacekeeping Operations. All the other political and peace-building missions are directed by the Department of Political Affairs.

The following missions were completed in 2005.

1 UNOMB: United Nations Observer Mission in Bougainville: 1 January 2004-30 June 2005.

2 UNAMIS: United Nations Advanced Mission in Sudan: 11 June 2004 until 24 March 2005 when it was absorbed into UNMIS: United Nations Mission in Sudan.

Current number of Missions, 10

Personnel:

International Civilians, 666

Military and civilian police advisers and liaison officers, 107

Local civilian personnel, 1,492

UN volunteers, 79

Total number of personnel serving in political and peacebuilding missions, 2,334

Sources: UN Political and Peace-Building Missions background note: 30 November 2005 and the UN website.

the Alliance agreed in 2005 to provide logistic and training support to the African Union's involvement in Darfur, Sudan (see pp. 202-03). In response to a request from UN disaster relief officials, NATO decided in October on a battalion-sized deployment to Pakistan, to assist with post-earthquake relief. Medical teams and a field hospital were deployed, NATO engineer units helped to clear roads, and logistics specialists assisted UN staff (see pp. 278-79). More unusually, naval and air components of the NRF were also deployed in response to a US request for assistance in the aftermath of Hurricane Katrina (see pp. 121-24).

Some 2,000 NATO troops were sent to Afghanistan to support National Assembly and provincial council elections, and it was indeed Afghanistan that was to become NATO's most important operational concern during 2005 (see p. 265). In February it had been agreed that all US and European troops in Afghanistan—some 18,000 US troops deployed on "Operation Enduring Freedom" (OEF), together with a further 11,000 in NATO's International Security Assistance Force (ISAF)—would come under NATO command. This would be achieved incrementally into 2006. But doubts were raised as to whether these two very different missions—NATO's mission of peacekeeping and stabilisation on the one hand, and the higher intensity US counter-insurgency and counter-terrorism deployment along the Afghanistan-Pakistan border on the other—could be combined under one command. At a more general level, some wondered whether NATO had transformed sufficiently to undertake a large-scale deployment of this sort, so far from Europe. In some European governments, such as the Netherlands, there was concern that the amalgamation of the two missions would see ISAF-oriented troops becoming vulnerable to OEF-style attack; troops prepared for peacekeeping and reconstruction operations might prove to be inadequate in the face of a serious insurgent adversary. Among the more vehemently anti-US critics in Europe, some claimed that European forces were being dragged into a combat role in order either to validate the US-led "war on terror", or to release US troops to be deployed elsewhere. Towards the end of the year, commentators (and even some officials) in the USA expressed concern that their European allies were succumbing to the so-called "body-bag syndrome"; increasingly casualty averse and unwilling to undertake combat deployments in Afghanistan or elsewhere.

For the EU's security and defence organisation, 2005 saw yet more experience being gained in military, police, and rule of law deployments. In December 2004 it had been agreed that NATO's Stabilisation Force (SFOR) commitment to Bosnia & Herzegovina would be taken over by a new organisation known as European Force (EUFOR, see AR 2004, pp. 373-74). Although help would still be needed from NATO, the EU-led deployment, known as "Operation Althea", would be the biggest test so far of the EU's military aspirations. Spain, Italy, France, the Netherlands, and Portugal also agreed in 2005 to establish a European Gendarmerie Force, to be launched in January 2006. On the military front, EU Defence Ministers, meeting in May, sought to put more flesh on the plan for deployable battlegroups. It was agreed that there would be fourteen such units, each with about 1,500 troops, on call to act as rapid reaction forces, preparing the ground for larger-scale deployments by other organisations such as the UN. The Defence Ministers' goal was to be able, by 2007, to mount two such deployments simultaneously. As had so often been the case with EU military aspirations, however, critics were quick to note that the EU still lacked the necessary command and control and strategic transport to make even these limited deployments a realistic goal.

Scepticism, bordering on cynicism, had often attended discussion of the EU's security and defence plans. Yet during 2005 it seemed to some observers that the EU was at last developing its own particular (some might say peculiar) so-called "strategic culture"; the political and organisational capacity to use organised armed force. Policy analysts had become accustomed to describing the EU as an institution relying on the "soft power" of trade, finance, and diplomacy, and as far as possible from the military "hard power" offered by NATO. But during 2005, some began to ask whether the EU was emerging as something altogether different, perhaps a "soft power-plus"? The EU was already established as a mature international actor with political, economic, industrial, cultural, and even historical authority. Now, although the EU's battlegroups might seem insignificant when compared to NATO's many divisions and overwhelming firepower, they might offer precisely the level of military capacity needed to make the EU a fully-rounded international organisation able to act on at least some level in every area of international policy. If so, then perhaps the EU was on the verge of becoming an organisation far better suited than NATO to the multi-level diplomacy, coercion, and even confrontation of the 21st century? Given that transatlantic divisions over Iraq had plainly not subsided, and given that some concerns were expressed in 2005 that the NATO-EU institutional rivalry of the early- and mid-1990s was about to resume, then the notion that the EU might have begun to acquire its own version of a strategic personality became especially significant. Although the EU could not be said during 2005 to have rivalled NATO militarily—nor would it ever for as long as NATO remained intact—neither could it be said any more to be a mere paper tiger; the EU's increasing ability to act across the political-economic-military spectrum would give it a breadth of international capacity which NATO could not match.

Yet the clearest lesson of 2005, for both NATO and the EU, was the need for a co-operative relationship between the two organisations, in which the strengths of each could be exploited. It was with this in mind that, in January 2005, the US administration announced the appointment of a new homeland security attaché to the EU, to enable direct and constant US-EU communication at the operational level. Following the terrorist attacks in London in July (see pp. 14-15), it was clear that institutional differences could not be allowed to undermine security. A co-operative relationship between NATO and the EU could help to bridge the conceptual divide between the USA and Europe. On one side lay the US democratic interventionist argument, to the effect that the absence of democracy was the cause of international terrorism, and democratisation the solution. The more sceptical European approach, on the other hand, was far less confrontational; Europeans had, after all, experienced terrorist attacks for decades and tended to argue for a more nuanced approach to terrorism, one which could take account of poverty in many areas of the Islamic world and other grievances such as that over Palestine. Least of all did Europeans accept the idea that democracy could be spread through the deployment and use of armed force. Thus, throughout 2005, European critics of US foreign and security policy concerned themselves with the possibility that the USA might decide to use armed force to "democratise" either Syria or Iran, or both. The alarming—but no less real—prospect that a terrorist group might in time acquire and use chemical, biological, radiological or even nuclear (CBRN) weapons presented the most impressive case for effective co-operation between the USA and Europe, and between NATO and the EU. Important aspects of the CBRN challenge were broadly military in character, and when a high-grade military response was required, NATO should plainly be the preferred institution. But other areas, such as the management of the nuclear fuel cycle and the regulation of chemical and biological industries, were more a matter of risk management, and this was where the EU would, some argued, be far better suited.

As 2005 came to an end, it was clear that the relationship between NATO and the EU's Common Security and Defence Policy was unresolved and that tensions persisted between the two organisations. But it was also clear that a functioning relationship of some sort was essential. Confronted by terrorism and by the possibility of CBRN proliferation, and faced with growing demand for humanitarian intervention operations around the world, an effective security partnership between the USA and the EU was arguably more necessary than for many years. In other words, both NATO and the EU were necessary, but neither alone would be sufficient.

Elsewhere in the world, security and defence organisations continued to develop. The Asia-Pacific region still lacked an effective multilateral security organisation, but there were signs of progress in 2005, even to the extent of the ASIA PACIFIC ECONOMIC COMMUNITY (APEC) taking on some sort of security role. For the USA this was a welcome development that could improve maritime and port security and contribute to the overall effort to control CBRN proliferation. An important step forward was taken in July, when the Australian government declared its intention to sign the ASSOCIATION OF SOUTH-EAST ASIAN NATIONS (ASEAN) Treaty of Amity and Cooperation (1976) (see p. 289). Previously, Australia had been reluctant to joint the treaty, arguing that the ASEAN agreement could clash with its mutual defence pact with the USA. Efforts were also made in 2005 to make the ASEAN REGIONAL FORUM (ARF) better able to undertake preventive action and conflict resolution, and to deal with the proliferation of CBRN and delivery systems. Once again the USA, a member of the ARF, welcomed this development. The ARF's security agenda expanded considerably during 2005, to include terrorism, human trafficking and smuggling, the proliferation of small arms and light weapons, transnational crime, civil-military relations, missile defence, and export licensing. With global security increasingly requiring a consolidated global response, the USA also called for a closer relationship between the ARF and the OSCE.

Little progress was made in 2005 by the SOUTH ASIAN ASSOCIATION FOR REGIONAL CO-OPERATION (SAARC). In November 2005 Afghanistan was admitted as the eighth member of SAARC, but security co-operation within the organisation remained low-level and tentative. Much was made of the need for improved confidence-building measures and for co-operation in the face of terrorism. The SAARC region saw a great deal of terrorist activity during 2005, and much associated cross-border activity. This led to tensions within the organisation; India, in particular, was convinced that many of its terrorist problems were exacerbated by the weak policies of its neighbours, such as Bangladesh, Pakistan, and Nepal (see pp. 280-82).

For the SHANGHAI CO-OPERATION ORGANISATION (SCO), 2005 proved to be a busy year. The SCO's security agenda had expanded in the late 1990s to include terrorism and the smuggling of narcotics, people, and arms. In July 2005 the SCO admitted India, Iran, and Pakistan to observer status and further developed its Regional Anti-Terrorist Structure (RATS), a small co-ordination body with no operational role based in Tashkent, Uzbekistan. The SCO's National Security Council Group examined the possibility of a regional agreement on stability and security, and supported practical activities such as joint anti-terror exercises and training, and the compilation of a list of terrorist organisations and individuals operating in the SCO region. Yet for all this co-operation and co-ordination, the prospect of a joint, operational response to terrorist attacks remained distant. Still more remote was the possibility that the SCO might one day become a politico-military alliance along the lines of NATO. China remained adamant that this should not occur, observing that the SCO charter would not permit it. Nevertheless, it became increasingly clear during 2005 that the SCO had developed a small but comprehensive bureaucratic infrastructure and that the organisation had become a factor for security dialogue in the region. Among all the security and defence organisations around the world, the SCO was the one most likely to acquire more political weight; if and when Mongolia, India, Iran, and Pakistan acquired full membership, the SCO would encompass approximately 50 per cent of the world's population (see pp. 271-72).

In Africa, members of the AFRICAN UNION (AU) continued to pursue the goal of a deployable military capability for peacekeeping and intervention operations across the troubled continent. Movement towards establishing an African Standby Force (ASF) had begun in 2004, with the intention that the ASF would act under the auspices of the AU to intervene in border wars and internal conflicts. The ASF would consist of five regionally based brigades of 3,000-4,000 troops, with a sixth headquarters establishment in Addis Ababa, Ethiopia. The intention was that initial operating capability would be achieved by the end of 2005, with full operating capability by 2010 when the AU would be in a position to manage a complex peacekeeping operation. By June 2005 it was intended that the ASF would be able at least to deploy and manage monitoring missions. With this in mind, the AU planned to have on call 300-500 military observers and 240 police officers at fourteen days' notice to move. It was also expected that the ASF would be able to draw on other regional security initiatives, such as the ECONOMIC COMMUNITY OF

WEST AFRICAN STATES (ECOWAS) Cease-Fire Monitoring Group and the security initiative of the Southern Africa Development Community (SADC). The 2003 SADC summit in Tanzania had agreed on a mutual defence pact and had made the first moves towards establishing deployable force structures for intervention and peacekeeping operations, which it was intended would result in a SADC standby brigade. For both the AU and SADC, however, budgetary constraints placed severe limitations on what could be achieved in 2005; as was the case, after all, for many of the world's defence and security organisations.

ECONOMIC ORGANISATIONS

International Monetary Fund (IMF)

DATE OF FOUNDATION: 1945 HEADQUARTERS: Washington DC, USA
OBJECTIVES: To promote international monetary co-operation and to assist member states in establishing sound budgetary and trading policies
MEMBERSHIP (END-'05): 184 members
MANAGING DIRECTOR: Rodrigo Rato y Figaredo (Spain)

World Bank (International Bank for Reconstruction and Development (IBRD) and International Development Association (IDA))

DATE OF FOUNDATION: 1945 HEADQUARTERS: Washington DC, USA
OBJECTIVES: To make loans on reasonable terms to developing countries with the aim of increasing their productive capacity
MEMBERSHIP (END-'05): 184 members
PRESIDENT: Paul Wolfowitz (USA)

World Trade Organisation (WTO)

DATE OF FOUNDATION: 1995 (successor to General Agreement on Tariffs and Trade, GATT)
HEADQUARTERS: Geneva, Switzerland
OBJECTIVES: To eliminate tariffs and other barriers to international trade and to facilitate international financial settlements
MEMBERSHIP (END-'05): 150 acceding parties
DIRECTOR GENERAL: Pascal Lamy (France)

Organisation for Economic Co-operation and Development (OECD)

DATE OF FOUNDATION: 1965 HEADQUARTERS: Paris, France
OBJECTIVES: To promote economic growth in member states and the sound development of the world economy
MEMBERSHIP (END-'05): Australia, Austria, Belgium, Canada, Czech Republic, Denmark, Finland, France, Germany, Greece, Hungary, Iceland, Ireland, Italy, Japan, South Korea, Luxembourg, Mexico, the Netherlands, New Zealand, Norway, Poland, Portugal, Slovakia, Spain, Sweden, Switzerland, Turkey, UK, USA (total 30)
SECRETARY GENERAL: Donald Johnston (Canada)

Organisation of the Petroleum Exporting Countries (OPEC)

DATE OF FOUNDATION: 1960 HEADQUARTERS: Vienna, Austria
OBJECTIVES: To unify and co-ordinate member states' oil policies and to safeguard their interests
MEMBERSHIP (END-'05): Algeria, Indonesia, Iran, Iraq, Kuwait, Libya, Nigeria, Qatar, Saudi Arabia, United Arab Emirates, Venezuela (total 11)
SECRETARY GENERAL: (acting) Adnan Shihab-Eldin (Kuwait)

THE WORLD BANK, the WTO, and the OECD all appointed new leaders in 2005 amid the perennial controversy over the procedures for selecting them. In 2004 such controversy had surrounded the selection of the new managing director of the IMF, but in 2005 it was focused on the choice of Paul Wolfowitz, the former deputy Defence Secretary of the USA, as president of the World Bank. Much of the controversy related to his earlier involvement in US policy towards Iraq, but there were also familiar objections to the lack of transparency in the manner of his selection and to the continued US monopoly over the post. In 2001, an IMF-World Bank working group had recommended the creation of a panel that would vet the professional competence of all applicants "whether or not there are any understandings regarding the nationality of the president [of the World Bank] or the managing director [of the IMF]". Nevertheless, the top posts continued to be filled, as they were in most international organisations, as a result of horse-trading among the major economic powers.

WORLD TRADE ORGANISATION (WTO). In mid-January an expert group appointed by the Director-General, Supachai Panitchpakdi, and chaired by the WTO's first Director-General, Peter Sutherland, published a report on the functioning of the organisation together with an assessment of threats to the multilateral trading system. Among the institutional issues discussed was the consensus rule which allowed any member to block any action, a rule that some critics held responsible for the lack of progress in the current trade negotiations. The expert group defended the rule as it helped to protect the poorest countries from being dictated to by the rich, but in order to overcome some of the difficulties it suggested (i) reviving the former GATT system of codes and agreements to which not all members need adhere; (ii) the setting of broad rules in certain areas that would allow countries to make varying commitments according to their circumstances (and as provided for in the General Agreement on Trade in Services); and (iii) obliging a country exercising a veto to explain why. (Many developing countries, while supporting the principle of consensus, had argued that the obscure manner in which it emerged from informal consultations actually favoured the interests of the richest countries). The group judged the WTO dispute settlement to have proved effective. On the sometimes fraught relations with non-governmental organisations (NGOs), they cautiously recommended improving communications with the NGOs and suggested that the proceedings of dispute settlement panels be opened to the public, subject to the agreement of the parties to a dispute.

The new Director-General, Pascal Lamy, the former EU Trade Commissioner, took up his post on 1 September. In his "candidacy speech" earlier in the year he spoke favourably of the Sutherland report but also of the need to rebalance the international trading system in favour of developing countries.

The major preoccupation of the WTO throughout 2005 continued to be the Doha round of trade negotiations, due to be completed by the end of 2006. Early in the year the Director-General listed the areas in which progress had to be made by July if there were to be a substantial advance at the ministerial meeting in Hong

Kong in December. These included agreeing the modalities of negotiation in agriculture and non-agricultural market access (NAMA); a critical mass of opening offers in services; significant progress in rules and trade facilitation; and a "proper reflection" of the promised "development round". By July there was no substantial progress and the Director-General declared "the negotiations are in trouble". In the event, the December talks did not collapse, as many had predicted, but the outcome was meagre and imbalanced in favour of the rich countries. The EU tentatively agreed to eliminate its agricultural export subsidies, but only from 2013 and only if the modalities for the negotiations were agreed. The USA similarly pledged to end its export subsidies to cotton in 2006 but made no commitment to end the much larger subsidies to its cotton producers which had already been ruled illegal. The major concessions at Hong Kong were made by the developing countries which, divided by their different interests and the differentiated offers made to them by the EU and the USA, agreed to negotiating modalities that would expose them to considerable pressure to open up their key service sectors to foreign companies and to make large cuts in their industrial tariffs.

WTO membership rose to 150 in December with the accession of Saudi Arabia (11 December) and Tonga (15 December). Accession negotiations remained at various stages for Russia, Vietnam, Iran, São Tomé and Príncipe, Cape Verde, Yemen, Montenegro, and Serbia, separate applications from the last two being accepted in February.

INTERNATIONAL MONETARY FUND. In its *World Economic Outlook* in September the IMF emphasised the resilience of the world economy despite a long series of natural disasters and heightened economic risks. Although its forecasts remained largely unchanged from the spring, there was concern at the large and growing global current account imbalances. The orderly correction of these, it was suggested, required a more co-operative response by the international community, including a medium-term fiscal correction in the USA, structural reforms in Europe and Japan to accelerate economic growth, and a combination of greater exchange rate flexibility and reform of financial institutions in the emerging economies of Asia. Increasing investment would help to reduce the high level of savings in Europe and Asia.

In 2004 the Fund started to review its medium-term strategy and priorities, the first results of which were presented to the annual meeting by the Managing Director. The review admitted that the organisation had been pulled too far from its original purpose of safeguarding international monetary stability and financing temporary balance of payments deficits. Changes in priorities, management, and organisational structure were recommended to meet the challenges of globalisation and, not least, of the institution's prospect of falling income. (New loans were at their lowest since the late 1970s and the Fund's outstanding loan book fell by more than one-quarter between April 2004 and November 2005). The proposed course of action included strengthening the Fund's surveillance of countries in a regional and global context; improving its capacity to anticipate and prevent financial crises; and adopting a more circumspect approach to capital account liberalisation. The Managing Director acknowledged that the present allocation of "quotas and voice" damaged the legitimacy of the Fund as a universal institution, and remarked that the "governance and ownership balances in the Fund now rival the current account imbalances. Neither is sustainable."

THE WORLD BANK. The Bank's lending in fiscal 2005 was US$22.3 billion, just over 11 per cent more than in 2004. The increase was due to lending by the International Bank for Reconstruction and Development (IBRD), the "hard window" of the Bank; International Development Association (IDA) finance on concessional terms fell. The largest increase in lending (46 per cent) was to South Asia, in part because of emergency support to the Maldives, Sri Lanka, and India in the wake of the tsunami disaster of December 2004. In East Asia, the Bank put together a multi-donor trust fund of US$500 million of grants for reconstruction in Indonesia, to which were added other Bank grants and credits. Nevertheless, Latin America continued to be the largest borrower both in terms of its share of total Bank lending (23 per cent) and of loans per capita (US$10.3); Africa—regarded as a major challenge for the Bank—took just over 17 per cent of the total or US$5.6 per head, all of it in IDA finance.

The Bank's largest exposure to a single borrower was to China (US$11.1 billion in total) although in mid-2005 this was still below the single borrower limit of US$13.5 billion. The Bank was criticised for continuing to lend to China, which had rapidly increasing resources and an overseas aid programme of its own, but the president defended the policy on the grounds that China still accounted for some 18 per cent of the world's population living in absolute poverty and that the development of civil society needed support.

The Bank was losing borrowers in middle-income countries which had turned increasingly to the international capital markets for funds: this was more costly but the conditions were fewer and less intrusive and there was less bureaucracy involved. Between 2001 and 2005, the Bank's outstanding loan book fell by 12 per cent and its loan income by nearly 50 per cent.

The new president reaffirmed the Bank's poverty reduction strategy which stressed improvement in the investment climate and empowering civil society. The Bank's *World Development Report* for 2005 focused on the importance of equity in the development process and underlined the necessity of providing equal opportunities and of ensuring that deprivation in levels of education, health, and income was not left aside. The second issue of the Bank's annual *Global Monitoring Report* warned that without a rapid acceleration in the rate of progress the UN's millennium development goals would not be achieved, the shortfall being particularly marked in Africa.

The Bank faced increasing demands for reform at the time of its annual meeting in September. These included demands that it stop stretching its resources over too many areas of policy; that the impact of its lending on development be subject to independent, external evaluation; that its governance be more transparent and that membership of the board of governors be rebalanced (Europe, for example, had eight seats and Africa only two); and that the selection of the president be more transparent, competitive, and not restricted to nationals of the USA.

ORGANISATION FOR ECONOMIC CO-OPERATION AND DEVELOPMENT. The theme of the OECD ministerial council in May was "enabling globalisation". The ministers regarded globalisation as inevitable and desirable, but a major task was to make it inclusive and sustainable. Ministers strongly supported the WTO's Doha round of trade negotiations (see above), arguing that success would provide a powerful boost to global growth and poverty reduction, but secretariat studies stressed that the benefits would depend on liberalisation being accompanied by active policies to ease adjustment.

One objective of the OECD was to deepen understanding of, and seek co-operation with, non-OECD economies. In 2005 this was reflected by the launch of a "good governance for development" programme with the states of the Middle East and North Africa, the first *OECD Economic Survey of China*, and the first review of agricultural policies in Brazil. The OECD also introduced a new, annual publication in 2005, *Economic Policy Reforms: Going for Growth*. This complemented the *OECD Economic Outlook* by focusing on the structural impediments to growth and addressing such questions as why, instead of converging, some countries had moved ahead in terms of income and prosperity while others continued to lag behind.

The annual *Employment Outlook* also called for better labour market policies in order to withstand competition from emerging economies and to address the rising sense of job insecurity in many OECD countries. Failure to tackle the problems of workforce adjustment, it argued, could erode public support for liberal trade policies.

Another source of personal insecurity in the OECD countries was the uncertain outlook for retirement pensions. The recent history of financial scandals prompted the OECD to approve in April a new set of guidelines for insurers and pension funds in order to strengthen confidence that the latter would be better protected from fraud and mismanagement. The OECD also launched a drive for the better financial education of citizens who were expected to bear increasing responsibility for financing their retirement.

The OECD's November *Economic Outlook* presented a picture of robust and resilient growth in the OECD area, but the downside risks were considered to be substantial and, because most of them involved financial variables, difficult to assess. The title of the chief economist's editorial neatly captured the assessment: "Less robust than meets the eye?".

At the end of November the OECD announced the appointment of Ángel Gurria, former Foreign Minister and Finance Minister of Mexico, as Secretary General of the Organisation from 1 June 2006, in succession to Donald Johnston of Canada.

ORGANISATION OF THE PETROLEUM EXPORTING COUNTRIES. The ministerial meeting in March (the 135th meeting) was held in Iran, the first time that OPEC had met in that country in thirty-four years. The meeting agreed that OPEC members should increase their official production ceiling by 500,000 barrels per day (b/d) to an overall quota of 27.5 million b/d. This was largely a token decision, as OPEC members were already thought to be producing significantly above their quotas at around 27.7 million b/d. A further rise in production of 500,000 b/d was agreed at the 136th (extraordinary) meeting in Vienna in June, but this had little impact on the market, the price of US crude reaching a record US$60 per barrel by 23 June. OPEC members noted that the high oil price was mainly due to the inability of global refining capacity to meet strong demand, rather than a shortage in the supply of crude oil.

No further increases in quotas were agreed over the remainder of the year, although in September OPEC agreed to make available spare capacity of around 2 million b/d for a period of three months, in response to the continued rising oil price which briefly reached US$70 per barrel in the aftermath of Hurricane Katrina in the USA.

OTHER WORLD ORGANISATIONS

THE COMMONWEALTH

DATE OF FOUNDATION: 1931   HEADQUARTERS: London, UK
OBJECTIVES: To maintain political, cultural and social links between (mainly English-speaking) countries of the former British Empire and others subscribing to Commonwealth democratic principles and aims
MEMBERSHIP (END-'05): Antigua & Barbuda, Australia, The Bahamas, Bangladesh, Barbados, Belize, Botswana, Brunei, Cameroon, Canada, Cyprus, Dominica, Fiji, The Gambia, Ghana, Grenada, Guyana, India, Jamaica, Kenya, Kiribati, Lesotho, Malawi, Malaysia, Maldives, Malta, Mauritius, Mozambique, Namibia, Nauru, New Zealand, Nigeria, Pakistan, Papua New Guinea, St Kitts & Nevis, St Lucia, St Vincent & the Grenadines, Samoa, Seychelles, Sierra Leone, Singapore, Solomon Islands, South Africa, Sri Lanka, Swaziland, Tanzania, Tonga, Trinidad & Tobago, Tuvalu, Uganda, UK, Vanuatu, Zambia (total 53)
SECRETARY-GENERAL: Don McKinnon (New Zealand)

THOSE who argued in the first years of the 21st century for the importance of the Commonwealth pointed to the spread and mix of its membership from some of the smallest to the largest countries in the world. In 2005 two events underlined the point: the rapid development of India as a global economic powerhouse, and the holding of the biennial Commonwealth Heads of Government Meeting (CHOGM) in the smallest member country so far given this honour: Malta. Lawrence Gonzi, who had been Malta's Prime Minister for only twenty-two months, found himself chairing a global summit as well as becoming chairperson-in-office of the Commonwealth for the next two years, succeeding in that role President Olusegun Obasanjo of Nigeria.

India's role in Commonwealth affairs had diminished under the government of the Bharatiya Janata Party (BJP). The return of a Congress-led government in 2004 promised renewed interest by Prime Minister Manmohan Singh. This began to show itself when India raised its contribution to the Commonwealth Fund for Technical Co-operation (CFTC) and other Commonwealth funds, including a special fund to support a Commonwealth action programme for the digital divide. However, Singh was not at the CHOGM; he sent a key colleague, Commerce Minister Kamal Nath, instead. Also absent was Paul Martin of Canada, whose government fell during the CHOGM (see p. 129). It was only the second time that Canada had not sent its Prime Minister to a Commonwealth summit. The summit (on 25-27 November) was attended by thirty-eight heads of government, with only Nauru unrepresented. It was notable for major changes in format. These included, for the first time, a two-day meeting of Foreign Ministers and a longer retreat of the heads of government, returning to the style introduced by Canadian Prime Minister Pierre Trudeau in 1973. The only officials present at the retreat were Secretary-General Don McKinnon and his assistant, and the hotel venue was isolated from all other CHOGM activity. The greater informality led to a more productive summit than of late.

The discussions centred mainly upon trade, in particular the forthcoming World Trade Organisation (WTO) meeting in Hong Kong. A statement on multilateral trade drew attention to the most distorted sector—agriculture—and called for all export subsidies to be eliminated by 2010. The adverse implications for small countries of the EU's reform of its sugar regime were condemned. Commonwealth Trade Ministers met in Hong Kong on the eve of the WTO meeting (11 December) to reinforce the CHOGM input, but McKinnon said that he was deeply disappointed at the Hong Kong outcome: trade issues needed statesmanship and political will, and should not be left to technocrats (see pp. 356-57).

Days before the CHOGM the opposition leader in Uganda was arrested (see p. 220). The uncertain political future in that country caused special concern because Uganda's capital, Kampala, was scheduled to host the 2007 CHOGM. Leaders in Malta voiced their anxieties informally to President Yoweri Museveni. This and other Commonwealth sensitivities about holding the line on governance were reflected in the summit communiqué, which also repeated the stand on Pakistan, namely, that the offices of head of state and chief of army staff held by General Pervez Musharraf must be separated by the end of his presidential term in 2007. Pakistan—suspended from the Commonwealth from 1999-2004—was represented at the CHOGM by Prime Minister Shaukat Aziz, who tried to prevent reiteration of the demand for the separation of posts, which had also been made by the Commonwealth ministerial action group (CMAG) at three meetings during 2005. He failed.

The Commonwealth secretariat's good offices work was stepped up. Election observers and expert teams were sent for polls in Lesotho, Bougainville in Papua New Guinea, Lesotho, Nauru, Sri Lanka, Vanuatu, and Zanzibar in Tanzania.

At the second meeting of Commonwealth Tourism Ministers, held in Abuja, Nigeria, on 28-29 April, Malaysia offered to set up and finance for three years a Commonwealth tourist centre to enhance promotion. The 50th Commonwealth law conference held in London on 1-15 September was followed by a meeting of Law Ministers in Accra, the Ghanaian capital, on 17-20 October. Finance Ministers held their annual meeting in Barbados on 18-20 September; Health Ministers met in Geneva, Switzerland, on 15 May.

In mid-year the Commonwealth secretariat celebrated its 40th birthday. The secretariat had been set up at the June 1965 meeting of Commonwealth Prime Ministers, chaired by UK Prime Minister Harold Wilson, with Canadian Arnold

Smith as the first Secretary-General (see AR 1965, p. 60). Mark Collins succeeded Colin Ball, who retired as director of the Commonwealth Foundation.
Collins was director of the UN Environment Programme world conservation monitoring centre in the UK.

The UK government switched UK£6 million of its budget for overseas missions
from six high commissions in order to open embassies in areas regarded as central to the "war on terror". The British high commissions in Vanuatu, Tonga, Kiribati, Bahamas, Lesotho, and Swaziland, and consulates in Brisbane, Perth, Auckland, and Douala were closed.

FRANCOPHONE AND PORTUGUESE-SPEAKING COMMUNITIES

International Organisation of Francophonie (OIF)

DATE OF FOUNDATION: 1997   HEADQUARTERS: Paris, France
OBJECTIVES: To promote co-operation and exchange between countries wholly or partly French-
    speaking and to defend usage of the French language
MEMBERSHIP (END-'05): Albania (associate member), Andorra (associate member), Belgium, French-
    speaking community of Belgium, Benin, Bulgaria, Burkina Faso, Burundi, Cambodia,
    Cameroon, Canada, New Brunswick (Canada), Québec (Canada), Cape Verde, Central African
    Republic, Chad, Comoros, Democratic Republic of Congo, Republic of Congo, Côte d'Ivoire,
    Djibouti, Dominica, Egypt, Equatorial Guinea, France, Gabon, Greece (associate member),
    Guinea, Guinea-Bissau, Haiti, Laos, Lebanon, Luxembourg, Macedonia (associate member),
    Madagascar, Mali, Mauritania, Mauritius, Moldova, Monaco, Morocco, Niger, Romania,
    Rwanda, St Lucia, São Tomé & Príncipe, Senegal, Seychelles, Switzerland, Togo, Tunisia,
    Vanuatu, Vietnam (total 52)
SECRETARY GENERAL: Abdou Diouf (Senegal)

Community of Portuguese-Speaking Countries (CPLP)

DATE OF FOUNDATION: 1996   HEADQUARTERS: Lisbon, Portugal
OBJECTIVES: To promote political, diplomatic, economic, social and cultural co-operation between
    member-states and to enhance the status of the Portuguese language
MEMBERSHIP (END-'05): Angola, Brazil, Cape Verde, East Timor, Guinea-Bissau, Mozambique,
    Portugal, São Tomé & Príncipe (total 8)
EXECUTIVE SECRETARY: Luís de Matos Monteiro da Fonseca (Cape Verde)

ALTHOUGH 2005 was an off-year for the ORGANISATION INTERNATIONALE DE LA FRAN-
COPHONIE (OIF), in that there was no summit, it was still a year with a variety of
significant events. Most important of these was the 21st annual ministerial meeting, held on 21-23 November in Antananarivo, capital of Madagascar.

This meeting had a symbolic importance in that it saw the adoption of a definitive version of the organisation's charter which incorporated a number of reforms
undertaken in the previous ten years. These included the establishment of the
office of Secretary-General in 1997, and the adoption of the organisation's current
name in 1998. The drafting of the text of the revised charter was undertaken by
the OIF's secretariat under Secretary-General Abdou Diouf, with the objective of
creating a stronger "juridical personality". Apart from rationalising the structure
of the secretariat and reinforcing and clearly defining the powers of the Secretary-
General, the charter incorporated what it called the "new strategic missions" of the

OIF. It also indicated clearly the motor role of the political body, the council of ministers, as well as the different capacities of the permanent council of Francophonie, which was chaired by the Secretary-General and prepared important meetings as well as having a watchdog role over the institution and the implementation of policies. The charter, although immediately operational, was due to be ratified by member states in time to be fully adopted by the next summit in Bucharest, capital of Romania, in the autumn of 2006. Luc Dehaime, a new administrator responsible to the Secretary-General, would replace Roger Dehaybe, the Belgian national who had headed the OIF's co-operation agency—with considerable autonomy—for eight years.

The ministerial meeting also adopted a special resolution on the issue of the UNESCO (United Nations Educational, Cultural, and Scientific Organisation) convention on the protection and promotion of cultural diversity. Lobbying for this project, which was adopted by UNESCO in October, had been one of the core activities of the OIF, even if it was clear that the whole project had also been close to the heart of France's government because of its concerns for the survival of the French language in a world increasingly dominated by English. In the protracted UNESCO meetings and debates on the subject, the issues had frequently been presented as part of the international movement against globalisation—and on occasion had been fuelled by anti-Americanism—in an attempt to broaden the battle lines. The Antanarivo resolution said that in view of the "success of the mobilisation of member states and governments of La Francophonie" in contributing to the adoption of the UNESCO cultural diversity convention, which would help the creation of a "vast juridical space" for the "development of cultural identities and industries", members were urged to ratify the convention urgently.

The meeting also broadly endorsed the position of developing countries at the important ministerial meeting of the World Trade Organisation (WTO) in mid-December in Hong Kong (see pp. 356-57). Francophone ministers held a consultation on the eve of the meeting, at which particular support was given to the "cotton four" (Mali, Burkina Faso, Benin, and Chad) in their campaign to force the US government to reduce subsidies to its cotton farmers. This met with some success, but although the overall ending of international agricultural subsidies by 2013 received general support there was no evidence that any Francophone countries were part of the diplomatic effort to cut by three years the deadline for the EU to reduce its cotton subsidies, which some states had tried to secure with UK support against France's opposition.

These moves dovetailed with parallel higher-profile actions at the Africa-France summit in Bamako, capital of Mali, in early December which, as far as France was concerned, was a major focal point of diplomatic effort (see p. 230). Although not structurally linked to the OIF, the summit's agenda shared many of the same concerns as would have been on the agenda of a Francophone summit and included many of the same participants. This was particularly true of trade issues, where a statement on the WTO was bland on subsidies in general, but forceful in relation to US cotton subsidies. France's President Jacques Chirac used his speech in

Bamako to call on the USA to remove subsidies to its cotton producers "as the EU has undertaken to do".

The OIF trend towards a higher political profile was also seen in a greater interest in security issues and it was decided that a ministerial meeting on the subject would be held in Canada in the first part of 2006. Of UN troops, 10 per cent were Francophones. Diouf, as a former national leader of Senegal, was not afraid to take political positions in line with the OIF's 2002 Bamako declaration on democracy (see AR 2004, p. 384). Thus, the attempt in February by the army in Togo to force a dynastic succession on the country was strongly resisted by the OIF, which suspended the country until the decision was reversed after three weeks (see pp. 232-34). Elections followed, and observers from the OIF overcame earlier misgivings (expressed at the end of March) to give the poll a qualified approval in April.

There were other Francophonie election observation missions, such as that in Burkina Faso in November, and the OIF's newly-established electoral observatory was closely involved in the UN-supervised processes for the return to democracy in Democratic Republic of Congo and Haiti. However, the difficulties of generalising about democracy in Africa were underlined by the military coup in Mauritania in August (see pp. 229-30). The condemnation by the OIF of the coup was also short-lived once it transpired that it had been genuinely popular and had removed a sham democracy.

Although observers sought to detect important differences between the OIF and the Commonwealth—notably in the former's great emphasis on the defence and propagation of the French language—it was noted that in the past decade the two organisations had increasingly come to resemble each other. As with the Commonwealth, there was a proliferation of lower-level grassroots activities in la Francophonie.

The year saw the COMMUNITY OF PORTUGUESE-SPEAKING COUNTRIES (CPLP) preoccupied with the political uncertainty surrounding Guinea-Bissau (see pp. 238-39). The year ended as it had begun with task forces being mobilised to observe the conduct of elections and to assist in the maintenance of political stability within the country. Close collaboration with the UN led to an accord pledging €1.4 million to aid the reform of the military and the consolidation of peace and democracy. CPLP observers deemed the second round of voting in disputed presidential elections on 24 July to have been conducted in a fair and transparent manner. An independent candidate, João Bernardo "Nino" Vieira, emerged victorious from this vote and was sworn in as President on 1 October. However, with Prime Minister Carlos Gomes Junior allegedly refusing to accept his authority, the new President dismissed the government on 30 October, thus plunging the country into further turmoil. To assist with a return to political normality, a CPLP task force headed by Executive Secretary Fonseca visited Guinea-Bissau on 10-12 December.

Despite these overarching difficulties, the CPLP did not ignore its social responsibilities. In 2005, the organisation promoted an HIV/AIDS conference in Luanda, capital of Angola; supported a Portuguese-language book fair in Dili,

East Timor; and hosted a major conference on industrial activity in Funchal, Madeira. In April, the CPLP announced the establishment of a centre of excellence in public administration at a location close to Maputo in Mozambique. The year ended on a bright note with intensive preparations being made for the July 2006 staging of the biennial conference of CPLP heads of states in Bissau.

NON-ALIGNED MOVEMENT AND DEVELOPING COUNTRIES

Non-Aligned Movement (NAM)

DATE OF FOUNDATION: 1961   HEADQUARTERS: rotating with chair
OBJECTIVES: Originally to promote decolonisation and to avoid domination by either the Western industrialised world or the Communist bloc; since the early 1970s to provide an authoritative forum to set the political and economic priorities of developing countries; in addition, since the end of the Cold War, to resist domination of the UN system by the USA
MEMBERSHIP (END-'05): 114 countries (those listed in AR 1995, p. 386, plus Belarus, the Dominican Republic, St Vincent and the Grenadines, East Timor; minus Cyprus, Malta, Yugoslavia)
CHAIRMAN: Abdullah Ahmad Badawi, Malaysia (since Oct '03)

Group of 77 (G-77)

DATE OF FOUNDATION: 1964   HEADQUARTERS: UN centres
OBJECTIVES: To act as an international lobbying group for the concerns of developing countries
MEMBERSHIP (END-'05): 132 developing countries (those listed in AR 1996, p. 385, plus China, Eritrea, Palau, East Timor, Turkmenistan; minus Cyprus, Malta, South Korea, Yugoslavia)
CHAIRMAN: Percival J Patterson (Jamaica)

THE main meeting of developing countries in 2005 was the second south summit of the GROUP OF 77 (G-77), in Doha, Qatar, on 14-16 June. In April, the Indonesian government hosted celebrations to honour the 50th anniversary of the Bandung Asian-African conference of 1955, which was widely seen as the forerunner to the NON-ALIGNED MOVEMENT (NAM) (see AR 1955, pp. 165-66). The NAM held a ministerial meeting on the advancement of women, in Putrajaya, Malaysia, on 7-10 May, and the sixth conference of Ministers of Information, in Kuala Lumpur, Malaysia, on 19-22 November. There were also the annual meetings of the G-77 and the NAM in New York at the UN in September.

The summit in Doha was similar to the first south summit held in Havana, Cuba, in that it achieved only a low level of attendance (see AR 2000, p. 394). It adopted a Doha plan of action, which was modelled on the Havana programme, mainly endorsing general aspirations for South-South co-operation rather than specific practical proposals. The reasons for the lack of progress in the intervening five years were evident in the failure of the follow-up committee to meet annually, the lack of mechanisms to implement potentially useful proposals, and the failure of members to provide the minuscule levels of funding requested to sustain a G-77 secretariat in New York. Despite the frank acknowledgement of these problems in the final section of the Doha plan, there was no reason to suppose that a working group established "to study possible ways and means to strengthen the G-77 and its secretariat . . . as well as innovative approaches to address resource and personnel requirements" would generate the necessary political will to support the planned activities. In contrast to this pessimistic assessment of the G-77 as an institution, a UN report pointed to the rapid growth in South-South trade, increased levels of regional co-operation, the growth of developing country transnational corporations, and the vitality of networking between non-governmental organisations (NGOs).

The Bandung celebrations resulted in the declaration of a new Asian-African strategic partnership (NAASP) to promote political solidarity, economic co-operation, and socio-cultural relations between the two continents. This was to be institutionalised through a summit every four years and a ministerial meeting every two years. However, it was difficult to see what this might add to the existing work of the G-77.

The Putrajaya meeting on the advancement of women was attended by seventy-four of the 114 members of the NAM; it endorsed a wide-ranging programme of action, containing 111 proposals on poverty eradication, political participation, education, health, disasters, and awareness of gender issues. The programme was surprisingly radical in its call for gender equality, but most proposals were relatively general and would require significant economic resources that were unlikely to become available. The declaration ended by welcoming the Malaysian proposal to establish a NAM centre on gender and development, and recommending further ministerial meetings every two years.

The NAM Ministers of Information were meeting nine years after their previous conference and five years after it had been agreed that they should meet again. Work in this field had declined after the vigorous leadership provided by the Yugoslavs had been lost when they were expelled from the Movement in 1992. The conference noted that the Non-Aligned news agency pool had been inactive due to declining support from member countries. It was agreed to accept the Malaysian offer to replace the pool with a new mechanism, in the form of an Internet-based news network, to be managed by the Bernama news agency.

During the south summit, the NAM ministers met on the sidelines to adopt a declaration on preparations for the UN "world summit" in September. They expressed fears that UN reform would not be agreed in a manner that was "inclusive, open-ended and transparent". The Movement was not able to adopt a collective position on increasing the size of the Security Council nor on whether to create a human rights council. The declaration was hostile to the concept of a "responsibility to protect" people suffering from violent oppression by their own government and rejected the corresponding expansion of the authority of the UN Security Council. However, three months later in New York, many of the Non-Aligned, notably African members, actively supported giving the Security Council the right to authorise the use of force against governments who were unwilling or unable to prevent gross violations of human rights. Only Venezuela, Cuba, and Belarus voiced their objections on this question when the summit's outcome document was adopted (see pp. 334-36).

Throughout the year, UN reform dominated the work of the Non-Aligned in New York, to the point of limiting their initiatives on other questions. It was quite exceptional that the NAM ministers in September did no more than review the outcome of the debate on reform of the UN. Normal activities on behalf of the Palestinians were at a low level, until after the UN summit. However, Malaysia's Foreign Minister did attend in July, on behalf of the NAM, an event in Ramallah to commemorate the International Court of Justice ruling on the illegality of the Israeli security wall in Palestine (see AR 2004, pp. 387; 443-44; text, pp. 147-50). The NAM troika (the Foreign Ministers of Malaysia, South Africa, and Cuba) visited the Iranian capital, Teheran, in November and made a qualified statement of support for Iran in its dispute with the USA over the processing of nuclear fuel. This was balanced by the NAM's endorsement of the work of the International Atomic Energy Agency (IAEA), the EU, and Russia to ensure that Iran did not develop nuclear weapons.

At the end of 2005 Jamaica handed the chairmanship of the Group of 77 to South Africa for 2006. There was no change in the membership of either the NAM or the G-77 in 2005.

ORGANISATION OF THE ISLAMIC CONFERENCE (OIC)

DATE OF FOUNDATION: 1969   HEADQUARTERS: Jeddah, Saudi Arabia
OBJECTIVES: To further co-operation among Islamic countries in the political, economic, social, cultural and scientific spheres
MEMBERSHIP(END-'05): Afghanistan, Albania, Algeria, Azerbaijan, Bahrain, Bangladesh, Benin, Brunei, Burkina Faso, Cameroon, Chad, Comoros, Côte d'Ivoire, Djibouti, Egypt, Gabon, the Gambia, Guinea, Guinea-Bissau, Guyana, Indonesia, Iran, Iraq, Jordan, Kazakhstan, Kuwait, Kyrgyzstan, Lebanon, Libya, Malaysia, Maldives, Mali, Mauritania, Morocco, Mozambique, Niger, Nigeria, Oman, Pakistan, Palestine, Qatar, Saudi Arabia, Senegal, Sierra Leone, Somalia, Sudan, Suriname, Syria, Tajikistan, Togo, Tunisia, Turkey, Turkmenistan, Uganda, United Arab Emirates, Uzbekistan, Yemen (total 57)
SECRETARY GENERAL: Ekmeleddin Ihsanoglu (Turkey)

THE OIC's third extraordinary summit meeting in Mecca, Saudi Arabia, on 7-8 December was held under the banner "meeting the challenges of the 21st century, solidarity in action". Addressing the opening session, newly-appointed Secretary General Ekmeleddin Ihsanoglu (see AR 2004, p. 389) reviewed the current situation of the OIC and the place it was aspiring to occupy on the international scene. Taking into account "huge global developments" and the need for "strategic planning" in order to stay abreast of these developments, Ihsanoglu called on the Muslim world to preserve its identity, civilisation, and "lofty human values".

In a final communiqué, the summit reaffirmed that Islam was "a religion of moderation" which rejected "bigotry, extremism, and fanaticism". It stressed that dialogue among civilisations "based on mutual respect, understanding, and equality between people", was "a prerequisite for establishing a world marked by tolerance, co-operation, peace, and confidence among nations". It called for "combating pseudo-religious and sectarian extremism" and reaffirmed the need "to deepen dialogue and promote restraint, moderation and tolerance, and issuance of fatwas by those not eligible to issue them".

The summit expressed its concern at rising hatred against Islam and Muslims and condemned the "desecration" of the image of the Holy Prophet Mohammad in "the media of certain countries", a reference to the twelve caricatures of the Prophet published in a Danish newspaper, *Jyllands-Posten*, on 30 September. It stressed the responsibility of all governments to ensure full respect for all religions and religious symbols and "the inapplicability of using the freedom of expression as a pretext to defame religions". It underlined the need to counter Islamophobia, defamation of Islam and its values, and desecration of Islamic holy sites, and to co-ordinate effectively with states as well as regional and international organisations to urge them to criminalise this phenomenon as a form of racism.

The summit stressed the need to condemn terrorism and declared its "solidarity with member states which have been victims of terrorism". It called for the implementation of the recommendations adopted by the international counter-terrorism conference, held in the Saudi Arabian capital, Riyadh, in February 2005, including the creation of an international centre for combating terrorism.

Finally, the summit stressed the importance of the question of Palestine as "the central cause of the Muslim ummah" (community or people). It discussed the developments in Iraq and expressed the hope that the forthcoming legislative elections (see pp. 185-88) would lead to a constitutional Iraqi government in order to safeguard the country's unity and territorial integrity.

OIC Foreign Ministers convened for their 32nd session in Sana'a, the capital of Yemen, on 28-30 June. Tourism Ministers held their fourth session in Dakar, the capital of Senegal, on 28-30 March. The 21st session of the standing committee for economic and commercial co-operation of the OIC was held in Istanbul, Turkey, on 22-25 November.

EUROPEAN UNION

DATE OF FOUNDATION: 1952   HEADQUARTERS: Brussels, Belgium
OBJECTIVES: To seek ever-closer union of member states
MEMBERSHIP (END-'05): Austria, Belgium, Cyprus, Czech Republic, Denmark, Estonia, Finland, France, Germany, Greece, Hungary, Ireland, Italy, Latvia, Lithuania, Luxembourg, Malta, Netherlands, Poland, Portugal, Slovakia, Slovenia, Spain, Sweden, United Kingdom (total 25)
SECRETARY GENERAL: President of European Commission: José Manuel Durao Barroso (Portugal)

THE most significant unfinished business at the start of the year was ratification of the European Convention, the treaty which had finally been signed in October 2004 and which would give the EU its own constitution, change the make-up of the European institutions to allow for a Union of up to thirty or so member countries, and strengthen emerging areas of policy such as external relations, and justice and home affairs (see AR 2004, pp. 391-94). The deadline for ratification was October 2006.

Each member state had to decide whether to allow a popular vote through a referendum or to give the responsibility for approving the treaty to its national legislature alone. Fourteen member countries opted for the latter course, with Sweden undecided. Of these fourteen, eleven had ratified the treaty by the end of June with only marginal opposition from fringe political parties. In the Austrian Nationalrat (the lower chamber), for instance, the vote was 181 in favour and one against; in Greece the vote was 268 to seventeen; in Italy 217 to sixteen; and in Slovakia 116 to twenty-seven.

The decision of the UK government to consult the electorate directly over the issue put pressure on President Jacques Chirac to offer the French people a similar opportunity, and a referendum was duly scheduled for May. Spain, Luxembourg, and the Netherlands also decided to hold referendums in the first half of the year. (The UK government had opted for the last possible date, late summer 2006.) The Spanish electorate voted in February and approved the treaty, which went to the legislature for formal ratification (see pp. 60-61). Thereafter things began to go wrong, as it became clear that in France and the Netherlands the electorate had serious doubts. The French went to the polls on 29 May. They voted by 55 to 45 per cent against ratification, on a turnout of 69 per cent (see p. 40). On 1 June the Dutch voted 61.5 to 38.5 per cent against, in a 63 per cent turnout (see p. 48).

The outcome in these two countries revealed a sharp divergence between popular sentiment and the assumptions of the political elites. As the referendum campaigns got under way there were signs that, at least in France and the Netherlands, the European treaty was associated with issues that provoked deep unease amongst the population, such as high levels of unemployment, outsourcing of jobs, the threat to generous social support systems, the level of immigration, and fear of globalisation, as well as the general unpopularity of national politicians. Some argued that it was national issues alone which had determined the outcome, but there was little doubt that the terms of the treaty were perceived—with some justification—as agents of change which the people did not welcome.

The 2004 enlargement was one telling factor, reminding people as it did of the likely accession of Turkey in another ten years: not a popular cause among the population of Europe as a whole. The myth of the Polish plumber snatching work from local tradesmen became common currency in France, coupled with fear over proposals for a free market in services. In the Netherlands the prospects of further expansion of the EU encouraged a negative vote.

The double referendum result rocked the confidence of European leaders. Some insisted that the process of ratification should continue in those member countries which had yet to decide, but at the June EU summit in Brussels it became clear that this would not be acceptable. It was agreed that a "time for reflection" was appropriate before deciding the next step. The Czech Republic, Denmark, Ireland, Poland, Portugal, and the UK all postponed their referendums indefinitely, seeing no need to confront popular sentiment. It spared the UK government, in particular, the prospect of a difficult referendum campaign requiring a fundamental shift in popular sentiment (see p. 21).

Members of the European Parliament, which would have secured some additional powers and responsibilities if the treaty had been ratified, were critical of the national politicians. "The campaigns were poorly prepared and poorly executed", said UK Liberal MEP Andrew Duff. "They should be seen as rehearsals. Practice makes perfect." He joined with Austrian Green MEP Johannes Voggenhuber to produce a report for the Parliament's constitutional affairs committee called *The period of reflection: the structure, subjects, and context for an assessment of the debate on the European Union*. In September Voggenhuber attacked Commission President José Manuel Barroso for his mild response to the crisis, to which the President retorted: "We don't need a philosophical debate on the future of Europe; we need to get Europe back to work." The Parliament's report was due to be published early in 2006.

THE EUROPEAN BUDGET. The crisis of confidence triggered by the referendum votes in France and the Netherlands was a difficult backdrop to crucial negotiations to settle the European budget for 2007-13: the seven-year financial perspective. Decisions were required by the end of 2005 and it was generally anticipated that the process would be painful and divisive. It would be a major challenge for Luxembourg, in the chair of the European Council until the end of June, and then for the UK in the second half of the year, in the absence of a June settlement.

In political terms the task was daunting: new resources had to be found to boost investment in the ten East European and Mediterranean countries which had joined the EU in the 2004 enlargement, plus Bulgaria and Romania which were expected to join in 2007; yet the main contributing countries had already said that the EU budget should not exceed 1 per cent of GDP. The UK was intent on defending the budget rebate formula which had been won by Prime Minister Margaret Thatcher some twenty years earlier, but France refused to countenance any reduction in the 2002 commitment to maintain farm spending at existing levels. The Netherlands and Sweden were pressing for a reduction in their contribution, while Poland and the other new members were insisting that their future budget receipts should not be whittled away in order to help fund the UK's rebate.

In the run-up to the June European Council meeting in Brussels there was much talk of the dire consequences for the EU of failing to reach a budget agreement. The pressure mounted on the UK government, which was seen as the main obstacle to progress. "If we don't achieve this, the Union will be involved in permanent crisis and paralysis", said the European Commission President. For Germany's Chancellor Gerhard Schröder there was no longer any genuine justification for the UK rebate. President Chirac, fresh from his failure in the French referendum, went on the offensive in advance of the summit, associating the intransigence of the UK on the budget with France's general hostility to the "Anglo-Saxon" economic model.

The British Prime Minister upped the ante in return, telling the UK (Westminster) Parliament in advance of the June summit that "the UK rebate will remain and we will not negotiate it away. Period." The UK government was clear that when, in 2002, it had accepted a Franco-German deal maintaining farm spending for the 2007-13 period (see AR 2002, pp. 415-16), it had also been clear that the British rebate would be untouched. Stung by the comments of the French President, Blair thus demanded a reform of the common agricultural policy as a prime condition for any compromise. There were suggestions that his hands were being tied by the hostility of Chancellor Gordon Brown to any change in the rebate, and even that the UK Treasury had refused to co-operate with their Foreign Office colleagues during the June negotiations.

At the June meeting in Luxembourg, Prime Minister Jean-Claude Juncker presented new proposals in an effort to find a compromise. He suggested a total budgetary ceiling of €871 billion for the seven years, representing 1.07 per cent of EU GDP, compared with the original European Commission proposal of 1.24 per cent. The British rebate would be frozen at the average of 1997-2003, amounting to €4.3 billion as compared with the 2005 figure of €5 billion.

The UK government and others rejected this formula and—to nobody's surprise—the incoming UK presidency inherited the issue on 1 July, chairing the search for a compromise while also being the major protagonist in the dispute. Its starting position was a budget ceiling of 1.03 per cent of GDP, while its stance on the rebate would have meant a significant cut in the funds available for the new accession countries of Eastern Europe. As the strongest advocate of EU enlargement to embrace the countries of the old Communist bloc, this put the British Prime Minister in an embarrassing position.

During the autumn and early winter the British presidency kept its counsel, giving no indication of where it would be willing to move, but continuing to stress that the common agricultural policy would require fundamental reform. The defeat of Gerhard Schröder in the September elections in Germany and the installation of Angela Merkel as Chancellor introduced some change in the chemistry among EU leaders (see pp. 35-39). She had said in June that while the British would have to soften their position, others would also have to show flexibility. This had led the then Chancellor Schröder to accuse her of undermining Germany's negotiating position.

Expectations were low in the run-up to the December European Council meeting. In an unprecedented alliance, the Foreign Ministers of France and Poland published a joint letter to the *Financial Times* on 16 December, in which they wrote that that the UK's compromise proposals were unacceptable. They would make victims of poor member states and could not become the basis of an agreement. "The UK has been a champion of enlargement. We trust it will also be willing to cover the costs it presents", they wrote.

The tactic of the British presidency was to work out an interlocking pattern of concessions to be put to EU leaders when they met in Brussels on 16-17 December. Intensive bilateral and trilateral meetings were held to seek a compromise, culminating in a meeting between Blair, Chirac, and the new German Chancellor Merkel, to be joined later by Luxembourg's Juncker and Austria's Prime Minister Wolfgang Schüssel. Germany's new leader was credited with making a major contribution to the fashioning of the final agreement. "Sober, pragmatic and down-to-earth", in the words of Wolfgang Schüssel. She gave Germany's approval for a higher budget total, and persuaded Chirac of the need to make concessions. Romanian President Traian Băsescu was generous in his praise:

"she brokered the deal from start to finish. She was the first to break the deadlock with a proposal."

In the ultimate settlement UK Prime Minister Blair agreed to an overall budget ceiling of 1.045 per cent of GDP, amounting to €862 billion over the seven years. He offered a further €2.5 billion reduction in the British rebate, which would mean that the UK net contribution would rise by 63 per cent over the period. The key political element for the UK government in agreeing to a settlement was the review clause attached. This invited the European Commission to undertake a "full, wide-ranging review covering all aspects of EU spending, including the common agricultural policy, and of resources, including the UK rebate, to report in 2008-09". This commitment gave Blair the justification he needed to claim in the UK that the settlement was acceptable. Commission President Barroso stressed that the Commission would undertake the review "without restrictions or taboos". Unmentioned was the fact that the review would take place after the next presidential elections in France, and probably with a new British Prime Minister as well.

The budget settlement would mean that French net contributions would rise by 116 per cent over the seven years. The contributions of the Netherlands and Sweden would be somewhat reduced. The detailed budget was constructed in such a way that the new member countries would not be expected to contribute to the UK rebate.

In outlining the agreement to the European Parliament following the Brussels meeting, Blair underlined that he did believe in the need for a larger EU budget, but that this could only be achieved in the context of a reformed budget structure. The European Parliament would now have to decide whether to demand fundamental changes to the negotiated settlement, but this debate was reserved for 2006.

ECONOMIC REFORM. A summit in March agreed a package of measures to re-launch the Lisbon strategy, a programme of economic reform which had been agreed in 2000 to make the European economy a world leader (see AR 2000, p. 404), but which had thereafter failed to produce tangible results. Europe's leaders committed themselves to maintain a target of 3 per cent of domestic GDP for research and development, to introduce tax incentives for private investment in innovation, and to create a European research council to support cutting-edge and basic research, although a proposal to establish a European technology institute was "noted" but not launched. The summit decisions contained the customary shopping list of sometimes contradictory ambitions, calling for a reduction in regulatory administrative burdens and red tape for business, while asking business to "develop its sense of social responsibility". There was emphasis on the need to raise employment rates and extend working life with measures to reconcile working and family life. It was agreed that member states should draw up their own national reform programmes to make a more practical contribution to growth and employment.

In the wake of the disappointments of the referendums and the impasse over the EU budget, the UK presidency was charged with trying to breathe new life into the European project. Prime Minister Blair issued the invitation for an informal meeting of heads of government, to be held at Hampton Court on 27 October (see p. 22). His invitation said the purpose of the meeting was "to consider together the strategic issues facing Europe in the years ahead . . . to uphold the European ideals in which we believe, in the modern world . . . to demonstrate to our citizens that we are addressing the issues and challenges they really care about". In virtually his last appearance as German Chancellor, Gerhard Schröder was scathing about the British approach at Hampton Court. "We are standing before a fundamental debate in Europe", he said. "Should markets and calls for ever-greater liberalisation be the final measure for political action? . . . It boils down to which direction Europe should take."

In spite of the Chancellor's sceptical approach, the Hampton Court meeting did appear to remove some of the bitter divisions over the nature of Europe—polarised between the Franco-German model and the more liberal British-Irish model—and identify some areas for positive action. The European Commission presented a document on European values in the globalised world, which outlined specific areas of concern such as increased research and development, reform of the university system in Europe, the demographic challenge, growing dependence on energy imports, and immigration. "We are moving from analysis to action", Commission President Barroso said after the meeting. The commitment to the development of European energy policy and investment in a European energy grid was particularly striking.

EUROPEAN MONETARY UNION. The budgetary disciplines set out under the Stability and Growth Pact, which were intended to be the bedrock of monetary union, continued to lose authority as the big member countries of the eurozone continued to ignore the rules and sought to water down the conditions under which participating countries could be penalised for exceeding the 3 per cent limit on public debt.

Finance Ministers met to negotiate reforms to the pact in February, but were subject to serious lobbying from certain Prime Ministers. German Chancellor Schröder, for instance, in a *Financial Times* article, demanded a return to "national sovereignty", provoking the Dutch Finance Minister Gerrit Zalm to warn against such interference.

At the March European Council meeting there was agreement on measures to "improve the implementation" of the Stability and Growth Pact. The Council agreed that a "rules-based system is the best guarantee for commitments to be enforced", but said that "an enriched common framework with a stronger emphasis on the economic rationale of its rules" would better allow for differences between member states. A key passage of the new undertakings allowed for greater flexibility and "room for budgetary manoeuvre". The impact of an ageing population—with its far-reaching implications for pension provision—was a pervasive argument in favour of this.

France and Germany remained committed to reducing their budget deficits. Italy was a different case. In April the Italian government was warned that the Commission would start formal action under the revised Pact in light of the escalation in its national deficit, which was forecast by the Commission to be 3.6 per cent of GDP in 2005 and 4.6 per cent in 2006. The Italian position was further weakened by the refusal of Eurostat—the institution charged with overseeing national budget statistics under economic and monetary union (EMU)—to certify Italy's budget data from 2003 and 2004, which it regarded as seriously understated (see p. 43). The results of the referendums on the European treaty in May and June introduced further political uncertainty. The euro fell to an eight-month low against the US dollar. It was all the more important to show that discipline still applied; in June, Monetary Affairs Commissioner Joaquín Almunia attacked Italy's profligacy. He accused the government of disguising its actual deficits through faulty statistics and predicted excessive deficits for 2005 and 2006. He also noted that Italy's public debt was 106 per cent of GDP compared with an EMU target of 60 per cent. To add to market uncertainty, Italian Welfare Minister Roberto Maroni proposed that his country should temporarily quit the eurozone, to which Commissioner Almunia responded that the euro was like an old-fashioned marriage, with no provision for divorce.

On the evening of 6 June, the twelve Finance Ministers from the euro-currency countries met over dinner in Luxembourg to discuss the crisis. The European Commission determined that Italy should reduce its deficit below 3 per cent by 2007. Portugal was also instructed to deal with its deficit, estimated at above 6 per cent of GDP (see p. 65). Pressure mounted on the European Central Bank to reduce interest rates in the light of poor economic growth in some member states, but the ECB resisted and kept rates unchanged at 2 per cent until 1 December, when a rise of one-quarter of 1 per cent was decided.

EXTERNAL RELATIONS. The electoral success of President Viktor Yushchenko in December 2004 (see AR 2004, pp. 113-15) opened the way for a new relationship between the EU and Ukraine. Commissioner for External Relations Benita Ferrero-Waldner attended Yushchenko's inauguration in January together with Javier Solana, the EU's foreign policy representative, and on 21 February the Ukrainian leader visited Brussels to plead the case for closer ties and agreement that his country could plan negotiations for EU membership. The EU was not willing to go so far, but did sign a three-year action plan, agreeing to some visa relaxation and efforts to give Ukraine market economy status, while setting out the main areas for reform which the EU would require. The European Commission gave its backing to Ukraine's bid to join the World Trade Organisation (WTO).

A high priority of the UK presidency was to fulfil the commitment made twelve months earlier to begin negotiations with Turkey for EU membership. The meeting of Foreign Ministers in Luxembourg on 3-4 October was the key date. Austria was facing fierce popular opposition to Turkey's membership and continued, until late on the first day, to refuse to give its consent, arguing that some form of favoured nation status should be offered instead, an option which the Turkish government consistently refused. Austria was also pressing for the opening of membership negotiations with Croatia, frozen because of that country's failure to co-operate in the hunt for alleged war criminals. Late in the evening Carla del Ponte, the chief prosecutor at the UN's International Criminal Tribunal for the Former Yugoslavia (ICTY), declared Croatia "in full co-operation" with the Tribunal. This meant that the Croatian application could go ahead, clearing the way for Austrian agreement to begin talks with Turkey (see pp. 72; 95). Abdullah Gul, Turkey's Foreign Minister, flew into Luxembourg to join his EU colleagues on the evening of 3 October. "This is an historic moment", he said. "Turkey is stepping into a new era."

The chill in relations between the USA and several European countries, including France and Germany, showed remarkably rapid warming in the first weeks of the new year, following the inauguration of US President George W. Bush for his second term. Decisions had clearly been taken in Washington DC that it was time to end the stand-off and try to establish stronger personal and working relationships. A feature of the new approach was the attention given by the USA to the EU and its institutions, as well as to individual governments. Early in February, US Secretary of State Condoleezza Rice visited Brussels to meet the European Commission and the Council in order to prepare for the President's visit later in the month. A meeting with UK Prime Minister Blair and a dinner with France's President Chirac were early appointments in Bush's Brussels visit. There were visits to the headquarters of NATO and the European institutions, and the visit concluded with a press conference flanked by Luxembourg Prime Minister Juncker and Commission President Barroso before the US President flew to Mainz for a meeting with the German Chancellor. "Europe and America have reconnected", was the comment of Barroso.

Transatlantic relations were relatively calm for most of the year following the Bush visit, although contentious trade issues continued to arise, including the question of subsidies to the aircraft manufacturer Airbus and the announced intention of the EU to allow exports of military equipment to China. The US refusal to join the Kyoto process on climate change remained a divisive issue. There was some souring of relations over the alleged "rendition" of terrorist suspects and rumours of the existence of secret detention camps across Europe. In December leaders of the European Parliament decided to launch an investigation, despite a statement by Condoleezza Rice, made just before travelling to Berlin and Brussels, that nothing had been done outside the knowledge of European governments and denying that the USA condoned the use of torture (see p. 121).

TRADE NEGOTIATIONS. Despite sending four ministers to a specially convened Foreign Ministers meeting in October, France failed to persuade EU ministers to withdraw the negotiating mandate of EU Trade Commissioner Peter Mandelson for the crucial December meeting of the Doha WTO round in Hong Kong. The German government supported Mandelson. The mandate gave the Commissioner scope to negotiate on agricultural matters within the limits of the reforms of the common agricultural policy. The Hong Kong meeting ended with a whimper, but the EU did commit itself to the elimination of export subsidies on agricultural goods by 2013, three years later than the USA had demanded (see p. 357). EU Commissioners Mandelson and Fischer Boel called the agreement "a genuine advance for the agriculture negotiations and for the development goals of the Doha round".

The looming shadow of world trade talks led to a partial reform of the subsidies paid to European sugar producers. Ministers agreed in November to a 36 per cent cut in the guaranteed price of sugar over four years—twice the time originally proposed by the Commission—and accompanied by substantial direct subsidies to soften the blow to producers.

EUROPEAN ORGANISATIONS

THE COUNCIL OF EUROPE

DATE OF FOUNDATION: 1949   HEADQUARTERS: Strasbourg, France
OBJECTIVES: To strengthen pluralist democracy, the rule of law and the maintenance of human rights
    in Europe and to further political, social and cultural co-operation between member states
MEMBERSHIP(END-'05): Albania, Andorra, Armenia, Austria, Azerbaijan, Belgium, Bosnia &
    Herzegovina, Bulgaria, Croatia, Cyprus, Czech Republic, Denmark, Estonia, Finland, France,
    Georgia, Germany, Greece, Hungary, Iceland, Ireland, Italy, Latvia, Liechtenstein, Lithuania,
    Luxembourg, Macedonia, Malta, Moldova, Monaco, Netherlands, Norway, Poland, Portugal,
    Romania, Russia, San Marino, Serbia & Montenegro, Slovakia, Slovenia, Spain, Sweden,
    Switzerland, Turkey, Ukraine, UK (total 46)
SECRETARY GENERAL: Terry Davis (UK)

THE leaders of the member countries of the Council of Europe met in Warsaw, the capital of Poland, on 16-17 May for a rare summit. Three subjects dominated the agenda: the legal framework for dealing with terrorism; the problem of people-trafficking; and the relationship between the Strasbourg institution with its forty-six member countries and the newly enlarged European Union with twenty-five members, all of them in the Council of Europe. An action plan was approved in Warsaw which included a commitment to sustain the European Court of Human Rights, condemned terrorism, and undertook to combat corruption and organised crime. Three conventions were opened for signature: against traffic in human beings; on the prevention of terrorism; and on laundering, search, seizure, and confiscation of the proceeds of crime. Peter Hammarberg, formerly Secretary General of the human rights organisation, Amnesty International, was appointed human rights commissioner.

There was a growing feeling that the Council of Europe was losing ground to the EU in areas which were formerly its own preserve, raising long-term questions about its future. The Warsaw summit, therefore, called on the Council of Europe to strengthen its relations with the EU and appointed Luxembourg's Prime Minister Jean-Claude Juncker to prepare a political report on the issue to be delivered in 2006. Symbolic of the relationship between the two European organisations was the joint ceremony held in November to celebrate the 50th anniversary of the European flag—twelve gold stars on a blue background—a symbol of European unity first flown by the Council of Europe and formally adopted by the EU in 1985.

The need to protect civil liberties in the face of terrorist threats was an abiding theme of the year. In the words of the Council of Europe Secretary General, Terry

Davis, "We cannot allow our societies to find themselves under attack at the same time not only from terrorists but also from governments, however well motivated, restricting freedom and civil liberties for the sake of security."

Detention by the USA of so-called "enemy combatants" at the US military detention centre at Guantánamo Bay, Cuba, provoked a strong reaction in the Parliamentary Assembly of the Council of Europe, which adopted a resolution in April calling on the US government to cease torturing and maltreating detainees and challenging the administration either to try them or release them. This issue took on new force as reports multiplied of the alleged "rendition" of prisoners by the CIA (the US Central Intelligence Agency) to camps in Europe and Asia (see pp. 121; 418). On 7 November the legal affairs committee appointed its chairman, Dick Marty (Switzerland), as rapporteur to examine the allegations. Article 52 of the European Convention on Human Rights was invoked, authorising the Council formally to request information from member countries as part of a broader enquiry into reports of rendition and secret camps.

The Council entered other sensitive territory in observing elections in Chechnya, while its Venice commission of eminent lawyers (the Commission for Democracy through Law) was asked to give an opinion on the conditions under which part of a country could seek its own independence, with particular reference to Montenegro and its relationship with Serbia (see pp. 98-99).

ORGANIZATION FOR SECURITY AND CO-OPERATION IN EUROPE (OSCE)

DATE OF FOUNDATION: 1975   HEADQUARTERS: Vienna, Austria
OBJECTIVES: To promote security and co-operation among member states, particularly in respect of the resolution of internal and external conflicts
MEMBERSHIP(END-'05): Albania, Andorra, Armenia, Austria, Azerbaijan, Belarus, Belgium, Bosnia & Herzegovina, Bulgaria, Canada, Croatia, Cyprus, Czech Republic, Denmark, Estonia, Finland, France, Georgia, Germany, Greece, Holy See (Vatican), Hungary, Iceland, Ireland, Italy, Kazakhstan, Kyrgyzstan, Latvia, Liechtenstein, Lithuania, Luxembourg, Macedonia, Malta, Moldova, Monaco, Netherlands, Norway, Poland, Portugal, Romania, Russian Federation, San Marino, Serbia & Montenegro, Slovakia, Slovenia, Spain, Sweden, Switzerland, Tajikistan, Turkey, Turkmenistan, Ukraine, UK, USA, Uzbekistan (total 55)
CHAIRMAN-IN-OFFICE (2005): Dimitrij Rupel (Slovenia)

THE Slovenian Foreign Minister, Dimitrij Rupel, the Chairman-in-Office, opened his year's term with a powerful call for the "revitalisation, reform and rebalancing" of the Organisation, responding to the criticism by Russia that it had favoured the interests of Western members and disadvantaged those of others (see AR 2004, pp. 400-01). Russia had particularly perceived OSCE criticism of elections in Georgia (2003) and Ukraine (2004) as contributing to public protests which had brought about changes of government deleterious to Russia's relations with those states. Consequentially, Russia blocked agreement on the Organisation's budget, complaining that it bore an inequitable share of contributions. The impasse was broken by an informal agreement reached in

Moscow in April, whereby reforms would be elaborated and members' contributions to budgets in 2007 would be kept in the 2004 proportions.

The review was conducted by a panel of eminent persons, chaired by Knut Vollbeaek, a former Norwegian Foreign Minister and OSCE Chairman. His report in June—*Common Purpose: Towards a More Effective OSCE*—comprised more than seventy recommendations. These included strengthening the role of the Secretary General without weakening that of the rotating Chairman, who should focus on creating consensus and the political handling of urgent crises. A new Secretary General, Marc Perrin de Brichambaud, who had been director for strategic affairs at the French Foreign Ministry since 1998, took office in the same month for a three-year term; his predecessor, Jan Kubis of Slovenia, had served two such terms.

At a ceremony commemorating the thirty years since the Helsinki Final Act (the Final Act of the Conference on Security and Co-operation in Europe of 1 August 1975: see AR 1975, p. 319; for text see pp. 474-79), Rupel said that "the CSCE/Helsinki process was a key element in ending the Cold War and making Europe safer and more united". He looked forward to the OSCE's becoming "a fully-fledged international organisation with member states rather than participating states and with a legal personality". Such institutional strengthening was an objective of an agreement signed with the Council of Europe during the latter's Warsaw summit in May (see p. 376). The two bodies pledged to co-operate, as Rupel observed, "in the protection of persons belonging to national minorities, combating trafficking in human beings, and in the fight against terrorism". Another agreement between the two agencies (17 November) underwrote their joint efforts to foster compliance with international standards by local governments in south-east Europe. A further stage in inter-agency collaboration was marked at the session of the OSCE's permanent council (Vienna, 3 November) addressed by NATO's Secretary General, Jaap de Hoop Scheffer.

By the end of his year in office (at a ministerial council in Ljubljana, Slovenia, on 5-6 December), Rupel could point to twenty important decisions. These included, notably, moves towards the resolution of conflicts in the southern Caucasus, specifically in Georgia and Nagorno-Karabakh. However, the anticipated progress on Kosovo had not been achieved, and Rupel perceived "back-pedalling on reforms in Uzbekistan". Specifically, he requested monitoring by the OSCE's Office for Democratic Institutions and Human Rights (ODIHR) of the closed-court trials arising from the violence in Andijan in May (see pp. 267-68). Rupel was, however, optimistic for a resolution of disputes over the status of Kosovo and the Transdniester region in Moldova, and determined that the OSCE adapt to changes in the nature of conflict, notably in its counter-terrorism activities. That the latter should be conducted with due regard to protecting civil liberties was the topic of a joint declaration in December by special rapporteurs of the OSCE, the UN, and the Organisation of American States on freedom of expression on the Internet.

The annual ministerial council failed to agree a resolution approving the operations of the ODIHR in monitoring elections, once again because of Russia's complaints of pro-Western bias. Russia cited as evidence the report on Kazakhstan's presidential election in December, the shortcomings of which included campaigning restrictions and outsiders' interference at polling stations (see p. 269). Other elections monitored included presidential elections in Kyrgyzstan in June ("tangible progress. . . though not without flaws"), and Romania in December ("potential multiple voting addressed"). Legislative elections were also monitored in Tajikistan in February ("widespread irregularities"); Moldova in March ("generally complied with OSCE standards [but] unequal campaign conditions and constrained media coverage"); Kyrgyzstan in February and April ("undermined by vote-buying, de-registration of candidates, interference with media"); Bulgaria in June ("confirms credible progress"); Albania in July ("complied only partially with international commitments"); and Azerbaijan in November ("progress in the pre-election period was undermined by deficiencies in the count"). Missions were also sent to monitor local elections in Macedonia in March and April ("well-conducted generally [but] ballot-box stuffing . . . intimidation of voters and election-board members"); Moldova in July ("calm, but not without shortcomings"); Albania in October ("improvements . . . and . . shortcomings"); and Azerbaijan in December ("fell short of a number of international standards").

EUROPEAN BANK FOR RECONSTRUCTION AND DEVELOPMENT (EBRD)

DATE OF FOUNDATION: 1991 HEADQUARTERS: London, UK
OBJECTIVES: To promote the economic reconstruction of former Communist-ruled countries on the basis of the free-market system and pluralism
MEMBERSHIP(END-'05): Albania, Armenia, Australia, Austria, Azerbaijan, Belarus, Belgium, Bosnia-Herzegovina, Bulgaria, Canada, Croatia, Cyprus, Czech Republic, Denmark, Egypt, Estonia, European Investment Bank, European Union, Finland, France, Georgia, Germany, Greece, Hungary, Iceland, Ireland, Israel, Italy, Japan, Kazakhstan, Kyrgyzstan, South Korea, Latvia, Liechtenstein, Lithuania, Luxembourg, Macedonia, Malta, Mexico, Moldova, Mongolia, Morocco, Netherlands, New Zealand, Norway, Poland, Portugal, Romania, Russia, Serbia & Montenegro, Slovakia, Slovenia, Spain, Sweden, Switzerland, Tajikistan, Turkey, Turkmenistan, Ukraine, UK, USA, Uzbekistan (total 62)
PRESIDENT: Jean Lemierre (France)

IT was a measure of the EBRD's "quiet diplomacy" that its 4,000th trade facilitation transaction was effected in August by the issue of a US$391,000 letter of credit by Ineximbank of Kyrgyzstan to Russia's Vneshtorgbank for the import of KAMAZ lorries. The EBRD's trade facilitation programme (TFP) freed banks' working capital by building track records of participating banks and guaranteeing their trade-finance instruments. It was an important contributor to the EBRD's initiative for early transition countries (ETC), launched in 2004 for its "seven neediest members" (see AR 2004, p. 402). Eleven of the high-income member-states joined ETC as donors, and each of the seven recipient states had projects funded by the initiative. To emphasise the initiative's significance in the EBRD's strategy, the Bank's President, Jean Lemierre, himself joined the Georgian investment council, which had been established in March to promote private-sector development and investment in Georgia and which was expected to become self-financing in eighteen months.

High priority was accorded to lending to small and medium enterprises (SMEs) and to development schemes in rural areas. The Bank's medium-sized co-financing facility shared with local banks the risks of lending, and its operation was exemplified by a US$3 million co-financing facility provided to the Armenian Economy Development Bank, Arcomeconombank, in which it had had a stake since December 2004. Correspondingly, the Bank's Russia small business fund had advanced US$1.97 billion to more than 230,000 borrowers since inception in 1994. In April a majority of shares in KMB, a bank which had played a crucial role in expanding the fund, was taken over by Italy's Banca Intesa, thereby injecting new capital into Russia's leading small-business bank, with the largest regional network of any foreign-owned bank.

The EBRD's business advisory services and its turnaround management programme used more than €120 million of donor funding for 4,000 enterprises in twenty-seven of the Bank's countries. SMEs were not the only recipient, for the Bank supported mortgage lending where, as in Kazakhstan, long-term funding was not readily available: it was to lend US$10 million over ten years to BTA Ipoteka, with half earmarked for mortgages elsewhere than the major cities of Almaty and Astana. Lemierre underscored the importance of this sector by signing two innovative microfinance deals in Tajikistan in June, and bringing that country into the TFP.

New country strategies were formulated for Armenia ("partial isolation will continue to impede economic development"); Azerbaijan ("progress . . . has been slow and uneven and many challenges remain"); Bosnia & Herzegovina; Croatia ("despite strong GDP growth . . . much remains to be done"); the Czech Republic ("enhance the competitiveness of the economy"); Latvia ("broadly favourable, but rising inflation"); Moldova ("prosperity will depend on renewed efforts to implement structural reform"); Romania; Tajikistan ("macroeconomic conditions have improved"); Ukraine ("taking important steps towards integrating into the European and world economy"); and Uzbekistan ("prospects for quick political liberalisation remain remote").

The annual meeting and business forum (Belgrade, Serbia, 22-23 May) attracted 3,000 participants, with opening statements by Lemierre and UK Prime Minister, Tony Blair. Steven Kaempfer, vice-president, finance, reported a significant surpassing of operational and financial targets but warned that the policy of financing more projects in poorer countries would "almost certainly entail greater risk". When subsequently nine-months results were published, new commitments in 2005 were €2.02 billion, compared with €2.27 billion in the same period of 2004, reflecting a trend towards more and smaller projects. Good performance on the Bank's equity portfolio was reflected in a rise in profit, after provisions, to €822 million, against €267 million the previous year. The meeting had been preceded by more regional seminars: in Tirana, Albania, on energy in February; and in Skopje, Macedonia, on private-sector financing in March.

Personnel changes included the resignation of Willem Buiter as the Bank's chief economist, to return to the London School of Economics. He was replaced by Erik Berglof, director of the Stockholm Institute of Transition Economics. The Bank conceded most of the staff council's demands in a dispute over pensions, at an annual additional cost of €3.9 million, under 2 per cent of the operating budget.

OTHER EUROPEAN ORGANISATIONS

European Free Trade Association (EFTA)

DATE OF FOUNDATION: 1960   HEADQUARTERS: Geneva, Switzerland
OBJECTIVES: To eliminate barriers to non-agricultural trade between members
MEMBERSHIP (END-'05): Iceland, Liechtenstein, Norway, Switzerland (total 4)
SECRETARY GENERAL: William Rossier (Switzerland)

Visegrad Group

DATE OF FOUNDATION: 1991   HEADQUARTERS: rotating
OBJECTIVES: Reducing trade barriers between members with a view to their eventual membership of the European Union
MEMBERSHIP (END-'05): Czech Republic, Hungary, Poland, Slovakia (total 4)
ROTATING PRESIDENCY: 2004-05: Poland; 2005-06: Hungary

Central European Initiative (CEI)

DATE OF FOUNDATION: 1992   HEADQUARTERS: rotating
OBJECTIVES: To promote the harmonisation of economic and other policies of member states
MEMBERSHIP (END-'05): Albania, Armenia, Belarus, Bosnia & Herzegovina, Bulgaria, Croatia, Czech Republic, Hungary, Italy, Macedonia, Moldova, Poland, Romania, Slovakia, Slovenia, Ukraine, Serbia and Montenegro (total 17)
DIRECTOR GENERAL: Harald Kreid (Austria)

IN the course of a busy year the EUROPEAN FREE TRADE AREA (EFTA) steadily worked towards broadening the range of countries with which it held trade agreements. Successful negotiations with South Korea led to the signing of an agreement in Hong Kong in December. An agreement was also concluded with the Southern Africa Customs Union and negotiations were opened with Thailand. EFTA and Indonesia embarked on a feasibility study of the prospects for formal negotiations. Agreement was reached with the USA on conformity assessments, certificates, and markings. Moves were made towards closer trade relations with Japan, China, and Russia. Bulgaria and Romania applied to become contracting parties to the European Economic Area agreement.

The year also brought membership for EFTA countries of the European Network and Information Security Agency and the European Railway Agency. A recurring preoccupation was to find ways of improving participation in EU advisory committees. Among issues the Council of Ministers addressed, and on which they attempted to influence EU policy, were the organisation of European air space and the open skies policy. It opposed proposals for additional charges or taxes on air travel and energetically pressed its views on the EU's approach to the World Trade Organisation (WTO) negotiations (see pp. 357; 375-76). Ministers also discussed the fight against terrorism and the reform process of the Organisation for Security and Co-operation in Europe (OSCE) (see p. 378). Finally, they embarked on a review of the organisation's own committee structure and financing.

The Prime Ministers of the four VISEGRAD countries met in June at Kazimierz Dolny in Poland. The meeting was held in the immediate wake of the London suicide bombings and the French and Dutch referendums on the EU constitution (see pp. 14-18; 40; 48). While making an unqualified condemnation of the bombings, the meeting's main concern lay with the implications of the twin rejection of the EU treaty. While considering that the reasons lay more with extraneous factors than with any deficiencies in the treaty itself, they acknowledged this as a "very serious challenge" to the EU, one that called for the European dream to be "rediscovered and revitalised". It was the responsibility of the leaders of the EU to provide Europe's citizens with a positive vision. And the group endorsed the vain hope that the ratification process should proceed. It also reiterated its support for further EU enlargement.

The group welcomed the commitment of the new government of Ukraine to reform and closer relations with the EU. Ministers confirmed their commitment to the EU-Ukraine action plan and lent support to measures facilitating Ukraine's accession to the WTO and to negotiations for a free trade agreement between the EU and Ukraine (see p. 374).

Meeting in Budapest at the opening of the Hungarian presidency in July, Foreign Ministers addressed the presidency's priorities: bringing Visegrad co-operation closer to the people, strengthening the Group's cohesion, and promoting modernisation. Underlying this was a desire to increase members' influence on EU policy. A particular concern was to win early and concrete results on the financial framework for 2007-13 (see pp. 370-72). Now tacitly accepting that early progress on a European constitution was unlikely, Visegrad ministers again insisted that further enlargement was a key factor in achieving a stable, secure and prosperous Europe.

The group extensively explored possible fields of co-operation with the Benelux countries, including a range of joint activities. In particular the V4 countries, as they termed themselves, hoped to draw on the Benelux experience in such fields as the Schengen agreement, implementation of EU regulations, structural funds, spatial planning, environmental policy, and labour market issues.

The CENTRAL EUROPEAN INITIATIVE claimed to be the oldest and largest of the European sub-regional groups. Under the presidency of Slovakia and, subsequently, Albania, 2005 was hailed as a record year for CEI activity. Much of this was detailed and technical, building up to the annual summit economic forum in the Slovak capital, Bratislava, in November. The conference focused on the reforms needed to become competitive, with particular reference to improving the business environment and the development of telecommunications and transport infrastructures. Also at Bratislava, the relatively little known Parliamentary Assembly concentrated on seeking ways in which the CEI's parliamentary dimension might be strengthened.

ARAB, AFRICAN, ASIA-PACIFIC, AND AMERICAN ORGANISATIONS

ARAB ORGANISATIONS

League of Arab States

DATE OF FOUNDATION: 1945   HEADQUARTERS: Cairo, Egypt
OBJECTIVES: To co-ordinate political, economic, social and cultural co-operation between member states and to mediate in disputes between them
MEMBERSHIP (END-'05): Algeria, Bahrain, Comoros, Djibouti, Egypt, Iraq, Jordan, Kuwait, Lebanon, Libya, Mauritania, Morocco, Oman, Palestine, Qatar, Saudi Arabia, Somalia, Sudan, Syria, Tunisia, United Arab Emirates, Yemen (total 22)
SECRETARY GENERAL: Amre Moussa (Egypt)

Gulf Co-operation Council (GCC)

DATE OF FOUNDATION: 1981   HEADQUARTERS: Riyadh, Saudi Arabia
OBJECTIVES: To promote co-operation between member states in all fields with a view to achieving unity
MEMBERSHIP (END-'05): Bahrain, Kuwait, Oman, Qatar, Saudi Arabia, United Arab Emirates (total 6)
SECRETARY GENERAL: Abdulrahman al-Attiya (Qatar)

Arab Maghreb Union (AMU)

DATE OF FOUNDATION: 1989   HEADQUARTERS: Casablanca, Morocco
OBJECTIVES: To strengthen "the bonds of brotherhood" between member states, particularly in the area of economic development
MEMBERSHIP (END-'05): Algeria, Libya, Mauritania, Morocco, Tunisia (total 5)
SECRETARY GENERAL: Habib Boulares (Tunisia)

The LEAGUE OF ARAB STATES (ARAB LEAGUE) held its seventeenth summit meeting in Algiers, the capital of Algeria, on 22-23 March. The summit took place against a backdrop of dramatic changes in the Middle East. In Iraq, despite the bloody insurgency against US-led occupying forces, efforts were underway to build democracy after elections in January (see pp. 184-90). In Lebanon, prompted by the assassination in February of former Prime Minister Rafik al-Hariri, thousands of people were demonstrating for greater democracy and the withdrawal of Syrian troops after three decades (see pp. 182-83). And on the Israeli-Palestinian issue, both sides had reached an uneasy truce as peace efforts intensified following the election of the moderate Mahmoud Abbas as the successor to Palestinian leader Yassir Arafat (see pp. 173-77). Yet despite these significant developments, and increasingly vocal calls for Arab leaders to assume responsibility for their peoples' expectations, the summit achieved little. Only thirteen of the twenty-two Arab League leaders attended and few resolutions were passed. Jordan's King Abdullah II, Lebanese President Emile Lahoud, and Saudi Arabia's then de facto ruler Crown Prince Abdullah ibn Abdul Aziz were among those absent.

The crisis in Lebanon was not mentioned in the summit's official communiqué, but support was given to Syria against "foreign intervention". In an address to the summit, UN Secretary-General Kofi Annan said that he was encouraged by a Syrian pledge to "comply fully" with UN Security Council resolutions demanding its withdrawal from Lebanon. Annan, who held talks with Syrian President Bashar al-Assad at the summit, said earlier that the latter had promised to draw up a precise timetable for withdrawal of all Syrian troops and intelligence agents during April. In his speech to the summit, Libya's leader Colonel Moamar Kadhafi defended Syria's role in Lebanon and launched an attack on the UN Security Council's double standards, calling it a "terrorist organisation". On the question of the Israeli-Palestinian peace process, Arab League Secretary General Amre Moussa said that "commitment should be only in return for commitment". Israel, Moussa said, "still imagines that rights will be forgotten . . . that the Arabs will normalise relations without any equivalent worth mentioning. It cannot happen."

The Arab League's interim parliament held its inaugural session in Cairo (the capital of Egypt) on 27 December. The eighty-eight-member body was made up of four delegates chosen from the legislatures or advisory councils of each Arab League member state. The interim parliament was to be based in Syria and would meet twice a year in order to draft the arrangements for a permanent Arab parliament by 2011. The interim parliament had no legislative powers and its inauguration provoked widespread scepticism, as analysts noted that many countries had sent deputies from un-elected bodies while others had excluded any opposition participation.

The creation of the Arab parliament was part of a package of institutional changes promoted by Secretary General Moussa as a way of modernising the sixty-year-old institution and improving its lacklustre image. Other recommendations from the Arab League, such as the establishment of a regional security council and court of justice, had not been endorsed by heads of state. The interim parliament elected Mohammad Jassim al-Saqr, a Kuwaiti liberal, as its Speaker.

The 26th summit meeting of the GULF CO-OPERATION COUNCIL (GCC) took place in Abu Dhabi, in the United Arab Emirates (UAE), on 18-19 December. The summit was named the "King Fahd summit" in honour of King Fahd ibn Abdul Aziz of Saudi Arabia who had died in August (for obituary see pp. 537-38). In a final communiqué, the GCC Supreme Council noted with "satisfaction" the efforts exerted and measures adopted by the member states to combat terrorism on both the regional and international levels. It welcomed the outcome of the international anti-terrorism conference hosted by Saudi Arabia in February. It was agreed to hold the 27th summit in Riyadh, the Saudi capital, in December 2006.

Abd al-Rahman Mohammed Shalgam, the Libyan Secretary for Foreign Liaison and International Co-operation, announced on 25 May that the seventh summit of the largely moribund ARAB MAGHREB UNION (AMU), scheduled to be held in Libya in late May, had been postponed for "objective reasons that convinced everybody". The sixth AMU summit had been held in Tunisia in 1994. The postponement came after King Mohammed VI of Morocco had announced that he would not attend because of Algeria's recent "surprising stances" over the issue of Western Sahara (see p. 210). Algeria supported the pro-independence Polisario Front.

The first ARAB-SOUTH AMERICA SUMMIT was held in Brasilia, the capital of Brazil, on 10-11 May and was attended by sixteen heads of state and government, high-level ministers from another eighteen countries, and officials from sub-regional blocs. The unprecedented summit was attended by twenty-two Arab delegations (Algeria, Bahrain, Comoros, Djibouti, Egypt, Iraq, Jordan, Kuwait, Lebanon, Libya, Mauritania, Morocco, Oman, the Palestine National Authority (PNA), Qatar, Saudi Arabia, Somalia, Sudan, Syria, Tunisia, the UAE, and Yemen); twelve South American delegations (Argentina, Bolivia, Brazil, Chile, Colombia, Ecuador, Guyana, Paraguay, Peru, Suriname, Uruguay, and Venezuela); and delegations from the Arab League, the GCC, Mercosur (the South American Common Market), and the Andean Community (CAN). The Brasilia declaration, issued at the end of the summit, expressed "deep concern" over unilateral sanctions imposed on Syria by the USA in May 2004 (see AR 2004, pp. 191-92), saying that these violated principles of international law. The declaration reaffirmed the need to reach "a just, durable and comprehensive peace in the Middle East on the basis of the principle of land for peace". It also called on the UK and Argentina to resume negotiations to reach "a peaceful, fair and lasting solution" to the sovereignty dispute over the Falklands (Malvinas) Islands. The declaration also contained sections on cultural and economic co-operation, international trade, and sustainable development. It was agreed that a meeting of Foreign Ministers would be held in Argentina in 2007 and that a second summit would take place in Morocco in 2008.

AFRICAN ORGANISATIONS AND CONFERENCES

African Union (AU)
DATE OF FOUNDATION: 2001　　HEADQUARTERS: Addis Ababa, Ethiopia
OBJECTIVES: To promote the unity, solidarity and co-operation of African states, to defend their
　　sovereignty, to promote democratic principles, human rights and substainable development
　　and to accelerate the political and socio-economic integration of the continent
MEMBERSHIP (END-'05): Algeria, Angola, Benin, Botswana, Burkina Faso, Burundi, Cameroon, Cape
　　Verde, Central African Republic, Chad, Comoros, Congo, Côte d'Ivoire, Democratic Republic
　　of Congo, Djibouti, Egypt, Equatorial Guinea, Eritrea, Ethiopia, Gabon, Gambia, Ghana,
　　Guinea, Guinea-Bissau, Kenya, Lesotho, Liberia, Libya, Madagascar, Malawi, Mali,
　　Mauritania, Mauritius, Mozambique, Namibia, Niger, Nigeria, Rwanda, Sahrawi, São Tomé &
　　Príncipe, Senegal, Seychelles, Sierra Leone, Somalia, South Africa, Sudan, Swaziland,
　　Tanzania, Togo, Tunisia, Uganda, Zambia, Zimbabwe (total 53)
CHAIRMAN: President Olusegun Obasanjo (Nigeria)

Economic Community of West African States (ECOWAS)
DATE OF FOUNDATION: 1975　　HEADQUARTERS: Abuja, Nigeria
OBJECTIVES: To seek the creation of an economic union of member states
MEMBERSHIP (END-'05): Benin, Burkina Faso, Cape Verde, Côte d'Ivoire, Gambia, Ghana, Guinea,
　　Guinea-Bissau, Liberia, Mali, Niger, Nigeria, Senegal, Sierra Leone, Togo (total 15)
SECRETARY GENERAL: Executive Secretary: Mohamed ibn Chambas (Ghana)

Southern African Development Community (SADC)
DATE OF FOUNDATION: 1992　　HEADQUARTERS: Gaboro, Botswana
OBJECTIVES: To work towards the creation of a regional common market
MEMBERSHIP (END-'05): Angola, Botswana, Democratic Republic of Congo, Lesotho, Madagascar,
　　Malawi, Mauritius, Mozambique, Namibia, South Africa, Swaziland, Tanzania, Zambia,
　　Zimbabwe (total 14)
EXECUTIVE SECRETARY: Tomaz Augusto Salomão (Mozambique)

MEETINGS of African heads of state under the umbrella of the AFRICAN UNION
(AU) became even more frequent in 2005. Because of the crisis in western
Sudan (Darfur) the AU moved its July summit from Khartoum, the Sudanese
capital, to the Libyan city of Sirte, and instead of the Sudanese President
becoming the new chairman of the AU, Nigeria's President Olusegun Obasanjo
remained in office for an extra six months until the next of what were becoming
biannual summits.

A special summit was held in Addis Ababa, Ethiopia, in August to discuss the
issue of African representation on an enlarged UN Security Council. Much time
and lobbying was spent on this before the UN meeting in September (see pp.
334-36), especially by the three countries thought to be in contention for a seat
on an enlarged council: Egypt, Nigeria, and South Africa. The AU insisted that
at least two African countries should sit on the Security Council, that the AU
should select which ones, and that the holders of the African seats should have
all the prerogatives and privileges of permanent membership, including the
power of veto. This latter precondition did not help the case for reform, and the
year ended without any progress on the issue. Similarly, the AU's efforts to
secure reform of other global multinational institutions, including the IMF and
the World Trade Organisation (WTO), got nowhere.

President Thabo Mbeki of South Africa agreed at the request of the AU chairman to mediate on behalf of the AU in the conflict resolution process in Côte d'Ivoire, after the ECONOMIC COMMUNITY OF WEST AFRICAN STATES (ECOWAS) had failed to end the civil war there. After visits by the main political leaders of Côte d'Ivoire to South Africa, and by Mbeki to Côte d'Ivoire, eventually an agreement was reached on a new Prime Minister (see pp. 231-32).

The AU sent a multinational peacekeeping force of 7,000 to Darfur, although the bulk of the cost of the operation was borne by international donors, and the USA in particular wanted the AU force in Darfur to be brought under UN control. The Sudanese government, however, would not agree to an armed UN presence on its soil. At the beginning of the year it was one of the lesser-known regional organisations under the AU, the Intergovernmental Authority on Development (IGAD), which had long been a mediator in the conflict between the Sudanese government and the southern rebel Sudan People's Liberation Movement (SPLM), that successfully brokered a peace deal for southern Sudan (see pp. 201-03).

While the AU had a policy of not recognising governments that came to power as a result of a coup, it waived this in the cases of Mauritania and the Central African Republic in 2005 because the new governments in those two countries were clearly better than their ousted predecessors (see pp. 229-30; 236).

All AU operations suffered from funding constraints, but the Pan African Parliament (PAP) was particularly badly hit. Funded almost entirely by its host country, South Africa, its third session took place in April, and a fourth in a new building at Midrand, between Johannesburg and Pretoria, in September. The PAP sent missions to Côte d'Ivoire and the Democratic Republic of Congo, but largely remained an expensive talking-shop.

The AU's most critical intervention was the voluntary African Peer Review Mechanism (APRM) set up under the New Partnership for Africa's Development (NEPAD). The aim was to show foreign and local investors that countries were committed to good governance, accountability, and investor-friendly economic policies. A panel of eminent persons appointed by the AU was charged with the implementation and oversight of the process; the chairperson was Adebayo Adedeji of Nigeria, and other members included Graca Machel of Mozambique and individuals from Senegal, Kenya, Algeria, Cameroon, and South Africa. Though more countries signed up for peer review during the course of the year, by the end of 2005 fewer than half of Africa's fifty-three states had put themselves forward, and those that had were not the ones which most needed investigation. The first peer review reports—on Ghana and Rwanda—were completed, but not yet published. In late 2005, South Africa was preparing a self-assessment as part of the review that would take place in 2006. After complaints from civil society organisations in South Africa that they had not been sufficiently consulted, ten of the fifteen places on the APRM governing council set up by the South African government were given to them. However, critics of the APRM maintained that there was not the capacity to carry out any major in-depth investigation and pointed out that there were no means to enforce any recommendations that came out of the APRM process.

The AU's credibility was severely tested over its failure to condemn the gross example of poor governance in Zimbabwe and the anti-democratic practices of the absolute monarchy of Swaziland. A member of the eleven-person African Commission on Human and People's Rights (ACHPR, an agency of the AU) was sent to Zimbabwe in July to investigate the controversial urban clean-up campaign there, "operation murambatsvina" (see pp. 252-53); another ACHPR member went to Mauritania after the coup there. Though the Zimbabwe opposition demanded that its government comply with the SOUTHERN AFRICAN DEVELOPMENT COMMUNITY (SADC) electoral guidelines, SADC did nothing to ensure that these were observed. At the end of 2005, the ACHPR did at last condemn Zimbabwean President Robert Mugabe's human rights record and found that the Zimbabwean government had violated the AU's charter, but it remained to be seen what impact the report would have; the one previous critical report from the Commission, in 2002, had been sidelined.

ASIA-PACIFIC ORGANISATIONS

Association of South-East Asian Nations (ASEAN)

DATE OF FOUNDATION: 1967   HEADQUARTERS: Jakarta, Indonesia
OBJECTIVES: To accelerate economic growth, social progress and cultural development in the region
MEMBERSHIP (END-'05): Brunei, Burma (Myanmar), Cambodia, Indonesia, Laos, Malaysia, Philippines, Singapore, Thailand, Vietnam (total 10)
SECRETARY GENERAL: Ong Keng Yong (Singapore)

Asia-Pacific Economic Co-operation (APEC)

DATE OF FOUNDATION: 1989   HEADQUARTERS: Singapore
OBJECTIVES: To promote market-oriented economic development and co-operation in the Pacific Rim countries
MEMBERSHIP (END-'05): Australia, Brunei, Canada, Chile, China, Hong Kong, Indonesia, Japan, South Korea, Malaysia, Mexico, New Zealand, Papua New Guinea, Peru, Philippines, Russia, Singapore, Taiwan, Thailand, USA, Vietnam (total 21)
EXECUTIVE DIRECTOR: Choi Seok Young (South Korea)

South Asian Association for Regional Co-operation (SAARC)

DATE OF FOUNDATION: 1985   HEADQUARTERS: Kathmandu, Nepal
OBJECTIVES: To promote collaboration and mutual assistance in the economic, social, cultural and technical fields
MEMBERSHIP (END-'05): Afghanistan, Bangladesh, Bhutan, India, Maldives, Nepal, Pakistan, Sri Lanka (total 8)
OBSERVER MEMBERS: China, Japan (total 2)
SECRETARY GENERAL: Q.A.M.A Rahim (Bangladesh)

Pacific Islands Forum (PIF)

DATE OF FOUNDATION: 1971 (as South Pacific Forum)   HEADQUARTERS: Suva, Fiji
OBJECTIVES: To enhance the economic and social well-being of the people of the Pacific, in support of the efforts of the members' governments
MEMBERSHIP (END-'05): Australia, Cook Islands, Fiji, Kiribati, Marshall Islands, Federated States of Micronesia, Nauru, New Zealand, Niue, Palau, Papua New Guinea, Samoa, Solomon Islands, Tonga, Tuvalu, Vanuatu (total 16)
SECRETARY GENERAL: Greg Urwin (Australia)

Pacific Community (PC)

DATE OF FOUNDATION: 1947 (as South Pacific Commission)   HEADQUARTERS: Noumea, New Caledonia
OBJECTIVES: To facilitate political and other co-operation between member states and territories
MEMBERSHIP (END-'05): American Samoa, Australia, Cook Islands, Fiji, France, French Polynesia, Guam, Kiribati, Marshall Islands, Federated States of Micronesia, Nauru, New Caledonia, New Zealand, Niue, Northern Mariana Islands, Palau, Papua New Guinea, Pitcairn Islands, Samoa, Solomon Islands, Tokelau, Tonga, Tuvalu, UK, USA, Vanuatu, Wallis & Futuna Islands (total 27)
DIRECTOR GENERAL: Jimmie Rodgers (Solomon Islands)

Asian Development Bank (ADB)

DATE OF FOUNDATION: 1966   HEADQUARTERS: Manila, Philippines
OBJECTIVES: To improve the welfare of the people in Asia and the Pacific, particularly the 1.9 billion who live on less than $2 a day
MEMBERSHIP (END-'05): REGIONAL MEMBERS: Afghanistan, Armenia, Australia, Azerbaijan, Bangladesh, Bhutan, Burma (Myanmar), Cambodia, China, Cook Islands, East Timor, Fiji, Hong Kong, India, Indonesia, Japan, Kazakhstan, Kiribati, Kyrgyzstan, Laos, Malaysia, Maldives, Marshall Islands, Federated States of Micronesia, Mongolia, Nauru, Nepal, New Zealand, Pakistan, Palau, Papua New Guinea, Philippines, Samoa, Singapore, Solomon Islands, South Korea, Sri Lanka, Taiwan, Tajikistan, Thailand, Tonga, Turkmenistan, Tuvalu, Uzbekistan, Vanuatu, Vietnam (total 46); NON REGIONAL MEMBERS: Austria, Belgium, Canada, Denmark, Finland, France, Germany, Italy, Luxembourg, the Netherlands, Norway, Portugal, Spain, Sweden, Switzerland, Turkey, UK, USA (total 18)
PRESIDENT: Haruhiko Kuroda (Japan)

THE eleventh summit meeting of the ASSOCIATION OF SOUTH-EAST ASIAN NATIONS (ASEAN) was held on 12-14 December in Kuala Lumpur, the capital of Malaysia, along with the related ASEAN+3 (China, Japan, and South Korea) and meetings with India and Russia. The most significant act of the summit was a call by other ASEAN leaders for Burma to release political prisoners and to show that it was making progress towards restoring democracy. Such explicit criticism indicated increasing impatience by other ASEAN members towards Burma's ruling military junta. At a meeting of ASEAN Foreign Ministers in Vientiane (the capital of Laos), on 26 July, Burma had announced that it would forgo its scheduled 2006 chairmanship of ASEAN and would instead focus on democratisation and national reconciliation. On the eve of the meeting, both the EU and the USA had threatened to boycott meetings chaired by Burma, but it was thought that discreet pressure from fellow ASEAN members Thailand, Malaysia, and the Philippines had prompted Burma's withdrawal (see pp. 289-90).

The first EAST ASIA SUMMIT (EAS) was held in Kuala Lumpur on 14 December on the margins of the eleventh ASEAN summit. In addition to the ten ASEAN members, the summit was attended by representatives from Australia, China, India, Japan, South Korea, and New Zealand. The EAS was intended as a forum for the discussion of "broad strategic, political and economic issues of common interest" and was planned as an annual event. However, China and some ASEAN countries were believed to be uneasy with the inclusion of India and the "Western" influence of Australia and New Zealand within the grouping. Apart from a general commitment to the promotion of peace, stability, and prosperity, the summit's closing statement also pledged co-operation in preventing an avian influenza epidemic (see p. 289).

A summit meeting of leaders of the ASIA-PACIFIC ECONOMIC CO-OPERATION (APEC) forum was held on 18-19 November in Pusan, South Korea. The meeting produced two closing statements. One specifically concerned free trade, and called for a concerted effort at the ministerial meeting of the World Trade Organisation in Hong Kong in mid-December, to revive the stagnating Doha round of talks on multilateral trade liberalisation, due for completion in 2006 (see pp. 356-57). Australia, Canada, and the USA wanted to include specific criticism of the EU for its reluctance to cut agricultural subsidies, but this was diluted by other participants to a general call for all WTO members to show more flexibility. The summit's general communiqué covered a wide range of themes, including avian influenza, terrorism, corruption, and closer economic co-operation.

Leaders of the SOUTH ASIAN ASSOCIATION FOR REGIONAL CO-OPERATION (SAARC) held their thirteenth summit meeting on 12-13 November in Dhaka, the capital of Bangladesh. Whilst some leaders expressed frustration at the association's lack of concrete achievement since its formation in 1985, analysts noted that improving relations between India and Pakistan gave grounds for hope that this might change. The meeting's closing declaration called for a "decade of implementation" of aims and principles. This included a determination to make the planned South Asia Free Trade Area (SAFTA) operational by 1 January 2006; directives to implement a SAARC action plan for poverty alleviation; the coming into force of an additional protocol to the SAARC convention on terrorism; and the adoption of Bangladesh's proposal for region-wide afforestation programmes. The summit decided to admit Afghanistan as the eighth SAARC member.

The 36th meeting of the PACIFIC ISLANDS FORUM (PIF) was held on 25-27 October in Port Moresby, the capital of Papua New Guinea, together with the retreat of Madang. The leaders endorsed the Kalibobo Road Map (KRM) for implementing the Pacific Plan regional co-operation accord which had been first agreed in 2004 (see AR 2004, p. 414). The KRM consisted of twenty-four initiatives under the four pillars of the plan. Under economic growth there were seven initiatives, including the expansion of trade in goods through the 1980 South Pacific regional trade and co-operation agreement (SPARTECA), the 2001 Pacific Island Countries trade agreement (PICTA), and the Pacific agreement on closer economic relations (PACER). Under sustainable development there were eight initiatives, largely concerning environmental protection and the harmonisation of health measures, including the implementation of a strategy to combat HIV/AIDS. There were five initiatives under good governance, such as the building of leadership codes, anti-corruption institutions, and judicial training. The four initiatives under security included the mitigation and management of natural disasters.

The fourth conference of the PACIFIC COMMUNITY (PC) was held in Koror, the capital of Palau, on 18 November. The conference appointed Jimmie Rodgers from the Solomon Islands as the new Director General in place of Lourdes Pangelinan.

At the conclusion on 6 May of the 38th annual meeting of the ASIAN DEVEL-OPMENT BANK (ADB) board of governors in Istanbul, Turkey, ADB President Haruhiko Kuroda confirmed the bank's commitment to institutional change and renewal. Kuroda said that the ADB was "firmly committed" to reducing poverty and achieving the UN's millennium development goals in the Asia and Pacific region.

AMERICAN AND CARIBBEAN ORGANISATIONS

Organisation of American States (OAS)

DATE OF FOUNDATION: 1951   HEADQUARTERS: Washington DC, USA
OBJECTIVES: To facilitate political, economic and other co-operation between member states and to defend their territorial integrity and independence
MEMBERSHIP (END-'05): Antigua & Barbuda, Argentina, Bahamas, Barbados, Belize, Bolivia, Brazil, Canada, Chile, Colombia, Costa Rica, Cuba (suspended), Dominica, Dominican Republic, Ecuador, El Salvador, Grenada, Guatemala, Guyana, Haiti, Honduras, Jamaica, Mexico, Nicaragua, Panama, Paraguay, Peru, St Kitts & Nevis, St Lucia, St Vincent & the Grenadines, Suriname, Trinidad & Tobago, United States of America, Uruguay, Venezuela (total 35)
SECRETARY GENERAL: José Miguel Insulza (Chile)

Rio Group

DATE OF FOUNDATION: 1987   HEADQUARTERS: rotating
OBJECTIVES: To provide a regional mechanism for joint political action
MEMBERSHIP (END-'05): Argentina, Bolivia, Brazil, Chile, Colombia, Costa Rica, Dominican Republic, Ecuador, El Salvador, Guatemala, Guyana, Honduras, Mexico, Nicaragua, Panama, Paraguay, Peru, Uruguay, Venezuela (total 19)

Association of Caribbean States (ACS)

DATE OF FOUNDATION: 1994   HEADQUARTERS: Port of Spain, Trinidad
OBJECTIVES: To foster economic, social and political co-operation with a view to building a distinctive bloc of Caribbean littoral states
MEMBERSHIP (END-'05): Caricom members plus Aruba, Colombia, Costa Rica, Cuba, Dominican Republic, El Salvador, France, Guatemala, Honduras, Mexico, Netherlands Antilles, Nicaragua, Panama, Venezuela; minus Montserrat (total 28)
SECRETARY GENERAL: Rubén Arturo Silié Valdez (Dominican Republic)

Southern Common Market (Mercosur)

DATE OF FOUNDATION: 1991   HEADQUARTERS: Montevideo, Uruguay
OBJECTIVES: To build a genuine common market between member states
MEMBERSHIP (END-'05): Argentina, Brazil, Paraguay, Uruguay (total 4)
ASSOCIATE MEMBERS: Chile, Bolivia, Peru, Venezuela (total 4)
SECRETARY GENERAL: Administrative Secretary: Santiago Gonzalez Cravino (Argentina)

Andean Community of Nations (Ancom/CAN)

DATE OF FOUNDATION: 1969   HEADQUARTERS: Lima, Peru
OBJECTIVES: To promote the economic development and integration of member states
MEMBERSHIP(END-'05): Bolivia, Colombia, Ecuador, Peru, Venezuela (total 5)
ASSOCIATE MEMBERS: Argentina, Brazil, Paraguay, Uruguay (total 4)
SECRETARY GENERAL: Allan Wagner Tizón (Peru)

Caribbean Community and Common Market (Caricom)

DATE OF FOUNDATION: 1973   HEADQUARTERS: Georgetown, Guyana
OBJECTIVES: To facilitate economic, political and other co-operation between member states and to
    operate certain regional services
MEMBERSHIP(END-'05): Antigua & Barbuda, Bahamas, Barbados, Belize, Dominica, Grenada,
    Guyana, Haiti (suspended), Jamaica, Montserrat, St Kitts & Nevis, St Lucia, St Vincent & the
    Grenadines, Suriname, Trinidad & Tobago (total 15)
ASSOCIATE MEMBERS: Anguilla, Bermuda, British Virgin Islands, Cayman Islands, Turks & Caicos
    Islands (total 5)
SECRETARY GENERAL: Edwin Carrington (Trinidad & Tobago)

Organisation of Eastern Caribbean States (OECS)

DATE OF FOUNDATION: 1981   HEADQUARTERS: Castries, St Lucia
OBJECTIVES: To co-ordinate the external, defence, trade and monetary policies of member states
MEMBERSHIP (END-'05): Anguilla, Antigua & Barbuda, British Virgin Islands, Dominica, Grenada,
    Montserrat, St Lucia, St Kitts & Nevis, St Vincent & the Grenadines (total 9)
DIRECTOR GENERAL: Len Ishmael

INTERNAL divisions within the ORGANISATION OF AMERICAN STATES (OAS) came to
the fore during the year over who should replace Miguel Rodríguez Echeverría as
Secretary General (see AR 2004, p. 416). Two candidates stood for election on
11 April: Luis Ernesto Derbez, Foreign Minister of Mexico, and José Miguel
Insulza, Interior Minister of Chile. A third candidate, Francisco Flores—a former
President of El Salvador, who had the support of the USA—withdrew prior to the
vote. When the election was held, both Derbez and Insulza received seventeen
votes and despite attempts to break the deadlock no resolution was possible. The
pattern of voting seemed to indicate a division between North and Central American states on the one hand (supporting Derbez) and the South American and
Caribbean states on the other (supporting Insulza). Because of the failure to
choose a new Secretary General in April, a re-run election was organised for 2
May. However, in a surprise move prior to the vote, Derbez withdrew his candidacy "in order to prevent a breakdown of hemispheric relations". This left Insulza
as the sole candidate for the post, and he was duly elected.

The nineteenth summit of the RIO GROUP was held on 25-26 August, but without the Presidents who were scheduled to attend. Rather the summit was downgraded to a meeting of Foreign Ministers and other officials. A spokesman for
the Argentinian Foreign Ministry, which hosted the gathering, denied that the
absence of heads of state indicated a lack of interest on the part of members.
Nevertheless, little of substance was achieved at the summit. Of more interest
were two meetings that the Rio Group held with Russia and the EU. On 17 February, counter-terrorism experts from the Rio Group and Russia met in Trinidad
& Tobago and discussed their respective experiences in dealing with terrorist
threats. They also agreed to strengthen their co-operation in this area. Subsequently, on 26-27 May, the twelfth ministerial meeting of the Rio Group and the
EU was held in Luxembourg. Issues discussed included the progress made in
deepening integration and co-operation between the two regions, the situation in
Haiti, and the fight against poverty.

The ASSOCIATION OF CARIBBEAN STATES (ACS) celebrated its tenth anniversary in 2005, and held its fourth summit of heads of state and/or government in Panama at the end of July. In the "declaration of Panama", which was released at the end of the summit, a number of rather bland commitments and observations were made. Among the more interesting were a call to strengthen co-operation with the EU, an appeal to the US government to end its embargo against Cuba, a pledge to take the necessary measures to ensure that the Caribbean sea was recognised by the UN as a special area of sustainable development, and a promise to support greater economic and trade co-operation amongst ACS member states.

At a meeting of SOUTHERN COMMON MARKET (MERCOSUR) states on 8-9 December in Uruguay it was agreed that Venezuela would become the fifth full member of the organisation. However, no time frame was given for the country's accession, and questions were raised in some quarters about Venezuela's likely adherence to Mercosur's principles of open trade, private sector-led integration, and democracy. Later in December, Mercosur announced that Bolivia would be invited to join the organisation as a full member.

On 7 July the ANDEAN COMMUNITY OF NATIONS (ANCOM/CAN) granted associate membership status to Argentina, Brazil, Paraguay, and Uruguay (the member countries of MERCOSUR). Andean Community Secretary General Allan Wagner Tizon welcomed the move and stated that it was "highly symbolic and a matter of the greatest importance for the convergence of the two subregional blocs". In other news, it was announced that the volume of trade between CAN members reached a record high in 2004.

A summit meeting of CARIBBEAN COMMUNITY AND COMMON MARKET (CARICOM) heads of government took place on 3-6 July in St Lucia, and reviewed the state of readiness of Caricom members to participate fully in the Caribbean single market and economy (CSME) by the end of December. Despite firm assurances that all Caricom members—with the exception of the Bahamas, Haiti, and Montserrat—would join on time, only six states had become full members of the CSME by the end of the year: Barbados, Belize, Guyana, Jamaica, Suriname, and Trinidad & Tobago. It was expected that countries belonging to the ORGANISATION OF EASTERN CARIBBEAN STATES would join the CSME by March 2006. Membership of the CSME allowed for the free movement of goods, services and skilled workers.
In other developments, the long-planned Caribbean Court of Justice (CCJ) was launched on 16 April in Trinidad & Tobago. The CCJ operated as a court to deal with matters arising from the CSME, and as a final court of appeal for civil and criminal cases, thereby replacing the London-based Privy Council. Its first case was held on 7 November. In early December, the second Cuba-Caricom summit was held, and produced a call for greater regional integration and closer co-operation. Earlier in the year, Caricom Foreign Ministers had recom-

mended that the region's relationship with Brazil be formalised. The continued international pressure against the region's sugar and banana industries reinforced Caricom's desire for stronger links within the hemisphere.

The 41st meeting of the Authority of the ORGANISATION OF EASTERN CARIBBEAN STATES (OECS) was held in June. At the gathering, a range of issues was discussed including membership of the CSME, and the need to establish a regional development fund to enable the small states of the OECS to liberalise their markets without undue harm. An agreement was subsequently reached in December. In other developments the OECS established its technical mission to the World Trade Organisation in late June, and in September the sub-region jointly participated in the Grand Pavois Boat Show in France to secure new business opportunities for its yachting sector.

XII THE INTERNATIONAL ECONOMY IN 2005

THE growth of the world economy slowed sharply in 2005, from just over 5 per cent in 2004 to around 4.3 per cent, but the general picture was one of resilient growth which was only marginally affected by rising prices for oil and other commodities and by an exceptional series of natural disasters including two hurricanes that caused extensive damage to the infrastructure, including oil and refinery installations, of the south-eastern seaboard of the USA.

The USA continued to be the main driver of the world economy, but the continued rapid development of China and India was an increasingly important influence, not least on other developing countries. The growth of the developing countries slowed somewhat, to around 5.6 per cent in 2005, still more than twice as much as the developed countries although for many of them it remained below what was required if they were to meet the UN's millennium development goals.

A major concern in 2005 was the continued rise in the price of crude oil which reached a peak of around US$70 per barrel following Hurricane Katrina at the end of August. It then fell back to around US$60 by the end of the year. The growth of demand for oil was much smaller than in 2004, but the medium-term outlook was for continued pressure on available capacities, which left the price very sensitive to disruptions of supply, actual or threatened. Non-fuel commodity prices also rose in 2005, but by much less than in 2004 (roughly 10 per cent against 20 per cent) and they tended to decelerate through the year. Whether measured in current US dollars or SDRs (special drawing rights), these prices were still below their levels of the early 1980s.

Accompanying the slowdown in output growth, the volume of world trade grew by just 7 per cent compared with 11 percent in 2004. The growth of import demand fell sharply in the USA and China, and despite the appreciation of the euro it also weakened in the eurozone. There was some partial offset from increased import demand by oil exporters, but producers in the Middle East were reckoned to be saving more of their increased oil revenues than after the oil shocks of the 1970s. The total value of world trade rose by about 13 per cent (20 per cent in 2004), mainly reflecting higher commodity prices since those for manufactures were more or less flat.

The higher oil prices of 2004-05 led to some acceleration in worldwide inflation rates but this was limited and there was little sign of second-round effects on wage growth and core inflation. The latter was partly due to the offsetting price weakness of manufactured goods subject to intense international competition, exchange rate appreciation in some cases, and more generally to well-anchored expectations that monetary policy would react to any acceleration in prices. A worry for policy makers, however, was whether this benign prospect would survive a continued steady rise in oil prices or a severe supply-side shock to oil supplies.

Two weak features of the world economy in 2005 were investment and employment. Despite high levels of corporate profits, stronger balance sheets, and historically low, long-term interest rates, non-residential fixed investment across the globe showed little dynamism. There was no general agreement as to the causes of this. The second feature—partly related to the first—was the persistently limited impact even of high rates of economic growth in creating new jobs and absorbing high levels of both unemployment and underemployment.

One of the most pressing concerns in 2005 was the continued deterioration in the global distribution of current account balances and the lack of any consensus among political leaders on how to ensure an orderly adjustment, or on whether co-ordination was even needed. The current account deficit of the USA increased to more than US$800 billion—over 6 per cent of its GDP—and this was matched by larger surpluses in Europe, East Asia, and the oil-exporting countries. The largest surplus was that of the oil producers (OPEC, Norway, and Russia) which together reached some US$400 billion and was about double that of East Asia. There was disagreement over the origin of the imbalances. Some analysts and policy makers, especially in the USA, argued that they reflected a global, structural imbalance between savings and investment propensities, partly driven by demographic factors, and that therefore there was no need to worry about the continued financing of the US deficit. Outside the USA, and including the major international economic institutions, the imbalances were largely seen as the result of one-sided growth in the US economy where household expenditure had persistently run ahead of disposable income, thanks to a boom (or bubble) in house prices that supported rising levels of household indebtedness. Since household indebtedness must have a limit, the fear was that when the US consumer stopped borrowing and increased savings the fall in demand would not be offset elsewhere, thus risking a global recession. Against this background, the warnings of the governments of Japan and of several members of the eurozone to their central banks against a hasty move to higher interest rates had obvious implications for the global adjustment process.

WESTERN EUROPE was again the slowest growing region in the world economy in 2005. Although GDP growth and business confidence were improving for much of the year, there was a very sharp showdown in the last quarter, especially in France and Germany. The net result was an annual increase of 1.6 per cent, against some 2.25 per cent in 2004. In the eurozone growth was even weaker, at 1.3 per cent. The dampening effect of higher oil prices played a role, but the continuing caution of households towards spending and the moderate rate of fixed investment were also important; the main support to output thus continued to come from exports. Outside the eurozone growth slowed sharply in the UK, from 3.2 per cent in 2004 to 1.8 per cent and thus the offset that it had provided to the weakness of the eurozone in the previous four years was greatly reduced (see pp. 23-26). Denmark and Sweden continued to grow faster than the west European average, with household consumption and investment in both countries responding to lower interest rates. In Norway the mainland economy was booming on the back of surging oil revenues and strong domestic demand.

The new EU members in CENTRAL EUROPE AND THE BALTIC REGION maintained their dynamism in 2005, GDP growth averaging more than 4 per cent. This was less than in 2004 but most of the slowdown was due to Poland. The Baltic states retained their sobriquet of the "tigers" of central Europe with growth rates of 7 to 9 per cent. Growth was generally driven by external demand. Better than expected improvements in fiscal deficits and low inflationary pressures allowed interest rates to be cut, a move that was also intended to check currency appreciation. Improvements in the labour markets were marginal: employment rose slightly and unemployment fell a little. Unemployment rates of 17-18 per cent in Slovakia and Poland were by far the highest in the EU, although in the other new members they were below the average for the eurozone.

The economies of SOUTH-EAST EUROPE (THE BALKANS) grew rapidly in 2005, on average by some 5 per cent. Bulgaria, Croatia, and Romania benefited from their status as candidates for accession to the EU; investor and consumer confidence rose; foreign direct investment flowed in, contributing to restructuring and the expansion of export capacities. Elsewhere, post-conflict reconstruction together with macroeconomic stabilisation underpinned expansion. Growth was largely driven by private consumption and fixed investment and although exports increased considerably, import growth was even stronger. This pattern led to increases in already large current account deficits, and although normal for rapidly growing, emerging economies it left them vulnerable to external shocks. Inflation rates continued to fall under the influence of tight macroeconomic policies and increased competition in domestic markets. Unemployment rates fell in the three EU candidate countries but in the rest of the region (except Romania), they remained in double digits.

The COMMONWEALTH OF INDEPENDENT STATES (CIS) remained one of the most dynamic regions of the world economy in 2005 but after two years of exceptionally strong growth there was a deceleration to just over 6 per cent. The aggregate was heavily influenced by the two largest economies in the region: Russia, where oil production was affected by bottlenecks, and Ukraine, where the slowdown was particularly marked (from 12 to 4 per cent) partly because of a large deterioration in exports, especially of steel. Most of the smaller countries continued to grow rapidly despite many of them being net oil importers. Macroeconomic policies were generally expansionary, partly reflecting the attempts of commodity exporters to prevent an excessive appreciation of real exchange rates. Inflation rates in 2005 averaged around 12 per cent, higher than in 2004 and above government targets. There was little improvement in the labour markets: growth was relatively concentrated in capital-intensive sectors and there still appeared to be high levels of labour hoarding by enterprises. The current account surplus of the CIS as a whole rose from US$63 billion in 2004 to about US$105 billion.

In EAST ASIA AND THE PACIFIC GDP growth slowed somewhat from 8.3 per cent in 2004 to just under 8 per cent in 2005. Excluding China, the deceleration was from 6 to 5 per cent. The Chinese economy continued to expand rapidly, GDP increasing by 9.6 per cent following 10 per cent growth in 2004. (In December the national economic census in China concluded that the economy was some 17 per cent larger than previously estimated, largely because of the systematic under-recording of private services. Consequently, annual growth rates from 1993 to 2004 were raised, on average by 0.5 percentage points). Domestic demand in China slowed considerably in 2005 following administrative controls on state-controlled investments, but the subsequent lifting of constraints on private invest-ment and selective tax cuts led to a recovery from the third quarter: imports accel-erated, export growth slowed, and the reduced contribution of net exports to growth suggested that the trade surplus (over US$100 billion for the year as a whole) would eventually start to level out.

Although the slowdown in China was relatively slight, it had—in combination with weaker global demand for electronic products—a major impact on the other economies in the region. The growth of China's imports from them was roughly half as much as in 2004. Higher oil prices led to large terms of trade losses for some of the oil importing countries, reducing GDP growth by 0.5 percentage points or more. Other negative factors included the slump in tourism following the December 2004 tsunami disaster (Hong Kong and Thailand especially) and the outbreaks of avian influenza. The latter were significant for countries such as Thailand, Vietnam, and the Philippines, where the poultry sector accounted for between 0.6 to 2 per cent of GDP.

Inflation picked up in the second half of the year but the acceleration was slight thanks in part to currency appreciation against the US dollar. Higher oil prices led to some reduction in the region's large current account surplus. Although this partly reflected the weakness of investment, the role played by over-investment in the 1997 financial crises deterred governments from boosting it. Low interest rates led to a boom in property prices and this—also with echoes of 1997—was another reason for tightening monetary policy. Among the other worries of gov-ernments at the end of 2005 were fears of more protectionism in the EU and the USA against clothing and textiles, the possibility of further increases in oil prices, the risk of outbreaks of avian influenza causing considerable loss of life and eco-nomic damage, and concern that a disorderly adjustment of the global imbalances could have major consequences for East Asian exports and growth.

After years of deflation and virtual stagnation, the economy in JAPAN picked up strongly in the first half of 2005 following a slowdown in the second half of 2004 that had raised doubts about the sustainability of the recovery. But 2005 ended with unexpectedly strong output growth in the last quarter and for the year as a whole it was 2.8 per cent. The recovery was broadly based, with business invest-ment, private consumption, and net exports all rising. There were still doubts as to whether deflation had been truly defeated and, for this reason, the government and a number of commentators were anxious that the Bank of Japan should not move too quickly to raise interest rates.

In SOUTH ASIA the average growth of GDP in 2005 was more or less the same as in 2004. The Indian economy—the largest in the region—grew by about 7 per cent, the expanding middle class sustaining the booming demand for consumer goods which, in turn, supported the rapid growth of the manufacturing sector. Information technology services and tourism also grew strongly. Pakistan was the victim of a massive earthquake in October that caused huge loss of life but had little impact on national output. Pakistan's GDP actually accelerated in 2005, an important source of growth—as in Bangladesh, India, and Sri Lanka—being textiles and clothing which were less affected than feared by the ending of quotas in the main importing countries. Economic growth in the smaller countries of the region generally weakened under the impact of higher oil prices, the effects of the tsunami disaster (earnings from tourism fell in the Maldives and Sri Lanka), flooding (Bangladesh), and political instability (Bangladesh and Nepal). Unemployment and underemployment remained a major problem in the region where the growth of the population of working age was greater than the capacity of the formal sector to absorb them. Inflation rates increased and monetary policies were generally tightened, but fiscal policies tended to remain expansionary as a result of spending on infrastructure, health and education. Most countries had current account deficits, but these were easily financed, largely by workers' remittances, foreign portfolio capital, and foreign direct investment.

Most of WESTERN ASIA enjoyed boom conditions in 2005 as a result of surging oil prices, the oil exporting countries growing by around 6 per cent and the oil importers by around 4.5 per cent. The latter benefited from remittances from workers in the Arabian Gulf and from increased tourism. Growth was especially strong in the six members of the Gulf Co-operation Council, with consumption, investment, and trade surpluses all rising. Despite some debt relief for Iraq by the Paris Club of sovereign creditors, the dilapidated state of its infrastructure, energy shortages, violence, and a weak rule of law all contributed to maintaining high levels of unemployment and poverty and to undermining economic activity in general. The exodus of skilled Iraqis benefited Jordan and Syria. Unemployment continued to be a major problem throughout the region, with rates averaging around 15 per cent and youth unemployment well over 20 per cent. The average rate of inflation (excluding Iraq) picked up to 4 per cent, a modest acceleration due to the prevalence of exchange rates pegged to the US dollar and subsidised energy prices in the oil-importing countries. Oil export revenues were estimated to have reached some US$300 billion in 2005 and the IMF reckoned that governments were saving about 70 per cent of their extra revenues.

Estimates by the UN's economic commission for LATIN AMERICA AND THE CARIBBEAN at the end of 2005 put the region's growth at 4.3 per cent, somewhat down on 2004 (5.6 per cent). The slowdown was almost entirely due to the two largest economies: Brazil, where high interest rates, and Mexico, where weaker export growth, were responsible. There were large differences, however, among countries: in some of the oil and mineral exporters—Chile, Peru, Venezuela, for example—GDP grew by between 6 and 9 per cent. The countries of the Caribbean averaged some 4 per cent growth, with Haiti virtually stagnant at 1.5 per cent. The trend of export-led growth continued in 2005, with strong Asian demand for primary commodities and the lagged effect of real exchange rate depreciations among the major influences. The region was in current account surplus for the third year running, most of it accruing to South America.

Many Latin American governments were able to strengthen their fiscal balances, reduce public debt burdens, and restructure their external debt. Argentina and Brazil announced at the end of the year that they would pre-pay their outstanding debts to the IMF. The extent to which inflationary pressures in the region were contained varied quite widely: in Brazil and Mexico fiscal policy was tightened and inflation targets set for monetary policy; in Central America and the Southern Cone countries, inflation rates were higher than in 2004. Two years of strong growth in Latin America led to some improvement in labour markets. Increases in employment, together with a weaker supply of labour, led to a fall in the average unemployment rate to 9.3 per cent, a percentage point lower than in 2004 and the lowest rate in eight years. There was also an increase in the share in the total of formal employment, and a reduction in the incidence of severe poverty to around 40 per cent. Among the issues worrying policy makers at the end of the year were the risks of a disorderly adjustment of global imbalances, the sustainability of China's demand for primary products, and the policy dilemmas presented by appreciating currencies.

Growth in AFRICA was relatively strong over the past five years and in both 2004 and 2005 averaged just over 5 per cent. Much the same factors were at work in both years: large production increases in the oil-exporting countries, improvements in agriculture, greater macro-economic stability, increased political stability, and commitment to reform (twenty-three countries had signed up to the African Union's African peer review mechanism (APRM) by November). GDP growth in the net fuel exporters was nearly 6 per cent, although there was some deceleration through the year as capacity limits were approached in some of them and as a result of local unrest disrupting Nigerian output. The slowdown in the oil-importing countries was surprisingly mild, from 4.8 to 4.5 per cent.

In contrast to oil and other primary producing sectors, Africa's manufacturing output fell sharply following the termination of the World Trade Organisation (WTO) agreement on textiles and clothing (ATC) in January and the exposure of textile and clothing exporters to fierce competition from Asian producers. There was a large fall in exports and considerable job losses in some half a dozen countries. Even in South Africa—the largest economy in the region with a growth rate of nearly 6 per cent—the opportunities for alternative employment were very limited.

Although macroeconomic stability had markedly improved, the average rate of growth still fell short of the 7 per cent that the World Bank and the UN economic commission for Africa (UNECA) judged to be the minimum required if poverty was to be halved by 2015. Growth tended to be relatively capital intensive with little impact on poverty reduction or employment. UNECA put unemployment at some 10-11 per cent of those actively seeking work, but this ignored all those who had simply given up hope of finding employment, as well as the millions of workers in the informal sector living on less than US$1 a day.

DISSATISFACTION WITH NEO-LIBERALISM IN 2005. Since the early 1980s the major thrust of economic policy, as promoted by the governments of the G-7 group of developed economies and the major international economic institutions, was to remove as far as possible all obstacles and restraints to the international movement of goods, services, and capital and to give the fullest possible play to market forces in determining the allocation of global resources. This neo-liberal agenda, which for many economists lay at the heart of what was meant by globalisation, had always been contested but there were a number of developments in 2005 which suggested that resistance to it had increased significantly.

One sign of this resistance was the resurgence of economic nationalism in many parts of the world, not least in the G-7 countries themselves. In Europe, the rejection of the European constitution in the spring was widely interpreted as a protest against neo-liberal policies. The opposition to the EU services directive, the refusal by twelve of the "old" member countries to allow unrestricted access to their labour markets to workers from the new member states, opposition by the European Parliament and street demonstrations against proposals to foster greater competition in European ports, the revival of the idea of "national champions" in some countries as a principle of industrial policy, and the growing hostility to cross-border take-overs, all testified in varying degrees to dissatisfaction with the globalisation model. This was not confined to Europe: resistance to cross-border takeovers, for example, was also evident in the USA, Japan, Russia, China, and several other East Asian economies. Attitudes and policies towards immigrants were almost everywhere ambiguous: controls were tightened in many of the rich countries but exceptions made for skilled personnel, particularly in areas such as healthcare where the rich countries had failed to invest sufficiently in the required human capital.

To some extent these developments reflected a general policy failure to deal effectively with the problems of adjustment and equity: the re-imposition of controls on imports of clothing from China by the EU and the USA in the first half of 2005 was one indication of this. More broadly indicative, however, was the continuing weakness of most economies in combining output growth with adequate rates of job creation and reductions in inequality. In many developing and transition economies, high rates of structural unemployment (and underemployment) were left largely untouched by high rates of growth and unresolved by current policies. As a result, unemployment rates in 2005 were still generally higher than they were before the global downturn in 2001-02, implying limited reductions in poverty and increased numbers of marginalised people, especially among the young. In the rich, developed economies, unemployment remained high in many of them, income inequalities had risen sharply in some of them, and in most of them population ageing added to the sense of insecurity as a result of the fiscal pressures on social safety nets, the growing number of company pension funds in deficit in 2005, and the threatening prospect for many of poverty in old age.

Growing dissatisfaction with liberalisation, at least on the terms dictated by the EU and the USA, was also a major factor behind the limited progress in the Doha round of trade negotiations in 2005. Although the reluctance of the EU

and the USA to eliminate agricultural subsidies was widely seen as the major
sticking point, the more fundamental issue was that in return for relatively small
improvements in agricultural access, which would benefit only a limited
number of countries, the rich countries were demanding major cuts in the developing countries' industrial tariffs and a significant opening of their service sectors to foreign companies. Just before the WTO ministerial meeting in Hong
Kong, the World Bank published estimates of the benefits that were likely to
result from significant cuts in agricultural and industrial tariffs: of the gain in
global income of just US$96 billion in 2015, only 17 per cent would accrue to
the developing countries. In December the developing countries surprisingly
made significant concessions on the negotiating modalities for industrial tariffs
and services, but the prospect of such meagre gains suggested that another large
extension of market liberalisation might prove problematic (see pp. 356-57).

Developing countries were also resisting the globalisation agenda by reducing their financial dependence on the IMF, the World Bank, and the G-7 countries. The growing political strength of indigenous peoples' movements in Latin
America reflected to a large extent a backlash against the policies promoted by
the international financial institutions. What emerged more clearly in 2005 was
that a growing number of developing countries were becoming more confident
about challenging the ruling international financial system and the governance
structures of the multilateral institutions that were among the leading vectors for
the diffusion of neo-liberal policies.

The NOBEL PRIZE FOR ECONOMICS in 2005 was awarded to Thomas C.
Schelling of Harvard, and Robert J. Aumann of the Hebrew University of
Jerusalem "for enhancing our understanding of conflict and co-operation
through game-theory analysis".

XIII THE SCIENCES

SCIENTIFIC, INDUSTRIAL AND MEDICAL RESEARCH

SPACE AND ASTRONOMY. In January the European Space Agency's *Huygens* probe, from the US National Aeronautics and Space Administration (NASA) spacecraft *Cassini*, landed on Titan, the largest moon orbiting Saturn, after leaving Earth nearly seven years earlier (see AR 1997, p. 454; AR 2004, p. 427). From what was described as a "splat-down" landing onto a "crème brûlée" of soft mud with a crusty topping, *Huygens* sent back photographs of a hilly landscape, looking remarkably similar to that of Earth, but with rivers of liquid methane depositing icy debris. Elsewhere, the mobile rovers *Spirit* and *Opportunity*, launched by NASA in 2003 (see AR 2003, p. 477; AR 2004, p. 427), continue to relay detailed information and photographs from the surface of Mars where they operated throughout the year. There was increasing evidence that this planet had once been warmer, with a more dense atmosphere and salty, acidic water. The team behind the UK-built craft *Beagle 2*, which was lost when it landed on Mars in 2003, claimed in December that they had located it in a crater, but communication with the lander was not restored (see AR 2004, p. 427). Data from *Voyager 1*, launched in 1977, indicated that it was approaching the edge of the solar system.

During the year there were two deliberate collisions with asteroids. The US *Deep Impact* probe collided with the asteroid Tempel 1 on 4 July, sending back pictures of large circular craters on the fourteen-kilometre-wide surface of ice and rock. Japan's *Hayabusa* probe became the first spacecraft to land on an asteroid when it touched down briefly on 26 November on the asteroid Itokawa, hopefully harvesting rock samples which would be brought back for analysis upon its return to Earth in 2007. NASA was unable to solve the foam-shedding problem that had dogged its shuttle launches in 2003, leading to the *Columbia* disaster of that year (see AR 2003, p. 473). When the same problem recurred whilst launching *Discovery*, the agency announced in December that it would no longer use foam air shields on the fuel tank. NASA failed, however, to explain how it would protect electrical cables and pressurisation lines during take-off.

First results were announced on 2 June from the millennium simulation, the largest ever model of the Universe. The Virgo consortium—an international group of astrophysicists from the UK, Germany, Japan, Canada, and the USA—created a simulated universe (requiring 25 million megabytes of computer data) which represented 20 million galaxies, an area of space 2 billion light years across. Physicists claimed that results from the model were already showing the role that quasars and black holes played in the formation of galaxies. The "big bang" theory of the origins of the Universe, accepted by most physicists, had always had its critics who were concerned about the poorly understood concepts—such as dark matter and dark energy—which were needed to explain it, and about the tolerance towards discrepancies in the data. Controversy reared its head in July with a conference in Portugal entitled "crisis in cosmology", although this failed to shake mainstream confidence in the theory.

PHYSICS, CHEMISTRY AND MATERIAL SCIENCE. The December 2004 tsunami in the Indian Ocean, hurricanes in the USA, and the Kashmir earthquake focused attention on forecasting risk areas and timing. Work began in June to update the Indian Ocean monitoring network of seismographic and sea level information, and by the end of the year details could be relayed by satellite to twenty-six tsunami-warning centres. Pressure sensors were being laid on the ocean floor to detect changes of sea level.

Sharp increases in energy prices, coupled with continued steady growth in energy demand (around 4 per cent globally) made energy supply a continuing concern. Developing countries, particularly China, were driving the bulk of the growth. Political uncertainty in key Middle East countries pushed oil and gas prices to record levels. Increased emphasis on climate change furthered concern over carbon emissions. Whilst renewable energy use was growing, many countries found that deployment was falling behind targets. As a result of these environmental and supply concerns, several countries began looking once again at nuclear energy. In the UK, an energy policy review was scheduled for early 2006 and it was widely expected that the UK would follow Finland, where construction of the West's first new nuclear reactor for many years began in mid-2005.

A decision was finally made on the location of the world's first fusion reactor. It was to be built in France, following fierce competition from Japan. The deadlock was broken after a deal was brokered whereby Japanese scientists would be allocated 20 per cent of the research posts, whilst Japan would provide only one-tenth of the costs of the project. Operation of the US$12 billion international thermonuclear experimental reactor, which would reach temperatures of 100 million degrees Centigrade, should begin in 2016.

Nanotechnology continued to be the most rapidly developing area of materials chemistry. The latest successful commercialisation was the fuel additive EnviroxTM (nanoparticles of cerium oxide catalyst), which was put into use by the Stagecoach Group public transport company in the UK, after commercial evaluation showed more than 5 per cent reduction in fuel consumption and a consequent decrease in vehicle emissions. Other nanotechnology products, such as self-cleaning glass and stain-repellent clothes, had become widely accepted. There had been widespread suspicion of this technology, culminating in 2004 in a recommendation that nanoparticles be classified as new entities requiring new safety testing, but public confidence seemed to be growing and, after a shaky start, the industry was looking increasingly profitable and ambitious. In October scientists at the Centre for Oxide-Semiconductor Materials for Quantum Computation announced a method for creating semiconductor quantum dots smaller than ten nanometres in scale. These germanium dots would be placed on the surface of silicon with two-nanometre precision and were reportedly capable of confining single electrons. This development was hailed as the first step towards a quantum computer.

Contamination of food products with a banned colouring triggered the largest ever product recall (more than 500 branded products) in the UK and many other countries. Sudan 1—a red azo dye used as a colouring in solvents, oils, waxes, petrol, and shoe and floor polish—had been illegal as a food additive in the EU since 2003 because it had been shown to cause cancers in animals. In February chilli powder from India was found to be adulterated with the dye. Despite official announcements that the risk to health was very small, especially as it was present in a condiment that was added to food only in small quantities, there was widespread public concern.

SCIENCE COMMUNICATION. It was a particularly good year for science communication. Einstein year, marking the 100th anniversary of the publication of his most influential papers, was celebrated across the globe; there was even physics on stage at the Glastonbury music festival. Amazon, the US Internet-based bookseller, announced that its Christmas bestseller was *Does Anything Eat Wasps?*, a collection of readers' questions and answers from the *New Scientist* magazine. Hester Blumenthal, a German chef working in the UK, who was famous for his snail porridge and sardine-on-toast ice cream and who had a laboratory associated with his restaurant and a PhD student working for him, was named chef of the year by the industry. *March of the Penguins*, a film about emperor penguin breeding and nurture, was a surprise hit at the box office; and Sudoku, a Japanese puzzle of logic and reasoning, took the public by storm in almost every country.

MEDICAL AND BIOLOGICAL SCIENCES. The exciting breakthrough in the field of cloning, stem cell and genetic research, reported by the team of South Korean and US scientists at the University of Seoul (see AR 2004, pp. 429-30), regrettably turned out to be a false dawn. The creation of eleven embryonic stem cell lines, from eleven different donors, as published in *Science* in May, was claimed to be the world's first example of human embryonic stem (ES) cells cloned from the cells of real people. It thus had the potential for major advances in the replacement of damaged tissue without the risk of rejection by the body's immune system, a process known as therapeutic cloning. A US co-researcher raised doubts on two scores: firstly that the eggs used were unethically donated by junior researchers, and secondly that the stem cell lines were not authentic. A subsequent independent investigation confirmed these suspicions and verified that Professor Hwang Woo Suk had not created a single cloned stem cell. His shame highlighted the pressure placed on him by the expectations of the South Korean government (see pp. 315-16). Even his claim in *Nature* in August that he had cloned an Afghan hound named Snuppy was cast into doubt and was still awaiting full DNA verification. Although the advances in therapeutic cloning of stem cells had taken a significant setback, work continued with the application of ES cells derived from surplus embryos left over from in-vitro fertilisation treatments.

The world's first facial transplant was performed by a French surgical team led by Professor Jean-Michel Dubernard in late November at Amiens university hospital. The recipient's face had been severely mauled by a dog. She received a new nose, lips, and chin from a donor. Facial transplantation had long been recognised as technically challenging but clinically possible. Reluctance by ethical committees to sanction the procedure hinged upon the benefit in terms of improvement of function, aesthetics, and psychology against the risk of long term immunosuppression. The three main global facial transplant groups favoured different technical approaches (nose, lips, and chin in France, and whole face reconstruction following severe burns in the USA and the UK). The level of immunosuppression was considered to be less than that required for renal transplantation and was about equivalent to a hand transplant. The psychological effects of the procedure should be beneficial, although there were some who were concerned about the risks of altered identity.

The epidemic of avian influenza (H5N1 virus) affecting poultry and humans spread from South-East Asia to the threshold of Eastern Europe, with human deaths reported in Romania, Turkey, and Cyprus. All these cases arose from bird-to-human contact. As yet, the lack of sustained human-to-human transmission suggested that the H5N1 avian virus did not currently have the capacity to cause a human pandemic, but the potential for antigenic shift could result in rapid human transmission leading to global spread. In the meantime governments continued to stockpile antiviral drugs and to encourage the development of vaccines against avian influenza.

Work by Keith Cheng and Mark Shriver (USA), published in *Science*, explained genetically the evolution from dark to light skin as humans moved out of Africa and migrated into northern latitudes, thus exhibiting and supporting the theory that lighter skin evolved as an adaptation to the weaker sunlight of northern climes, thus making easier the essential manufacture of vitamin D.

The medical application of robots extended to the introduction of "Sister Mary and Dr Robbie", both remote presence (RPG) robots which allowed medical experts visually to examine and communicate with a patient from anywhere in the world via the machine using wireless technology. The robots were trialled at St Mary's hospital, London.

Scientists in the USA recorded ultrasonic squeaks made by male mice when they smelled a female, showing for the first time that these were far from random but were actually a form of recognisable song, thus adding the mouse to the small list of currently-known singing mammals, comprising only whales, bats, and human beings.

The ethics of end of life continued to attract the world's attention. In the USA, Terri Schiavo, who suffered from permanent brain damage resulting from heart failure, finally had her life-sustaining feeding tube removed and died at the end of March thus raising the temperature of the euthanasia debate (see p. 128).

ARCHAEOLOGY AND ANTHROPOLOGY. Brain scans of the skull of *Homo floriensis*, the small "Hobbit-like" creature found on Flores, Indonesia, in 2004 (see AR 2004, p. 431), confirmed that it was indeed a new species distinct from *Homo erectus*, not simply an early human with brain deformity as some critics had claimed. Palaeontologists' views of the relationship between mammals and dinosaurs were revolutionised by two fossil discoveries in Lianoning, northern China, from the early Cretaceous period. One of these, a new species of mammal named *Repeno-mamus gigantus*, was much larger than expected. Mammals in this period had been thought to be small—the size of mice or rats—but this was a carnivore around a metre in length and weighing thirteen kilogrammes. Even more surprising was a fossilised primitive mammal, *Repenomamus robustus*, whose stomach contents showed that it ate young pscittacoaur dinosaurs. Until this discovery it had been assumed that dinosaurs were always the predator. In Mungo national park, Australia, more than 450 human footprints were uncovered from tribes dating back to the Pleistocene era, 20,000 years ago.

"Creationism" (also known as "intelligent design", the theory that the world was created by a being rather than through evolution) was controversially highlighted in 2005 following a dramatic court case in Pennsylvania, USA, where a federal judge ruled in December that a school board was wrong to include "intelligent design" in its biology class. There was also concern in the UK that two privately sponsored, but state run, schools were teaching creationism as fact.

NOBEL PRIZES. Professor Barry Marshall and Dr Robin Warren (Australia) shared the 2005 Nobel Prize for Physiology or Medicine for their discovery of "the bacterium *Helicobacter pylori* and its role in gastritis and peptic ulcer disease". The pair's initial attempts to culture the bacteria from stomach biopsies were unsuccessful but in the tradition of Alexander Fleming they unintentionally tripled the incubation time of a set of plates and thereby produced an abundant growth of the microbe known as *H. pylori*. To answer the question as to whether the organism caused the inflammation or whether it was the inflammation that permitted *H. pylori* to develop, Barry Marshall deliberately infected himself, developed gastritis, and then underwent endoscopy and stomach biopsy with the result that *H. pylori* was detected in the samples. The pair's work led to the simple eradication of *H. pylori* by antibiotics and acid secreting inhibitors, thus relieving many duodenal and gastric ulcer sufferers of the need for surgery. One half of the Prize for Physics was awarded to Roy J. Glauber (USA) for "his contribution to the quantum theory of optical coherence". The other half was awarded jointly to John L. Hall (USA) and Theodor W. Hänsch (Germany) "for their contributions to the development of laser based precision spectroscopy, including the optical frequency comb technique". Their research made it possible to measure frequencies with an accuracy of fifteen digits, which had an application in the development of extremely accurate clocks and improved global positioning by satellite technology. The Prize for Chemistry was jointly awarded to Yves Chauvin (France), Robert H. Grubbs (USA), and Richard R. Schrock (USA) "for the development of the metathesis method of organic synthesis". Metathesis (changing places) was a way of producing new organic compounds by regrouping atoms using catalysis rather than high pressures, high temperatures, and noxious solvents. These new systems were much more environmentally friendly, reducing waste, pollution, and energy usage. This process was a great step forward for "green chemistry" and was an example of the importance of the application of basic science for the benefit of man, society, and environment.

INFORMATION TECHNOLOGY

SOFTWARE PATENTS. In Europe, the controversy surrounding the patentability of computer software (see AR 2004, pp. 434-35) continued into the new year. The tone remained much the same, with the European Commission continuing to press for the legal recognition of software patents (via the EU Directive on Computer Implemented Inventions, informally known as the directive on software patents) and the European Parliament in opposition to the bill. Hungary, Latvia, The Netherlands, Poland, and Cyprus having declared their intention formally to oppose the Directive, the European Parliament's committee on legal affairs (known as JURI) voted overwhelmingly for a restart, meaning that all matters relating to the Directive would have been renegotiated from the beginning. Nevertheless the European Council of Ministers decided to ignore the restart request and allow the bill to continue to the next stage in its journey towards adoption (that stage being a second reading in the Parliament). The Council's decision to ignore the European Parliament's restart request and the general opposition to the Directive was widely criticised, especially given that both the Council and the Commission were appointed bodies whereas the Parliament was elected. The Parliament, however, eventually made its will known in July when deputies voted by 648 votes to fourteen with eighteen abstentions to scrap the Directive entirely. With the option for a restart lost, future attempts at implementing software patents would have to come from a completely new directive.

GALILEO. In December, the first satellite to form part of the Galileo project was launched on a Russian *Soyuz* rocket from Baikonur, Kazakhstan. The Galileo project—a joint venture by the EU and the European Space Agency (ESA)—aimed to deliver the world's second global positioning system (GPS) by 2008. Consisting of thirty satellites in orbit around the Earth, the Galileo GPS was designed to enable users to fix their position on the Earth to within one metre. At the time of writing, the only GPS system available was that run by the US military which gave an accuracy of only 100 metres for civilians or twenty-two metres for military users. The initial satellite was to be used to test critical systems, on which the final constellation would depend, and to secure the frequencies allocated to the Galileo system by the International Telecommunications Union. Despite reaching this milestone, agreement between the participating European countries on issues such as project funding beyond the initial two test satellites and the location of the various ground control stations was still proving difficult to achieve.

THE DIGITAL DIVIDE. The second phase of the UN-sponsored world summit on the information society took place in November in Tunis (see pp. 206-07). The first phase was held in Geneva in 2003 (see AR 2003, p. 484). Whilst the first phase attempted to develop a common political will with regard to creating an "information society" for all nations, the purpose of the second phase was to take concrete steps towards implementing this common will. However, before delegates could even address the summit's agenda, there were heated negotiations over the control of the Internet. Pressure from countries such as China and Iran to move management of the Internet to an international body under UN control threatened to disrupt the summit, but a last minute agreement saw the Internet remain under the control of the Internet corporation for assigned names and numbers (ICANN), a US corporation. ICANN's most important areas of responsibility included the allocation of internet protocol (IP) addresses and the management of the top level domain name system, which combined to give it effective control over all Internet traffic.

The highlight of the summit was the demonstration of a prototype laptop computer by Professor Nicholas Negroponte of the "one laptop per child" association. Intended for use as an educational tool by children and teachers in developing countries, and costing only US$100, the laptop was powered by a hand-wound crank and was capable of participating in ad hoc wireless community networks.

DUAL CORE. Intel and AMD's so called "dual-core" processors began to gain momentum in 2005. A dual-core processor effectively put two processors on a single piece of silicon, allowing a machine with a single physical processor to perform at speeds comparable to a computer with two physical processors. The concept was essentially a reaction to the inability of computer processor manufacturers to improve computer performance by increasing the speed at which a processor performed computations (known as its clock speed). At high clock speeds, processors became increasingly difficult to power and to cool effectively. By using only a single piece of silicon, dual-core processors delivered the performance of a two processor computer, whilst consuming the power, and producing the heat, of only one.

APPLE. Apple's iPod continued its rise as the world's most popular portable digital music player, with more than 30 million players sold by the end of the year. Apple introduced three new models, two with flash-based memory (instead of a miniature computer hard disc) and one which was capable of playing video. More significant for the long term future of Apple, however, was its announcement in June of its intention to switch the central processing unit in all its computers from the IBM/Motorola PowerPC to Intel models. Such a move came with considerable cost and risk, as all software which ran on the computer would have to be rebuilt (or "compiled") for the new processor. It was thought that the reasons for the switch to Intel were IBM's reluctance to expand the range of PowerPC chips that it manufactured and its inability to produce a version of the chip that would be suitable for use in Apple's more high powered laptops.

Rising in tandem with the popularity of digital music players was the habit of downloading radio programmes after their first broadcast and listening to them at a later time (PODCASTS). Although not a necessary component in the process, the success of Apple's iPod also made it the most popular device for listening to pre-recorded radio, and caused the practice to be dubbed "podcasting" (as opposed to broadcasting). Podcasting could be seen as the reinterpretation of several existing technologies, doing for radio what the video cassette recorder (VCR) had done for television. In addition, Podcasting had a democratising effect on the medium of radio, similar to the effect that "blogging" (web logging) was having on journalism, with people recording their own digital audio programmes and publishing them on the Internet.

GAMING. The year saw an increase in the popularity of computer games with fast Internet connections enabling thousands of players to interact with one another in a virtual fantasy environment. These so called "massively multiplayer online role-playing games" (MMORPG) received public attention when actions in these virtual worlds began to have tangible and often adverse effects in the real world.

Real economies believed to be worth between US$100 million and US$1 billion had grown around these virtual worlds, where imaginary items (which had use only in these virtual worlds) were traded for real money; in Japan a man was arrested on suspicion of mugging (using unbeatable, software controlled, characters) MMORPG players of virtual items which were then sold for real money. Even more remarkable was the imprisonment in June of a man in Shanghai, China, for the murder of another man over the theft of a virtual sword. Further fatalities occurred throughout the year, with a Russian teenager and a South Korean man dying of stroke and heart failure respectively after playing MMO-PRGs for up to fifty hours without a break.

EBAY. Online auction company EBay agreed to buy the Internet communications company Skype for US$2.6 billion in September. Skype, which provided a type of a communications infrastructure known as voice over internet protocol (VOIP), allowed users to make free computer-to-computer calls and low cost calls to landlines and mobile telephones by routing all or part of the call over the Internet. At the end of the year, Skype had 53 million registered users.

WEB 2.0. One of the most talked about areas of information technology during the year surrounded the perceived maturation of the World Wide Web from a collection of static web pages to a computing platform capable of delivering to end users applications comparable in features and responsiveness to desktop applications.

Collectively referred to as "Web 2.0", these new types of more powerful applications used several technologies developed in the late 1990s—such as asynchronous javascript and XML (AJAX), web services, and syndication—to move more of the application logic from the web server to the client's browser and to allow easier interaction across different web sites. The net effect of these changes was a much richer user experience, with users able to achieve more within a single web application before being slowed by either having to move between web sites or wait for a web page to be reloaded (both common occurrences with first generation web applications).

Some of the best examples of Web 2.0 came from Internet search company Google, which in February launched Google Maps. Whilst there existed many web sites which could supply users with maps, Google Maps could give the user directions between any two points and allow them to search for local businesses in a given area, and do so with a responsiveness not previously seen in a web-based application.

Web 2.0 applications found particular success within community-based, collaboration services as the quality of these increased with the number of participants and the number of different web services involved. Some of the most popular services of this type were Flickr and del.icio.us which allowed users to upload and share photographs and World Wide Web bookmarks respectively.

PEER-TO-PEER. In a significant blow to creators of peer-to-peer software (which allowed for the swapping of files over the Internet), the US Supreme Court overturned various lower court decisions (see AR 2004, pp. 432-33), and ruled unanimously that the creators of peer-to-peer software could be held responsible for piracy which took place using their software.

In delivering the ruling, Justice David Souter said, "We hold that one who distributes a device with the object of promoting its use to infringe copyright, as shown by clear expression or other affirmative steps taken to foster infringement, is liable for the resulting acts of infringement."

The decision had the potential to supersede the 1984 Sony Betamax ruling on which previous judges had relied in declaring peer-to-peer software legal (as this had legal as well as illegal uses). Despite the potential conflict between these two rulings, no detailed clarification of the Sony Betamax case was made and it was unclear how these two rulings would interact. The decision was passed back to the lower courts for them to review, in its light, the ongoing litigation between peer-to-peer software companies such as Grokster and Streamcast Networks and recording industry bodies the Motion Picture Association of America (MPAA) and the Recording Industry Association of America (RIAA).

THE ENVIRONMENT

THE challenge posed by climate change constituted the most pressing environmental question in 2005. However, 2005 was also a year in which the impact of a number of other human activities—not all directly related to the burning of fossil fuels—was shown to have produced near-critical effects on the environment.

THE POLITICS OF CLIMATE CHANGE. The only existing international legal instrument for mitigating global warming caused by human activities—the 1997 Kyoto Protocol to the 1992 UN Framework Convention on Climate Change (UNFCCC)— came into force on 16 February, ninety days after Russia had ratified the protocol in October 2004 (for text see AR 1997, pp. 568-72). Russia's ratification fulfilled the condition that those states which together accounted for at least 55 per cent of the global emissions of six carbon-based greenhouse gases which trapped heat in the atmosphere (including carbon dioxide) should be parties to the treaty. The

Protocol thus acquired legal force, despite the continuing intransigent opposition of the USA—which had rejected the Protocol—to its mandatory targets that required the thirty-eight states ratifying its Annexe I to reduce emissions by 2012 by an average of 5.2 per cent of their 1990 levels. The twin objections of the US government to the Kyoto provisions—apart from its continued, increasingly isolated insistence that the science of climate change was too uncertain to be sure that industrial emissions were responsible for global warming—were firstly that meeting the mandatory targets would have a severe adverse effect on the US economy, and secondly that the Protocol set no targets for a group of rapidly industrialising economies, especially China and India. However, the closing communiqué of the G-8 summit meeting in Scotland in July did include the statement that climate change posed a threat to a stable world, that human activities played a major role in it, and a generalised commitment to reduce emissions of greenhouse gases. UK Prime Minister Tony Blair had made forging a strategy for combating climate change one of the two priorities of his 2005 chairmanship of the G-8, alongside the relief of African poverty and developing country debt. Later that month the USA, Australia, China, India, Japan, and South Korea announced the formation of the Asia-Pacific partnership on clean development and climate (APPCDC), which aimed to co-operate in reducing emissions through the development of cleaner technologies for energy generation, principally new coal-based technology and nuclear power, and the capture and storage of carbon emissions. It was planned that the APPCDC would be formally inaugurated by a ministerial meeting in Australia in November, but this was postponed until January 2006. Although the US government described the new partnership as complementary to the Kyoto mechanism, sceptical environmental critics saw it as intended to undermine negotiations on a second stage of the Kyoto pact which would extend beyond the 2012 commitments.

The eleventh conference of the parties to the UNFCCC (COP-11) was held in Montreal, Canada, between 28 November and 10 December. With the entry into force of the Kyoto Protocol, the conference became the first meeting of the parties (COP/MOP). The USA played a largely obstructive role at the conference, unwilling to contemplate any extension of Kyoto, but came under great pressure to continue discussions within the framework of the convention to which it was still a party. The pressure on the US government was by no means all external; many US cities and businesses, and some states, had already set their own emissions reduction targets independently of the federal government. A report produced in April by the US Energy Department found that the cost to the US economy of reducing US greenhouse gas emissions by 4 per cent by 2015 and by 7 per cent by 2025 would be 0.15 per cent of GDP, far less than previous estimates. During the conference a group of twenty-five prominent US economists, including three Nobel laureates, urged US President George W. Bush to drop his opposition to mandatory emissions cuts, saying that the cost to the US economy of fully implementing Kyoto would be only 1 per cent of GDP. The US-based International Climate Change Task Force had issued a report in January recommending urgent policy decisions to reduce emissions and to invest in "cleaner" technology if climate change were not to become irreversible within ten years (see pp. 478-79). Former US President Bill Clinton, addressing a meeting at the conference, suggested that Bush was out of touch with US public opinion on the issue. Eventually some of the USA's allies, including China, India, Australia, and Saudi Arabia, made its isolation at the conference more complete by committing themselves to further negotiations within the UNFCCC/Kyoto framework on reducing emissions, with the Chinese delegation indicating that it strongly supported the Kyoto process. The upshot was that the USA signed a last-minute commitment to join the other parties to the convention in talks beginning in 2006 on the future of the UNFCCC, although the US delegation stipulated that these should not be "formalised" or lead to negotiations on mandatory targets. At the same time the countries that had ratified the Protocol would begin a second track of talks on a second phase of commitments after 2012.

The conference also agreed to reform the clean development mechanism (CDM) under which industrialised countries could gain carbon credits by funding projects to transfer low-carbon technology for power generation to developing countries. It was also agreed to explore the potential of carbon capture and storage technology, and to support poor countries in finding ways to adapt to climate change, which most analysts now saw as inevitable even if the most stringent forms of mitigation were to be adopted. COP-11 also agreed to include in the CDM payments to tropical zone countries as an incentive to preserve their rainforests as repositories of carbon dioxide ("carbon sinks"), in addition to their role in maintaining biodiversity. A private international investment scheme had already over the past year established eight carbon trading partnerships to regenerate rainforest in countries such as Brazil, India, and Uganda. There was now a wide consensus that hopes of mitigating climate change lay in the adoption of a range of approaches, with the enforcement of regulation complemented by the development of new technology and market-based mechanisms.

ENVIRONMENTAL SCIENCE. Although many scientific uncertainties remained, evidence accumulated throughout the year confirming a recent rise in temperatures. Additionally, in some cases feedback mechanisms were identified, whereby one phenomenon of climatic change could trigger other factors not previously envisaged, increasing the complexity of the situation. Three pieces of research published in the journal *Science* in August suggested a resolution of a major anomaly in climatology: the contrast between plentiful evidence of rising temperatures on the surface of the Earth and the apparent stability of temperature in the atmosphere over a forty-year period. All three studies concluded that the discrepancy was the result of misinterpretation of data collected by weather balloons and satellites on temperatures in the troposphere.

There were several studies in 2005 of the Arctic and Antarctic regions, which were particularly sensitive to changes in temperature, and which also provided an uncontaminated record of past climatic conditions, because they were relatively undisturbed by local human activity. In April it was reported that scientists of the ten-country European project for ice-coring in Antarctica (EPICA) had succeeded in extracting an ice core drilled to a depth of 3,270.2 metres near the project's base at Dome C in eastern Antarctica. The deepest ice extracted was some 900,000 years old. Analysis of air bubbles trapped in a core drilled to a depth of 3,139 metres extracted in 2004 showed that the current proportion of carbon dioxide in the atmosphere was higher than the average for previous interglacial periods, and the highest for some 440,000 years. In studies published in *Science* in November analysis of samples from the new core dating back 650,000 years found that the current level of atmospheric carbon dioxide, reckoned at 380 parts per million (ppm), was 27 per cent higher than at any time over the period analysed, and the level of methane—a more potent greenhouse gas than carbon dioxide—was 130 per cent higher. The studies concluded that the levels of carbon dioxide, methane, and nitrous oxide were increasing 200 times faster than could be accounted for by natural processes alone.

Research carried out by the UK National Oceanography Centre, published in the journal *Nature* in December, provided fresh evidence of changes in the Atlantic thermohaline system which conveyed currents of warm water from the Gulf of Mexico to the north-east Atlantic (the Gulf Stream), thereby giving parts of north-west Europe, especially the British Isles, a much milder climate than parts of North America at the same latitude. It was found that the rate of flow of ocean currents at a latitude 25 degrees north of the Equator had dropped from a 1992 measurement of 20 Sverdrups (Sv—million tonnes of water per second) to 14Sv. It was estimated that if the slower turnover of water was maintained, average temperatures in the UK would drop by 1 degree Celsius over twenty years, but if the currents weakened drastically, causing a complete shutdown of the Gulf Stream—which was thought unlikely—UK temperatures would drop by between 4 degrees and 6 degrees Celsius, leading to winter conditions comparable to those in Newfoundland, Canada. It was thought that the phenomenon was caused by increased melting of Arctic freshwater ice, diluting the salinity and density of the Gulf Stream when it met the colder northern waters, making it slower to sink and impairing the formation of the deepwater return current.

Although, as all environmental scientists pointed out, it was impossible to attribute a single weather event to climate change, Hurricane Katrina, which killed over 1,200 people in the USA in late August, served to focus attention on the proposition that a warmer climate would generate more extreme weather conditions (see pp. 121-24). Research by Professor Kerry Emanuel of the Massachusetts Institute of Technology (MIT) on tropical cyclones of the past thirty years, published in *Nature* in August, found that there was a correlation between increased severity and duration of tropical storms and an increase of 0.5 degrees Celsius in average surface sea temperatures. A further study, by the Georgia Institute of Technology, published in *Science* in September, found that the overall frequency of tropical storms since the 1970s was unchanged, but that the number of the most severe storms—category 4 and 5 hurricanes—had almost doubled.

ENVIRONMENTAL IMPACTS AND BIODIVERSITY. Owing to their unique and pristine geophysical environments, the polar regions were the areas of the Earth's surface that registered the most rapidly increasing temperatures. A study of the Kangerdlugssuag glacier in eastern Greenland reported in July that the glacier was both shrinking in area and moving at a rate of 13.9 kilometres per year, compared with 5.9 kilometres per year between 1988 and 1996, as a result of surface melting that lubricated the ice. Satellite data released in September by the US National Aeronautical and Space Administration (NASA) and the University of Colorado found that surface air temperatures over the Arctic Ocean were 2-3 degrees Celsius higher than the average for 1955-2004 and that the extent of Arctic sea ice in September was about 20 per cent less than the long-term average. It constituted the lowest area on record, having fallen for four consecutive summers; the winter recovery of ice in 2004-05 had also been the smallest on record. Scientists identified this phenomenon as a probable feedback factor that would itself accelerate climate change, because the shrinkage of the area of white ice that reflected heat back into space would allow faster warming of the ocean.

A study published in the journal *Science* in April, by the British Antarctic Survey (BAS) and the US Geological Survey, of 244 Antarctic glaciers, based on satellite imagery and aerial photographs dating back to the 1940s, found that 87 per cent of them had shrunk significantly, by an average of 600 metres, over the past fifty years. The rate of retreat of the glaciers was found to have accelerated over the past five years. A new study produced by the BAS in October found that the average summer sea temperature west of the Antarctic peninsula had risen by 1.2 degrees Celsius between 1955 and 1994, which could have serious consequences for the survival of temperature-sensitive creatures such as molluscs and krill, the staple diet of many fish and marine mammal species at higher levels of the Antarctic food chain. The loss of sea ice also adversely affected the reproductive cycle of krill and meant a loss of breeding grounds for penguins and seals. Furthermore, an international study, partly based on computer modelling, published in *Nature* in September, found that the absorption by the oceans of current and likely future levels of atmospheric carbon dioxide would increase seawater acidity, especially in the Southern Ocean and the subarctic Pacific Ocean, to levels that by 2100 would threaten populations of shellfish.

A study conducted by scientists of Tomsk and Oxford universities, published in August, found that an area of 1 million square kilometres of permafrost in Siberia was thawing for the first time since its formation some 11,000 years ago. It was estimated that the frozen peat bogs contained some 70 billion tones of methane, which could be released in its entirety into the atmosphere if the thawing continued over the next 100 years, constituting another feedback factor to accelerate global warming. There was speculation that the thawing of the permafrost represented a "tipping point", beyond which climate change was uncontrollable no matter what measures were taken to reduce greenhouse gas emissions.

The most comprehensive study of the world's ecosystems—the UN's millennium ecosystem assessment (MEA), launched in 2001—published its report, produced by 1,500 scientists, in March. It concluded that economic development over the past fifty years had radically altered the world's ecosystems, at a high environmental cost. Some 60 per cent of the Earth's ecosystem "services" that supported life—such as fresh water, arable land, and air—were being degraded by pollution or used unsustainably, and continuation of current practices threatened the planet's ability to sustain future generations. The report recommended numerous changes of policy in order to avert such a future, including the development of new technologies, changes in the patterns of consumption, trade reforms, and factoring the environmental cost into the price of food and other goods.

Another large-scale survey of the "human footprint" was published in December, in the form of global maps produced by the University of Wisconsin-Madison that combined satellite imagery with world-wide agricultural census data. The research showed that about 40 per cent of the Earth's land surface was being used in 2000 for agriculture or farm animal grazing, compared with 7 per cent in 1700. The study concluded that very little uncultivated land remained on which crops could be grown, without destroying the remaining tropical rainforests of Africa and South America.

The campaigning group Greenpeace in October published a report on the environmental consequences of China's headlong drive for economic growth. Greenpeace projected that, at a continuing rate of 8 per cent growth, by 2031 China's grain consumption would be two-thirds of the world's current production level and its demand for oil would exceed the current global production total.

EU fisheries ministers meeting in December agreed on cuts of up to 15 per cent of the catch quotas for four species (including cod) but failed to act on scientific advice that a complete ban on cod fishing in the North Sea and the Baltic Sea was needed to allow stocks to recover to sustainable levels.

Copious information was made public in 2005 on the many and varied threats to biodiversity, but there seemed little prospect of determined, coherent action to counter these. A possible exception was a declaration signed in September in Kinshasa, capital of the Democratic Republic of Congo (DRC), at an unprecedented intergovernmental meeting on great apes attended by four donor countries and twenty-three "range states" containing ape populations, and supported by UN agencies. The declaration committed the signatories to a range of measures to attempt to protect the four great ape species from extinction. The total population of great apes was estimated to have declined from 2 million to 350,000 over the past fifty years. A report compiled by fifty specialists and published in April by Conservation International said that 25 per cent of the 625 primate species and subspecies were at risk of extinction, mainly from destruction of habitat by farming or logging, and from hunting, both subsistence and commercial. The report's list of twenty-five most critically endangered species included two kinds of African gorilla and the Sumatran orang-utan.

The phenomenon of deforestation in countries such as Brazil, Indonesia, the Philippines, and Papua New Guinea was difficult to monitor, and the regulation of legal logging and the prevention of illegal logging often seemingly impossible to enforce, given the resources available. Official figures suggested that the rate of deforestation in Brazil's Amazon rainforest was slowing, but a study published in

Science in October, using enhanced satellite technology, discovered the damage caused by a previously undetected practice of selective logging, the authors concluding that the resultant rate of deforestation was twice that previously estimated (see pp. 153-54).

A report published by the UN environment programme (UNEP) challenged the widely held view that deforestation contributed heavily to severe floods and landslides, maintaining that this applied only to small-scale flooding. However, advocates of the efficacy of natural protection from hazards were supported by a study conducted by US and Sri Lankan researchers of the effects of the December 2004 Indian Ocean tsunami (see map p. 296), which found that the illegal mining of offshore coral reefs had left the coast of Sri Lanka more exposed to the force of the tsunami, resulting in greater loss of life and destruction. By contrast, healthy coral reefs had protected the low-lying islands of the Maldives, where the tsunami had caused relatively few casualties and less damage.

XIV THE LAW

INTERNATIONAL LAW

THE "war on terrorism" continued to give rise to legal debate concerning the appropriate scope of protection of human rights, in particular about the USA's treatment of "unlawful combatants" held in detention, and about the practice and definition of torture. On 28 October the Inter-American Commission on Human Rights (an autonomous body of the Organisation of American States, the OAS) indicated precautionary measures regarding inmates at the US detention centre at Guantánamo Bay in Cuba. It requested that the USA take immediate measures to have the legal status of the detainees effectively determined by a competent tribunal, and that it investigate, prosecute, and punish instances of torture or mistreatment. The USA denied that the Commission could assert jurisdiction over issues concerning the laws of war or that it could address requests for precautionary measures against non-state parties. The Commission rejected these arguments.

Towards the end of the year allegations were made by Human Rights Watch that the USA was running or had run a system of secret prisons, including some in Europe, and that it was following the practice of "extraordinary rendition" whereby the USA apprehended terrorist suspects and transferred them to countries which may use torture. The Council of Europe initiated investigations into these allegations (see pp. 121; 377).

At the end of the year the INTERNATIONAL COURT OF JUSTICE had eleven cases from all regions on its docket: two involving African states, one between Asian states, four between European, three between Latin American, and one inter-continental. One new case was brought, by Costa Rica against Nicaragua, concerning navigational and related rights on the San Juan River.

The most important case decided by the Court was *Armed Activities on the Territory of the Congo* (Democratic Republic of Congo (DRC) v Uganda). The DRC accused Uganda of illegal use of force, intervention, looting and plundering its natural resources, and violation of the laws of war and of human rights during the 1998-2003 conflict in the DRC. Uganda counter-claimed that the DRC was itself responsible for armed attacks against Uganda, and that it had maltreated Ugandan nationals and diplomats. Uganda admitted the use of force by its troops in the DRC, but argued that they had acted on the basis of consent and/or in self-defence against armed attacks from the DRC's territory. The Court rejected Uganda's arguments and found that, although the DRC had initially consented to Ugandan counter-insurgency operations in the border area, this limited consent had been withdrawn by 8 August 1998 at the latest (see pp. 220; 242). The 1999 Lusaka Peace Agreement did not subsequently constitute consent to the presence of Ugandan troops in the DRC.

As regards Uganda's claim that it was acting in self-defence, the Court found that its operations went far beyond this: the taking of towns and airports hundreds of miles from the border could not qualify as self-defence. Moreover, Uganda had not reported its actions to the UN Security Council as self-defence, as required by the UN Charter. Nor was there any armed attack against Uganda attributable to the DRC; Uganda had claimed that there was a conspiracy between the DRC, a Ugandan rebel group, and Sudan, but failed to prove this allegation. There had been attacks from the DRC's territory against Uganda, but Uganda had not shown that the DRC government was involved in these. The Court did not go into the controversial question of whether contemporary international law provided for a right of self-defence against attacks by non-state actors.

The Court went on to rule that Uganda had also intervened illegally in the DRC through its support for rebel groups. Uganda became an occupying power as its forces had substituted their authority for that of the DRC government; it was therefore under a duty to restore and maintain order and to secure respect for the applicable rules of international humanitarian law and human rights law. It was responsible for the atrocities by its own troops and also for its failure to prevent violations of humanitarian law by rebel groups. Although it had not been proved that the Ugandan government had pursued a policy of plundering the DRC's rich mineral resources, Ugandan army officers had engaged in looting and plundering in breach of humanitarian law and Uganda was responsible for this. The Court upheld only one of Uganda's counter-claims: that the DRC was liable for its attacks on the Ugandan embassy and maltreatment of diplomats.

A Chamber of the Court decided the *Frontier Dispute* between Benin and Niger. It determined the course of the boundary between the two parties in the River Niger, decided which islands belonged to which party, and fixed the boundary line on two bridges over the river. The judgment upheld the principle of *uti possidetis*, to secure respect for the territorial boundary at the time of independence. The Court also decided the *Case concerning Certain Property* between Liechtenstein and Germany. This was a complex case, arising out of the confiscation of Liechtenstein-owned property after World War II. The Court found that it had no jurisdiction to decide the merits of the case. The Convention giving jurisdiction to the Court covered only disputes arising before 1980. Germany argued that the crucial events took place after this date and the Court agreed (see p. 59).

Ronny Abraham (France) was elected on 15 February as a new member of the Court to replace Judge Gilbert Guillaume. On 5 November five members were elected for nine years, to begin on 6 February 2006. Judge Thomas Buergenthal (USA) was re-elected; Judges Mohamed Bennouna (Morocco), Sir Kenneth Keith (New Zealand), Bernardo Sepulveda Amor (Mexico), and Leonid Skotnikov (Russia) were elected.

An arbitration tribunal made an award under the UN Convention on the Law of the Sea in a case concerning land reclamation between Malaysia and Singapore. Following the indication of provisional measures by the International Tribunal for the Law of the Sea, the parties had established a group of independent experts to determine the effects of Singapore's land reclamation and to propose measures to address any adverse effects. This study had been submitted to the parties in 2004. On 26 April the parties agreed on a settlement, terminating the case on agreed terms. The Tribunal accordingly made a binding award on this basis, agreeing on the boundary for land reclamation, compensation for fishermen, and joint mechanisms to discuss the environment and to monitor water quality and ecology. Maritime boundary issues were to be resolved through amicable negotiations.

The Eritrea-Ethiopia Claims Commission at the Permanent Court of Arbitration in The Hague, established to decide claims arising out of the 1998-2000 war between Eritrea and Ethiopia, continued its work (see p. 215). It made awards in three cases. First, it dismissed Ethiopia's claim for injuries caused by the closing of Eritrean ports to Ethiopian trade in 1998. The Commission upheld the right of a party to an international armed conflict to restrict or terminate trade or commerce between itself and another party. Second, it accepted Eritrea's claims for Ethiopia's failure to prevent rape and for damage caused by looting and destruction of buildings. However, it rejected Eritrea's claims for displacement of civilians, as this did not in itself constitute a violation of international humanitarian law. The third award was the most controversial: this concerned Ethiopia's claims on the illegal use of force. The Commission found that it had jurisdiction to decide such claims, even though the determination of liability for the use of force had been assigned by the arbitration agreement to an independent and impartial body to be established by the UN Secretary-General. The Commission determined that Eritrea was responsible for a violation of Article 2(4) of the UN Charter and could not claim to be acting in self-defence, even though it had used force to seize what was subsequently determined by the Boundary Commission in 2002 to be its own territory (see AR 2002, p. 472). Its reasoning on this important question was very brief and its approach was very different from that of the International Court of Justice in the *Cameroon/Nigeria* case (see AR 2002, pp. 471-72). The UN Security Council repeatedly expressed deep concern at the continued lack of progress in the implementation of the 2002 Boundary Commission ruling, at Ethiopia's refusal to comply with the boundary award, and at Eritrea's subsequent refusal to co-operate with the UN peacekeeping mission.

The UN Compensation Commission set up to arbitrate reparations claims after Iraq's invasion of Kuwait held its 56th and final session and approved four final reports. This marked the end of twelve years of claims processing. Over 2,680,000 claims for a total of US$354 billion had been made, leading to awards of US$52.5 billion.

A wide range of treaties was adopted or came into force. The Kyoto Protocol on climate change came into force on 16 February, binding over thirty industrialised countries to targets of reduced emissions of greenhouse gases during 2008-12 (see p. 411). On 23 May the World Health Assembly, the governing body of the World Health Organisation (WHO), approved extensive revisions of the WHO health regulations, to enter into force on 15 June 2007 unless states opted out. These were designed to strengthen the WHO's right of intervention and to increase international co-operation to deal with potential risks. International reporting was to be mandatory for any disease outbreak that may have serious public health impact, such as polio, smallpox, SARS (severe acute respiratory syndrome), Ebola fever, and avian influenza. The WHO Framework Convention on Tobacco Control came into force on 27 February. This quickly became one of the most widely accepted UN treaties: a hundred states had ratified it by the end of the year. It required parties to restrict tobacco advertising, sponsorship, and promotion, to set new labelling standards, and to clamp down on tobacco smuggling.

The International Convention for the Suppression of Acts of Nuclear Terrorism was unanimously adopted by the UN General Assembly on 13 April. It was the first such convention adopted since the 11 September 2001 terrorist attacks on the USA; it complemented the other twelve universal conventions on terrorism. It created new offences of possession of radioactive material or devices and of threats to use such devices. However, the General Assembly failed to reach agreement on a comprehensive convention on terrorism. A major disagreement was over the exemption of armed resistance groups involved in struggles against colonial domination and foreign occupation (see p. 335).

The UN Firearms Protocol entered into force on 6 July, the third supplementary protocol to the UN Convention against Transnational Organised Crime. This was the first legally binding treaty on small arms adopted at the global level, to promote co-operation among states in preventing the illegal manufacture and trafficking in firearms and ammunition. The UN Convention against Corruption entered into force on 14 December. This was the first global instrument to assist states to fight corruption in public and private sectors; it included a mechanism to allow states to recover stolen assets. However, only two EU states ratified it and the USA did not do so. The UNESCO Convention on Cultural Diversity was adopted on 20 October; it gave states the right to protect and promote the diversity of cultural expression within their territory. It also allowed special measures to protect cultural expression (such as films, magazines, music) when such expression was at risk of extinction. Only the USA and Israel objected to this convention.

The European Convention on Human Rights system continued to operate under enormous pressure, with over 80,000 cases pending. The EUROPEAN COURT OF HUMAN RIGHTS decided nearly 1,000 cases in 2005, covering a very wide range of subjects, from rent control in Poland to the regulation of sadomasochistic practices in Belgium. Other cases dealt with freedom of political speech and conditions of detention in Ukraine, the rights of asylum seekers in several states, the failure by France to prevent the servitude of illegal immigrants, and the treatment of Roma in Bulgaria and Romania. The largest number of cases were those brought against Russia, Poland, Turkey, and Romania.

The Court gave its first judgment on claims arising out of the armed conflict in Chechnya for the extra-judicial execution of civilians by Russian forces in indiscriminate bombing. This was a controversial decision as cases arising from armed conflict were traditionally governed primarily by the laws of internal armed conflict rather than by human rights law. The Court acknowledged that the Russian government had the right to use force and that its air strikes were a legitimate response to the threat of attack, but held that they were not planned and executed with the requisite care for the life of civilians; it accordingly found a violation of the right to life.

The Grand Chamber upheld earlier judgments in two cases against Turkey. In *Sahin* the Grand Chamber held by sixteen to one that the prohibition of the headscarf at Istanbul University did not violate the applicant's right to freedom of religion. The restriction was necessary in a democratic society as it was adopted to uphold the principle of secularism (see AR 2004, p. 446). The Grand Chamber also confirmed the earlier decision by a Chamber of the Court in *Öcalan* that Turkey's judicial procedure had violated the right to a fair trial, and that the imposition of the death penalty amounted to inhuman treatment. Several cases on the right to life were brought against Turkey, including one arising from the shooting of a Greek Cypriot by a Turkish soldier in the buffer zone between northern and southern Cyprus; the Court held that any remedies in the Turkish Republic of Northern Cyprus could not be regarded as domestic remedies for Convention purposes and rejected Turkey's argument that the applicant had not exhausted local remedies.

Among the cases against the UK the Grand Chamber held in *Hirst* that the total bar on all convicted prisoners from voting violated the Convention; this general, automatic and indiscriminate restriction on a vitally important Convention right was outside any acceptable margin of appreciation.

The Statute of the INTERNATIONAL CRIMINAL COURT (ICC) received its one hundredth ratification. The Court issued its first arrest warrants, against leaders of the Ugandan rebel Lord's Resistance Army (LRA) for crimes against humanity and war crimes committed in northern Uganda since July 2002 (the date of entry into force of the Rome Statute of the ICC). The ICC made it clear that it intended to prosecute only those senior leaders alleged to bear the greatest responsibility for the most serious crimes.

As regarded the situation in Sudan, the International Commission of Inquiry on Darfur set up in 2004 reported to the UN that the government of Sudan and the Janjawid militias were responsible for crimes under international law (see pp. 480-89). Although the government had not pursued a policy of genocide, the crimes against humanity and war crimes that had been committed in Darfur were nevertheless extremely serious. The Security Council accordingly decided to refer the Darfur situation to the Prosecutor of the ICC; this was the first use of Article 13(b) of the Rome Statute. The USA abstained in the vote, rather than using its veto, thus abandoning its previous total opposition to resort to the ICC (see p. 203). The Prosecutor carried out a comprehensive fact-finding mission and reported that there were admissible cases involving the killing of thousands of civilians, widespread destruction and looting of villages, leading to the displacement of about 1.9 million civilians.

On 7 January the Central African Republic referred the situation of crimes on its territory since 1 July 2002 to the Court; the Prosecutor was to decide whether to initiate an investigation.

Serbia & Montenegro and the Republika Srpksa in Bosnia & Herzegovina began to co-operate with the INTERNATIONAL CRIMINAL TRIBUNAL FOR THE FORMER YUGOSLAVIA (the ICTY) and for the first time surrendered indicted suspects to it. Several other indicted Bosnian Serb suspects also surrendered themselves. The Croatian General Ante Gotovina was surrendered to the Tribunal; Croatia's earlier failure to arrest and transfer him had harmed its EU and NATO prospects (see pp. 94-95). The Prime Minister of Kosovo, Ramush Haradinaj, surrendered voluntarily to the Tribunal after his indictment for war crimes as a former senior commander of the Kosovo Liberation Army, the KLA (see p. 100). There was a significant increase in the number of people awaiting trial. However, the most-wanted accused—Bosnian Serb leaders Ratko Mladic and Radovan Karadzic—remained at large.

Several important cases were decided on the doctrine of command responsibility. *Sefer Halilovic*, a founder and supreme commander of the army of Bosnia & Herzegovina who had voluntarily surrendered to the Court on 25 September 2001, was acquitted of murders committed in 1993; the prosecution had not shown that he had effective control over his subordinates at the time the crimes were committed. Judgment was also given in *Vidoje Blagojevic* and *Dragan Jokic* for their part in crimes against Bosnian Muslims during the fall of Srebrenica in July 1995. Blagojevic by virtue of his position of command had participated in the forcible transfer of women and children and the detention and execution of prisoners and was found guilty of complicity to commit genocide and other crimes through aiding and abetting. Jokic had assisted in the planning and carrying out of the burials involved in the murder operation. He successfully appealed on the grounds that concurrent convictions for individual and superior responsibility in relation to the same counts based on the same facts constituted a legal error; he was acquitted of any superior responsibility but his original sentence was maintained for the other charges. Also *Pavle Strugar*, a retired Lieutenant-General of the Yugoslav People's Army, the JNA, was found guilty of the crimes of devastation and destruction of cultural property in the course of unlawful shelling of the historic town of Dubrovnik in Croatia in 1991, as a superior responsible for the criminal conduct of the forces under his command. The tribunal issued its first judgment on crimes in Kosovo; two commanders of the KLA were acquitted and one, *Haradin Bala*, was found guilty of torture, cruel treatment, and murder for maintaining inhumane conditions as a guard at a prison camp.

The INTERNATIONAL CRIMINAL TRIBUNAL FOR RWANDA made steady progress. The number of accused in completed and ongoing cases reached fifty-two and included a former Prime Minister, eleven former ministers, four prefects, and many other prominent figures. The strategy of referral of cases to national jurisdictions began implementation; by the end of the year thirty files had been handed over to the Rwandan authorities. The Tribunal was on course to complete its trials by the end of 2008 (see p. 245).

Judgments were delivered in three cases, and three appeals were decided. In *Rutaganira*, the defendant was found guilty of a crime against humanity for aiding and abetting attacks at Mubuga church that resulted in thousands of deaths. As a local councillor, Vincent Rutaganira had knowledge of the planned massacre and did not use his authority to prevent the population from participating in attacks. The *Muhimana* judgment was a significant contribution to jurisprudence on sexual offences. Mikaeli Muhimana participated directly, and aided and abetted others, in genocide, rape, and murder as crimes against humanity. He was sentenced to life imprisonment. In *Simba*, the defendant was found guilty of genocide and crimes against humanity and sentenced to twenty-five years' imprisonment; as a retired army officer and former member of Parliament, Aloys Simba had not been an architect of the massacres but had distributed weapons and given encouragement and approval to the assailants.

EUROPEAN UNION LAW

THE change in the character of European Union (EU) law, which had been noticeable for some time, became absolutely clear in 2005. It would, henceforth, be pointless to think of it as lawyers of the 1980s or 1990s had done. Although lawyers were still treating competition law as their bread and butter, it had become increasingly marginalised at EU level.

This development affected commercial law and constitutional law as well as the rapidly growing new fields of criminal law, family law, and the administration of justice. The emphasis was no longer on the creation of a new legal system and the establishment of a fully working, continent-wide mercantile law (both now essentially complete); it was, rather, on the operation of a system of power, analogous to that within nation states, where law-making would represent positive political and social choices at all levels.

This change was reflected in a new attitude to enlargement and to action in the international arena; in the originating of most of the important law-making in the European Council instead of the European Commission; and in the resurgence into a leading role of the member state governments and leaders, as the

European Council took a more active role in law-making. Even the European Commission was focusing its legislative effort on advancing legal policy in areas where political or social policy pressures were exerted, rather than on protecting and advancing the integrity of the Community and on ironing out hindrances to its effective functioning.

Regarding enlargement, the signature in April of the Sixth Accession Treaty, with Bulgaria and Romania, was accompanied by misgivings. Uniquely, the date set for accession (2007) could, in certain circumstances, be postponed to 2008 if one or both of the candidate states were held to be unready for membership. This was followed by anguished debate on the long-standing application of Turkey for EU membership. That too was at last, but reluctantly, agreed and accession negotiations were authorised to begin in October. Both of these events, but especially the latter, gave rise to a growing suggestion that enlargement of the EU should be closed after Bulgaria and Romania. That notwithstanding, it was agreed that Croatia should also join the queue (see pp. 72; 94-95).

The unease over further expansion of the EU reflected a new uncertainty over the future of the Union in general. That was dramatically expressed in the failure of the referendums in France and the Netherlands for ratification of the previous year's constitutional treaty and the catatonic trance which followed (see pp. 368-70).

Fragmentation was a different matter. It dated from the mid-1970s when the UK had joined the Community and the 1968 judgments convention had had to be amended. The new version applied only to those member states which ratified it, the others remaining bound by the old version. That anomaly occurred after every subsequent accession and was not ended even when the convention (requiring ratification) was replaced by a regulation (which did not), since Denmark disputed the validity of the legal basis for adopting the regulation and used its opt-out (agreed at Maastricht) to evade the regulation and stay with the convention. This was solved in 2005 by a special treaty between the European Community (EC) and Denmark under which the latter agreed to apply the contents of the regulation.

The same happened under the 1997 convention on the service of judicial documents, which in fact never came into force. It too was replaced, in 2000, by a regulation, the validity of which was denied by Denmark. A similar treaty between the EC and Denmark was signed in October, whereby the contents of the regulation would apply in Denmark. In both cases, however, it was expressly provided that compliance with the treaty would be a matter of international law and not Community law.

The second, and more far-reaching, example of fragmentation was the Schengen treaty, which was originally concluded in 1985 between five of the original six member states. Providing for enhanced movement over internal borders and concomitant transnational police powers, it was gradually extended to most of the other member states; but Ireland, the UK, and Denmark remained outside. It was also extended to some non-member states: Norway, Iceland, and Switzerland. In May the first two Schengen treaties (1985 and 1990) were supplemented by a third, signed at Prüm by the five original Schengen signatories plus Spain and Austria.

While the Commission continued to produce important legislation, such as the cross-border company mergers directive 2005/56, adopted in October, and the continuing saga of the highly controversial Bolkestein directive on the free movement of services within the EU, its energies were mostly diverted into legislation which the member states wished to see enacted in the fields of criminal law and the justice system.

Of particular importance were the two money laundering directives. One of these (framework decision 2005/212), issued in February under the third pillar, "police and judicial co-operation in criminal matters", finally put paid to the pretence that the offence was merely the washing of proceeds from crime. Instead, the framework decision went on to provide for confiscation of such proceeds and, where the proceeds had been spent, confiscation of assets of an estimated equivalent value. The second (directive 2005/60), issued in October under the first pillar, codified and rationalised the existing money laundering law into an elaborate and elegantly expressed system, while at the same time extending it to cover, inter alia, the financing of terrorist activities.

Also in February came two further important criminal law texts, both framework decisions under the third pillar. The first, the computer data crimes framework decision 2005/222, related to hacking and other crimes against computer systems but was drafted in such a way that it would also apply to accessing a database in breach of the intellectual property rights of the rights holder. The second, the financial penalties recognition framework decision 2005/214, was part of the Union's aim to unify the member states' criminal justice systems through the principle of mutual recognition, a civil justice principle introduced by the 1968 judgments convention. It provided for the automatic enforcement of fines and related orders imposed by a court in another member state. It was a companion to the European arrest warrant (EAW) framework decision 2002, and contained parallel provisions on double criminality and grounds for non-recognition and non-execution; like the EAW, it made no mention of jurisdiction. The other proposed companion to the EAW would have introduced minimum standards of criminal procedure and trial practice throughout the EU. However, during 2005 it was revealed that this had been quietly dropped in view of the objections of several member states, on the pretext that any defects in national procedure would be covered by the European Convention on Human Rights.

The European Court of Justice (ECJ) too began to consider issues of criminal justice and other third pillar issues. Its judgment of January, in case C-257/01, *Commission v Council*, considered the position of the Schengen rules in the Union system: the case turned on the technicalities of self-delegation, where the European Council delegated implementing powers to itself, thereby evading Parliament and Commission interference. Normally, under the "comitology" legislation, this procedure was only permissible "in specific and substantiated cases". The Court held that the origins and character of Schengen did, for the present, constitute such a specific case.

A highly controversial judgment was delivered in September by the Court of First Instance (CFI) in case T-306/01 and another, *Yusuf and Kadi v Council and Commission*, concerning the freezing of funds of suspected terrorists pursuant to decisions of the UN Security Council sanctions committee. The EC Treaty empowered the European Council to impose economic sanctions specifically on third states. The CFI held that this could be expanded to include sanctions on individuals. Its reasoning depended on a somewhat naïve view of international law and the relations between the UN and the EU, and also a complacent view of the protective value of the international law concept of *jus cogens* ("compelling law" which may not be violated by any country). The judgment was heavily attacked by academics and was appealed to the ECJ.

At national level, too, a potentially explosive situation was narrowly averted. In *Oakley Inc. v Animal Ltd*, the English High Court had, in a very closely argued judgment in February, queried the validity of a statutory instrument promulgated under section 2(2) of the European Communities Act to implement an EC directive on the harmonisation of registered designs law. If upheld, this would have imperilled a large part of the UK legislation implementing EC directives. However, the day was saved in October when the Court of Appeal in three careful opinions unanimously allowed the appeal (see pp. 428-29).

Finally, the Civil Service Tribunal, instituted in 2004 as part of the ECJ court system (see AR 2004, p. 449), completed all its set-up processes during the year and in December was declared duly constituted and ready for business.

LAW IN THE UNITED KINGDOM

The Constitutional Reform Act 2005 brought major changes in the way that judges were appointed in England. The old system of "secret soundings" by the Lord Chancellor gave way to appointment by a judicial appointments commission, made up of a mixture of judicial, legal-professional and lay members, and chaired by a layman. Appointment was to be made solely on merit, although the commission was to have regard to the need to "encourage diversity" in the range of people available for selection, subject to that requirement. The Lord Chancellor's judicial role was formally abolished too. The Lord Chief Justice took over as head of the judiciary, with new presidents for each division of the High Court. The Act declared that it did not affect "the existing constitutional principle of the rule of law" and reaffirmed the need for the Lord Chancellor and other government ministers to uphold the independence of the judiciary. Furthermore, the Act provided for a new UK Supreme Court, to replace the appellate committee of the House of Lords in accordance with the alleged constitutional requirement of the separation of powers. However, the Court would not come into being until (or unless) the Lord Chancellor certified that suitable accommodation existed for it. With ongoing wrangles over the suitability, and cost of conversion, of the mock-Tudor Middlesex Guildhall into a "21st century Supreme Court", this seemed unlikely to happen in the immediate future (although the government hoped that the first sitting would be in 2008).

The year saw a number of important constitutional decisions. In *A and others v Secretary of State for the Home Department*, the House of Lords held that evidence procured by torture was not admissible, in an appeal under the Anti-Terrorism, Crime and Security Act 2001, even though the evidence had been obtained by the acts of a foreign state without the complicity of the UK government (see p. 18). The suggestion that such evidence could be heard flew in the face of 500 years of English legal history, throughout which the common law had set its face against torture: this had more the status of high constitutional principle than a mere rule of evidence. The common law position was bolstered by public international law, and the European Convention on Human Rights. Lord Bingham of Cornhill professed himself "startled, even a little dismayed, at the suggestion (and the acceptance by the Court of Appeal majority) that this deeply-rooted tradition and an international obligation solemnly and explicitly undertaken can be overridden by a statute and a procedural rule which make no mention of torture at all".

In *Regina (Jackson) v Attorney-General*, the House of Lords had to consider the validity of the Parliament Act 1949, and the statutes enacted using its provisions, notably the Hunting Act 2004 (see AR 2004, p. 451). Thus to question a statute was an "unusual, and in modern times probably unprecedented" task (Lord Woolf). The applicants had strenuously argued, however, that in 1949 it had been unlawful to extend the power conferred on the King and House of Commons by the Parliament Act 1911 through a legislative process which bypassed the House of Lords (viz. using the 1911 Act to enact the 1949 Act). This contention was unanimously rejected by the appellate committee. The only limitation contained in the Parliament Act 1911 was that the King and Commons could not pass a statute to prolong the life of a Parliament (and delay a general election) beyond five years. There was no warrant to read in further restrictions, whether to prohibit major constitutional changes (as the Court of Appeal had thought), or simply to prevent amendment of the 1911 Act using its own procedure. The principle that a delegate could not unilaterally extend the power delegated to him was inapt: statutes enacted using the Parliament Acts were statutes in the full sense; it was an "absurd and confusing mis-characterisation" to describe such Acts as "delegated legislation" (Lord Nicholls of Birkenhead). Moreover, the validity of the Parliament Act 1949 had long been assumed, and relied upon to pass several statutes, including the Hunting Act.

In *Oakley Inc. v Animal Ltd* the English High Court had ruled that when making use of the option contained in an EU directive to retain in force certain provisions of domestic British law, the government was not acting to "implement" any EU "obligation", and thus lacked the power to legislate by statutory instrument under the European Communities Act 1972. Such decisions of policy should be made by primary legislation (an Act of Parliament), said the judge. "Henry VIII powers" (viz. to amend primary legislation by statutory instrument) were to be construed narrowly and strictly against the government. The Court of Appeal in 2005, however, allowed the appeal on the basis that this narrow construction of ministerial powers under the 1972 Act was "illogical", "practically absurd" and "obviously wrong". Since EU directives (as opposed to regulations) always gave some discretion as to implementation to member states, the powers in the 1972 Act would be rendered a dead letter for directives' translation into domestic law. Parliament could not have intended such a result (see p. 427). Elsewhere, the government introduced the draft legislative and regulatory reform bill, which if enacted would confer yet more extensive "Henry VIII" powers upon ministers. The bill was very widely condemned by constitutional commentators.

The Human Rights Act 1998 (HRA) continued to make its influence felt across virtually every department of the law. In *Beaulane Properties v Palmer*, the acquisition of title by adverse possession ("squatter's rights") under the Land Registration Act 1925 was held to be unlawful confiscation of property contrary to the European Convention on Human Rights (ECHR). The court remedied this by interpreting "adversity" in an older, narrower sense, summoning up the ghosts of pre-1833 adverse possession law. The Land Registration Act 2002 was to solve these problems in due course. The courts continued to rely upon the ECHR to develop a tort of invasion of privacy in all but name, strictly, a "new sub-species" of the action for breach of confidence, although the Court of Appeal admitted the artificiality of this in *Douglas v Hello! Magazine (No. 3)*. In that case, the claimants were not barred from recovering damages in respect of invasion of privacy simply because they had sold the rights to publish their wedding photographs to another, rival magazine. That magazine (*OK!*) had no claim against *Hello!* of its own, however.

Many other HRA claims were unsuccessful. Paying a lower jobseeker's allowance to those under twenty-five years of age was not unlawful discrimination: *Regina (Reynolds) v Work and Pensions Secretary*. The rule that, in defamation, loss is presumed and need not be proved did not constitute an undue restriction on newspapers' freedom of expression: *Jameel v Wall Street Journal*. Nor did the rule requiring a newspaper to pay the costs of a successful defamation claimant: *Campbell v MGN (No. 2)*. The importance of jury confidentiality to the criminal process justified a finding of contempt of court when a juror passed information about those deliberations to the defendant's lawyers: *Attorney-General v Scotcher*. It was not "inhuman and degrading treatment" to deport an alien with HIV/AIDS back to a state where the standards of medical care for the disease were very much lower than in the UK: *N v Home Secretary*. The right to life under the ECHR did not oblige the National Health Service (NHS) to provide a particular, experimental treatment for cancer: *Regina (Rogers) v Swindon NHS Trust*. The common law crime of public nuisance was sufficiently certain and predictable to comply with the ECHR: *Regina v Rimmington*. Even when HRA claims did succeed, the House of Lords emphasised that courts must award damages only where causation of financial loss was positively proved, or there were exceptional circumstances. A finding of breach of the ECHR should normally of itself suffice to vindicate the claimant's rights: *Regina (Greenfield) v Home Secretary*.

In criminal law, the Privy Council reaffirmed an objectively determined level of self-control for the defence of provocation in murder cases to be made out: *Attorney-General of Jersey v Holley*. The High Court ruled that to permit grown adults to swim unsupervised in a lake did not expose the landowner to prosecution under the Health and Safety Act 1974. The swimmers knowingly took the risks upon themselves: *Hampstead Heath Winter Swimming Club v Corporation of London*. Elsewhere, the House of Lords refused the invitation to limit the temporal effect of its rulings to act prospectively only. Such "prospective over-ruling" was inconsistent with the traditional conception of the judicial role, and would alter the courts' constitutional function. On the other hand, in a case where grave disruption and injustice would be caused by a retrospective ruling, the House of Lords might feel compelled to depart from established practice. This, however, was not such a case, and accordingly the question would have to wait for another day: *Re Spectrum Plus Ltd*.

LAW IN THE USA

IN 2005 the US Supreme Court did not render any significant decisions on federalism, the allocation of powers between the federal and state governments. Chief Justice William Hubbs Rehnquist, who, during the prior ten years, had led in the Court's decisions that expanded the immunity of state governments from federal regulation, dissented, along with Justice Thomas, in *Gonzalez v Raich*, which held that federal legislation which prohibited the sale of marijuana pre-empted a California law that permitted the sale of marijuana to be used for medicinal purposes, even though the marijuana was grown, sold, and used solely within the state of California. Chief Justice Rehnquist died in 2005 and was replaced with Judge John Roberts (see p. 116).

The scope of the US President's power, under the constitution and the "authorisation for the use of military force" (AUMF)—the joint resolution adopted by the US Congress (the legislature) on 14 September 2001—continued, in 2005, to raise the most controversial legal and policy questions. Following the decision in 2004 by the Supreme Court that the President could not detain indefinitely as an "enemy combatant" Yasser Hamdi, a US citizen who was taken prisoner in Afghanistan by the US armed forces, Hamdi was deported to Saudi Arabia in 2005 (see AR 2004, p. 453). In February, a federal district court, in *Padilla v Hanf*, ruled that the President did not have authority to detain José Padilla—a US citizen who was arrested in Chicago and detained as an enemy combatant, based on allegations that he had plotted to build and detonate a radiological dispersal device in a major US city—because the AUMF authorised only the detention of those captured on the battlefield. In September, the Fourth

Circuit Court of Appeals reversed that decision, holding that the President did have authority under the AUMF to detain Padilla. Padilla appealed against that decision to the Supreme Court, but in November he was charged by the federal government with "with providing—and conspiring to provide—material support to terrorists, and conspiring to murder individuals who are overseas", and he was transferred from military to civilian custody. In December the Court of Appeals held that the President did not have authority to transfer Padilla to civilian custody. In response to claims by the President that he had authority under the Constitution and the AUMF to use torture during the interrogation of detainees, Congress passed a bill prohibiting the use of cruel, inhumane or degrading treatment or torture of detainees. When he signed this bill into law, however, the President issued a signing statement, stating, in part: "The executive branch shall construe [the law] in a manner consistent with the constitutional authority of the President [. . .] as Commander in Chief", implying that the President's authority had not been restricted by this law (see p. 121).

The Supreme Court's decision in *Kelo v City of New London* confirmed that the clause in the fifth amendment of the US constitution which prohibited taking property without due process did not prohibit a municipal government from the condemnation of privately owned property for the purpose of transferring it to a private developer as part of a programme that promoted the economic rejuvenation of the area in which such property was located. Four justices dissented from the decision, which was one of the most significant rulings, in fifty years, on when private property may be taken for "public use", because the property had been taken to transfer it to a private developer.

The Supreme Court's decisions in *Rompilla v Beard* and *Roper v Simmons* were an indication that a majority of the Court was inclined to restrict the use of capital punishment. In the first case, the Court held that a defendant in a capital case was denied effective representation when his counsel failed to review his file for evidence that mitigated the gravity of his crime. In the second, the Court held that capital punishment was a cruel and unusual punishment when applied to offenders who were under the age of eighteen when they had committed the crime for which they would be executed.

The tobacco companies achieved significant milestones in the lawsuits against them. In one of the most important decisions in the history of such suits, the Supreme Court of Illinois voided a US$10 billion judgment awarded in 2003 in a class action lawsuit against Philip Morris USA for deceiving smokers in its marketing campaign, because the federal trade commission had authorised Philip Morris to use the words "light" and "low tar" to describe cigarettes (see AR 2003, p. 504). In the civil prosecution by the United States of the tobacco companies for violation of the anti-racketeering laws, the US District Court of Appeals held that the United States could not recover US$280 billion in penalties as the illegal profits of the tobacco companies' past actions. The United States appealed the decision to the Supreme Court. Subsequently, the United States, in its closing argument before the judge presiding over the prosecution of the tobacco companies, requested only US$10 billion to pay the costs of anti-smoking campaigns over a five-year period. In response to this decision by the United States, organisations which were not parties to the case asked for and received the right to submit memoranda and briefs proposing appropriate remedies in the case. A decision by the judge presiding over the prosecution was expected in 2006.

In January the Supreme Court ruled, in *Ileto v Glock*, that a lawsuit against gun manufacturers by the victims of a shooting—which alleged that the manufacturers were negligent and created a public nuisance by the manufacture and distribution of guns—could proceed. Subsequently, Congress enacted the Protection of Lawful Commerce in Arms Act which gave the manufacturers and sellers of guns protection from lawsuits for the damages caused by illegal use of firearms or ammunition, with a few narrow exceptions applicable to sellers only.

XV RELIGION

Notwithstanding periodic media comment about "the clash of civilisations", and connections made between religion and political struggles in the Middle East, religious events in 2005 were conspicuous more for turmoil or debate within the major faiths than between them.

CHRISTIANITY. The most publicised event of 2005 within Christianity was the death of Pope John Paul II, leader of the world's 1.1 billion Roman Catholics. After many years of declining health he died on 2 April, aged eighty-four, his twenty-seven-year reign constituting the second longest documented pontificate in history (for obituary see p. 456). John Paul II's promotion of peace and inter-religious harmony through the years of the ending of the Cold War was coupled with centralisation of the papal office, the severe loss of political influence by the Roman Catholic church, and declining numbers of clergy in Europe and North America.

The Bavarian Cardinal Joseph Ratzinger, Dean of the College of Cardinals and Prefect of the Congregation for the Doctrine of the Faith from 1981, was announced as the next Pope on 19 April, three days after his seventy-eighth birthday, making him the oldest pope on his appointment for over a century (see pp. 58-59). He took the name of Benedict XVI. Well known as the Vatican's chief defender of orthodoxy and opponent of liberalism, Benedict was expected by most commentators to follow the line of his predecessor, whom he had called "John Paul the Great": in May he initiated the beatification process, dispensing with the usual five-year rule. In August he gave a strong media performance at the Cologne World Youth Congress. However, some commentators were surprised that his first months as pope were marked by a relative silence on moral and doctrinal issues. There was much media speculation about the content of his first encyclical, expected early in 2006.

High-profile scandals involving sex and corruption caused the Orthodox Church in Greece to be in the news throughout 2005. Archimandrite Yiosakis was imprisoned for embezzlement and illegally selling antiques. Other revelations involved compromising photographs of the ninety-one-year old Metropolitan Stefanos of Trifyllia and Olympia, and the broadcast of apparently dishonest conversations between Metropolitan Panteleimon of Attica and a high-ranking judge. Further allegations of financial corruption led to Panteleimon's suspension, dramatically announced by Archbishop Christodoulos of Athens and all Greece live on television. Some prominent Greek politicians, including a member of the European Parliament, John Varvitsiotis, called for a separation of church and state.

In Jerusalem the Greek Orthodox Patriarch, Ireneos I, leader of the largest Christian denomination in Israel and Palestine, was deposed by the Holy Synod in May on the grounds that he was "incorrigibly caught up in a syndrome of lying, religious distortions, degradation of the Patriarchate, and irresponsible mishandling of Patriarchate property". One of the main charges against him was that he had sold off property to Jews, which incensed many Arab members of his community. His successor, Theophilus III, sworn in on 22 November, was opposed by the state of Israel.

Other churches continued to be divided over moral issues, particularly the question of homosexuality. In November, for instance, the bishops of the American United Methodist church affirmed that homosexuality was not a bar to membership of the church, only two days after a court had supported a pastor's decision to refuse a gay man admission to his congregation. Several leaders of the Anglican Communion called for a tougher stance on homosexuality. The primates' meeting in February in Northern Ireland considered, as its most pressing business, the "Windsor report" commissioned in 2004 which proposed a more centralised structure for the Anglican community (see AR 2004, p. 455). The Communion appointed an officer to listen to the experience of homosexual people; however, in what some commentators saw as the initiation of a split within the Anglican communion, the primates also requested that the North American churches (the Episcopal Church (USA) and the Anglican Church of Canada) "voluntarily withdraw their members from the Anglican consultative council for the period leading up to the next Lambeth Conference" due in 2008, and "consider their place within the Anglican Communion". In November a critical letter sent to the Archbishop of Canterbury from leaders of the "global south" Anglican church backfired after it was disowned by a number of its purported signatories. A further sign of the redirection of Anglicanism away from its historic European base was the appointment of the first black archbishop in the Church of England, John Sentamu, originally from Uganda, who was enthroned at York (see p. 19).

The Christian world was shocked by the murder in his Burgundy church on 17 August of Brother Roger of Taizé, aged ninety. He had led the ecumenical community over a long period, during which time large numbers of people were inspired by his teaching. June saw the death of the Philippine Cardinal Jaime Sin, who had played an important role in the overthrow of the Marcos dictatorship (for obituary see pp. 549-50). The same month marked the final crusade in New York of the veteran evangelist, Billy Graham, which was attended by over 240,000 people.

Christianity continued to influence public life in many and varied ways. While Pat Robertson, television evangelist and founder of the American Christian coalition, called in August for the assassination of the Venezuelan President, Hugo Chávez (see pp. 166-67), others adopted a more pacifist tone, including the Christian Peacemaker Teams, four of whose members were abducted in Iraq in November (see p. 192). A degree of unity emerged among Christians after the devastation following Hurricane Katrina, even though some attributed it to divine retribution for the liberal policies of the New Orleans city council.

HINDUISM. There was further controversy over the 69th Shankaracarya (chair) of the Kanchi Mutt (monastery), Sri Jayendra Saraswati (see AR 2004, p. 456). Having been accused in 2004 of arranging a murder, he and some devotees were now said to have stolen an image of the god Shiva (Shivalingam) from an ancient temple at Periyakudi in Tiruvarur district of Tamil Nadu, India. Anticipating arrest, he and his disciples surrendered to the judicial magistrates court. He was granted bail.

The presentation of Hinduism, particularly in the context of education, continued to be of concern to Hindus. A particular focus was the historical problem of whether groups calling themselves aryans migrated into, or even invaded, India in the first or possibly second millennium BC. Some Indian scholars, particularly those influenced by Hindu nationalism, saw this concept as a purely Western construction and a relic of colonialism. Others opposed this "Hinduness" (*hindutva*) camp on archaeological and philological grounds. The issue came to a head in December over a textbook in the state of California, USA, which Harvard University indologist Professor Michael Witzel had recommended altering, on the grounds that its contents distorted the history of India in favour of a Hindu nationalist agenda. His emendations were rejected by some Hindus and not all were accepted by the California board of education.

Elsewhere, it was reported that the UK government was to spend UK£10 million on the country's first Hindu school, a primary school to be completed within the next five years. Welcoming the move, Ramesh Kallidai, secretary-general of the Hindu Forum of Britain, noted that there had long been Christian, Muslim, and Jewish state schools in the UK but hitherto no Hindu school; the project would increase parental choice and contribute to the development of the Hindu community. The development contributed to the wider context of the ongoing debate over faith schools in Britain and whether or not they promoted sectarianism and racism.

Hindus everywhere expressed outrage after it was reported that Archbishop Nikon of Ufa and Sterlitamak of the Russian Orthodox church, seeking to prevent the construction in Moscow of a Hindu temple, had, in a November letter to the Moscow mayor Yury Luzhkov, called the Hindu god Krishna an "evil demon, the personified power of hell opposing God".

India continued to recover from the tsunami of December 2004 (see map, p. 296). One story was seen as a symbol of hope. A small figurine image of a deity was found in January floating on a raft in Meyyurkuppam village on the Tamil Nadu coast. Meyyurkuppam was less damaged than many coastal villages, and its inhabitants attributed this to the deity in question. The image turned out, in fact, to be that of a Buddhist deity, Jalagupta, which had floated a thousand kilometres from Burma (Myanmar), where it had been released in mid-December in a local ritual. It was planned to build a temple to the deity with help from the Burmese government.

ISLAM. Against the backdrop of the ongoing war in Iraq, tensions persisted between mainstream and radical tendencies within Islam. Symptomatic of this was a series of assassinations of religious leaders in Afghanistan by suspected Taliban members; these claimed the lives, most notably, of Muhammad Gul, a member of the ulema council, the national council of Muslim clerics, and Nur Ahmad Khan, head of the scholars' council in Kunar province.

In Iraq a similar polarisation was evident, with the association of Sunni ulema playing a key role in mediating between Sunni radicals and traditionalists. The association, formed immediately after the US-led invasion of 2003, grew in importance during the year under the leadership of Harith al-Dari. While opposing the more extreme Wahhabi factions, the mixed Arab and Kurdish association declared in February that, because of a Sunni boycott of national elections, the new Iraqi government had no right to frame the country's constitution. Frustrated by its self-imposed marginality, the council changed its stance, and towards the end of the year described voting in the 15 December elections as a "religious duty" (see pp. 185-88). Although its mediation successfully secured the release of several Western hostages, the association failed to reduce the level of Wahhabi terrorism, and by the end of the year the Interior Minister, Bayan Jabr, had acknowledged that Iraq had become the major training ground for international terrorists.

In Central Asia Islamic expression continued to be under pressure from secular governments. In May up to a thousand protestors were killed by Uzbek security forces during a demonstration in favour of imprisoned members of Akromiya, an Islamic group (see pp. 267-68). In neighbouring Turkmenistan further mosque closures were reported, and the country's only remaining centre for training imams, the theology faculty in Ashgabat, was merged with the history faculty and downgraded in size. President Saparmurat Niyazov announced close controls on religious rituals, and ordered that his own book, the *Ruhnama*, be given equal prominence with the Qur'an in mosques.

In July a major conference held in Amman, Jordan, sought to capitalise on Muslim reactions to the rise of terrorism in Iraq and elsewhere by issuing an ambitious joint statement on Muslim unity. The highest religious figures of forty countries, including the Shaykh al-Azhar Ali Goma (Egypt), and Grand Ayatollah Ali Sistani (Iraq), present at the "international islamic conference", passed a religious edict (fatwa) which sought to end the disorder which they felt had crept into Islamic law and ethics in the previous two decades. With an eye on sectarian violence in Iraq and Pakistan, they declared that the eight most widely-followed Islamic schools (*madhhabs*) were all valid, and the rulings given by their accredited leaders were to be respected by all Muslims. These schools were the four main Sunni tendencies (Maliki, Shafi'i, Hanbali, and Hanafi), and the two Shi'ite schools of the Ja'faris and the Zaydis, together with the small Ibadi school, and the Zahiri school (now largely defunct). The Wahhabi school was not included on the list of valid denominations, but the fatwa forbade Muslims to consider the Wahhabis as apostates. The conference's second major achievement was to call on the members of each school to regularise their internal mechanisms for delivering authoritative judgments. It stated that "no-one may issue a religious ruling without adhering to the methodology of the schools of jurisprudence." This was no doubt an attempt to disown the rulings of radicals, such as Osama bin Laden, who rejected the authority of Islam's traditional leadership and methodology.

The Amman fatwa was widely welcomed across the Islamic world as an historic step towards Muslim unity. While it did not seek to reduce the established doctrinal and jurisprudential differences, it provided a binding articulation of the informal atmosphere of mutual respect prevalent among most scholars. Individual participants at the conference—particularly those concerned by the Sunni-Shi'ite divide—launched further initiatives to consider ways of reducing the substantial doctrinal differences which separated them.

Partly in the wake of the Amman fatwa, an extraordinary summit meeting of the fifty-seven member states of the Organisation of the Islamic Conference (OIC) took place in Mecca, Saudi Arabia, in December, with a mandate to articulate a common Muslim stance against terrorism (see pp. 367-68). This time involving political rather than religious leaders, the final declaration stated that "we are determined to develop our national laws and legislations to criminalise every single terrorist practice", in the light of "our unwavering rejection of terrorism and all forms of extremism and violence". The OIC states adopted a "ten-year action plan", mostly to co-ordinate responses to terrorism, but also with a remit to focus Muslim policies on greater support for Palestinian rights and for the victims of poverty in Africa. There were strong echoes of the Amman fatwa in the OIC's call for controlling the proliferation of unqualified preachers and for retrieving earlier levels of mutual respect among the religion's major denominations.

JUDAISM. On 27 January world leaders and religious representatives joined survivors at a ceremony in Auschwitz, Poland, to mark the 60th anniversary of the liberation of the Nazi concentration camps. With the survivors aging, this was seen as one of the last opportunities there would be to ponder the horrors of the Nazis' "final solution" with those who had personally experienced them. In the light of various contemporary anti-Semitic incidents in Europe, the importance of remembering and learning the lessons of the concentration camps was reiterated.

In September Simon Wiesenthal, the famed hunter of Nazi war criminals, died, aged ninety-six (for obituary see pp. 551-52). His work, *The Sunflower: On the possibilities and limits of forgiveness*, encapsulated the difficulties of constructing Jewish-Christian relations in a post-Holocaust context, when interpretations of religious terms often differed markedly.

Celebrations in October marked the 40th anniversary of *Nostra Aetate*, the declaration issued at the Second Vatican Council by Pope Paul VI regarding the Roman Catholic church's relations with non-Christian religions. *Nostra Aetate* condemned anti-Semitism. It rejected the teaching that the Jewish people could collectively be charged with deicide and recalled the Jewish origins of much of Christian thought. The perception of the relationship between Judaism and the Christian church as that of root and branch was presented as a basis for efforts to increase understanding between the two. In the intervening years a number of additional statements had been issued by the Vatican, in an attempt to clarify further the Catholic church's position regarding Judaism and the manner in which it was portrayed in Christian teachings and liturgy. The resultant inter-faith dialogue formed part of joint efforts to overturn 2,000 years of what has been termed the church's "teaching of contempt".

The 25th annual Limmud conference in Nottingham, UK, in December marked a different kind of anniversary, primarily, though not exclusively, within Anglo-

Jewry. As an educational movement focused chiefly around a winter conference, Limmud was designed to create the widest possible range of Jewish learning opportunities, in which Jews with affiliation to any or no denomination of Judaism could freely gather and share a platform. In 2005 the conference attracted some 2,000 participants, who were able to choose from around 1,000 different sessions.

At the opposite end of the spectrum of Jewish study, the completion of the (US) ArtScroll publishing house's fifteen-year project of translating the Babylon Talmud was celebrated in March. The seventy-three volume work was beneficial in facilitating access in translation to this central Jewish text, an issue that had exercised Orthodox Judaism since the late eighteenth century. Yet it also formed part of a wider mission by ultra-Orthodox publishers to inculcate a narrow view of Judaism based on strict interpretations and not necessarily concerned to shed a comprehensive light upon the material they presented. Thus, explanations or viewpoints at variance with the publisher's agenda were excluded, even when these were found acceptable in other sectors of Orthodoxy.

XVI THE ARTS

OPERA—MUSIC—BALLET & DANCE—THEATRE—CINEMA—TELEVISION & RADIO

OPERA

It was a curiously unsettling year for opera. Companies around the world maintained service as usual, including the premieres of many important new works. But governmental policy decisions and management upsets left those who cared about the art form with a deep sense of foreboding.

In Italy, birthplace of opera, the government of Prime Minister Silvio Berlusconi announced a 20 per cent cut in arts subsidies. The Minister of Culture threatened to resign, but failed to do so. Italian companies cancelled productions and shortened their seasons. The experienced and respected sovrintendente of the San Carlo theatre in Naples, Gioacchino Lanza Tomasi, said "we are staring disaster in the face". Results in the 2006 Italian election were awaited with much nervousness. In the UK, a cut of UK£34 million in overall arts subsidy and a funding standstill (i.e. a cut) for three years caused much gloom. The Scottish Parliament ordered Scottish Opera to go "dark" for a year (see AR 2004, p. 461). The distinguished Scottish critic Andrew Clark described this as "one of the biggest acts of philistinism ever seen in Europe". The Belgian Culture Minister threatened to disband Flemish Opera's orchestra, but had second thoughts in the face of protests.

There was a serious blip in the field of private sponsorship, on which many companies had been forced to rely. The dot.com billionaire Alberto Vilar, lavish in his donations to companies from Los Angeles to Saint Petersburg, was arrested in May on charges of fraud and, unable to raise his US$4 million bail, spent three weeks in prison. But there was one piece of good news: the Metropolitan Opera in New York found a new sponsor, Toll Brothers, for the worldwide Saturday matinee broadcasts previously supported by Texaco. These broadcasts reached an estimated 11 million listeners in forty-two countries.

In the UK, there threatened to be more drama at management level in English National Opera than on stage. The company's director of marketing loudly booed the conductor, Paul Daniel, at his final performance as music director. Daniel left, the marketing man stayed. Towards the end of the year, the chief executive and artistic director, Séan Doran, left the company somewhat abruptly. His successors, John Berry (artistic director) and Loretta Tomasi (executive director), were appointed from within by the controversial chairman of the board, Martin Smith, without outside advertisement and to the publicly expressed disapproval of the Arts Council of England. The incoming music director, Oleg Caetani, was "let go". In the last days of the year, Smith himself resigned as chairman, citing a press campaign against him as one reason. His post was advertised. Under his chairmanship seat prices had risen sharply, against the founding principles of Lilian Baylis's "people's opera". All the above suggested to pessimists that opera was reverting to being a trophy art form, "too good for the average man".

Nevertheless, ENO had a good year on stage, with fine new productions of *On the Town*, *Billy Budd*, and *Madama Butterfly*. Daniel conducted the final segment of Phyllida Lloyd's *Ring* production, *Twilight of the Gods*. The company also gave the premiere of Gerald Barry's *The Bitter Tears of Petra von Kant*, an all-female drama based, too closely many thought, on Fassbinder's play of the same name. Welsh National Opera moved into its new home, the Wales Millennium Centre, with a new production by Richard Jones of *Wozzeck*, followed by *Don Carlos* (sung in the original French), and ending the year with a depressingly limp *Merry Widow*. London's Royal Opera had a good year, with further instalments of Keith Warner's *Ring* staging enjoying a mixed reception, colourful new productions of Rossini's *Barbiere di Siviglia* and *Il turco in Italia*, an outstanding concert performance of Donizetti's virtually unknown last opera, *Dom Sébastien*, and the premiere of Lorin Maazel's *1984*, based on Orwell. This last proved controversial in that the composer-conductor paid up to half the production costs, in default of Vilar's promised contribution, and this smacked to many of the equivalent of vanity publishing.

Worldwide, new operas included John Adams's *Doctor Atomic* (San Francisco), a study of J. Robert Oppenheimer and the Manhattan Project, received with respect rather than boundless enthusiasm. Tobias Picker's *An American Tragedy* was given a lavish launch at the Met. Philip Glass's new work, *Waiting for the Barbarians*, to a libretto by Christopher Hampton drawn from J.M. Coetzee's novel, was premiered in Erfurt. Mark Adamo's *Lysistrata*, loosely based on Aristophanes, was a success for Houston Grand Opera. Richard Danielpour's *Margaret Garner*, set in a nineteenth-century slave plantation, was successfully premiered in Detroit. In Europe, Giorgio Battistelli's *Richard III* (Antwerp) and Philippe Boesmans's *Julie* (based on Strindberg, premiered in Brussels) were significant contributions to the form.

Notable stagings of old operas included *Tristan und Isolde*, by Peter Sellars and the video artist Bill Viola in Paris; the revival of Alfano's *Cyrano de Bergerac* as a vehicle for Plácido Domingo at the Met; Peter Stein's production of Henze's *The Bassarids* in Amsterdam; and an affectionate and sensitive *Cenerentola* at Glyndebourne, directed by Peter Hall. Glyndebourne also staged David McVicar's riotously colourful—too much so for some purists—version of Handel's *Giulio Cesare*. Other festival productions included *Così fan tutte* by Patrice Chéreau (Aix) and Christoph Marthaler's *Tristan und Isolde* (Bayreuth), both surprisingly conservative. There was an important revival of Schreker's *Die Gezeichneten* at Salzburg.

There were many changes of management in a turbulent year. After much politicking, Riccardo Muti resigned as artistic director of La Scala, Milan; he was replaced by Aix's Stéphane Lissner. Houston Grand Opera's David Gockley moved to San Francisco and was replaced by Welsh National Opera's Anthony Freud.

The year's "scandals" included Calixto Bieito predictably treating *Madama Butterfly* as a drama about sex tourism, with Cio-Cio-San failing to commit suicide but shooting her child (Berlin); Opera Ireland having to postpone rehearsals of *La traviata* because the sets imported from Germany were found to contain 13lbs of cocaine, and a *Rigoletto* directed by Doris Dörrie in which all the cast were *Planet of the Apes*-style primates (Munich).

The year's obituary included the conductors Carlo Maria Giulini (see p. 533) and Gary Bertini, the sopranos Victoria de los Angeles and Birgit Nilsson (see pp. 529-30; 543), the tenor James King, the baritones Theodor Uppman (creator of Billy Budd) and Piero Cappuccilli, and the impresarios Leonard Ingrams and Patric Schmid.

MUSIC

THE vitality and life-force of classical music, and its power to evolve and to change in the face of diverse global challenges, particularly in popular culture, were apparent in the high level of musical activity in 2005, which manifested itself in contrasting ways in different traditions.

The American musical tradition, multi-ethnic and idealistic, gave readier acceptance to living composers than its British counterpart. Every major US orchestra had its permanent composer-in-residence; smaller orchestras pooled their resources in a collaborative network of much sought-after commissions. One such project led to performances of *Made in America* by Joan Towers, spread over two seasons, in each of the fifty states. Performances of other composers' works of whatever nationality occurred as a matter of course. The Australian composer Brett Dean was a prominent example, and his two commissions of 2005 were collaborative. His *Viola Concerto*, with himself as soloist, was commissioned jointly by the Los Angeles Philharmonic and the BBC in London, and proved a highly colourful display of instrumental virtuosity. His *Parteitag*, heard at the Holland Festival in June, was less orthodox, and had the Royal Concertgebouw Orchestra spread in uncomfortable groups round the Wester gas works in Amsterdam and used in combination with video projections to make a political point about the use of power in the modern world.

The 80th birthday of the American composer Gunther Schuller was marked by a festival "I hear America: Gunther Schuller at 80" at the New England Conservatory in Boston, where he had served as president for ten years. *Grand Concerto for Percussion and Keyboards*, first heard in August at Tanglewood, featured eleven musicians playing 150 instruments, and was followed by *Spectre* with the Boston Symphony Orchestra.

But the chief focus of 2005 was on the grand old man of American music, Elliott Carter, and the sustained, rich flowering of his late works. Two pieces for ensemble were premiered in Europe: *Mosaic* for ensemble—really a miniature harp concerto—was given in London by the Nash Ensemble; and *Reflexions*, a light-hearted tribute to the eighty-year-old Pierre Boulez, was played in Paris and on tour by the Ensemble Intercontemporain. The rattling of stones (*pierres*) greatly pleased its dedicatee. Two of Carter's pieces for orchestra were premiered in the USA, on the same day, 6 October: *Soundings* by the Chicago Symphony under Daniel Barenboim; and *Three Illusions* by the Boston Symphony under James Levine. *Soundings*, like *Reflexions*, was light-hearted. Beginning and ending with resonating piano chords, from which the harmony was derived, it was directed from the keyboard by Barenboim. *Three Illusions* originated from an altogether more fantasy-centred creative impulse. The first illusion, *Micomicón*, was an imaginary kingdom in Cervantes's *Don Quixote*. The second, *Fons Juventatis*, came about when Youth was turned into a fountain by Jupiter, and had the power to make old people young again. The third, *Utopia*, used the music as a metaphor for an ideal, non-existent form of society, with absolute order and absolute freedom. The work ended abruptly, a reference to the beheading of Thomas More.

That most typically American initiative, *The Silk Road Project* (see AR 2001, p. 507), continued to bear rich fruit in 2005. Its purpose was to foster cultural exchange by uniting artists from Asia, the Middle East, and the West in creative collaborations. The words of its founder, Yo-Yo Ma, applied not just to American musical culture, with its diverse ethnic strands, but to all living traditions: "by examining the cultural mosaic of the silk road, we seek to illuminate the cultural heritages of its countries, and identify the voices that represent these traditions today".

In 2000 new chamber works were commissioned from twenty composers from silk road lands, and heard in a festival at Tanglewood in July that year. By 2005 American composers associated with the project had achieved great international prominence. Tan Dun's opera *Tea: A Mirror of Soul* was issued on DVD (Deutsche Grammophon), and was a musical mixture of East and West. By contrast, the idealistic theme of Richard Danielpour's *Washington speaks*, for narrator and orchestra, was one of reconciliation between different faiths and religious tolerance. Danielpour's work took the declaration of the Second Vatican Council of 1965, *Nostra Aetate*, as the start of dialogue between Christianity and Judaism. To mark the declaration's 40th anniversary in 2005 (see p. 437) he set it against words by the first US President, George Washington. The performance took place in Washington DC, at the wish of Pope John Paul II.

By contrast, the British musical tradition, less visionary than the American, centred more on the performer than on the composer. This was a year of several centenaries, the best known being Michael Tippett's, whose works were widely celebrated, particularly the operas. A sumptuous performance of *The Midsummer Marriage* was given at Covent Garden under Richard Hickox, who also conducted the less familiar choral work *The Vision of Saint Augustine*. The ENO mounted the first staged version of *A Child of Our Time*, and *The Knot Garden* was performed—in its reduced version—in Vienna under Walter Kobéra. That left the most radical and violent of Tippett's operas, *King Priam*, to be given a less than ideal performance in Manchester at the Royal Northern College of Music. Nevertheless Tippett fared much better than other major British composers born in 1905, such as Constant Lambert and Alan Rawsthorne.

In such a prevailing mood, one of cautious non-commitment, individual achievements shone out all the more. Chief among these was a major retrospective at the Barbican in January, when the music of the Scottish composer James MacMillan revealed his discovery of a many-layered idiom, a synthesis of new ideas of tonality and sonority. June saw the launch in Birmingham of IgorFest, a four-year project covering nothing less than Stravinsky's complete output, presented by the Birmingham Royal Ballet and the CBSO under Sakari Oramo. Among the classical festivals of 2005, the most exploratory was that at Aldeburgh, where Thomas Adès put together, under the umbrella of Purcell/Britten/Stravinsky, a patchwork of composers of many styles and trends. Other distinctive performances in 2005 included two American works: John Adams conducted his *Harmonium* for chorus and orchestra, to words on the theme of love and death by John Donne and Emily Dickinson, and thereby earned an ovation; and a much acclaimed series of performances by the ENO at the Coliseum of Leonard Bernstein's musical *On the Town* had to be extended to meet popular demand. The greatest unexpected success of the year for a British composer came with the little-noticed premiere by Sinfonia da Camera, at the University of Illinois, under the English conductor Ian Hobson, of the brilliant, virtuosic *Overture in E* by Samuel Wesley, composed in 1830.

As for the record industry in 2005, the supply of music far outstripped the capacity of audiences, and of a declining market. Thus, the record companies fell back on familiar promotional techniques: "complete" series, collections, musicians' portraits, visual aids such as DVDs, and, particularly, anniversaries. It was the 50th anniversary of the Beaux Arts Trio, also of the death of Wilhelm Fürtwangler, who was commemorated along with Arturo Toscanini. Daniel Barenboim was prominent on Warner Classics; "great recordings of the century" was the slogan favoured by EMI; "critics' choice" by Decca, DG, and Philips. In a comparatively lean year, each category produced some distinctive work. In early music, there was Haydn, *The Paris Symphonies* (Deutsche Harmonia Mundi); John Jenkins, *Consort Music* (Naïve); William Byrd, *Consort Songs and Pieces* (Harmonia Mundi USA); and Guillaume Dufay, *Quadrivium* (Glossa). From the classical nineteenth-century repertoire there was Beethoven's *Complete Symphonies* (Bis); and Bruckner's *Symphonies* NDRSO / Wand (TDK DV-COWAND 1-4). From the classical 20th and 21st centuries, there was Penderecki, *A Polish Requiem* (Naxos); Unsuk Chin, *Fantaisie Mécanique, Double Concerto, Acrostic-Wordplay* (DG); Steve Reich, *Different trains, Triple Concerto, The Four Seasons* (Naïve), *Drumming* (Canteloupe Music); Brett Dean, *Beggars and Angels, Amphitheatre, Ariel's Music* (ABC Classics); James MacMillan, *Seven Last Words from the Cross, On the Annunciation of the Blessed Virgin, Te Deum* (Hyperion); Elliott Carter, *Night Fantasies, Two Diversions* (Warner Classics); *Dialogue, Boston Concerto, Cello Concerto* (Bridge Records); Constant Lambert, *Piano Con-*

certo No. 1, Romeo and Juliet (Hyperion); *The Art of Constant Lambert* (Dutton); Christian Darnton, Howard Ferguson, and Roberto Gerhard, *Piano Concertos* (Naxos).

Those who died in 2005 included the composers Arnold Cooke and David Diamond; the pianist Lazar Berman; the violinists Isidore Cohen and Norbert Brainin; the cellists Christopher Bunting and Siegfried Palm; the conductors Carlo Maria Giulini (see p. 533) and Marcello Viotti; the sopranos Ghena Dimitrova and Victoria de los Angeles (see pp. 529-30); the baritone Piero Cappuccilli; and the organ builder Noel Mander.

BOOKS OF THE YEAR. *The New Oxford History of Western Music (5 vols.)*, ed. by Richard Taruskin; *Britten on Music*, Paul Kildea (ed.); *Letters from a Life: selected letters of Benjamin Britten*, Donald Mitchell, Philip Reed, Mervyn Cooke (eds); *The Cambridge History of Twentieth-Century Music*, Nicholas Cook, Anthony Pople (eds); *An Improbable Life: Memoirs*, by Robert Craft; *Shostakovich and His World*, Laurel E. Fay (ed.); *Music and the Aesthetics of Modernity*, Karol Berger, Anthony Newcomb (eds).

BALLET AND DANCE

THE year saw the usual balance between creations and the revival of heritage works. The work of three choreographers—August Bournonville, Frederick Ashton, and Robert Cohan—was celebrated. The eternally popular *Swan Lake* was presented in a variety of styles, and choreographers tackled a wide range of topics in their new productions. London saw frequent visitors such as Merce Cunningham who presented a lively series of events for a week at the Barbican, each with changing choreography and music on a stage decorated by the work of a different eminent artist, while the rarely seen Paris Opera Ballet brought over Angelin Preljocaj's *Le Parc* as a highlight of the French-orientated "dance umbrella". *Le Parc* revealed man's conquest of woman in a formal, classical style to music by Mozart with the final pas de deux showing seduction at its most erotic. The work, apparently set in pre-Revolutionary France, evoked the world of Choderlos Laclos's *Liaisons Dangereuses* far more effectively than Adam Cooper's ballet based on that novel, which was first performed in Japan in January. Although superbly designed by Lez Brotherston, with rooms of tarnished panels, the choreography failed to live up to the visual images. Cooper's charisma enhanced the role of Vicomte de Valmont, while his wife, Sarah Wildor, brought authority to the innocent widow, the Présidente de Tourvel. For Christmas 2005 Matthew Bourne presented his long-awaited *Edward Scissorhands*, inspired by the film. The production was slick and, like Cooper's ballet, benefited from Brotherson's designs, but it seemed like nothing so much as a musical without songs.

In the field of revivals, the most significant event was the nine-day season in June by the Royal Danish Ballet in Copenhagen celebrating the two-hundredth anniversary of the birth of August Bournonville. The company performed the full range of his surviving ballets, including a selection of divertissements at the closing gala. Several of the ballets—*La Sylphide, La Ventana, The Kemesse in Bruges,* and *The King's Volunteers of Amagar*—were presented in recent stagings by Nikolaj Hübbe, Frank Andersen, Lloyd Riggins, and Anne Marie Vessel Schlüter, respectively. Andersen, the company's artistic director, felt strongly that Bournonville's ballets needed to be kept up-to-date to maintain the interest of local audiences and dancers. Yet there was a balance between old and new, as the Royal Danish Ballet also presented on stage, and on a remarkable DVD, the full "Bournonville school" (the system of training codified after Bournonville's death), showing the technique and style required to dance his ballets. Altogether there was a striking array of publications and events to support the anniversary, including books, a collection of nine CDs by Aalborg Symphony Orchestra conducted by Peter Ernst Lassen, and a fine and informative exhibition of costumes and designs for Bournonville ballets.

Three ballets stood out. *Napoli,* the celebration of Italian joie de vivre; *A Folk Tale,* enlivened now that the original markings in the musical score were being adhered to; and the complete *Le Conservatoire, or a Newspaper Courtship,* a gem of a character work. The hero of this Bournonville festival was Thomas Lund whose vivid characterisation and perfect technique enhanced his roles, whether comic or romantic. Lund also led a group of dancers on an international tour so that audiences elsewhere, including London, tasted performances of Bournonville's choreography in fine interpretations. He was deservedly acclaimed as danseur of the year in London.

Copenhagen was also celebrating the bi-centenary of the birth of Hans Christian Andersen. *Papirklip,* by Pär Isberg, performed by students of the Royal Danish Ballet School, was a collage of biographical events (including the storyteller's dream of becoming a dancer) and episodes from his *Tales.* It showed off the young dancers effectively and its swift, varied action kept its young audience absorbed. The Bournonville bi-centenary was also celebrated by The Royal Ballet in London which mounted its first complete *La Sylphide.* Johan Kobborg, responsible for its staging, researched the ballet's evolution, restoring some "lost" details and imparting the Bournonville style to his dancers. Alina Cojocaru, Tamara Rojo, and Sarah Lamb were notable as the elusive sylph and both Sorella Englund and Gary Avis brought drama to the vengeful Madge.

Throughout the first half of 2005 the centenary of Ashton's birth continued to be celebrated by The Royal Ballet. *Ondine* and *Enigma Variations* were revived along with a noteworthy programme of *Les Biches* by Ashton's mentor, Bronislava Nijinska, and his own contrasting masterpieces, the non-narrative *Symphonic Variations,* and his distillation of Ivan Turgenev's play *A Month in the Country.* Rojo also made a memorable debut as the vulnerable dying Marguerite Gautier in *Marguerite and Armand.*

Revivals of older ballets dominated The Royal Ballet's programmes. While revivals of Andrée Howard's *La fête étrange* and John Cranko's *The Lady and the Fool* were welcome, neither received the performance it deserved. The former showed no understanding of its source, an episode from Alain Fournier's novel evoking lost innocence; the latter, by Birmingham Royal Ballet, had elaborate new designs which were completely out of touch with the society portrayed in Cranko's jeu d'esprit. The Royal Ballet's new creations were few, Kim Brandstrup's *Two Footnotes to Ashton* being most memorable. Sylvie Guillem consequently developed her work with Russell Maliphant in sell-out independent programmes allowing his work the profile and audience it deserved.

As ever, *Swan Lake* featured in various forms. The UK saw three noteworthy productions by visiting companies. Australian Ballet's production, which amalgamated a Charles-Diana-Camilla triangle with the sophisticated society of Cecil Beaton and the final days of the Hapsburg Empire, was visually and emotionally effective, although the Dégas-inspired interpretation by Christopher Wheeldon for the Philadelphia Ballet, which was presented at the Edinburgh Festival, seemed a superficial gloss. Next to the freshness and enthusiasm with which the Australians and Americans presented the ballet, the Kirov's *Swan Lake* looked tired. Indeed theirs was a disappointing season. Their principal novelty—a full-evening of William Forsythe's choreography—seemed mundane and their Balanchine ballets miscast. This was particularly true of *The Prodigal Son* where the predatory Siren was performed by unusually short dancers (although the role was designed for tall ballerinas).

Early in 2005 *Giselle* received two very different treatments. English National Ballet restaged Mary Skeaping's 1971 carefully researched production based on the 1841 original ballet, while Michael Keegan-Dolan created an imaginative new version for Fabulous Beast Dance Theatre. This was set in a dysfunctional community in Ireland in which line-dancing was a popular pastime. Initially poles apart from the romantic conception, by its close it had faded into the recognisable ballet and the fate of Daphne Strothmann's Giselle was every bit as moving as in the original work. Having proved its ability in romantic ballet, English National Ballet also toured Kenneth MacMillan's production of the challengingly academic *The Sleeping Beauty* and rose to the task. This was one of Matz Skoog's final commissions before handing over the directorship of the company to Wayne Eagling.

Robert Cohan's 80th birthday was celebrated over a weekend in May, culminating with a performance of three contrasting works: *Forest* danced by Phoenix (their director, Darshan Singh Bhuller, had become keeper of Cohan's flame); *Eclipse* by Richard Alston Company; and *Stabat Mater* by Ballet Theatre Munich. Cohan continued to be active and presented a tantalising sketch as part of The Place's "White Christmas" season. Seeing his works reminded audiences just how influential he had been in establishing modern dance in Britain.

Zero Degrees, first performed in July, was one of the productions of the year: a collaboration involving two choreographer-dancers, British-Bangladeshi Akram Khan, and Flemish-Moroccan Sidi Larbi Cherkaoui; life-size, articulated casts of the dancers by Antony Gormley; and an original score by Nitin Sawhney. The subject of *Zero Degrees*, concerning experiences on a journey to India and inter-racial harmony, gained in resonance as its premiere coincided with the suicide bombings in London in July (see pp. 14-18). Michael Clark's reconstructed *O* (inspired by George Balanchine's *Apollo*) was disappointing, as the 2005 cast—with the exception of statuesque Kate Coyne—was not of the calibre of dancers in 1994. This production seemed to have diminished in stature while Clark's *Swamp*, brilliantly performed by Rambert Dance Company, continued to rise. Rambert, under Mark Baldwin, performed several new creations. Rafael Bonachela's *Curious Conscience* showed him using a formal musical score rather than a created soundscape and Christopher Bruce, having created the Jimi Hendrix-inspired *Three Songs, Two Voices*, for The Royal Ballet, made the "new-age" work, *A Steel Garden*, for Rambert. The most successful of the Rambert creations was Baldwin's witty *Constant Speed*, created in collaboration with the Institute of Physics to mark the centenary of the publication of Einstein's theories. It was science as fun. Set to a selection of music by Einstein's contemporary, Franz Lehar, the audience had no need to understand Brownian Motion or the photoelectric effect to enjoy the work; non-physicists appreciated the colour, energy, and the quality of the dancers.

THEATRE

WHO would have thought that a rigorous Henrik Ibsen play about a doomed teenager called Hedwig could be the year's great theatrical event in London, a city whose capacity for on-stage surprise is ever boundless? But with barely three weeks to go before 2005 gave up the ghost, along came the ceaselessly prolific English director Michael Grandage with a new production of *The Wild Duck* at the small Covent Garden venue, the Donmar Warehouse, run by Grandage, and suddenly, the town was agog. In a London theatre year unusually alive and alert to classic texts—albeit generally in new productions that seemed to refashion them afresh—this *Wild Duck* was the most wondrous: an uncompromising, scrupulous account of evil cloaked in charisma and smiles and ostensible concern. With knockout performances by a company of fine British stage veterans, though none one might call stars, David Eldridge's new version of Ibsen's play seemed both timely and timeless, its account of the sabotage quietly wreaked daily by human beings sometimes drolly funny, where necessary, and ultimately wounding, too.

Ibsen was the scribe of the moment on the English stage during 2005, starting in the spring with the dynamic, fearless Eve Best as Hedda Gabler, the general's daughter with a gift for self-mockery and a keen sense of her stultifying life. As directed by the National Theatre's onetime leader, Richard Eyre, a potentially overproduced play was shorn of parody and emerged like a canvas newly cleaned, Best's unbeatable Hedda matched at every turn by a gratifyingly un-buffoonish portrayal of her husband, Tesman, from rising star Benedict Cumberbatch. Far less well known, though almost as exciting, was director Marianne Elliott's reclamation for the National Theatre of *Pillars of the Community*, which starred Damian Lewis as an archetypally Ibsenesque man of the people ripe for a fall.

Making her National debut, Elliott charged through a three-hour text with great, broad brushstrokes in keeping with a play that has its share of bluster, the epic nature of this staging an intriguing antithesis to the miniaturist skill that Grandage, the English theatre's finest anatomist, brought to bear on *The Wild Duck*.

Ibsen wasn't the only classical game in town, even if it sometimes seemed that way. An even less likely candidate for commercial production (two of the three Ibsens were sensible enough to stay in the not-for-profit arena) was the German dramatist Friedrich Schiller, who was represented not once but twice on Shaftesbury Avenue, the heartland of London's West End. *Don Carlos*, a transfer into London from the enterprising Crucible Theatre in Sheffield, arrived first, giving Sir Derek Jacobi his finest role for some time as the deep-voiced, fearsome Philip II, father to the crown prince of the title in an intrigue-laden sixteenth-century Spain. Even better was the transfer from the Donmar of Phyllida Lloyd's electrifying take on a better-known Schiller text, *Mary Stuart*, with Janet McTeer as the eponymous, doomed Scottish queen and a fascinatingly reined-in Harriet Walter—winner of the *Evening Standard* best actress prize in November—as Mary's cousin, Queen Elizabeth I. In reality, the two women never actually met, but they do so in this play: the encounter in the second act did not let audiences down, a rain-swept face-off between two formidable female monarchs in a society that was still unsure what to do with women, even at the highest level. In that way and others (references to an age of terror seemed eerily apt for the contemporary world), the show benefited hugely from a new adaptation of the original text by Peter Oswald, a writer more frequently glimpsed in the al fresco reaches of Shakespeare's Globe, the summer theatre in Bankside, south-east London.

What of the Bard? He was to be found, as he always is, startlingly so in two totally different takes on that fiendishly difficult tragedy, *Macbeth*. Max Stafford-Clark's touring production of the play relocated a Scottish saga to an unnamed African country, where a black Macbeth and his white Lady moved uneasily amongst a landscape that made particular sense of the three witches, here three shamanistic practitioners of a most exotic ritual. Later in the year, the Tony-winning actor Stephen Dillane divided the critics with what, to this observer, was a total revelation: a solo interpretation of the play with Dillane fearlessly assuming all of the voices. Appearing barefoot on a largely empty stage, accompanied only by some chamber musicians, Dillane peered far into the heart of darkness of this most daunting play, with Macbeth's qualities as an utterly and recognisably modern-day nihilist thrown into sharp relief.

Away from London, Sir Peter Hall, now well into his seventies, offered up a beautiful *Much Ado About Nothing* as the high point of his annual summer residency at the Theatre Royal, Bath, the elegant Regency theatre in the spa city west of London. Janie Dee and the effortlessly engaging Aden Gillett played the sparring pair at the play's bruised yet buoyant heart. Less special, though solidly enough packed with star names—including Diana Quick and Edward Fox—to command a West End transfer in the autumn, was Hall's production of *You Never Can Tell*, George Bernard Shaw's droll if unexceptional comedy of dentistry, familial reckoning, and some unexpectedly wise waiters.

Bigger noises, inevitably, came from (where else?) the musicals. The ubiquitous Michael Grandage interlaced his Schiller and Ibsen with the first new staging in London in twenty-three years of the immortal Frank Loesser classic song-and-dance show, *Guys and Dolls*. US choreographer Rob Ashford's fiery work put the emphasis in this production firmly on dance, although it was the stage musical debut of international film name Ewan McGregor that accounted for queues around the block for the first seven months of the run. And it was considered somehow unpatriotic not to fall for the year's original musical behemoth, *Billy Elliot—the musical*, even if Stephen Daldry's stage version of his rightly acclaimed 2000 film lacked the movie's charm, sweetness, and lightness of touch. The show's main "improvement" on the film was a score by Sir Elton John: until, that is, one actually heard songs amounting to as derivative a set of tunes as any major show had boasted in years. The music, too, meant asking any of three Billys—rotating in the title role of a ballet-minded miner's son in England's industrial north—not just to act and dance but also sing, a challenging task, albeit one that the opening lead, the pint-sized Liam Mower, ably met. Somehow, for all its ostensible grit and heart, claims for *Billy Elliot* as an instant musical classic seemed both chauvinistic and premature.

If London couldn't get enough of the classics, Broadway seemed determined to send the American canon packing, and briskly, too. Two-time Oscar winner Jessica Lange, braving the New York theatre for the second time, proved second time unlucky. Her portrayal of Amanda Wingfield in *The Glass Menagerie* was not much better received than had been her 1992 Broadway debut as Blanche du Bois in *A Streetcar Named Desire*. As was true the first time around, Lange proved incapable of dishonesty or fakery on stage, her firmly spoken Amanda being far and away the best aspect of an ill-conceived and miscast staging from Englishman David Leveaux, who had done fine work before with American dramatists such as Eugene O'Neill. (Co-star Christian Slater, in the crucial role of Amanda's errant son, Tom, was a late recruit, drafted in after the originally-cast Dallas Roberts parted company with the production amidst considerable intrigue.) US critics found Lange too pretty for a seminal Tennessee Williams heroine famously originated by the less elegant, frumpier Laurette Taylor. The actress, meanwhile, could take scant solace in the equally frosty reviews afforded to Broadway's latest Blanche, *Cabaret* Tony award-winner Natasha Richardson, an erstwhile New York theatre darling who was generally cold shouldered on this occasion. Tackling Williams's most demanding role for a limited run at Studio 54 (the onetime disco), Richardson was deemed too "actressy" for the part of the famously neurasthenic, man-hungry, self-deluded Blanche.

One theory making the rounds was that New York did not need all of these British directors tampering with their classics, thank you very much: besides Leveaux, this list included Edward Hall, making his Broadway debut as the director of the Richardson-John C. Reilly *Streetcar*. Rising above the ruckus was previous Tony-winner Anthony Page, another Englishman, who staged the first New York production in nearly thirty years of *Who's Afraid of Virginia Woolf?* and found a renewed fury in Edward Albee's defining 1962 play of marital discord.

His leading lady was 1980s screen queen Kathleen Turner (*Body Heat, Romancing the Stone*), who had long spoken of wanting to play Albee's blowsy faculty wife Martha before she turned fifty, and was given the role within weeks of that very birthday. And at last, Turner—an actress whose career had sometimes bordered on camp—found a part made to order for her larger-than-life demeanour and singularly husky voice. If anything, her co-star, New York theatre veteran Bill Irwin, was even better, lending a reptilian froideur to the part of the henpecked George, famously played in the 1966 movie by the late Richard Burton, opposite the Martha of his on-again-off-again wife, Elizabeth Taylor. Irwin was the thoroughly deserving, if somewhat surprising, winner of the best actor prize at the Tony awards in June and took to the podium to speak with unusual eloquence about the life and lot of the American theatre actor. But for all the acclaim heaped on the show—co-stars David Harbour and Mireille Enos, playing George and Martha's hapless guests, included—US audiences seemed not to want to know; the production closed earlier than was hoped at a financial loss, with only the prospect of a 2006 West End run in London to buoy up its creative team's morale.

Elsewhere, and hardly for the first time, the musical ruled Broadway, especially once the finest new play to reach New York in many a season—the Anglo-Irish writer Martin McDonagh's scarily brilliant *The Pillowman*, directed, as in London, by John Crowley—closed in the autumn at (happy news) a financial profit. Unusually, however, all four of the Tony nominees for best musical in June were still running six months later at the year's end: *Dirty Rotten Scoundrels*, with John Lithgow and Tony-winner Norbert Leo Butz in the roles that had been played in the movie of the same name by Michael Caine and Steve Martin; *The Light In the Piazza*, a reflective, beautifully designed show that marked the Broadway coronation, so to speak, of composer Adam Guettel, the grandson of Broadway great Richard Rodgers of *Carousel* and *Oklahoma!* composing renown; *The 25th Annual Putnam County Spelling Bee*, a sweet, slight William Finn musical about that most American of institutions embedded in its title; and *Monty Python's Spamalot*, the deliriously silly stage musical adaptation of the movie *Monty Python and the Holy Grail*, directed by the septuagenarian Broadway veteran, Mike Nichols, who won a Tony for his efforts. Containers of Spam and coconut shells were amongst the merchandise uniquely available at this production.

Also lasting until the end of the year, and well beyond, was the Broadway transfer of *Moonstruck* Oscar-winner John Patrick Shanley's ninety-minute four-hander *Doubt: a Parable*, starring Cherry Jones and Brian F. O'Byrne as a nun and a priest in 1964 who face off over the latter's possible molestation of a student at the Bronx Catholic school run by Jones's character, Sister Aloysius. Shanley's play—the first in an apparent trilogy—dominated the non-musical categories at the Tonys, bringing New York favourite Jones her second trophy for best actress. So what if the "parable" itself—a comment on the current American climate as refracted through events some forty years before—seemed fairly specious to not a few observers? Broadway at last had an indigenous serious play which mainstream audiences were ready and happy to debate. Of that there was no doubt, and a sometimes frivolous theatrical neighbourhood seemed all the richer for it.

CINEMA

ANYONE viewing the 2006 Oscar nominations would be forgiven for thinking that American cinema was in a very healthy state. There was not a single unworthy film among the list. The surprise winner, Paul Haggis's *Crash*, which examined racial bigotry and corruption in Los Angeles, was certainly worthy, although Ang Lee's audacious and beautifully made Western, about two gay cowpokes, was perhaps even better. The list of nominees also included Steven Spielberg's *Munich*, controversially examining the Israeli attempt to assassinate the terrorists who killed their Olympic athletes at the Munich games in 1972; George Clooney's *Good Night, and Good Luck*, which showed how Ed Murrow, the famous broadcaster, stood up to Senator McCarthy's witch-hunting; *Capote*, which won the best actor award for Philip Seymour Hoffman as Truman Capote, the author of *In Cold Blood*; *Walk The Line*, a lively biography of singer Johnny Cash; and David Cronenberg's clever latterday film noir, *The History of Violence*.

Only two of these films, however, *Munich* and *Walk The Line*, could justifiably be called Hollywood products. The rest were made for about a quarter of the budget typically expended on Hollywood epics and could truly be described as independent movies. They dealt with difficult subject matter and did not expect huge box-office appeal.

The real Hollywood movies were considerably less distinguished. Huge epics like Oliver Stone's *Troy*, the Disney version of C.S. Lewis's *The Witch And the Wardrobe*, or Ridley Scott's *The Kingdom of Heaven* varied from bad to moderate. Time after time, the box-office receipts for these films proved slightly disappointing, though *The Witch and the Wardrobe* profited from being the first in what seemed likely to be a long list of Narnia stories to be screened. It seemed that, either because the films were not good enough or because many decided to wait and rent the DVDs (or even simply pull down the films from pirated versions on the Internet), the young crowd who formed the base audience in commercial cinemas were getting sated by lavish expenditure on films of no great artistic value apart from their swingeing computerised special effects. Even Peter Jackson's three-hour version of *King Kong*, made for well over US$100 million, failed to ignite the box-office as hoped. Though Hollywood often employed young directors with good work behind them to make these big budget films, success was not ensured. The older directors seemed to have shot their bolt, with the honourable exception of Tim Burton, whose *Willy Wonka and the Chocolate Factory* and animated *Corpse Bride* were at least considerable fun.

Thus, Hollywood considered itself in trouble and, though pleased to distribute the kind of upmarket fare which the Academy Awards celebrated, the powers-that-be within the industry were under no illusion that such intelligent films were the way ahead. These made money only because they cost much less to produce. No studio could survive on them and few studios were eager to finance them in the first place.

Britain held its head up fairly high during 2005. With the help of US money, yet another of J.K. Rowling's Harry Potter films, *Harry Potter and the Goblet of Fire*, did well all over the world. More audaciously, there was *The Constant Gardener*, about the way that the pharmaceutical companies exploited the African poor, and one of the very best of the John Le Carré film adaptations. A new version of *Pride and Prejudice* also proved successful, and the prolific British director Michael Winterbottom made one of his best films in *A Cock And Bull Story*, an ironic tale about the impossibility of adapting Laurence Sterne's *Tristram Shandy* to the screen. There was also Nick Park's *Wallace and Gromit: The Curse of the Were-rabbit*, which won the British director his fourth Oscar as the best animated film of the year. Generally, though, the average run of British films did even more disappointingly at the box-office in their own country than those from Hollywood did in the USA.

France also suffered from fading returns for the average French film, though at least three were of outstanding quality. The Austrian director Michael Haneke's *Caché (Hidden)*, about a bourgeois French couple terrified by videos and messages left at their house by unknown hands, was one of his best. It won the European Film Academy's premier award and also the European critics' prize. Also from France came Jacques Audiard's *The Beat My Heart Skipped*, in which actor Romain Duris distinguished himself as a young property developer who wants to become a concert pianist but gets in too deep with the Russian mafia to pursue his new career. There was an even better performance from Michel Bouquet, the veteran French star, as President Mitterrand in *The Last Mitterrand*, a film about his final days when, dying from cancer, the President tries to justify his career to a Jewish journalist.

Sophie Scholl, a film about the young student executed by the Nazis for spreading dissent, was by some way the best German production of 2005 and it seemed that at last the dormant German industry was beginning to awake once more. In Italy, there were several good films, but nothing outstanding and, in what we used to call Eastern Europe, financial restraints prevented much from happening at all. Far and away the best film from this area came from Romania, where Chrsti Puiu, with hardly any money, made *The Death of Mister Lazarescu*, an extraordinarily powerful story about a poverty-stricken and eccentric old man taken to hospital and allowed to die through neglect. It seemed to be a moral tale, often funny but also very moving, about the way we treat old people in Europe.

Another outstanding film was Jean-Pierre and Luc Dardenne's *L'Enfant*, which won the Palme D'Or at the Cannes festival. Made in Belgium, it told the story of a young couple and their baby, and what happens when the feckless father sells the baby for a wad of money and then desperately tries to get him back when the mother collapses with shock. This was the second time that the Belgian brothers had won Cannes, and they seemed extraordinarily adept at making humanist films about those whom society often ignores.

There were no outstanding films from Russia or from its neighbours. But at least there was good news about indigenous films doing better at the box-office than for some years past, even if most of them were about crime and corruption in high places, and made as commercially as possible. More ambitious film-makers found, however, that few were interested in financing productions that were more likely to succeed at the many film festivals across the world rather than in their home territory.

From Australia came John Hillcoat's *The Proposition*, a Western in all but name about the violent birth pangs of that country. Very well filmed and acted, it seemed like a latter-day movie from Sam Peckinpah, full of a kind of iconic power and a capacity for myth-making. Latin America continued its revival with good films from Mexico, Argentina, and Brazil, among which was the delightful *BomBon Le Perro*, about an old man who buys a huge dog in the hope of breeding from it but finds the animal cannot find a bitch that he fancies. This was as much a sympathetic treatise about poverty as about the animal itself, but the recalcitrant dog undoubtedly helped it to sell all over the world.

As last year, some of the most impressive films came from the East, with South Korea leading the way. There were at least a dozen exceptional films from this source, with Park Chan-wook leading the way with *Old Boy* and *Sympathy for Lady Vengeance*, two thrillers of great originality and power. But perhaps the best of the eastern films came from Hong Kong. Wong Kar-Wai's romantic and stylish *2046*, using some of the same characters as in his previous *In The Mood For Love*, proved the director to be one of the finest in the world.

Deaths in 2005 included Eddie Albert, Hollywood actor; Parveen Babi, Bollywood star; Anne Bancroft, American actress noted for her role as Mrs Robinson in *The Graduate* (see p. 524); Constance Cummings, Hollywood star of the 1930s; Ossie Davis, black American actor and director; Sandra Dee, Hollywood star; Sunil Dutt, famous Indian actor and politician; June Haver, Hollywood musical star; Li Li-li, star actress of the Chinese cinema; Matsumura Tatsuo, Japanese actor; Virginia Mayo, blonde star of Hollywood romances; Sir John Mills, leading British actor (see pp. 541-42); Brigitte Mira, German actress for Rainer Werner Fassbinder; Dan O'Herlity, who played the lead in Bunuel's *Robinson Crusoe*; Richard Pryor, black American comedian and actor; Maria Schell, Austrian actress; Simone Simon, the great French star; Teresa Wright, Hollywood actress; Ahmed Zaki, prominent Egyptian actor; Guy Green, acclaimed British cinematographer; Tonino Delli Colli, who shot films for Pasolini, Fellini, and Sergio Leone; Omer Kavur, well-known Turkish director; Alberto Lattuada, respected Italian director; Charles Gormley, Scottish film-maker; Wolf Rilla, British film-maker; Robin Spry, Canadian film-maker; Pastor Vega, Cuban film-maker; Robert Wise, director of *West Side Story* and *The Sound of Music* (see p. 552); Humbert Balsam, French actor turned successful producer; John Brabourne, British producer of a series of Agatha Christie films; Debra Hill, pioneer American woman producer; Ismail Merchant, director and producer for James Ivory (see pp. 540-41); and Marc Lawrence, American actor who appeared in 200 films from 1932 until his death.

TELEVISION AND RADIO

Both the volume and nature of the pictures and emails that flooded into the offices of the UK's broadcasters on the morning of 7 July were unprecedented. Many thousands of messages were received and with them digital pictures from the heart of the London Underground bombings sent from mobile phones. Although broadcasters had used pictures taken by members of the public from time to time over the years, this was a different phenomenon. The coverage of the London bombings by members of the public was seen as the moment when "citizen journalism" came of age. The impact was dramatic because so many of those trapped in the bombed carriages had mobile phones able to take pictures, and the location, deep underground, meant that it was impossible for professional cameramen to get close. Later that month a member of the public earned an estimated UK£80,000 in a joint deal with ITV News and the *Daily Mail* for an exclusive film of the arrest of alleged would-be bombers (see pp. 14-16).

"The genie is out of the bottle and things will never be the same again," commented Richard Sambrook who managed the BBC World Service and was former head of BBC News. There were worries about everything, from issues of copyright and privacy, to the safety of would-be citizen journalists who might take unnecessary risks to get their pictures. Yet Sky, ITN, the BBC, and international broadcasters such as CNN, all wanted viewers to send in pictures if they suddenly became involved in breaking news stories. The London bombings further demonstrated the power of 24-hour television news channels. Much to its surprise, the BBC found that the audience to the main *10 O'Clock News* did not rise by nearly as much as expected on 7 July. The likely explanation was that by the evening most people had already watched hours of live coverage on the news channels. The growing importance of 24-hour news channels was underlined when Peter Horrocks, the newly appointed head of BBC Television News, declared that in future BBC News 24 would be the heart of the Corporation's television news coverage.

The big picture for the BBC, however, involved the renegotiation of its royal charter for the ten years from 1 January 2007. In March Culture Secretary Tessa Jowell made it clear in a green paper that the BBC would get a new ten-year charter and that the Corporation would continue to be funded by a universal licence fee until 2016. The BBC governors would, however, be abolished in their present form and replaced by a "new, transparent and accountable BBC trust". The Corporation would be run by a new executive board responsible for delivering BBC services within a framework set by the trust. Although the licence fee would be retained throughout the new charter period, there would be a review before the charter expired to see whether other ways of funding the BBC, such as subscription, should be introduced after 2016.

During the year support grew for a BBC proposal to make greater use of independent production. In addition to the 25 per cent independent "quota" required by legislation, a further 25 per cent would go into a "window of creative opportunity" (WOC). In the WOC both independents and in-house producers could compete for programme commissions and revenue. The aim for the BBC was to be able to commission the best ideas while still protecting the Corporation's own production capacity. The BBC plan, and rulings from communications regulator Ofcom, creating better terms of trade for independents, encouraged several to float on the stock exchange. Thus, the owners of Shed, producers of *Bad Girls* and *Footballer's Wives*, and of RDF, the company behind *Wife Swap*, became multi-millionaires.

In October the BBC finally set out its case for an increased licence fee to pay for developments sought by the government, such as building the transmitter network that would allow the UK to move completely to digital broadcasting by 2012. The BBC independently costed the "wish list", which also included new digital services, enhanced programmes, and the launch of new local services. The switchover to digital alone would, the BBC said, cost UK£500 million. The total extra investment over the period came to UK£6 billion but the BBC would raise UK£3.9 billion through greater efficiency and staff cuts. To fund the remaining gap the BBC concluded that it would need a licence fee 2.3 per cent higher than general inflation. This would mean that the licence fee would reach UK£150.50 at 2005 prices in 2013. The licence fee was increased to UK£126.50 in April. Newspapers were quick to point out that this rise could mean a UK£180 licence fee by 2013 at actual prices. The BBC claim was met with scepticism and its new licence fee, to be announced in summer 2006, was expected to be noticeably less than the BBC was seeking.

The BBC did catch the public imagination with dramatisations such as *Bleak House*, and new versions of old ideas with programmes like *Dr Who* and a second series of *Strictly Come Dancing*. The person responsible, however, BBC One controller Lorraine Heggessey, left to become chief executive of TalkBack Thames, the UK's largest independent producer. In one of the most remarkable job swaps in British broadcasting, the TalkBack Thames chief executive Peter Fincham went the other way and became controller of BBC One.

Channel 4 had a strong financial year and was widely praised for campaigning programmes such as *Jamie's School Dinners* and remarkable live cricket coverage of England beating Australia to win the Ashes. As a result, the fact that rights to live Test Cricket were scooped up by BSkyB, the satellite broadcaster, and would no longer be on terrestrial television, rapidly became a political issue. Channel 4 provided the most memorable programme moment of the year when, during a *Big Brother* broadcast, the dissident (and former Labour) MP George Galloway risked derision by going on all fours, purring, and pretending to lick cream from the hands of actress Rula Lenska.

In October, Channel 4 launched More4, a new digital channel specialising in factual programming and aimed at the BBC Four audience, reflecting the growing important of digital broadcasting. By the end of the year 66 per cent of the population was able to receive digital television in some form.

During the year ITV and ITN both marked their 50th anniversaries with grand parties. For many commentators the events, and a television history of

ITV presented by Melvyn Bragg, served to highlight the way in which competition from multi-channel television had forced ITV to focus increasingly on the obviously popular. ITV chief executive Charles Allen made himself popular in the city by persuading communications regulator Ofcom to reduce greatly the cost of ITV licence payments to the Treasury. Before the Ofcom review the ITV companies and Channel Five had been expected to pay around UK£180 million for their licences in 2005. The regulator said that the sum was being reduced to around UK£90 million, reflecting the increased competition within the market.

ITV, formed from the merger of Carlton and Granada, went through a painful management restructuring with around half of the executives being replaced, including many of the programme commissioners. The aim was to prepare ITV for the move from analogue to digital. The plan was to launch more digital channels and seek other streams of revenue to compensate for the fact that the main flagship channel, ITV 1, would inevitably face intensifying competition. As part of the strategy review in December, the commercial broadcaster pulled out of the 24-hour television news business by closing ITV News, despite its numerous scoops. The channel had never made money and was languishing in third place behind both BBC News 24 and Sky News. Just before ITV News closed, ITV made a big move into the business of Internet advertising by agreeing to pay up to UK£175 million for the "friends reunited" web site. Both ITV and Channel 4 were so interested in launching new advertising-funded digital channels because of the continuing success of Freeview, the free-to-air digital terrestrial television service. As many as 10 million of the simple Freeview receivers had been sold and a total of 6.4 million UK homes had them. With the one-time cost of the boxes down to UK£40, the number of Freeview homes was expected to overtake Sky in the next couple of years.

BSkyB did meet its target of reaching 8 million homes with satellite receivers by the end of 2005, and said that it hoped to be in 10 million homes by 2010. The success of PVRs (personal video recorders) had given a significant boost to BskyB, and the company hoped that the planned launch of its high definition service in time for the 2006 football world cup would also help to drive subscription growth. BSkyB, like other broadcasters also showed signs of embracing the Internet by acquiring the search engine company Easynet. One cloud on the horizon for Sky came from the European Commission, which made it clear that at least one of the packages of live Premiership football rights—all currently held by Sky—must go to another broadcaster next time.

In September Tessa Jowell finally confirmed at the Royal Television Society convention in Cambridge that the UK would move from analogue to digital in phases from 2008 to 2012. "There will be no more rural communities effectively cut off from the media world that the rest of us inhabit. The disabled pensioner will have the same access to digital as the city broker," she promised. Before the end of the year, viewers in the first area to go completely digital—the Border television region straddling the border between England and Scotland—received letters explaining the changes to come. HTV Wales, Westcountry, and Granada regions would follow in 2009, with London, Meridian, Tyne-Tees, and Ulster bringing up the rear in 2012.

Just like television, radio was being increasingly influenced by the spread of digital. Nearly 500,000 digital radios were sold in the Christmas period, taking the total number of digital sets sold so far in the UK to 2.7 million. With digital radios available for less than UK£50, sales were expected to accelerate. Despite the rise of digital broadcasting, Ofcom continued to advertise new analogue radio licences everywhere from Manchester and Edinburgh to the Solent region and Belfast. The new Belfast licence was won by UTV, the commercial television operator for Northern Ireland, and the company emphasised its interest in being a major UK radio player by paying UK£100 million for The Wireless Group. The company, founded by former *Sun* editor Kelvin MacKenzie, was best known for its national station TalkSport. MacKenzie made UK£7 million from the deal.

On a larger scale, the UK£700 million merger of the two biggest commercial radio companies, GWR and Capital, was approved and the new company, GCAP, began trading on the stock market. The shares plummeted over worries concerning the management structure and a weak advertising market. David Mansfield, former chief executive of Capital, then departed from GCAP, leaving former GWR executive chairman Ralph Bernard firmly in charge. The turmoil in commercial radio may have helped the BBC, which recorded its highest ever share of total listening—55.1 per cent—in the fourth quarter. The BBC also scored in "podcasting" the downloading of programmes to computers or iPods (see pp. 409-10).

As well as the arrival of citizen journalism, podcasting, and video iPods, the pace of technological change in the broadcasting market showed no signs of slowing. The telephone company BT was among those promising to launch IPTV—television and films delivered over the Internet—turning the competitive screw even tighter.

VISUAL ARTS—ARCHITECTURE

VISUAL ARTS

War-like conditions in Iraq continued to wreak havoc with its patrimony. The British Museum recorded damage to the archaeological site of Babylon caused by the construction of a major US (then Polish) military base there. On the other hand, the military did at least prevent the looting that was taking place elsewhere of ancient Iraqi sites. The museums, including the National Museum of Antiquities in Baghdad, ransacked by Iraqis just after the allied invasion in 2003, remained closed.

In the West, the tide began to turn decisively against the trade in illegally excavated antiquities, with Switzerland—hitherto a major entrepot in such commerce—passing a law to ratify the 1970 UNESCO (UN Educational, Scientific, and Cultural Organisation) convention on the means of prohibiting and preventing the illicit import, export and transfer of ownership of cultural property. The

Italian state brought a criminal law suit against the Getty Museums curator of antiquities, Marion True, accusing her of knowingly acquiring illicitly traded works. Italy also formally lodged claims to pieces in other US museums, including the Metropolitan Museum, New York, and the Museum of Fine Arts, Boston. Greece followed suit shortly afterwards. The International Criminal Tribunal for the Former Yugoslavia (ICTY) in The Hague showed that it would enforce the The Hague convention for the protection of cultural property in the event of armed conflict (1954) by sentencing Pavle Strugar, a former lieutenant-general in the Yugoslav People's Army (the JNA), to eight years in prison for his role in shelling the historic centre of Dubrovnik in 1991 (see p. 423).

The July terrorist attacks in London led to a 25 per cent fall in attendance figures to the capital's museums, with Tate Britain and Tate Modern most seriously affected (see p. 25). In November the river Arno came within a few feet of bursting its banks, reminding Florentines of the disastrous 1966 flood which caused serious damage to hundreds of works of art, including a great Cimabue *Crucifix*. It was revealed that none of the twenty measures planned to prevent the recurrence of such an event was in place. The outward looking director of the Museum of Contemporary Art in Teheran, the Iranian capital, Ali-Reza Sami Azar, resigned in September due to the hostile cultural climate after the election of the hardline Islamist, Mahmoud Ahmadinejad, as President (see pp. 261-62). Just before leaving the museum, Dr Azar put on display a large part of the collection of modern Western art bought in the 1970s on instruction from the then Empress, including works by Pollock, Bacon, Warhol, Twombly and others. These had been in store since 1979 and large crowds of Iranians came to see them

With a different kind of internationalism, the British Library and the Monastery of St Catherine in Egypt signed an agreement to collaborate on digitally reassembling the *Codex Sinaiticus*, the earliest known version of the Bible, of which the greater part was in London and twelve leaves in the desert monastery. This required differences over ownership to be set aside (the manuscript was taken to Russia in the nineteenth century in suspect circumstances). The British Museum transferred its Ethiopian tabots (sacred tablets) to a church in London on long loan, since they were considered so holy that they should only be seen by priests.

Despite a week-long hunger strike by the curators, the Russian government evicted the State History and Architecture Museum from the former Ipatievsky Monastery 100 miles north of Moscow. The monastery, founded in the thirteenth century, was to be returned to the Russian Orthodox Church, and the eviction of the Museum left 400,000 works of art without a home. In the meanwhile, Russian millionaires made themselves felt in the Western art market. Sotheby's April sale of Russian paintings and objects in New York totalled US$35.2 million, making the sale the auction house's third biggest earner after the impressionist and modern, and the contemporary art auctions, both established market leaders.

In step with its booming economy, China was also a strong influence on the market, with the new millionaires buying the kind of art a pre-revolutionary prince, mandarin, or scholar might have acquired. This led to a reversal of the centuries-old flow of porcelain from East to West, encouraged also by the Chinese government's policy of allowing Chinese art and antiquities that had been legally exported in the past to be brought back for auction on the mainland, and re-exported if bought by an overseas buyer.

French billionaire François Pinault abandoned plans to build a €150 million museum on an island in the Seine, three miles downstream from the Eiffel Tower. He decided instead to take a lease on part of the Palazzo Grassi in Venice, previously adapted by the Fiat car manufactures to be an exhibition centre. He would show parts of his valuable collection of contemporary art there in rotation, as well as mounting other shows. Pinault cited an unhelpful bureaucratic climate in France as the reason for his change of plans, but it may also have been due to the 5 per cent import tax that he would have had to pay in France on any art he brought in permanently from the USA or elsewhere outside the EU.

More and more money chasing fewer and fewer iconic works of art drove the market to unprecedented heights: Brancusi's sculpture *Bird in Space* sold for US$27.4 million; Damien Hirst's shark in formaldehyde sold to US hedge-fund tycoon Steve Cohen for US$12 million; and the first-rate Canaletto painting of the Grand Canal from Palazzo Balbi sold for UK£18.6 million, with five buyers in contention at the auction. The art market as a reliable investment was, nonetheless, rejected by the Dutch bank ABN/AMRO, which in 2004 had launched a fund of art funds. On closer study of the existing art investment enterprises, it decided that, with very few exceptions, these were not succeeding in attracting enough investors and that only the smaller, more specialised ones run by skilled dealers were likely to give a good return. The way in which the art market could be skewed in a specialist area by the anomalous behaviour of even a single buyer was shown by the removal from the market of Sheikh Saud al-Thani, cousin of the Emir of Qatar and for three years an obsessive, big-spending collector in many fields, but especially that of Islamic art (see AR 2004, p. 480). He was arrested on orders of the Emir in March (released later in the year and allowed to start buying again) for alleged misuse of public funds, with the consequence that subsequent Islamic auctions slumped. A booming market and many very rich people made the role of a museum director no easier in the USA, where museums were judged by how much they could grow their endowment funds, attract valuable acquisitions, and increase their visitor figures. No fewer than twenty directorships were standing vacant in the spring, with most scholars unwilling to exchange their careers as curators for a life of fund-raising.

If one new work had to be singled out this year, it might be the Richard Serra bought by the Basque government for US$15 million. The difficulties experienced by the curators of the famous Bilbao museum, with its swooping outlines and curved internal walls, over how to display the art were solved by installing this magnificent, walk-through sculpture of curving, oxidised steel walls, called *A Matter of Time*. At the Venice Biennale, curated this year for the first time by two women, the Spaniards Maria de Corral and Rosa Martinez, there were many works explicitly on social or feminist themes, such as the video by the Guatemalan artist, Regina José Galindo, of the surgical recreation of a hymen. It was, by common consent, a better organised and more coherent Biennale than had been seen for years in Venice, and more nations than ever were competing for attention, including Iran, with work also by women artists. The Turner Prize, awarded annually to a British artist by the Tate, went to Simon Starling for his shed that turned into a boat and back into a shed. "It's about trying to retard the incredible speed at which we live," he explained.

The exhibition of the Japanese woodblock artist, Hokusai, at the Tokyo National Gallery, attracted the largest attendance figures for the year, with an average of 9,436 visitors a day. The most successful exhibitions in the West, were, as so often, of late nineteenth-century artists: 6,571 visitors a day flocked to see drawings by Van Gogh at the Metropolitan Museum; 6,387 came to view Cézanne and Pissarro at the Museum of Modern Art, New York; and 6,343 to Turner, Whistler and Monet at the Grand Palais, Paris.

Deaths during the year included Philip Johnson, US architect (see p. 536); Harald Szeemann, Swiss curator of contemporary art; Sir Eduardo Paolozzi, British sculptor (see p. 544); Patrick Caulfield, British painter; and Arman (Armand Pierre Fernandez), French sculptor.

ARCHITECTURE

THE Venice Architecture Biennale of 2004 was curated by Harvard Professor Kurt Forster, and entitled "Metamorph". Forster described the prevalence of digital technology—computer aided design, and computer-generated pre-fabrication techniques, such as laser cutting—as the logical result of "transformations over the past several decades", that "have been so profound as to mark a marvellous passage in the evolution of architecture". If modernism in architecture represented a belief in social progress through the application of new technology and the dominance of functionalist design composition, then Forster's comments marked a high water mark in the rehabilitation of technico-instrumental thinking.

Foreign Office Architects Yokohama ferry terminal exemplified this attitude. Completed in 2003, it formed the basis of an exhibition in the British pavilion at Venice, as well as at the Institute of Contemporary Arts in London in 2004. The firm had described its work as "hi-tech plus theory". Similarly, the mass misapplication of pseudo-scientific terms such as "logarithmic unpredictability", "field condition", "data-scapes", and "machinic landscapes" influenced the recent work of students at the Architectural Association. Zaha Hadid's Phaeno Science Centre at Wolfsburg and BMW factory offices at Leipzig also celebrated the "force of flow" and the energy of industry. Whilst these buildings lacked facades and were brutishly sensual, Hadid's modernism replaced social critique with blind faith in the dynamism of capitalism. Similarly, Peter Eisenmann, the star of Venice in 2004, built a Jewish memorial in Berlin out of a hectare of gently undulating concrete blocks arranged in the fashionable "landscape flow" style.

The difficulty of practising modern architecture in a consumerist society was also made clear in the frosty reception received by Enric Miralles's posthumously delivered Scottish Parliament building in Edinburgh. Despite winning the Royal Institute of British Architects (RIBA) Stirling prize for 2005, the project was hated—and loved—by the Scots, topping a BBC poll of buildings that the public wished to see demolished. Miralles's design evoked the "soft undulations of the Highlands" and an image of upturned boats, in lieu of any architectural precedents. His death, together with that of Scotland's First Minister Donald Dewar, also in 2002, left the project administrators with massive organisational problems. The finished scheme was twice as large as the competition-winning design and it cost ten times the initial estimated budget of UK£40 million (see AR 2004, p. 29).

Internally the building was a triumph of luxuriantly crafted material surfaces. Grand ramps led the public and the elect to the vast debating hall, conceived of as a clearing beneath a forest of oak beams. Situated at the end of the Royal Mile, beside the Palace of Holyrood, the Parliament garden merged with wild hillsides. Less successful were the main facades to the formal entrances. They were the same height as neighbouring buildings, whilst playing an abstract game of non-figurative architecture: South African granite panels hung from the new facades in an expensively ambivalent gesture of deference to, and disrespect for, the local tradition of slate roofs and stone walls. Modernist architects seemed able to embrace context only when it was conceived of as nature recast in the language of scientific metaphors ("flows", "gravity wells", "turbulence"). Yet the actual presence of the history of architectural culture (older buildings, streets, squares) seemed to paralyse even the most gifted, ostensibly avant-garde form makers. All of the architects mentioned above sought to turn their buildings away from the complexity and contradiction of the historic city towards the comforting clichés of science fiction imagery and the romantic inspiration of nature.

The UK's Lord Norman Foster was seventy in 2005. His tower for Swiss Re in the city of London—the first "ecologically sustainable office building" to be made of steel and glass—won the Stirling prize in 2004. The post-geodesic form created an atmospheric vacuum around itself that sucked air through the offices on a few days each year; and in place of the medieval street pattern, the resulting cyclone created a windswept corporate plaza all year round. Lord Richard Rogers, architecture adviser to the Mayor of London, declared in *Building Design* magazine that "the only thing limiting the height of tower blocks in London is technology". Mayor Ken Livingstone awarded himself special planning powers and granted consent for seventeen new towers.

It seemed that we were all threatened with virtual architectural vacuums. Culture Minister Tessa Jowell proposed that listed buildings should be demolished and virtual versions of them stored on the Internet, in order not to halt "the development of our talented young architects". How remarkable that Bennetts Associates, which won building design architect of the year 2005, and Lynch architects, which took the young architect of the year award, did so without the benefits of such government condescension. Japanese architect Toyo Ito was awarded the RIBA gold medal 2005 and Rem Koolhaas in 2004. The Pritzker prize 2005 went to US citizen Tom Mayne, who, in common with the recipient the previous year, Zaha Hadid, had built little but drawn much.

The UK's New Labour government privatised public building projects through the private finance initiative (PFI), which had been devised by the Conservative government in 1992. All schools, hospitals, university buildings and "public" buildings would be built using private developers' finance, and leased from them by the state. Design build contracts, whereby the architect became a design consultant paid to get planning consent but was not responsible for the delivery of the detailed masterpiece, would be used unilaterally. British architecture seemed to be imitating US attitudes towards professionalism and commerce alongside a fragile adherence to a European view of modernism—as a social contract—that no-one wanted to pay for. Whilst British television was awash with house makeovers, the ambiguous attitude towards public buildings reflected a wider cultural confusion.

In contrast, the critics' favourite for the Stirling prize 2006, designed by Irish pair Sheila O'Donnell and John Tuomey, was paid for by Lewis Glucksman, a US citizen happy to provide University College Cork with an art gallery to rival Louis Kahn's Yale Art Gallery and Le Corbusier's Carpenter centre at Harvard. Set on columns amongst treetops beside the River Lee, this curvaceous oak-clad pavilion acted as a gatehouse which spoke to both town and gown.

Outside the UK the status of architects was not significantly threatened and the historically attuned and technically astute nature of the training in Spain, Portugal, and Switzerland meant that architects there continued to control the production of buildings with the aid of traditionally trained craftsman. The 1990s hegemony of Dutch architecture—a colourful brand of what critic Peter Buchanan called "cartoon modernism"—had been replaced by what *The Architectural Review* called the "new materiality". This nascent movement was inspired by the writing and buildings of Swiss architects such as Peter Zumthor and Andrea Deplazes, who were interested in the history of construction and in vernacular buildings' relationships with place. Young Spanish architects Luis Mansilla and Emilio Tuñón, trained by Rafael Moneo, preserved their tradition of innovative civic urbanism. Renzo Piano continued to divide opinion with a grandiose cathedral in Italy, a ground-hugging museum in Switzerland and a Romanesque art gallery in Dallas, USA. Rem Koolhaas's Casa da Musica in Oporto and the Dutch embassy in Berlin showed that even buildings designed primarily as diagrams now attempted to relate to their context, if only in presenting the context as a spectacle. Similarly Jean Nouvel's extension to the Reina Sofia museum in Madrid reflected the city back to itself via a vast mirrored ceiling, whilst blocking the streetscape with ventilation ducts.

In Chile and Japan necessity led to the proliferation of a number of quirky, cheap dwellings typified by imaginative responses to difficult site conditions— tiny urban plots or cliff edges—approaches that were perhaps lacking in the Western scene. Steel supplies worldwide were scarce, due to the explosive rate of China's building boom.

The US scene continued to be enlivened only by high profile public buildings designed by foreign architects. Koolhaas built a public library in Seattle which, like his Dutch embassy, was one long corridor wrapped around itself to form a building; Hadid's private art gallery in Cincinatti arranged a collection of window-less "white cubes" in various shades of concrete connected by escalators; and Tadao Ando built an art gallery next to Louis Kahn's masterly Kimbell gallery in Fort Worth, Texas, that suffered from the comparison. Frank Gehry announced his retirement and the closure of his practice, which had energetically applied bent metal facades to various building types throughout the world. The competition to redesign "ground zero" (the site of the twin towers in New York destroyed on 11 September 2001) was won by Daniel Libeskind only for the project to be usurped by SOM; the political and financial wrangles rumbled on, seemingly oblivious to the architecture. Meanwhile, in San Fancisco, the De Young Museum—by Swiss architects Jacques Herzog and Pierre de Meuron—sat submerged in a park like a modern Inca temple nestling amongst trees, scanning the city with its periscopic tower. The overall impression one gained from these recent phenomena was of architects trying hard to work out where they were, and whether architecture could presume to address anything other than the present.

LITERATURE

The year will be remembered for the number of significant writers who died. Without question Arthur Miller will be regarded as one of the major playwrights of modern times, arguably as re-defining a figure in the history of stage tragedy as was Ibsen in the nineteenth century. Miller is likely to be seen as the key modern author who revealed that a work of literature could still be tragic in scope in an age that had eschewed a general consensus about the relationship of God to man (for obituary see p. 541).

No less a figure who departed the American canvas was Saul Bellow, a Nobel laureate whose novels were outstanding evocations of twentieth-century *mores* and psychological obsessions. Many regarded *Herzog* as the greatest American novel of its time and elevated Bellow, like Miller with whom he shared a Jewish inheritance, as the conscience of modern America (for obituary see pp. 525-26).

Still to be given their final weighting in the story of American literature, August Wilson and Hunter S. Thompson both died too. Wilson's death removed the first black playwright to conquer international theatre with more than a single play. He had just completed his grand project of a decathlon of plays covering every decade of the twentieth century. It was a premature death and a great blow to contemporary drama. By contrast, Thompson died at his own hand, an end somehow commensurate with the bleakness of his fiction. *Fear and Loathing in Las Vegas* was one of the iconic novels of the last century (for obituary see p. 550). The death of the crime writer Ed McBain removed another figure around whom a cult had gathered. Other American authors who died included the feminist Andrea Dworkin and the Civil War historian Shelby Foote.

This was also a year in which British drama lost some important names. Though deeply out of fashion, some works of the verse dramatist Christopher

Fry—*The Lady's Not for Burning*, for example—seemed destined to be minor classics, wittily artificial (for obituary see pp. 532-33). Fry was part of the generation ousted by the "angry young men" of the 1950s. Among these were Anthony Creighton, who was best remembered for a play he co-wrote with John Osborne, and which the London theatre coincidentally revived during the year, *Epitaph for George Dillon*. A third playwright to leave the stage for ever was Willis Hall, whose war play, *The Long and the Short and the Tall*, and whose role in creating the quintessential working-class fantasist Billy Liar (co-written with life-long friend and collaborator Keith Waterhouse), made him one of the writers who helped to shape the character of post-war Britain.

John Fowles had a unique following among British novelists. Though he had been almost silent for several years, his death took many by surprise, perhaps because of the vibrancy of his writing. *The French Lieutenant's Woman*, though essentially pastiche, was one of the most celebrated of twentieth-century novels in English, and other works, such as *The Magus*, caught the slightly spurious mysticism that attracted many readers in the late twentieth century, possibly as a substitute for religion (for obituary see p. 532).

A number of prominent literary critics died in 2005. Among them were David Daiches (also an authority on Scotch whisky); poet and scholar Philip Hobsbaum; the biographer of W.B. Yeats and virtual inventor of Commonwealth literary studies A.N. Jeffares; the Shakespearian essayist Derek Traversi; and the Wordsworth scholar Robert Woof, who had done so much to transform Dove Cottage from being just the birthplace of the Romantic poet into a centre for serious Romantic research.

Eugene Laguerre, Puerto Rico's most celebrated modern writer (though little known elsewhere), and the Canadian writer of short stories, Norman Levine, were among other notable authors to die during the year.

It was, of course, not only a year of mourning the passing of talent. As always, the major literary prizes honoured the vitality of contemporary authors. The award of the Nobel prize for literature to Harold Pinter was generously received on the whole, though there were some in the media who felt that his selection was intended as a political snub to the architects of the Iraq war, which Pinter had always roundly condemned. Such comments seriously undervalued his place in the development of the form of modern drama, as innovative in its way as Samuel Beckett had been.

The Man Booker prize, still the most publicised of British literary awards, went to a controversial choice, the Irish writer John Banville, for *The Sea*. Though it had its champions, there were many who felt this to be the weakest of the six short-listed novels. Martyn Goff, the octogenarian administrator of "the Booker" almost since its conception, retired amid plaudits, and speculation as to what his anticipated memoirs might contain, since this was regarded as a literary prize that had thrived on gossip and nuance.

No indiscretions attended the jury of the Man Booker international prize, which was chosen in Edinburgh. This new award sought to acknowledge the best of international fiction over a lifetime. The choice of Albanian writer

Ismail Kadare was thought judicious and especially appropriate at a politically sensitive moment in the relationship between Islam and Christianity. Another major international award, the Commonwealth writers' prize, went to Andrea Levy for *Small Island*. This was possibly the most honoured book of the year, winning a number of major trophies and selling in large numbers. It was good to see an experienced but previously unfeted author achieving such success, since in recent years many prizes had gone to new writers attracting immediate attention with their first books and then fading rapidly. Levy's humorous, affectionate, but perceptive look at the founding generation of black Caribbean life in Britain seemed to appeal to almost everyone.

Islands were in vogue during the course of the year. Much publicity surrounded the re-publication of *Our Island Story*, a history of the British Isles which had long been considered reactionary. It seemed to herald the return of a kind of history which made heroes and heroines more important than social movements or economic trends. The distinguished Canadian essayist John Ralston Saul wrote of a new insularity in world affairs in his penetrating discussion, *The Collapse of Globalism*.

Inevitably, given world politics during the year, books about the Middle East and Iraq made particular waves. Outstanding among these was Robert Fisk, the most trenchant of observers in this part of the world, who was on top form with *The Great War for Civilisation: The conquest of the Middle East.*

It was another outstanding year for fiction. Julian Barnes produced one of his best novels, the Sherlock Holmesian *Arthur and George*. The Canadian mistress of the short story, Alice Munro, had another outstanding collection, *Runaway*. Three Nobel laureates added to their corpus: Nadine Gordimer, J.M. Coetzee, and Gabriel Garcia Márquez, though none of them were felt to be writing at their peak. On the other hand, Kazuo Ishiguro with *Never Let Me Go*, Ian McEwan with his post 11 September 2001 novel *Saturday*, and Salman Rushdie, with *Shalimar the Clown*, decidedly were. In more popular mode, the octogenarian P.D. James had another great success with *The Lighthouse*, as did J.K. Rowling with *Harry Potter and the Half-Blood Prince*, although there were the first signs that the Potter boom might at last be on the wane as this immensely long book did not generate quite the frenzy of its predecessors. It was good to see some younger writers consolidate their reputations, among them Dave Eggers and Ali Smith. Outstanding new novelists included Tash Aw, the first new name of substance in Malaysian writing for many years; Uzodinma Iweala, and Tarun J. Tejpal. Well over seventy years of age, the playwright Arnold Wesker wrote his first novel, *Honey*, and it was no less heartening to see Zadie Smith return to form with her extraordinary novel *On Beauty*, which seemed both about herself and a most intelligent critique of E.M. Forster.

In the world of poetry Christopher Logue was highly praised for the fifth volume of his re-telling of Homer, *Cold Calls*. Carol Ann Duffy wrote in *Rapture* a deeply moving account of the break-up of a relationship. Derek Walcott was admired for *The Prodigal* and many readers were happy to have Anne Stevenson's rather underrated poems collected in a volume simply entitled *Poems 1955-2005*. It was good to have Philip Larkin's posthumous *Early Poems and Juvenilia*, though critics acidly spoke of them as, indeed, juvenile. Mark Haddon was invited to stick to surrealistic fiction rather than attempt more verse, and J.H. Prynne's *Poems* went barely noticed except by the small number of plausible readers who regarded him as the poetic genius of our time.

The outstanding biography of the year was Jung Chang's and her husband Jon Halliday's *Mao: The unknown*. This book did not conceal its opinions. There was no doubt that the authors believed Mao Zedong to have been one of the most evil tyrants in history. Some historians felt that they had bowed to prejudice, but none doubted that this would be a very influential account of its subject for a long time to come. It was unlikely that Christopher Meyer's *DC Confidential* would enjoy the same enduring reputation, but as a fly-on-the-wall view of the Anglo-American political relationship between 11 September 2001 and the invasion of Iraq it stirred up much controversy.

There were two outstanding books about Shakespeare: Peter Ackroyd's and James Shapiro's, but the Elizabethan literary study that produced the most favourable response was Park Honan's brilliant life of Christopher Marlowe. Among more obscure biographical subjects, Harriet O'Brien's life of the Saxon Queen Emma was outstanding. So, too, was Kathryn Hughes's life of Isabella Beeton, the great Victorian home-maker. Increasingly, however, devoted research of the kind that lay behind these works was giving way to the lives of contemporary celebrities. It was to be expected, for example, that a biography of the new Pope Benedict XVI, would appear with weeks of his election, and sure enough it did, in an acceptable but hardly over-informed book by Rupert Shortt.

2005 saw the 250th anniversary of the publication of Samuel Johnson's *Dictionary of the English Language*. This was celebrated in many ways, all of them reminders that lexicography is at the root of any civilisation. In a year that saw Winston Churchill voted "greatest Briton" in a BBC poll, as good a case should have been made for the melancholic Dr Johnson.

This was a year in which issues of freedom of expression were publicly aired and contentiously legislated. There was an emerging view, as crude as it was dangerous, that it was only in Western culture that free speech was properly understood. If there was one overriding need evident in the world of literature it was for more translations of the great works of Islamic and Arab culture. This prospect, however, remained on the distant horizon. Meanwhile many writers continued to suffer for their beliefs. Among them was the novelist Orhan Pamuk, who was threatened with trial for his supposed traducing of the Turkish state through his reference to the killing of a million Armenians within the Ottoman Empire in 1915-17 (see p. 73). His case received more publicity than all the other imprisoned writers around the world put together, but there was value in this. In a celebrity-obsessed world, it was possible for the story of one person to speak for many. Pamuk's situation drew international attention back to a general plight. Once again, it seemed that threats across the world to free expression were both real and growing.

Among the books published in 2005, the following, indicated with their UK publishers, were of particular note:

FICTION. Leila Aboulela, *Minaret* (Bloomsbury); Michael Arditti, *Unity* (Maia); Margaret Atwood, *Oryx and Crake* (Virago); Tash Aw, *The Harmony Silk Factory* (Fourth Estate); Paul Auster, *The Brooklyn Follies* (Faber); John Banville, *The Sea* (Picador); Julian Barnes, *Arthur and George* (Cape); Sebastian Barry, *A Long Long Way* (Faber); Stefan Chin, trans. Philip Boehm, *Death in Danzig* (Secker and Warburg); J.M. Coetzee *Slow Man* (Secker and Warburg); Rachel Cusk, *In the Fold* (Faber); Marie Darrieussecq, trans. Ian Monk, *White* (Faber); Dave Eggers, *How We Are Hungry* (Hamish Hamilton); Michael Faber, *The Fahrenheit Twins* (Canongate); John Fuller, *Flawed Angel* (Chatto and Windus); Nadine Gordimer, *Get a Life* (Bloomsbury); Abdulrazak Gurnah, *Desertion* (Bloomsbury); Michel Houellebecq, trans. Gavin Bowd, *The Possibility of an Island* (Weidenfeld); Kazuo Ishiguro, *Never Let Me Go* (Faber); Frances Itani, *Leaning, Leaning Over Water* (Sceptre); Uzodinma Iweala, *Beasts of No Nation* (John Murray); Dan Jacobson, *All for Love* (Hamish Hamilton); P.D. James, *The Lighthouse* (Faber); Delia Jarrett-Macauley, *Moses, Citizen and Me* (Granta); Elias Khoury, trans. Humphrey Davies, *Gate of the Sun* (Harvill Secker); Benjamin Kunkel, *Indecision* (Picador); Andrey Kurkov, trans. George Bird, *A Matter of Death and Life* (Harvill); David Leavitt, *TheStories of David Leavitt* (Bloomsbury); Penelope Lively, *Making It Up* (Viking); Hilary Mantel, *Beyond Black* (Fourth Estate); Gabriel García Márquez, trans. Edith Grossman, *Memories of My Melancholy Whores* (Cape); Valerie Mason-John, *Borrowed Body* (Serpent's Tail); Ian McEwan, *Saturday* (Cape); Patrick McGrath, *Ghost Town* (Bloomsbury); Zakes Mda, *The Whale Caller* (Viking); Magnus Mills, *Explorers of the New Century* (Bloomsbury); Alice Munro, *Runaway* (Chatto and Windus); Haruki Murakami, trans. Philip Gabriel, *Kafka on the Shore* (Vintage); Joyce Carol Oates, *Rape: a love story* (Atlantic Books); Cynthia Ozick, *The Bear Boy* (Weidenfeld and Nicolson); Chuck Palahniuk, *Haunted* (Cape); Tim Parks, *Rapids* (Secker and Warburg); Caryl Phillips, *Dancing in the Dark* (Secker); J.K. Rowling, *Harry Potter and the Half-Blood Prince* (Bloomsbury); Salman Rushdie, *Shalimar the Clown* (Cape); Ali Smith, *The Accidental* (Hamish Hamilton); Zadie Smith, *On Beauty* (Hamish Hamilton); Amy Tan, *Saving Fish from Drowning* (Fourth Estate); Tarun J. Tejpal, *The Alchemy of Desire* (Picador); Adam Thorpe, *The Rules of Perspective,* (Cape); Rose Tremain, *The Darkness of Wallis Simpson and Other Stories* (Chatto); Dubravka Ugresic, trans. Michael Henry Heim, *The Ministry of Pain* (Saqi); John Updike, *Villages* (Hamish Hamilton); Jane Urquhart, *A Map of Glass* (Bloomsbury); Arnold Wesker, *Honey* (Scribner); Tim Winton, *The Turning* (Macmillan)

POETRY. Moniza Alvi, *How the Stone Found Its Voice* (Bloodaxe); John Ashbery, *Where Shall I Wonder* (Carcanet); Sebastian Barker, *The Matter of Europe* (Menard); Adrian Blamires, *The Effect of Coastal Processes* (Two Rivers Press); Carol Ann Duffy, *Rapture* (Picador); Paul Durcan, *The Art of Life* (Harvill); Mark Haddon, *The Talking Horse and the Sad Girl and the Village Under the Sea* (Picador); David Harsent, *Legion* (Faber); Geoffrey Hill, *Scenes from Comus* (Penguin); Jackie Kay, *Life Mask* (Bloodaxe); David Kinloch, *In My Father's House* (Carcanet); Philip Larkin (ed. A.T. Tolley), *Early Poems and Juvenilia* (Faber); Christopher Logue (after Homer), *Cold Calls* (Faber); Peter Manson, *Adjunct, An Undigest* (Edinburgh Review); Sinéad Morrissey, *The State of the Prisons* (Carcanet); Alice Oswald, *Woods etc* (Faber); Clare Pollard, *Look, Clare! Look!* (Bloodaxe); Richard Price, *Lucky Day* (Carcanet); J.H. Prynne, *Poems* (Bloodaxe); Alan Ross, *Poems* (Harvill Press); Anne Stevenson, *Poems 1955-2005* (Bloodaxe); Matthew Sweeney, *Sanctuary* (Cape); Derek Walcott, *The Prodigal* (Faber); Gerard Woodward, *We Were Pedestrians* (Chatto and Windus);

AUTOBIOGRAPHY AND BIOGRAPHY. Peter Ackroyd, *Shakespeare: The biography* (HarperCollins); Sybille Bedford, *Quicksands A Memoir* (Hamish Hamilton); Andrew Biswell, *The Real Life of Anthony Burgess* (Picador); Stephen Bourne, *Elisabeth Welch: Soft lights and sweet music* (Scarecrow Press); Elias Canetti, trans. Michael Hofmann, *Party in the Blitz: The English years* (Harvill); Virginia Spencer Carr, *Paul Bowles: A life* (Peter Owen); Jung Chang and Jon Halliday, *Mao: The unknown* (Cape); David Crane, *Scott of the Antarctic: A life of courage and tragedy in the extreme south* (HarperCollins); Lisa Chaney, *Hide-and-Seek with Angels: a Life of J.M. Barrie* (Hutchinson); Terry Coleman, *Olivier* (Bloomsbury); Max Egremont, *Siegfried Sassoon: a biography* (Picador); Marc Eliot, *Cary Grant* (Aurum); Jane Fonda, *My Life So Far* (Ebury); Lyndall Gordon, *Mary Wollstonecraft: A new genus* (Virago); Saskia Hamilton (ed.), *The Letters of Robert Lowell* (Faber); Christina Hardyment, *Malory: the life and times of King Arthur's chronicler* (HarperCollins); Claire Harman, *Robert Louis Stevenson: A biography* (HarperCollins); Douglas Haig, ed. Gary Sheffield and John Bourne, *War Diaries and Letters 1914-18* (Weidenfeld); Park Honan, *Christopher Marlowe: Poet and spy* (O.U.P.); Kathryn Hughes, *The Short Life and Long Times of Mrs Beeton* (Fourth Estate); Kathleen Jamie, *Findings* (Sort of Books); Rebecca Jenkins, *Fanny Kemble* (Simon and Schuster); Ian Kelly, *Beau Brummell: the ultimate dandy* (Hodder and Stoughton); Roger Knight, *The Pursuit of Victory: The life and achievements of Horatio Nelson* (Allen Lane); Gwyneth Lewis, *Two in a Boat: A marital voyage* (Fourth Estate); Simon Louvish, *Mae West: It ain't no sin* (Faber); Mary S. Lovell,

Bess of Hardwick: First Lady of Chatsworth (Little Brown); Christopher Meyer, *DC Confidential: The controversial memoirs of Britain's ambassador to the US at the time of 9/11 and the Iraq war* (Weidenfeld); John McGahern, *Memoir* (Faber); Harriet O'Brien, *Queen Emma and the Vikings: a history of power, love and hgreed in eleventh-century England* (Bloomsbury); Garry O'Connor, *Universal Father: a life of Pope John Paul II* (Bloomsbury); Fintan O'Toole, *White Savage: William Johnson and the invention of America* (Faber); Roger Pearson, *Voltaire Almighty: A life in pursuit of freedom* (Bloomsbury); George Perry, *James Dean* (Dorling Kindersley); Sue Prideaux, *Edvard Munch: Behind the Scream* (Yale); Jane Robinson, *Mary Seacole* (Constable); Bernice Rubens, *When I Grow Up* (Little, Brown); Vikram Seth, *Two Lives* (Little, Brown); James Shapiro, *1559: a Year in the life of William Shakespeare* (Faber); Rupert Shortt, *Benedict XVI: Commander of the Faith* (Hodder and Stoughton); Paul Webb, *Ivor Novello* (Haus); Alison Weir, *Isabella: She-Wolf of France, Queen of England* (Cape); Edmund White, *My Lives* (Bloomsbury); Charles Williams, *Pétain* (Little, Brown).

OTHER. Robert Fisk, *The Great War for Civilisation: The conquest of the Middle East* (HarperCollins); Tom Holland, *Persian Fire: The First World Empire and the battle for the West* (Little, Brown); Bruce Lawrence (ed.), *Messages to the World: The Statements of Osama bin Laden* (Verso); Eleanor Mills (ed.), *Cupcakes and Kalashnikovs: 100 years of the best journalism by women* (Constable); Nicholas Ostler, *Empires of the Word: A language history of the world* (HarperCollins); John Ralston Saul, *The Collapse of Globalism* (Atlantic); Simon Schama, *Rough Crossings: Britain, the slaves and the American Revolution* (BBC Books); Colin Tudge, *The Secret Life of Trees: How they live and why they matter* (Allen Lane); A.N. Wilson, *After the Victorians* (Hutchinson).

XVII SPORT

FOOTBALL. The international year was dominated by qualification for the 2006 World Cup. Nearly all the leading nations made it to Germany, though not without some wobbles along the way, including a shock 1-0 defeat for England by Northern Ireland in Belfast. England duly qualified for the final tournament, however, an achievement which proved beyond all the other countries from the British Isles. The Republic of Ireland's failure to qualify cost Brian Kerr his job as manager. Walter Smith inspired an upturn in Scotland's fortunes after his appointment in succession to Berti Vogts, but was unable to earn qualification. Elsewhere, Trinidad & Tobago, Ukraine, Angola, Ghana, Côte d'Ivoire, and Togo all qualified for their first-ever World Cup finals.

Brazil confirmed their status as favourites when they won the Confederations Cup, beating Argentina in the final and Germany, the hosts, in the semi-finals. The tournament, a mini dress rehearsal for the following year's extravaganza, went smoothly, but Germany received less welcome publicity through a match-fixing scandal involving referees. Robert Hoyzer, who admitted fixing games in co-operation with a Croatian betting ring, was sentenced to two years and five months in prison. Dominik Marks, another referee, was given a suspended sentence.

Liverpool won the European Cup (formally entitled the UEFA Champions League) for the fifth time after an extraordinary comeback against Milan in the final in Istanbul. The Italians led 3-0 at half-time, but Liverpool took the game into extra time after scoring three goals in a remarkable six-minute spell in the second half. Liverpool, who had played in the qualifying competition and were within minutes of being knocked out at the group stage, won the penalty shoot-out 3-2. In the semi-finals Liverpool had knocked out Chelsea. Arsenal and Manchester United went out in the first knock-out round. Chelsea, Liverpool, Arsenal, and Rangers all qualified for the knock-out stages of the 2005-06 Champions' League, but Manchester United failed to progress for the first time in a decade. CSKA Moscow became the first Russian club to win a major European trophy when they beat Sporting Lisbon on their own ground in the Uefa Cup final.

Chelsea won the English Premiership, their first league title for fifty years. Their defence, with Petr Cech outstanding in goal and captain John Terry leading by example, was the meanest in the Premiership, while their England midfielder, Frank Lampard, who scored nineteen goals in all competitions, was "footballer of the year". Chelsea's continuing financial muscle was shown by the publication of accounts which showed a loss of UK£87.8 million in a single year's trading. However, the club's recruitment policies regularly came under fire. Chelsea were censured for talking to Arsenal's Ashley Cole without permission, and Tottenham Hotspur successfully sought substantial compensation after their director of football, Frank Arnesen, was lured to Chelsea. Although Chelsea won a protracted chase for the Lyon midfielder, Michael Essien, they failed in their pursuit of

Steven Gerrard, who signed a new contract with Liverpool. Moreover, the greatest transfer coup by a premiership club was Newcastle United's signing of Michael Owen from Real Madrid for UK£16 million.

Chelsea won the Carling Cup by beating Liverpool 3-2 in extra time but were knocked out of the FA Cup by Newcastle. Arsenal won the latter competition, beating Manchester United in the first final to be decided by a penalty shoot-out. Malcolm Glazer, a US entrepreneur, completed a UK£812 million takeover of Manchester United. Some fans were so disgusted that they formed a new club, FC United, which joined the North West Counties League, nine rungs below the Premiership. In the autumn Manchester United agreed to release Roy Keane, their influential captain, who had not been happy at the club. He joined Celtic.

In an extraordinary finish to the Scottish Premier League season, Celtic conceded two late goals at Motherwell to hand the title to Rangers by one point. Celtic found some consolation by beating Dundee United to win the Scottish Cup final. Gordon Strachan was appointed Celtic manager in succession to Martin O'Neill, who stepped down in order to look after his sick wife. Strachan's first competitive match ended in a humiliating 5-0 defeat away to Artmedia Bratislava in the second qualifying round of the Champions' League. Rangers beat Motherwell in the final of the CIS Insurance Cup.

In an agreement likely to have major financial implications for the English game, the Premier League told the European Commission that it would not offer all its future television rights to one broadcaster. The Commission had been concerned about the lack of competition (see p. 456). Meanwhile Brian Barwick, a former television executive, took over as chief executive of the Football Association.

Germany won the women's European Championship for the fourth time in a row, beating Norway 3-1 in the final. England, the hosts, failed to qualify for the semi-finals, finishing bottom of their group. However, with large crowds attending games the tournament was seen as a success.

CRICKET. England won the Ashes for the first time in eighteen years in one of the greatest series of all time. Australia came to England as the world's leading cricket nation, but, despite stirring performances from their two bowling veterans, Shane Warne and Glenn McGrath, they were unable to hold a team inspired by Michael Vaughan's leadership, Andrew Flintoff's heroics with bat and ball, and the batting flair of Kevin Pietersen, who had surprisingly ousted Graham Thorpe from the team. It was no surprise when Flintoff won the BBC's sports personality of the year award. The same eleven England players would have appeared in every Test had Paul Collingwood not replaced the injured Simon Jones at the Oval.

The first day of the first Test at Lord's set the tone for a series in which runs were scored briskly and fortunes swayed regularly. Steve Harmison took five wickets as Australia crumbled under England's fearsome bowling attack and were dismissed for 190. By the end of the day, however, England were ninety-two for seven as McGrath took five wickets, bringing his overall Test tally to 504. When

Australia won the first Test by 239 runs it seemed that the old order was still in place, but England responded magnificently in the second Test at Edgbaston, scoring 407 runs on the first day and holding their nerve to win by two runs in an extraordinarily tight finish. Australia hung on for a draw in another dramatic finale at Old Trafford, and at Trent Bridge it was England who held their nerve, winning by three wickets after being set a modest target of 129 runs. England eventually won the series 2-1 thanks to a draw in the final Test at the Oval.

England had begun the year in promising fashion, completing their first series victory in South Africa for forty years. Vaughan's team won the series 2-1, despite losing the third Test at Cape Town to end a long unbeaten run. However, England lost the one-day series 4-1. England thrashed Bangladesh in an embarrassingly one-sided two-Test series at the start of the English summer and the early weeks of Australia's tour hinted at what might be ahead. Beaten by 100 runs in the inaugural Twenty20 international against England, Australia went on in a NatWest Series qualifier to lose to Bangladesh, who had won only two of their previous seventy-four completed one-day internationals. However, Ricky Ponting's team recovered to tie the final against England in a nail-biting finish and also won the NatWest Challenge one-day series against England.

In the autumn England were quickly brought back down to earth when they lost a three-Test series 2-0 in Pakistan. England lost the first Test by twenty-two runs in Multan. They drew the second Test in Faisalabad, but Pakistan won by an innings and 100 runs in Lahore to secure the series. Pakistan won the one-day series 3-2. Australia completed a clean sweep in a three-Test series against the West Indies, for whom Brian Lara became the most prolific Test batsman of all time when he passed Allan Border's total of 11,174 runs.

Honours were spread around in English county cricket. Nottinghamshire won the county championship for the first time since 1987, while Essex won the Totesport League, lifting the one-day crown for the first time in twenty years. Hampshire won the Cheltenham and Gloucester Trophy, beating Warwickshire in a high-scoring final at Lord's by eighteen runs, while Somerset won the Twenty20 Cup, beating Lancashire in the final.

Australia lifted the women's World Cup in South Africa, beating India in the final, and beat England in a one-day series and a Twenty20 international. However, they were beaten 1-0 by England in a two-match Test series.

RUGBY. Wales won rugby union's Six Nations Championship in emphatic style, playing thrilling, attacking rugby in the country's best traditions (see p. 28). Mike Ruddock's team never looked back after opening the tournament with a dramatic late victory over England in Cardiff. Another comeback, after they had trailed 15-3 in the first half, saw the Welsh win 24-18 in Paris to stay firmly on course for their first grand slam for twenty-seven years, which they duly secured. France finished runners-up, Ireland third, and England fourth. England lost 18-17 to France at Twickenham and Andy Robinson's team made it three defeats in three games when they lost to Ireland in Dublin before saving face with home wins over Italy and Scotland. The Scots faded badly after making a promising start, when they were unlucky to lose 16-9 to France in Paris. Matt Williams, the coach, was later sacked and replaced by Frank Hadden.

New Zealand underlined their position as favourites for the 2007 World Cup with a resounding series victory over the Lions. Graham Henry's team played some thrilling rugby, winning the three Tests 21-3, 48-18, and 38-19. The All Blacks were superior in every department and in Daniel Carter, their brilliant fly half, they had a player capable of turning matches on his own. Clive Woodward, the Lions coach, was under fire from the moment he named his initial squad, which included twenty Englishmen but only ten Welshmen, despite the fact that Wales had won the grand slam and England had finished fourth in the Six Nations Championship. There was also frequent criticism of Alastair Campbell, former director of communications for UK Prime Minister Tony Blair, who was the Lions' media adviser. After the tour Woodward went on to a new career in football, working on Southampton's coaching staff.

New Zealand won the Tri Nations and confirmed their global supremacy in the autumn internationals, when they showed the strength in depth of their squad. They thrashed Wales 41-3 in Cardiff and beat Ireland 45-7 in Dublin with their second string a week later. It was much tighter against England, who lost 23-19 at Twickenham, but victory over Scotland at Murrayfield meant the 2005 All Blacks became only the seventh overseas side to complete a clean sweep of the four countries. England had a good autumn, beating Australia and Samoa, although the latter match was tarnished by the red card shown to Lewis Moody, who became the first England player ever to be sent off at Twickenham after he punched an opponent. Australia lost to France, England and Wales, winning only in Dublin. After the tour Eddie Jones, their long-serving coach, was sacked. In other significant results in the autumn Scotland lost to Argentina, and Wales were beaten by South Africa. In a controversial decision, the international rugby board ignored Japan's claims and awarded the 2011 World Cup to New Zealand (see p. 327).

Toulouse, emphatic winners at Leicester in the semi-finals, beat Stade Français in the Heineken Cup final after extra time. Sale Sharks won the European Challenge Cup, beating Section Paloise in the final. Wasps beat Leicester to win the Premiership final at Twickenham, condemning Martin Johnson to defeat in his final match before retirement. On a dramatic last day of the regular Premiership season, Harlequins were relegated after losing 23-22 at home to Sale. Leeds caused a major upset in the Powergen Cup final, beating Bath 20-12. The Ospreys won the Celtic League, with Munster winning the Celtic Cup thanks to a 27-16 victory over Llanelli Scarlets at Lansdowne Road.

In rugby league, Bradford Bulls could finish only third in the regular season but went on to win the grand final, beating Leeds 16-5 with their twelfth successive victory. Hull won the Challenge Cup final, beating Leeds, the overwhelming favourites, 25-24. Australia won the Tri-Nations tournament in the autumn, Great Britain taking the wooden spoon after losing three of their four matches. Andy Farrell, the Great Britain captain, moved from league to union, but the start of his new career with Saracens was delayed by injury.

TENNIS. Although Roger Federer failed to win either of the first two grand slam events, the Swiss confirmed his status as the best player in the world by winning both Wimbledon and the US Open. He won his third successive Wimbledon title in imperious style, beating Andy Roddick in a final display which many regarded as one of the best in the history of the game. Federer won the sixth major of his career when he beat the evergreen Andre Agassi in four sets in the US Open final. However, his year ended in defeat in the Masters Cup final in Shanghai, when he was beaten over five epic sets by David Nalbandian, a result which ended his sequence of twenty-four successive victories in finals.

Marat Safin won the Australian Open after beating Lleyton Hewitt in four sets in the final. The Russian beat Federer in five sets in the semi-finals in one of the greatest matches ever played at Melbourne. Rafael Nadal dominated the clay court season and won the French Open, beating Federer on his way to victory over Argentina's Mariano Puerta in the final. Puerta was later banned for eight years after testing positive for a banned stimulant after the final.

Andy Murray began the year ranked outside the world's top 400 and with a defeat in his first senior match. By the end of it, he was Britain's leading player in all but name, had played in his first Association of Tennis Professionals (ATP) final and was firmly established in the world's top 100. Having become the youngest player ever to represent Britain in the Davis Cup, Murray beat Taylor Dent—ranked more than 300 places above him—in his first senior tournament in Britain, the Stella Artois Championships at Queen's Club, before losing a tight match against Thomas Johansson, the world number twenty. At Wimbledon he beat George Bastl and Radek Stepanek, the number fourteen seed, before losing a five-set thriller to Nalbandian. At the US Open Murray beat Andrei Pavel in five dramatic sets before losing another five-set thriller to Arnaud Clément. Although Murray could not prevent Britain losing their Davis Cup tie against Switzerland in September, by the end of the year he had reached his first ATP final, losing to Federer in the Thailand Open, and had won his first match against the British number one, Tim Henman, in Basle.

Henman had a poor year. In the Australian Open he lost in the third round to Nikolay Davydenko, winning only eight games, and he went out in the second round of the French Open and Wimbledon (where he was beaten by Dmitry Tursunov, the world number 152) and the first round of the US Open. Greg Rusedski, the British number two, returned from injury to make a steady climb up the world rankings and won a grass court tournament in Newport, Rhode Island. Croatia won the Davis Cup for the first time, beating Slovakia in the final.

Serena Williams, having beaten Maria Sharapova in the Australian Open semi-finals, went on to beat Lindsay Davenport in the final. Justine Henin-Hardenne triumphed in the French Open, beating Mary Pierce in the final. Venus Williams, whose career had appeared to be in decline, won Wimbledon for the third time when she beat Davenport in an epic final, having disposed of Sharapova, the holder, in the semi-finals. Sharapova went out at the same stage and to the eventual champion in the US Open when she lost to Kim Clijsters, who beat Pierce in the final to crown her recovery from injury. The Belgian had appeared in four previous grand slam finals but lost them all.

GOLF. Tiger Woods underlined his position as the world's best golfer by winning two of the year's majors, taking his overall tally to ten. Woods won the Masters after a titanic struggle with a fellow American, Chris DiMarco, who led the first two rounds and lost in a play-off. Woods dominated the Open at St Andrews from start to finish, winning by five strokes. Britain's Colin Montgomerie finished second, with Fred Couples and Jose Maria Olazabal joint third. Jack Nicklaus played his last ever round in a major when he bowed out with a seventy-two after thirty-six holes at St Andrews. Michael Campbell celebrated his first major when he won the US Open by two strokes from Woods at Pinehurst, while Phil Mickelson won his second, a birdie at the last hole securing the PGA Championship at Springfield. Montgomerie crowned a fine year by winning the European Order of Merit for the eighth time, while Luke Donald enhanced his reputation as Britain's most promising young player. He finished joint third in the Masters.

The United States won the Walker Cup after Nigel Edwards missed a putt on the final green that would have given Britain and Ireland victory. The Americans also triumphed in the women's team professional event, the Solheim Cup, beating Europe by three points. Ian Woosnam was named as Europe captain for the 2006 Ryder Cup.

Annika Sorenstam won her ninth major when she won the LPGA Championship at Bulle Rock in Maryland. The Korean Birdie Kim won the US Open at Cherry Hills Country Club in Denver. Korea's Jeong Jang, who had never won a professional tournament before, took the British Open by four strokes. Michelle Wie, the Korean prodigy, turned professional at sixteen but suffered embarrassment in her first tournament, the Samsung World Championship. She thought she had finished fourth but was disqualified for taking an incorrect drop from a bush.

ATHLETICS. Justin Gatlin was the star of the world championships in Helsinki, becoming only the second man to win the world sprint double. His winning margin of three metres in the 100 metres was the biggest in the history of the championships. Asafa Powell of Jamaica, who had broken the world 100 metres record at the Athens Olympic Games in 2004 with a time of 9.77sec, pulled out of the Helsinki event with injury. Two Americans, Lauryn Williams and Allyson Felix, won the women's 100 metres and 200 metres respectively.

Rashid Ramzi, representing Bahrain, completed the middle-distance double at 800 metres and 1,500 metres, while Ethiopia's Tirunesh Dibaba became the first woman to win the 5,000 metres and 10,000 metres world championships double. Cuba's Osleidys Menendez beat her own world javelin record to win gold, while Russia's Yelena Isinbayeva set a world record in winning the pole vault.

A marathon gold medal for Paula Radcliffe on the final day could not hide the paucity of British talent. The British team won only two other medals—relay bronzes—while Tim Benjamin was the only British male to reach an individual track final. Earlier in the year the British men's team were relegated from the top flight of the European Cup for the first time since the competition became divisional in 1983, although there was some consolation when Britain's women won promotion back to the elite group with an impressive victory in Portugal. Although Britain won seven medals at the European indoor championships, there were several disappointments and only one gold, Jason Gardener leading Mark Lewis-Francis home in a British one-two in the men's sixty metres. Lewis-Francis later lost his medal after testing positive for cocaine, though he escaped a possible two-year ban after blaming passive smoking.

Radcliffe won the London Marathon, while Kenenisa Bekele broke his own world record for 10,000 metres by more than two seconds at a grand prix meeting in Brussels.

Victor Conte, head of the Bay Area Laboratory Co-Operative (BALCO)in the USA, was sentenced to four months in jail and four months of house arrest for his part in a scheme to provide athletes with undetectable performance-enhancing drugs. Tim Montgomery and Chryste Gaines, the US sprinters, were both banned for two years following an investigation into BALCO (see AR 2003, p. 537; 2004, p. 492).

MOTOR SPORT. Fernando Alonso became the youngest world champion in the history of Formula One when he lifted the drivers' crown at the age of twenty-four. The Spaniard secured the title in only his 68th race when he finished third in Brazil. He won seven races in total and his victory in the final race in Shanghai ensured that Renault would also win the manufacturers' title. However, it came as a blow to Renault when Alonso later announced that he would join McLaren in 2007.

McLaren's Kimi Raikkonen was Alonso's closest challenger. The Finn finished twenty-one points behind the winner, but fifty points ahead of third-placed Michael Schumacher, whose Ferrari team had a miserable season by their own high standards. Raikkonen's team-mate, Juan Pablo Montoya, won the British Grand Prix from Alonso. There were farcical scenes at the United States Grand Prix in Indianapolis, where only three teams raced after a dispute over tyre safety. Britain's Jenson Button failed to win a grand prix, did not finish on the podium until the end of July, and found himself embroiled in a legal wrangle between BAR, his employers, and Williams, who had an agreement to recruit him for the 2006 season. It was resolved when Williams accepted a UK£18 million settlement, enabling Button to stay with BAR.

Dan Wheldon became the first British driver since Graham Hill in 1966 to win the Indianapolis 500. He also became the first Briton to win the American ILR IndyCar Championship. The Dane Tom Kristensen became the first driver to win seven Le Mans 24-hour titles when his Audi triumphed by two laps. France's Sébastien Loeb, driving a Citroen, successfully defended his world rally championship title. On two wheels, Valentino Rossi won his seventh world title when he won the MotoGP Championship, while Australia's Troy Corser won the World Superbike Championship.

HORSE RACING. Kieren Fallon replaced Jamie Spencer as Aidan O'Brien's number one jockey at Ballydoyle and promptly rewarded his new employers with a Newmarket double, Footstepsinthesand winning the 2,000 Guineas and Virginia Waters the 1,000 Guineas. Godolphin's Dubawi, ridden by Frankie Dettori, won the Irish 2,000 Guineas. Saoire, ridden by Mick Kinane and trained by Frances Crowley, won the Irish 1,000 Guineas.

The Derby was won, for once, by a trainer from outside the select top group. Michael Bell's Motivator, ridden by Johnny Murtagh, beat Walk in the Park by five lengths. Hurricane Run, ridden by Fallon and trained by André Fabre, won the Irish Derby and went on to triumph in the Prix de l'Arc de Triomphe at Longchamp. Scorpion, ridden by Dettori and trained by Aidan O'Brien, won the St Leger at Doncaster. Kinane rode John Oxx's Azamour to victory in the King George VI and Queen Elizabeth Diamond Stakes, which was staged at Newbury during the rebuilding of Ascot.

The National Hunt Festival's expansion to four days at Cheltenham was regarded as a success, despite the absence of Best Mate, who ruptured a blood vessel; later in the year Best Mate died of a heart attack during a race at Exeter. Kicking King, ridden by Barry Geraghty, took Best Mate's Gold Cup crown in style, winning by five lengths. Hardy Eustace won the Champion Hurdle, while Moscow Flyer regained the two-mile chasing crown with victory in the Queen Mother Champion Chase. Hedgehunter, ridden by Ruby Walsh and trained by Willie Mullins, won the Grand National.

BOXING. In a year when the best known boxer of modern times announced his retirement, the sport welcomed the largest champion in its history. Mike Tyson, the former world heavyweight title holder, quit on his stool at the end of the sixth round against Kevin McBride, a journeyman fighter, and said he would not fight again. Meanwhile Nikolay Valuev, a seven foot tall Russian weighing twenty-three stone and three pounds, became the tallest and heaviest world champion in history when he beat the American John Ruiz.

Danny Williams beat Audley Harrison on points in a British heavyweight championship bout which aroused considerable interest, but Ricky Hatton and Amir Khan were the country's best known fighters. Hatton enjoyed the best victory of his career when he beat the odds-on favourite, Kostya Tszyu, to win the International Boxing Federation's world light-welterweight title and recognition as the planet's best fighter in the ten stone division. Khan turned professional after gaining revenge over Mario Kindelan, the Cuban who had denied him gold at the 2004 Olympics, in his last fight as an amateur. Joe Calzaghe retained his World Boxing Organisation super-middleweight title when he beat Mario Veit in six rounds. Scotland's Scott Harrison beat Michael Brodie of Manchester and Australia's Nedal Hussein to retain his WBO featherweight title.

MISCELLANEOUS. Lance Armstrong extended his record as the greatest cyclist in Tour de France history, winning the race for the seventh time in a row before retiring. Britain's track cyclists continued to excel, winning four gold medals at the world championships in Los Angeles in the men's team pursuit, men's sprint relay, madison, and women's sprint.

Shaun Murphy, a 150-1 outsider who had to qualify to play in the tournament, won the world snooker championship at Sheffield, beating Matthew Stevens in the final.

Britain finished third in the medals table at the world rowing championships after winning two golds, in the men's coxless four and the women's quad. Oxford won the Boat Race by two lengths and in the third fastest time with the heaviest crew in the race's history.

In sailing, Ellen MacArthur broke the record for the fastest solo circumnavigation of the globe, in seventy-one days, while Bruno Peyron set a new mark of fifty days for a crewed circumnavigation.

Britain claimed their sixth consecutive team gold at the European Three-Day Event Championship at Blenheim. Zara Phillips won the individual gold medal. Pippa Funnell, riding Primmore's Pride, won the Badminton horse trials for the third time in four years.

In American football, the New England Patriots beat the Philadelphia Eagles 24-21 to record their third Super Bowl success in four years, while in basketball the San Antonio Spurs won the NBA finals for the third time in seven years, beating the Detroit Pistons 4-3. The Chicago White Sox won baseball's World Series for the first time since 1917 when they beat the Houston Astros.

XVIII DOCUMENTS AND REFERENCE

MEETING THE CLIMATE CHALLENGE: RECOMMENDATIONS OF THE INTERNATIONAL CLIMATE CHANGE TASKFORCE

Published below are the foreword and the summary of the main recommendations of the International Climate Change Taskforce, issued in January 2005, which called on governments worldwide to take action to reduce global warming.

FOREWORD

The vast majority of international scientists and peer-reviewed reports affirm that climate change is a serious and growing threat, leaving no country, however wealthy, immune from the extreme weather events and rising sea levels that scientists predict will occur, unless action is taken.

By reducing anthropogenic emissions of carbon dioxide and other greenhouse gases that are currently being emitted into the atmosphere, we can mitigate climate change as well as have a real opportunity to enhance energy security and drive technological modernisation in both an economical and environmentally friendly way. The development of clean, climate-friendly energy technologies will provide new business opportunities and new avenues of prosperity for both developed and developing countries alike.

As the causes of climate change are global, however, the challenge can only be met with all the countries of the world working together. The politics involved are difficult, but we believe progress can be made.

To develop solutions as to how to move forward, the International Climate Change Taskforce was established by three leading think tanks - the Institute for Public Policy Research in the United Kingdom (UK), the Center for American Progress in the United States (US), and The Australia Institute. It is a unique international cross-party, cross-sector collaboration, including leaders from public service, science, business, and civil society in both developed and developing countries.

The Taskforce's recommendations are to all governments and policymakers worldwide. They are published in the year when the UK holds the presidencies of the G8 and EU, during which the UK's Prime Minister Tony Blair has pledged to make climate change an agenda priority as one of the most serious and far-reaching challenges of the twenty-first century. It is also the year in which the Kyoto Protocol comes into force and nations start discussions on future global action on climate change.

The strength of our recommendations is that we have been able to find common ground. We have set out a pathway to engage all countries in concerted action on climate change, including those not bound by the Kyoto Protocol and major developing countries. We have not been able to consider every aspect of this complex problem, but this is not our final word. Later this year, we plan to publish a report that will further elaborate on our recommendations.

We believe that our proposals can become the foundation for action and a blueprint for moving forward. The prize is precious - to bequeath to all our children a world as rich in life and opportunity as the one we inherited. But time is short. Action is required now if we are to win the battle against climate change.

Rt Hon. Stephen Byers MP   Senator Olympia J. Snowe
Co-Chair   Co-Chair

SUMMARY OF MAIN RECOMMENDATIONS

1. A long-term objective be established to prevent global average temperature from rising more than 2°C (3.6°F) above the pre-industrial level, to limit the extent and magnitude of climate-change impacts.

2. A global framework be adopted that builds on the UNFCCC and the Kyoto Protocol, and enables all countries to be part of concerted action on climate change at the global level in the post-2012 period, on the basis of equity and common but differentiated responsibilities.

3. G8 governments establish national renewable portfolio standards to generate at least 25% of electricity from renewable energy sources by 2025, with higher targets needed for some G8 governments.

4. G8 governments increase their spending on research, development, and demonstration of advanced technologies for energy-efficient and low- and zero-carbon energy supply by two-fold or more by 2010, at the same time as adopting near-term strategies for the large-scale deployment of existing low- and no-carbon technologies.

5. The G8 and other major economies, including from the developing world, form a G8+ Climate Group, to pursue technology agreements and related initiatives that will lead to large emissions reductions.

6. The G8+ Climate Group agree to shift their agricultural subsidies from food crops to biofuels, especially those derived from cellulosic materials, while implementing appropriate safeguards to ensure sustainable farming methods are encouraged, culturally and ecologically sensitive land preserved, and biodiversity protected.

7. All developed countries introduce national mandatory cap-and-trade systems for carbon emissions, and construct them to allow for their future integration into a single global market.

8. Governments remove barriers to and increase investment in renewable energy and energy efficient technologies and practices through such measures as the phase-out of fossil fuel subsidies and requiring Export Credit Agencies and Multilateral Development Banks to adopt minimum efficiency or carbon intensity standards for projects they support.

9. Developed countries honour existing commitments to provide greater financial and technical assistance to help vulnerable countries adapt to climate change, including the commitments made at the seventh conference of the parties to the UNFCCC in 2001, and pursue the establishment of an international compensation fund to support disaster mitigation and preparedness.

10. Governments committed to action on climate change raise public awareness of the problem and build public support for climate policies by pledging to provide substantial long-term investment in effective climate communication activities.

UN DARFUR REPORT: SUMMARY, CONCLUSIONS AND RECOMMENDATIONS

Published below are the Executive Summary, together with the Conclusions and Recommendations, of the Report of the International Commission of Inquiry on Darfur to the UN Secretary-General. The report was published in Geneva on 25 January 2005. It established that the government of Sudan and the Janjawid militia were responsible for serious violations of human rights against the people of Darfur, amounting to crimes under international law. However, it concluded that genocidal intent was not present. The commission identified possible perpetrators—in a sealed file submitted to the UN Secretary-General—whom it recommended should be brought before the ICC.

INTERNATIONAL COMMISSION OF INQUIRY ON DARFUR
REPORT TO THE SECRETARY-GENERAL
EXECUTIVE SUMMARY

Acting under Chapter VII of the United Nations Charter, on 18 September 2004 the Security Council adopted resolution 1564 requesting, *inter alia*, that the Secretary-General 'rapidly establish an international commission of inquiry in order immediately to investigate reports of violations of international humanitarian law and human rights law in Darfur by all parties, to determine also whether or not acts of genocide have occurred, and to identify the perpetrators of such violations with a view to ensuring that those responsible are held accountable'.

In October 2004, the Secretary General appointed Antonio Cassese (Chairperson), Mohamed Fayek, Hina Jilani, Dumisa Ntsebeza and Therese Striggner-Scott as members of the Commission and requested that they report back on their findings within three months. The Commission was supported in its work by a Secretariat headed by an Executive Director, Ms. Mona Rishmawi, as well as a legal research team and an investigative team composed of investigators, forensic experts, military analysts, and investigators specializing in gender violence, all appointed by the Office of the United Nations High Commissioner for Human Rights. The Commission assembled in Geneva and began its work on 25 October 2004.

In order to discharge its mandate, the Commission endeavoured to fulfil four key tasks: (1) to investigate reports of violations of international humanitarian law and human rights law in Darfur by all parties; (2) to determine whether or not acts of genocide have occurred; (3) to identify the perpetrators of violations of international humanitarian law and human rights law in Darfur; and (4) to suggest means of ensuring that those responsible for such violations are held accountable. While the Commission considered all events relevant to the current conflict in Darfur, it focused in particular on incidents that occurred between February 2003 and mid-January 2005.

The Commission engaged in a regular dialogue with the Government of the Sudan throughout its mandate, in particular through meetings in Geneva and in the Sudan, as well as through the work of its investigative team. The Commission visited the Sudan from 7-21 November 2004 and 9-16 January 2005, including travel to the three Darfur States. The investigative team remained in Darfur from November 2004 through January 2005. During its presence in the Sudan, the Commission held extensive meetings with representatives of the Government, the Governors of the Darfur States and other senior officials in the capital and at provincial and local levels, members of the armed forces and police, leaders of rebel forces, tribal leaders, internally displaced persons, victims and witnesses of violations, NGOs and United Nations representatives.

The Commission submitted a full report on its findings to the Secretary-General on 25 January 2005. The report describes the terms of reference, methodology, approach and activities of the Commission and its investigative team. It also provides an overview of the historical and social background to the conflict in Darfur. The report then addresses in detail the four key tasks referred to above, namely the Commission's findings in relation to: i) violations of international human rights and humanitarian law by all parties; ii) whether or not acts of genocide have taken place; iii) the identification of perpetrators; and iv) accountability mechanisms. These four sections are briefly summarized below.

I. Violations of international human rights law and international humanitarian law

In accordance with its mandate to 'investigate reports of violations of human rights law and international humanitarian law', the Commission carefully examined reports from different sources including Governments, inter-governmental organizations, United Nations bodies and mechanisms, as well as nongovernmental organizations.

The Commission took as the starting point for its work two irrefutable facts regarding the situation in Darfur. Firstly, according to United Nations estimates there are 1,65 million internally displaced persons in Darfur, and more than 200,000 refugees from Darfur in neighbouring Chad. Secondly, there has been large-scale destruction of villages throughout the three states of Darfur. The Commission conducted independent investigations to establish additional facts and gathered extensive information on multiple incidents of violations affecting villages, towns and other locations across North, South and West Darfur. The conclusions of the Commission are based on the evaluation of the facts gathered or verified through its investigations.

Based on a thorough analysis of the information gathered in the course of its investigations, the Commission established that the Government of the Sudan and the Janjaweed are responsible for serious violations of international human rights and humanitarian law amounting to crimes under international law. In particular, the Commission found that Government forces and militias conducted indiscriminate attacks, including killing of civilians, torture, enforced disappearances, destruction of villages, rape and other forms of sexual violence, pillaging and forced displacement, throughout Darfur. These acts were conducted on a widespread and systematic basis, and therefore may amount to crimes against humanity. The extensive destruction and displacement have resulted in a loss of livelihood and means of survival for countless women, men and children. In addition to the large scale attacks, many people have been arrested and detained, and many have been held *incommunicado* for prolonged periods and tortured. The vast majority of the victims of all of these violations have been from the Fur, Zaghawa, Massalit, Jebel, Aranga and other so-called 'African' tribes.

In their discussions with the Commission, Government of the Sudan officials stated that any attacks carried out by Government armed forces in Darfur were for counter-insurgency purposes and were conducted on the basis of military imperatives. However, it is clear from the Commission's findings that most attacks were deliberately and indiscriminately directed against civilians. Moreover even if rebels, or persons supporting rebels, were present in some of the villages - which the Commission considers likely in only a very small number of instances - the attackers did not take precautions to enable civilians to leave the villages or otherwise be shielded from attack. Even where rebels may have been present in villages, the impact of the attacks on civilians shows that the use of military force was manifestly disproportionate to any threat posed by the rebels.

The Commission is particularly alarmed that attacks on villages, killing of civilians, rape, pillaging and forced displacement have continued during the course of the Commission's mandate. The Commission considers that action must be taken urgently to end these violations.

While the Commission did not find a systematic or a widespread pattern to these violations, it found credible evidence that rebel forces, namely members of the SLA and JEM, also are responsible for serious violations of international human rights and humanitarian law which may amount to war crimes. In particular, these violations include cases of murder of civilians and pillage.

II. Have acts of genocide occurred?

The Commission concluded that the Government of the Sudan has not pursued a policy of genocide.

Arguably, two elements of genocide might be deduced from the gross violations of human rights perpetrated by Government forces and the militias under their control. These two elements are, first, the *actus reus* consisting of killing, or causing serious bodily or mental harm, or deliberately inflicting conditions of life likely to bring about physical destruction; and, second, on the basis of a subjective standard, the existence of a protected group being targeted by the authors of criminal conduct. However, the crucial element of genocidal intent appears to be missing, at least as far as the central Government authorities are concerned. Generally speaking the policy of attacking, killing and forcibly displacing members of some tribes does not evince a specific intent to annihilate, in whole or in part, a group distinguished on racial, ethnic, national or religious grounds. Rather, it would seem that those who planned and organized attacks on villages pursued the intent to drive the victims from their homes, primarily for purposes of counter-insurgency warfare.

The Commission does recognise that in some instances individuals, including Government officials, may commit acts with genocidal intent. Whether this was the case in Darfur, however, is a determination that only a competent court can make on a case by case basis.

The conclusion that no genocidal policy has been pursued and implemented in Darfur by the Government authorities, directly or through the militias under their control, should not be taken in any way as detracting from the gravity of the crimes perpetrated in that region. International offences such as the crimes against humanity and war crimes that have been committed in Darfur may be no less serious and heinous than genocide.

III. Identification of perpetrators

The Commission has collected reliable and consistent elements which indicate the responsibility of some individuals for serious violations of international human rights law and international humanitarian law, including crimes against humanity or war crimes, in Darfur. In order to identify perpetrators, the Commission decided that there must be 'a reliable body of material consistent with other verified circumstances, which tends to show that a person may reasonably be suspected of being involved in the commission of a crime.' The Commission therefore makes an assessment of likely suspects, rather than a final judgment as to criminal guilt.

Those identified as possibly responsible for the above-mentioned violations consist of individual perpetrators, including officials of the Government of Sudan, members of militia forces, members of rebel groups, and certain foreign army officers acting in their personal capacity. Some Government officials, as well as members of militia forces, have also been named as possibly responsible for joint criminal enterprise to commit international crimes. Others are identified for their possible involvement in planning and/or ordering the commission of international crimes, or of aiding and abetting the perpetration of such crimes. The Commission also has identified a number of senior Government officials and military commanders who may be responsible, under the notion of superior (or command) responsibility, for knowingly failing to prevent or repress the perpetration of crimes. Members of rebel groups are named as suspected of participating in a joint criminal enterprise to commit international crimes, and as possibly responsible for knowingly failing to prevent or repress the perpetration of crimes committed by rebels.

The Commission has decided to withhold the names of these persons from the public domain. This decision is based on three main grounds: 1) the importance of the principles of due process and respect for the rights of the suspects; 2) the fact that the Commission has not been vested with investigative or prosecutorial powers; and 3) the vital need to ensure the protection of witnesses from possible harassment or intimidation. The Commission instead will list the names in a sealed file that will be placed in the custody of the UN Secretary-General. The Commission recommends that this file be handed over to a competent Prosecutor (the Prosecutor of the International Criminal Court, according to the Commission's recommendations), who will use that material as he or she deems fit for his or her investigations. A distinct and very voluminous sealed file, containing all the evidentiary material collected by the Commission, will be handed over to the High Commissioner for Human Rights. This file should be delivered to a competent Prosecutor.

IV. Accountability mechanisms

The Commission strongly recommends that the Security Council immediately refer the situation of Darfur to the International Criminal Court, pursuant to article 13(b) of the ICC Statute. As repeatedly stated by the Security Council, the situation constitutes a threat to international peace and security. Moreover, as the Commission has confirmed, serious violations of international human rights law and humanitarian law by all parties are continuing. The prosecution by the ICC of persons allegedly responsible for the most serious crimes in Darfur would contribute to the restoration of peace in the region.

The alleged crimes that have been documented in Darfur meet the thresholds of the Rome Statute as defined in articles 7 (1), 8 (1) and 8 (f). There is an internal armed conflict in Darfur between the governmental authorities and organized armed groups. A body of reliable information indicates that war crimes may have been committed on a large-scale, at times even as part of a plan or a policy. There is also a wealth of credible material which suggests that criminal acts were committed as part of widespread or systematic attacks directed against the civilian population, with knowledge of the attacks. In the opinion of the Commission therefore, these may amount to crimes against humanity.

The Sudanese justice system is unable and unwilling to address the situation in Darfur. This system has been significantly weakened during the last decade. Restrictive laws that grant broad powers to the executive have undermined the effectiveness of the judiciary, and many of the laws in force in Sudan today contravene basic human rights standards. Sudanese criminal laws do not adequately proscribe war crimes and crimes against humanity, such as those carried out in Darfur, and the Criminal Procedure Code contains provisions that prevent the effective prosecution of these acts. In addition, many victims informed the Commission that they had little confidence in the impartiality of the Sudanese justice system and its ability to bring to justice the perpetrators of the serious crimes committed in Darfur. In any event, many have feared reprisals in the event that they resort to the national justice system.

The measures taken so far by the Government to address the crisis have been both grossly inadequate and ineffective, which has contributed to the climate of almost total impunity for human rights violations in Darfur. Very few victims have lodged official complaints regarding crimes committed against them or their families, due to a lack of confidence in the justice system. Of the few cases where complaints have been made, most have not been properly pursued. Furthermore, procedural hurdles limit the victims' access to justice. Despite the magnitude of the crisis and its immense impact on civilians in Darfur, the Government informed the Commission of very few cases of individuals who have been prosecuted, or even disciplined, in the context of the current crisis.

The Commission considers that the Security Council must act not only against the perpetrators but also on behalf of the victims. It therefore recommends the establishment of a Compensation Commission designed to grant reparation to the victims of the crimes, whether or not the perpetrators of such crimes have been identified.

It further recommends a number of serious measures to be taken by the Government of the Sudan, in particular (i) ending the impunity for the war crimes and crimes against humanity committed in Darfur; (ii) strengthening the independence and impartiality of the judiciary, and empowering courts to address human rights violations; (iii) granting full and unimpeded access by the International Committee of the Red Cross and United Nations human rights monitors to all those detained in relation to the situation in Darfur; (iv) ensuring the protection of all the victims and witnesses of human rights violations; (v) enhancing the capacity of the Sudanese judiciary through the training of judges, prosecutors and lawyers; (vi) respecting the rights of IDPs and fully implementing the Guiding Principles on Internal Displacement, particularly with regard to facilitating the voluntary return of IDPs in safety and dignity; (vii) fully cooperating with the relevant human rights bodies and mechanisms of the United Nations and the African Union; and (viii) creating, through a broad consultative process, a truth and reconciliation commission once peace is established in Darfur.

The Commission also recommends a number of measures to be taken by other bodies to help break the cycle of impunity. These include the exercise of universal jurisdiction by other States, re-establishment by the Commission on Human Rights of the mandate of the Special Rapporteur on human rights in Sudan, and public and periodic reports on the human rights situation in Darfur by the High Commissioner for Human Rights.

• • •

SECTION V
CONCLUSIONS AND RECOMMENDATIONS

626. The people of Darfur have suffered enormously during the last few years. Their ordeal must remain at the centre of international attention. They have been living a nightmare of violence and abuse that has stripped them of the very little they had. Thousands were killed, women were raped, villages were burned, homes destroyed, and belongings looted. About 1,8 million were forcibly displaced and became refugees or internally-displaced persons. They need protection.

627. Establishing peace and ending the violence in Darfur are essential for improving the human rights situation. But real peace cannot be established without justice. The Sudanese justice system has unfortunately demonstrated that it is unable or unwilling to investigate and prosecute the alleged perpetrators of the war crimes and crimes against humanity committed in Darfur. It is absolutely essential that those perpetrators be brought to justice before a competent and credible international criminal court. It is also important that the victims of the crimes committed in Darfur be compensated.

628. The Sudan is a sovereign state and its territorial integrity must be respected. While the Commission acknowledges that the Sudan has the right to take measures to maintain or re-establish its authority and defend its territorial integrity, sovereignty entails responsibility. The Sudan is required not only to respect international law, but also to ensure its respect. It is regrettable that the Government of the Sudan has failed to protect the rights of its own people. The measures it has taken to counter the insurgency in Darfur have been in blatant violation of international law. The international community must therefore act immediately and take measures to ensure accountability. Those members of rebel groups that have committed serious violations of human rights and humanitarian law must also be held accountable.

629. Measures taken by all parties to the internal conflict in the Sudan must be in conformity with international law.

I. FACTUAL AND LEGAL FINDINGS

630. In view of the findings noted in the various sections above, the Commission concludes that the Government of the Sudan and the Janjaweed are responsible for a number of violations of international human rights and humanitarian law. Some of these violations are very likely to amount to war crimes, and given the systematic and widespread pattern of many of the violations, they would also amount to crimes against humanity. The Commission further finds that the rebel movements are responsible for violations which would amount to war crimes.

631. In particular, the Commission finds that in many instances Government forces and militias under their control attacked civilians and destroyed and burned down villages in Darfur contrary to the relevant principles and rules of international humanitarian law. Even assuming that in all the villages they attacked there were rebels present, or at least some rebels were hiding there, or that there were persons supporting rebels - a fact that the Commission has been unable to verify for lack of reliable evidence - the attackers did not take the necessary precautions to enable civilians to leave the villages or to otherwise be shielded from attack. The impact of the attacks on civilians shows that the use of military

force was manifestly disproportionate to any threat posed by the rebels. In addition, it appears that such attacks were also intended to spread terror among civilians so as to compel them to flee the villages. From the viewpoint of international criminal law these violations of international humanitarian law no doubt constitute large-scale war crimes.

632. The Commission finds that large scale destruction of villages in Darfur has been deliberately caused, by and large, by the Janjaweed during attacks, independently or in combination with Government forces. Even though in most of the incidents the Government may not have participated in the destruction, their complicity in the attacks during which the destruction was conducted and their presence at the scene of destruction are sufficient to make them jointly responsible for the destruction. There was no military necessity for the destruction and devastation caused. The targets of destruction during the attacks under discussion were exclusively civilian objects. The destruction of so many civilian villages is clearly a violation of international human rights law and international humanitarian law and amounts to a very serious war crime.

633. The Commission considers that there is a consistent and reliable body of material which tends to show that numerous murders of civilians not taking part in the hostilities were committed both by the Government of the Sudan and the Janjaweed. It is undeniable that mass killing occurred in Darfur and that the killings were perpetrated by the Government forces and the Janjaweed in a climate of total impunity and even encouragement to commit serious crimes against a selected part of the civilian population. The large number of killings, the apparent pattern of killing and the participation of officials or authorities are amongst the factors that lead the Commission to the conclusion that killings were conducted in both a widespread and systematic manner. The mass killing of civilians in Darfur is therefore likely to amount to a crime against humanity.

634. It is apparent from the information collected and verified by the Commission that rape or other forms of sexual violence committed by the Janjaweed and Government soldiers in Darfur was widespread and systematic and may thus well amount to a *crime against humanity* . The awareness of the perpetrators that their violent acts were part of a systematic attack on civilians may well be inferred from, among other things, the fact that they were cognizant that they would in fact enjoy impunity. The Commission finds that the crimes of sexual violence committed in Darfur may amount to rape as a crime against humanity, or sexual slavery as a crime against humanity.

635. The Commission considers that torture has formed an integral and consistent part of the attacks against civilians by Janjaweed and Government forces. Torture and inhuman and degrading treatment can be considered to have been committed in both a widespread and systematic manner, amounting to a crime against humanity. In addition, the Commission considers, that conditions in the Military Intelligence Detention Centre witnessed in Khartoum clearly amount to torture and thus constitute a serious violation of international human rights and humanitarian law.

636. It is estimated that more than 1.8 million persons have been forcibly displaced from their homes, and are now hosted in IDP sites throughout Darfur, as well as in refugee camps in Chad. The Commission finds that the forced displacement of the civilian population was both systematic and widespread, and such action would amount to a crime against humanity.

637. The Commission finds that the Janjaweed have abducted women, conduct which may amount to enforced disappearance as a crime against humanity. The incidents investigated establish that these abductions were systematic and were carried out with the acquiescence of the State, as the abductions followed combined attacks by Janjaweed and Government forces and took place in their presence and with their knowledge. The women were kept in captivity for a sufficiently long period of time, and their

whereabouts were not known to their families throughout the period of their confinement. The Commission also finds that the restraints placed on the IDP population in camps, particularly women, by terrorizing them through acts of rape or killings or threats of violence to life or person by the Janjaweed, amount to severe deprivation of physical liberty in violation of rules of international law. The Commission also finds that the arrest and detention of persons by the State security apparatus and the Military Intelligence, including during attacks and intelligence operations against villages, apart from constituting serious violations of international human rights law, may also amount to the crime of enforced disappearance as a crime against humanity, as these acts were both systematic and widespread.

638. In a vast majority of cases, victims of the attacks belonged to African tribes, in particular the Fur, Masaalit and Zaghawa tribes, who were systematically targeted on political grounds in the context of the counter-insurgency policy of the Government. The pillaging and destruction of villages, being conducted on a systematic as well as widespread basis in a discriminatory fashion appears to have been directed to bring about the destruction of livelihoods and the means of survival of these populations. The Commission also considers that the killing, displacement, torture, rape and other sexual violence against civilians was of such a discriminatory character and may constitute persecution as a crime against humanity.

639. While the Commission did not find a systematic or a widespread pattern to violations committed by rebels, it nevertheless found credible evidence that members of the SLA and JEM are responsible for serious violations of international human rights and humanitarian law which may amount to war crimes. In particular, these violations include cases of murder of civilians and pillage.

II. DO THE CRIMES PERPETRATED IN DARFUR CONSTITUTE ACTS OF GENOCIDE?
640. The Commission concluded that the Government of the Sudan has not pursued a policy of genocide. Arguably, two elements of genocide might be deduced from the gross violations of human rights perpetrated by Government forces and the militias under their control. These two elements are, first, the *actus reus* consisting of killing, or causing serious bodily or mental harm, or deliberately inflicting conditions of life likely to bring about physical destruction; and, second, on the basis of a subjective standard, the existence of a protected group being targeted by the authors of criminal conduct. Recent developments have led members of African and Arab tribes to perceive themselves and others as two distinct ethnic groups. The rift between tribes, and the political polarization around the rebel opposition to the central authorities has extended itself to the issues of identity. The tribes in Darfur supporting rebels have increasingly come to be identified as "African" and those supporting the Government as "Arabs". However, the crucial element of genocidal intent appears to be missing, at least as far as the central Government authorities are concerned. Generally speaking the policy of attacking, killing and forcibly displacing members of some tribes does not evince a specific intent to annihilate, in whole or in part, a group distinguished on racial, ethnic, national or religious grounds. Rather, it would seem that those who planned and organized attacks on villages pursued the intent to drive the victims from their homes, primarily for purposes of counter-insurgency warfare.

641. The Commission does recognize that in some instances, individuals, including Government officials, may commit acts with genocidal intent. Whether this was the case in Darfur, however, is a determination that only a competent court can make on a case-by-case basis.

642. The conclusion that no genocidal policy has been pursued and implemented in Darfur by the Government authorities, directly or through the militias under their control, should not be taken as in any way detracting from the gravity of the crimes perpetrated in that region. Depending upon the circumstances, such international offences as crimes against humanity or large scale war crimes may be no less serious and heinous than genocide. This is exactly what happened in Darfur, where massive atrocities were perpetrated on a very large scale, and have so far gone unpunished.

III. WHO ARE THE PERPETRATORS?

643. As requested by the Security Council, to "identify perpetrators" the Commission decided that the most appropriate standard was that requiring that there must be "a reliable body of material consistent with other verified circumstances, which tends to show that a person may reasonably be suspected of being involved in the commission of a crime." The Commission therefore has not made final judgments as to criminal guilt; rather, it has made an assessment of possible suspects that will pave the way for future investigations, and possible indictments, by a prosecutor, and convictions by a court of law.

644. Those identified as possibly responsible for the above-mentioned violations consist of individual perpetrators, including officials of the Government of the Sudan, members of militia forces, members of rebel groups, and certain foreign army officers acting in their personal capacity. Some Government officials, as well as members of militia forces, have also been named as possibly responsible for joint criminal enterprise to commit international crimes. Others are identified for their possible involvement in planning and/or ordering the commission of international crimes, or of aiding and abetting the perpetration of such crimes. The Commission also has identified a number of senior Government officials and military commanders who may be responsible, under the notion of superior (or command) responsibility, for knowingly failing to prevent or repress the perpetration of crimes. Members of rebel groups are named as suspected of participating in a joint criminal enterprise to commit international crimes, and as possibly responsible for knowingly failing to prevent or repress the perpetration of crimes committed by rebels. The Commission has collected sufficient and consistent material (both testimonial and documentary) to point to numerous (51) suspects. Some of these persons are suspected of being responsible under more than one head of responsibility, and for more than one crime.

645. The Commission decided to withhold the names of these persons from the public domain. This decision is based on three main grounds: 1) the importance of the principles of due process and respect for the rights of the suspects; 2) the fact that the Commission has not been vested with investigative or prosecutorial powers; and 3) the vital need to ensure the protection of witnesses from possible harassment or intimidation. The Commission instead will list the names in a sealed file that will be placed in the custody of the United Nations Secretary-General. The Commission recommends that this file be handed over to a competent Prosecutor (the Prosecutor of the International Criminal Court, according to the Commission's recommendations), who will use that material as he or she deems fit for his or her investigations. A distinct and very voluminous sealed file, containing all the evidentiary material collected by the Commission, will be handed over to the High Commissioner for Human Rights. This file should be delivered to a competent Prosecutor

646. The Commission's mention of the number of individuals it has identified should not, however, be taken as an indication that the list is exhaustive. Numerous names of other possible perpetrators, who have been identified on the basis of insufficient evidence to name them as suspects can be found in the sealed body of evidentiary material handed over to the High Commissioner for Human Rights. Furthermore, the Commission has gathered substantial material on different influential individuals, institutions, groups of persons, or committees, which have played a significant role in the conflict in Darfur, including on planning, ordering, authorizing, and encouraging attacks. These include, but are not limited to, the military, the National Security and Intelligence Service, the Military Intelligence and the Security Committees in the three States of Darfur. These institutions should be carefully investigated so as to determine the possible criminal responsibility of individuals taking part in their activities and deliberations.

IV. THE COMMISSION'S RECOMMENDATIONS CONCERNING MEASURES DESIGNED TO ENSURE THAT THOSE RESPONSIBLE ARE HELD ACCOUNTABLE

1. Measures that should be taken by the Security Council

647. With regard to the judicial accountability mechanism, the Commission strongly recommends that the Security Council should refer the situation in Darfur to the International Criminal Court, pursuant to Article 13(b) of the Statute of the Court. Many of the alleged crimes documented in Darfur have been widespread and systematic. They meet all the thresholds of the Rome Statute for the International Criminal Court. The Sudanese justice system has demonstrated its inability and unwillingness to investigate and prosecute the perpetrators of these crimes.

648. The Commission holds the view that resorting to the ICC would have at least six major merits. First, the International Court was established with an eye to crimes likely to threaten peace and security. This is the main reason why the Security Council may trigger the Court's jurisdiction under Article 13 (b). The investigation and prosecution of crimes perpetrated in Darfur would have an impact on peace and security. More particularly, it would be conducive, or contribute to, peace and stability in Darfur, by removing serious obstacles to national reconciliation and the restoration of peaceful relations. Second, as the investigation and prosecution in the Sudan of persons enjoying authority and prestige in the country and wielding control over the State apparatus, is difficult or even impossible, resort to the ICC, the only truly international institution of criminal justice, which would ensure that justice be done. The fact that trials proceedings would be conducted in The Hague, the seat of the ICC, far away from the community over which those persons still wield authority and where their followers live, might ensure a neutral atmosphere and prevent the trials from stirring up political, ideological or other passions. Third, only the authority of the ICC, backed up by that of the United Nations Security Council, might impel both leading personalities in the Sudanese Government and the heads of rebels to submit to investigation and possibly criminal proceedings. Fourth, the Court, with an entirely international composition and a set of well-defined rules of procedure and evidence, is the best suited organ for ensuring a veritably fair trial of those indicted by the Court Prosecutor. Fifth, the ICC could be activated immediately, without any delay (which would be the case if one were to establish ad hoc tribunals or so called mixed or internationalized courts). Sixth, the institution of criminal proceedings before the ICC, at the request of the Security Council, would not necessarily involve a significant financial burden for the international community.

649. The Security Council should, however, act not only against the perpetrators but also on behalf of victims. In this respect, the Commission also proposes the establishment an International Compensation Commission, consisting of fifteen (15) members, ten (10) appointed by the United Nations Secretary-General and five (5) by an independent Sudanese body.

2. Action that should be taken by the Sudanese authorities

650. Government of the Sudan was put on notice concerning the alleged serious crimes that are taking place in Darfur. It was requested not only by the international community, but more importantly by its own people, to put an end to the violations and to bring the perpetrators to justice. It must take serious measures to address these violations. The Commission of Inquiry therefore recommends the Government of the Sudan to:

(i) end the impunity for the war crimes and crimes against humanity committed in Darfur. A number of measures must be taken in this respect. It is essential that Sudanese laws be brought in conformity with human rights standards through *inter alia* abolishing the provisions that permit the detention of individuals without judicial review, the provisions granting officials immunity from prosecution as well as the provisions on specialized courts;

(ii) respect the rights of IDPs and fully implement the Guiding Principles on Internal Displacement, particularly with regard to facilitating their voluntary return in safety and dignity;

(iii) strengthen the independence and impartiality of the judiciary and to confer on courts adequate powers to address human rights violations;

(iv) grant the International Committee of the Red Cross and the United Nations human rights monitors full and unimpeded access to all those detained in relation to the situation in Darfur;

(v) ensure the protection of all the victims and witnesses of human rights violations, particularly those who were in contact with the Commission of Inquiry and ensure the protection of all human rights defenders;

(vi) with the help of international community, enhance the capacity of the Sudanese judiciary through the training of judges, prosecutors and lawyers. Emphasis should be laid on human rights law, humanitarian law, as well as international criminal law;

(vii) fully cooperate with the relevant human rights bodies and mechanisms of the United Nations and the African Union, particularly, the special representative of the United Nations Secretary-General on human rights defenders; and

(viii) create through a broad consultative process, including civil society and victim groups, a truth and reconciliation commission once peace is established in Darfur.

3. Measures That Could be Taken by Other Bodies
651. The Commission also recommends that measures designed to break the cycle of impunity should include the exercise by other States of universal jurisdiction, as outlined elsewhere in this report.

652. Given the seriousness of the human rights situation in Darfur and its impact on the human rights situation in the Sudan, the Commission recommends that the Commission on Human Rights consider the re-establishment of the mandate of the Special Rapporteur on human rights in the Sudan.

653. The Commission recommends that the High Commissioner for Human Rights should issue public and periodic reports on the human rights situation in Darfur.

UN INVESTIGATION COMMISSION ON KILLING OF HARIRI: SUMMARY AND CONCLUSIONS

Published below are the summary and conclusions of the UN International Independent Investigation Commission into the bombing on 14 February 2005 that killed former Lebanese Prime Minister Rafik Hariri and 22 others. In this first report of 19 October 2005, the Commission pointed to converging evidence of the involvement of both Syrian and Lebanese forces in the bombing, and noted limited co-operation by the Syrian security agencies in the investigation.

Report of the International Independent Investigation Commission established pursuant to Security Council resolution 1595 (2005)
 Detlev Mehlis, Commissioner
 Beirut, 19 October 2005

SUMMARY

The Security Council, by its resolution 1595 (2005) of 7 April 2005, decided to establish an International Independent Investigation Commission based in Lebanon to assist the Lebanese authorities in their investigation of all aspects of the terrorist attack which took place on 14 February 2005 in Beirut that killed former Lebanese Prime Minister Rafik Hariri and others, including to help identify its perpetrators, sponsors, organizers and accomplices.

The Secretary-General notified the Council that the Commission began its full operations with effect from 16 June 2005. The Commission was granted an extension to the initial period of investigation mandated by the Council, until 26 October 2005.

During the course of its investigation, the Commission received extensive support from the Government of Lebanon and benefited from expert inputs from a number of national and international entities.

The main lines of investigation of the Commission focused on the crime scene, technical aspects of the crime, analysis of telephone intercepts, the testimony of more than 500 witnesses and sources, as well as the institutional context in which the crime was committed.

The full case file of the investigation was transmitted to the Lebanese authorities during October 2005.

The present report sets out the main lines of enquiry of the investigation conducted by the Commission, its observations thereon, and its conclusions, for the consideration of the Security Council. It also identifies those matters on which further investigation may be necessary.

It is the Commission's view that the assassination of 14 February 2005 was carried out by a group with an extensive organization and considerable resources and capabilities. The crime had been prepared over the course of several months. For this purpose, the timing and location of Mr. Rafik Hariri's movements had been monitored and the itineraries of his convoy recorded in detail.

Building on the findings of the Commission and Lebanese investigations to date and on the basis of the material and documentary evidence collected, and the leads pursued until now, there is converging evidence pointing at both Lebanese and Syrian involvement in this terrorist act. It is a well known fact that Syrian Military Intelligence had a pervasive presence in Lebanon at the least until the withdrawal of the Syrian forces pursuant to resolution 1559 (2004). The former senior security officials of Lebanon were their appointees. Given the infiltration of Lebanese institutions and society by the Syrian and Lebanese intelligence services working in tandem, it would be difficult to envisage a scenario whereby such a complex assassination plot could have been carried out without their knowledge.

It is the Commission's conclusion that the continuing investigation should be carried forward by the appropriate Lebanese judicial and security authorities, who have proved during the investigation that, with international assistance and support, they can move ahead and at times take the lead in an effective and professional manner. At the same time, the Lebanese authorities should look into all the case's ramifications including bank transactions. The 14 February explosion needs to be assessed clearly against the sequence of explosions which preceded and followed it, since there could be links between some, if not all, of them.

The Commission is therefore of the view that a sustained effort on the part of the international community to establish an assistance and cooperation platform together with the Lebanese authorities in the field of security and justice is essential. This will considerably boost the trust of the Lebanese people in their security system, while building self-confidence in their capabilities.

• • •

VI. Conclusions

215. It is the Commission's view that the assassination on 14 February 2005 was carried out by a group with an extensive organization and considerable resources and capabilities. The crime had been prepared over the course of several months. For this purpose, the timing and location of Rafik Hariri's movements had been monitored and the itineraries of his convoy recorded in detail.

216. Building on the findings of the Commission and Lebanese investigations to date and on the basis of the material and documentary evidence collected and the leads pursued until now, there is converging evidence pointing at both Lebanese and Syrian involvement in this terrorist act. It is a well-known fact that Syrian military intelligence had a pervasive presence in Lebanon at the least until the withdrawal of the Syrian forces pursuant to resolution 1559 (2004). The former senior security officials of Lebanon were their appointees. Given the infiltration of Lebanese institutions and society by the Syrian and Lebanese intelligence services working in tandem, it would be difficult to envisage a scenario whereby such a complex assassination plot could have been carried out without their knowledge.

217. It is also the Commission's view that the context of the assassination of Mr. Hariri was one of extreme political polarization and tension. Accusations and counter-accusations targeting mainly Mr. Hariri over the period preceding his assassination corroborate the Commission's conclusion that the likely motive of the assassination was political. However, since the crime was not the work of individuals but rather of a sophisticated group, it very much seems that fraud, corruption and money-laundering could also have been motives for individuals to participate in the operation.

218. The Commission considers that the investigation must continue for some time to come. In the short time period of four months more than 400 persons have been interviewed, 60,000 documents reviewed, several suspects identified and some main leads established. Yet, the investigation is not complete.

219. It is the Commission's conclusion that the continuing investigation should be carried forward by the appropriate Lebanese judicial and security authorities, who have proved during the investigation that, with international assistance and support, they can move ahead and at times take the lead in an effective and professional manner. At the same time, the Lebanese authorities should look into all the ramifications of the case, including bank transactions. The 14 February explosion needs to be assessed clearly against the sequence of explosions which preceded and followed it, since there could be links between some, if not all, of them.

220. The Commission is therefore of the view that, should the Lebanese authorities so wish it, a sustained effort on the part of the international community to establish an assistance and cooperation platform together with the Lebanese authorities in the field of security and justice is essential. This will considerably boost the trust of the Lebanese people in their security system, while building self-confidence in their capabilities.

221. The recent decision to proceed with new senior security appointments was hailed by all the Lebanese parties. It was an important step towards improving the integrity and credibility of the security apparatus. However, it took place after months of a security vacuum and extensive sectarian-political debate. Much needs to be done to overcome sectarian divisions, disentangle security from politics and restructure the security apparatus to avoid parallel lines of reporting and duplication and to enhance accountability.

222. It is the Commission's conclusion that, after having interviewed witnesses and suspects in the Syrian Arab Republic and establishing that many leads point directly towards the involvement of Syrian security officials with the assassination, it is incumbent upon the Syrian Arab Republic to clarify a considerable part of the unresolved questions. While the Syrian authorities, after initial hesitation, have cooperated to a limited degree with the Commission, several interviewees tried to mislead the investigation by giving false or inaccurate statements. The letter addressed to the Commission by the Foreign Minister of the Syrian Arab Republic proved to contain false information. The full picture of the assassination can be reached only through an extensive and credible investigation conducted in an open and transparent manner to the full satisfaction of international scrutiny.

223. As a result of the Commission's investigation to date, a number of people have been arrested and charged with conspiracy to commit murder and related crimes in connection with the assassination of Mr. Hariri and 22 others. The Commission is of course of the view that all people, including those charged with serious crimes, should be considered innocent until proven guilty following a fair trial.

INDEPENDENT INQUIRY COMMITTEE INTO THE UN OIL-FOR-FOOD PROGRAMME

Published below are the preface, the general conclusions and the major recommendations of the Volcker Committee—the Independent Inquiry Committee into the United Nations Oil-for-Food Programme for Iraq—published on 7 September 2005. The Committee concluded that the Programme revealed the need for fundamental reform of the UN; and that, despite achieving notable successes in helping to ensure minimum standards of health and nutrition for the Iraqi people and to deprive Saddam Hussein of weapons of mass destruction, the Programme fell victim to corruption and inefficiency within the UN organisation.

MANAGEMENT OF THE OIL-FOR-FOOD PROGRAMME
VOLUME I - PREFACE TO REPORT OF THE COMMITTEE

PREFACE

In April of 2004, the Independent Inquiry Committee was charged by the Secretary-General and the Security Council with the task of thoroughly reviewing the management of the United Nations Oil-for-Food Programme.

That Programme was certainly the largest, most complex, and most ambitious humanitarian relief effort in the history of the United Nations Organization. In the Programme's administration, the Organization had to deal with a mixture of political, security, financial, and economic concerns. Almost every part of the United Nations family was involved, beginning with the Security Council, the central Secretariat under the Secretary-General, and nine of the UN-related Agencies, with varying degrees of financial and operational independence.

The Committee Report provides a broad and intensive review and analysis of the Programme. It reflects more than a year's work by dozens of experienced attorneys, seasoned investigators, and forensic specialists drawn from twenty-eight countries. Constraints of time, concerns for personnel security in Iraq, and lack of full cooperation by some member states and individuals, means that examination of some parts of the Programme has been less detailed than others. However, the Committee firmly believes that its investigation and this Report provide a solid base for fairly evaluating the Programme's administration. Moreover, given the breadth of the Programme, and the involvement of so many arms of the United Nations, the difficulties encountered—the politicization of decision-making, the managerial weaknesses, the ethical lapses—are symptomatic of systemic problems in United Nations administration. Consequently, the lessons drawn are broadly applicable to the Organization as a whole.

The main conclusions are unambiguous.

The Organization requires stronger executive leadership, thoroughgoing administrative reform, and more reliable controls and auditing.

At stake is the United Nations' ability to respond promptly and effectively to the responsibilities thrust upon it by the realities of a turbulent, and often violent, world. In the last analysis, that ability rests upon the Organization's credibility—on maintaining a widely-held perception among member states and their populations of its competence, honesty, and accountability.

It is precisely those qualities that too often were absent in the administration of the Oil-for-Food Programme.

Conceived as a means for reconciling strong sanctions against a corrupt Iraqi regime with needed supplies of food and medicines to an innocent and vulnerable population, the Programme did achieve important successes. Its existence helped maintain the international effort to deprive Saddam Hussein of weapons of mass destruction. Furthermore, a new study commissioned by the Committee confirms that minimal standards of nutrition and health were maintained in the face of a potential crisis.

Those were real accomplishments. They were achieved despite uncertain, wavering direction from the Security Council, pressures from competing political forces in Iraq, and endemic corruption on the ground.

Sadly, those successes fell under an increasingly dark shadow. As the years passed, reports spread of waste, inefficiency, and corruption, even within the United Nations itself. Some was rumor and exaggeration, but much—too much—has turned out to be true.

The Committee Report documents how differences among member states impeded decision-making, tolerated large-scale smuggling, and aided and abetted grievous weaknesses in administrative practices within the Secretariat. An adequate framework of controls and auditing was absent. There were, in fact, instances of corruption among senior staff as well as in the field. As a result, serious questions have emerged about the United Nations' ability to live up to its ideals.

One perspective is that the United Nations Organization was simply asked to do too much, too soon, without any clear sense of how long the Programme would continue; it was authorized only in six-month increments. As time passed, the huge flow of funds far exceeded that of ordinary United Nations operations. Thousands of staff were hired and deployed in the field, overtaxing weak management oversight and accountability.

The Committee's investigation clearly makes the point that, as the Programme expanded and continued, Saddam Hussein found ways and means of turning it to his own advantage. For the UN-related

Agencies, the work went beyond their core competencies—from monitoring, planning, and consulting—to rebuilding of infrastructure, thereby multiplying problems. Nor was there much success in coordinating so large a program among the Agencies, which are accustomed to defending zealously their individual autonomy.

In the light of those failures, the Committee has asked itself a simple question: Should the United Nations—the Secretariat and its Agencies—simply put their collective feet down, and refuse to take on such costly and complicated operational programs for which it is ill-equipped?

Of course, a realistic answer cannot be so simple. Fresh emergencies, cutting across particular agency missions will surely recur. Differences in political priorities among members of the Security Council are a fact of life. In the absence of the United Nations, no other organization or nation, or no grouping of organizations or nations, may be readily available, or available at all, to take on the complex missions cutting across national boundaries and diverse areas of competence. And, singly or together, the Agencies do have skills and experience—and a presumption of legitimacy—difficult or impossible to match.

Interestingly, in at least one large area, peacekeeping and nation-building, the United Nations is called upon more and more frequently. The "blue helmets" do convey a sense of international legitimacy, and the United Nations over time has built some infrastructure and professional management. In the case of the Oil-for-Food Programme, no similar structure, no adequate capacity for planning within or among the Agencies, and no adequate control or auditing framework was in place.

The basic lessons the Committee has drawn from its review are both pointed and broad. In sum:

1. However well-conceived the Programme was in principle, the Security Council failed to define clearly the practical parameters, policies, and administrative responsibilities. Far too much initiative was left to the Iraqi regime in the Programme's design and subsequent implementation. Compounding that difficulty, the Security Council, in contrast to most past practice, retained within its own sanctions committee of national diplomats substantial elements of operational control. Neither the Security Council nor the Secretariat leadership was clearly in command. That turned out to be a recipe for the dilution of Secretariat authority and evasion of personal responsibility at all levels. When things went awry—and they surely did—when troublesome conflicts arose between political objectives and administrative effectiveness, decisions were delayed, bungled, or simply shunned.

2. The administrative structure and the personnel practices of the Organization— certainly within the Secretariat—were simply not fit to meet the truly extraordinary challenges presented by the Oil-for-Food Programme, or even programs of much lesser scope. The Committee Reports reveal serious instances of illicit, unethical, and corrupt behavior within the United Nations, but the pervasive administrative difficulties were not only, or even primarily, related to personal malfeasance. As will become evident in the Committee's next, and final, report, the wholesale corruption within the Programme took place among private companies, manipulated by Saddam Hussein's government.

   The United Nations Charter designates the Secretary-General as Chief Administrative Officer. Whatever the founders had in mind, the Secretary-General—*any* Secretary-General—has not been chosen for his managerial or administrative skills, nor has he been provided with a structure and instruments conducive to strong executive oversight and control. That is most clearly evident in the area of personnel management, where professional competence must compete with, and often take second place to, the narrow political interests of member states.

The reality is that the Secretary-General has come to be viewed as chief diplomatic and political agent of the United Nations. The present Secretary-General is widely respected for precisely those qualities. In these turbulent times, those responsibilities tend to be all consuming. The record amply reflects consequent administrative failings.

3. Most notable among the United Nations' structural faults is a grievous absence of effective auditing and management controls. In both areas, the General Assembly has taken steps to develop competence and accountability, but that belated effort has fallen far short of what is needed. The Oil-for-Food Programme has exposed chronic weakness of planning, sorely inadequate funding, and the simple absence of enough professional personnel to implement controls and auditing. That remained true even as the Programme grew exponentially in its financial magnitude, eclipsing in size ordinary United Nations operations. As important was the palpable absence of authority for the auditors and the lack of clear, if any, reporting lines to "the Top." As a consequence, needed independence was absent. Line managers could and did divert auditing initiatives. Follow-up to critical findings was erratic or non-existent.

4. The isolated instances of corruption detailed in the earlier Committee Reports extend to the top of the Programme administration—one important reflection of the managerial weaknesses. Those egregious lapses signal the absence of a sufficiently strong organizational ethic—an ethic that should permeate its leadership and staff if the United Nations is to command the respect upon which its work depends.

Corrosive corruption—private and public—has been far too common, not least in member states in which the United Nations has programs of economic and humanitarian assistance. In that environment, the evidence clearly demonstrates that the General Assembly, the Security Council, and the Secretariat management have been insufficiently conscious of the need to seize the Organization's unique opportunity to exemplify and encourage the highest standards of conduct in international affairs.

5. Finally, the particular nature of the Oil-For-Food Programme placed in stark relief the difficulties of effective cooperation among United Nations Agencies. There was and is no simple way accurately to track Programme expenditures across agency lines. The presumption of central budgetary authority for the Oil-for-Food Programme was not matched by an ability to assess actual spending (much less the effectiveness of spending), or to insist on uniform accounting standards or treatment. Surely the difficulties perceived should not be tolerated in any other programs, however large or small.

The inescapable conclusion from the Committee's work is that the United Nations Organization needs thoroughgoing reform—and it needs it urgently.

That is not surprising. It is a central point in all recent studies of the United Nations, including those initiated by the Secretary-General himself.

The work of the Independent Inquiry Committee into the United Nations Oil-for-Food Programme does bring new dimensions to the discussion. Its investigation is unprecedented in its breadth and depth. It has involved not only the Security Council and the Secretariat in New York, but has touched directly upon nine other members of the United Nations family.

The urgent need for action can be summarized in four broad recommendations:

- The Security Council, in making decisions about United Nations intervention in critical areas, should *clarify each program's purpose and criteria.* The *execution* should be delegated to the Secretariat and appropriate Agencies, with clear lines of reporting responsibility.

- To provide the *needed focus for the administrative responsibilities* of the Secretariat, there should be a Chief Operating Officer ("COO"), nominated by the Security Council and approved by the General Assembly. While ultimately reporting to the Secretary-General, the new COO should have access to the Security Council, and should have clear authority for planning and for personnel practices that emphasize professional and administrative talent over political convenience.

- A strong *"Independent Auditing Board"* with adequate staff support, must be built. That Board should go well beyond financial audits to full review of the staffing and budgeting of accounting and auditing services. Auditing, control, and investigatory staffs should have direct access to that Board and be subject to its oversight.

- In programs extending over more than one agency, *effective coordination* should be required from the start by clear and agreed memoranda of understanding and enforced by common accounting and auditing standards.

Most of these measures could be accomplished by decision of the General Assembly, the Security Council, the Secretariat, and the individual Agencies. But if changes in the Charter are required to implement reform and to *underscore* its importance, then member states should not shrink from that effort.

What is important—*what has been recognized by one investigation after another*—is that real change take place, and change over a wide area.

Clear benchmarks for measuring progress must be set. The General Assembly should insist, in its forthcoming meeting, that key reforms be put in place no later than the time of its regular meeting in 2006.

To settle for less, to permit delay and dilution, will invite failure, further erode public support, and dishonor the ideals upon which the United Nations is built.

The time for action is now.

Paul A. Volcker	Richard J. Goldstone	Mark Pieth
Chairman	Member	Member

• • •

XI. GENERAL CONCLUSIONS

Broadly, the Committee's conclusions address the adequacy of political oversight and direction, the capacity of the Secretariat to administer its responsibilities under the Programme, the United Nations' ability to provide financial oversight and control to the Programme, and the question of persuading the entities in the United Nations' highly decentralized system to work effectively and efficiently together in an enterprise of this complexity and size.

The Committee's conclusions and recommendations are generally consonant with recommendations by others who have urged and are urging early action on United Nations reform. However the Committee cannot help but note that many of these recommendations, some of which are both detailed and holistic, have in large measure lain fallow for long periods of time, some for over a decade.

The Committee makes two contributions to the reform debate. First, the depth to which the Committee has analyzed the Programme leads uniquely to a detailed background from which the Committee's recommendations have come. Second, the Committee's analysis of the Programme confirms that reform is urgent. It suspects that the weaknesses in structure and ethic within the Programme may well be symptomatic of a wider malaise throughout the United Nations.

In short, this investigation leads to the firm belief that reform is necessary if the United Nations is to regain and retain the measure of respect among the international community that its work requires. As important, the Committee believes that action must be taken now. The urgency to pursue fundamental reform of the Organization is heightened by a sense that, in this volatile world, roughly analogous situations demanding sanctions, enforcement of sanctions, and/or humanitarian relief are more than likely to recur.

A. THE SECURITY COUNCIL STRUGGLED

The Security Council struggled in clearly defining the broad purposes, policies, and administrative control of the Programme. Resolution 986 followed prior failed efforts to engage the Government of Iraq in an oil-for-food program. As a result, there appears to have been conflicting sentiments between treating Iraq with enough "flexibility" to get its agreement to a program and a concern to retain sufficient control that any program would not become a doorway to the clandestine reinvigoration of Iraq's ambitions for weapons of mass destruction. In the end, on one hand, far too much initiative and decision-making was left to the Iraqi regime while on the other, the Security Council took the extraordinary step of retaining, through its 661 Committee, substantial elements of administrative, and therefore operational, control. That turned out to be a recipe for the dilution of individual and institutional responsibility. When things went awry—and they did—when troublesome questions of conflict between political objectives and administrative effectiveness arose, decisions were delayed, bungled, or simply avoided—no one was in charge.

B. ADMINISTRATIVE AND PERSONNEL STRUCTURE NOT ADEQUATE

The Committee recognizes that the United Nations was faced with an extraordinary challenge, replete with conflicting political pressures, for which it was ill-equipped in terms of experience and administrative capacity.

Indeed, the Committee believes that "professional disciplines" at the United Nations are weak and eroded. As a consequence, the Secretariat, from its most senior levels, proved unable to deal effectively with the political pressures. There also appears to be a pervasive culture resistant to accountability and prone to escaping responsibility. The Secretariat was also hampered in effectively carrying out its functions under the Programme through an absence, at the time, of suitable administrative infrastructure for dealing with the sudden demands of this exceptionally large and complex "temporary" humanitarian program.

From what it has seen of the Programme's operations, the Committee considered whether the United Nations could reasonably limit operational responsibility to such areas as peacekeeping, where experience has led to the creation of some degree of permanent infrastructure. Ultimately, the Committee was convinced that, in a world where a myriad of considerations inform crises in a volatile and often violent environment, that approach would deprive the world of a needed resource.

If the United Nations is to fulfill that mission, the fault lines and flaws uncovered during the investigation clearly demand that the Organization's administrative capacity be strengthened. To this end, the Committee has made a series of recommendations, which are outlined elsewhere in this Report. The key point is that the Organization and its Secretary-General need a stronger structure at the top. A Secretary-General is, de facto, the Organization's chief political and diplomatic officer. In unsettled times, those responsibilities tend to be all consuming. The present Secretary-General, widely respected for precisely those very qualities, has regrettably been undercut by lapses in the administration of the Organization.

The United Nations Charter designates the Secretary-General as Chief Administrative Officer. But whatever the founders had in mind, the Secretary-General—any Secretary-General—has not been chosen for managerial or administrative skills, nor has he been provided with the instruments needed for strong executive control, most clearly in the area of personnel, where professional competence must compete with the political demands of member states.

A Secretary-General needs stronger support. That need has been recognized, in part, by the creation in 1998 of the new post of Deputy Secretary-General. However, the results of the investigation suggest that the role of Deputy Secretary-General as "Chief Operating Officer" must be strengthened and made more explicit. The Committee proposes that the Deputy Secretary-General be appointed by the General Assembly on the recommendation of the Security Council, as is the case with the Secretary-General.

While ultimately responsible to the Secretary-General, the Chief Operating Officer should have direct authority for personnel, budgeting, and other key administrative functions with access to the Security Council and General Assembly as needed.

C. LACK OF EFFECTIVE CONTROLS
Most notable among the administrative failures of the Programme was a grievous absence of effective controls and audits. In both areas, the Organization has in recent years worked to develop competence, but it has been from a standing start. The Oil-for-Food Programme exemplified the weakness of planning, the lack of adequate funding, and the paucity of manpower, even after the Programme went on and on. As important structurally was a palpable absence of authority and clear, if any, reporting lines, especially to the Secretariat's senior management. As a consequence, needed independence was lost. Line managers could and did divert auditing initiatives, and follow-up to critical findings was erratic at best.

D. INSTANCES OF CORRUPTION REFLECT CONTROL WEAKNESSES
The instances of corruption detailed in the Committee Reports—corruption that reached to the top of the Programme management—are an important reflection of control weaknesses. The Committee's concern is that these influences are symptomatic of an absence of a strong institutional ethic—an ethic that should reflect the unique and crucial role of the United Nations system in exemplifying and encouraging the highest standards in which corrosive corruption— private and public—has been far too common. The General Assembly, Security Council, and Secretariat have been insufficiently conscious of the serious risks posed by not enforcing ethical standards, both to the Organization's credibility and to its internal morale.

E. LACK OF INTER-AGENCY COORDINATION
The particular nature of the Oil-For-Food Programme placed in stark relief the difficulties of effective cooperation across the Agencies. There was and is no simple way accurately to track Programme expenditures across agency lines. The presumption of central budget authority was not matched by an ability to assess actual spending (much less the effectiveness of spending), or to insist on common accounting standards or treatment. Clearly, the demand for inter-agency action inherent in the Oil-for-Food Programme was exceptional. Arguably, such demands are unlikely to be repeated in so dramatic a fashion. But surely the difficulties perceived should not be tolerated in lesser programs.

XII. MAJOR RECOMMENDATIONS

A. CREATE THE POSITION OF CHIEF OPERATING OFFICER

Create the position of Chief Operating Officer ("COO"). The COO would have authority over all aspects of administration and would be appointed by the General Assembly on the recommendation of the Security Council. The position would report to the Secretary-General, and the United Nations Charter should be amended as appropriate.

Creation of this position would serve to better insulate United Nations administrators from political pressures distorting management decisions. It would provide sufficient authority for effective management discipline and would free the Secretary-General of some of the duties inherent in the role of the chief administrative officer.

B. STRENGTHEN INDEPENDENCE OF OVERSIGHT AND AUDITING

Establish an Independent Oversight Board ("IOB") with a majority of independent members and an independent chairman. In discharging its mandate, the IOB should have functional responsibility for all audit, investigation, and evaluation activities, both internal and external, across the United Nations Secretariat and agencies substantially funded by the United Nations and whose leadership is appointed by the Secretary-General. The IOB should be particularly concerned with overseeing and monitoring:

1. Implementation of risk-based planning across the United Nations system;
2. Implementation of oversight, audit, and investigation best practices;
3. Implementation of a consistent framework for assessing findings and recommendations and bringing significant oversight issues to the attention of the Secretary-General/Director-Generals and the General Assembly/Governing Bodies;
4. Investigations and improvements in the ethics and integrity of the Organization; and
5. The efficiency and effectiveness of the oversight function.

In the interests of transparency, there should be annual disclosure from the IOB to the General Assembly of the planned audit coverage and the actual results of oversight activity. IOB oversight reports should be publicly accessible. The IOB should consult with and coordinate as appropriate with all UN-related agencies.

C. IMPROVE COORDINATION AND THE OVERSIGHT FRAMEWORK FOR CROSS-AGENCY PROGRAMS

The Programme demonstrated the need for significant improvements in the oversight of cross-agency programs, particularly regarding common principles, planning, transparent financials, and resources. The IOB should provide the needed coordination.

1. Establish high level coordinating bodies for all major cross-agency relief and emergency programs and provide them with real decision making ability, agreed to by all participating entities; these coordinating bodies should be empowered to set, implement, and enforce principles and policies;
2. Improve the following aspects of cross-agency programs by:
   • Promulgating, subject to audit, appropriate policies and procedures;
   • Documenting processes for rapid deployment and rapid response projects identifying areas of risk and applicable critical controls necessary to be in place to mitigate exposure; and
   • Developing standard audit plans for programs;
3. Ensure that each program has consolidated financial statements that are subject to external and internal audit; and

4. Make sufficient oversight resources available immediately and integrate them into the management and implementation of a new program. Mandate the creation of a rapid deployment audit program with investigatory presence ("rapid integrity") that allows oversight to begin at the inception of a new program.

D. REFORM AND IMPROVE MANAGEMENT PERFORMANCE

Strong and effective leadership and management is essential to the success of the United Nations' mission. There is a need for the United Nations to strengthen the quality of its management and management practices. To this end:

1. Improve the scope and quality of the internal management review processes by mandating periodic, high-level executive reviews against clear objectives of all major initiatives and activities;
2. Ensure that senior management and professional staff adhere to the highest standards of accountability and transparency in their performance, and remove those who do not meet these performance requirements;
3. Seek opportunities for peer review of management performance; and
4. Overhaul the management hiring, promotion, evaluation, and reward methodology basing each on key tasks, and agreed measures of performance.

E. EXPAND CONFLICT-OF-INTEREST AND FINANCIAL DISCLOSURE REQUIREMENTS

The financial disclosure requirement must extend well below the current Assistant Secretary-General level within the Organization and should also specifically include the Secretary-General and the Deputy Secretary-General. Financial disclosure requirements must include all United Nations staff who have any decision-making role in the disbursement or award of United Nations funds (e.g., Procurement Department, Office of the Controller).

A strong financial disclosure program is an integral part of creating an institutional culture that recognizes and understands actual, potential, and apparent conflicts of interest. The United Nations' conflict-of-interest rules and regulations need to be expanded and better defined so that they encompass actual, potential, and apparent conflicts of interest.

F. COST RECOVERY

The Committee recognizes that fair compensation to third parties is necessary to enable the United Nations to complement its core resources with competent outside specialists, such as the Agencies. However, the United Nations should ensure that such compensation does not result in egregious profits.

Agencies involved in the Programme should return up to $50 million in excess compensation secured as a result of work performed under Security Council Resolution 1483.

TEXT OF THE DRAFT IRAQI CONSTITUTION

Published below is the text of the draft Iraqi constitution (translated from the Arabic by the Associated Press), which was read out to the National Assembly on 28 August and was approved by referendum on 15 October. It replaced the law of administration for the transitional period, implemented by the US-led Coalition Provisional Authority. The constitution, drafted by a seventy-one-member constitutional committee, was opposed by most Sunnis, who feared that it could lead to the creation of Kurdish and Shi'ite autonomous areas, and was approved by only a narrow margin in the referendum.

"Verily we have honored the children of Adam" (Qur'an 17.70)

We the sons of Mesopotamia, land of the prophets, resting place of the holy imams, the leaders of civilization and the creators of the alphabet, the cradle of arithmetic: on our land, the first law put in place by mankind was written; in our nation, the most noble era of justice in the politics of nations was laid down; on our soil, the followers of the prophet and the saints prayed, the philosophers and the scientists theorised and the writers and poets created.

Recognizing God's right upon us; obeying the call of our nation and our citizens; responding to the call of our religious and national leaders and the insistence of our great religious authorities and our leaders and our reformers, we went by the millions for the first time in our history to the ballot box, men and women, young and old, on January 30 2005, remembering the pains of the despotic band's sectarian oppression of the majority; inspired by the suffering of Iraq's martyrs - Sunni and Shiite, Arab, Kurd and Turkomen, and the remaining brethren in all communities - inspired by the injustice against the holy cities in the popular uprising and against the marshes and other places; recalling the agonies of the national oppression in the massacres of Halabja, Barzan, Anfal and against the Faili Kurds; inspired by the tragedies of the Turkomen in Bashir and the suffering of the people of the western region, whom the terrorists and their allies sought to take hostage and prevent from participating in the elections and the establishment of a society of peace and brotherhood and cooperation so we can create a new Iraq, Iraq of the future, without sectarianism, racial strife, regionalism, discrimination or isolation.

Terrorism and "takfir" (declaring someone an infidel) did not divert us from moving forward to build a nation of law. Sectarianism and racism did not stop us from marching together to strengthen our national unity, set ways to peacefully transfer power, adopt a manner to fairly distribute wealth and give equal opportunity to all.

We the people of Iraq, newly arisen from our disasters and looking with confidence to the future through a democratic, federal, republican system, are determined - men and women, old and young - to respect the rule of law, reject the policy of aggression, pay attention to women and their rights, the elderly and their cares, the children and their affairs, spread the culture of diversity and defuse terrorism.

We are the people of Iraq, who in all our forms and groupings undertake to establish our union freely and by choice, to learn yesterday's lessons for tomorrow, and to write down this permanent constitution from the high values and ideals of the heavenly messages and the developments of science and human civilization, and to adhere to this constitution, which shall preserve for Iraq its free union of people, land and sovereignty.

CHAPTER ONE: BASIC PRINCIPLES

Article (1): The Republic of Iraq is an independent, sovereign nation, and the system of rule in it is a democratic, federal, representative (parliamentary) republic.
Article (2):
1st   - Islam is the official religion of the state and is a basic source of legislation:
    (a) No law can be passed that contradicts the undisputed rules of Islam.
    (b) No law can be passed that contradicts the principles of democracy.

(c) No law can be passed that contradicts the rights and basic freedoms outlined in this constitution.

2nd - This constitution guarantees the Islamic identity of the majority of the Iraqi people and the full religious rights for all individuals and the freedom of creed and religious practices.

Article (3): Iraq is a multiethnic, multi-religious and multi-sect country. It is part of the Islamic world and its Arab people are part of the Arab nation.

Article (4):

1st - Arabic and Kurdish are the two official languages for Iraq. Iraqis are guaranteed the right to educate their children in their mother tongues, such as Turkomen or Assyrian, in government educational institutions, or any other language in private educational institutions, according to educational regulations.

2nd - the scope of the phrase "official language" and the manner of implementing the rules of this article will be defined by a law that includes:

(a) issuing the official gazette in both languages.

(b) speaking, addressing and expressing in official domains, like the parliament, Cabinet, courts and official conferences, in either of the two languages.

(c) recognition of official documents and correspondences in the two languages and the issuing of official documents in them both.

(d) the opening of schools in the two languages in accordance with educational rules.

(e) any other realms that require the principle of equality, such as currency bills, passports, stamps.

3rd - Federal agencies and institutions in the region of Kurdistan use both languages.

4th - The Turkomen and Assyrian languages will be official in the areas where they are located.

5th - Any region or province can take a local language as an additional official language if a majority of the population approves in a universal referendum.

Article (5): The law is sovereign, the people are the source of authority and its legitimacy, which they exercise through direct, secret ballot and its constitutional institutions.

Article (6): Government should be rotated peacefully through democratic means stipulated in this constitution.

Article (7):

1st - Entities or trends that advocate, instigate, justify or propagate racism, terrorism, "takfir" (declaring someone an infidel), sectarian cleansing, are banned, especially the Saddamist Baath Party in Iraq and its symbols, under any name. It will be not be allowed to be part of the multilateral political system in Iraq, which should be defined according to the law.

2nd - The state will be committing to fighting terrorism in all its forms and will work to prevent its territory from being a base or corridor or an arena for its (terrorism's) activities.

Article (8): Iraq shall abide by the principles of good neighbourliness and by not intervening in the internal affairs of the other countries, and it shall seek to peacefully resolve conflicts and shall establish its relations on the basis of shared interests and similar treatment and shall respect its international obligations.

Article (9):

1st -

(a) The Iraqi armed forces and security apparatuses consist of the components of the Iraqi people, keeping in consideration their balance and representation without discrimination or exclusion. They fall under the command of the civil authority, defend Iraq, don't act as a tool of oppression of the Iraqi people, don't intervene in political affairs and they play no role in the rotation of power.

(b) Forming military militias outside the framework of the armed forces is banned.

(c) The Iraqi armed forces and its personnel - including military personnel working in the Defence Ministry and in any offices or organizations subordinate to it - are not allowed to run as candidates in elections for political office. They should not engage in election campaigning for candidates and should not take part in activities forbidden by the regulations of the Defence Ministry. This ban includes the activities of the previously mentioned individuals acting in their personal or professional capacities, but does not include their right to vote in the elections.

d) The Iraqi national intelligence service shall gather information and assess threats to national security and offers advice to the Iraqi government. It is under civilian control; it is subjected to the supervision of the executive authority; it operates according to the law and to recognized human rights principles.

e) The Iraqi government shall respect and implement Iraq's international commitments regarding the non-proliferation, non-development, non-production, and non-use of nuclear, chemical, and biological weapons. Associated equipment, material, technologies, and communications systems for use in the development, manufacture, production, and use of such weapons shall be banned.

2nd - Military service shall be regulated by a law.

Article (10): The holy shrines and religious sites in Iraq are religious and cultural entities. The state is committed to maintain and protect their sanctity and ensure the exercising of (religious) rites freely in them.

Article (11): Baghdad is the capital of the republic of Iraq.

Article (12):

1st - The flag, emblem and national anthem of Iraq shall be fixed by law in a way that symbolizes the components of the Iraqi people.

2nd - Medals, official holidays, religious and national occasions and the official calendar shall be fixed by law.

Article (13):

1st - This constitution shall be considered as the supreme and highest law in Iraq. It shall be binding throughout the whole country without exceptions.

2nd - No law that contradicts this constitution shall be passed; any passage in the regional constitutions and any other legal passages that contradict this constitution shall be considered null.

CHAPTER TWO: RIGHTS AND FREEDOMS

PART ONE: RIGHTS FIRST: Civil and political rights.

Article (14): Iraqis are equal before the law without discrimination because of sex, ethnicity, nationality, origin, colour, religion, sect, belief, opinion or social or economic status.

Article (15): Every individual has the right to life and security and freedom and cannot be deprived of these rights or have them restricted except in accordance to the law and based on a ruling by the appropriate judicial body.

Article (16): Equal opportunity is a right guaranteed to all Iraqis, and the state shall take the necessary steps to achieve this.

Article (17):

1st - Each person has the right to personal privacy as long as it does not violate the rights of others or general morality.

2nd - The sanctity of the home is protected. They cannot be entered or searched or violated except by judicial decision and in accordance with the law.

Article (18):

1st - An Iraqi is anyone who has been born to an Iraqi father or an Iraqi mother.

2nd - Iraqi nationality is a right to all Iraqis and it is the basis of their citizenship.

3rd -

(a) It shall be forbidden to withdraw the Iraqi citizenship from an Iraqi by birth for any reason. Those who have had their citizenship withdrawn have the right to reclaim it and this should be regulated by law.

(b) Iraqi citizenship shall be withdrawn from naturalized citizens in cases stated by law.

4th - Every Iraqi has the right to carry more than one citizenship. Those who take a leading or high-level security position must give up any other citizenship. This shall be regulated by law.

5th - Iraqi citizenship may not be granted for the purposes of a policy of population settlement disrupting the demographic makeup in Iraq.

6th - Citizenship regulations shall be determined by law, and the proper courts should hear suits arising from the regulations.

Article (19):

1st - The judiciary is independent, with no power above it other than the law.

2nd - There is no crime and no punishment except by the text (of law). And there is no punishment except for an act that the law considers a crime at the time of its commission. No punishment can be enacted that is heavier than the punishment allowed at the time of the crime's commission.

3rd - Trial by judiciary is a right protected and guaranteed to all.

4th - The right to defence is holy and guaranteed in all stages of investigation and trial.

5th - The accused is innocent until his guilt is proven in a just, legal court. The accused cannot be tried for the same accusation again after he has been freed unless new evidence appears.

6th - Every individual has the right to be treated in a just manner in all judicial and administrative procedures.

7th - Court sessions will be open unless the court decides to make them secret.

8th - Punishment is for individuals.

9th - Laws do not apply retroactively unless otherwise has been legislated, and this exception does not include laws of taxes and duties.

10th - Punitive law shall not be applied retroactively unless it is best for the defendant.

11th - The court shall appoint an attorney to defend defendants charged with a felony or a misdemeanour who don't have an attorney and it shall be at the state's expense.

12th -

(a) (Arbitrary) detention shall not be allowed.

(b) Arrest or imprisonment is not allowed in places other than those designated for that according to prison laws that are covered by health and social services and are under the control of the state.

13th - Preliminary investigation papers shall be shown to the concerned judge no later than 24 hours from the time of the detention of the accused and cannot be extended except once and for same duration.

Article (20): Citizens, male and female, have the right to participate in public matters and enjoy political rights, including the right to vote and run as candidates.

Article (21):

1st - An Iraqi shall not be handed over to foreign bodies and authorities.

2nd - Political asylum to Iraq shall be regulated by law and the political refugee shall not be turned over to a foreign body or forcefully returned to the country from which he has fled.

3rd - Political asylum shall not be granted to those accused of committing international or terror crimes or to anyone who has caused Iraq harm.

SECOND: Economic, social and cultural rights
Article (22):
1st   -   Work is a right for all Iraqis in a way that guarantees them a good life.
2nd -   The law regulates the relation between employees and employers on an economic basis, while keeping in consideration rules of social justice.
3rd   -   The state guarantees the right to form or join syndicates or professional unions. This shall be regulated by law.
Article (23):
1st   -   Private property is protected and the owner has the right to use it, exploit it and benefit from it within the boundaries of the law.
2nd -   Property may not be taken away except for the public interest in exchange for fair compensation. This shall be regulated by law.
3rd   -

    (a) An Iraqi has the right to ownership anywhere in Iraq and no one else has the right to own real estate except what is exempted by law.

    (b) Ownership with the purpose of demographic changes is forbidden.
Article (24): The state shall guarantee the freedom of movement for workers, goods and Iraqi capital between the regions and the provinces. This shall be regulated by law.
Article (25): The state shall guarantee the reforming of the Iraqi economy according to modern economic bases, in a way that ensures complete investment of its resources, diversifying its sources and encouraging and developing the private sector.
Article (26): The country shall guarantee the encouragement of investments in the different sectors. This shall be regulated by law.
Article (27):
1st   -   Public property is sacrosanct, and its protection is the duty of every citizen.
2nd -   Regulations pertaining to preserving and administrating state property, the conditions set for using it and the cases when giving up any of the property may be allowed shall be regulated by law.
Article (28):
1st   -   Taxes and fees shall not be imposed, amended, collected or eliminated except by law.
2nd -   Low-income people should be exempted from taxes in a way that guarantees maintaining the minimum level necessary for a living. This shall be regulated by law.
Article (29):
1st   -

    (a) The family is the foundation of society and the state should preserve its (the family's) existence and ethical and religious value.

    (b) The state shall guarantee the protection of motherhood, childhood and old age and shall take care of juveniles and youths and provide them with agreeable conditions to develop their capabilities.
2nd -   Children have the right to upbringing, education and care from their parents; parents have the right to respect and care from their children, especially in times of want, disability or old age.
3rd   -   Economic exploitation of children in any form is banned and the state shall take measures to guarantee their protection.
4th   -   Violence and abuse in the family, school and society shall be forbidden.
Article (30):
1st   -   The state guarantees social and health insurance, the basics for a free and honourable life for the individual and the family - especially children and women - and works to protect them from illiteracy, fear and poverty and provides them with housing and the means to rehabilitate and take care of them. This shall be regulated by law.

Article (31):

1st   - Every Iraqi has the right to health service, and the state is in charge of public health and
        guarantees the means of protection and treatment by building different kinds of hospitals
        and health institutions.

2nd   - Individuals and associations have the right to build hospitals, dispensaries or private clin-
        ics under the supervision of the state. This shall be regulated by law.

Article (32): The state cares for the disabled and those with special needs and guarantees their rehabilitation to integrate them in society. This shall be regulated by law.

Article (33):

1st   - Every individual has the right to live in a correct environmental atmosphere.

2nd   - The state guarantees protection and preservation of the environment and biological diversity.

Article (34):

1st   - Education is a main factor for the progress of society and it is a right guaranteed by the
        state. It is mandatory in the primary school and the state guarantees fighting illiteracy.

2nd   - Free education is a right for Iraqis in all its stages.

3rd   - The state encourages scientific research for peaceful purposes in a way that benefits human-
        ity and it promotes excelling, creativity and the different manifestations of excellence.

4th   - Private and national education is guaranteed and regulated by law.

PART TWO: FREEDOMS

Article (35):

1st   -

        (a) The freedom and dignity of a person are protected.

        (b) No one may be detained or investigated unless by judicial decision.

        (c) All forms of torture, mental or physical, and inhuman treatment are forbidden. There
            is no recognition of any confession extracted by force or threats or torture, and the
            injured party may seek compensation for any physical or mental injury that is inflicted.

2nd   - The state is committed to protecting the individual from coercion in thought, religion or
        politics, and no one may be imprisoned on these bases.

3rd   - Forced labour, slavery and the commerce in slaves is forbidden, as is the trading in women
        or children or the sex trade.

Article (36): The state guarantees, as long as it does not violate public order and morality:

1st   - the freedom of expressing opinion by all means.

2nd   - the freedom of press, publishing, media and distribution.

3rd   - freedom of assembly and peaceful protest will be organized by law.

Article (37):

1st   - Freedom to establish and belong to political organizations and parties is guaranteed, and
        it will be organized by law.

2nd   - No person can be forced to join or remain a member of a political party or organization.

Article (38): The freedom of communications and exchanges by post, telegraph, telephone and by
electronic and other means is guaranteed. They will not be monitored or spied upon or revealed except
for legal and security necessity in accordance with the law.

Article (39): Iraqis are free in their adherence to their personal status according to their own religion,
sect, belief and choice, and that will be organized by law.

Article (40):

1st   - The followers of every religion and sect are free in:

        (a) the practice of their religious rites, including the (Shiite) Husseiniya Rites.

        (b) the administration of religious endowments and their affairs and their religious insti-
            tutions, and this will be organized by law.

2nd - The state guarantees freedom of worship and the protection of its places.

Article (41): Every individual has freedom of thought and conscience.

Article (42):

1st - The Iraqi citizen has freedom of movement and travel and residence within Iraq and outside it.

2nd - No Iraqi can be exiled or forced out or forbidden to return to his nation.

Article (43):

1st - The state is keen to strengthen the role of civil society groups and to support, develop them and preserve their independence in accordance with peaceful means to realize legitimate goals. This shall be regulated by law.

2nd - The state is keen to advance Iraqi tribes and clans and it cares about their affairs in accordance with religion, law and honourable human values and in a way that contributes to developing society and it forbids tribal customs that run contrary to human rights.

Article (44): All individuals have the right to enjoy the rights stated in international human rights agreements and treaties endorsed by Iraq that don't run contrary to the principles and rules of this constitution.

Article (45): Restricting or limiting any of the freedoms and liberties stated in this constitution may only happen by, or according to, law and as long as this restriction or limitation does not undermine the essence of the right or freedom.

CHAPTER THREE: THE FEDERAL AUTHORITIES
PART ONE: THE LEGISLATIVE AUTHORITY

Article (47): The federal legislative authority is made up of the Council of Representatives and the Council of Union.

FIRST: The Council of Representatives (Parliament).

Article (48):

1st - The Council of Representatives is made up of a number of members at a proportion of one seat for every 100,000 people from the population of Iraq. They represent the entire Iraqi people and are elected by general, direct, secret ballot, and they take care to represent all groups of people.

2nd - A candidate for membership in the Council of Representatives must be a fully qualified Iraqi.

3rd - Conditions for candidates and voters and everything connected to elections will be regulated by law.

4th - The Council of Representatives will promulgate a law dealing with replacing of its members when they resign or are removed or die.

5th - It is not permitted to hold membership in the Council of Representatives and another official position.

Article (49): Members of the Council of Representatives shall take the constitutional oath in front of the council before starting their work, as follows:

"I swear by God almighty to carry out my legal duties and responsibilities with dedication and devotion and to preserve the independence and sovereignty of Iraq and to look after the interests of its people and to see to the safety of its land, sky, water, wealth and democratic, federal system and to work to preserve the public and private freedoms and the independence of the judiciary and to abide by honestly and impartially implementing the legislation. God is the witness of what I say."

Article (50): The Council of Representatives shall establish an internal system to regulate its work.

Article (51):

1st - The Council of Representatives should determine the correctness of the membership of a member by a two-third majority within 30 days of the registering of an objection.

2nd - The council's decision may be challenged before the Supreme Federal Court within 30 days of the day it was issued.

Article (52):

1st - Sessions of the Council of Representatives shall be public unless it is necessary to do otherwise.

2nd - Sessions reports shall be published in the way the council sees fit.

Article (53): The president of the republic calls on the council to convene by a presidential decree within 13 days of the date that the results of the general elections have been certified. The session shall be held under the chairmanship of the oldest member, to elect the president of the council and his deputies. Extensions for more than the previously mentioned period are not allowed.

Article (54): In its first session, the council shall elect by absolute majority its president, then a first deputy and a second deputy by direct, secret balloting.

Article (55):

1st - The duration of the council's cycle is four calendar years, starting with the first session and ending by the end of the fourth year.

2nd - The election of a new Council of Representatives takes place 45 days before the cycle ends.

Article (56): The Council of Representatives has two legislative seasons a year, running for eight months. Internal rules will determine how they shall be held. The season in which the general budget is submitted to the council shall not end before it is approved.

Article (57):

1st - The president of the republic, the prime minister, the president of the Council of Representatives or 50 members of the council may call for an extraordinary session, and the meeting shall be confined to the issues that have made it necessary to call for the session.

2nd - The legislative season for the Council of Representatives may be extended for no longer than 30 days to accomplish the tasks that require this, based on a request from the president of the republic, the prime minister, the president of the Council of Representatives or 50 members.

Article (58):

1st - Quorum for sessions of the Council of Representatives shall be reached by the attendance of the absolute majority of its members.

2nd - Decisions shall be made in the Council of Representatives by simple majority, as long as it has not been stated otherwise.

Article (59): The Council of Representatives is given the following duties:

1st - Legislating federal laws.

2nd -

(a) Examining draft laws submitted by 10 of the council's members or by one of its specialized committees.

(b) Examining draft laws suggested by the president of the republic and the prime minister.

3rd - Overseeing the performance of the executive authority.

4th - Certifying treaties or international agreements by a two-thirds majority of the members of the Council of Representatives, as will be regulated by law.

5th - Approving the appointments of:

(a) the head and members of the Federal Cassation Court, the head of the General Prosecutors Office and the head of the Judiciary Inspection Department by absolute majority, based on the recommendation of the Supreme Judicial Council.

(b) ambassadors and those with special ranks, based on the recommendation of the Cabinet.

(c) the army chief of staff, his deputies and those who hold the title of division leader and up, the head of the intelligence service, based on the recommendation of the Cabinet.

6th -

    (a) Questioning the president of the republic based on a request that mentions the reason for questioning, passed by an absolute majority of the Council of Representatives.

    (b) Relieving the president of the republic of his duties by absolute majority of the members of the Council of Representatives after he has been convicted from the Supreme Federal Court in one of the following cases:

        1 - Violating the constitutional oath.

        2 - Violating the constitution.

        3 - Grand treason.

7th -

    (a) A member of the Council of Representatives has the right to ask the prime minister and the ministers questions about any subject that falls under any their specialties, and each has the right to answer the members. He/she who asks the question is the only one who has the right to comment on the answer.

    (b) At least 25 members of the Council of Representatives may propose a general topic for discussion to clarify the policy or performance of the Cabinet or one of the ministries, and it is then presented to the president of the Council of Representatives, and the prime minister or the ministers set a date to come before the Council of Representatives to discuss it.

    (c) A member of the Council of Representatives, with the approval of 25 members, may direct an interpellation to the prime minister or the ministers to hold them accountable for the affairs under their specialty. Discussing the interpellation may not take place before seven days from the date it was submitted.

8th -

    (a) The Council of Representatives may withdraw confidence from a minister by absolute majority, and he/she is considered removed from the date of the withdrawal of confidence. The issue of confidence in a minister can only be put forth at his request or because of a request signed by 50 members as a result of discussing an interpellation directed to him. The council may not decide on the request except after at least seven days from the day it has been submitted.

    (b)

        1 - The president of the republic may submit a request to the Council of Representatives to withdraw confidence from the prime minister.

        2 - The Council of Representatives, based on a request from one-fifth of its members, may vote to withdraw confidence from the prime minister. This request may not be submitted except after an interpellation directed to the prime minister and after at least seven days from the submission of the request.

        3 - The Council of Representatives decides the withdrawal of confidence from the prime minister by absolute majority of its members.

    (c) The Cabinet shall be dissolved in the case that confidence is withdrawn from the prime minister.

    (d) In the case of a vote withdrawing confidence from the whole Cabinet, the prime minister and ministers remain in their positions to run the daily affairs for a period no longer than 30 days until a new Cabinet is formed.

    (e) The Council of Representatives has the right to question and relieve the officials of independent associations from their duties according to the procedures relating to the ministers and by absolute majority.

9th -

    (a) Approving the declaration of war and a state of emergency by a two-thirds majority, based on a joint request by the president of the republic and the prime minister.

(b) The state of emergency may be declared for 30 days, which may be extended by approving it each time.

(c) The prime minister shall be given the necessary powers to enable him to run the country's affairs during the period of a declaration of war or a state of emergency. These powers shall be regulated by law in a way that does not run contrary to the constitution.

(d) The prime minister presents to the Council of Representatives the measures adopted and the results during the period of a declaration of war or a state of emergency within 15 days from the time they have ended.

Article (60):

1st - The Cabinet presents the general budget bill and the final accounting statement to the Council of Representatives for approval.

2nd - The Council of Representatives has the right to rearrange between the parts of the general budget, reduce its total amount of money and it may, when necessary, propose to the Cabinet to increase general costs.

Article (61):

1st - The rights and privileges given to the president of the Council of Representatives and his deputies and the members of the council shall be fixed by law.

2nd -

    a) A member of the Council of Representatives enjoys impunity that covers the opinions he expresses during the time of convening (the council); he shall not be sued before courts for this.

    b) A member may not be arrested during the duration of the council's cycle unless he is accused of a felony and by the approval of the absolute majority of the members that he be stripped of his immunity or if he was arrested red-handed.

Article (62):

1st - The Council of Representatives shall be dissolved by the absolute majority of its members, based on a request from third of its members or a request from the prime minister and with the approval of the president of the republic. The council may not be dissolved while interpellating the prime minister.

2nd - The president of the republic calls for a general election in the country no later than 60 days after the council of representatives has been dissolved. In that case, the Cabinet is considered dissolved and it continues to run the daily affairs.

SECOND: The Council of Union

Article (63):

1st - A legislative council called the "Council of Union" will be established and will include representatives of regions and provinces to examine bills related to regions and provinces.

2nd - The makeup of the council, the conditions for membership and all things related to it will be organized by law.

PART TWO: THE EXECUTIVE AUTHORITY

Article (64): The federal executive authority consists of the president of the republic and the Cabinet. It carries out its authorities based on the constitution and the law.

FIRST The President

Article (65): The president of the republic is the president of the country and the symbol of the nation's unity and represents the sovereignty of the country and oversees the guarantees of adherence to the constitution, the preservation of Iraq's independence and unity and the security of its territory, in accordance to the law.

Article (66): The candidate for the president's post must:

1st - be Iraqi by birth from Iraqi parents.

2nd - be legally competent and have reached the age of 40.

3rd - have a good reputation and political experience and be known for his integrity, rectitude, justice and devotion to the homeland.

4th - not have been convicted of a crime that violates honour.

Article (67): The rules of nomination for the president's post shall be regulated by law.

Article (68):

1st - The Council of Representatives selects from among the candidates a president of the republic by a two-thirds majority.

2nd - If no single candidate gets the required majority, the two candidates with the highest votes will compete and whoever wins a majority of votes in the second round is declared president of the republic.

Article (69): The president of the republic is sworn in in front of the Council of Representatives, using the wording mentioned in article 49 in the constitution.

Article (70):

1st - The term of president of the republic is limited to 4 years.

2nd - The Council of Representatives elects a new president for the republic, three months before the end of the former president's term.

Article (71): The president of the republic enjoys the following powers:

(a) issuing special amnesty, upon a recommendation from the prime minister, to pardon those convicted in international crimes, terrorism, financial or administrative corruption or crimes against personal rights.

(b) endorsing treaties and international agreements following approval by the Council of Representatives.

(c) endorsing and issuing laws enacted by the Council of Representatives. They are considered validated 15 days after the date they were sent to him.

(d) calling for the elected Council of Representatives to convene within a period not exceeding 15 days from the date that election results are ratified, and in other cases stated in the constitution.

(e) awarding medals and badges upon recommendation of the prime minister and in accordance with the law.

(f) receiving ambassadors.

(g) issuing republican protocols.

(h) endorsing execution verdicts issued by the proper courts

(i) taking leadership of the armed forces for ceremonial and commemoration purposes.

(j) practicing any other presidential powers mentioned in the constitution.

Article (72): The law determines the salary and allowances for the president of the republic.

Article (73):

1st - The president of the republic can present a written resignation to the prime minister, and it is considered valid after seven days of the date it is lodged to the Council of Representatives.

2nd - A «deputy» of the president of the republic replaces the president during his absence.

3rd - The deputy of the president of the republic replaces the president of the republic when the post is empty for any reason, and the Council of Representatives has to elect a new president within a period not exceeding 30 days from the date the post is vacant

4th - In the case when the post of the president of the republic is vacant, the president of the Council of Representatives replaces the president if there is no deputy for him, and a new president should be elected in a period not exceeding 30 days from the time the position is vacant, according to the laws of the constitution.

SECOND The Cabinet.

Article (74):

1st - The president assigns the candidate of the parliamentary majority to form a Cabinet during the first 15 days from the date of the first session of the Council of Representatives.

2nd - The prime minister is assigned to name members of his Cabinet within a period of 30 days, at the longest, from the date of the assignment.

3rd - The president assigns a new candidate to be the prime minister within 15 days if the prime minister assigned form the cabinet during the period mentioned in the 2nd Clause fails.

4th - The assigned prime minister presents the names of the members of his cabinet and its ministerial platform to the Council of Representatives. He is considered to have won confidence when his ministers are approved individually and his ministerial platform is approved by an absolute majority.

5th - The president will take up the assigning of another candidate to form a cabinet within 15 days if the Cabinet does not win confidence.

Article (75):

1st - The prime minister must meet the conditions set for the president of the republic. He must have a university degree or an equivalent and must be no younger than 35.

2nd - Ministers must meet the same conditions set for candidates to the Council of Representatives. A minister must have a university degree or an equivalent.

Article (76): The prime minister is the direct executive responsible for the general policy of the nation, the general commander of the armed forces and carries out the administration of the Cabinet and presides over its sessions. The prime minister has the right to remove ministers, with the consent of the Council of Representatives.

Article (77): The prime minister and the ministers carry out the constitutional oath of office before the Council of Representatives in the manner laid out in Article (49) of the constitution.

Article (78): The Cabinet carries out the following duties:

1st - planning and implementing the general policy of the state; general plans; supervising the work of the ministers and offices not subordinate to a ministry.

2nd - proposing draft laws.

3rd - issuing regulations, instructions and decisions to implement the laws.

4th - preparing the draft of the general budget and the final accounting statement and development plans.

5th - recommending to the Council of Representatives for approval the appointments of under-secretaries of ministers, ambassadors, those who have special ranks; the army chief of staff, his deputies and those who are division leaders or higher; the head of the national intelligence service and the heads of the security apparatuses.

6th - negotiating treaties and international agreements and signing them or designating someone to sign.

Article (79):

1st - The president of the republic becomes the acting prime minister when the position is empty for any reason.

2nd - The president of the republic must name another prime minister within no more than 15 days and in accordance with the provisions of Article 74 in this constitution.

Article (80): The salaries and allowances of the prime minister and the ministers and those at their rank shall be fixed by law.

Article (81): The responsibility of the prime minister and the ministers before the Council of Representatives shall be collective and personal.

Article (82):

1st - The work of the security apparatuses and the intelligence service shall be fixed by law; their duties and powers shall be specified and they shall work according to the principles of human rights and shall be subjected to the supervision of the Council of Representatives.

2nd - The national intelligence service is tied to the Cabinet.

Article (83): The Cabinet shall lay down a system of internal rules to regulate its work.

Article (84): The forming of ministries and their functions and responsibilities and the powers of the minister shall be regulated by law.

Article (85): The judiciary is independent and will be represented by courts of different kinds and levels, and they will issue their rulings according to law.

Article (86): Judges are independent, with no authority over them in their rulings except the law. No authority can interfere in the judiciary or in the affairs of justice.

Article (87): The federal judiciary will include the Supreme Judiciary Council, the Supreme Federal Court, the Federal Cassation Court, the Prosecutor's Office, the Judiciary Inspection Department and other federal courts that are organized by law.

FIRST: The Supreme Judiciary Council

Article (88): The Supreme Judiciary Council will administer judicial affairs in accordance with the law.

Article (89): The Supreme Judiciary Council will exercise the following powers:

1st - administering and supervising the federal judiciary system.

2nd - nominating the head and members of the Supreme Federal Court and presenting their names to parliament for endorsement.

3rd - nominating the head of the Federal Cassation Court, the chief prosecutor and the head of the Judiciary Inspection Department, and presenting them to parliament for approval.

4th - proposing the annual budget for the federal judiciary system and presenting it to parliament for approval.

SECOND: The Supreme Federal Court

Article (90):

1st - The Supreme Federal Court is an independent judicial body, financially and administratively, its work and its duties will be defined by law.

2nd - The Supreme Federal Court will be made up of a number of judges and experts in Sharia (Islamic Law) and law, whose number and manner of selection will be defined by a law that should be passed by two-thirds of the parliament members.

Article (91): The Supreme Federal Court will have the following duties:

1st - overseeing the constitutionality of federal laws before they are issued.

2nd - overseeing the constitutionality of the laws and standing regulations.

3rd - interpreting the text of the constitution.

4th - ruling in cases that emerge from the implementation of federal laws.

5th - ruling in disputes between the federal government and the governments of the regions and the provinces and local administrations.

6th - ruling in disputes between the governments of the regions or provinces.

7th - ruling in accusations against the president of the republic, the prime minister and the ministers.

8th - endorsing the final results of parliamentary general elections.

Article (92): Resolutions of the Supreme Federal Court are binding for all authorities.

THIRD: General Provisions:

Article (93): Establishing private or exceptional courts is forbidden.

Article (94): The law shall regulate the establishment of courts, their kinds, degrees, duties and the means of appointing judges, members of the General Prosecutors Office, the provisions for disciplining them and moving them into retirement.

Article (95): Judges shall not be impeached except in the cases determined by law; the law will also specify the rules pertaining to them and regulate disciplinary actions against them.

Article (96): It is forbidden for a judge or a member of the prosecution to:

1st   - Simultaneously hold a judicial position and a legislative or executive position or any other job.

2nd - Belong to any party or political organization or engage in any political activity.

Article (97): The military judiciary shall be fixed by law and the responsibilities of the military courts, which are limited to crimes with a military nature committed by members of the armed forces and security forces, shall be specified within the limits of the law.

Article (98): It is forbidden to legislate into a law provisions protecting any administrative action or decision from being challenged in court.

Article (99): It is permissible by law to establish a state council to handle the tasks of the administrative judiciary, advising, phrasing, representing the state and all other public associations in front of the judiciary, except what the law exempts.

PART FOUR: INDEPENDENT ASSOCIATIONS

Article (100): The Supreme Commission for Human Rights and the Supreme Independent Commission for Elections and the Integrity Agency are considered independent associations subject to the supervision of the Council of Representatives. Their work is regulated by law.

Article (101):

1st   - The Iraqi Central Bank, the Financial Inspection Office, the media and communications agency, and the offices of (religious) endowments are considered financially and administratively independent associations. Each of their activities is regulated by law.

2nd - The Iraqi central bank is responsible before the Council of Representatives, and the Financial Inspection Office and the media and communications agency are tied to the Council of Representatives.

3rd   - Offices of endowments are affiliated to the Cabinet

Article (102): An agency shall be established called the Institution of the Martyrs, affiliated to the Cabinet, and its operations and powers will be regulated by law.

Article (103): A public agency will be founded to guarantee the right of the regions and of provinces that do not belong to a region to fair participation in the administration of the various federal state institutions, missions, fellowships, delegations and regional and international conferences. It shall be made up of representatives of the federal government, regions and provinces that do not belong to a region, and it shall be regulated by law.

Article (104): A general body shall be established by law to monitor and allocate federal incomes; the body shall consist of experts from the federal government, the regions and the provinces and representatives from them. It should shoulder the following responsibilities:

1st   - verifying fairness in distribution of international grants, aid and loans based on what the regions and the provinces that do not belong to a region deserve.

2nd - ensuring that federal financial resources are being used and distributed in the best way.

3rd   - ensuring transparency and justice when allocating money to the regional governments and provinces according to the decided ratios.

Article (105): A council, to be called the federal public service council, shall be established and it shall be responsible for regulating the affairs of the federal public office, including appointments and promotions. Its formation and responsibilities shall be regulated by a law.

Article (106): It is allowed to establish other independent associations according to need and necessity and by law.

CHAPTER FOUR: POWERS OF THE FEDERAL AUTHORITIES

Article (107): The federal authority will maintain the unity of Iraq, its integrity, independence, sovereignty and its democratic federal system.

Article (108): The federal authorities will have the following exclusive powers:

1st - drawing up foreign policy, diplomatic representation, negotiating international accords and agreements, negotiating and signing debt agreements, drawing up foreign sovereign economic and trade policies.

2nd - drawing up and executing national defence policy including setting up and operating the armed forces to ensure the protection and security of Iraq's borders and its defence.

3rd - drawing up financial and customs policy, issuing currency, organizing trade policy among regions and provinces in Iraq, setting the general budget for the nation, drawing up currency policies and establishing and administering a central bank.

4th - organizing issues of weights and measures.

5th - organizing issues of nationality and naturalization, residence and asylum rights.

6th - organizing a policy of broadcast wavelengths and the mail.

7th - setting the general and investment budgets.

8th - planning policies connected to water resources from outside Iraq and guaranteeing levels of water flow into Iraq, according to international law and custom.

9th - conducting the general census of the population.

Article (109): Oil and gas is the property of all the Iraqi people in all the regions and provinces.

Article (110):

1st - The federal government will administer oil and gas extracted from current fields in cooperation with the governments of the producing regions and provinces on condition that the revenues will be distributed fairly in a manner compatible with the demographical distribution all over the country. A quota should be defined for a specified time for affected regions that were deprived in an unfair way by the former regime or later on, in a way to ensure balanced development in different parts of the country. This should be regulated by law.

2nd - The federal government and the governments of the producing regions and provinces together will draw up the necessary strategic policies to develop oil and gas wealth to bring the greatest benefit for the Iraqi people, relying on the most modern techniques of market principles and encouraging investment.

Article (111): All that is not written in the exclusive powers of the federal authorities is in the authority of the regions. In other powers shared between the federal government and the regions, the priority will be given to the region's law in case of dispute.

Article (112): The following duties will be shared by the federal and regional authorities:

1st - administering and organizing customs, in coordination with the regional government, and this will be regulated by law.

2nd - organizing and distributing the main electrical power resources.

3rd - drawing up environmental policy to guarantee the protection of the environment from pollution and the preservation of its cleanliness, in cooperation with the regions.

4th - drawing up general planning and development policies.

5th - drawing up general health policy, in cooperation with the regions.

6th - drawing up general education and childrearing policy, in consultation with the regions.

CHAPTER FIVE: AUTHORITIES OF THE REGIONS

Article (113): The federal system in the republic of Iraq is made up of the capital, regions, decentralized provinces, and local administrations.

Article (114):

1st - The regions comprise one province or more, and two regions or more have the right to join into one region.

2nd - One province or more have the right to form a region, based on a request for a referendum, which can be presented in one of two ways:

    a) a request by a third of the members of each of the provincial councils in the provinces that desire to form a region.

    b) a request by 1/10 (one-tenth) of the voters in each of the provinces that desire to form a region.

3rd -

    a) The general referendum is held among the residents of the particular provinces concerned with what is referred to in «1st» of this article. The referendum takes place when the provincial councils are in session, and the referendum is considered a success with the agreement of the majority of voters.

    b) the referendum is not repeated, unless 2/3 (two-thirds) of the members in each of the provincial councils, or 1/4 (one-quarter) of the concerned provinces' residents, put forward a request for a new referendum.

Article (115): The authorities of each region include legislative, executive and judicial authorities.

Article (116):

1st - The governments of regions have the right to practice legislative, executive and judicial powers according to this constitution, except in what is listed as exclusive powers of the federal authorities.

2nd - The regional authority has the right to amend the implementation of the federal law in the region in the case of a contradiction between the federal and regional laws in matters that do not pertain to the exclusive powers of the federal authorities.

3rd - It is permissible to delegate the authorities practiced by the federal government to the regional governments and vice versa, with the approval of both.

4th - A fair share of the revenues collected federally is designated to regions, in a way that suffices their duties and obligations, taking into consideration the (region's) resources and needs.

5th - Offices for regions and provinces are to be established in embassies and diplomatic missions to follow up on cultural, social and local development affairs.

PART ONE: LEGISLATIVE AUTHORITIES OF THE REGION.

Article (117): The legislative authority of a region consists of one council called the National Council for the Region.

Article (118): Members of the National Council for the Region are elected by residents of the region through universal direct secret ballot.

Article (119):

1st - The National Council for the Region devises the regional constitution, stipulates laws, in a way that does not contradict with this constitution and the federal laws.

2nd - The regional constitution is put up for a referendum to the residents of the region and becomes effective after approval by a majority and its publication in the official newspaper.

PART TWO: EXECUTIVE AUTHORITIES OF THE REGION.

Article (120): The executive authority is made up of the president of the region and the regional cabinet.

Article (121): The executive authority carries out its responsibilities as designated in the regional constitution, in a way that does not contradict this constitution.

FIRST: The president of the region

Article (122): The president of the region is the highest executive president in the region.

Article (123): The president of the region is elected according to the constitution of the region.

Article (124): The constitution of the region determines the responsibilities of the president and the authorities designated to the regional constitutional agencies in a way that does not contradict this constitution.

SECOND: The Cabinet of the region

Article (125): The Cabinet is the highest executive authority in the region and practices its authorities under the supervision and guidance of the president of the region.

Article (126): The Cabinet consists of the prime minister and a number of ministers set according to the constitution of the region.

Article (127): The Cabinet practices the authorities accorded to it following the constitution of the region.

Article (128):

   1st - The revenues of the region are made up of its designated share from the state budget and from the region's local resources.

   2nd - The Cabinet of the region prepares the annual budget for the region and the final expense account, and a law is issued for them by the National Council for the Region. The Cabinet presents a copy of the region's general budget and the final expense account to the federal finance ministry, after they are approved by the National Council for the region.

Article (129): The region's government is responsible for all that is required to manage the region, in particular establishing and organizing internal security forces for the region such as police, security and regional guards.

PART THREE: JUDICIAL AUTHORITIES OF THE REGION

Article (130): The judicial authority of the region consists of the judicial council of the region, the courts, the prosecutor's offices, and the regional court of cassation is considered the highest judicial authority in the region.

Article (131): The types of courts, their levels and specializations are organized according to the judicial authority law of the region, provided it does not contradict this constitution.

PART FOUR: PROVINCES NOT ORGANIZED INTO A REGION

Article (132):

   1st - Provinces consist of districts, counties and villages.

   2nd - Provinces that were not included into a region are given extensive administrative and financial authorities to enable them to self-manage according to the principal of administrative decentralization, and this is regulated by law.

   3rd - The provincial governor, who is elected by the provincial council, is considered the highest executive president of the province to carry out the responsibilities designated to him by the council.

   4th - The election of the provincial council, the governor and their authorities will be regulated by law.

   5th - The provincial council is not subject to the domination or the supervision of any ministry or any party unrelated to a ministry, and it has its independent finances.

Article (133): It is permissible to delegate the federal government's authorities to the provinces or vice versa, with the two parties' approval, and this is regulated by law.

PART FIVE: THE CAPITAL

Article (134): Baghdad with its administrative boundaries is the capital of the republic of Iraq, and it consists of the province of Baghdad with its administrative boundaries, and its status is regulated through a law.

PART SIX: LOCAL ADMINISTRATIONS

Article (135): This constitution guarantees the administrative, political, cultural, educational rights for the various ethnicities such as Turkomen, Chaldeans, Assyrians, and the other components, and this is regulated through a law.

CHAPTER SIX: FINAL AND TRANSITIONAL GUIDELINES

FIRST: Final Guidelines

Article (136):

1st - The president of the republic and the Cabinet together, or one- fifth of the members of the Council of Representatives, can suggest amending the constitution.

2nd - The basic principles of the constitution mentioned in Chapter One of this constitution cannot be amended, except after two consecutive parliament cycles and based on the consent of two-thirds of the members of the Council of Representatives, a public referendum and the endorsement of the president of the republic within seven days.

3rd - Other items not covered by the 2nd clause of this article can only amended by two-thirds of the members of the Council of Representatives, the consent of the people in a general referendum and the endorsement of the president within seven days.

4th - No amendment is allowed that lessens the powers of the regions that are not among the exclusive powers of the federal authority, except with the agreement of the legislative council of the concerned region and the consent of a majority of its population in a general referendum.

5th - An amendment is considered in effect upon the date of its publication in the official gazette.

Article (137): It is not permitted for the president of the republic, the prime minister and Cabinet, the president of the Council of Representatives and its members and delegates, members of the judicial authority and holders of special positions to use their influence to buy or rent anything from the finances of the state or to sell or rent to the state anything from their own finances or to bring suit against the state over these things or to strike contracts with the state in their capacity as concessionairies, importers or contractors.

Article (138): Laws and judicial rulings are issued in the name of the people.

Article (139): Laws are published in the official gazette, and are in effect from the publishing date as long as it is not legislated otherwise.

Article (140): Legislation remains in effect as long as it is not nullified or amended in accordance to the rules of this constitution.

Article (141): Every referendum mentioned in this constitution is passed by a simple majority unless mentioned otherwise.

SECOND: Transitional Guidelines

Article (142):

1st - The state guarantees the welfare of political prisoners and those who were harmed by the practices of the former dictatorial regime.

2nd - The state guarantees compensation to the families of martyrs and those who were wounded by terrorist acts.

3rd - What is provided for in these first and second clauses will be regulated by law.

Article (143): The Council of Representatives shall rely in its first session on the internal organization of the Transitional National Assembly until its own internal organization is decided.

Article (144): The Supreme Iraqi Criminal Court will continue its activities as an independent judicial agency, looking into the crimes of the dictatorial regime and its leading figures. The Council of Representatives can dissolve it by law once its work is finished.

Article (145):

1st - The National De-Baathification Committee will continue its work as an independent body in coordination with the judiciary and the executive authorities in the framework of law regulating its work. The committee is linked to the Parliament.

2nd - The Council of Representatives can dissolve the committee after it finishes its work.

3rd - It is a condition upon candidates for the positions of president of the republic, prime minister, ministers, parliament speaker and parliament members, head of the Federal Council and its members and all similar posts in the regions, and members of the judiciary and other posts included under de-Baathification, that they not be included under the provisions of de-Baathification.

4th - The condition mentioned in the 3rd clause of this article will remain in effect until it is abolished by law.

Article (146):

1st - The Property Claims Agency will continue its operations as an independent body in coordination with judicial authorities and executive bodies in accordance with the law, and it is linked to the Council of Representatives.

2nd - The Council of Representatives can dissolve the agency by a two-thirds majority.

Article (147): Rules in articles concerning the Council of Union wherever they appear in this constitution will not come into effect until a decision is reached by the Council of Representatives, with a two-thirds majority, in its second cycle following the enactment of this constitution.

Article (148):

1st - The phrase (Presidential Council) replaces the phrase (President of the Republic) wherever it appears in this constitution, and regulations concerning the president of the republic will come into effect after one session following the enactment of this constitution.

2nd -

(a) The Council of Representatives will elect a president for the nation and two deputies for him to form a council called the Presidential Council. It will be elected in one list with a two-thirds majority.

(b) The rules for removing the president of the republic in this constitution apply to the president and members of the Presidential Council.

(c) The Council of Representatives can remove any member of the Presidential Council for reasons of lack of competence or integrity with a three-quarters majority vote by its members.

(d) If any position in the Presidential Council should come empty, the Council of Representatives shall elect a replacement by a two-thirds majority.

3rd - Members of the Presidential Council must meet the same conditions as those for a member of the Council of Representatives, that they must:

(a) have reached 40 years of age.

(b) possess a good reputation, integrity and uprightness.

(c) have left the dissolved party at least 10 years before its fall if they were members in it.

(d) not have participated in the repression of the 1991 uprising or the Anfal Campaign or have committed any crime against the Iraqi people.

4th - The Presidential Council must take its decisions unanimously, and any member can delegate his position to one of the other two members.

5th -

(a) Laws and resolutions passed by the Council of Representatives are sent to the Presidential Council for approval by unanimity, to be issued within 10 days of the date of their arrival at the council.

(b) If the Presidential Council does not approve, the laws and resolutions are returned to the Council of Representatives to examine the aspects that were objected to and to vote on them once more by majority, whereupon they are sent again to the Presidential Council for approval.

(c) If the Presidential Council does not approve the laws or resolutions again with 10 days of their arrival, they are returned to the Council of Representatives which can adopt them by a three-fifths majority of its members. This cannot be opposed and it is considered approved.

6th - The Presidential Council practices the powers provided for the president of the republic until the issuing of a decision by the Council of Representatives as provided for in the 1st clause of this article.

Article (149):

1st - The executive authority will take the necessary steps to complete implementation of the requirements of Article (58) of the Transitional Administration Law for the Iraqi State, with all its clauses.

2nd - The responsibilities placed on the executive authority provided for in Article (58) of the Transitional Administration Law for the Iraqi State are extended to and will continue for the executive authority until the completion of (normalization, census, ending with a census in Kirkuk and other disputed areas to determine the will of the people) in a period no longer than 12/31/2007.

Article (150): Laws legislated in Kurdistan since 1992 remain in effect, and decisions made by the government of the Kurdistan region - including contracts and court decisions - are effective unless they are voided or amended according to the laws of the Kurdistan region by the concerned body, as long as they are not against the constitution.

Article (151): A proportion of no less than 25 percent of the seats in the Council of Representatives is specified for the participation of women.

Article (152): The Transitional Administration Law for the Iraqi State and its appendix are voided upon creation of the new government, except for what appears in paragraph (a) of Article (53) and Article (58) of the Transitional Administration Law.

Article (153): This constitution comes into effect after its approval by the people in a universal referendum and its publication in the official newspaper and the election of the Council of Representatives in accordance with its provisions.

UNITED KINGDOM LABOUR GOVERNMENT

(as at 31 December 2005)

Members of the Cabinet

Prime Minister, First Lord of the Treasury and Minister for the Civil Service	Rt Hon. Tony Blair, MP
Deputy Prime Minister and First Secretary of State	Rt Hon. John Prescott, MP
Chancellor of the Exchequer	Rt Hon. Gordon Brown, MP
Secretary of State for Foreign and Commonwealth Affairs	Rt Hon. Jack Straw, MP
Secretary of State for Environment, Food and Rural Affairs	Rt Hon. Margaret Beckett, MP
Secretary of State for Transport and Secretary of State for Scotland	Rt Hon. Alistair Darling, MP
Secretary of State for Defence	Rt Hon. Dr John Reid, MP
Lord Privy Seal and Leader of the House of Commons	Rt Hon Geoff Hoon, MP
Secretary of State for Health	Rt Hon Patricia Hewitt, MP
Secretary of State for Culture, Media and Sport	Rt Hon. Tessa Jowell, MP
Parliamentary Secretary to the Treasury and Chief Whip	Rt Hon. Hilary Armstrong, MP
Secretary of State for the Home Department	Rt Hon Charles Clarke, MP
Secretary of State for Northern Ireland and Secretary of State for Wales	Rt Hon Peter Hain, MP
Minister without Portfolio	Rt Hon. Ian McCartney, MP
Leader of the House of Lords and Lord President of the Council	Rt Hon. Baroness Amos
Secretary of State for Constitutional Affairs and Lord Chancellor	Rt Hon. Lord Falconer of Thoroton, QC
Secretary of State for International Development	Rt Hon. Hilary Benn, MP
Secretary of State for Trade and Industry	Rt Hon. Alan Johnson, MP
Secretary of State for Education and Skills	Rt Hon. Ruth Kelly, MP
Secretary of State for Work and Pensions	Rt Hon John Hutton, MP
Chancellor of the Duchy of Lancaster (Minister for the Cabinet Office)	vacant
Chief Secretary to the Treasury	Rt Hon. Des Browne, MP
Minister of Communities and Local Government	Rt Hon David Miliband, MP

Also attending Cabinet

Lord Chief Whip, Lords, Captain of the Honourable Corps of Gentlemen-at-Arms	Rt Hon. The Lord Grocott
Attorney General	Rt Hon. The Lord Goldsmith
Minister of State for Europe in the Foreign and Commonwealth Office	Rt Hon. Douglas Alexander, MP

Law Officers

Solicitor General	Mike O'Brien, MP
Advocate General for Scotland	Baroness Clark, QC

UNITED STATES REPUBLICAN ADMINISTRATION

(as at 31 December 2005)

Members of the Cabinet

President	George W. Bush
Vice President	Richard B. Cheney
Secretary of Agriculture	Mike Johanns
Secretary of Commerce	Carlos Gutierrez
Secretary of Defence	Donald Rumsfeld
Secretary of Education	Margaret Spellings
Secretary of Energy	Samuel W. Bodman
Secretary of Health and Human Services	Michael O. Leavitt
Secretary of Homeland Security	Michael Chertoff
Secretary of Housing and Urban Development	Alphonso Jackson
Secretary of Interior	Gale Norton
Attorney General and Head of Department of Justice	Alberto Gonzales
Secretary of Labour	Elaine Chao
Secretary of State	Condoleezaa Rice
Secretary of Transportation	Norman Mineta
Secretary of the Treasury	John Snow
Secretary of Veterans' Affairs	Jim Nicholson

Cabinet Rank Members

Director of Office of Management and Budget	Joshua B. Bolten
Administrator of Environmental Protection Agency	Stephen Johnson
White House Chief of Staff	Andrew H. Card Jr
United States Trade Representative	Ambassador Rob Portman
Director of Office of National Drug Control Policy	John Walters

Other Leading Executive Branch Officials

Chairman of Council of Economic Advisers	Ben S. Bernanke
Chairman of Council on Environmental Quality	James L. Connaughton
Director of National Economic Council	Allan Hubbard
Director of White House Office of Faith Based and Community Initiatives	Jim Towey
Director of Office of National AIDS Policy	Carol Thompson
Director of Office of Science and Technology Policy	John Marburger
Chairman of President's Foreign Intelligence Advisory Board	Lt.-Gen. (rtd) Brent Scowcroft
Director of USA Freedom Corps	Desiree T. Sayle
Director of White House Military Office	Rear Adml Mark I. Fox
Director of Central Intelligence Agency	Porter J. Goss
Director of National Intelligence	John Negroponte

INTERNATIONAL COMPARISONS: POPULATION, GDP AND GROWTH

The following table gives population, gross domestic product (GDP) and growth data for the main member states of the Organisation for Economic Co-operation and Development plus selected other countries. (Source: World Bank, Washington)

	Population		GDP ($000mn)		GDP growth %	
		Avg. annual % growth			Avg. annual % growth	Avg. annual % growth
	2004 mn	1990-2004	2003	2004	1990-2000	2000-2004
Algeria	32.4	1.8	66.5	84.6	1.9	4.8
Argentina	38.4	1.2	129.6	153.0	4.3	-0.1
Australia	20.1	1.2	522.4	637.3	3.9	3.5
Austria	8.2	0.4	253.1	292.3	2.4	1.2
Bangladesh	139.2	2.1	51.9	56.6	4.8	5.2
Belgium	10.4	0.3	301.9	352.3	2.1	1.4
Brazil	183.9	1.5	492.3	604.0	2.9	2.0
Canada	32.0	1.0	856.5	978.0	3.1	2.6
Chile	16.1	1.4	72.4	94.1	6.6	3.7
China	1,296.2	0.9	1,417.0	1,931.7	10.6	9.4
Colombia	44.9	1.8	78.7	97.7	2.8	2.9
Denmark	5.4	0.4	211.9	241.4	2.5	1.1
Egypt	72.6	1.9	82.4	78.8	4.7	3.4
Finland	5.2	0.3	161.9	185.9	2.6	2.3
France	60.4	0.4	1,757.6	2,046.6	2.0	1.5
Germany	82.5	0.3	2,403.1	2,740.6	1.8	0.6
Greece	11.1	0.6	172.2	205.2	2.2	4.2
Hungary	10.1	-0.2	82.7	100.7	1.6	4.0
India	1,079.7	1.7	600.6	691.2	6.0	6.2
Indonesia	217.6	1.4	208.3	257.6	4.2	4.6
Iran	67.0	1.5	137.1	163.4	3.5	6.0
Irish Republic	4.1	1.1	153.7	181.6	7.5	5.1
Italy	57.6	0.1	1,468.3	1,677.8	1.6	0.8
Japan	127.8	0.2	4,300.9	4,622.7	1.3	0.9
Kenya	33.5	2.5	14.4	16.1	2.2	2.7
South Korea	48.1	0.8	605.3	679.7	5.8	4.7
Malaysia	24.9	2.4	103.7	118.3	7.0	4.4
Mexico	103.8	1.6	626.1	676.5	3.1	1.5
Netherlands	16.3	0.6	511.5	579.0	2.9	0.5
New Zealand	4.1	1.2	79.6	99.0	3.2	4.0
Nigeria	128.7	2.5	58.4	72.1	2.5	5.4
Norway	4.6	0.6	220.9	250.1	4.0	1.6
Pakistan	152.1	2.4	82.3	96.1	3.8	4.1
Philippines	81.6	2.1	80.6	84.6	3.4	3.9
Poland	38.2	0.0	209.6	242.3	4.6	2.8
Portugal	10.5	0.4	147.9	167.7	2.7	0.3
Russia	143.8	-0.2	432.9	581.4	-4.7	6.1
South Africa	45.5	1.8	159.9	212.8	2.1	3.2
Spain	42.7	0.7	838.7	1,040.0	2.6	3.0
Sweden	9.0	0.4	301.6	346.4	2.2	2.0
Switzerland	7.4	0.7	320.1	357.5	1.0	0.6
Thailand	63.7	1.1	143.0	161.7	4.2	5.4
Turkey	71.7	1.7	240.4	302.8	3.8	4.2
United Kingdom	59.9	0.3	1,794.9	2,124.4	2.7	2.3
USA	293.7	1.2	10,948.5	11,711.8	3.5	2.5
Venezuela	26.1	2.0	85.4	110.1	1.6	-1.2
Vietnam	82.2	1.5	39.2	45.2	7.9	7.2

XIX OBITUARY

al-Hariri, Rafik (b. 1944), Prime Minister of Lebanon who guided the recovery of his country following the civil war but was later assassinated. Born in Sidon to Sunni Muslim parents, Hariri was educated in Egypt and at the Arab University in Beirut, leaving after a year to take a job in accountancy. He moved to Saudi Arabia where he founded a construction company and began to make his fortune. He became a Saudi citizen in 1978, but returned to Lebanon in 1983, acting as a mediator between various militias and becoming Prime Minister for the first time in 1992 when he formed a government that restored some confidence in the country's economy and finances. After returning to office for the second time in 2000, he resigned when Syria forced the Lebanese parliament to extend President Emile Lahoud's term for three years beyond its constitutional limit. Al-Hariri was intending to stand again in the elections of May 2005, but was killed when the car in which he was travelling in Beirut was blown up by a bomb, with suspected Syrian involvement. Died 14 February.

Azcona del Hoyo, José Simeón (b. 1927), former President of Honduras who campaigned against military intervention in politics and helped bring an end to civil war in Central America. Born in La Ceiba, he studied engineering at the University of Tegucigalpa and the Technical Institute at Monterrey in Mexico, returning to Tegucigalpa to set up a construction company concentrating on low-cost housing. After joining the Honduran Liberal Party he won a seat in Congress in 1980, was appointed Minister of Communications, Public Works and Transport, and elected President three years later. He soon found himself in conflict with the Sandinista government of Nicaragua, which accused Honduras of conniving with the USA in the organisation of Contra activity against it. At the summit of Central American governments in 1987 Azcona agreed to expel the Contras from Honduras, and though this was not immediately carried out the Contra campaign had effectively ended by 1990, when he retired from the presidency. Died 24 October.

Bancroft, Anne (b. 1931), US actress who won one Oscar and was nominated for four more, as well as two Tony and three British Academy awards for stage performances. Born Anna Maria Louisa Italiano in the Bronx district of New York, she trained at the American Academy of Dramatic Art and appeared in several local television productions before moving to Hollywood, where she made her film debut (with the name Anne Bancroft) in *Don't Bother to Knock* in 1952. After a series of fifteen unsuccessful films she returned to the stage in New York to play in *Two for the Seesaw* and *The Miracle Worker*, for both of which she won Tony awards. She repeated her role as Annie Sullivan in the film of *The Miracle Worker*, for which she won an Oscar as best actress. She was nominated again for her next film, *The Pumpkin Eater*, in 1964, when she met and married the director Mel Brooks, and once more in 1968 for *The Graduate*, in which she played a frustrated American housewife who seduces her neighbour's son. She continued to make many more films (writing, directing and acting in one called *Fatso*), as well as appearing in some stage and television dramas, but none had quite the impact of *The Graduate*. Died 6 June.

Barber, Lord (b. 1920), British Chancellor of the Exchequer during the early 1970s. Born in Hull, Anthony Barber was educated at Retford Grammar School before serving in the Second World War. Commissioned in the Royal Artillery, he was evacuated from Dunkirk and seconded to the RAF, flying on photo-reconnaissance missions until, in 1942, he was taken prisoner after ditching his Spitfire into the sea when it ran out of fuel. While a prisoner he gained a first class degree in law by means of a correspondence course, then after release gained a First in PPE at Oriel College, Oxford. As Conservative candidate he won the Doncaster seat in 1951 by 284 votes, was appointed a junior whip in 1957 and parliamentary private secretary to the Prime Minister, Harold Macmillan, in 1958. He became economic secretary to the Treasury in 1959, financial secretary in 1962 and Minister of Health, with a seat in the Cabinet, in 1963. He lost his parliamentary seat in 1964, but won Altrincham and Sale in a by-election in 1965. He was made party chairman in 1967 and, when Edward Heath became Prime Minister after the 1970 election, Chancellor of the Duchy of Lancaster, but became Chancellor of the Exchequer when Iain Macleod died shortly after the election. Committed by Heath to a dash for growth, Barber soon found himself faced with inflation, recession and the introduction of a prices and wages freeze, leading to the miners' strike and the election of 1974, which the Conservatives lost. He was appointed a life peer, retired from politics and became chairman of the Standard Chartered Bank, a post he held until 1987. Died 16 December.

Barker, Ronnie, OBE (b. 1929), English actor, writer and comedian. Born in Bedford, Barker was brought up in Oxford and after working briefly as a bank clerk gave it up in favour of the stage, where, after spells with several repertories, he was brought into Peter Hall's 1955 production of *Mourning Becomes Electra* at the Arts Theatre, followed by roles in other West End productions. In 1959 he was given a part in the BBC radio comedy series, *The Navy Lark*, performing in it for nine years while also moving into television with a series of satirical sketches in *The Frost Report* and *Frost on Sunday*, programmes for which he also wrote scripts under the pseudonym of Gerald Wiley. In 1971 he and his friend Ronnie Corbett were given their own show, *The Two Ronnies*, which was an instant success. Twelve series were made during the next sixteen years, Barker writing most of the material, while he also starred in two situation comedies: *Porridge*, in which he played an habitual criminal with an intimate knowledge of the prison system, and *Open All Hours*, in which his character was a stammering Yorkshire shopkeeper. Barker formally announced his retirement in 1987, though he was later persuaded to take part in a few television plays. Died 3 October.

Bellow, Saul (b. 1915), US novelist who was awarded the Nobel Prize for Literature in 1976 for his "exuberant ideas, hilarious comedy and burning compassion". Born in Canada, Solomon Bellows was the fourth child of Russian immigrant Jews and was brought up and educated in Chicago. He moved to New York, taking a variety of jobs until, in 1944, he served in the Merchant Marine, joining up in the year which saw publication of his first novel, *Dangling Man*, the story of a graduate waiting to be drafted into the forces. After leaving the Merchant Marine Bellow began teaching English at the University of Minnesota, publishing his second novel, *The Victim*, in 1947 before moving to Paris to write the book that made his name, *The Adventures of Augie March*, whose celebrated opening lines ("I am an American, Chicago born—Chicago, that sombre city—and go at things as I have taught myself, free-style") set a new genre of writing. In 1964 Bellow's reputation was enhanced with *Herzog*, the story of an academic confronted with his wife's adultery with his best friend. His next major novel, *Humboldt's Gift* (1975), describing the decline of a poet and reflecting some of Bellow's own disillusion with the world around him, won the Pulitzer Prize. He continued to write, mostly a series of shorter novels, even after, in 1995, a bout of food poisoning nearly killed him. His last novel, *Revelstein,* was published in 2000. Like many of his works it included some personal experience (in this case the food-poisoning incident). Others reflected some of his own marital experiences (he was married five times). Died 5 April.

Benenson, Peter (b. 1921), British lawyer who founded the human-rights organisation Amnesty International. Privately tutored by the poet W.H. Auden before going to Eton and to Balliol College, Oxford, Benenson served during World War II in the Intelligence Corps. Called to the Bar after the war, he stood as Labour candidate in four parliamentary elections, first for Streatham and then for Hitchin, but failed to win either seat. He was sent by the Labour Party as an observer at the trial of Basque nationalists in Spain and his experience there and at other trials he witnessed or read about inspired him to launch an Appeal for Amnesty. He wrote an article, "The Forgotten Prisoners", for *The Observer* newspaper in May 1961, calling for common action to draw attention to the plight of the individual "who had been imprisoned, tortured or executed because his opinions or religion were unacceptable to his government". The response was fast. By the end of the year Amnesty had case files from more than

thirty countries. Benenson was appointed its president in 1964, and though he formally withdrew two years later he continued to campaign and speak on its behalf. He refused to accept an honour for himself from any government, but Amnesty International was awarded the Nobel Peace Prize in 1977. Died 25 February.

Best, George (b. 1946), footballer of brilliance whose early success, fame and good looks led to the life of a playboy and alcoholism. Born in Belfast, he was sent to the local grammar school but as it only played rugby football and Best was obsessed with soccer he was transferred to a secondary modern, where he was recruited by a Manchester United scout. Turning professional on his seventeenth birthday, Best began to play for United's first team and soon made his presence felt. In 1965 United won the league championship and in 1966 reached the semi-final of the European Cup, Best scoring twice in the opening ten minutes of the quarter-final against Benfica. In 1967 United won the league again and in 1968 secured the European Cup, Best scoring in every round, including the final against Benfica. Still only twenty-two, he found it difficult to cope with his celebrity status, turning to alcohol and womanising, failing to turn up for games, and finally leaving Manchester United in 1974, having scored 178 goals for the team, as well as playing for Northern Ireland thirty-seven times. He went to the USA, playing occasionally in the North American League, then returned to Britain to play for a number of teams with occasional flashes of his old brilliance. But he continued to be dogged by alcoholism. He was sent to prison for drunk driving, was admitted to hospital in 2000, given a liver tansplant in 2002, but again returned to drink. Died 25 November.

Bethe, Professor Hans (b. 1906), physicist who worked on the atomic bomb and was awarded the Nobel prize for his carbon cycle theory of the generation of energy in the stars. Born in Strasbourg, he was educated at the Goethe Gymnasium in Frankfurt and at the universities of Frankfurt and Munich. In 1932 he was appointed assistant professor at the university of Tubingen, but lost his job when Hitler came to power. He emigrated first to England and then to the USA, where in 1935 he went to Cornell University to work on the theory of nuclear reactions. In 1939 he published his paper *Energy production in Stars* in which he explained that most of the energy produced by stars derived from a series of six nuclear reactions in which hydrogen was the fuel and carbon the catalyst. For this, the first elucidation of stellar and solar energy, he was awarded the New York Academy of Science's Morrison Prize and eventually, in 1967, the Nobel Prize for Physics. In 1943 Bethe went to Los Alamos to work on the Manhattan Project, witnessing the first nuclear test in New Mexico, which he found both exhilarating and terrifying. He subsequently became one of the Emergency Committee of Atomic Scientists, headed by Albert Einstein, which set out to educate the public about atomic energy. He warned that H-bomb fall-out could destroy life on earth, and eventually wrote to US President Bill Clinton urging him to ban all experiments whose primary purpose was to design new types of nuclear weapons. Died 6 March.

Bondi, Professor Sir Hermann, FRS (b. 1919), scientist and mathematician who helped develop the steady-state theory of the universe. Born in Vienna, he was educated at the Realgymnasium and at Trinity College, Cambridge. Interned and sent to Canada when World War II broke out in 1939, he was allowed to return to Britain three years later to work for the Admiralty, testing equipment for spotting submarines from the air. Appointed a Fellow of Trinity College, he teamed up with Thomas Gold and Fred Hoyle after the war to produce the steady-state theory, which held that the universe had always existed and would have no end. In 1952 Bondi published the theory in detail in his book *Cosmology*, but it began to be challenged when research into galaxies and quasars suggested that the universe had once been much hotter, and following the discovery of a cosmic background of microwave radiation Bondi accepted that the Big Bang theory was a more likely explanation of the origin of the universe. After leaving Cambridge he was appointed Professor of Mathematics at King's College, London, and director of the European Space Research Organisation (later absorbed into the European Space Agency). In 1971 he became chief scientific adviser to the Ministry of Defence, in 1980 chairman and chief executive of the National Environment Research Council, and in 1983 Master of Churchill College, Cambridge. Died 10 September.

Callaghan of Cardiff, Lord (b. 1912), British Prime Minister from 1976 to 1979, James Callaghan was born in Portsmouth, educated at the local primary and grammar schools, and started work with the Inland Revenue at the age of seventeen. He subsequently became branch secretary and a member of the executive of the Inland Revenue Staff Federation, quickly developing into a skilled union negotiator. After war service in the Royal Navy, he won Cardiff South as Labour Party candidate in the 1945 election and was appointed a junior minister in 1947, first at Transport and then at the Admiralty. When Labour went into opposition in 1951 he became spokesman for colonial affairs. In 1963 he stood against Harold

Wilson and George Brown for party leader, and when Wilson became Prime Minister in 1964 Callaghan was appointed Chancellor of the Exchequer. Confronted with a succession of balance of payments crises he was eventually forced, in 1967, to devalue the pound. He was moved to the Home Office, sent troops to try to keep the peace in Northern Ireland, while running into trouble with Wilson for refusing to go along with the union reforms proposed in the white paper, "In place of strife". When Labour returned to power in 1974, Callaghan was appointed Foreign Secretary, securing a favourable vote in the referendum of 1975 following some minor renegotiation of the terms of entry into the EEC. When Wilson suddenly resigned in the following year, Callaghan won the leadership contest against Michael Foot and Denis Healey and became Prime Minister. For the first two years of his administration he seemed in firm control, but after a series of industrial strikes he lost a vote of confidence in the House of Commons, and the subsequent election. He remained in the Commons until 1987, when he was made a life peer, but in retirement he stayed mainly at home looking after his wife Audrey, whom he had married sixty years earlier and who died eleven days before him. Died 26 March.

Carson, Johnny (b. 1925), television presenter whose late-night show ran for twenty-nine years in the USA. Born in Corning, Iowa, Carson was brought up in Nebraska and was educated locally before being called up into the US Navy during the Second World War. On demobilisation he went to the University of Nebraska, completing a thesis on comedy writing while paying his way with work at the local radio station. He was given a TV show of his own by CBS, but it was soon closed and Carson moved to New York, where he was taken on

to front the ABC-TV quiz show *Who Do You Trust?*, which he did from 1957 until 1962, when he moved to NBC-TV to host the *Tonight Show*, which ran five nights a week from 11.30 until 1 o'clock in the morning. As host Carson was modest and affable, seldom allowing his quick wit to upstage his guests, with the result that he was never short of distinguished people to interview. By 1978 he had doubled the programme's audience to about 17 million, had won four Emmy awards, and become very wealthy. He was awarded the presidential medal of freedom in 1992, living quietly in retirement with his fourth wife. Died 23 January.

Charles, Dame Eugenia, DBE (b. 1919), Prime Minister of Dominica, one of the Windward Islands, who became known as the "Iron Lady of the Caribbean". Born at Pointe Michel in Dominica , Mary Eugenia Charles was educated at convents in Dominica and Grenada, at the University of Toronto and finally at the London School of Economics. She was called to the Bar in London in 1947 and from 1950 practised in Dominica and Barbados. When Dominica obtained internal self-government in 1967 she was drawn into politics by opposing the attempt by the ruling Dominica Labour Party to introduce a bill limiting freedom of expression. She became a founder member of the Dominica Freedom Party and in 1975 was elected to the House of Assembly, where she became leader of the opposition. She retained this role when Dominica achieved full independence in 1978, but became Prime Minister when the Freedom Party won the election of 1980. She held the post for fifteen years, surviving several attempted coups, riots in the capital of Roseau, and opposition to her efforts to eradicate corruption. She strongly supported US military intervention following the coup in Grenada and, as chairman of the

Eastern Caribbean States, championed the banana producing countries against European attempts to remove the old colonial preferences. She was appointed DBE in 1991 and retired at the end of her third term of office in 1995. Died 6 September.

Cook, Robin, PC (b. 1946), British Labour Party politician and Cabinet minister who resigned over the decision to invade Iraq. Born in Belshill near Glasgow and educated at Aberdeen Grammar School and Edinburgh University, he was attracted by Labour politics, winning the marginal seat of Edinburgh Central in 1974 and moving to the safer seat of Livingston in 1983. After the Labour defeat that year Cook was elected to the shadow cabinet and was made front bench spokesman successively on Europe, Trade, Health, and Foreign Affairs. His greatest triumph in opposition came in 1996, when the Scott report on arms to Iraq was put before the House of Commons. Given less than three hours in a locked room to digest 1,800 pages, Cook tore apart the government's credibility and helped pave the way for the success of New Labour in the 1997 election. He was appointed Foreign Secretary, but his reputation suffered from the revelation that he had been having an affair with his secretary, which prompted a very public divorce. His tenure at the Foreign Office was at times equally disconcerting. Declaring that he intended to pursue "an ethical foreign policy" he was embarrassed to find that arms sales continued to a number of countries likely to use them for questionable purposes. He also contrived to upset the Indian and the Israeli governments by unwise comments made during official visits to those countries. After the election in 2001 Cook was removed from his ministry and appointed Leader of the House of Commons, a clear demotion but a role which he accepted and carried out with typ-

ical energy, reforming the hours of work in the Commons but failing in his attempt to reform the House of Lords. When the decision came to go to war with Iraq, Cook left the government with a memorable resignation speech. Died 6 August.

Cowling, Maurice (b. 1926), Cambridge political historian who was a major influence on Conservative thought. Born in south London, he was educated at Battersea Grammar School and Jesus College, Cambridge, interrupted by war service which he spent as an infantry officer with the Queen's Royal Regiment, returning to Cambridge to complete a double first. He tried a number of non-academic careers, including the foreign service and journalism on *The Times* and the *Daily Express*, from both of which he was fired. After gaining a fellowship at Jesus and a university lectureship in history he wrote a number of books, the first being *The Nature and Limits of Political Science* (1963), in which he suggested that too much philosophy could be an impediment to political action, which was basically concerned with party- or self-interest. He moved to Peterhouse in 1963, writing a number of other political books, including *The Impact of Labour* (1970) and *The Impact of Hitler* (1975), before embarking on his major work, *Religion and Public Doctrine in Modern England*, published in three volumes between 1980 and 2000, in which he offered a conservative and Christian view of the nineteenth and 20th centuries in place of what he saw as the current progressive doctrines. Died 24 August.

de los Angeles, Victoria (b. 1923), Spanish lyric soprano who was one of the great opera and concert singers of her time. Born in Barcelona, Victoria Gomez Cima had a troubled education because of the Spanish Civil War, but she eventually went to the Barcelona Conservatorium to study singing and the piano. She gave her first public concert in 1944 and made her formal operatic debut, as the Countess in the *Marriage of Figaro*, in 1945. Two years later she won first prize in the Geneva Concours International and from then on, with her chosen new name, her career was assured. She made her debut at the Paris Opera in 1949, as Marguerite in Gounod's *Faust*, and at Covent Garden in 1950 as Mimi in Puccini's *La Boheme*, which she followed with an outstanding recital at the Wigmore Hall and two Promenade concerts which included a series of Spanish songs for which she became renowned. She retired from opera in 1979 and from concert work twenty years later. Died 15 January.

Donaldson of Lymington, Lord (b. 1920), Engish barrister who became Master of the Rolls and president of the National Industrial Relations Court. Educated at Charterhouse and Trinity College, Cambridge, John Donaldson served during World War II with the Royal Armoured Corps Signals. He was called to the Bar in 1946, developing a practice in commercial law. He was junior counsel at the bank rate inquiry of 1957 and junior counsel to the Registrar of Restrictive Trading Agreements 1959-61. Appointed QC in 1961 he was leading counsel at the Vassal spy tribunal in 1962 and became a judge of the High Court in 1966. He helped draft the Industrial Relations Act of 1971 and became first president of the National Industrial Relations Court in that year, discarding wig and robes in the hope of giving the proceedings a relaxed atmosphere. He failed to win the trust of the trade unions and the court was abolished when the Labour Party returned to power in 1974. Donaldson was appointed to the Court of Appeal in 1979 and Master of the Rolls in 1982, where he rapidly reduced the Court of Appeal's backlog of cases, but his reputation suffered when the interim report into the trial of the Maguire Seven concluded that he had failed to appreciate the significance of critical evidence in the original trial of 1976. Donaldson stood down from the Bench in 1992, but remained active in public life as a crossbencher in the House of Lords. Died 31 August.

Duisenberg, Wim (b. 1935), Dutch politician who became president of the European Central Bank and was blamed by some for the early troubles of the euro. Born in Heereveen, Willem Frederik Duisenbeg was educated at Groningen University, and remained there for some years as an assistant teacher. In 1966 he joined the IMF, taking a one-year stint at the Nederlandsche Bank in 1969 and then three years at the University of Amsterdam, where he taught economics. In 1973 he was appointed Netherlands Finance Minister, where he initially increased public spending to counter recession but later introduced new fiscal controls to curb inflation. Resigning in 1977, he joined Rabobank before returning to the Nederlandsche Bank to become its governor. He was appointed first president of the European Central Bank in 1998, presiding over the introduction of the euro with skill and efficiency, but once it was introduced he seemed to fall into the habit of making spontaneous and unhelpful public comments which enabled others to blame him for the euro's initial weakness. In office he was dogged by the question of his retirement date. The post had a statutory period of eight years, but the French believed it to have been cut by half when they agreed to his appointment. Duisenberg eventually retired in 2003, after more than five years in the post. Died 31 July.

Ellis, Alice Thomas (b. 1932), British writer whose novels, she once said, were mainly an attack on the 1960s, while her other writings were deeply critical of changes in the Roman Catholic Church. Born in Liverpool, Anna Margaret Lindholm became a Catholic at the age of nineteen, spending six months as a postulant nun until she slipped a disc and had to leave. She wrote her first novel, *The Sin Eater*, under the pseudonym Alice Thomas Ellis, in 1977. Her second, *The Birds of the Air*, was published in 1980 and her third, *The Twenty-Seventh Kingdom*, which was short-listed for the Booker prize, in 1982. All were witty books about chaotic lives which, like others to follow—including the trilogy *The Clothes in the Wardrobe* (1987), *The Skeleton in the Cupboard* (1988), and *The Fly in the Ointment* (1989)—contained elements critical of modern life, which she saw as developments of the 1960s, "free love and drugs and beads and flowers and crap". In 1985 she began writing a column for *The Spectator*, then in 1989 for *The Universe* and, in 1991, for *The Catholic Herald* from which she was dismissed in 1996 after writing a column critical of David Warlock, the reformist Roman Catholic Archbishop of Liverpool, three months after his death. She was fiction editor for Duckworth, the publishers for which her husband, Colin Haycraft, was a managing director. Together they founded an arts centre at their house in Wales. Died 8 March.

Eyadéma, Gnassingbé (b. 1935), President of Togo since 1967, when he seized power in a coup and tolerated no opposition thereafter. Born in the village of Pya, in the French colony of Togoland, Etienne Eyadéma was educated locally before joining the French Army, serving in Indochina and Algeria before returning to what had become the independent state of Togo in 1962. Adopting the first name of Gnassingbé, he joined in a rebellion against the head of state, Sylvanus Olympio, who was killed. Eyadéma was appointed chief-of-staff by the new President, Nicolas Grunitzky, but seized power for himself in 1967, taking control of the army and banning all political parties until he formed a new one, the Rassemblement du Peuple Togolais, the only party allowed in what became a one-party state. He was the only candidate in the presidential elections of 1979 and 1986. Aid from the EU was suspended in 1993 in protest at his abuse of human rights. In 1998 he agreed to a new presidential election, but many opponents were killed and the poll was abandoned. In 1999, under pressure from France, Eyadéma agreed not to stand for election again, but abandoned his pledge and was re-elected in 2003. Died of a heart attack 5 February.

Fitt, Lord (b. 1926), founder and former leader of the Social Democratic and Labour Party (SDLP) in Northern Ireland. Born into a Catholic family in Belfast, Gerry Fitt left school at fourteen and joined the Merchant Navy, sailing with convoys to Russia during the Second World War. Back in Belfast afterwards, he joined the Irish Labour Party and won a seat in the Northern Ireland House of Commons in 1962. Four years later he was elected to the Westminster Parliament for West Belfast. Always a target for sympathisers of the Provisional IRA (Irish Republican Army) he was beaten up while leading a civil rights march in Londonderry in 1968, and subsequently threatened with death. In 1970 he and others formed the SDLP to represent the fears of the Catholics in Ulster, but opposing violence and urging the British government to send in troops to control the situation. He was a member of the constitutional convention in 1975-76 and in 1979, though a socialist, played a part in bringing down the Labour government by voting against its bill for Scottish devolution. Later in the same year he resigned the leadership of the SDLP after failing to persuade his colleagues to take part in a conference on devolution for Nothern Ireland. In 1983 he lost his House of Commons seat to the Sinn Féin candidate, Gerry Adams. Three weeks later his house in Belfast was destroyed by IRA supporters. Fitt was made a life peer, and he and his family moved permanently to England. Died 26 August.

Fowles, John (b. 1926), English author whose often complex novels commanded critical attention as well as securing substantial sales. Born in Leigh-on-sea, Essex, he was educated at Bedford School and served in the Royal Marines in 1945-46 before going on to New College, Oxford, where he read modern languages. He taught for a while in France and then at a school on the Greek island of Spetses before returning to teach in England while working on his first two novels, *The Collector*, published in 1963, and *The Aristos*, in 1964. The first, a story of a man's obsession with a girl he imprisons in a cellar, became a bestseller, was made into a film, and provided Fowles with an income that allowed him to give up teaching and move to a fairly reclusive life in Lyme Regis. The second was less a work of fiction than an intellectual portrait of its author. His third book, *The Magus* (1966), which was set on a Greek island, was a complex fable with Shakespearean allusions which he later regretted adapting for a film. He published a revised version of the book in 1977 some years after achieving his greatest critical and popular success, *The French Lieutenant's Woman* (1969), a love story set in Victorian times, complicated at times by the author's commentary and the presentation of alternative endings. The

book won the WH Smith literary award, sold in large numbers, and was successfully adapted as a film by Harold Pinter. The expectations raised by the success of this book were never quite realised by his later novels, but he did not stop writing, producing some local histories, adaptations, and memoirs. Died 5 November.

Fry, Christopher (b. 1907), English playwright whose optimistic verse plays were welcomed in the immediate aftermath of war but later seemed dated and irrelevant. Born in Bristol, Christopher Harris (he took his mother's maiden name, Fry, because of its Quaker associations) was educated at Bedford Modern School and, though starting to write poetry in his teens, did not do so seriously until he was asked to write a drama in verse for a church jubilee. The play was *The Boy With A Cart,* which was performed by amateurs in the Sussex village where he lived in 1938, and by professionals at the Lyric Theatre, Hammersmith, in 1950. As a Quaker, Fry was a conscientious objector during World War II, serving as a non-combatant while also a director of the Oxford Repertory Players. In 1946 he wrote a verse play, *A Phoenix Too Frequent*, which was produced at the Mercury Theatre, and after joining the Arts Theatre in London he wrote *The Lady's Not for Burning*, which was produced there in 1948, then transferred to the Globe Theatre with John Gielgud in the lead as a soldier disillusioned by war and wanting to commit suicide and Pamela Brown as a girl about to be burned as a witch bur desperate to stay alive. The play's combination of optimism, wit, and verbal fireworks was gratefully received by audiences weary of war and austerity, as was the second in the tetralogy of the seasons, *Venus Observed* (1950), with Laurence Olivier playing the lead; the two that followed, *The Dark is Light Enough* (1954) and *A Yard of Sun*, which was not completed until 1970, seemed not just out of fashion but lacking in inspiration. Fry turned to translation and scriptwriting for films and television. Died 30 June.

Garang de Mabior, Lieutenant-General John (b. 1945), rebel leader who became Vice-President of Sudan. Garang was born in the Upper Nile region, into a Christian family of cattle herders. Orphaned, he was sent to school by relatives and won a scholarship to Grinnell College, Iowa, USA. He returned to Sudan, where he had already been involved in the rebel southern movement in the 1960s. With the peace agreement of 1972 that offered the south autonomy from the Arabic north, he joined the Sudanese armed forces, travelling to the USA for advanced military training in Fort Benning, Georgia, and to take a PhD in economics at Iowa State University, before returning to Sudan in 1981. When the peace agreement collapsed in 1983 with moves to impose Islamic (Sharia) law throughout the country, Garang joined the southern rebels and, with Ethopian backing, became head of the Sudan People's Liberation Army which he built into a significant military force and, eventually, into a political organisation. In 2002 Garang entered peace negotiations with Sudanese President Omar Bashir in a bid to end two decades of civil war. Under the terms of the comprehensive peace agreement of January 2005 he became Vice President of Sudan on 9 July but was killed three weeks later in a helicopter crash. Died 30 July.

Giulini, Carlo Maria (b. 1914), leading Italian conductor whose striving for perfection limited his operatic repertoire. Born in Barletta, he attended the Santa Cecilia Academy in Rome, joining the Augusteo Orchestra as viola player at the age of eight-

een. He was conscripted into the Italian Army during World War II but deserted and remained in hiding until war ended. In 1946 he became principal conductor of the Italian Radio Orchestra in Rome, and in 1950 founded the Radio Orchestra in Milan. He made his opera debut with Verdi's *La Traviata* at Bergamo in 1951, with Maria Callas singing Violetta. He worked with Callas again in Gluck's *Alceste* after he moved to La Scala as principal conductor in 1953. He made his debut at Covent Garden with Verdi's *Don Carlos* in 1956, and in the same year became guest conductor of the British Philharmonia orchestra, making many recordings with it, including one of Mozart's *Marriage of Figaro* for which he required more than 100 hours of rehearsal. From 1973 to 1976 Giulini was principal guest conductor of the Chicago Symphony Orchestra, and in 1978 moved to Los Angeles, after the Symphony Orchestra there agreed to give him proper rehearsal time. His failure to get sufficient rehearsal time from opera houses caused him to abandon opera for fourteen years until 1982, when he was persuaded to conduct *Falstaff* in Los Angeles, Covent Garden, and Florence. Died 14 June.

Goncalves, Vasco dos Santos (b. 1921), Portuguese General who was Prime Minister during the aftermath of the 1974 "Carnation Revolution". Educated at the Military College, Goncalves joined the Portuguese Army in 1942, rising to the rank of colonel in the 1960s and becoming one of the leaders of the Movement of the Armed Forces, a group of officers from the Portuguese army stationed in Africa. They launched a successful coup against the dictator, Marcelo Caetano, in 1974, when soldiers handed out carnations to people celebrating in the streets. Goncalves, appointed Prime Minister in 1974, embarked on a policy of decolonisation, beginning with Mozambique and Guinea-Bissau, followed by Angola and East Timor, and pursued Marxist policies at home, handing over private property to farmers' co-operatives and nationalising banks. It was a period of turmoil, and he was soundly defeated by the Socialist party of Mario Soares in 1976. Though no longer actively involved in Portguese politics, he continued to defend his policies, which even his supporters came to accept would not have been in Portugal's best interests had they all been put into practice. Died 11 June.

Goodpaster, Andrew (b. 1915), US General who was Supreme Allied Commander in Europe 1969-74. Born in Granite City, Illinois, he was educated locally and at West Point, commanding an engineer battalion in North Africa and Italy during World War II, when he was twice wounded and was awarded the distinguished service cross, a silver star and two purple hearts. When General Dwight Eisenhower went to Paris as NATO's Supreme Commander in Europe in 1950, Goodpaster was appointed assistant to his chief-of-staff, and on becoming President in 1953 Eisenhower made Goodpaster his defence liaison officer. He remained in the White House for the rest of Eisenhower's term, and for a short time in 1955, when the President was recovering from a stroke, was said to be virtually running the country. He was appointed assistant to the Joint Chiefs of Staff in 1962 and its director in 1966. Soon after President Richard Nixon took office he was appointed Supreme Allied Commander in Europe, his knowledge of the way Washington worked standing him in good stead with Congress at a time when there were strong moves to cut the US contribution to NATO. After his retirement Goodpaster became chairman of the Atlantic Council, and in 1996 he joined with some other retired generals and admirals from the USA, Russia, and Britain in calling for the elimination of all nuclear arsenals. Died 16 May.

Gray, Louis Patrick (b. 1916), acting director of the FBI whose career was wrecked by the Watergate scandal. Born in St Louis, he was educated at Rice University and the US Naval Academy, serving in the Pacific during the Second World War and as a submarine captain during the Korean War. After retiring from the Navy he practised law, and was appointed head of the civil division of the Justice Department and assistant Attorney-General in 1971 and acting head of the Federal Bureau of Investigation (FBI) in 1972, succeeding J. Edgar Hoover a few months before the Watergate break-in became public. Gray provided the US presidency with FBI files on the investigation, but refused demands to dismiss his deputy, W. Mark Felt, on suspicion of leaking secrets to the press. When he came before the Senate to be confirmed in his appointment Gray revealed that the White House counsel, John Dean, had sat in on FBI interviews with White House suspects, which gave new impetus to the Watergate investigation. Gray's nomination as director of the FBI was withdrawn and he resigned in 1973. He was indicted for alleged conspiracy in 1978, but the indictment was dismissed in 1980 at the request of the prosecution. It was only revealed that Felt was "deep throat"—the main source of the *Washington Post*'s revelations—shortly before Gray's death. He attributed his deputy's actions to resentment at being passed over for the FBI directorship. Died 6 July.

Haynes, Johnny (b. 1934), footballer who played for Fulham and captained England on twenty-two occasions. Born in Kentish Town, London, Haynes demonstrated his talent at an early age, joining the ground staff at Fulham at the age of fifteen and making his debut with the first team—then in the second division—in 1952. He played for the England team two years later. An inside forward and brilliant passer of the ball, Haynes was capped fifty-six times, scoring eighteen goals including a hat-trick against the Soviet Union in 1958 and two in a 9-3 victory against Scotland in 1961. He captained England in the world cup in Chile in 1962, but the team lost in the quarter finals to the eventual champions, Brazil. Later in 1962 Haynes was badly injured in a car crash, and did not play for England again, though he recovered sufficiently to return to the domestic game for Fulham. Aside from his football skill, he will be remembered as the first player in the English game to be paid more than £20 a week, which was the maximum allowed until his colleague, Jimmy Hill, successfully campaigned against it. Haynes became the first to benefit when the Fulham chairman, Tommy Trinder, agreed to pay him £100. Died 18 October.

Heath, Sir Edward KG, PC, MBE (b. 1916), British Prime Minister who took the country into the EEC but whose administration foundered in the misery of the three-day week. Born in Broadstairs, Heath was educated at Chatham House grammar school in Ramsgate and at Balliol College, Oxford, where he gained an organ scholarship. Though musically accomplished, his main concern at Oxford was politics. He was president of the Union and of the University Conservative Association, but opposed the policy of appeasement and the Munich agreement. When war broke out he fought with the Royal Artillery, was mentioned in dispatches, appointed MBE (military), and left with the rank of lieutenant-colonel. As Conservative candidate he won the marginal Bexley seat in 1950 and within

a year had been appointed an assistant whip. He became joint deputy chief whip during Churchill's last government and chief whip under Anthony Eden. He joined the Cabinet as Minister of Labour under Harold Macmillan and held a succession of other ministerial posts until the 1964 election, which the Conservatives lost. In 1965 he defeated Reginald Maudling for the party leadership and became Prime Minister after the 1970 election. He saw his immediate task as that of getting Britain into Europe, which he succeeded in doing in 1972. Life at home was more difficult. In Northern Ireland the Parliament at Stormont was suspended as terrorist activity increased, while strikes by dockers and miners forced the declaration of two states of emergency and the introduction of a three-day working week. The almost inevitable result was the calling of an election on the theme of "who governs Britain?". When it came, in February 1974, Labour won four seats more than the Conservatives and were confirmed in office with a more convincing win in the second election that year. Heath was now seen as a loser, and was challenged, and defeated, for the party leadership by Margaret Thatcher. He remained a critical and somewhat resentful presence in the House of Commons until 2001, when he retired as Father of the House. Outside politics he was an enthusiastic sailor, winning the Sydney-Hobart race in his yacht *Morning Cloud* in 1969 and captaining the British team (when he was Prime Minister) to win the Admiral's Cup in 1971. He also took great solace in music. He was appointed a Knight of the Garter in 1992. Died 17 July.

Heckmair, Anderl (b. 1906), mountaineer who led the first successful ascent of the north face of the Eiger. Born in Munich, Heckmair was raised in an orphanage after his father had been killed in World War I. Eschewing regular work, he spent his youth as an impoverished climber, and by the mid-1930s had conquered a number of challenging European peaks. In 1937 he served as a mountain guide for the film-maker Leni Riefenstahl and the two developed a close relationship thereafter. Through her he met Hitler, although Heckmair showed no interest in politics and did not join the Nazi party. In 1938 he took up a post at the Ordensburg (physical training colleges for Nazi elite) at Sonthofen where he teamed up with fellow climber Ludwig Vörg. The two men embarked upon their ascent of the Eiger's north face, a sheer 5,905ft wall of crumbling limestone, on 22 July 1938. Using 12-point crampons for the first time (which were to revolutionise ice climbing by negating the need to cut each step with an ice axe) the German pair moved with remarkable speed and soon caught up with a pair of Austrian climbers—Heinrich Harrer and Fritz Kasparek—who had set off the previous day. The four men teamed up—a decision seen as personifying the recent Anschluss—with Heckmair taking the lead. They reached the summit on 24 July and were subsequently feted as heroes by the Nazi regime. After the outbreak of war Heckmair, who was considered politically unreliable, was posted to the Eastern front (where Vörg was killed) but was later transferred to a mountain training unit near Innsbruck for the remainder of the war. Afterwards he worked as a mountain guide in the Bavarian resort of Oberstdorf and helped found Germany's professional mountain and ski guides' association. He wrote several books on mountaineering and undertook further climbs in Europe and the Americas. Died 1 February.

Johnson, Philip (b. 1906), controversial US architect, museum curator, and critic. Born in Cleveland, Ohio, to a wealthy family

Philip Johnson was educated privately and at Harvard, interrupted by prolonged visits to Europe, where he came under the influence of the art historian Alfred Barr, who in 1928 was commissioned to create the Museum of Modern Art in New York. Johnson was appointed its first director of architecture, in 1932 arranging an exhibition on modern architecture for the museum, following it up two years later with *The Machine Age*, which celebrated the design of modern household and industrial objects. Back in Europe in 1933, Johnson was present at Hitler's Potsdam rally, became sympathetic to fascism and formed a political party modelled on Hitler's National Socialists. It was, as Johnson later described it, a time when he lost his mind. He recovered it in 1940 by returning to Harvard to study architecture, and after two years in the US Army set up a practice in New York. His first significant building was the Glass House which he built for himself in Connecticut with walls of glass supported by steel pillars. In 1956 he collaborated with Ludwig Mies van der Rohe on the Seagram building in New York, later forming a partnership with John Burgee to produce buildings such as the Crystal Cathedral in California, the AT&T building (later the Sony building) in New York, and the 1986 office block popularly known as the Lipstick Building, before setting up on his own in 1992, at the age of eighty-six. Died 25 January.

Kennan, George (b. 1904), US diplomat who, as a specialist in Russian affairs, devised the policy of "containment" of Stalin's Soviet Union in the immediate postwar years. Born in Milwaukee he was educated at St John's Military Academy in Wisconsin and at Princeton University, joining the foreign service in 1926 and being posted to Moscow in 1933. When war broke out he was sent to Berlin as first secretary, and was interned for six months when the USA entered the war. After his release he served in Lisbon and in Moscow again in 1944-46, and it was there, as minister-counsellor, that he wrote what came to be known as the "long telegram", an 8,000 word dispatch warning that the Soviet Union was hostile to the USA because it wished to expand Communist influence, and suggesting that this threat should be met by containment rather than by confrontation. As part of this policy, the Marshall Plan was devised to help countries threatened by Communist takeover, and Kennan was put in charge of the planning process. Posted to Moscow again as ambassador in 1952, he was declared persona non grata and left in 1953, retiring from the service. He continued to make his influence felt through teaching, through speeches and lectures (he delivered the Reith Lectures for the BBC in 1957) and through articles and books — he was awarded Pulitzer prizes in 1956 for his book *Russia Leaves the War* in 1956 and again for his *Memoirs 1925-1950* published in 1967, some years after he had rejoined the foreign service for a short time as ambassador to Yugoslavia. Kennan was awarded the presidential medal of freedom in 1989. Died 17 March.

Kilby, Jack (b. 1923), US physicist who won the Nobel Prize for his invention of the microchip. Born in Missouri and brought up in Grand Bend, Kansas, he was educated at the University of Illinois, interrupted by war service, which he spent in the US Army. After completing his degree he went on to the University of Wisconsin to study electrical engineering, working at the same time for an electronic components manufacturer in Milwaukee. In 1958 he moved to Dallas, Texas, to work for Texas Instruments where he developed an integrated circuit (the microchip), which made possible the revolution in information technology. Kilby

moved on to develop military systems and computers incorporating integrated circuits, as well as working on the first pocket calculator and thermal printer, and in the development of silicon technology for the generation of electricity from solar power. From 1978 to 1984 he was professor of electrical engineering at Texas A&M University, remaining as consultant with Texas Instruments. He shared the Nobel Prize for Physics for his revolutionary work in electronics in 2000, and held more than sixty patents during his lifetime. Died 20 June.

King Fahd ibn Abdul Aziz Al Saud, (b. about 1922), ruler of Saudi Arabia who maintained absolute control of his wealthy country until a stroke forced him to hand over power. Born in Riyadh, Fahd was the tenth son of the emir Abdul Aziz ibn Saud, who proclaimed himself king of Jedda (later Saudi Arabia) after defeating the Hashemite Sharif Hussein of Mecca. Fahd was appointed governor of the northern province of Jauf in 1942 and later Minister of Education and, when Crown Prince Faisal had come to power, Minister of the Interior. When Faisal was assassinated in 1975 and Prince Khalid became king, Fahd was appointed Crown Prince, taking advantage of the country's new oil-based wealth to build new cities and industries with modern communications as well as schools, universities, and hospitals. He also promised political reform, but when he succeeded to the throne in 1982 he acted for the most part as absolute ruler. When, in 1993, he finally created a consultative assembly (thirty years after it had been promised), it was composed solely of members he appointed. On the other hand, Fahd did always consult with other princes, which often led to lengthy delays in decisions, notably at the time of the Iraqi invasion of Kuwait, though once he made up his mind Saudi Arabia opened the country to US and British troops in spite of widespread Arab support for Saddam Hussein. Even when the oil market was depressed, Fahd continued to increase spending on defence, and the inevitable cuts in social spending provoked opposition (mainly aimed at western targets), and the rise of al-Qaida terrorism. When he suffered a stroke in 1995 Fahd handed over most of his powers to his half-brother, Crown Prince Abdullah, though he was still consulted on major issues. Died 1 August.

King of Wartnaby, Lord (b. 1917), British industrialist who turned British Airways into a profitable airline. Born in Farnborough, Oxfordshire, John King was educated in the village school at Banbury and, when the family moved to Surrey, at Dunsfold. In 1945 he bought a motor repair business, merged it with another, Pollard, and moved the works to Ferrybridge, near Pontefract in Yorkshire, concentrating the business on the production of ball-bearings. The business was successful and made King a millionaire, a fortune which was greatly increased when Pollard was sold. In 1972 he became chairman of Babcock and Wilcox (subsequently the Babcock International Group) and in 1979 was brought in to supervise the dismantling of the National Enterprise Board. He was appointed chairman of the state-owned British Airways in 1981 at a time when it was a demoralised organisation, badly run and making huge losses. King reduced the staff level by more than one-third, replaced many senior managers and sold unwanted aircraft and other assets. By 1983 BA had been brought back into profit and in 1987 was successfully floated as a public company. Though King's ruthlessness had paid off, he at times overstepped the mark, as with a "dirty tricks" attempt to put Virgin Airlines out of business, which ended

in court with BA being forced to pay large damages and costs, and King having to apologise. He gave up the chairmanship soon afterwards, becoming president emeritus, and retired to farm his large estate in Leicestershire, where he also hunted with the Belvoir, of which he was Master for some fourteen years. He was created a life peer in 1983. Died 12 July.

Lane, Lord, PC, AFC (b. 1918), Lord Chief Justice of England 1980-92. Born in Derby, Geoffrey Dawson Lane was educated at Shrewsbury School and Trinity College, Cambridge. He served as a pilot in the RAF during the war and was awarded the Air Force cross. On D-Day he flew a Dakota carrying paratroops to the landing beaches, and later towed a glider on the operation at Arnhem. He was called to the Bar in 1946, took silk in 1962 and was recorder for Bedford from 1963 until 1966, when he was appointed a High Court judge. He was a member of the parole board 1970-72, went to the Court of Appeal in 1974 and was made a lord of appeal in ordinary in 1979. In the following year he succeeded Lord Widgery as Lord Chief Justice. During his time in this office he worked to improve the administration of the courts, set up guidelines for sentencing, and put an end to the law that ruled that a man could not be guilty of raping his wife, while concentrating mainly on criminal work. When he dismissed the appeal of the Birmingham Six in 1988, and in the following year that of the three men imprisoned for the murder of PC Keith Blakelock—decisions that were both reversed in subsequent appeals—Lane became associated in the public mind with inadequacies in the justice system. There was a call by more than 100 MPs for his resignation, and soon after the Royal Commission on Criminal Justice was set up, in 1991, Lane retired. Died 22 August.

Lange, David, CH (b.1942), New Zealand lawyer and politician who was Prime Minister from 1984 to 1989. Born in Auckland, he worked as a barrister and solicitor at the New Zealand Supreme Court before setting up a legal practice in Auckland. He was elected to the House of Representatives in 1977 as a member of the Labour Party, and within two years became deputy leader. He was elected party leader in 1983 and Prime Minister after winning the election of 1984. Faced with a run on the New Zealand dollar he devalued the currency, reduced government spending, and imposed wage restraints but remained popular in his country, largely because of his stand against nuclear weapons, which brought him into conflict with the USA and the formal removal of New Zealand from Anzus. Lange was re-elected in 1987 but his popularity declined as his party split over his economic policies. He resigned as Prime Minister in 1989 and retired from Parliament in 1996. Died 13 August.

Lichfield, the Earl of (b. 1939), English aristocrat who became a highly successful photographer. The son of Viscount Anson and his wife Anne (née Bowes-Lyon, who subsequently married Prince George of Denmark), Thomas Patrick John Anson was brought up at the family seat, Shugborough Hall in Staffordshire, and educated at Harrow and Sandhurst. Commissioned into the Grenadier Guards in 1959 he succeeded to the title, as fifth earl, in 1960, on the death of his grandfather (his father having died in the previous year), remaining in the army until 1962, when he began work as a professional photographer, specialising in portraits of debutantes, attractive women, and the royal family. He quickly built up a portfolio which was reproduced in a number of books, including *The Most Beautiful Women* (1981), *Lichfield on Photography* (1981), *A Royal Album* (1982), *Lichfield on Travel Photography* (1986), and an autobiography *Not The Whole Truth* (1986). In 1992 he was seriously hurt in a fall at his house on the island of Mustique, where he spent much of his time when not at his apartment at Shugborough Hall (now owned by the National Trust). Died 11 November.

Liu Binyan (b. 1925), Chinese journalist whose criticisms of the Communist regime forced him into exile. Born in Changchun in north-east China, he was educated at the local school in an area that was then under Japanese control. Liu joined the Communist Party and, when the People's Republic was established in 1949, joined the staff of *China Youth News*, the official organ for Chinese youth. When he wrote articles drawing attention to official corruption he was condemned as a "rightist" and sent to live in the country. He was brought back after the death of Mao Zedong in 1976 and began again to write articles exposing corruption among party officials, becoming vice-chairman of the Chinese writers' association when it was permitted to elect its own leaders. His continuing complaints about the slow pace of political reform, as opposed to the economic, began to incur the anger of Deng Xiaoping and he was one of those on whom Deng publicly imposed silence. Eventually Liu was allowed to leave the country, settling in the USA, where he continued to write critically of events in China. He was never allowed to return home. Died 5 December.

Maskhadov, Aslan (b. 1951), commander of the Chechen separatist army who became the republic's first elected President. Born in exile in Kazakhstan, Maskhadov returned with his family in 1957, when the Chechen-Ingush republic was established, and was educated locally before attending the Tbilisi Artillery Academy. He served with the Soviet Army until the break-up of the Soviet Union in 1992, returning to Chechnya, which had declared its independence from Moscow. When Russian troops crossed into Chechnya in 1994 Maskhadov organised the resistance, avoiding pitched battles after the Russians had captured Grozny, but harassing them with guerrilla attacks until the capital was recaptured in 1996, when he signed a ceasefire. In elections held in 1997 Maskhadov was elected President and in May signed a peace treaty with the Russian President, Boris Yeltsin, but he was unable to maintain control over some of the radical elements in Chechnya and some fundamentalist Muslims. The subsequent breakdown in law and order paralysed Maskhadov's attempts to attract foreign investment and recognition of Chechnya's independence, and when in 1999 Russian troops were sent across the border by Yeltsin's successor, Vladimir Putin, Maskhadov went into hiding with a price on his head. He was shot by Russian special forces. Died 8 March.

McCarthy, Eugene (b. 1916), US Senator who ran unsuccessfully for the presidency on three occasions. Born in Watkins, Minnesota, he was educated at St John's University, Collegeville, and at Minnesota University before training initially as a Benedictine monk, then as a secular priest but finally becoming a professor of economics at St John's. From there he entered politics, becoming a Democratic congressman in 1949. Ten years later he won a tough campaign, against two rivals from his own party as well as a two-term Republican incumbent, for the Senate. With his political blood up he campaigned in 1968 for the Democratic presidential nomination, first against Robert Kennedy and then, after Kennedy's assassination, against Hubert Humphrey, who won the nomination but

lost the election to Richard Nixon. McCarthy then ran for the presidency twice more, in 1976 and 1992, as a Liberal Independent. In addition to his political preoccupations McCarthy also had a literary bent. He was a director of the publishers Harcourt Brace Jovanovich and wrote poetry as well as a number of political books, notably *Frontiers in American Democracy* (1960), *The Limits of Power: America's Role in the World* (1967), and *Up 'Til Now: A Memoir of the Decline of American Politics* (1987). Died 10 December.

Merchant, Ismail, (b. 1936), Indian film producer who, with James Ivory, was responsible for a series of successful period films. Born in Bombay, Ismail Abdul Rehman (Merchant was adopted later) was educated at St Xavier's College and at New York University. An avid film-goer, he was determined to make his own and began, when working with an advertising agency in New York, with a short, *The Creation of Woman*, in 1960. Nominated for an Academy Award as the best short film and shown at the Cannes Film Festival, its success took him to Los Angeles, where he joined up with the US director James Ivory to set up Merchant Ivory Productions. Together they persuaded the writer Ruth Prawer Jhabvala to adapt her novel *The Householder* for a film they made in 1963, and she went on to write scripts for most of their films. The next was *Shakespeare Wallah* (1965) the story of an acting troupe travelling through India. Subsequent films on Indian subjects were less successful and it was not until they turned to making detailed, often slow-moving, period pieces that they achieved lasting success. They began with an adaptation of the Henry James novel *The Europeans* (1979), followed by *Heat and Dust* (1981), *The Bostonians* (1983), by three E.M. Forster adaptations—*A Room With a*

View (1985), *Maurice* (1987), and *Howard's End* (1992), which between them won six Oscars—and by *The Remains of the Day* (1993), from the novel by Kazuo Ishiguro. In some later films Merchant took to directing, including *The Mystic Masseur* (2001), and in 2002 he wrote a memoire, *My Passage from India*. Died 25 May.

Miller, Arthur (b. 1915), US playwright whose early plays, *Death of a Salesman* and *The Crucible*, established his reputation and continue to be revived. Born on the upper east side of New York he was brought up in Brooklyn. After trying a number of jobs he went to the University of Michigan to study English, taking a job in the Brooklyn Navy Yard when he graduated, while also writing scripts for CBS radio. His first play, *The Man Who Had All the Luck*, was produced on Broadway in 1944 but ran for only four performances. This was followed in 1947 by *All My Sons*, which won the New York drama critics' award and a Tony award, and, in 1949, by *Death of a Salesman*, which ran for more than eighteen months on Broadway, was made into a film and won him a Pulitzer Prize. Both plays were essentially family dramas, whereas his next, *The Crucible*, first produced in 1953, had a broader political base, retelling the story of the seventeenth-century Salem witch-hunt with obvious reference to Senator McCarthy's investigation of Communist activities in the 1950s. Miller was called before the House committee on unAmerican activities in 1956 and was cited for contempt of Congress when he refused to name people he had seen at a Communist writers' meeting. Fined and given a suspended prison sentence, his conviction was overturned on appeal to the Supreme Court. Meanwhile Miller was hitting the headlines for another reason. While on a visit to Hollywood he had met the actress Marilyn Monroe and

married her after divorcing his first wife in 1956. The very public marriage lasted five years, during which time Miller adapted his short story, *The Misfits*, as a screenplay which was to become Monroe's last film. Miller continued to write plays, including the semi-autobiographical *After the Fall* (1964), but none had the success of the earlier dramas. Died 10 February.

Mills, Sir John, CBE (b. 1908), British actor renowned for his portrayal of the average decent Englishman. Born in North Eltham, Suffolk, he had his first taste of acting at Sir John Leman School in Beccles (Puck in *A Midsummer Night's Dream*, a role he was to repeat professionally at the Old Vic in 1939). He started professionally as a song-and-dance man but soon joined a repertory company touring the far east, where he was seen by Noel Coward who gave him a part in the London production of *Cavalcade*. Mills made his first mark in films in 1935 with *Brown on Resolution*, the C.S. Forester story of an able seaman holding up a German warship with a rifle. After briefly serving in the Army at the outbreak of war Mills was invalided out and soon began, with Coward's *In Which We Serve* (1942), a series of war films which established his heroic reputation, among them *This Happy Breed*, *The Way to the Stars*, *Above Us the Waves*, *The Colditz Story*, *Ice Cold in Alex*, and *Tunes of Glory*. In 1968 he gave a memorable performance as Field Marshal Haig in the film version of *Oh! What a Lovely War* and there were other demanding roles in films that enhanced his distinction as an actor, including Pip in *Great Expectations*, Alfred Polly in *The History of Mr Polly*, and the village idiot in *Ryan's Daughter*, for which he was awarded an Oscar as best supporting actor in 1971. In spite of his film succcesses Mills did not desert the stage, performing in Terence Rattigan's *Separate*

Tables at the Apollo London in 1977 and at the National Theatre in Brian Clark's *The Petititon* in 1986. Died 23 April.

Montefiore, the Right Reverend Hugh (b. 1920), former Bishop of Birmingham whose intellectual energy and original thinking often aroused controversy. Born in Bayswater to a Jewish family, he converted to Christianity while at Rugby School. He spent a year at St John's College, Oxford, until war broke out, when he was commissioned in the Royal Artillery and saw service in India. Returning to Oxford he read theology and moved on to Westcott House, Cambridge, to prepare for holy orders. After two years in a parish in the north of England he returned to Westcott as chaplain and tutor, and in 1953 as vice-principal. From 1954 to 1963 he was fellow and dean of Caius College and in 1963 became vicar of Great St Mary's, the university church in Cambridge, where he maintained its tradition of originality and new Christian thinking, but also caused offence by suggesting, at a conference in 1967, that Jesus might have been homosexual in nature. The controversy this aroused might have kept him from further advancement, but his energy and constantly inquiring mind made him someone the Church could not ignore. He was elected to the Convocation of Canterbury in 1966, appointed an honorary canon of Ely Cathedral in 1969, consecrated suffragan bishop of Kingston in 1970, and Bishop of Birmingham in 1978 in spite of the opposition of some local MPs and media, who feared his radicalism. He held the post with distinction until he felt compelled to retire early (in 1987) because of his wife's illness, though he continued to write, his later books including *Credible Christianity* (1992), *Oh God, What Next?* (1994), and *On Being a Jewish Christian* (1998). Died 13 May.

Motley, Constance Baker (b. 1921), staunch supporter of the civil rights movement of the 1960s, she was the first black woman to become a US federal judge. Born in New Haven, Connecticut, she was educated at a black college in Nashville, at New York University, and at Columbia Law School. She became legal counsel for the National Association for the Advancement of Coloured People, working as attorney in many school desegregation cases in the southern states, including that of James Meredith, the black student who in 1962 sought to gain admission to the University of Mississippi, finally winning the case after a court battle lasting some sixteen months. In the following year she successfully represented a thousand black children in Birmingham, Alabama, who had been suspended from school for taking part in civil rights demonstrations. Motley was appointed a judge in the southern district of New York in 1966 and became chief judge there in 1982. She was installed in the US national women's hall of fame in 1993. Died 21 September.

Mowlam, Mo, PC (b. 1949), Labour MP who was Secretary of State for Northern Ireland 1997-98. Born in Watford, christened Marjorie but always known as Mo, she was educated locally and Durham University, then went to the USA to obtain a doctorate at Iowa University. She taught for a while at Florida State University before returning to the UK to lecture on politics. She joined the Labour Party and in 1987 was elected to Parliament as member for Redcar, and within a year had been appointed opposition spokesman on Northern Ireland and subsequently on city and corporate affairs. She became a member of the shadow Cabinet in 1992 and of the party's national executive in 1997 and, when Labour was returned to power that year, was appointed Secretary of

State for Northern Ireland, at a time when she had just completed a course of radiotherapy for a benign brain tumour. During her time in the office she restored the IRA (the Provisional Irish Republican Army) ceasefire and brought Sinn Féin into talks about the political future, her energy and determination raising hopes that real progress was about to be made. However she lost the confidence of the Ulster Unionists and much of the work that led to the "Good Friday" agreement of 1998 was done directly with the Prime Minister's office. Later in that year she was moved to the position of Minister for the Cabinet Office and Chancellor of the Duchy of Lancaster, but was dissatisfied with the post and retired from Parliament in 2001, publishing her memoirs, *Momentum*, in 2002. Died 19 August.

Narayanan, Kocheril Raman (b. 1920), Indian diplomat who was President of his country 1997-2002. Born a Dalit (formerly "untouchable") in the village of Uzhavoor in Kerala, he was educated at the University of Travanscore and at the London School of Economics. He joined the Indian Foreign Service in 1949, serving in Rangoon, Tokyo, London, Canberra, and Hanoi, before becoming ambassador to Thailand in 1967, to Turkey in 1973, to China in 1976, and to the USA in 1980. He was elected to the Lok Sabba, the Indian parliament, in 1984, was appointed Minister for Planning in 1985, for External Affairs in 1985, and for Science and Technology in 1986. He became Vice-President of India in 1992 and President in 1997. Though normally a ceremonial post it became, during Narayanan's time, more politically involved because many of his governments were coalitions, and he had twice during his term to dissolve the Lok Sabba because no politician could retain its confidence. He retired from the presidency in 2002. Died 9 November.

Nilsson, Birgit (b. 1918), Swedish soprano whose powerful voice excelled in Wagnerian operas. Born in Vastra Karup, on the coast near Malmo, she studied at the Royal Academy of Music in Stockholm and made her formal debut in 1947 with the role of Lady Macbeth in the Verdi opera, with Fritz Busch conducting. She made her UK debut at Glyndebourne in 1951, as Electra in Mozart's *Idomeneo*, and began a long association with Bayreuth in 1954 as Elsa in Wagner's *Lohengrin*. In 1955 she sang Brunnhilde in a complete *Ring* cycle at Munich, returning to Bayreuth to sing Sieglinde, Brunnhilde, and Isolde in succeeding years, her pure, unforced voice soaring comfortably and with precision through the great orchestras. In addition to the Wagnerian roles she particularly excelled in Puccini's *Turandot*, Richard Strauss's *Elektra*, and as Leonore in Beethoven's *Fidelio*. Nilsson retired from the stage in 1982, but she left memorable recordings of the *Ring* cycle, with the Vienna Philharmonic Orchestra, of Strauss's *Salome* and *Elektra*, and of *Turandot*. Died 25 December.

Obote, Milton (b. 1924), former President of Uganda who led his country to independence but was twice forced into exile. Born in Akokoro in the Lango district of northern Uganda, he was educated locally and at Makerere College in Kampala, which he left without taking a degree. In 1957 he set up a branch of the Uganda National Congress (UNC) in Lango and in 1958 was elected to represent the district in the country's Legislative Council. He left the UNC in 1959 to form the Uganda People's Congress (UPC) and an uneasy alliance with the Kabaka of Buganda. When Uganda achieved independence in 1962 Obote became Prime Minister, later adding the portfolios of Defence and Foreign Affairs. He appointed Idi Amin to take charge of the army and himself to be President with full powers and, when the Kabaka objected, ordered Amin to attack his palace, forcing the Kabaka to flee. A five-year development plan was launched and Uganda seemed set on a period of stability when, in 1970, while Obote was attending a conference in Singapore, Amin seized power, imposed martial law, and instituted his reign of terror. Obote went into exile in Tanzania until, in 1979, Amin was overthrown by the Tanzanian army. Obote resumed his presidency when the UPC won elections in the following year. Another development plan, including currency flotation, the return of Asians expelled by Amin, and a programme of privatisation, was introduced, but growing disorder throughout the country, fuelled by alleged vote-rigging, led in 1985 to a second coup against Obote, who was eventually given asylum in Zambia. Died 10 October.

Packer, Kerry, AC (b. 1937), Australian businessman, media proprietor, and sportsman who revolutionised international cricket. Born in Sydney, Packer was educated at Cranbrook School in Sydney and at Geelong Grammar in Victoria, taking control of the Packer media interests in newspapers, television, radio, and magazines on the death of his father, which with other business and property assets quickly established him as his country's wealthiest man. He was also a gambler, winning and losing huge sums of money at the races and at blackjack. His impact on international cricket began in 1977, when thirty-five of the world's best cricketers signed contracts with him to play a series of one-day matches in Australia. The games, which came to be called World Series Cricket, set a new style, many of the matches being played at night to ensure a large television audience, but they were opposed by the cricket authorities, who imposed a ban on Packer players. Taken to court, their action was ruled illegal, and one-day cricket became immensely popular. In 1979 a compromise was reached: Packer disbanded his World Series and was given exclusive rights to televise cricket in Australia, and an undertaking that no player would be victimised. Packer then took up polo in a typically grand way, but suffered a heart attack on the field in 1991, and was affected by further cardiac and other health problems for the rest of his life. He was appointed a Companion of the Order of Australia in 1983. Died 26 December.

Paolozzi, Sir Eduardo, CBE (b. 1924), sculptor who liked to find a use for everything and was one of the initiators of pop art. Born to Italian parents in Edinburgh, he was educated locally but spent most of his holidays in Italy, and when war broke out he was interned for three months before serving in the Pioneer Corps. He later studied at the Slade School of Art and left for Paris in 1947 after holding a one-man exhibition in London. Though he consorted with many French artists, and began his association with surrealism, he found the going hard until he returned to London in 1950. Here he developed the style of sculpture most associated with him, using odd bits of machinery and other discarded objects, often casting them in aluminium and then welding them together, as well as producing collages that developed pop art images from advertisements, comic strips, and other popular culture. He was given major exhibitions at the Museum of Modern Art in New York in 1964 and at the Tate in London in 1971, and his commissioned work included cast-aluminium doors for the Hunterian Art Gallery in Glasgow, the mosaic redecoration of Tottenham Court Road underground station, and the bronze of Sir Isaac Newton in the forecourt of the British Library. He was knighted in 1989. Died 22 April.

Parks, Rosa (b. 1913), US black woman whose refusal to give up her seat to a white man on an Alabama bus set alight the civil rights movement. Born in Tuskegee, Alabama, Rosa Louise McCauley was educated locally and at Alabama State College. She worked as a seamstress, marrying, in 1932, Raymond Parks, a local barber. Both worked at times for civil rights causes, but the incident that made Rosa Parks famous was not a deliberate act of civil rights defiance. On a December evening in 1955 she had boarded a bus in downtown Montgomery and, as was the custom, took a seat at the back. When the front seats reserved for whites became full, and a white man was left standing, the bus driver ordered Parks to give up her seat, which meant that she would have to stand, as the seats for blacks were also full. She refused, the police were summoned, she was arrested and fined US$14, which she refused to pay. Her arrest set off a year-long boycott of Alabama's buses, organised by the Montgomery Improvement Association, of which the young Martin Luther King became leader. The case ultimately went to the Supreme Court, which ruled, in December 1956, that the state's segregation laws were illegal. Popularly known as the "mother of the civil rights movement", Parks was awarded the presidential medal of freedom in 1996 and the congressional gold medal in 1999. Died 24 October.

Parrinder, Edward Geoffrey Simons (b. 1910), scholar of world religions and venerable contributor to *The Annual Register*. Born into a Methodist family, Geoffrey Parrinder attended school at Leighton-on-Sea, Essex, but left aged sixteen to work as a railway clerk. After training for the Wesleyan Methodist ministry, he went to French West Africa in 1933, where his missionary work continued intermittently until 1946. During this time he took London University degrees externally, completing a PhD from his empirical research on the indigenous religions of West Africa. His book *Religion in an African City* (1953) earned him a doctorate of divinity from London University. Between 1949 and 1958 he was lecturer and senior lecturer in the department of religious studies at University College, Ibadan, Nigeria; he then became reader in comparative religion at King's College, London, where he taught the future Archbishop Desmond Tutu. He was awarded a personal chair in 1970, was dean of the faculty of theology in 1972-74, and retired in 1977. Parrinder was a member of the World Congress of Faiths. In addition to his twenty-nine books and numerous other writings, he contributed to *The Annual Register* for forty-five years, first writing the article on religion in 1958 and producing his last piece for the 2002 volume. Died 16 June.

Philips, Frits (b. 1905), Dutch engineer and businessman who was president of his family's international electronics firm. Born near Delft, he was educated at the town's technical university. He spent a year in military service before joining the firm as an engineer, becoming managing director of the engineering works in 1939. After the German occupation of Holland in 1940, Philips was left to run the business while other directors went to the USA to take care of the company's international interests. Philips was made to open a workshop in a concentration camp, contriving to keep alive a large proportion of the Jews who were forced to work there, for which he subsequently received an award from Israel. He was imprisoned for five months when there was a national strike against the occupying forces, and later went into hiding until the war ended. After the war the company expanded rapidly with the development of new products such as electric shavers, hair driers, tape recorders, and television sets. Philips became president in 1961, opening works in South America and Asia, including a cathode-ray tube factory in Japan. He retired in 1971. Died 5 December.

Pope John Paul II (b. 1920), the first non-Italian Pope for more than four centuries, he was a compassionate but often uncompromising pontiff. Born Karel Jozef Wojtyla, in Wadowice, southern Poland, he was educated at the local grammar school and at Jagiellonian University in Cracow. He began to write and perform plays, but following the German invasion was sent to work in a stone quarry. During this time he began to train for the priesthood, but could not reveal this openly until the Soviet Army freed Poland from the Germans. He was ordained in Cracow in 1946 and went to study in Rome. Returning to Poland two years later he began to teach at the Catholic University in Lublin. In 1958 he was appointed auxiliary bishop of Cracow and five years later elevated to Archbishop by Pope Paul VI. Wojtyla used his position to strengthen the Church's influence in Poland, including the creation of new parishes, holding covert ordinations, and organising community work for Catholics under the suspicious eyes of the Communist regime. In 1967 he was elected Cardinal, which involved regular trips to Rome as well as tours in other countries. He was summoned to help with *Humanae Vitae*, the Pope's encyclical prohibiting artificial contraception, and to preach at the Vatican's Lenten. Two years later, when the Pope's death was followed quickly by that of his successor, John Paul I, Wojtyla was elected Pope on the eighth ballot. He soon displayed a missionary zeal, setting off to Poland "as a pilgrim" (the first Pope to enter a Communist country) and visiting 129 countries during his twenty-six years, generally drawing huge crowds to addresses and celebrations of Mass in open-air locations such as Victory Square in Warsaw and the Yankee Stadium in New York. He became the first Pope to visit the UK, in 1982—the year after he had survived an assassination attempt in Rome—taking the opportunity to warn that democratic and capitalist socieities could, without fundamental values, reduce human beings to economic units, as Communism did. He aroused concern within the Catholic community by resisting change in church doctrine on issues such as birth control, abortion, and the ordination of women, arguing in his encyclicals that temptations had to be resisted in the 21st century, as in the first, and that authority had to be obeyed. In spite of increasing frailty (he suffered from Parkinson's disease, an intestinal tumour, and other complaints that took him frequently into hospital) he continued with a punishing schedule of public activities until the last year of his life. Died 2 April.

Porter, Sir Leslie (b. 1920), businessman who became chairman of the Tesco supermarket chain. Born in Holloway, he left school at the age of fourteen to work in a garage. During World War II he joined the King's Royal Rifle Corps, serving in North Africa and Europe, and on demobilisation in 1946 joined his father's textile business, becoming managing director in 1953. He had married Shirley Cohen, daughter of Sir Jack Cohen, founder and chairman of Tesco, in 1949, and was persuaded to join the board of Tesco in 1959, specifically to advise on its expansion into the sale of non-food items. He joined the company full-time in the following year and in 1973 became chairman. He did not have an easy initiation and he and his father-in-law, who stayed on as president, were reported to have come to blows on several occasions as Porter tried to emphasise that he was now in charge. Tesco continued to grow in size and profits under his chairmanship, but by the time he retired in 1985 it was his wife, Shirley Porter, who was making headlines as Westminster council leader and mayor, becoming embroiled in the "homes for votes" scandal, which attempted to gerrymander votes for the Conservatives by selling off council houses to likely Tory voters. The Porters left London to live in Israel as the row developed, and a large part of their assets was frozen until, in 2004, they finally agreed to pay a settlement of UK£12.3 million (of the UK£42 million owed) to Westminster council. In Israel Leslie Porter became chancellor of Tel Aviv University. He was knighted in 1983. Died 20 March.

Rainier III, Prince of Monaco (b. 1923), whose fifty-five year reign brought new prosperity to his 482-acre principality. Born Rainier Louis Henri Maxence Bertrand Grimaldi, he was educated at Summerfields School in England, at Montpellier University, and the Ecole Libre des Sciences Politiques in Paris. He enlisted in the Free French Army in 1944 and was cited for bravery and awarded the croix de guerre. He succeeded his grandfather, Prince Louis II, in 1949, becoming the thirty-first member of the House of Grimaldi to run the principality, which, when he took over, depended on gambling for more than 90 per cent of its income. Rainer began at once to alter this by developing industries, particularlly tourism, as well as encouraging sport and scientific research. Besides developing its economy he was also concerned to provide the principality with heirs, and in the early 1950s his eye fell on the US film star, Grace Kelly, when she attended the Cannes film festival. Rainier went to the USA in 1955, and, after

persuading her to give up her film career, was able to announce their engagement. They were married in 1956, had their first child, Caroline, in 1957, a son Albert in 1958, and a second daughter, Stephanie, in 1965. Meanwhile Rainier ran into difficulties with his National Council, which began demanding constitutional reforms. He responded by suspending the constitution, prompting a political crisis that was only resolved when he set up a new legislative body. The death of Princess Grace in a car crash in 1982 was a devastating blow, only aggravated by his daughters' difficulties with marital and other highly-publicised relationships. Died 6 April.

Rehnquist, William (b. 1924), US lawyer who was Chief Justice of the Supreme Court from 1986. Born in Milwaukee, Wisconsin, he was educated at the local high school and Stanford University, California, and, after serving with the US Army Air Force during World War II, at Harvard. He opened a private law practice in Arizona, while also becoming active in Republican party politics, working for the presidential campaigns of Barry Goldwater and Richard Nixon. In 1971 he joined the Supreme Court as an associate justice, often finding himself championing the minority view, as in the *Roe v Wade* judgment legalising abortion. There was strong opposition to his appointment as Chief Justice—a third of the Senate voting against him—but his court tended to be less conservative than he, and was generally disposed not to interfere with decisions taken at state level. In 1999 Rehnquist presided over the impeachment trial of President Bill Clinton, subsequently announcing his acquittal, and in the presidential election of 2000 he was one of five justices who stopped the ballot re-counts in Florida, effectively ensuring the election of George W. Bush. Although diagnosed with thyroid cancer, he continued to work until shortly before his death. Died 3 September.

Roll of Ipsden, Lord, KCMG, CB (b. 1907), economist, British civil servant who became an international banker as chairman of SG Warburg. Born in Czernowitz, which later became part of Ukraine, Eric Roll was educated first in a gymnasium in Vienna, where the family lived during the First World War, and later at Birmingham University. In 1930 he took British citizenship and taught at the University College of Hull, becoming in 1935 professor of economics and commerce. During the Second World War he became deputy head of the British food mission in the USA, and was subsequently one of the team working on the administration of the Marshall Plan. In 1962 he worked on the negotiations over Britain's entry into the Common Market, and when these failed he was sent to Washington as UK Economic Minister. In 1964 he was appointed permanent under-secretary at the Labour government's new Department of Economic Affairs, retiring, when it failed to establish itself, to become deputy chairman (later chairman) of Warburgs, together with a host of other appointments, including a directorship of the Bank of England. He had first published *A History of Economic Thought* in 1954, which he continually updated, with a fifth edition in 1995, as well as many books and articles on economics, concluding with *Where Did We Go Wrong?* in 1995 and *Where Are We Going?* in 2000. He was appointed a life peer in 1977. Died 30 March.

Rotblat, Sir Joseph, KCMG, FRS (b. 1908), scientist who worked on the atomic bomb in Los Alamos but left for reasons of conscience, later being awarded the Nobel Prize for Peace. Born in Warsaw, he studied physics at Warsaw University and after

completing a doctorate joined Liverpool University. In 1944 he travelled to the USA to join the Manhattan Project developing the atom bomb, believing that it was to be only a deterrent, but later he asked to leave and returned to Liverpool, taking British citizenship in 1946. Three years later he went to St Bartholomew's Hospital Medical College in London to work on the possible medical applications of nuclear physics. While there he joined other scientists concerned with the proliferation of nuclear weapons, taking part in the first Pugwash meeting in Canada in 1957, and in all subsequent meetings that came to be known as the Pugwash conferences. It was for his consistent stand on nuclear disarmament that he was awarded, in 1995, the Nobel Peace Prize, jointly with Pugwash (of which he was president from 1988 to 1997). Died 31 August.

Rothschild, Dame Miriam, DBE, FRS (b. 1908), naturalist and parasitologist whose six-volume catalogue of fleas was compiled over thirty years. Born at Ashton Wold, the house built by her father in Northamptonshire, she was educated at home, quickly developing an interest in fleas, on which her father was an expert. She published *Fleas, Flukes and Cuckoos*, an erudite and witty analysis of bird parasites, in 1952, and the first volume of the *Catalogue of the Rothschild Collection of Fleas in the British Museum* in 1953 and the sixth in 1983. She also campaigned constantly as a conservationist, urging gardeners not to battle against nature but to let everything flourish, particularly wild flowers, which she also sought to grow in parks and on motorway verges, marketing her packets of seed for the purpose, which she called "Farmers' Nightmare". She mixed wild with cultivated plants in her own garden at Ashton Wold, and helped to sow a wild flower meadow for Prince Charles at Highgrove. She wrote *The But-*

terfly Gardener in 1983 and *Butterfly Cooing Like a Dove* in 1990, as well as many scientific papers and several other books; was a trustee of the Natural History Museum from 1967 to 1975, and appointed DBE in 2000. Died 20 January.

Saunders, Dame Cicely, OM, DBE (b. 1918), British nurse who founded the modern hospice movement. Born in Barnet, North London, she was educated at Roedean and St Anne's, Oxford, but abandoned her studies during World War II to become a nurse. After completing her degree she went to St Thomas's Hospital as an almoner, where she met a young Pole dying of cancer. Through him, she discovered that pain could be alleviated by modern drugs, and suffering made more tolerable by a form of care not available in hospitals. She went on to qualify as a physician and, after much planning and a hard struggle to find the money, she set up St Christopher's, first as a registered charity and, in 1967, as a hospice. Here she put into practice her belief that care should provide the relief not just of physical pain but also of the patients' mental, social, and spiritual suffering. Largely as a result of her efforts, and of the books she wrote about pain relief — including *The Management of Terminal Disease* (1978) and *Living with Dying* (1983) — palliative medicine was accepted as a medical speciality by the Royal College of Physicians. Saunders retired as medical director of St Christopher's in 1985, and in 2002 launched the Cicely Saunders Foundation to promote research into all aspects of palliative medicine. She was appointed DBE in 1980 and to the Order of Merit in 1989. Died, at St Christopher's Hospice, 14 July.

Sheppard of Liverpool, the Right Reverend Lord (b. 1929), England cricket captain who became Bishop of Liverpool. Born

in Chelsea, he was educated at Sherborne and at Trinity Hall, Cambridge, distinguishing himself on the cricket field at both school and university, and subsequently for Sussex and England. In his last year at Cambridge he scored seven centuries for the university, two for Sussex and one for England, heading the national averages. After playing for Sussex for one more full season in 1953 he began to prepare for ordination at Ridley Hall theological college, but the call of cricket was still strong, and he captained England for two Tests against Pakistan in 1954. Ordained in the following year, he was given time off to play for England again in 1956, and for two more Tests in 1957. By this time he had been appointed warden of the Mayflower family centre in east London, but came back to play a final tour for England in Australia in 1962, while accepting invitations to preach on Sundays in all the Australian state capitals. In 1969 Sheppard was appointed suffragan bishop of Woolwich, where his experience of the poor and disadvantaged confirmed his determination that things needed to be changed. He was appointed Bishop of Liverpool in 1975, arriving to find his new see in some crisis, with high unemployment culminating in an explosion of riots in Toxteth in 1981. Sheppard, one of whose first undertakings had been to establish a close co-operation with Derek Worlock, the Roman Catholic Archbishop of Liverpool, joined with Worlock in urging the city council to take more account of the poorest sections of the community, and the two men collaborated on three books on the theme of reconciliation in church and society. Sheppard retired in 1997 and was created a life peer. Died 5 March.

Sin, Cardinal Jaime (b. 1928), Archbishop of Manila who helped to bring down President Ferdinand Marcos. Born on Panay island in the central Philippines, he was ordained in 1954, spent three years as a diocesan missionary in Capiz Province, and the next ten as rector of a seminary in Panay. He was appointed auxiliary bishop of Jaro in 1967, Archbishop of Jaro in 1972, created Cardinal in 1976, and Archbishop of Manila in 1984. Assuming this office shortly after the assassination of the opposition leader Benigno Aquino, Sin was publicly critical of the regime and, when Marcos had been returned in the rigged election of 1986, called on people to rectify the situation by non-violent means. When two military officers came out in support of the opposition candidate, who was Aquino's widow, Sin broadcast an appeal urging people to protect the officers and their camps. Thousands of unarmed Filipinos took to the streets to provide a human shield round the camps, and when the regime collapsed Mrs Corazon Aquino became President. Sin became politically involved again in 1999, criticising José Estrada, who had succeeded Aquino as President, for trying to control the media; later he called for the President's resignation after an attempt to impeach him had collapsed. Once more crowds took to the streets, forcing Estrada to resign. Sin retired in 2003. Died 21 June.

Thompson, Hunter S. (b. 1937), US journalist famous for his acerbic first-person reporting, dubbed "gonzo journalism", and for his drug-fuelled lifestyle, which came together in his best-known work, *Fear and Loathing in Las Vegas*. Born in Louisville, Kentucky, into a middle-class family, Thompson rebelled after his father's death when he was fourteen and by the age of eighteen was serving time in prison for robbery. He joined the US Air Force in 1956, where he became a sports journalist, a profession which he continued on his discharge in 1958. He branched into political journalism with his first election report in 1964,

and reported on the Hells Angels counter-culture for *Rolling Stone* magazine in 1965 in an article which established his reputation. His invention of "gonzo journalism", in which the reporter put himself at the centre of the story, came about because, he claimed, he was late for a deadline and was too drugged to write. Sending the pages of his notebook containing his rambling report of the Kentucky Derby direct to the printer, he was sure that he had ended his career; instead he caused a sensation with what was described as "a breakthrough in journalism". Thompson went on to produce his account of a hallucinatory road trip, *Fear and Loathing in Las Vegas* (originally a 1972 article for *Rolling Stone*), and numerous other books and articles. He died from a self-inflicted gunshot wound at his home in Colorado. Died 20 February.

Tueni, Gebran (b. 1957), Lebanese journalist who championed his country's independence and was assassinated while driving in Beirut. Born in the capital, he was educated locally and in France, obtaining a degree at the Ecole Supérieure de Journalisme. Tueni's grandfather had founded and edited the liberal newspaper *An-Nahar* in 1933 and the paper had remained in the family, Tueni taking over as editor from his father in 1993. Before this, when the Syrians invaded Lebanon, he had returned to Paris where he set up a political weekly, *An-Nahar Arab and International*. Returning to Lebanon while the Syrians were still in control he eventually wrote an editorial calling for the withdrawal of their forces and when, in February 2005, the former Prime Minister Rafik al-Hariri was assassinated (see p. 182) Tueni organised the demonstrations that eventually forced Syrian troops off the streets. He was elected to the Lebanese Parliament in May, but fled to France when his name was found on a list of people to be eliminated. Tueni went back to Beirut but was killed on the day after his return. Died 12 December.

Weizman, Ezer (b. 1924), Israeli airman and military commander who became his country's President. Born in Tel Aviv, he was educated in Haifa, and at the RAF Staff College, having volunteered, at the age of eighteen, to fight for the RAF. He served as a Spitfire pilot in Egypt and India during World War II. In 1958 he commanded the Israeli Air Force and in 1966 was head of the general staff of the Israeli Defence Forces and second-in-command to Yitzhak Rabin during the Six Day War. In 1969 he joined the Herut Party and was appointed Minister of Transport in the coalition government, but lost the job when the party withdrew from the government. In 1977 he ran the party's victorious election campaign and was appointed Minister of Defence, resigning in 1980 to form his own Yahad party, but in the negotiations that followed the indecisive 1984 election he pledged his support to Labour and was appointed Minister Without Portfolio and subsequently Minister for Science and Technology in the coalition government. He was forced to leave the inner Cabinet when it was revealed that he had been having unauthorised contacts with Arab organisations (he was always more keen on negotiating peace than many of his colleagues), and he retired in 1992. In the following year he was elected by the Knesset as President of Israel, was re-elected in 1998, but resigned in 2000 following allegations that he had been paid by businessmen while a member of the Knesset. No charges were brought. Died 24 April.

Westmoreland, William (b. 1914), US General who commanded the land forces in the Vietnam War. Born in South Carolina, he was trained for the US Army at West Point. During World War II he served in North Africa and Sicily, was at Utah Beach during the Normandy landings, and fought his way up to the Elbe. He was appointed chief-of-staff of the 82nd Airborne Division at Fort Bragg in 1947 and returned to active service in Korea, where he commanded an airborne brigade. In 1964 he was posted to Vietnam, first as deputy commander then, later that year, as commander. The US strength at that time comprised only 15,000 men, but in the next four years, under Westmoreland's command, it increased to more than half a million (which was less than half the number he said he needed to defeat the North Vietnamese and Vietcong). His plan was to win by attrition, killing the enemy more quickly than they could be replaced, but the enemy proved too elusive to be caught in set-piece battles. Westmoreland was recalled in 1968 after the Tet offensive, which, though it did not succeed militarily, changed attitudes in the USA. He was appointed Chief-of-Staff of the Army on his return, and retired in 1972. Died 19 July.

Wiesenthal, Simon (b. 1908), survivor of German concentration camps who tracked down many Nazi war criminals. He was born in Buczacz in the Galicia region of the Austro-Hungarian Empire, but during the First World War his family moved to Vienna, where he studied architecture. For a while he worked in Lvov, but when the Germans invaded in 1942 he was sent to labour camps, ending up at Mauthausen, near Linz, where he was in the death block when it was liberated in 1945. He had already begun compiling a list of those operating the camps, and soon afterwards set up his Jewish historical documentation centre assembling dossiers on Nazi war criminals. When he finally ceased his work, in 2003, he was credited with having provided evidence that helped to bring more than 1,000 war criminals to justice, including Adolf Eichmann, Franz Strangl (commandant of the Treblinka extermination camp in Poland), and Hermine Brunsteiner (camp guard at Majdanek). Died 20 September.

Wise, Robert (b. 1914), versatile US film editor, producer, and director who won Academy Awards for two musicals. Born in Winchester, Indiana, his education was cut short by the depression when he went to work at the RKO studios in Hollywood, where he eventually became a film editor. Two of the early films he edited were *Citizen Kane* (1941) and *The Magnificent Ambersons* (1942), both directed by Orson Welles. Wise went on to direct two horror films and then, more notably, *The Set-Up* (1949), a gritty film about a boxer fighting corruption, which won the critics' prize at the Cannes film festival. He continued directing films at the rate of one a year during the 1950s, for a number of different studios, including *The Day the Earth Stood Still* (1951), *Executive Suite* (1954), and *I Want to Live* (1958), which won an Oscar for Susan Hayward playing a prostitute faced with the gas chamber. In 1961 Wise turned to musicals, first working with the choreographer Jerome Robbins on *West Side Story* (1961), for which he and Robbins shared an Oscar, and then directing *The Sound of Music* (1965), for which he won another Oscar and which for a time was the biggest grossing movie. None of his later films was very successful. Died 14 September.

Yakovlev, Aleksandr (b. 1923), Soviet politician who supported Mikhail Gorbachev and was known as the "ideologue of *perestroika*" and the "godfather of *glasnost*" for his role in those reforms. Born in the Yaroslavl region east of Moscow, he was invalided out of the army after being seriously wounded during World War II. He joined the Communist Party after completing his education at the Yaroslavl Pedagogical Institute, enrolled at the Academy of Social Sciences, and became a leading member of the Central Committee after spending a year at Columbia University in New York as an exchange student. He upset conservative Committee members in 1972 with an article in *Literaturnaya gazeta* attacking Russian nationalism, and was sent to Canada as Soviet ambassador. When Gorbachev became General Secretary of the Communist Party in 1985, Yakovlev was appointed head of the propaganda department of the Central Committee, and by 1987 had become a voting member of the Politburo, supervising ideology. He was a major influence behind the policy of non-intervention in Eastern European countries, was responsible for rehabilitating many Soviet citizens who had suffered from past purges, and in 1990, when Gorbachev was elected Soviet President, became a member of the new Presidential Council. Yakovlev took to the barricades to defend Gorbachev during the attempted coup of 1991, and when the Soviet Union collapsed in December of that year he became an advisor to Boris Yeltsin and, for a short while, head of the Ostankino television station. He published *A Century of Violence in Soviet Russia* in 2002 and a volume of memoirs in 2003. Died 18 October.

Yao Wenyuan (b. 1931), Chinese politician who was the last surviving member of the Cultural Revolution's "gang of four". Born in Shanghai, Yao came to prominence as a member of the Shanghai party committee and, more significantly, as a polemical writer who edited the Shanghai paper *Liberation Daily* and was instrumental in providing support for the removal of leaders who Chairman Mao Zedong believed to have turned against the Cultural Revolution. Yao became a member of the Cultural Revolutionary Group, which also comprised Mao's wife, Jiang Qing, who died in 1991, Zhang Chunqiao, who died in May 2005 (see below), and Wang Hongwen, who died in 1992, and who between them sought to justify and implement Mao's revolution. The four were arrested and charged with treason soon after Mao's death, and Yao was sentenced to twenty years in prison. On his release, in 1996, he lived quietly in Shanghai. Died 23 December.

Zhao Ziyang (b. 1919), former Chinese Communist Party leader who was ousted in 1989 and remained under house arrest for the rest of his life. Born in Hehan province, in central China, he joined the Young Communists during his schooldays and soon after the People's Republic was formed in 1951 was put in charge of land reform in Guangdong province. He was dismissed during the Cultural Revolution and sent to work in Inner Mongolia, but was later rehabilitated and appointed party secretary in Sichuan, where he successfully introduced industrial and agricultural reforms. In 1980 he was brought to Beijing to join the Politburo and was appointed Premier of the State Council, where he began the process of opening the country to foreign trade and investment. In 1987 he became Communist Party General Secretary, but when, at the party congress, he proposed separating the party from government he was dismissed as Premier and succeeded by Li Peng, who introduced the martial law act that sparked student unrest and led to the massacre in Tiananmen Square in 1989. Zhao, who was accused of supporting the turmoil and splitting the party, was dismissed by Deng Xiaoping, and did not appear in public again. Died 17 January.

Zhang Chunqiao, (b. 1917), Chinese politician who was a member of the "gang of four" who did much of the dirty work for the Cultural Revolution. Born in Shandong province, Zhang joined the League of Chinese Writers in 1936 and became a member of the Communist Party in 1940. When the revolution began, he worked with other members of the "gang of four" to remove reactionaries from Shanghai and establish himself, as some described him, as a revoutionary warlord and potential successor to Mao Zedong. When the gang was arrested and put on trial after Mao's death, charged with anti-party activities and responsibility for the deaths of 35,000 people, Zhang refused to say a word and was sentenced to death, later commuted to life imprisonment. He was released on medical grounds in 1998. Died 21 April.

Zhvania, Zurab (b. 1963), Prime Minister of Georgia who was once an ally of President Eduard Shevardnadze but later took part in his overthrow. Born in Tbilisi, he was educated at the Ivane Dzhavakhishvili State University. After joining the Green Party in 1988 he was elected to the Georgian National Parliament in 1992. He was appointed chairman of Shevardnadze's Union of the Citizens of Georgia in 1993, but left in 2002 to join the reformist party (Kmara) which initiated the "rose revolution" forcing the Shevardnadze government from power. Zhhvania became Prime Minister after free elections had been held, declaring that he would not leave politics until there was no danger of controls being imposed on freedom of speech and the press. He was found dead at his home, apparently killed by a gas leak, on 3 February.

XX CHRONICLE OF PRINCIPAL EVENTS IN 2005

JANUARY

1 **Uganda**: President Yoweri Museveni ordered the resumption of military operations against the rebel Lord's Resistance Army (LRA) following the failure of peace talks in December 2004 to secure a long-term ceasefire.

4 **Chile**: the Supreme Court upheld the ruling of a lower court that the former dictator General (retd) Augusto Pinochet Ugarte was mentally fit to stand trial on charges relating to cases of kidnapping and murder during his rule in the 1970s.

7 **Democratic Republic of Congo (DRC)**: the UN Office of Internal Oversight Services released a report on the "serious and ongoing" problems of sexual abuse by UN peacekeepers in the DRC

Pakistan: an outbreak of tribal unrest in the south-western province of Baluchistan followed the alleged rape by the military of a female doctor working at the country's major gas field. In skirmishes between tribesmen and the army up to fifteen people died and gas pipelines were seriously damaged, cutting off supplies to the rest of the country for weeks.

Somalia: Prime Minister Ali Mohammed Gedi on 7 January named a new forty-seven-member Cabinet, revised from his choice in December 2004; the new list was subsequently endorsed by the transitional legislature.

9 **Palestine**: Mahmoud Abbas was elected President of the Palestine National Authority (PNA) with over 62 per cent of the vote in an election contested by six other candidates. Although the election was boycotted by Hamas and Islamic Jihad, turnout was reported to be around 73 per cent.

Sudan: First Vice President Ali Osman Taha signed a comprehensive peace agreement with John Garang, leader of the Sudan People's Liberation Movement (SPLM), to end a civil war in southern Sudan that had lasted some twenty-one years.

Uzbekistan: run-off elections were held to the 120-seat Legislative Assembly, with all five contending parties supporters of President Islam Karimov because no opposition parties had been allowed to register.

10 **Israel**: the Knesset (the unicameral legislature) vote fifty-eight to fifty-six to approve a new coalition government, led by Prime Minister Ariel Sharon of the Likud party, that also included the Labour Party and the United Torah Judaism party, thus enabling Sharon to carry through his controversial plan to dismantle all Israeli settlements in the Palestinian Gaza Strip.

Russia: mass protests by old-age pensioners began against pension reforms that came into force on 1 January, substituting cash payments for numerous free or subsidised services.

12 **EU**: the European Parliament endorsed the treaty to introduce an EU constitution, by 500 votes to 137 with forty abstentions.

Georgia: in the self-declared republic of Abkhazia, former Abkhaz Prime Minister Sergei Bagapsh won an overwhelming victory in a repeat presidential election with over 90 per cent of the vote.

13 **Equatorial Guinea**: Sir Mark Thatcher, son of former UK Prime Minister Baroness (Margaret) Thatcher, pleaded guilty in a South African court to unwittingly aiding a failed coup attempt in Equatorial Guinea by financing the chartering of a helicopter intended by the conspirators for use in the coup.

Nicaragua: the National Assembly passed a bill of constitutional reforms aimed at limiting the power of President Enrique Bolaños Geyer, in defiance of a ruling by the Central American Court of Justice (an institution whose jurisdiction was recognised only by El Salvador and Nicaragua).

14 **Serbia & Montenegro**: US ambassador Michael Polt announced that the USA was cutting aid to Serbia & Montenegro because of its government's persistent failure to co-operate with the International Criminal Tribunal for the Former Yugoslavia (ICTY) at The Hague.

Singapore: the government signed an agreement with Malaysia on the basis of a solution to a long-running dispute between the two states over Singapore's offshore land reclamation works.

15 **Bosnia & Herzegovina:** the Bosnian Serb entity, Republika Srpska, for the first time delivered a war crimes suspect from the 1992-95 Bosnian war to the ICTY. Improved relations with the ICTY followed the appointment on 8 January of new Republika Srpska Prime Minister Pero Bukejlovic.

16 **Croatia:** in the second round of a presidential election, the incumbent reformist and pro-EU President Stipe Mesic was elected with nearly 65 per cent of the vote, defeating Jadranka Kosor, candidate of the ruling Croatian Democratic Union (HDZ). Mesic and Kosor had emerged as the two leading candidates in the first round held on 2 January.

17 **China:** Zhao Ziyang, deposed as general secretary of the Chinese Communist Party (CPP) in 1989 for opposing the use of force to crush the pro-democracy demonstrations in Tiananmen Square, died aged eighty-five.

18 **Australia:** leader of the opposition Australian Labor Party (ALP) Mark Latham resigned following his electoral defeat October 2004. Former leader Kim Beazley was endorsed unopposed as party leader later in the month.

Indonesia: the government held the first peace talks with the separatist Free Aceh Movement (GAM) since the failure of negotiations with the rebels in May 2003.

20 **USA**: in the inaugural address for his second successive term of office President George W. Bush asserted that the survival of freedom in the USA was increasingly dependent on "the success of liberty in other lands", and that the USA would support "the growth of democratic movements and institutions in every nation and culture".

22 **Maldives**: in elections to the People's Majlis (the unicameral legislature), independent candidates backed by the exiled opposition Maldivian Democratic Party (MDP) claimed to have won eighteen of the forty-two popularly elected seats. However, President Maumoon Abdul Gayoom, who himself appointed eight additional legislators, said that the government had won thirty seats.

23 **Ukraine**: Viktor Yushchenko, winner of the re-run presidential election in December 2004, was inaugurated as independent Ukraine's third President after the Supreme Court rejected appeals by rival candidate and outgoing Prime Minister Viktor Yanukovych against the election result. Yushchenko nominated as his Prime Minister Yuliya Tymoshenko, who had played a prominent role in the popular movement that brought him to power.

25 **UK**: the four remaining UK Muslim nationals held in the US detention camp at Guantánamo Bay in Cuba as "enemy combatants" were released and flown back to the UK. The men were released from UK police custody the next day.

26 **UK**: Home Secretary Charles Clarke introduced in the House of Commons (the lower house of Parliament) amendments to the 2001 Anti-Terrorism Act in response to the December 2004 law lords' ruling that detention without trial of foreign terrorist subjects under the Act was discriminatory and disproportionate. Detention in prison would be replaced by "control orders", a form of house arrest.

27 **Bangladesh**: the killing in a grenade attack of widely respected former Finance Minister A.M.S. Kibria at an opposition Awami League rally focused international concern over spreading lawlessness in Bangladesh.

28 **Bolivia**: President Carlos Mesa signed a decree authorising the direct election of regional governors and the holding of referendums on 12 June on autonomy for the country's nine regions. The decree followed a wave of strikes and protests in the region of Santa Cruz and two other regions.

30 **African Union (AU)**: the AU began its fourth two-day summit in Abuja, the capital of Nigeria; the closing communiqué called on the G-8 (Group of Eight) countries to cancel all debts of African countries.

Iraq: elections were held to a 275-member National Assembly, governing councils for Iraq's eighteen provinces and, in the northern Kurdish-controlled area, deputies to the autonomous Iraqi Kurdistan National Assembly. Although there were some 260 attacks by insurgents on election day, killing some thirty-four people, they failed to disrupt the voting. However, there was a low turnout in Sunni Muslim areas.

FEBRUARY

1 **Nepal**: King Gyanendra dismissed Prime Minister Sher Bahadur Deuba and the government he had led since June 2004, assuming direct control of government himself and declaring a state of emergency in which civil liberties were suspended and many politicians detained.

Sudan: an independent report to the UN on the widespread crimes against the inhabitants of the Darfur region principally blamed the government and its Janjawid militia for the violence that had caused tens of thousands of deaths and displaced some 1.8 million people, but stopped short of describing it as genocide.

2 **Northern Ireland**: the Irish Republican Army (IRA) withdrew its offer to decommission all its weapons, in reaction against allegations by the UK and Irish governments of its involvement in a major bank robbery in December 2004.

3 **Chad**: Moussa Faki Mahamat resigned as Prime Minister, to be replaced by Pascal Yoadimnadji, hitherto Minister of Agriculture.

Georgia: Prime Minister Zurab Zhvania died of apparent accidental carbon monoxide poisoning from a faulty gas heater. Some Georgian politicians, however, blamed his death on interference by "external forces". President Mikheil Saakashvili on 8 February named Zurab Noghaideli as the new Prime Minister.

4 **Ukraine**: President Viktor Yushchenko's choice of Yuliya Tymoshenko as the new Prime Minister was confirmed by a 373-0 vote in the Verkhovna Rada (the unicameral legislature). On the same day the Rada endorsed Tymoshenko's Cabinet and programme of reforms.

5 **Togo**: President Gnassingbé Eyadéma, who had ruled the country since 1967, died, aged sixty-nine, following which the military high command installed his son, Faure Gnassingbé, as President, in contravention of the constitution. International pressure forced Gnassingbé's resignation on 25 February and his replacement by interim President Abass Bonfoh.

6 **Thailand**: in elections to the 500-seat House of Representatives (the lower house of the legislature) the ruling Thai Rak Thai (TRT—Thais Love Thais) party won a landslide victory, with 377 seats, securing an unprecedented second consecutive term for the government of President Thaksin Shinawatra.

7 **Kenya**: the resignation of John Githongo, the country's senior anti-corruption official, was a damaging blow to the reputation of President Mwai Kibaki's government and was followed by the suspension of both US and German aid to the country's anti-corruption programme.

8 **Denmark**: in a general election to the 179-seat Folketing (the unicameral legislature) the three-party ruling right-wing coalition led by the Liberal party retained power, winning a total of ninety-four seats. Prime Minister Anders Fogh Rasmussen announced a new Cabinet on 18 February.

Greece: veteran socialist and former Foreign Minister Karolos Papoulias, seventy-five, was elected to the largely ceremonial post of President by 279 votes out of 300 deputies in the Vouli (the unicameral legislature).

10 **Saudi Arabia**: in the first round of elections to municipal councils 127 non-partisan councillors were elected, the first step in a programme to increase public participation in government. Although turnout was about 65 per cent, the proportion of citizens that had registered to vote was as low as 10 per cent.

12 **Brazil**: the murder by gunmen of US-born nun, environmentalist and human rights activist Dorothy Stang in the state of Pará led to local protests and international condemnation that prompted the government to send 2,000 troops to the region and create two rainforest conservation areas in the state totalling some 4 million hectares of land.

13 **Iraq**: the Independent Electoral Commission released the final results of the 30 January elections to a 275-seat transitional National Assembly, showing the main Shi'ite Muslim coalition, the United Iraqi Alliance, to have won a narrow majority with 140 seats and 48 per cent of the vote. Although national turnout was 58 per cent it was much lower in many predominantly Sunni Muslim areas where the insurgency was most active.

14 **Lebanon**: businessman and former Prime Minister (1992-98; 2000-04) Rafik al-Hariri was killed by a car bomb in Beirut, the capital, along with nineteen others. It was widely suspected that Syria was responsible for his murder.

20 **Cyprus**: in elections to the fifty-seat Republican Assembly (unicameral legislature) of the self-proclaimed Turkish Republic of North Cyprus (TRNC), Prime Minister Mehmet Ali Talat's ruling Republican Turkish party (CTP) increased its number of seats from nineteen to twenty-four, in what was seen as an endorsement of Talat's proposals for reunification of the island.

Portugal: in elections to the 230-seat Assembly of the Republic (the unicameral legislature) the Socialist Party (PS) defeated the incumbent coalition, securing a majority with 120 seats. PS leader José Sócrates became the country's fourth Prime Minister in three years.

Spain: in a referendum some 77 per cent of voters approved the treaty establishing a constitution for the EU, making Spain the first member country to endorse the constitution. Only 42 per cent of the electorate participated in the plebiscite.

21 **Anguilla**: in elections to the House of Assembly (the unicameral legislature) the ruling Anguilla United Front (AUF) coalition led by Chief Minister Osbourne Fleming won four out of the assembly's seven elected seats, securing a second successive term in government.

27 **Egypt**: President Mohammed Hosni Mubarak announced that he would propose to the legislature a reform to allow multiple candidates to stand for direct presidential elections. The necessary constitutional amendment would be subject to a referendum.

Kyrgyzstan: elections to a new unicameral legislature, the Supreme Assembly, were criticised by monitors from the Organisation for Security and Co-operation in Europe (OSCE), who alleged widespread vote-buying, intimidation of the media, and violations of the secrecy of the ballot.

Lebanon: the government led by pro-Syrian Prime Minister Umar Karami resigned, giving way to the demands of thousands of demonstrators protesting against the assassination of the former Prime Minister Hariri.

Tajikistan: in elections to the sixty-three-member Assembly of Representatives (the lower house of the legislature) President Imamoli Rahmonov's People's Democratic Party of Tajikistan (PDPT) won thirty-eight of the forty-one seats whose results were decided, with around 80 per cent of the vote. Run-off elections would be held for the remaining twenty-two seats.

28 **Burundi**: in a national referendum 92 per cent of voters approved a new constitution in place of the country's 1992 constitution, paving the way for the replacement of the transitional government.

Iraq: a suicide bomb attack targeted on a police and army recruitment centre killed at least 125 people in the mainly Shi'ite city of Hilla, south of Baghdad. It was said to be the deadliest single bombing since the US-led invasion of Iraq in March 2003. About 220 other people were killed during the month in resurgent violence since the January elections.

MARCH

1   **Democratic Republic of Congo (DRC)**: a force of Pakistani peacekeepers of the UN's MONUC mission launched an offensive in Ituri province, where nine Bangladeshi UN peacekeepers had been killed by militants of the Lendu tribe. About fifty Lendu militiamen were killed in the operation. UN peacekeepers had hitherto been accused of passivity in the face of aggressive Congolese militias, and failure to protect civilians.

   USA: the Supreme Court ruled five to four that the imposition of the death penalty on murderers who were below the age of eighteen when they committed the crime of which they were convicted was unconstitutional and represented "cruel and unusual" punishment.

3   **French Polynesia**: Oscar Temaru was elected President by twenty-nine votes in the fifty-seven-member Legislative Assembly against twenty-six for Gaston Tong Sang . Temaru had held the presidency for four months in 2004 before being ousted by a no-confidence vote.

   Indonesia: a court in Jakarta, the capital, convicted radical Muslim cleric Abu Bakar Bashir, the alleged spiritual leader of the Islamic militant group Jemaah Islamiah (JI), of playing an indirect role in the conspiracy that resulted in the bombings on the island of Bali in October 2002 that killed 202 people.

4   **Italy**: the death of a secret service agent, Nicola Calipari, killed in Iraq by US gunfire as he accompanied an Italian hostage, Giuliana Sgrena, on the journey to Baghdad airport after he had helped to secure her release, caused a temporary diplomatic crisis between Italy and the USA, but no withdrawal of Italian forces from the US-led coalition in Iraq.

   Portugal: Prime Minister José Sócrates announced a new Cabinet, following the victory of his Socialist Party (PS) in February.

6   **Moldova**: in legislative elections the Communist Party of Moldova (PCM) won a majority with fifty-six out of 101 seats in the Parlamentul (the unicameral legislature), but fell short of the sixty-one seats needed to re-elect President Vladimir Voronin, whom the opposition parties rejected. Voronin was later confirmed in office on 4 April.

7   **Lebanon**: at a meeting in Damascus, the capital of Syria, Lebanese President General Émile Lahoud and Syrian President Bashar al-Assad agreed that Syrian troops in Lebanon would be redeployed to the eastern Bekaa valley by the end of the month.

   USA: President George W. Bush nominated under-secretary of state John Bolton as US permanent representative at the UN, a choice regarded both abroad and domestically as controversial because of Bolton's hawkish and unilateralist tendencies.

8   **Federated States of Micronesia (FSM):** elections were held to the ten two-year seats in the fourteen-seat FSM Congress (the unicameral legislature).

   Russia: Chechen separatist leader Aslan Maskhadov was killed by Russian forces during a raid in northern Chechnya.

   Serbia and Montenegro: Ramush Haradinaj resigned as Prime Minister of the disputed province of Kosovo and the next day surrendered to the International Criminal Tribunal for the former Yugoslavia (ICTY) at The Hague.

10 **Hong Kong:** Tung Chee-hwa, Chief Executive of the Hong Kong Special Administrative Region resigned with two years of his term still to run. His deputy, Donald Tsang, took over as interim Chief Executive.

11 **UK**: the Prevention of Terrorism bill providing for the imposition of domestic "control orders" on terrorist suspects who could neither be tried nor deported became law, the government having accepted amendments that all restriction orders should be made by a judge and that the law should be subject to review after twelve months.

13 **Central African Republic (CAR):** in the first round of presidential elections incumbent President François Bozizé led with nearly 43 per cent of the vote, but because he failed to reach the 50 per cent threshold necessary for outright victory would have to contest a second round on 1 May, against the runner-up, Martin Ziguélé.

Liechtenstein: in legislative elections Prime Minister Otmar Hasler's ruling Progressive Citizens' Party (FBP) lost its overall majority in the twenty-five-seat Landtag (the unicameral legislature), its representation falling from thirteen to twelve seats.

Tajikistan: in a second round of elections to the Assembly of Representatives (the lower house of the legislature) the ruling People's Democratic Party of Tajikistan (PDPT) consolidated its success in the first round in February, winning an additional fourteen seats, giving it a total of fifty-two seats in the sixty-three-member assembly.

16 **Iraq:** the inaugural meeting was held of the transitional 275-member National Assembly elected in January. However, as no agreement had been reached by the main Shi'ite Muslim and Kurdish blocs of legislators on the formation of the government, no business was transacted at this meeting or at a second on 29 March.

17 **Tonga:** elections were held to eighteen seats of the non-partisan thirty-member Fale Alea (the unicameral legislature). In announcing a new Cabinet Prime Minister Prince Ulukalala Lavaka Ata made the innovation of naming four additional Cabinet ministers drawn from the Fale Alea (two nobles and two commoners), which necessitated them resigning their seats as legislators.

21 **Namibia:** Hifikepunye Pohamba of the ruling South West African People's Organisation, who was elected with 76 per cent of the vote in November 2004, was sworn in as the new President of Namibia.

UN: Secretary-General Kofi Annan presented to the General Assembly a report proposing far-reaching reforms of the UN, including the expansion of the Security Council from fifteen to twenty-four members and the adoption of new guidelines on the authorisation of military action.

USA: President Bush signed legislation allowing the federal courts to intervene in the highly publicised case of Terri Schiavo, a woman who had been in a persistent vegetative state since 1990, whose husband had asked doctors in the state of Florida to withdraw her feeding tube. However, both the Florida and federal supreme courts refused to consider the case and Schiavo died on 31 March.

23 **EU:** at the end of a two-day summit EU leaders endorsed a major relaxation of the rules relating to national budget deficits and public debt levels of the Stability and Growth Pact that governed participation in the euro single currency.

Italy: the Senate (the upper house of the legislature) approved a constitutional reform bill that strengthened the executive powers of the Prime Minister and increase autonomy for the country's twenty regions.

Netherlands: Deputy Prime Minister Thom de Graaf resigned, weakening the three-party centre-right coalition government, following the defeat of his electoral reform bill in the upper house of the Staten Generaal (the legislature).

24 **Kyrgyzstan:** President Askar Akayev was effectively deposed by anti-government demonstrators besieging the presidential compound. He escaped Bishkek, the capital, by helicopter. An interim government under acting President Kurmanbek Bakiev was sworn in on 25 March.

Sudan: the UN Security Council adopted resolution 1590 (2005) replacing the UN Advance Mission in Sudan (UNAMIS) by the UN Mission in Sudan, which would deploy 10,000 troops and over 700 policemen to reinforce a January peace agreement in the south and also support the African Union peacekeepers in the western region of Darfur.

UK: the royal assent was given to a constitutional reform bill providing for the establishment of a Supreme Court separate from the House of Lords.

26 **Bhutan:** the government published a thirty-four-article draft constitution to replace a 1953 royal decree giving the monarch absolute power. Under the proposed constitution King Jigme Singye Wangchuk could be forced to abdicate by a three-quarters vote of the joint legislature, the lower house of which would now be elected under a two-party system.

29 **Bosnia & Herzegovina**: High Representative of the Bosnian Peace Implementation Council Lord (Paddy) Ashdown dismissed Dragan Covic from his post as ethnic Croat member of the three-member joint Bosnian presidency. On the next day Covic went on trial for customs evasion, corruption and abuse of office.

Nicaragua: the regional Central American Court of Justice (CACJ) dismissed a package of constitutional reforms passed by the Nicaraguan National Assembly in January, arguing that the reforms should have been approved by a constituent assembly, not the legislature. On the next day President Enrique Bolaños, said that he would abide by the CACJ ruling, but the Nicaraguan Supreme Court of Justice said that the regional court had exceeded its powers.

30 **Czech Republic**: the centrist Christian Democratic Union-Czech People's Party (KDU-CSL) pulled out of the ruling coalition, citing a financial scandal concerning Prime Minister Stanislav Gross, leader of its coalition partner, the Czech Social Democratic party (CSSD).

31 **Estonia**: President Arnold Rüütel asked Andrus Ansip, leader of the Estonian reform party (ER) to form a new coalition government, following the resignation on 24 March of Prime Minister Juhan Parts after the adoption of a no-confidence motion in the Riigikogu (the unicameral legislature) against Justice Minister Ken-Marti Vaher.

Rwanda: an exiled ethnic Hutu rebel group, the Democratic Forces for the Liberation of Rwanda (FDLR), issued an unprecedented apology for the part it had played in the 1994 genocide of ethnic Tutsi Rwandans and said that it was halting "offensive operations" against Rwanda.

Sudan: the UN Security Council passed by a margin of eleven to zero (with four abstentions) Resolution 1593 (2005) deciding to refer any suspected perpetrators of war crimes in the Darfur region of Sudan to the UN's International Criminal Court (ICC).

Zimbabwe: in general elections to the 120-seat House of Assembly (the unicameral legislature) President Robert Mugabe's ruling Zimbabwe African National Union-Patriotic Front (ZANU-PF) won seventy-eight seats, sixteen more than in the June 2000 elections, whilst the main opposition party, the Movement for Democratic Change (MDC) correspondingly saw its number of seats fall from fifty-seven to forty-one.

APRIL

2 **Vatican**: Pope John Paul II (Karol Josef Wojtyla) died, aged eighty-four, following a steep decline in his health since February. A secret conclave of 115 cardinals on 19 April elected Cardinal Joseph Ratzinger, seventy-eight, of Germany, as John Paul II's successor; he was installed on 24 April as Pope Benedict XVI, the 265th Pope.

5 **Japan**: the approval by the Education Ministry of a new school history text book that omitted mention of Japanese war crimes in the 1930s and 1940s was condemned by the Chinese government and sparked major anti-Japanese demonstrations in several Chinese cities.

6 **Côte d'Ivoire**: after four days of talks in South Africa President Laurent Gbagbo signed an agreement with opposition and rebel leaders to end hostilities, begin disarmament, and to resolve a dispute over citizenship requirements for presidential candidates.

Iraq: the transitional National Assembly formed in late January elected as President of Iraq Jalal Talabani, leader of the Patriotic Union of Kurdistan (PUK). On 7 April Talabani and his two deputy presidents appointed former interim vice president Ibrahim al-Jaafari—leader of the Shi'ite Da'wa Party—as Prime Minister.

7 **India**: a bus service was successfully inaugurated between the Indian and Pakistani zones of the northern state of Jammu and Kashmir. The service was the most tangible fruit of fifteen months of negotiations between the two countries.

8 **Djibouti**: Ismael Omar Guelleh was re-elected unopposed as President, on an official turnout of over 78 per cent.

9 **South Africa**: delegates to the federal council of the New National Party (NNP), the successor to the National Party that ruled South Africa throughout the apartheid era, voted to disband the party.

11 **Kyrgyzstan**: the Supreme Assembly (the unicameral legislature) accepted the formal resignation of President Askar Akayev, who fled the country in March, effectively ousted by a popular uprising. The assembly also set a date in July for fresh presidential elections.

13 **Estonia**: a new three-party coalition government was sworn in, led by Prime Minister Andrus Ansip, who was appointed in March.

15 **Lebanon**: President Emile Lahoud appointed Najib Mikati as Prime Minister; by 19 April Mikati had assembled a Cabinet that included both pro-Syrian loyalists and opposition figures.

Nigeria: A Swiss court charged Abba Abacha, son of the late Nigerian dictator General Sani Abacha, with money laundering in connection with the embezzlement of Nigerian state funds.

20 **Ecuador**: Congress (the unicameral legislature) removed President Colonel Lucio Gutiérrez from office, replacing him with Vice President Alfredo Palacio. Months of public unrest had culminated in mass demonstrations against Gutiérrez.

Italy: Prime Minister Silvio Berlusconi tendered his resignation to President Carlo Azeglio Ciampi after the ruling coalition suffered serious losses in thirteen regional elections held on 3-4 April. However, on 22 April Ciampi asked Berlusconi to form a new government, which was sworn in the next day.

21 **Liechtenstein**: the Landtag (the unicameral legislature) elected a new government under Prime Minister Otmar Hasler, which revived the coalition between the Progressive Citizens' Party (FBP) and the Patriotic Union (VU) that had governed the principality from 1938 to 1997.

22 **Non-Aligned Movement (NAM)**: representatives of 106 countries met in Jakarta, the Indonesian capital, for a two-day Asian-African summit meeting to mark the 50th anniversary of the 1955 conference in Bandung, Indonesia, that was said to have led to the creation of the NAM.

USA: Zacarias Moussaoui, the only person to be charged in relation to the attacks on New York and Washington DC on 11 September 2001, pleaded guilty to charges of conspiracy, although he denied involvement in the 11 September plot itself.

24 **Andorra**: in elections to the twenty-eight-member General Council of the Valleys (the unicameral legislature) the ruling Liberal Party of Andorra (PLA) secured only fourteen seats, losing its overall majority.

Togo: a presidential election was won by Faure Gnassingbé, son of the late President Gnassingbé Eyadéma, the candidate for the Rally of the Togolese People (RPT), with over 60 per cent of the vote. Following the declaration of the result violent rioting broke out in Lomé, the capital, amid allegations of electoral fraud.

25 **Czech Republic**: President Václav Klaus appointed former Local Development Minister Jiri Paroubek of the Czech Social Democratic Party (CSSD) as the new Prime Minister, following the resignation of Prime Minister Stanislav Gross, who had been brought down by a financial scandal.

26 **Lebanon**: Syrian armed forces completed their withdrawal from Lebanon, having first entered the country in 1976 as peacekeepers in the Lebanese civil war.

29 **Nepal**: King Gyanendra announced the end of the state of emergency he imposed on 1 February, but many restrictions remained on political activity and freedom of the press.

30 **Niue**: elections were held to the twenty-seat non-partisan Fono (the legislature); the tenth Fono, elected in 2002, had been dissolved in March.

MAY

2 **Oman:** a court sentenced thirty-one members of a secret society to between one and twenty years' imprisonment for attempting to overthrow the government by force.

3 **Iraq:** a new Cabinet led by Prime Minister Ibrahim al-Jaafari was sworn in following approval by the National Assembly (the transitional legislature).

5 **Dominica:** in a general election the ruling Dominica Labour Party (DLP) won twelve of the twenty-one elected seats in the thirty-two-seat House of Assembly (the unicameral legislature), ensuring the continuation of the government led by Prime Minister Roosevelt Skerrit.

UK: in elections to the 646-seat House of Commons (the lower house of Parliament) the Labour Party led by Prime Minister Tony Blair won a third consecutive term, despite losing fifty-seven seats, with its share of the 61.5 per cent turnout dropping to 35.2 per cent from 40.7 per cent in 2001.

6 **Poland:** President Aleksander Kwasniewski refused to accept the resignations of Prime Minister Marek Belka and his Cabinet, saying that he wanted the minority government to stay in office until elections in the autumn.

7 **Burma:** three bombs exploding in Rangoon, the capital, killed at least nineteen people, although opposition sources later reported that about seventy people died. No organisation claimed responsibility but the State Peace and Development Council (SPDC—the military government) blamed a wide range of opposition groups.

Iraq: US forces launched their largest offensive operation for six months in the western province of Anbar with the intention of cutting off the route into Iraq of foreign Islamist suicide bombers.

8 **Central African Republic (CAR):** in the second round of a presidential election the incumbent President François Bozizé secured a further term in office with 64.6 per cent of the vote, against 35.4 per cent for his rival Martin Ziguélé. In simultaneous legislative elections Bozizé's supporters emerged as the largest group in the 106-member National Assembly with forty-two seats.

Nepal: seven of the leading political parties announced that they had reached a common agenda for the restoration of democracy, suspended since King Gyanendra seized power on 1 February.

10 **Egypt:** the People's Assembly (the unicameral legislature) voted 405 to thirty-four to endorse a constitutional reform proposed in February by President Hosni Mubarak to allow multiple candidates to compete for the presidency. The constitutional amendments were approved in a national referendum on 25 May.

11 **Cayman Islands:** in a general election the opposition People's Progressive Movement (PPM) defeated the ruling United Democratic Party (UDP), winning nine of the fifteen elected seats in the Legislative Assembly.

Slovakia: the National Council (the unicameral legislature) voted 116 to twenty-seven to ratify the treaty on a constitution for the EU.

13 **Democratic Republic of Congo (DRC):** the Chamber of Representatives (the lower house of the legislature) voted to approve a new constitution that would be subject to ratification by a popular referendum within six months.

14 **Uzbekistan:** hundreds of people died in the eastern city of Andizhan when troops fired on demonstrations against the government of President Islam Karimov. Thousands fled to neighbouring Kyrgyzstan and there were reports of protests in nearby towns.

15 **Ethiopia:** elections were held to both houses of the bicameral legislature, with the ruling coalition, the Ethiopian People's Revolutionary Democratic Front (EPRDF) winning 302 seats in the 548-member lower house, the Council of People's Representatives. The opposition Coalition for Unity and Democracy (CUD), which won 121 seats, claimed that there had been massive electoral irregularities.

Guinea-Bissau: former President Kumba Yalla retracted his September 2003 resignation, made under duress during a military coup, saying that he wished to complete his term of office. An attempt by Yalla later in the month to reoccupy the presidential palace was unsuccessful.

Saudi Arabia: three liberal reformers, including poet and critic Ali al-Damaini, received prison sentences of between six and nine years for "stirring up sedition" by launching petitions calling for elections and a constitution.

16 **Kuwait**: the National Assembly (the unicameral legislature) voted by thirty-five votes to twenty-three to amend the electoral law to allow women to vote and stand for election. Kuwait thus became the fourth Gulf state to grant women the vote, after Bahrain, Qatar, and Oman.

17 **Sudan**: a two-day African regional summit in Tripoli, the Libyan capital, ended with an agreement on the need for logistical assistance from the EU and NATO for the African Union peace-keeping mission in the western Darfur province of Sudan.

20 **Brazil**: legislators from the Green Party withdrew from the eight-party ruling coalition in protest at the government's failure to curb destruction of the Amazon rainforest, which reached its second-highest level ever in 2004.

Peru: Congress (the bicameral legislature) voted by fifty-seven votes to forty-seven against impeaching President Alejandro Toledo for electoral malpractice, despite the publication earlier in the month of a congressional report claiming that many of the signatures used for the registration of his Peru Possible party in the 2000 presidential election were forged.

22 **Germany**: the Social Democratic Party (SPD), the main governing party, was heavily defeated in a state assembly election in North-Rhine-Westphalia, the SDP's industrial heartland. Federal Chancellor Gerhard Schröder announced that he would seek to hold federal elections in the autumn, a year early.

Mongolia: Nambaryn Enkhbayar, a former prime minister, current speaker of the legislature and candidate of the ruling Mongolian People's Revolutionary Party (MAHN), won a presidential election with 53 per cent of the vote.

23 **Zimbabwe**: the government launched a crackdown on street traders in Harare and other major cities, evicting thousands of traders and their families from shanty towns that were subsequently burnt down by the authorities.

25 **Austria**: the Bundesrat (the upper house of the legislature) voted fifty-nine to three to ratify the treaty on an EU constitution.

Azerbaijan: the opening ceremony was held in Baku, the capital, of the 1,760 km Baku-Tbilisi-Ceyhan oil pipeline connecting the oil fields of the Caspian sea to the shipping terminal at Ceyhan on Turkey's Mediterranean coast.

Brunei: Sultan Hassanal Bolkiah, the head of state and government, made the first major reshuffle of his Cabinet for seventeen years.

Suriname: although the ruling New Front for Democracy coalition led by President Ronald Venetiaan suffered a major setback in elections to the fifty one-seat National Assembly (the unicameral legislature), no party secured a majority and it was unclear who would form the next government.

27 **Disarmament**: the seventh review conference of the parties to the 1970 Nuclear Non-Proliferation Treaty (NPT), begun on 2 May, ended without agreement on new measures to prevent the spread of nuclear weapons.

Germany: the Bundesrat (the upper house of the federal legislature) overwhelmingly approved the ratification of a treaty introducing a constitution for the EU; the Bundestag (the lower house) had already approved it on 12 May, voting for the treaty 569 to twenty-three.

Turkey: the Grand National Assembly (the unicameral legislature) voted 346-three to approve a revised penal code, a key requirement in Turkey's application to join the EU.

29 **France**: in a referendum over 54 per cent of voters rejected a treaty introducing a constitution for the EU, despite a strenuous campaign by the government for a "yes" vote. On 31 May President Jacques Chirac replaced Prime Minister Jean-Pierre Raffarin with Interior Minister Dominique de Villepin.

Lebanon: the first round of elections to the National Assembly (the unicameral legislature) was held in Beirut, the capital. Three further rounds were scheduled to be held in June.

31 **Russia**: Mikhail Khodorkovsky, founder and former chief executive of the formerly state-owned Yukos oil company, was found guilty on nine counts of fraud and tax evasion and sentenced to nine years' imprisonment after a trial lasting over eleven months.

JUNE

1 **Netherlands**: a proposal to ratify the treaty providing for an EU constitution was rejected in a referendum by 61.5 per cent of the electorate, an even larger "no" vote than in the French referendum days earlier that similarly rejected the treaty.

2 **Bolivia:** President Carlos Mesa, in an attempt to end anti-government protests, announced that the constitution would be rewritten by a new assembly to be elected in October. However, in the face of continuing protests by tens of thousands of farmers and workers, Mesa on 6 June tendered his resignation to Congress (the bicameral legislature), which on 9 June appointed as President head of the Supreme Court Eduardo Rodríguez.

India: eleven moderate separatist leaders from Indian-administered Kashmir were allowed for the first time since 1947 to cross the cease-fire line into Pakistan-administered Kashmir for talks with Pakistani Kashmiri leaders and senior members of the Pakistan government.

Latvia: the 100-member Saeima (the unicameral legislature) approved a treaty providing for an EU constitution by seventy-one votes to five.

3 **Andorra**: a new Cabinet was appointed under Albert Pintat as Head of Government.

Maldives: the People's Majlis (the legislature) voted to endorse a constitutional reform that would allow the registration of political parties.

6 **Chad**: a national referendum approved an amendment to the 1996 constitution that abolished the article limiting a president to two terms in office.

Papua New Guinea: results were announced of May elections of the first autonomous government of the island province of Bougainville. Former pro-independence rebel Joseph Kabui was elected President of Bougainville.

Sudan: Luis Moreno Ocampo, chief prosecutor of the UN International Criminal Court (ICC), announced that he had decided to open an investigation into alleged war crimes committed in Sudan's western Darfur province.

UK: Foreign and Commonwealth Secretary Jack Straw announced that the government was suspending a bill for a referendum on the treaty providing for an EU constitution in the light of the rejection of the treaty by the Dutch and French electorates.

7 **Hungary:** the 386-member National Assembly (the unicameral legislature) elected as President László Solyóm, a former president of the Constitutional Court and former anti-communist dissident, by 185 votes to 182.

12 **Kuwait**: Prime Minister Shaikh Sabah al-Amad al-Jabir al-Sabah appointed Ma'suma al-Mubarak as Kuwait's first female Cabinet minister, with the Planning portfolio.

14 **Argentina**: the Supreme Court ruled that two amnesty laws dating from 1986-87 and relating to the "dirty war" under military rule in the 1970s were unconstitutional.

South Africa: President Thabo Mbeki dismissed Vice President Jacob Zuma because of his connections with his former financial adviser Schabir Schaik, who was convicted on 2 June of corruption and fraud.

16 **Hong Kong:** former Chief Secretary Donald Tsang was confirmed as the new Chief Executive of the territory, completing the term of his predecessor Tung Chee-hwa, which would expire in 2007.

17 **EU**: a two-day EU summit in Brussels ended in deadlock on the 2007-13 budget, with UK Prime Minister Tony Blair refusing to agree to a reduction in the UK's post-1984 level of

budget rebate unless it were accompanied by other reforms, notably of the common agricultural policy.

18 **Sudan:** the government and the opposition umbrella organisation, the National Democratic Alliance (NDA), signed a national reconciliation agreement in Cairo, the Egyptian capital.

19 **Lebanon:** the last of four rounds of voting (begun in May) to elect the 128-seat National Assembly (the unicameral legislature) was held, with final results announced on 21 June. The "anti-Syrian" opposition alliance led by Future Movement won a majority with seventy-two seats. The legislature voted 128 to two on 30 June to appoint Future Movement candidate Fouad Siniora as the new Prime Minister.

Vietnam: Prime Minister Phan Van Khai began a six-day visit to the USA, the first Vietnamese head of government to be received at the White House since the communist victory that ended the Vietnam War in 1975.

21 **Palestine:** the second summit meeting between Palestinian President Mahmoud Abbas and Israeli Prime Minister Ariel Sharon was held in Jerusalem, but no progress was made on security matters related to the planned Israeli withdrawal from the Gaza Strip.

24 **Bulgaria:** in elections to the 240-seat National Assembly (the unicameral legislature) the opposition Coalition for Bulgaria won the largest number of seats, eighty-two, with the outgoing ruling National Movement Simeon II (NDSV) coming second with fifty-three seats.

Iran: in the second round of presidential elections conservative candidate Mahmoud Ahmadinejad, the mayor of Tehran, beat former President Ali Akbar Hashemi Rafsanjani with over 61.7 per cent of the vote. In the inconclusive first round on 17 June, contested by seven candidates, Rafsanjani had led with 21 per cent.

Sri Lanka: the government signed a long-delayed deal with the separatist Liberation Tigers of Tamil Eelam (LTTE) on the distribution of aid to areas of the country affected by the December 2004 tsunami that were effectively under LTTE control.

JULY

3 **Albania:** elections to the 140-seat People's Assembly (the unicameral legislature) resulted in victory for an opposition alliance of parties led by the centre-right Democratic Party of Albania (PDS), which itself won fifty-five seats in a bloc of seventy-three. The defeated Socialist Party of Albania (PSS), which won forty seats, had been in power since 1997. The PDS was led by former President Sali Berisha.

Mauritius: in elections to the seventy-seat National Assembly (the unicameral legislature) the opposition five-party Social Alliance (AS), winning forty-two seats, defeated the ruling coalition led by Prime Minister Paul Bérenger. A new Cabinet was sworn in on July 5, headed by Prime Minister Navin Ramgoolam of the Mauritius Labour Party (MLP).

4 **Burundi:** the country's first multi-party legislative elections since 1993 were won by the former rebel pro-Hutu National Council for the Defence of Democracy-Forces for the Defence of Democracy (CNDD-FDD), which secured sixty-four out of 118 seats in the National Assembly (the lower house of the legislature).

Georgia: Eduard Kokoity, self-declared president of the breakaway region of South Ossetia, appointed Russian national Yuri Morozov as the new South Ossetian Prime Minister.

5 **Japan:** the House of Representatives (the lower house of the Diet, the legislature) narrowly voted to pass six bills to privatise the state-owned post office (Japan Post) and its associated banking system.

6 **Burma (Myanmar):** the trial began of former Prime Minister General Khin Nyunt on corruption and bribery charges. It was reported on 22 July that Khin Nyunt, who was removed from office in October 2004, had been sentenced to forty-four years in prison, although the sentence was suspended and he continued to be held under house arrest.

7 **UK**: four suicide bombers, attacking three underground trains and one bus, killed fifty-two people in London apart from themselves and injured about 700 others.

8 **G-8**: at the end of a three-day summit meeting at Gleneagles, Scotland, the leaders of the G-8 (Group of Seven advanced industrialised economies and Russia) agreed on a plan for debt relief for eighteen mostly African least developed countries and for increased aid to the developing world.

10 **Luxembourg**: in a national referendum over 56 per cent of voters approved a treaty providing for a constitution for the EU.

   Russia: criminal investigations began against former Prime Minister Mikhail Kasyanov (2000-04), relating to corruption allegations. Following his dismissal in 2004 Kasyanov had been critical of the government and hinted at his ambitions to contest the presidency.

11 **Kyrgyzstan**: Acting President Kurmanbek Bakiev of the People's Movement of Kyrgyzstan was declared winner of a presidential election held on 10 July, with 89.5 per cent of the vote. Former opposition leader Bakiev was elected to a five-year term.

12 **Monaco**: Prince Albert II, forty-seven, was formally proclaimed ruler of the principality in a ceremony at the Cathedral of the Immaculate Conception, succeeding his father Prince Rainier III, who died on 6 April.

15 **Thailand**: Prime Minister Thaksin Shinawatra introduced an emergency powers decree to deal with a separatist insurgency in the country's three southern Muslim majority provinces, which had caused some 800 deaths since it began in January 2004.

16 **Iraq**: in a month which saw a steep escalation of insurgency-related violence a suicide bombing outside a mosque in the town of Musayyib, 70 kilometres south of Baghdad, killed at least ninety-eight people, the highest death toll in a single incident since the formation of a new government on 28 April.

17 **Iraq**: the Iraq Special Tribunal, a national court established to try former Iraqi leaders for war crimes and crimes against humanity, laid the first formal charges against former President Saddam Hussein.

19 **Lebanon**: a new Cabinet was announced, headed by Prime Minister Fouad Siniora, appointed in June.

21 **China**: the government announced that it was relaxing the fixed exchange-rate system that had pegged the yuan (renminbi) to the US dollar for eleven years.

   UK: another attempt was made to target London's public transport system, but the four bombs failed to detonate. On 22 July police shot dead Jean Charles de Menezes, a Brazilian, as he boarded an underground train, thinking that he was a suspect. It was quickly established that he had no connection with terrorism.

   USA: The House of Representatives (the lower house of the bicameral legislature) voted 257-171 permanently to extend fourteen provisions of the 2001 Patriot Act introduced in response to the 11 September 2001 attacks on the USA. Two of the Act's provisions, granting federal powers to conduct wiretaps and to spy on library borrowing records, were extended for ten years.

22 **Russia**: President Vladimir Putin signed into law a bill amending thirteen federal laws on the election system. The effect of many of the changes was to make it more difficult for small parties to gain representation in the State Duma (the lower house of the federal legislature).

23 **Egypt**: bomb attacks on three tourist hotels in the Red Sea resort of Sharm el-Sheikh killed at least sixty-four people and injured over 100. At least three Islamic militant groups claimed responsibility for the attacks.

24 **Guinea-Bissau**: former President João Bernardo "Nino" Vieira, standing as an independent, won the second round of a presidential election with over 52 per cent of the vote, defeating Malam Bacai Sanha of the ruling African Party for the Independence of Guinea-Bissau and Cape Verde (PAIGC). The first round had been held on 19 June.

25 **Ethiopia**: the authorities announced that fresh elections would be held in at least twenty constituencies of the 524-seat legislature, following opposition claims that the ruling party's vic-

tory in a May general election had been procured by vote rigging.

Philippines: opposition legislators submitted a formal motion to impeach President Gloria Macapagal-Arroyo for alleged vote rigging in the 2004 presidential elections.

26 **Nepal**: an anti-corruption court convicted former Prime Minister Sher Bahadur Deuba on corruption charges and sentenced him to two years' imprisonment.

North Korea: the six-party talks on negotiating the closure of North Korea's nuclear weapons programme resumed for the first time since June 2004, hosted by China. The other participants were the USA, Japan, Russia, and South Korea.

Space: the US National Aeronautics and Space Administration (NASA) successfully launched the space shuttle *Discovery* on a mission to the International Space Station (ISS), the first shuttle flight since the catastrophic loss of the *Columbia* in February 2003.

27 **New Zealand**: the House of Representatives (the unicameral legislature) voted 109 votes to nine to defeat a private bill to lift a ban, introduced in 1985, on nuclear powered or armed ships entering New Zealand's ports or territorial waters.

28 **Northern Ireland**: the Irish Republican Army (IRA), which had been observing a ceasefire since 1994, formally declared that its thirty-six-year armed campaign, designed to detach Northern Ireland from the UK and unite it with the Republic of Ireland, was over.

Uganda: in a national referendum over 92 per cent of voters favoured a return to multi-party politics to replace the no-party "movement" system established by President Yoweri Museveni in 1986.

30 **Sudan**: veteran leader of the rebel Sudan People's Liberation Army (SPLA) Lieutenant General John Garang, who was sworn in on 9 July as First Vice President of Sudan as part of a peace agreement signed in January, was killed in a helicopter crash in southern Sudan whilst returning from a visit to Uganda.

AUGUST

1 **Saudi Arabia**: King Fahd ibn Abdul Aziz died aged eighty-three or eighty-four, and was succeeded as King by his half-brother Crown Prince Abdullah ibn Abdul Aziz, eighty-two, who had been the de facto ruler of Saudi Arabia since Fahd suffered a stroke in 1995.

2 **Zimbabwe**: public prosecutor Florence Ziyambi announced that the state had dropped all treason charges, filed in June 2003, against Morgan Tsvangirai, leader of the opposition Movement for Democratic Change (MDC). No explanation was offered for dropping the charges.

3 **Mauritania**: President Maaouyia Ould Taya was overthrown in a bloodless coup by a group of army officers when he was out of the country. A new Cabinet headed by Prime Minister Sidi Mohammed Ould Boubacar was formed on 10 August.

Suriname: Ronald Venetiaan was elected for a third term as President by a joint session of the National Assembly (the unicameral) legislature) and regional councils.

5 **UK**: Prime Minister Tony Blair proposed twelve new measures to combat Islamic extremism, including new grounds for deportation and withdrawal of citizenship and a new offence of "condoning or glorifying terrorism".

8 **UK**: four Muslims of African origin were charged with attempting to bomb the London public transport system on 21 July. The authorities had applied for the extradition of a fifth suspect from Italy. No evidence had been found of a connection between the failed bombing attempts on 21 July and the attacks on 7 July, in which fifty-six people (including the bombers) died.

11 **Japan**: Prime Minister Junichiro Koizumi called a general election for 11 September following the defeat in the House of Councillors (the upper house of the legislature) of bills to privatise Japan's postal service, which had been narrowly passed in July by the lower house.

Peru: Prime Minister Carlos Ferrero Costa resigned in protest against the appointment of Fernando Olivera Vega—a close ally of President Alejandro Toledo—as Foreign Minister. Constitutionally, this obliged the whole Cabinet to resign. Toledo on 16 August announced a new Cabinet, which included neither Ferrero Costa nor Olivera.

12 **Sri Lanka**: an unidentified gunman assassinated Foreign Minister Lakshman Kadirgamar at his home in Colombo, the capital.

15 **Bulgaria**: the three largest political parties—the Bulgarian Socialist Party (BSP), the National Movement Simeon II (NDSV), and the mainly Turkish ethnic Movement for Rights and Freedoms (DPS)—agreed to form a coalition government led by BSP leader Sergei Stanishev.

Indonesia: negotiators for the government and the separatist Free Aceh Movement (GAM) signed a formal peace agreement in Helsinki, Finland, to bring to an end a conflict in the north Sumatran province of Aceh that began in 1976.

17 **Bangladesh**: nearly 500 small bombs exploded outside government offices and courts across the country, killing two people and injuring about 140. The co-ordinated bombings were seen as a significant show of strength by the Islamic fundamentalist group, Jamaat-ul Mujaheddin Bangladesh (JMB).

Western Sahara: the pro-independence Polisario Front released the last 404 Moroccan army prisoners of war, captured between 1975 and 1991, as a good-will gesture.

19 **Burundi**: Pierre Nkurunziza, candidate of the former pro-Hutu ruling National Council for the Defence of Democracy-Forces for the Defence of Democracy (CNDD-FDD) was elected President of Burundi by over 91 per cent of both houses of the legislature. Nkurunziza was the only candidate. He formed a new Cabinet on 30 August.

Germany: a court in Hamburg convicted Moroccan national Mounir Motassadeq of membership of a terrorist organisation and sentenced him to seven years' imprisonment, although he was acquitted on participation in the plot to mount the 11 September 2001 terrorist attacks on the USA. The case was a retrial after an appeals court in March 2004 had quashed Motassadeq's February 2003 conviction on the same charges.

Kazakhstan: the ruling Otan party won ten out of sixteen seats contested in elections to the Senate (the upper house of the legislature), which comprised thirty-two members elected by regional assemblies and seven appointed members.

22 **Maldives**: Mohammed Nasheed, chairman of the recently registered Maldivian Democratic Party (MDP) was charged with terrorism, having been arrested in August at a demonstration urging the release of political prisoners. The constitution had been amended in June to legalise political parties.

23 **Israel**: the evacuation of Israeli settlers from the Gaza Strip, begun on 15 August, was completed ahead of schedule, although the Israeli military remained in the Gaza Strip prior to handing over to the Palestine National Authority.

26 **India:** the official death toll in the devastating monsoon floods that hit the western state of Maharashtra in late July was reported to be 1,059.

28 **Iraq**: a draft constitution that would be put to a referendum on 15 October was read to the National Assembly (the interim legislature), despite the continued rejection of the final text by the 15 minority Sunnis on the seventy-one-member drafting committee.

29 **USA**: Hurricane Katrina hit the Gulf coast states of Louisiana, Mississippi, and Alabama, causing widespread and severe damage, having already killed seven people in Florida. About 80 per cent of the city of New Orleans was flooded by storm surges.

30 **Lebanon**: three former senior security officials with close links to Syria were arrested for questioning by a UN commission investigating the February assassination of former Prime Minister Rafik al-Hariri.

Zimbabwe: the House of Assembly (the unicameral legislature) voted 103 to twenty-nine to approve a bill of constitutional amendments, including a provision to establish a second legislative chamber, the Senate.

SEPTEMBER

1 **Albania**: final results of the July general election revised the number of seats won by the opposition centre-right coalition led by the Democratic Party of Albania (PDS) upwards from seventy-three to eighty in the 140-member People's Assembly (the unicameral legislature). A new Cabinet led by Prime Minister Sali Berisha was sworn in on 10 September.

3 **Nepal**: Comrade Prachanda, leader of the rebel underground Communist Party of Nepal-Maoist (CPN-M) announced a unilateral three-month ceasefire, widely seen as a preliminary move towards negotiations with the main political parties, excluded from government since King Gyanendra seized power in February.

5 **China**: EU Trade Commissioner Peter Mandelson and China's Commerce Minister Bo Xilai agreed the terms to release millions of Chinese textile items that had been held up in warehouses since June, when China exceeded its quota of textile exports to the EU.

Ethiopia: final results of May legislative elections gave the governing Ethiopian People's Revolutionary Democratic Front (EPRDF) 327 seats, a decisive majority in the 547-seat Council of People's Representatives (the lower house of the legislature).

Nicaragua: an emergency Central American summit meeting attended by the presidents of Costa Rica, El Salvador, Guatemala, and Honduras urged Nicaragua's National Assembly (the unicameral legislature) not to enact constitutional reforms passed in January that would restrict the powers of President Enrique Bolaños.

Russia: President Vladimir Putin announced a new social spending programme, with priority given to healthcare, education, agriculture, and housing.

6 **Philippines**: the House of Representatives (the lower house of the legislature) ratified by 158 votes to fifty-one a report by its justice committee rejecting a motion to impeach President Gloria Macapagal-Arroyo for alleged electoral malpractice.

7 **Egypt**: incumbent President Hosni Mubarak won the country's first direct presidential election with over 86 per cent of the vote, defeating nine other candidates. However, the turnout was extremely low at just under 23 per cent.

8 **Ukraine:** President Viktor Yushchenko dismissed Prime Minister Yuliya Tymoshenko and her government, amid mutual allegations of corruption from their respective factions. Yushchenko named Yury Yekhanurov as the new Prime Minister, but only secured endorsement of his nomination by the legislature on 22 September, following concessions to the opposition.

9 **Côte d'Ivoire**: UN Secretary-General Kofi Annan announced that presidential elections scheduled for 30 October—a key component of an April peace agreement—would not now take place because the rebel New Forces refused to accept further South African mediation in the crisis.

11 **Japan**: in elections to the 480-member House of Representatives (the lower house of the Diet, the legislature) the ruling Liberal Democratic Party (LDP) won 296 seats, the largest number won by a single party since the end of World War II.

12 **Norway**: in elections to the 169-seat Storting (the bicameral legislature) an alliance led by the Labour Party (AP) won eighty-seven seats, defeating the outgoing centre-right coalition led by Prime Minister Kjell Magne Bondevik.

Palestine: the Israeli army completed its evacuation of soldiers and civilians from the Gaza Strip.

14 **Chile**: the Supreme Court upheld the ruling in July of a lower court that former dictator General Augusto Pinochet Ugarte should be stripped of his immunity from prosecution in investigations into his alleged role in the killing of political opponents in 1975.

Iraq: in suicide bombings and other attacks in Baghdad some 160 people were killed and 500 wounded, in apparent retaliation for US-Iraqi military operations along the border with Syria in which US military sources claimed 156 insurgents were killed.

15 **Israel**: the Supreme Court ordered the government to consider changing the route of a section of its 600 kilometre security barrier on the West Bank, but rejected Palestinian appeals that the route of the barrier should follow Israel's 1949-67 border.

UK: Home Secretary Charles Clarke published a new terrorism bill, which included new offences of "preparing terrorist acts" and "encouraging" or "glorifying" such acts, and controversially extended the maximum period of detention without charge for terrorist suspects from fourteen days to ninety days.

16 **UN**: at the end of their three-day 60th anniversary "world summit", UN members approved a compromise declaration on UN reform and fulfilment of the UN's millennium development goals. Several of UN Secretary-General Kofi Annan's reform proposals were diluted, the General Assembly could not agree on a definition of terrorism, and the declaration omitted references to nuclear disarmament and non-proliferation.

17 **New Zealand:** in elections to the House of Representatives (the unicameral legislature) the Labour Party, led by Prime Minister Helen Clark, secured a third successive three-year term in office, but without an overall majority, winning fifty seats in the 121-seat House, compared with forty-eight seats for the main opposition National Party.

18 **Afghanistan**: in the first fully democratic elections since 1969, elections were held to the 249-seat House of the People (the lower house of the National Assembly, the new legislature) and to thirty-four provincial councils. Results announced in October revealed that at least half the seats in the House had been won by conservative Islamic figures and former fighters.

Germany: in elections to the Bundestag (the lower house of the bicameral legislature) the ruling coalition of the Social Democratic Party (SPD) and the Greens lost its overall majority, and whilst the Christian Democratic Union-Christian Social Union (CDU-CSU) alliance became the largest bloc of seats, it too failed to gain a majority.

19 **Iraq**: an incident in the southern city of Basra in which UK forces broke into a prison to free two arrested British soldiers, resulting in a clash with angry Iraqi crowds, appeared to demonstrate increasing tension in the hitherto relatively peaceful area of southern Iraq under UK control.

North Korea: a fourth round of six-party talks designed to bring to an end North Korea's nuclear weapons programme ended with North Korea committing itself in a joint statement to dismantling all nuclear weapons and existing nuclear programmes. In return the USA affirmed that it maintained no nuclear weapons in South Korea and that it had no intention of attacking the North.

20 **Sudan**: a government of national unity was formed in which the northern National Congress Party (NCP), hitherto the sole ruling and legislative party, shared power with the former rebel Sudan People's Liberation Movement (SPLM)—the political arm of the southern Sudan People's Liberation Army—and several other opposition and southern parties.

22 **Italy**: Economics Minister Domenico Siniscalco resigned in disgust over the government's inability to remove Antonio Fazio, governor of the Bank of Italy (the central bank), who had refused to resign over a favouritism scandal that had damaged the bank's reputation.

Nigeria: police arrested Alhaji Mujahid Dokuba-Asari, leader of the separatist Niger Delta People's Volunteer Force (NDVF), formally charging him with treason on 6 October.

23 **Aruba**: in elections to the twenty-one-seat Staten (the unicameral legislature) the People's Electoral Movement (MEP) won eleven seats, securing a second term of office for Prime Minister Nelson Oduber.

Poland: elections to both houses of the legislature produced landslide victories for the two main opposition centre-right parties—Law and Justice (PiS) and the Citizen's Platform (PO)—with 288 seats in the lower 460-seat Sejm and eighty-three seats in the 100-seat Senate.

24 **Iran**: the board of governors of the UN International Atomic Energy Agency (IAEA) approved by twenty-two to one, with twelve abstentions, a resolution to refer Iran to the UN Security Council for possible imposition of sanctions because of concealment of aspects of its nuclear energy programme.

26 **Northern Ireland**: the Irish Republican Army (IRA) announced that the process of decommissioning the organisation's weaponry was complete.

Spain: Europe's largest trial of Islamic extremists ended with the conviction of one man of conspiracy to commit murder in connection with the 11 September 2001 attacks on the USA, for which he was sentenced to twenty-seven years in prison, and of seventeen others for belonging to or aiding the al-Qaida terrorist network. Six other defendants were acquitted.

29　**Algeria**: a national referendum was held, endorsing President Abdelaziz Bouteflika's "charter for peace and national reconciliation", which included a partial amnesty for Islamic militants.

Somalia: the self-declared Republic of Somaliland held its first multi-party legislative elections since seceding from Somalia in 1991.

OCTOBER

1　**Indonesia**: suicide bombings killed twenty-three people on the island of Bali, three years after the 2002 bombings that killed 202 people. The Islamic militant group, Jemaah Islamiah (JI), was believed responsible.

El-Salvador: the country's largest volcano, Ilamatepec (Santa Ana) erupted after more than a century of lying dormant. Two people were killed; more than 2,000 people were forced to flee.

2　**Congo**: indirect partial elections to the Senate (the upper house of the bicameral legislature) resulted in victory for President Denis Sassou Nguesso's ruling Congolese Labour Party, which took twenty-three of the thirty contested seats in the sixty-six seat chamber.

3　**USA:** President George W. Bush nominated Counsel to the President Harriet Ellan Miers to succeed Supreme Court justice Sandra Day O'Connor, who had resigned in July. Miers withdrew her nomination on 27 October in the face of general consternation that she was insufficiently qualified.

4　**Croatia**: accession negotiations opened with the EU, following a statement by the International Criminal Court for the Former Yugoslavia (ICTY) that Croatia was "co-operating fully" over the indictment of the fugitive General (retd) Ante Gotovina.

Turkey: accession negotiations with the EU opened after Austria withdrew its veto in response to the start of negotiations with Croatia.

5　**Tajikistan**: the Supreme Court sentenced Mahmadruzi Iskandrov, leader of the opposition Democratic Party of Tajikistan, to twenty-three years' imprisonment on charges including terrorism and attempted murder, which his supporters claimed were politically motivated in advance of presidential elections scheduled for 2006.

6　**Peru**: former President Alberto Fujimori announced from self-imposed exile in Japan that he planned to contest the 2006 presidential elections.

Scientific research: the journals *Nature* and *Science* reported that the US Centres for Disease Control had genetically recreated the H1N1 influenza virus responsible for the 1918 pandemic of "Spanish flu". The researchers concluded that this had been an avian virus which had mutated to infect humans.

8　**Pakistan**: an earthquake devastated the whole of Pakistani-administered Kashmir and much of North-West Frontier Province; Indian-administered Jammu and Kashmir was also affected. The earthquake measured 7.6 on the Richter scale.

9　**Germany:** Angela Merkel, the leader of the Christian Democratic Union (CDU) would become Germany's first female Chancellor, following agreement between the CDU-Christian Social Union (CDU-CSU) alliance and the Social Democratic Party (SPD) to form a "grand coalition" under her leadership after the inconclusive results of the September legislative elections.

10　**Ethiopia:** Meles Zenawi was re-elected for a further five-year term as Prime Minister by the Council of People's Representatives (the lower chamber of the bicameral legislature).

11　**Liberia**: elections were held for the presidency and both houses of the bicameral legislature. The leaders in the presidential elections, George Weah of the Congress for Democratic Change (CDC) and Ellen Johnson-Sirleaf of the Unity Party, proceeded to a second round. Weah's CDC took the largest number of seats in the lower House of Representatives.

Nicaragua: President Enrique Bolaños and opposition leader Daniel Ortega announced an agreement to postpone, until the end of Bolaños's term in 2007, constitutional reforms enacted in January, which Bolaños had challenged, prompting a constitutional crisis.

12 **Space**: China's second manned space mission took off from the Jiuquan launch centre, carrying two *taikonauts* (astronauts). They landed successfully on 17 October.

Syria: Interior Minister Major General Ghazi Kenaan was found dead in his office, having apparently committed suicide in response to the conclusions of the forthcoming UN Hariri investigation. Kenaan had been intelligence chief in Lebanon from 1982 to 2002.

13 **Russia:** multiple co-ordinated attacks were carried out on targets in Nalchik, the capital of the North Caucasus republic of Kabardino-Balkariya, by fighters from the Chechen resistance movement and Yarmuk, a local Islamic militant group.

15 **Iraq**: a national referendum was held on a new constitution. Results, announced on 25 October, showed that the document had been approved by a narrow margin, and overwhelmingly rejected in the two main Sunni Arab provinces.

Malawi: President Bingu wa Mutharika announced a state of national disaster resulting from the country's food crisis. The World Food Programme had, in September, issued an appeal for US$88 million to help Malawi's population. US$76 million was still required as of 19 October.

17 **Brazil**: Congress (the bicameral legislature) commenced expulsion hearings against eleven legislators implicated in the bribery scandal that emerged in June.

Norway: a new centre-left coalition Cabinet was sworn in, under Prime Minister Jens Stoltenberg of the leftist Labour Party (AP).

18 **China**: US Defence Secretary Donald Rumsfeld began a visit to China, the first since his appointment in December 2000.

19 **Iraq**: the trial of former President Saddam Hussein opened in the capital, Baghdad, on charges against him and seven associates from the Ba'ath Party relating to the execution of at least 143 people from the mostly Shi'ite village of Dujail in 1982.

20 **Lebanon**: the preliminary conclusions of the UN commission investigating the February assassination of former Prime Minister Rafik al-Hariri alleged probable Syrian involvement and criticised the Syrian government for its lack of co-operation with the investigation.

Nigeria: the Paris Club of sovereign creditors signed an agreement with Nigeria providing for the cancellation of US$18 billion of the US$31 billion in sovereign debt and arrears it owed to foreign governments.

Venezuela: President Hugo Chávez Frías claimed in an interview with the BBC that he was in possession of intelligence reports that the US government was planning a military invasion of his country.

21 **Côte d'Ivoire**: the UN Security Council adopted resolution 1633 (2005) recommending that President Laurent Gbagbo's mandate should be extended for up to twelve months in recognition of the difficulty of organising presidential elections for 30 October as originally scheduled under the terms of the April peace agreement.

23 **Argentina**: President Néstor Kirchner's Front for Victory (FPV) faction within the ruling (Peronist) Justicialist Party (PJ) secured victory in mid-term partial legislative elections, taking 39 per cent of the overall vote

Poland: a second round of voting in presidential elections brought to power the mayor of Warsaw, Lech Kaczynski, of the conservative Law and Justice (PiS) party, with over 54 per cent of the vote.

28 **France**: rioting by young Muslims of north and west African descent broke out in the Paris suburbs, following the deaths of two young Muslims, reportedly from electrocution after they fled from the police into an electricity substation. Rioting spread from Clichy-sous-Bois to other suburbs on subsequent evenings.

29 **India**:three bombs exploded in New Delhi, killing at least fifty-nine people. The obscure Islami Inqilabi Mahaz (Islamic Revolutionary Group) claimed responsibility.
USA: chief-of-staff to Vice President Dick Cheney, I. Lewis "Scooter" Libby was indicted on five counts of obstruction of justice, making false statements to the FBI, and committing perjury before a federal grand jury. The indictments related to the alleged leaking to the press of the identity of Valerie Plame, an undercover CIA agent.

30 **Tanzania**: elections in the partially autonomous island of Zanzibar returned to power incumbent President Amani Abeid Karume of the ruling Chama Cha Mapinduzi (CCM). The CCM also won elections to the island's legislature. The opposition Civic United Front alleged fraud.

31 **Poland**: a seventeen-member Cabinet was appointed under the new Prime Minister Kazimierz Marcinkiewicz (chosen in preference to the leader of the ruling Law and Justice (PiS) party, Jaroslaw Kaczynski, who was the twin brother of the new President Lech Kaczynski). The Cabinet, dominated by PiS, included eight independents.

NOVEMBER

1 **Ethiopia**: violent protests broke out in the capital, Addis Ababa, after a day of peaceful demonstrations organised by the main opposition Coalition for Unity and Democracy against alleged vote-rigging during the legislative elections in May. Up to forty-two people were killed.

2 **Guinea-Bissau**: President João Bernardo "Nino" Vieira appointed Aristides Gomes as Prime Minister. He was a senior figure in the pro-Vieira faction of the ruling African Party for the Independence of Guinea-Bissau and Cape Verde (PAIGC).
USA: the *Washington Post* newspaper published allegations that the CIA had transferred suspected al-Qaida members to secret prisons in Eastern European countries (as well as Afghanistan and Thailand), where they were interrogated and held without charge, under the practice known as "extraordinary rendition".

3 **Brazil**: a congressional inquiry into bribery allegations that had emerged in June published its findings. The ruling Workers' Party (PT) had used public money for election campaigns and had paid legislators from two parties in the ruling coalition for their support in the legislature.

6 **Azerbaijan**: elections to the 125-seat Milli Majlis (unicameral legislature) produced victory for the New Azerbaijan Party of President Ilham Aliyev. The Azadlyq (Liberty) coalition of opposition parties claimed widespread irregularities. Results were annulled in four constituencies, and in a further six constituencies (including two won by opposition candidates) by the Constitutional Court on 1 December.

7 **Egypt**: the final stage of elections to the 444 elected seats in the 454-member People's Assembly (unicameral legislature) was held; overall results gave the National Democratic Party of President Hosni Mubarak 311 seats, whilst candidates of the banned Muslim Brotherhood, standing as independents, increased their representation six fold to eighty-eight seats.
India: K. Natwar Singh resigned as External Affairs Minister after he was named as a beneficiary of corruption in the UN's "oil-for-food" programme for Iraq, in the report published on 27 October by the Volcker committee investigating the affair.
Peru: former President Alberto Fujimori was arrested in Santiago, the capital of Chile, when the Peruvian authorities requested his extradition on charges of corruption and human rights abuses.
Trinidad & Tobago: the leader of the radical Islamic group, Jamaat-al-Muslimeen, Yasin Abu Bakr, was arrested and charged under the country's recent anti-terrorism act.

8 **China**: the country's Commerce Minister Bo Xilai signed an agreement with US Trade Representative Rob Portman, setting quotas to regulate trade in textiles and clothing until the end of 2008.
France: a twelve-day state of emergency was declared under a 1955 internal security law to deal with the rioting by mainly Muslim members of ethnic minority communities, which had

begun in late October. The initial period was extended by parliamentary vote for three months from 21 November.

Liberia: the second round of presidential elections produced victory for Ellen Johnson-Sirleaf, the runner-up in the first round (on 11 October) to George Weah of the Congress for Democratic Change. On her inauguration in January 2006, Johnson-Sirleaf would become Africa's first female president.

9 **Indonesia:** Azahari Husin, the chief suspect in the 2002 Bali bombings, as well as attacks in 2003, 2004, and the recent bomb attacks in Bali in October, was killed during a police siege. Azahari was thought to be a leading member of the Islamic militant network, Jemaah Islamiah (JI).

Jordan: three suicide bombings in the capital, Amman, killed sixty people, mostly Jordanians. The near simultaneous attacks, targeted on hotels frequented by Western security personnel and contractors, were claimed by the Iraqi branch of the al-Qaida network.

Macedonia: the European Commission recommended granting the status of candidate country, without, however, mentioning a starting date for accession talks.

UK: the Labour government of Prime Minister Tony Blair suffered its first defeat in the House of Commons (lower chamber of the bicameral Parliament) since it came to power in 1997 over the controversial provision in the new Terrorism Bill that extended the period during which terrorist suspects could be detained without charge from fourteen to ninety days. The vote was 322 to 291.

13 **Burkina Faso**: Captain Blaise Compaoré was re-elected as President with over 80 per cent of the vote. He had first seized power in a coup in 1987.

14 **Uganda**: opposition leader Colonel Kizza Besigye, the chairman of the Forum for Democratic Change, who had returned to Uganda from exile in the USA on 26 October, was arrested and charged with treason, concealment of treason, and rape. His trial opened on 19 December.

15 **Iraq:** elections were held to a unicameral legislature, the 275-member Council of Representatives, to replace the interim National Assembly elected in January. The provisional results announced on 20 December indicated that the religious Shi-ite Muslim alliance and the Kurdish alliance had won at least 150 seats, and the Sunni Arab alliance some thirty-five seats.

16 **Italy**: the Senate (upper house of the bicameral legislature) approved by 170 votes to 132 a controversial constitutional reform bill which would increase regional autonomy and the powers of the Prime Minister. The bill would become law if approved by a national referendum in 2006.

17 **Sri Lanka**: presidential elections were won by Mahinda Rajapakse of the Sri Lanka Freedom Party with 50.29 per cent of the vote, against 48.43 per cent for Ranil Wickremasinghe of the United National Party. Rajapakse on 21 November named Ratnasiri Wickremanayake as Prime Minister.

21 **Kenya**: voters rejected a proposed new constitution, with about 58 per cent of the vote cast against the draft which was strongly supported by President Mwai Kibaki.

22 **Bosnia & Herzegovina**: during ceremonies in Washington DC to mark the tenth anniversary of the signing of the Dayton accords, which had ended the civil war of 1992-95, the three members of the Bosnian collective presidency—Sulejman Tihic (Bosniak), Mirko Sarovic (Serb), and Ivo Miro Jovic (Croat)—announced an agreement to press for constitutional changes to institute a stronger national government.

Nepal: an alliance of seven major opposition parties announced that they had reached agreement with the rebel Communist Party of Nepal-Maoist on collaborating to end the autocratic rule of King Gyanendra.

23 **Chile**: former President General (retd) Augusto Pinochet Ugarte was placed under house arrest and charged with tax fraud. On 19 October the Supreme Court had upheld a lower court decision from June that he should be stripped of immunity from prosecution in the case. Investigations revealed the former dictator to have amassed a fortune of some US$27 million.

26 **Zimbabwe**: elections to the newly-created Senate (upper house of the legislature) produced overwhelming victory for the ruling Zimbabwe African Union-Patriotic Front (ZANU-PF) of President Robert Mugabe.

27 **Gabon**: Omar Bongo was elected for a further seven-year term as president, with some 80 per cent of the vote. Bongo was Africa's longest-serving leader, having become president in 1967.

Honduras: in presidential elections Manuel "Mel" Zelaya Rosales of the Liberal Party (PLH) won 49.9 per cent of the vote. Simultaneous elections to the 128-member National Congress (unicameral legislature) were also won by the PLH with sixty-two seats to the PNH's fifty-five.

28 **Canada**: the minority Liberal government of Prime Minister Paul Martin lost a vote of confidence, triggering fresh legislative elections which were set for 23 January 2006.

30 **Ecuador**: a new Supreme Court of thirty-one judges was inaugurated in Quito, the capital. The previous Court had been disbanded by Congress (the unicameral legislature) in April, which had also dismissed the then President Colonel Lucio Gutiérrez.

USA: President George W. Bush speaking at the Naval Academy in Annapolis, Maryland, said that US forces in Iraq would increasingly hand over operations against indigenous insurgents to the Iraqi security forces, whilst themselves concentrating on combating international terrorism in the country.

DECEMBER

3 **Taiwan**: the ruling Democratic Progressive Party (DPP) was heavily defeated by the opposition Kuomintang (KMT) in local-level elections, prompting the resignation of the DPP chairman, and the offer of resignation by Prime Minister Frank Hsieh, which President Chen Shui-bian rejected.

4 **Kazakhstan**: incumbent President Nursultan Nazarbayev won a further seven-year term, with 91.15 per cent of the vote.

Venezuela: legislative elections to the unicameral National Assembly were won by President Hugo Chávez Frias's Fifth Republic Movement (MVR) with 114 of the 167 seats.

5 **Côte d'Ivoire**: Charles Konan Banny, chairman of the West African Central Bank (BECAO), was appointed as Prime Minister, replacing Seydou Diarra, who had held the post since March 2003.

6 **UK**: David Cameron was elected by party members to the leadership of the opposition Conservative Party.

South Africa: former Deputy President Jacob Zuma (dismissed on corruption allegations in June) was formally charged with rape.

7 **Eritrea**: the expulsion from the territory of all European, US, Canadian, and Russian members of the UN Mission in Ethiopia and Eritrea (UNMEE) was ordered, prompting fears of a new border war between Eritrea and Ethiopia.

Croatia: fugitive war crimes suspect General (retd) Ante Gotovina was arrested in the Canary Islands by Spanish police. He was transferred to the International Criminal Tribunal for the Former Yugoslavia (ICTY) in The Hague on 10 December.

Kenya: President Mwai Kibaki appointed a new Cabinet, having dissolved the previous administration on 23 November following the defeat in a national referendum of a proposed new constitution which the President had strongly backed but a number of outgoing Cabinet ministers opposed.

8 **UK**: a panel of seven law lords ruled unanimously that there was an absolute prohibition (under English law and the UK's international commitments) to the use in court of evidence obtained under torture, thereby overturning an August 2004 Court of Appeal ruling that such evidence was admissible, provided that it was obtained abroad and that UK agencies had not connived in its procurement.

Zimbabwe: UN emergency relief co-ordinator Jan Egeland said at the end of a four-day visit that the country was in a state of "meltdown".

9 **Germany**: ex-Chancellor Gerhard Schröder, who had stepped down on 22 November, was appointed as a director of the Russian-dominated consortium constructing the North European Gas Pipeline, to consternation in Germany that he had used influence while in office to promote the project.

11 **Australia**: a race riot broke out in the Cronulla suburb of Sydney, the capital of New South Wales, when a crowd of some 5,000 attacked a group of Lebanese Muslims apparently in retaliation for several incidents on the beach. Lebanese youths retaliated with attacks on cars and property.

Chile: Michelle Bachelet Jeria of the Socialist Party of Chile (PSC), a faction of the ruling Concertación coalition, won 45.96 per cent of the vote in presidential elections, but not an absolute majority, necessitating a second round in January 2006.

14 **Tanzania**: presidential and legislative elections resulted in victory for the ruling Chama Cha Mapinduzi party and its candidate, Jakaya Kikwete, the Foreign Minister, who took 80.28 per cent of the vote.

15 **Bosnia & Herzegovina**: Christian Schwarz Schilling was formally approved as the international community's new High Representative in the country, replacing Lord (Paddy) Ashdown who had held the post since 2002.

16 **USA**: the *New York Times* reported that, according to government officials, President George W. Bush had signed a secret executive order in 2002 allowing the National Security Agency to monitor telephone and electronic communications by US citizens believed to be in touch with persons abroad, without a warrant from the Foreign Intelligence Surveillance Court as was required by 1978 legislation controlling domestic spying operations against US citizens.

17 **Bhutan**: King Jigme Singye Wangchuk announced that he would abdicate in favour of his eldest son in 2008, when, under the terms of constitutional reforms agreed in March, Bhutan was due to hold its first national elections.

EU: the summit in Brussels which opened on 15 December concluded with agreement on the EU budget for 2007-13, under which the UK would accept a cut in its budget rebate in return for a full budget review, including the common agricultural policy, starting in 2008.

18 **Bolivia:** presidential elections were won by Evo Morales of the Movement Towards Socialism (MAS), with 53.7 per cent of the vote. An Aymara Indian, Morales was the first indigenous person to be elected head of state. Simultaneous legislative elections also brought victory for the MAS.

Democratic Republic of Congo (DRC): a national referendum on the new constitution approved by the legislature on 13 May was overwhelmingly endorsed by voters with over 84 per cent in favour.

World Trade Organisation: a ministerial meeting in Hong Kong concluded with only limited progress in the Doha round of talks on trade liberalisation that began in 2001.

19 **Democratic Republic of Congo (DRC):** the International Court of Justice at The Hague ordered Uganda to pay reparations to the DRC relating to its occupation of eastern regions of the DRC from 1998 to 2003.

Italy: Antonio Fazio, governor of the Bank of Italy (the central bank) resigned over a scandal concerning alleged favouritism during a bank takeover. Fazio's earlier refusal to go had prompted the resignation in September of the Economics Minister; on 28 December new legislation was promulgated to curtail the Bank's powers.

25 **Greece**: the weekly newspaper *To Proto Thema* revealed the identities of alleged UK and Greek intelligence officers accused of abducting and abusing twenty-eight Pakistani-born terrorist suspects in connection with the London bombings in July. The allegations prompted the Justice Ministry to order an inquiry.

29 **Indonesia**: the last contingent of the 24,000 non-local troops that the government had agreed to withdraw left the province of Aceh in fulfilment of the August peace agreement; on 27 December the dissolution of the Free Aceh Movement (GAM) combat force was announced.

INDEX

Page references in bold indicate location of main coverage.